feedback from tomorrow

Research in Planning and Design

Series editor Allen J Scott

P Pion Limited, 207 Brondesbury Park, London NW2 5JN

feedback from tomorrow

A J Dakin

Pion Limited, 207 Brondesbury Park, London NW2 5JN

© 1979 Pion Limited

ISBN 0 85086 071 7

Printed in Great Britain by Page Bros (Norwich) Limited

For those who have encouraged
me to think in this mode

"He (Heinrich Hertz) was able to produce the first radio waves from oscillating electric circuits and to detect directly the passage of the associated changing patterns of electric and magnetic fields as they passed across the room from his transmitting to his receiving apparatus."

D J E Ingram

"Perhaps the best way to delimit modern ecology is to consider it in terms of *levels of organization* visualized as a sort of 'biological spectrum' ... . Interaction with the physical environment (energy and matter) at each level produces characteristic functional systems."

Eugene P Odum

"Early scientific thinking was holistic but speculative; the modern scientific temper reacted by being empirical but atomistic ... . We witness today another shift in ways of thinking: the shift toward rigorous but holistic theories."

Ervin Laszlo

"As our sciences develop, and with them our power, it seems to me there will be a greater variety of possible futures, depending on the use we make of this power ... . The idea of change is so germane to our time that all forms seem destined to change and are therefore objects of conjecture."

Bertrand de Jouvenel

"Men are qualified for civil liberty in exact proportion to their disposition to put moral chains upon their own appetites. Society cannot exist unless a controlling power upon will and appetite be placed somewhere, and the less of it there is within, the more there is without."

Edmund Burke

"If we should not succeed in keeping alive a vision of mature life, then indeed we are confronted with the probability that our whole cultural tradition will break down."

Eric Fromm

"All science ... depends on its *concepts*. These are the ideas that are given names ... . They are more fundamental than the theories, which are stated in terms of them."

George Thomson

This book has come into being as a result of a progressively acute realization that certain two major areas of knowledge and practice are now of paramount importance to the human enterprise. These are the handling of information and computation through the electronic technology and, second, our knowledge of ecology, which has now brought us to an understanding of how life is sustained in dynamic systems on Spaceship Earth. In order to be able to explore what these bodies of knowledge and practice may mean for our human future it is necessary to acquire a reasonably firm grasp of what they are about. The first, preparatory task of the book is therefore to attempt description of their key ideas and practices, and to interrelate them. As basic material for this I have used well-recognized sources in the two fields.

In recent years, but particularly since *The Limits to Growth* (Meadows et al, 1972) and *A Blueprint for Survival* (*The Ecologist*, 1972) appeared, our sense of the emerging globalism has broadened in comparison with the planetary perspective of the previous decade. A look back at the thinking of, say Reiser (1958) or Wagar (1963) brings a shock of surprise at the extent of the change. The new emphasis is very considerably attributable to the phenomenally fast growth and diffusion of our electronic technology and our understanding of ecosystems.

The motivating concern of the book is primarily neither descriptive nor didactic. It is to make explorations into how the applications of these bodies of knowledge may be developed to assist the human enterprise in its present dangerous but exciting threshold experience into globalism. The basic motivation is therefore to make a modest contribution to our emerging planetary initiatives.

To be able to do this the bodies of knowledge and practices mentioned above have to be related to human beings. In both bodies there is already a considerable literature making the link to human societies. For example, certain societal issues, such as privacy, police surveillance, and education, raised through the general diffusion of the electronic technology, and pollution, energy use, and exploitative behaviour raised by our new awareness of ecosystemic principles, are now very well aired, even if the questions they imply are not necessarily fully answered.

Very much less attention has been paid to the individual seen as a human being having certain qualities of personality, mind, and character profile and to his role as the key constituent unit of society. Most typical of our time is that very large masses of such individuals share the same qualities of character profile, the same levels of information, attitudes, and beliefs. It is such individuals, multiplied by many scores of millions, that make up our mass societies.

In view of the imbalance of approach to the relationship between our two bodies of knowledge and human beings it has seemed more useful at the present juncture to use some of the available material about the mass individual, as a way of tying our two bodies of knowledge into the human enterprise, rather than trying to push further along the more familiar societal approach.

Many writers in the nineteenth century, from Schopenhauer onwards, categorized the industrial mass individual as alienated. Almost all writers of the twentieth century, from novelists to psychologists to belletrists, have told us how we suffer from a sense of the meaninglessness of existence. From Kafka to Sartre, from Tillich to Fromm, the message is the same.

I intend neither to add to it nor recapitulate it. The mass individual has other characteristics and can be viewed as a total personality. Such an attempt to see him has long since been well done by Ortega y Gasset. I have relied considerably on the diagnosis he made nearly fifty years ago. The lapse of time is a safeguard against the dangers of ephemeral emphases.

Because the influence of the mass media is an obvious major factor in the development and maintenance of the character of the mass individual it is necessary to give an important place to the role which the media may have played in forming the present mass individual's character and mind. As a source for this I have used Elémire Zolla. He has attempted to describe the mass individual of today as in part heir to the bourgeois character of the industrial culture of the nineteenth century.

An age has its typical emphases of mind and feeling. This we may call its characteristic sensibility. Our age of the mass individual is no exception. If we wish to get as full an appreciation of the character profile and mind of the mass individual of our time we shall need a guide to his sensibility. For this I have taken as source material certain writings of George Steiner.

An exposition of the character profile and sensibility of the contemporary mass individual therefore constitutes the second major preparatory task of the book.

That the mass individual when aggregated becomes a mass society is not, however, to be forgotten. Attention is therefore given to selected societal questions. Perhaps the two most important of these are the evidence that the developed countries are already 'information societies', and that in these the linkage *production–job–wages–consumption* begins to assume quite new characteristics which we have yet to learn to conceptualize and handle.

The need to develop new conceptualizations and concepts becomes the next focus of attention. The most important area here is the attempt to generate conceptual links between our biological–ecological understandings and our mental processes and products (much enhanced by the electronic technology), and between the biological–ecological knowledge and socio-economic systems. Particularly to be stressed is the linkage through the mass individual's behaviour in relation to aggregated societal performance.

The last major focus of the book is on the attempt to move toward action in the context of the emerging nature of our human future. This leads not only to suggested action specifics but also to the identification of areas of thinking and acting which raise great difficulty.

The contribution of the book is confined to a limited 'intermediate' approach. It attempts neither a highly specialized point of departure from a single discipline nor an overall generalization seeking to cope inclusively with *all* foci of attention, or a supposed total system. It is a modest attempt to start from an understanding of essentially two bodies of knowledge, to relate them to each other and to certain perceived aspects of our human concern.

The book has a metamessage which is conveyed through its organization. This is the 'gradient' of the book. The movement of the thought is from the relatively uncomplicated statement of scientifically obtained knowledge and its direct or 'simple' application in human affairs, through to the very complex area of the application of this knowledge to the guidance of human societies in their ongoing development. Such applications are no longer 'simple', but what they will be and how they will be made, humanely or not, is of very great concern, and complexity, to decide. *The metamessage is that we have to think upwards along this gradient: we may not start at the top.*

In trying to find out how to bring areas of knowledge together I have found it essential to face the task of discriminating and making judgments about the importance of various items. Overall, this is unavoidable because my essential frame of reference is concern for the human enterprise; but in particular it is necessary to discriminate and emphasize what is deemed crucial in a body of knowledge because it is specifics, not vague generalities, that have to be brought into relation with each other if synergy is to take place and new avenues of thinking opened. I hope I do not offend too much with this required exercise of discrimination those whose interest and preference may lie in the analytical approach to knowledge. The overarching aim is synthesis.

I would like to thank the many individuals and organizations, too numerous to name, who have contributed by providing material, offering guidance on technical matters, giving direction toward sound sources from which to draw, and offering opportunity for discussion. I am particularly indebted to those who undertook specific chores, such as reading parts of the manuscript, providing very valuable criticism, and otherwise giving indispensable assistance: Professor Stafford Beer, consultant; Dr D C Coll, Carleton University; Mr L H Day, Bell Canada; The Grumman Ecosystems Corporation, New York; Dr S Komatsuzaki, Nippon Telegraph and Telephone, Tokyo; Mr W F Mason, The Mitre Corporation; Dr Y Masuda, Japan Computer Usage Development Institute, Tokyo; Dr E B Parker and Dr M Porat, Stanford University; Dr D F Parkhill, Assistant Deputy Minister, Communications Canada; Mr Paul Ryan, Earthscore Foundation, New York; Dr G R Slemon and Dr K C Smith, University of Toronto; Dr J Todd, The New Alchemy Institute, Massachusetts; and Mr P I Weintraub, Bell Canada.

I also owe a very great deal to the encouragement and initiative of Dr J B de Mercado, Department of Communications, Canada. He made possible for me formal research projects relating the telecommunications–computer technology to planning and environmental matters. These included the opportunity to work experimentally on the Wired City audio–video conferencing network in Carleton University, Ottawa. On the ecological side, Dr E Mattyasovszky, Department of Urban and Regional Planning in the University of Toronto, has provided information, guidance, and criticism over many years, and throughout the writing of the book. Without his patient reading of the manuscript, readiness to discuss difficult questions, and broad understanding of what was being attempted, I could not have brought the book to completion.

To Professor A J Scott, the editor of this series, I am most grateful for very careful evaluation of the manuscript in its intermediate draft and for his comments on the manuscript in its final stage. The broad approach of his commentary was invaluable in enabling me to reach the present order and balance of the book.

Once again I very gratefully acknowledge the contributions of Ms P M Manson-Smith, who has rendered much valued bibliographic assistance in advising and in searching and obtaining material, and of Ms A E Rowe, who has most patiently and competently typed the many drafts and the final document. I am also indebted to Dr A H Sessoms of Pion Limited for her careful subediting of the manuscript.

Finally I wish to thank my wife, whose patience in listening to many parts of the various versions of the manuscript over a number of years has been unfailing.

I would add the usual note that errors of fact and mistakes of judgment must be attributed to the author alone.

Since completion of the manuscript developments have taken place, particularly in areas of the electronic technology mentioned in the book. A list of Addenda briefly drawing attention to some of these is therefore provided.

A John Dakin
Professor Emeritus of Urban and Regional Planning
University of Toronto
Toronto, September 1977

Acknowledgements

I wish to thank the following authors, publishers, and organizations for permission to use their copyright material.

Athens Center of Ekistics, Athens
  (Calhoun: "Space and the strategy of life" from *Ekistics*; quote on page 317)

Avon Books, New York
  (Wiener: *The Human Use of Human Beings: Cybernetics and Society*; quote on page 29)

Basic Books, New York, and Weidenfeld and Nicolson, London
  (de Jouvenel: *The Art of Conjecture*; opening quotation)

Belknap Press of the Harvard University Press, Cambridge, Massachusetts
  (Wilson: *Sociobiology: The New Synthesis*; quote on page 414)

The British Post Office, London (photograph; figure 3.6)

William Collins and Sons Company Ltd, London, and Lady Collins
  (Teilhard de Chardin: *The Phenomenon of Man: The Future of Man*; quotes on page 289)

Victor Ferkiss, and George Braziller Inc., New York
  (Ferkiss: *The Future of Technological Civilization*; quotes on pages pages 250, 355)

Funk and Wagnalls Co., New York
  (Zolla: *The Eclipse of the Intellectual*; quotes on pages 261-264)

Gordon and Breach, Science Publishers, Inc., New York
  (Ryan: *Cybernetics of the Sacred*; quotes on pages 183, 184, 189, 190; figure 11.1)

Grumman Ecosystems Corporation, Bethpage, New York (diagram; figure 24.1)

Harper and Row, Publishers, Inc., New York
  (Drucker: *The Age of Discontinuity: Guidelines to Our Changing Society*; quote on page 249)
  (Fromm: *The Art of Loving*; opening quotation

The Institute of Electrical and Electronics Engineers Inc., New York
  (Masuda: "The conceptual framework of information economics" from *IEEE Transactions on Communications*; quotes on pages 165, 166)

The Institute of Management Sciences, Providence, Rhode Island
  (Boulding: "General systems theory—the skeleton of science" from *Management Science*; table 1.1)

Japan Computer User Development Institute, Tokyo (*The Plan for Information Society—A National Goal Toward Year 2000*; quotes on pages 160-164)

Julian Press, New York
  (Lilly: *Programming and Metaprogramming in the Human Biocomputer*; quotes on pages 191, 192)

The MIT Press, Cambridge, Massachusetts
  (McCulloch: *Embodiments of Mind*; quotes on pages 85, 185)

The Mitre Corporation, Washington, DC
    (Mason et al: *Urban Cable Systems*; quotes on pages 61, 63)
New American Library, New York; Pitman Publishing Ltd, London
    (Childe: *Man Makes Himself*; quotes on pages 218, 219)
W W Norton and Company Inc., New York; George Allen and Unwin Ltd, Hemel Hempstead, Herts
    (Ortega y Gasset: *The Revolt of the Masses*; quotes on pages 258–260)
Oxford University Press, Oxford
    (Ingram: *Radiation and Quantum Physics*; opening quotation)
E B Parker ("Social implications of computer/telecoms systems" from *Telecommunications Policy*; quote on page 338)
Penguin Books Ltd, Harmondsworth, Middx; Deborah Rogers Ltd, London
    (Editors of *The Ecologist: A Blueprint for Survival*; quotes on pages 172, 173, 175, 177)
M U Porat ("The information economy", privately circulated manuscript; data for figure 1.2)
Prentice-Hall Inc., Englewood Cliffs, New Jersey
    (Martin: *Future Developments in Telecommunications*; quotes on pages 143, 149, 246)
W B Saunders Company, Philadelphia, and E P Odum
    (E P Odum: *Fundamentals of Ecology* 3rd edition; opening quotation, quote on page 87; figure 20.3)
Solsearch Architects, Cambridge, Massachusetts; figure 6.4
Souvenir Press Ltd, London
    (Grenet: *Teilhard de Chardin: The Man and His Theories*; quote on page 299)
George Steiner, Faber and Faber Ltd, London, and Atheneum Publishers, New York
    (Steiner: *In Bluebeard's Castle: Some Notes Towards the Re-definition of Culture*; quotes on pages 268–272)
George Steiner, and The Canadian Broadcasting Corporation
    (Steiner: *Nostalgia for the Absolute*; quotes on pages 273–275)
J H Todd, The New Alchemy Institute, Woods Hole, Massachusetts; *Journal of the New Alchemists*; figure 6.1, figure 6.2, quote on page 111)
John Wiley and Sons Inc., New York
    (Beer: *Platform for Change*; figure 7.2)
    (H T Odum: *Environment, Power and Society*; quote on page 357)
Wired City Laboratory, Carleton University, Ottawa
    (Coll et al: *The Wired City Laboratory: Studies in Interactive Broadband Communications*, quotes on pages 39, 41, 42; figure 3.2, figure 3.3, figure 3.4, figure 3.5)
World Future Society, Washington, DC
    (Harman: "The coming transformation" from *The Futurist*; quotes on page 281)

Contents

Contents

Contents

List of figures

List of tables

1

Introduction

1.1 The new perception

If a date has to be given for the beginning of our new human situation we could take 1950 as convenient. To this date we can trace the emergence of the 'information society' which now appears well established in the developed countries, and the beginnings of our response to the concept of Spaceship Earth. It is, however, especially during the last five years that the new general way of looking at the human condition has gained fairly wide acceptance. This view is compounded chiefly of our rapidly having become alert to the finiteness of the world and its physical resources, of our having achieved an understanding of the systemic nature of our biological life support, and of our realization of the importance we must now attach to the relationships between populations, food supply, and resources of energy. Further, we have developed some sensitivity to the need to relate the behaviour of socioeconomies to these understandings. We must also add a sense of the profound cultural change that is closely connected with our very rapidly developed and developing electronic capability for handling information.

If a single word has to be selected to describe this emergent view we might take *globalism* or *planetism* as descriptive of the way in which we are coming to regard our world and ourselves. Globalism is, however, an objectivization. We should, therefore, be prepared to add to such an 'outward' oriented view a recognition of the contemporary human individual's uncertainty about his existential sense of himself. We have deep anxieties about what the new conditions mean to us as individual human beings.

This new perspective is encouraging the exploration of various ways of approaching the orderly study of the human condition. These include attempts to generate working hypotheses of a world system (for example Forrester, 1971; Meadows et al, 1972; Mesarovic and Pestel, 1974), extensions of ecological knowledge, including efforts to incorporate into a single whole both 'natural' and 'human' systems (for example H T Odum, 1971; E P Odum, 1969), futures studies (for example Gabor, 1969; Jantsch, 1967; *Human Futures: Needs, Societies and Techniques*, 1974), cultural and societal studies with focus on identified 'problems' and proffered 'solutions' (for example Harman, 1977; Bhagwati, 1974; F H George, 1970b; Brubaker, 1975), resources studies—food, energy, and minerals (for example L R Brown, 1975; Ehrlich and Ehrlich, 1970), and technological studies and forecasts of future developments and societal impacts (for example Martin, 1971; Helmer, 1966; Gabor, 1970).

In addition to such studies there now exist a considerable number of experiments or demonstration projects which have come directly out of this emerging view. For example, we find demonstrations of attempted self-sufficiency, or near so, in food and energy, projects for capturing renewable energy by new technologies, new applications of the electronic technology, designs for short, highly productive food chains, new socio-economic possibilities based on telecommunications–computer technology, and new techniques of mental interaction and decisionmaking, including electronically assisted socioeconomic planning and management (for example Beer, 1975).

Our new perception is intimately bound up with the emergence of transdisciplinary studies. Such studies, simultaneously involving groups of disciplines, have both assisted the growth of globalism and offered a way of thinking and acting within that conceptualization. We have discovered that many matters requiring study cannot be handled by a single specialist discipline and that many applications of knowledge—the space programme and defense planning are outstanding examples—simply cannot be achieved other than by techniques for combining knowledge and expertise from a wide variety of areas. We may also note the recent pervasive influence of certain particular bodies of knowledge through the whole range of intellectual disciplines. Cybernetics, ecology, and the electronic technology are remarkable in their ability to permeate thought and practice in many other fields. This transdisciplinary characteristic is a major subsidiary facet of our globalism.

1.2 Reasons for selecting the two areas of knowledge
Our ecological knowledge is chosen first and foremost because it deals with the very basis of life and can conceptually cope with it on local, world–regional, and global scales. It is of vital importance to the human race that it now knows some of the broad rules by which it has to live, and has come to realize that unwitting breaking of certain of them may threaten survival. We are handling here the absolutely cardinal matter of the conditions on which the global biological system will continue to support us in a situation of present and increasingly heavy population pressure. There can be no doubt about the importance of the branches of knowledge that deal with this—let us agree to call them ecology—as a point of departure for contributing to any enquiry into the human condition.

Although the general diffusion of ecological knowledge has occurred only within the last decade or so, the essential formulation is considerably older and the component parts are older still. Ecological knowledge is considered to have been drawn together by Tansley (1935), who stated in his paper of that date the essential principle of the ecosystem as it is conceived today. The key idea is that the organism (itself a system) *and* its environment must be seen as a whole. This is the holism of Jan Smuts, and others, that now underlies much contemporary thought. To quote Tansley: "... the more fundamental conception is ... the whole *system* (in the sense of physics), including not only the organism-complex, but also the whole complex of physical factors forming what we call the environment

of the biome—the habitat factors in the widest sense ... It is the systems
so formed which ... are the basic units of nature on the face of the earth ... .
These *ecosystems*, as we may call them, are of the most various kinds and
sizes. They form one category of the multitudinous physical systems of
the universe, which range from the universe as a whole down to the atom"
(Tansley, 1935, page 299; this range of systems is shown on the right of
figure 1.1).

The conceptualization that condensed and became clear under the
pressure of Tansley's synthesis of 'organism' and 'environment' is now a
major force in all our thinking about the world, even in thinking that stems
from, and appears to concentrate on, other foci of attention, such as the
disciplines that deal with human culture and society, human behaviour,
'mind', control systems of all kinds, management, and even the development
of knowledge. *We thus have, in ecology, not only an established discipline
based on firm, experimentally demonstrable, substantive knowledge that
enables us to reach a clear picture of the natural workings of the biosphere,
but also an already proved richly productive way of approaching enquiry
in many other areas of research, including those distant from what we still
for convenience call the 'world of nature'.*

We now turn to the importance of our discovery and use of the various
regions of the electromagnetic spectrum. This spectrum is the range of
frequencies over which electromagnetic radiation can be propagated. It
includes light, radiowaves, x-rays, gamma rays, etc. Figure 1.1 shows it in
very simplified form on the left side. Almost, but not quite all, regions
are now extensively used for human purposes that have to do with
'information'. It is necessary to place the word in quotation marks
because of its various meanings. These meanings, in both living and
electronic systems, include change in the flow of energy equally with
'knowledge' understood in the conventional sense of data available in
whatever form (for example as statistical statements or electrical pulses).
With our discovery of the different properties of the various regions of
the electromagnetic spectrum there has very rapidly developed the ability
to exploit their various capabilities. We have learned through these
exploitations how to transcend not only the natural limitations of the
human sense organs of sight and hearing but also certain limits of human
mental capability, and have, effectively, broken through into what is an
'informational' mode apparently common to the entire universe. The few
ounces of highly specialized cells in the human brain and nervous system,
originally restricted in their spatial sensory capabilities to very short-range
immediate communication (sight and hearing) have now gained access to
the universal mode operating over cosmic distances, with all that this
implies in our ability to manipulate space and time. As in the case of our
new ecological knowledge, this acquisition of command of the regions of
the electromagnetic spectrum is describable as a major breakthrough.

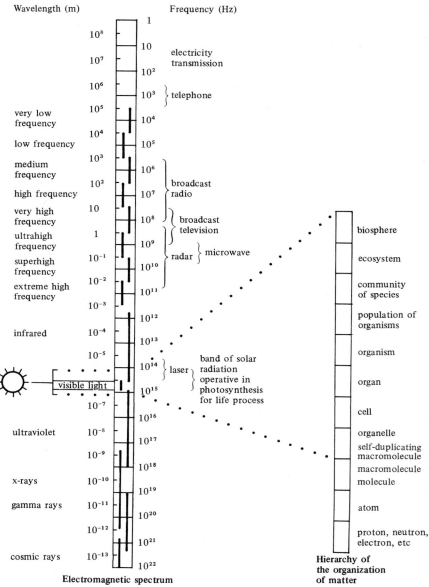

Figure 1.1. The relationship of radiation to life processes. On a clear day the process of photosynthesis, through which alone life is possible, operates through solar radiation in the approximate proportions of 45% visible light, 45% infrared and 10% ultraviolet frequencies. Life is dependent on only this very small 'window' in the total electromagnetic spectrum. On the radiation passing through this band the hierarchy of life systems, shown on the right, has developed and continues as an evolutionary process. In reading this diagram it is useful to bear in mind Boulding's (1956) hierarchy of systems given in table 1.1. The structure and functioning of matter (including living entities) moves from the simple to the complex. Life is based on relatively simple molecules capable of reproducing themselves (see Bronowski, 1973, page 316; 1970). Chemistry can now link all forms of life through the DNA molecule.

We are still only at the beginning of an understanding of the significance of this breakthrough in our comprehension of the cosmos, whether we think infinitely small or infinitely large. It has already caused very major changes: in transactions of almost all kinds, in behaviour patterns, in values and attitudes, in manufacturing processes, in business methods, in entertainment, in manipulation and application of resources, in the development and application of new knowledge, in the ways in which human activity is applied to the biosphere and the resultant effects on our human life support, and in our image of ourselves and the world.

Not only are the present applications of our knowledge of how to use the regions of the electromagnetic spectrum very generally diffused and of great influence—in the US about one-half of the work force is now employed in handling information (much of it electronically) and about one-half of every dollar spent goes to buy information—but also the potential for very rapid further development and application beggars the imagination. As we shall see in some detail, we are now at the beginning of the development of microprocessing and universal packet-switching. These allow common interchange of any kind of data, between equipment of any make, in any location, by any transmission mode. The organizational and protocol arrangements for such universalization of audio–video communication are already in place for working from Western Europe through North America to Japan. With the newly achieved satellite coverage of the three main oceans—Atlantic, Pacific, and Indian—this capability for universal communication is potentially global. It can safely be said that the electronic technology not only is a very major underpinning of society and culture in the developed countries but is at present of unmeasured, but large, potential for the management of all human societies, their affairs, and the life-support systems on which they depend. *The capability of the regions of the entire spectrum must now be seen as an extremely valuable global resource, which will need increasingly careful allocation since it is already under considerable pressure.*

Our two major areas of breakthrough in knowledge and application do not exist unrelated to each other. They are closely connected through two main linkages. These are, first, the common use of the properties of radiation, and, second, in terms of the human enterprise they constitute a binary or symbiotic pair. There are, of course, very many second-order linkages, such as the role of the telecommunications–computer technology in obtaining information about the state of ecosystems (for example Munn, 1973).

Radiation (the emission of rays, wave motion, or particles) from the sun is the energy source which daily creates and maintains the total living material of the world—the biomass which includes our food and our physical selves. The whole process of life essentially depends on the capacity of certain kinds of living material (vegetation and phytoplankton) to capture the energy of solar radiation and to use it, in conjunction with water, nutrients, etc, to create new living material and maintain existing material. This very complex process of photosynthesis, dependent on radiation, is the basis of all life. It is radiation that drives ecosystems. We shall see, however, that photosynthesis can work through only a very narrow wave band of the total electromagnetic spectrum. It is important to remember this, since the understanding of it indicates the significance of the breakthrough into all the other regions of the electromagnetic spectrum.

In the informational or communications perspective, radiation is to be regarded somewhat differently. For ecosystems it is essential energy, making possible the creation of new living material. For telecommunications–computer and other electronic systems it is better seen as a kind of vehicle capable of accepting a superimposition of human patterning. This super-imposition allows modifications to be made to the radiation so that we can capture the benefits of the various capabilities of the regions for human purposes—'seeing into' visually opaque material, sending and detecting signals over very small or galactic distances, transferring energy spatially, and using the heat generated by some wave propagation (fission), etc.

Our two breakthrough areas in knowledge and application are entirely dependent on radiation. This common dependency provides a unitary basis for new intellectual and imaginative approaches, such as the trans-disciplinary work of Bateson (1972) and McCulloch (1965) in the area of 'mind' and brain research, in which ecological knowledge—the principles of ecosystems—is related to the neurological and mental functioning of the organism[1] (see also Ashby, 1960; F H George, 1961).

The second major linkage joining our two areas of knowledge and practice is one of instrumentality or operations. The sequence of connections is this: human groups, as associations or whole societies, act upon ecosystems in order to obtain food and other materials, and in order to deflect ecosystemic energy toward themselves. They do this by developing technologies and techniques designed to achieve their purposes. But these means also produce unintended and unwanted effects in ecosystems. Their proper management therefore becomes important. Crucial to management is information about needs, intentions, the state of systems, commodity conditions (including markets), the behaviour of societies and groups, and the use of information to develop and implement plans of action. It is essentially the electronic technology which now collects, processes, makes the necessary information available, and even plays a major role in making possible the generation of new knowledge about ecosystems and matters impinging on them. The present relationships between human population concentrations and the ecosystems on which

---

[1] 'Brain' is used to indicate strictly the physical material and processes of the brain and nervous system. I have later separated out the physical material and termed it 'neuromass'. 'Mind' is the product—the total assembly of knowledge, ideas, feeling, etc, together with the dynamics of their relationships.

they depend could not be maintained at their present levels without the electronic technology and its associated manifestations.

As the population of the world increases and as the aspirations of the underprivileged rise, there will be increasing pressure on those ecosystems that are capable of producing food and other renewable resources, such as lumber, to produce more. This increasing pressure takes the form of further applications of technology directed at holding ecosystems in their 'young' phase so that maximum effort goes to producing new biomass and a minimum is expended on maintaining existing biological material. The pressure will also be typified by a global capability for applying any technology to any part of the world. Ecosystems thus will become very much more closely interrelated than at present. This global application and closer interrelatedness are products of, and are heavily reliant on, the telecommunications–computer technology. Information about the conditions of ecosystems is already collected globally, the basic documentation from which such data is extractable being updated for every part of the earth's surface every nine days (ERTS–LANDSAT; see section 7.1). As stricter ecosystem management is progressively forced upon us it is inevitable that the relationship between our understanding of ecosystems, our ability to apply that knowledge for ensuring the stability and long-term viability of ecosystems (including their human societies), and our uses and development of the electronic technology will become increasingly close and complex.

1.3 The link through radiation

The basic physical connection between our two key areas of knowledge through radiation can be shown at its simplest in the form of a diagram linking the range of the electromagnetic spectrum to a simplified hierarchy of living systems. The statement of the spectrum belongs essentially to physics; that of the living systems to biology (botany, zoology, etc). Ecology is essentially the study of the relationships between living systems and between them and the abiota (nonliving material) on which they depend for existence[2].

The interaction, which makes life possible, is shown in figure 1.1. On the left is the electromagnetic spectrum ranging from cosmic rays to alternating electric current. On the right we have the hierarchy of the systems of matter ranged from the simple to the more complex as we move upwards. The two ranges are joined by the cone of visible light, shown with dotted edges to indicate a certain variability in the marginal areas. *The principle expressed here is that of levels of systems, each upper system being unable to exist without the existence and functioning of*

[2] That a single organism (plant, animal, etc) can be described as a living entity is agreed. A group of such organisms is, however, less satisfactorily described as an organism. For this Tansley used 'quasi-organism'. It is probably a confusion to think of a society as an organism, but helpful to regard it as a system.

those below it yet each having capabilities not possessed by those below
(see Pattee, 1973). On the electromagnetic side of the diagram there is no
comparable hierarchy, and no interdependency between regions is implied.
The electromagnetic spectrum, however, is shown in the directional sense
of cosmic rays at the bottom and alternating current at the top as
acknowledgement of the fact that there are certain across-the-diagram
relationships, for example that between the radiation-propagating capabilities
of certain materials (for example, uranium) and the stability of the genetic
material of the living cell. Such relationships are omitted for clarity.

The various regions of the electromagnetic spectrum are describable by
their differences in frequency or wavelength. The wavelength measure is
conventionally in metres and frequency is given as the number of cycles
per second (hertz). The relationship between the two measures is that as
the wavelength increases, the number of cycles per second decreases. For
practical human purposes the regions of the spectrum are divided, under
international agreements, into frequency bands. A substantial group of
these (10 kilohertz to 300 gigahertz) are allocated to various uses—for
example, broadcast television (very high frequency and ultrahigh frequency)
is in the wavelength range of 10^{-1} to 10 metres. It is the very short
wavelength, very high-frequency radiation which can cause change in the
cells of living material, for example gamma rays at 10^{20} hertz (see OECD,
1973; Ingram, 1973).

Living material has evolved and is maintained in the world's biosphere
by radiation in only a relatively narrow band of the electromagnetic
spectrum. This is the span conventionally referred to as visible light, plus
part of the ultraviolet and the infrared bands. Radiation in this region
alone is the energy that drives the process of photosynthesis in vegetation
and phytoplankton. *On that process all life is dependent; other forms of
life, which cannot carry out photosynthesis themselves, must eat those
that can, or their dependents.* This chain of life dependency is inherent in
the range of living systems shown in figure 1.1, but is not explicitly stated
in order to keep the diagram simple.

The first part of our radiation link between the electromagnetic
spectrum and the range of life systems is, then, the primal one of life
itself. This is how organisms come to exist as living material. We might
take as the key organ of this link the specialized cell of the leaf that
carries out the function of receiving the radiation into the organism—the
first stage of the complicated set of subprocesses that we call photosynthesis.

There is a second radiation link between the two ranges. This is that
radiation serves as the vehicle for transmitting much of the information
that organisms need for surviving in a systemic situation in which the
organism can live only by capturing energy from outside itself, by competing
for light, for vegetation, or for the living material of those organisms who
have already been successful at incorporating these. To be able to compete,
the organism must be able to acquire and process information. Much of the

acquisition of information in the natural world is through an organ of sight
which depends, usually, on the radiation in the visible band of the electromagnetic spectrum. Nearly all mobile organisms depend heavily on this
information mode, frequently in close association with other sense processes
such as hearing (dependent on vibration in air or water, not on electromagnetic radiation), smell, touch, and sensing of heat. Thus for a very
large number of types of organism, including the human species, radiation
in the visible band and the infrared is the carrier of survival information,
and the organisms have developed the necessary specialized organs to be
able to accept radiation in this region. The most highly developed organ
for this purpose is the eye, which directly accepts radiation in the visible
light wave band.

The receiving of the radiation from outside the organism is matched by
an ability to process the information internally within the organism. The
processing determines how the organism will act: run away or fight, eat
or not eat, sleep or watch, etc. Making such decisions rests on a mental
function. This is the operation of logic. The processing side of information
is not as easy to describe as is the inputting of the radiation from the
environment into the organism because we have as yet no clear
understanding of what 'mind' is and have only the beginnings of knowledge
of the working of the brain and nervous system. However, it does appear
that electrical processes are involved in the functioning of the brain. The
outputting of the decision from the processing by logic and the operation
of the nervous system (information to, and activation of, muscles) seem
dependent on electrical impulses within the organism. These processes are
therefore describable in terms of the regions of the electromagnetic
spectrum at least in part.

A useful way to synthesize for our purpose is as follows. Solar radiation,
as an input of energy to the world system, has made life possible; a key
level in its evolutionary development has been that a stage was reached
when there appeared an upper-level system now capable of photosynthesis;
this made possible another and more complex level of evolution which has
included life, so to speak, being reared on life; *the upper-level species of
that hierarchy have developed by evolving organs that have enabled the
organisms to make their own specialized use of the properties of radiation
in the selfsame band as the one that sustains their life—the ability to
gather and process information about the environment. Thus photosynthesis
and information have been tightly bound together in the same wave band.*

*Human beings have taken this range of evolutionary development still a
stage further with regard to the electromagnetic spectrum. We have learned
how to extend this latter capability of using the visible radiation for
handling information to other regions than the visible band of the electromagnetic spectrum. These other regions have capabilities not possessed by
the visible band: infinite distances may be spanned, solid matter may be
penetrated, information may be stored indefinitely outside the human*

organism in modes that are universal, processing in certain regards vastly superior to human processing can be done outside the organism, and information transmitted by air (sound) can be converted into radiation and reconverted to sound. Together these culturally acquired capabilities give the human being a spatial and temporal mastery of certain sensory perceptions at a universal scale. This conversion, or extension capability, which is now essentially electronic, is one of the most important developments of our species. Its general diffusion has already brought us to an entirely new level of human development.

1.4 The operational link

The second major link between ecosystems and the capabilities of the regions of the electromagnetic spectrum is that of human operations. We shall deal with this very briefly here because the general idea that human beings have now a heavy dependency on the regions of the spectrum is general knowledge since there is common daily use of the spectrum's capacities by mass populations in the developed countries. It is therefore the detail that is most interesting.

If we restrict, for the moment, our ecological or life-support conceptualization to the strictly 'natural' world, we find the electronic technology already considerably developed for collecting data about certain aspects of the state of the world as a physical entity: typhoon and hurricane generation and transit, atmospheric conditions, surface ice, vegetation, ecosystem patterns, geological conditions, water conditions, etc.

The data obtained by monitoring physical conditions through the use of the electronic technology are also processed electronically. This part of the linkage to ecosystems consists of various levels, ranging from making the raw data available (for example, photographs of the eye of an emerging hurricane), through to sophisticated processing that can arrange the data specifically, or even electronically improve its basic quality, such as the computerized enhancing of the quality of photographs of the moon surface. These second-order and third-order processings include computer modelling of systems' performance. Models are used for comprehending systems and predicting their likely future behaviour (for example, weather prediction is now extensively systemically modelled).

Also at this level there is now a considerable use of the electronic technology for a similar kind of 'objective' monitoring of human affairs. These are treated in much the same way as natural phenomena. Statistical materials concerning certain characteristics of mass populations are produced in this way: census-taking and sampling, etc in relation to population, businesses, jobs, health, etc, are examples. In a developed country it would be impossible to achieve the necessary currentness of information of the kind now required for running the country or its major industries without heavy reliance on the data produced by this kind of electronic monitoring and processing. In including attention to monitoring human activities we are indicating that *we must now increasingly think of the 'natural' ecosystem and the 'human' system as parts of a single system.* We are just beginning to conceptualize this fusion at a global scale (see Clark and Cole, 1975) and to an extent in smaller entities such as the greater metropolitan region (see Dakin, 1973).

Turning now to transactions—interrelations between humans and humans or between humans and nonhuman entities—we find a variety of approaches possible. Many business transactions affect ecosystems. They cause physical resources, food, energy, people, technology, data, money, etc to be moved from one ecosystem to another. All the items mentioned are frequently moved and processed with the assistance of the electronic technology; some are very heavily dependent on electronic data movements. Governmental transactions, which become progressively similar to those of business, have the same dependency on the electronic technology, both for heavily and for sparsely populated areas (for example, the use of the ANIK satellites for relating the remote parts of Canada to the more populous parts— health, education, information, etc services).

The electronic technology plus the automotive vehicle in conjunction with the technologies that make agribusiness possible have effectively made populations almost entirely urban in their life-styles in the developed countries, whether technically classified as urban or as other. There is little distinction between the urban, the nonfarm rural, and the farm rural. All are bound into the general informational ambience of the electrobionic culture about equally. Rural populations may shortly be even superior to the urban populations in their electronic servicing, in part because of the explosion in mobile radio. This fact makes the transactional area covered by telephone, telex, radio, TV, film, disc, and tape common to whole continents and indeed associations of continents or their parts. The ecosystems which predominantly produce food are therefore culturally now strongly linked to the ecosystems which contain very large massed human populations. *This unification may be very important as it is a fundamental departure from the dichotomy that has hitherto existed between the ecologically sound practices of much traditional agriculture and the often ecologically dangerous behaviour of urban populations. That older distinction gave a protection to ecosystems that no longer exists since the action taken with regard to ecosystems for food production is based on the now ubiquitous urban values and is carried out through universally diffused technologies. We may well suspect that many of our ideas about the urban–rural distinction are now obsolete or irrelevant.*

A third form of operational linkage concerns that of purposeful action. This now considerably entails complicated planning procedures which precede the action itself but may also continue during the action. This includes the whole process of thinking about our human future, taking thought for shaping it, and carrying the thought out into action. As the population–food–energy linkage presses increasingly upon us through the dynamic of population growth (demand for food and the depletion of fossil fuels), planning and management, whether done nationally or by subnational groups, must grow in importance and sophistication.

Three areas of capability are now available in the electronic technology for achieving higher levels of effectiveness in planning and management than at present. These are already either operational or rapidly becoming so. They are: the computer conference, the computer modelling of real world situations capable of delivering on-line information of complex kinds, and the universalized telecommunications capability. Microprocessing technology will very rapidly cheapen and widely diffuse these capabilities.

The proposals of Kupperman et al (1975) and Sackman and Citrenbaum (1972), the impending experimental work of Turoff (1976), and Beer's (1974a; 1975) work in Chile are the beginnings of a new level of effectiveness in taking action upon the various components of systems, with reasonable hope of generating prior knowledge of possible adverse effects. *This means that in the telecommunications–computer technology we have new tools to help us plan action such that ecosystems can safely support larger human populations at a total world aggregate level on the one hand, coupled with the ubiquitous transactional capability, such that human behaviour may be guided so as not to upset the balance that must be held between the capacity of the total system to sustain human populations and its ability to continue to maintain its own integrity intact, on the other.* The reciprocal, systemic nature of the relationships becomes clear.

The present situation suggests that the operational linkages between our two bodies of knowledge and practice are rapidly becoming progressively closer. At this point we should perhaps say this in another way in order to think in a fruitful mode: *the role of information, particularly as played through the help of the electronic technology, is becoming rapidly a very major component of our conceptualization of a single world system accounting for both 'natural' and 'human' processes.*

1.5 The mass individual as key component

Enquiry into our ecological knowledge and electronic technology is intended to be related to our general human concern. It will therefore be necessary to bring those bodies of knowledge and practice into conjunction with some area of knowledge about human beings. On the one hand, humans as groups and as individuals are components of ecosystems; their activities have great impact on them, and human beings are completely dependent on ecosystems for food and energy. On the other hand, the electronic technology is widely in use instrumentally for human living, is very considerably itself an influence on human behaviour, and greatly enhances human capability for dominating ecosystemic processes. The tendency, therefore, to move from the bodies of knowledge themselves to a focus of attention that can be described as human is, not surprisingly, already taking place in thinking and action in both fields.

In this century we have given a great deal of attention to searching out the failures of various societal arrangements and applying remedial measures. The dominant feeling has been the need to redress injustice in the structure and working of society in the interest of fair shares for all. There has also been great attention paid to increasing the efficiency of the production of physical goods and services. This, too, has been approached at the societal level. As a result of these emphases there is considerable literature relating our two areas of knowledge to society and its perceived issues, needs, etc (for example, National Academy of Engineering, 1969). This book does not attempt to duplicate that literature.

It is notable in such approaches that society is frequently assumed to be passive, like a ball of putty to be shaped and onto which the new knowledge or technology is to be pressed in the expectation of an inert acceptance. An ecologist may formulate a new ethic to govern behaviour toward the life-support system and offer it for assimilation by the society but may totally neglect the question of the dynamics of its acceptance; or a new piece of electronic technology may be put on the market to perform a present task 'more efficiently' than existing equipment without the entrepreneur realizing that the relevant societal function itself may be thereby radically changed.

The individual exists as a *given* component of the system *society–individual* at any particular time in the history of a society. The attribute most important for describing him is not his national security number, economic status, or the number of years in university. If we are to see the individual as something other than a stereotyped cypher we must look at his values, attitudes, behaviour patterns, and the fundamental assumptions or beliefs held about the world and himself. The nature of these attributes may be of crucial importance in assessing how societies will handle life-support questions and what uses will be made of the electronic technology. *Reconstructions of societal frameworks will not be sufficient to achieve much improvement unless they and the character and sensibility of the individual either are in accord or can be brought into a workable symbiotic relationship.*

In the thinking of both our fields there is interest in the mass individual as having certain commonly possessed characteristics. In the ecological field the call for a survival ethic is recognition of the idea that the present behaviour of the mass individual in large populations may be self-destructive. The essential view here is systemic—the question is far larger than a 'problem'—in that the behaviour of the individual when aggregated into the numbers of our large populations is destructive of the system's stability. Seen in this way, alterations in society's behaviour are possible only on the basis of change in the individual's behaviour. *Hence, ecologically speaking, those factors already in the mass individual's character profile that strongly influence his behaviour are of key importance.*

On the side of the electronic technology, its instrumentality operates very much through the individual to aggregate into behaviour which may, or may not, strengthen the systemic relationships between the individual and the society. When the mass individual is in a passive situation with what the technology offers, he is liable to undergo a uniform influence: individuals tend to react identically. The mass becomes made up of similar individuals whose values, etc tend to be identically shaped. If we want identically responding individuals the electronic technology is the way to it, but even here it is the individual who must be approached. The mass is an abstraction in this perspective. On the other hand, if we wish to discourage the above tendency (perhaps inherent in the use of the electronic technology), it is toward the strengthening of the individual as a unique character that we must turn

Whether we look at the human aspects of our ecological concern or the practice of our electronic technology, and whatever perspective of intentionality we take, we find signs indicating that we could usefully focus attention of the mass individual in his aspects of character profile and sensibility. *If mass societies are going to be viable over the long term the mass individual must willingly behave so that his behaviour when aggregated at the mass level is stable within the capabilities of the life-support system. Potentially the electronic technology is a powerful means for assisting in the achievement of this. But is is also a means for enhancing the ecologically destructive elements in the mass individual's behaviour. The mere fact of a technology being able to deflect more energy toward the human species can no longer be accepted as a guarantee of survival.*

We shall need to look carefully at what we can find out about the values, attitudes, and sensibility of the mass individual who is now the basic building block of our developed mass societies, and to identify possible important linkages between the individual and the society in the context of our two areas of interest (Musil, 1968; Ortega y Gasset, 1957; Steiner, 1971; 1974; Zolla, 1968).

1.6 The 'information society'
One such linkage must be mentioned at once because of its multidimensional relevance. This example is provided by evidence that suggests we should now regard ourselves as already in the 'information society'—to use the jargon of the literature. The evidence comes from an analysis of the US work force designed to make visible the proportion of workers now employed in 'information' work ['knowledge work', in Drucker's (1968) terminology] in America (Porat, 1976; Parker, 1976a). The embedding of an information sector into a conceptualized input–output model gives a picture of the new informational socioeconomy.

The simplest statement of the Porat–Parker analysis for our purpose is shown in figure 1.2. In the USA—we shall know from an OECD project in a year or two the degree to which some other developed countries are

going the same route—the number of workers employed in the production
of physical goods (secondary industry) reached its apex about 1950. Since
then it has rapidly fallen and is still declining. During the same period the
number of those employed in the Parker–Porat category of 'information
sector' has very rapidly risen but growth is now slowing down. The
information sector today employs just under one-half of the total work
force (calculated by using median estimates). There are also other measures,
such as the proportion of the GNP and the National Income earned by the
information sector. These three measures give indication of the change
from a predominantly manufacturing society in, say, 1950 to a well-
established information society in 1975.

Figure 1.2 points to the very important question of job availability.
The growth in the information sector has been compensating for the loss
in the sector producing physical goods since about mid-century. As things
stand, that situation no longer obtains, and the indications are of continuing
fall in the latter and slowed growth in the former. The result would appear
to be an overall reduction in job availability. This would be extremely
serious because in the developed societies the individual is ecologically
'niched' into society in a *production–job–wages–consumption* linkage.
He has long ceased to be a subsistence farmer held in place in the society
by the production–consumption linkage. The repercussions of a serious
weakness developing in the present sustaining linkage of the developed
countries would heavily influence attitudes toward the questions emerging
about the stability and productivity of ecosystems, particularly those
producing large quantities of food. The mass individual may well react to
the conditions of job difficulty by showing great unwillingness to behave
as may be ecologically necessary—for example by resisting the idea of

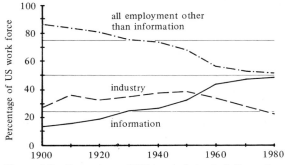

Figure 1.2. Percentage of US work force in information, industry, and all other than
information. The curves are based on median estimates of numbers of information
workers. The slackening of the information-worker curve between 1960 and 1970
and the projection of the same slower growth rate for 1970 to 1980 suggests that the
'information society' was essentially being generated in the period 1940–1960. The
present low gradient of the information curve coupled with the continued falling
gradient of the industry curve may be an important indicator of coming employment
difficulties (data from Porat, 1977).

'stabilizing' socioeconomies in their energy consumption or production of physical goods.

There is, therefore, need to pay attention to the increasingly strong relationships between the ecological demand on ecosystems, the behaviour and therefore values and sensibility of the mass individual, the nexus which holds the mass individual in the mass society, and the various linkages between these and the electronic technology. The latter, through its capacity to carry 'information' to the mass individual, can influence the individual's behaviour very considerably. At the same time its application drives us further into the information society by actually assisting the reduction of jobs in our present cultural–societal situation. Yet again, it is the one great medium which could hold mass populations to the required behaviour patterns by influencing the mass individual from outside himself. Seen in yet another perspective, the technology may actively prevent any such 'correcting' of the system's performance by allowing the mass individual to impose his attitudes upon the system to such an extent that the societal interest becomes submerged: the public will becomes the action, governments performing largely reactively.

There is, of course, no suggestion that the above comments can attempt to represent a full description of our condition. But it can be realistically maintained that the examination of such linkages must now be an important component of any attempt to say something useful about the present human situation. We have to think about our ecological concern in relation to a society which is transcending its traditional ways of relating the individual to the group and to its life support. In this nexus the role of the electronic technology is now crucial from the point of view of socioeconomic 'niching', 'control' of both societal and individual behaviour, the nature of the mass individual's character and sensibility, and the yet further development of information and its role. As we shall see, at least one country—Japan—has already done a great deal of thinking about these now very closely related matters.

The intermediate approach to our human concern has, therefore, three selected areas of origin: understanding of the life-support system, use of the capabilities of the regions of the electromagnetic spectrum, and the character profile and sensibility of the mass individual. These in their interrelationships generate secondary and tertiary foci of attention.

1.7 Degree of objectivization possible
Somewhat paradoxically we need also to be aware of difficulties in another direction. This is to question how far our technological rationality can be pushed, even in a context of the need for survival seen as possible only by the vigorous application of scientifically derived knowledge. Our dilemma can be expressed: only knowledge which is in accord with the working of the life-support system can possibly preserve that system, yet our motivation toward that kind of knowledge may not be adequate to

carry the process of application through at the required level. The acquisition and application of knowledge do not necessarily indefinitely inspire the motivation required for their own continued support. The assumption that they do is analogous to the mistaken eighteenth-century view that reasonable explanation would inevitably lead to reasonable action. In our global situation of population–food–energy pressure this misunderstanding could prove to be of tragic proportions. The systemic nature of 'mind' is of crucial importance in this context. The profile of the mass individual is already very possibly showing a diminishing tolerance for objective knowledge. We may already be facing the difficulty of knowing how to sustain our objectivity in a situation in which we feel its pursuit to have frozen out our individual sense of existential meaning. Some think a new kind of knowledge is required (for example Maslow, 1969). With this in mind I have taken a sceptical view of our contemporary naturalistic or 'mechanomorphized' approach to studying human beings[3].

1.8 A note on systems

The concept of system is a useful way of bringing items of knowledge together and of transferring knowledge across disciplinary boundaries. It has grown steadily since Bertalanffy's (1952; 1968) early work in the 1920s. The approach has been strengthened by Tansley's (1935) synthesis in ecology, the birth and explosive growth of cybernetics, and the application of the concept of system into fields ranging from the telecommunications–computer technology and operations research to neurological explorations and the ecological study of 'mind'. Today, the language of systems is a *lingua franca* linking many disciplines, and there is a considerable literature attempting unification under the concept of general system theory (see Bertalanffy, 1968). Such concepts as hierarchy or level of systems (see Feibleman, 1954), cyclicity, homeostasis, feedback, stability, diversity, telesis, etc are commonly used, with variations of detail, in a widening range of fields.

The idea of systems is closely related to the concept of hierarchical ordering. This is important to bear in mind since systems in a given hierarchy have different characteristics, increasing in complexity and capability as the hierarchy is ascended. We have seen this illustrated on the right of figure 1.1. The hierarchy can, however, be conceptualized in various ways. A useful way is to stress capability of function. In a well-known paper Boulding (1956) did this for the function of self-direction in systems. His range of systems is a helpful categorization for relating 'natural' and 'human' systems. (It is desirable to discontinue this dichotomy,

[3] Fromm (1968, page 94) very importantly points out that human character is a 'structure' which may take a variety of forms but has fixed parts in specific relationships. For example, if freedom is denied, resignation or aggression will be present. Thus in certain 'structures' objectivity may be seriously diminished. Our choice is between various kinds of 'structure'.

but it is still conventionally used.) Boulding's levels, in abbreviated form, are given in table 1.1, with the most complex at the top and the simplest at the bottom. As before, we should remember that no upper-level system can exist without the lower systems and that each upper level is capable of functions not possessed by the levels below; nor are the typical functions of an upper system inferable from the properties of a lower system. A system is greater than, or transcends, the sum of its parts (that is, of its lower systems).

Boulding uses his range of systems to indicate areas in which various disciplines do their work. Much of the thinking in physics, chemistry, economics, etc is conceptualized in level 2. In level 3 cybernetic controls are identified in living organisms and their societies as well as in automatic man-made machines. At the fourth level the entity is self-reproducing and is open in the sense that it exists only because of throughput of energy and information. As the range is further ascended, mobility and self-awareness increase in the organism until the top levels permit the grouping of organisms to form societies and consociations. Boulding concludes by expressing doubts as to whether "... we have as yet even the rudiments of theoretical systems" beyond level 4. Most of the theories in the social disciplines are in the second level and perhaps reaching into the third in

Table 1.1. Boulding's (1956) levels of systems.

Level	Key characteristics
9 Transcendental system	little known
8 Social organization	role of values, information, symbols, images
7 'Human' individual	self-reflexive capability, language, ability to interpret symbols, exists in time and history as self-knowing
6 'Animal' organism	increased mobility, teleological capability, specialized organs for handling information, highly developed nervous system with ability to structure complex information
5 Plant type of organism	division of labour by specialization of groups of cells, mutually interdependent, no highly specialized sense organs, very limited capacity for handling information
4 Open system	Self-maintaining structure, the cell, entity maintaining itself by throughput, self-reproduction
3 Cybernetic system	control mechanism, thermostat, simple equilibrium prescribed can be maintained, principle of homeostasis in natural and man-made systems [a]
2 Simple dynamic system	Clockworks, simple machines, equilibrium systems of the type of the solar system
1 Static structure system	Frameworks, anatomy, static constructions

[a] This designation of system at this level as cybernetic has not been generally adopted. All systems at and above this level have 'cybernetic' capability.

spite of the fact that the material they seek to handle is often in the eighth level. He goes on to comment that economics cannot yet conceptualize information as appearing in the third level, and cannot use concepts in levels beyond this. Fully workable theoretical models of systems can be regarded as reaching only up to level 4.

There are many reservations that can be made about Boulding's range of levels of systems but it remains a useful and readily accessible tool for our purpose.

The thought of this book owes a great deal to system concepts in several disciplines. The body of system thinking is used here, however, not so much with a descriptive emphasis as with an instrumental one: the general concept is used predominantly as a tool for thinking. System is a kind of metaphor, or model of thinking, which does nevertheless relate to the world outside human thought. Systems always include information, and always strive to preserve order and maintain negentropy.

Nevertheless, we should continuously bear in mind that ecosystems are descriptively systemic by the very nature of the discipline and its substance: *ecology describes a reality*. I have used also a descriptive assumption of the validity of systems thinking when trying to deal with the individual– society relationship; I tend to think of this, too, as a systemic reality.

To read the book it is not essential to be extensively knowledgeable about systems. The reader wishing to consult material in the field so as to reach a preliminary conclusion may like to look at the following: E P Odum (1969; 1975) for ecological systems, Porter (1969) for cybernetics, Bateson (1972) for 'mind' as system, Emery (1969) for a variety of disciplinary viewpoints on systems, and F H George (1970b) and Wiener (1967) for systems thinking about human societies. As systems approaches also very much include the application of knowledge to action, Churchman (1968), Mesarovic and Reisman (1972) and Beer (1975) are useful.

Although the background mode of thinking for the book is systemic, I am extremely cautious about the advisability of applying systems analysis techniques to societal matters in the present state of knowledge, and I have the very opposite standpoint to that which strives to make a system which is fixed and capable of being detailed in all its parts. There is here no system in the style of the Schoolmen, and certainly no notion whatever of an attempt to use or manufacture a framework of history after the manner of Mumford (1961), Sorokin (1957) or Reiser (1958). But broadly understood and used, systems approaches may help us to recapture some of the wonder—the $\theta\alpha\nu\mu\acute{\alpha}\zeta\epsilon\iota\nu$—with which the early Greeks looked out upon the world. That I take to be one of the most important likely benefits of systems approaches.

1.9 The need to be knowledgeable about the substance
In our present situation there is the ever greater danger of generating and implementing socioeconomic plans and policies based on inadequate

knowledge. The telecommunications–computer technology is capable of substantially helping us in this difficulty through improved information handling. Indeed, as Beer (1975) has already shown, the technology can be used to render workings of the socioeconomy 'transparent'—to borrow a piece of jargon from electronics. This means that the actual present state of the socioeconomy can be ascertained on a running basis pretty much in real time, eliminating the familiar lag in the currentness of information as at present used for governmental and business decisionmaking.

One of the implications of this on-line planning technique is the general need to be better informed. At present the major aspects of our two areas of new knowledge are not widely diffused, even among those who are responsible for plans and policies. Where there is a high level of familiarity with a body of knowledge there is generally a lack of information about other areas. Hence we find that those knowledgeable about the electronic technology usually know very little about ecology, and those well informed about ecology have little realization of what goes on in the field of the electronic technology. Familiarity with the substance is essential for the mind to be able to give sufficient weight to these bodies of knowledge *as substance* when their relationships with other matters are discussed, and action is planned.

1.10 A chain of reasoning

We might briefly define the underlying concern of the book as an attempt to probe the question of how to think about our emerging global condition in part describable in the following sequence:

1 Human beings must always live, in the long run, in ways that hold the behaviour of the society and the individual in an interrelationship that is workable within the ecological context (that is, in a single ecosystem or several interacting ecosystems).

2 At present this is achieved for large mass populations in the developed countries by the application of the very high-grade technologies connected with agribusiness and energy derived from ancient ecosystems. Very possibly this condition is not indefinitely maintainable, but to retreat to the food output and energy situation of an earlier time is equally unworkable without drastic falls in living standards, perhaps mass starvation and socioeconomic disintegration. We now know that we have an entirely new situation and perceive it globally.

3 *Not only is the mass individual geared to a certain pattern of behaviour, which aggregated to the level of society is causing whole populations to behave in ways probably destructive of their life support, but the socioeconomies are themselves weakened by their very technological successes.* The more the automation, the fewer the jobs, thus enfeebling the chief binding linkage of modern societies: production–job–wages–consumption. Present attempts to counteract that weakening tend to move in the direction of sharpening the ecological difficulty since there

is the temptation to allow, or create, socioeconomic activity at the risk of ecosystem degradation.

4 The well-tried way out of such difficulty has been traditionally the application of new knowledge in ever more sophisticated technology. This has meant an ever-increasing emphasis on objective knowledge. This has been very successful. We have found ways of increasing the world's output of food. *To achieve further increases, however, not only requires proportionally more inputs of energy than previous increases but will require much greater inputs of technological, managerial and other resources, which are all dependent on objective mental activity.*

5 But our pushing of the objective capability of the human being has already produced, in the developed countries, some revulsion and impairment of the motivation toward ecosystemically desirable behaviour. At the very moment when we urgently require the development of new knowledge and its application to the world system on behalf of the human enterprise we experience a reduction in that objective capability for learning and action, which are the only way we know to ensure our permanent viable survival in the life-support system of the world. *We do not know how far we can press a naturalistic view of the human being and society and still retain a strong will to action.*

6 Yet this crisis appears at a time when the human species has broken through the confining boundaries of its natural abilities, and has learned how to magnify enormously the power of both human muscle and human brainpower. Our capability for discovering what to do and carrying out the application is enormous and still growing fast. This, however, is no guarantee of our ability to reach a socioindividual nexus which will permit appropriate application on a global scale.

It is about such matters that we now have to think, learning how to keep them in mind simultaneously and seeing them in their interactions. For this, it is dangerous to think in 'problems' and 'solutions', and straight technological applications to supposed societal problems are no longer acceptable as necessarily workable. The view taken here is that present conventions in 'structuring questions or problems' should be viewed with scepticism; yet we have to feel for ways of generating structuralizations that are somewhere near the reality. To quote Stafford Beer (1974a, page 30) "... if we knew how to structure the problems properly, we could probably solve them, but we do not". We are constantly under the temptation to consider new situations in the perspective of outmoded structurings. The generated foci of attention in this book are therefore intended to serve as possible key areas of attention for future structuring. They are not all-inclusive and little attempt is made to weight them with any great precision. In our present condition I do not think that is possible, and it could well be damaging to the eventual development of an effective appreciation of relative values.

Part 1

Two areas of new knowledge

Two new areas of discovery and application are of great influence in the present phase of the human enterprise: the development of our ability to use the various areas of the electromagnetic spectrum, especially in communication and computation, and our understanding of the life-support system of the biosphere. These two areas progressively interact. The areas of knowledge are described and examples of the more important applications are examined.

Breakthrough: the electromagnetic spectrum

2.1 Key ideas

The view that the first half of the twentieth century achieved two humanly significant major breakthroughs in knowledge and practical application is a key idea of this study. The two areas of knowledge are:

1 The discovery and mastery of all the regions of the electromagnetic spectrum, encompassing a wide range of wavelengths, particularly those outside the wave band of human optical vision, especially important being the regions used for the computer–telecommunications technology.

2 The development of a firm understanding of the organization and workings of the life-support system of the earth. This knowledge lies in biology and ecology and may be referred to as the theory and comprehension of ecosystems, especially important being the potential application of this knowledge to the global condition.

A provisional hypothesis is that these two areas already strongly interact in ways as yet largely unexamined, that they will increasingly do so, and, further, that together they will make a very large contribution to a new stage of human cultural evolution which some think is already in its early phase. The coming stage can conveniently be referred to as *electrobionic* to the extent that it can be characterized by the dominance of these key ideas.

This chapter and the two following will look at the electromagnetic spectrum and the uses of certain regions, particularly focussing on electronic computation and communication.

2.2 Regions of the electromagnetic spectrum

Beginning with Hertz's 1888 demonstration that waves of electromagnetic energy could be propagated and would move outwards spatially from the point of propagation there was a series of discoveries concerned with radiation (Hertz, 1893). These discoveries aggregated into an understanding that there is a range, or spectrum, of wavelengths. As examples of applications we might take long-wave radio toward one end of the spectrum (say 10^3 metres) and gamma rays in nuclear fission reactors toward the other (10^{-12} metres). The energy transmitted varies with the wavelength. At the gamma ray end of the spectrum energy transmission is relatively high and can endanger living things. Atomic reactors usually have two metres of concrete protection against them. Danger to living tissue is generally thought to begin at the level of ultraviolet light. Very much less energy is transmitted at the long-wave radio frequency.

The regions of the electromagnetic spectrum can be described in order of increasing wavelength or decreasing frequency in cycles per second: cosmic rays, gamma rays, x-rays, ultraviolet light, visible light, infrared light, microwaves, radiowaves, and alternating current (when in a conductor).

Frequency is measured in the concept of *hertz* (Hz, after Heinrich Hertz), which combines time and cycle: one hertz is one cycle in one second; one megahertz (MHz) is one million cycles per second. The range is shown in figure 1.1 with the addition of the common uses of the various regions.

The properties and capacities of these regions are now well understood and our culture makes planned use of all of them except the cosmic ray region. Major significance for human beings lies in the fact that the capacities and capabilities of the different regions are varied, and what may be done in one region will not work at all in another. This is because, although the same laws apply, different properties predominate at different wavelengths. Radiation at the visible light wavelength is unable to penetrate most solid matter, but x-rays can. Gamma rays cannot be used for long-distance communication whereas those in the radiowave region are capable of being used over galactic distances. Human vision occurs along the range of the spectrum (as generally defined) at a wavelength of about 10^{-6} metres, or $10^{14 \cdot 5}$ hertz. The width of the visible region is very narrow compared with other regions.

During the long millenia of human development to the time when civilization emerged and during the relatively short period of those civilizations human beings have been able to use for communication, computational, and informational purposes only waves in air, in the form of spoken sound, and the narrow band of visible light. The use of the sound waves in air, which are not electromagnetic, was until recently restricted to immediate communication. Today tapes and discs break this restriction. Historically, in order to achieve permanency, conversion to the visible band in the electromagnetic spectrum has been used. This conversion is writing, and its receiving function, reading. To be able to shift communication in sound to communication via light was a major cultural step.

In civilizations before our own the conversion or transfer of information handling from sound to light enormously increased the scope of human culture, chiefly because it allowed systematic accumulation of precise information. But it also had limitations. The eye can see only a short distance and only at a certain scale. Although some modification was achieved by mechanical means, such as the telescope and the microscope, until recently civilizations have been limited in considerable degree to the possibilities permitted by human physical vision. This mode, together with mechanical means for reducing the spatial impediments to mental communication (for example, transportation), culminated in the Western civilization of, say, 1860. Information could be stored indefinitely on paper (light), and by mechanical means (train, boat, etc) the user and the document could be brought into operational physical relationship. At best the physical converter of information (the book, etc) had to be physically moved about. Only so could the shift from sound to light be effectively handled[1]. As the essential vehicle for information handling in all civilizations up to this time was the same narrow band of the electromagnetic spectrum through which the process of photosynthesis takes place, these civilizations might be termed *photobionic*.

Toward the end of the nineteenth century, on the basis of adumbrations shed by Newton, mathematically stated theory developed by Maxwell in 1865, and a series of demonstrations, researchers began to break into and master the capabilities of the whole electromagnetic spectrum. This ultimately placed in human hands the command of all its regions with their various potentials. The great period of discovery and operational mastery could be roughly given as 1900 to 1970.

2.3 Capabilities of the electromagnetic spectrum

It will be helpful to review briefly and in broad terms our already developed uses associated with the various regions of the electromagnetic spectrum.

2.3.1 Alternating current

Generation and mass transmission by copper or aluminium cable has been in widespread use since the beginning of this century. The making available of cheap electrical energy has produced major changes in industrial production, human settlement patterns, information handling, physical movement, business, and domestic life. It is the basis of much of our development of the other regions of the spectrum. The rapidly developing use of coaxial cable and waveguides also comes under this heading, and is very important because of the limited capacity of the regions of the spectrum for handling the rapidly growing volume of communication traffic if free radiation is used rather than radiation confined to cable or other guide.

2.3.2 Telecommunications

The capacity to transfer information across small or vast distances, either virtually instantaneously (at the velocity of light) or by using 'store and forward' techniques (hold and relay), depends at present on the use of wires (telegraph and telephone), various kinds of guides including coaxial cable, microwave (having relay stations in line of visibility every thirty miles or so), radio links, and satellites. This mixture of modes constitutes a worldwide system of very rapid intercommunication facilities of great flexibility. Waveguides, which are relatively expensive, are used for limited distances. Although these are physically more exacting than cable, these are capable of greatly increasing the number of circuits carried. The most important future development is likely to be in the use of the laser. The potential of fibre optics is already well appreciated. [The history of the

---

[1] The telegraph, however, gave an inkling of what was to come. General diffusion of it began in the 1840s. The telephone was invented in 1876. Radiotelegraphy effectively dates from Marconi, 1900.

growth of capacities of transmission modes is well illustrated in OECD (1973, Table 14).]

Material can be sent on these links in analogue or digital form, that is to say as a continuously variable signal like the voice, or as a discretely variable signal as for data characters. The trend is toward universal digitization—for audio, video, and data, including the voice on the telephone. Digitization of signal is extremely important for interlocking transmission facilities with the digital computer. It is the reduction of all signals to a common electrical pulse: a universal mode. *This ability to reduce all information to a single mode and send it over cosmic distances is one of the greatest achievements of our century.*

A major concept in telecommunications is that of trunks or highways joining large centres of population—successors to the grand trunk railways of an earlier age. Telecommunications have expanded very rapidly since the war. By using the Canadian Datran (OECD, 1973, page 149) transaction approach it is estimated the USA will experience a jump in transactions from 14 billion (14×10^9) in 1970 to 250 billion in 1980; calls will go from 3·7 to 32 billion, and the number of data terminals will increase from 185000 to 2·5 million. The arrival of public universal packet-switching with its capability for offering compatibility between all equipment and between national networks may make these estimates conservative.

2.3.3 Computation
It appears safe to state that by 1970 there were over 70000 computers in the world, representing with ancillary investment about US $100 billion. The number of computers does not, however, give an indication of usage. This is better shown by estimated compounded annual growth rate of remote data terminals. For example, the estimates for the increase in the USA are: 1970 to 1974—45% annually, and for 1974 to 1980—21%, aggregating in: securities, insurance, manufacturing, retailing, banking and finance, information services, health care (OECD, 1973, page 151). These figures mean that by 1980 there will be in the USA in those activities listed 2·5 million remote data terminals. The expected expenditures on digital computer systems and digital telecommunications systems between 1970 and 1980 in billions of US dollars are: USA 260, Japan 131, West Germany 78, UK 72, France 65, Canada 26, Switzerland 8.

The key benefit given by the computer is very rapid handling of very large quantities of data and their storage. Essentially this means not only an enormous increase in human computational ability and capacity to remember but also in ability to access information and to correlate data very rapidly. This greatly improved quantitative ability amounts to a qualitative improvement since computations that could not otherwise be tackled can be performed by the computer, allowing new areas of knowledge to be opened up. What is crucial, therefore, is the symbiosis between the computer—an artificial 'intelligence'—and the human brain.

Although based on the same breaking of the bond of time as was the invention of writing, the computer is perhaps a potentially more influential invention than writing for human cultural development, and perhaps comes second only to speech in human total development. Computers are now in rapidly expanding use from reserving air travel tickets to calculating precisely where a surgeon is to make an incision in the human cranium. Norbert Wiener (1967, page 89) had identified by 1950 the key significance of the digital computer: "... the sharpness of the decision between 'yes' and 'no' permits it to accumulate information in such a way as to allow us to discriminate very small differences in very large numbers".

The development of the miniaturization of circuits on silicon chips will very rapidly promote the diffusion of the microcomputer and will greatly increase the use of full-scale computers in the next decade. Changes may therefore be expected in the way computers are used, located, accessed, and owned. We shall have to revise our present conceptualizations of what a computer is, what it does, and how we use it. The present evidence suggests that location of the computer will be very much less important than it is at present, and that the microprocessor (microcomputer) will become ubiquitous in its uses both in its own right and as the access equipment to other electronic capabilities such as transmitting, computing, storing, and sophisticated processing of information.

2.3.4 Telecommunications and computers

During the 1960s scientific, technological, and entrepreneurial developments brought these two fields progressively together. This trend continues. Together they are a potential global cerebral cortex. In close combination, as they now are, they constitute not merely an immensely powerful group of interrelated tools, but in conjunction with the development of the electronic mass media, they are a new cultural environment. As Zolla (1968), McLuhan (1964), and others insist, these tools do not operate within the environment, nor do they describe it simply. They have become the environment.

Technically the most significant relationship between telecommunications and the computer is that all inputs to or outputs from the computer can be carried by the telecommunications networks. Therefore, in theory at least, all that the computer can do can be done anywhere there is access to the telecommunications system. The telecommunications capacity is a vast increase in the human sensory scope of hearing and seeing; the computer is an enormous addition to certain of our mental powers. The friction of space is capable of being eliminated as far as information handling is concerned. As both telecommunications and computers operate at the speed of light the traditional time lag for the processing and transfer of information hitherto inherent in the distances of terrestrial space may also be virtually eliminated. (The lag electronically is approximately one-quarter of a second for communication by satellite, and to the moon and back is two and one-half seconds.) Alternatively, time may be manipulated as we wish in the forward sense—material once processed may be accessed any time. The implications for the spatial and temporal aspects of transactions and therefore for the patterns of human behaviour and settlement are only just beginning to be examined. *These implications may be at least of the same order of magnitude for human cultural development as the neolithic breakthrough into settled agriculture, and the later invention and early diffusion of writing.* Compare Childe (1951).

2.3.5 Monitoring, control, and control systems

Through the greatly enhanced capacity to deal with information, the telecommunications and computer technology offers greatly improved ability to monitor and control. We can now store, process, and access information so that it can be brought to bear more effectively on changing situations. This improves the quality of decisionmaking, on the assumption that the better the knowledge on which it is based, the more likely is the decision to be effective. International-trade decisions can be improved by processing up-to-date information about commodity prices and currency rates, or better protection achieved against typhoon damage by picking up information from a satellite. The way is opened for very rapid decision-making based on up-to-the-minute information—the possibility of real-time on-line planning.

In addition to the generality of improved control there is the large field of control systems which use either or both of the technologies for control through the use of linked devices, concepts, or characteristics. Examples are: control systems used in manufacturing industry for producing goods through automated runs; automatic equipment such as elevators and telephone exchanges; accounting systems; signalling and totally automated control of trains; inventory and allocating systems; flight control of aircraft and spacecraft; quality control; homeostatic devices; traffic control; and control of learning (teaching machines), etc. Electronic control systems now touch virtually every aspect of life. Specifically, almost every technology we use is heavily dependent on them, whether it is baking bread or running an intensive care unit. This dependency will doubtless grow as technology becomes ever more sophisticated. These systems are noteworthy for their common use of every region of the electromagnetic spectrum, including gamma rays (used for medical photography), with the possible exception of the cosmic ray region. Very frequently they involve the capabilities of regions in combination so as to transfer information from one region to another. Very often it is precisely because of this capacity for transfer that the control can be achieved.

2.3.6 Broadcast diffusion

It is a sobering thought that the wave fronts of all the *I Love Lucy* shows still exist as they move outwards spherically from the earth into space.

Characteristically the spectrum regions used for radio and television allow the general diffusion of enough power for many receivers to pick up the signal. This has been exploited for informational, marketing, and entertainment purposes, reaching everyone in our dense metropolitan areas. These 'services' are regional and national, the latter being achieved by linking the transmitters in various regions together by land line. In general the physical range of radio transmitters is larger than that of TV stations because of reflection off the ionosphere. These services are expensive and have to be paid for by governments or commercial advertising or both. This factor of cost, together with other factors, brings in governments, who are aware of the societal aspects of these diffusion systems and try to exercise some control by means of quasi-public agencies like the British Broadcasting Corporation and the Canadian Radio and Television Commission[2].

An important factor here is that since the number of channels that can be used simultaneously in the radio (including TV) regions of the spectrum is limited, there have to be strict allocation rules which take into account the effective territorial extent of the diffusion from the point of propagation, the population being served, and the power of the transmitter. We have to think of a continent, therefore, as a geographically described collection of circles with their centres (the transmitters) located in the major urban areas, because this is where exist the mass markets whose mass audiences will buy the detergents that pay for the *Lucy* show. Some of these circles, particularly the TV ones, are linked and provide identical programmes. In North America the radio circles are local only, for the most part (an exception is the Canadian Broadcasting Corporation). They have learned to cater to specialized audiences. The TV stations are now probably entering this specialized phase of development. So far, radio and TV diffusion is a one-way process and the two systems are almost never used to support each other. Very small beginnings of interaction appear in the public being able to answer back through the use of hot lines—the invitation to the listener or viewer to telephone in to the programme while it is on the air. Very occasionally an FM channel may be used for the audio of a high-quality TV music programme, the viewer receiving the image on the TV but the sound through the radio set.

2.3.7 Cable TV (CATV) and other services

CATV consists of distributing the signals from several TV stations by land line to subscribers in a local area. It is a way of circumventing the limitation that the number of channels in the TV region of the spectrum is severely limited. Through CATV an area of dense population can have access to many more channels than it could have by direct diffusion. The cable company picks up the signals on a special antenna and distributes by coaxial cable that has a channel capacity considerably greater than the number of channels at present usually available. For example, the

[2] Now Canadian Radio-Television and Telecommunications Commission.

Metropolitan Toronto area (approximately two million population) of the Great Lakes by mid-1976 had on offer twenty-five channels, with some duplication of programmes. At that same date cable companies and the Canadian Radio and Television Commission were beginning to struggle with the probable addition of pay-TV to the cable systems. This might allow the subscriber about eight additional contemporary films per month on payment of a separate charge.

An interesting feature, in cultural terms, of cable companies is that their licences frequently require them to dedicate one channel to local community interests without charge. This is important because it opens the way to entirely new uses of TV capacities: public participation; locally produced programmes; routine information services such as weather reports, news, etc; and advertising by local firms—functions not possible on the national networks. Most importantly CATV offers the probability of the viewer being able to participate by answering back. Although there are difficulties of switching, multiple answering back could be coped with by the cable. It is also possible that telephone systems could provide a participatory service for TV programmes. Whichever way this comes, it will be a revolution in our present passive attitudes to TV. The unused cable capacity also makes the palms of entrepreneurs itch. What could it be used for? Education? Retailing? Monitoring of the environment? Political discussion? Public access to computers and databanks? All these, and other possibilities, are receiving close attention.

Up to the present almost no attention has been paid to the radio and TV diffusion services in planning our metropolitan regions. The absence of attention to this and to the telecommunications and computer technology suggests the question whether our metropolitan regional settlement patterns accord with the realities of everyday existence. Many transactions which at present require physical movement (for example, commuting to downtown) could be done wholly or in part electronically if computing and transmission facilities were more effectively used (see Harkness, 1973).

2.3.8 Locating spatially

Radiation in the microwave region of the spectrum can be used for measuring physical distance by a process of reflecting the emission back to the point of propagation. This is radar. It allows very rapid calculation of distance, and in conjunction with the computer delivers accurate information about the changing distance of a moving object like an aircraft or a speeding car that a policeman wishes to check. This technology is very important for air and sea navigation, weather information gathering, etc. It could be very valuable in developing traffic control techniques in large cities where vehicular congestion is an unsolved problem. Laser technology is also increasingly used for spatial measurement, and is the basis of modern survey technique.

2.3.9 Seeing into matter

Gamma ray, x-ray, and neutron photography and crystallophotography, are used to render the interior of material visible. Some of these techniques have extensive uses in medicine and industry, in both of which the technologies are used also for control purposes. In the ecological field multispectra techniques based on these capabilities are now of rapidly rising importance.

2.3.10 Conversion of sound

In addition to conversion from one region of the electromagnetic spectrum to another (for example from the x-ray to the visible), the technology can convert from sound (a wave motion in air) to waves in various regions of the spectrum. Thus the spoken word may be converted into analogue or digital form. It may be recorded on a light-sensitive sound track or a magnetic tape. This conversion of sound into the modes of the regions of the spectrum is, of course, extremely important because it ensures that the spoken word and vision can be related to each other and to the rest of the spectrum. This allows living, spoken communication to go anywhere in the world or out into space at the speed of light. The principle of conversion or extension is illustrated in figures 13.1 and 13.2.

2.3.11 Feedback and playback

The various regions of the spectrum are able to use the principle of the feedback loop. The study of feedback has become the recognized discipline of cybernetics, and has done much to help develop the concept of systems in other disciplines. The principle is used in control systems of all kinds, including societal systems. In terms of the human individual, playback of sound and vision of self-activity may amount to a very important tool for self-awareness and development (Ryan, 1974). In the technology, this is essentially storage and access—tapes, discs, and other highly manipulable devices for giving back on demand. It allows the individual to be a spectator of, and a participant in his own action. Thus the relationship between the actor and the audience is raised to a triadic level—the actor, the audience, and the actor-as-audience. The possibly great importance for human development of this technique of infolding is only just beginning to be probed. Biofeedback is of this kind.

2.3.12 Simulation

Electronic techniques offer remarkable opportunities for imitating or simulating conditions, relationships, or functions existing in the world. For example, it was early discovered that the thermionic valve, which will pass current in one direction only, could be used to make a yes–no choice or to mimic the working of the synapses of the nervous system (F H George, 1961). Thus certain mental functions, for example some aspects of memory and learning, can be simulated.

By using mathematical statements of relationships it is possible to simulate the functioning of quite complex systems that would otherwise be largely beyond our comprehension. Transportation models of large metropolitan areas which may assume a conceptual modal split of transportation movement between public transit and privately owned vehicles are of this kind. The 'system' is first conceptualized and then its working or functioning is simulated. In examining the simulation the analyst is looking at the system as conceptualized, not at the 'reality'. The match between system and reality can be checked, for some features, by comparison with the behaviour of the actual city. This type of combined conceptualization—simulation technique may perhaps be applicable to societies. Models of a national economy have already been attempted, and models of specific subsystems have now a considerable literature. Simulation is inevitably wrapped up with systems thinking, which, of course, provides the conceptualizations necessary for applying the techniques of simulation. The simulation is chiefly limited by the degree to which the system simulated is understood. That is, weaknesses in modelling may well lie not in the simulation but in our understanding of what we are trying to model.

2.3.13 Miniaturization

It is characteristic of electronic processes that they can take place in very small physical space. Electronic equipment gets smaller and smaller and, in Buckminster Fuller's phrase, gives "more for less". In 1950 about twenty cubic inches were usually required for one circuit. By 1960 a circuit occupied a cubic inch; by 1966 the same space would accommodate ten circuits (Martin and Norman, 1970, page 9). In addition the capacities of the circuits increased dramatically. During the 1960s the technology of the silicon chip carrying an integrated circuit with many components (large-scale integrated circuits—LSI) developed rapidly. Ten components on a single chip of less than one square centimetre were possible by the middle of the decade. By 1976 the same chip could carry an integrated circuit of over thirty thousand components. Still further miniaturization will take place in the near future. The development of integrated circuits on silicon chips has led to the invention of the microprocessor (1971, M E Hoff). This consists of the logical element of the computer being engraved on a single chip and combined with storage techniques such as the bubble memory. Microprocessors are microcomputers capable of computational functions in their own right, and also, most importantly, capable of interacting with other equipment, including full-scale computers. Microprocessors have made possible the virtual terminals and virtual circuits of universal shared packet-switching (section 4.3). An explosive growth of microprocessing may be expected as its applications proliferate, especially when coupled with telecommunications.

Along with reduction in size goes rapid fall in cost; so equipment becomes portable and cheap. A notable example in the last few years has been the electronic hand calculator. From being a $500 luxury in the early 1970s it has now become an essential tool from high school upwards. These two factors—portability and cheapness—are obviously of great potential cultural and societal importance. Hand-held radios, cassette tape recorders, buzz boys, calculators, and telephones (under test in New York, 1977), now fit into mass man's pocket. He can listen live, or in delayed time, to the tintinnabulations of his favourite rock group; he can be called up by his boss; he can record his sublime thought before it flits, or remember to bring home the milk, having accurately computed the small change. All this can be done as he walks or drives about, and some of these abilities may be combined.

2.3.14 New knowledge

The capabilities of the various regions of the spectrum assist the discovery of new knowledge at what is often described as an exponential rate. Not only has our technology become heavily dependent on the exploitation of the regions of the spectrum but so has science. In moving into this dependency both have become opaque to commonsense: our knowledge is no longer obviously comprehensible. Future developments in both science and technology will be likely to rely still more heavily on these capabilities, if only because the capabilities are mutually supportive. So although we have the expectation of a great growth in knowledge we also must expect that precise understanding of many key ideas and abilities will become less and less possible for ordinary people. Clearly scientists will have an increasing responsibility to explain what they do. Almost all growing edges of science now have a considerable dependency on expanding technologies based on our knowledge of radiation. Some of these edges are full of excitement. For example, Carl Sagan (1975b, page 153) comments: "There are new windows in the electromagnetic spectrum: Gamma-ray, x-ray, ultraviolet and certain kinds of infrared and radio astronomy are possible for the first time". Sagan is an exobiologist interested in life outside the earth.

2.4 Conclusion

To sum up, the major capabilities that the human species has been able to develop on breaking through into the whole range of the electromagnetic spectrum include: alternating current transmission; telecommunications; computer capacity; control systems; broadcast diffusion; cable distribution (CATV); spatial locating (radar and laser); seeing into matter; conversion of sound; feedback techniques; simulation; miniaturization; and the development of new knowledge. These capabilities are now highly developed, are generally used, and interact closely with each other. *Quietly they have become the very bases of our culture. It is not just that the medium is the message. It is that our mastery of the electromagnetic spectrum is very substantially the culture.* The ambience which the uses of its regions creates is a major component of our daily environment, directly through our uses of the equipment—telephone, TV, radio, computer, etc—and indirectly through the way in which these uses impose change in other things and in their relationships.

In the next two chapters we shall look at some of the more important areas of our mastery of the regions of the electromagnetic spectrum, beginning with teleconferencing. The reader requiring a more detailed but still readable overview may like to consult Martin and Norman (1970); this book deals with the technologies and some of their implications for society.

Computer and telecommunications technologies: 1

Various ways of interacting at a distance between humans and machines have been developed by using different applications of the electronic technology. Some of the more interesting techniques are examined in this chapter and the next because of their very important actual and potential effects on many aspects of contemporary life—work, leisure, education, government, business and industry, patterns of human settlement, and our images of ourselves[1]. In this chapter we shall look at teleconferencing.

All modes described have the characteristic that they are two-way although not necessarily carried on in on-line, real-time modes. They are thus clearly distinguishable from the mass media as at present developed. These are virtually exclusively one-way communication. The various techniques of teleconferencing to be described provide different degrees of interaction and have different theoretical approaches.

3.1 Audio teleconferencing

The simplest form of electronic meeting or teleconferencing uses sound only and consists of a variety of detailed ways of bringing individuals and groups together for live discussion by using the telephone system or other links.

Conferencing by telephone is generally available in the developed countries. Typically, several locations can be connected; handsets or loudspeaking phones and voice-switching are used. The Trans-Canada Telephone System offers up to eight locations with up to four participants at each. In Britain, Confraphone and certain specially developed services, such as 'remote meeting table' (for example, used by a department of government) and educational links, extend the use of the telephone to multiple participation. Special applications, such as the NASA conference system, the link between the Department of Communications Canada and the Communications Research Centre, the University of Quebec conference system, and the University of Wisconsin system for its educational extension services (173 locations) now result in a considerable variety of experience in relatively simple modifications of the typical one-to-one telephone service. Some techniques, for example the Canadian National/Canadian Pacific Telecommunications, use 'broadband' transmission. This allows a larger number of participants but appears to present certain user difficulties.

A good deal of attention has been paid to adding video to the telephone. A small monitor allows the speakers to see each other or display graphic and written material. These systems are called picturephone, videophone, viewphone, visiophone, etc. The quality of the picture is limited if

---

[1] An inventory of the various telecommunications-computer projects and experiments being initiated around the world is being undertaken by B Lefèvre on behalf of the French government. The list comprised over two thousand entries by fall 1976.

conventional slow-speed transmission is used, and the visual space is not a common space as provided by the Wired City Facility (see below). The participants cannot therefore work on the same document or display, but must each have a copy of the document. Early expectations of picture-phone do not now seem likely to be fulfilled. It is used for certain specialized purposes such as in medicine and engineering, where a certain level of visual display is commonly needed. Such uses are, however, somewhat restricted by the limitations of the technology for displaying visual material and computer-generated alphanumeric output. The band-width is about one-fifth of that used for broadcast TV. A switched-facility videophone for the general public does not at present appear viable.

Various areas of possible improvement in audio conferencing have been identified and further development seems very likely. So far, however, for reasons by no means entirely clear, audio conferencing has not come into widespread use. In the Apollo programme, NASA calculated that from three to five dollars in travel costs could be saved by each dollar spent in audio teleconferencing (Canada, Department of Communications, 1976b, volume 1, page 4). This suggests that the technique has a very considerable potential for reducing conferencing costs. Yet development appears slow. In Canada, for example, over the last twenty years only approximately 12000 conferences per year have taken place on the Trans-Canada Telephone System. Bell Canada's research shows that 20% of bus, rail, and air business trips might well be regarded as being capable of being substituted by telecommunications—in the opinion of the 30000 individuals actually taking trips who completed questionnaires (Bell Canada, 1972).

Under this heading we must also include citizens band (CB) radio. This allows the use of certain channels for two-way telephonic communication between members of the public. Transmission requires a licence. This is issued for a nominal fee and without any serious examination of skill or knowledge, as required for an amateur radio transmitter's licence (capability in morse code, etc). The US Federal Communications Commission has recently increased the CB channels from twenty-three to forty. The equipment can be freely purchased. It is commonly used by truck drivers, but in the last few years the general public interest in the mode has rapidly increased, particularly in the US.

The equipment sends out a signal broadcast in the same way as police, firefighting, etc radio nets. Any transmitter tuned to the wavelength being used can participate in the conversation. This is therefore a teleconferencing mode: several participants can interact two-way. Since anyone can have access for transmitting on any channel, interference in a teleconference is difficult to control. As range is generally relatively short—a few kilometres— this problem is settled informally; conventions for appropriate behaviour tend to develop. However, the use of a channel for a protracted discussion would seem difficult, particularly as the use of the mode grows and load on channels becomes heavier.

In spite of this difficulty the possibility of CB, or something very similar, becoming a way of serious teleconferencing needs to be kept in mind. It could be extremely useful for certain purposes. For example, on the campus of a large university the institution would probably be able to dominate the use of a good proportion of the total number of channels available, and control their use centrally. This would make possible interdepartmental seminars without individuals having to move between buildings. A channel would simply be booked in advance. The same equipment could be used for disseminating live material of common interest, such as lectures by outstanding speakers.

In conjunction with CB we should also note the possibility of directional rather than broadcast dissemination. This would reduce interference and allow simultaneous multiple use of a channel even in highly congested centres such as central business districts, campuses of government offices, research centres and universities.

In the US, Canada, and some other countries the demand for CB licences has increased very rapidly in the last two or three years. By early 1977 there was considerable evidence of the likelihood of a further very rapid growth. Technologically, mobile radio is developing very fast. Interaction with a remote computer is now possible and in 1977 experiments using pocket telephones with radio links to the general telephone system were being made in the New York area. Mobile radio and the use of fibre optics technology now seem likely to be able to provide very good telecommunications services to farming and rural nonfarm populations. Coupled with the slowing up of the growth of metropolitan areas it may prove influential in shaping new distribution patterns of population.

3.2 Audio-video teleconferencing: Wired City Facility
This is an experimental network located in the Systems Engineering Department of Carleton University in Ottawa, Canada. The original intention, crystalized in 1969, was to develop an experimental system "... oriented toward both the application and the technology of broadband communications" (Coll, 1973; Coll et al, 1974; Wired City Laboratory, 1974; D A George et al, 1975). The motivation for developing this particular technique included *the desire to explore the design and use of a two-way system of a kind that would avoid imposing rigid constraints and would allow maximum user control, such that the individual might be able to enjoy audio-video communication at will.* This would be the basic concept of a future wired city on the ground. The phrase 'wired city' implies extensive use of the electronic technology including coaxial cables such as are used for cable TV, etc.

This experimental network, which became operational in 1971, was developed in the context of many experiments going on all over the world, related to contemporary technological advances in this field. These included: videophone; cable TV; use of the cable system for shopping, information services, etc; teleconferencing; telemetering; the use of home terminals; interactive educational systems; and generally exploring the potential of the increasingly close relationship between the computer and telecommunications. The vision was of an emerging world in which the individual would become considerably reliant on this technology in normal daily living. A key concern, therefore, was to design a system which would *ensure maximum user choice*, thereby enhancing the effectiveness of communication. The devised network was multiuser and multipurpose, ranging in capability from formal information storage and retrieval capability, such as for library material, to person-to-person and group-to-group discussion. In concept the system would therefore truly be of the type required for the basic general all-purpose communications network of society—whether 'city' or other. The facility should be seen as capable of providing a general common level of service, in much the same light as we view the ubiquitous availability of electrical energy or the telephone.

After several years of experimental work covering a wide range of interests connected with audio–video conferencing and information

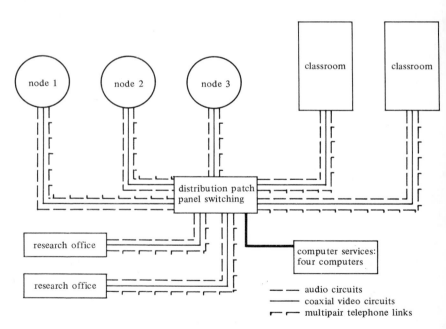

Figure 3.1. Wired City Project in Carleton University, Ottawa. The system generates a common audio–video electronic space in which all participants can see and hear each other continuously, and can show display material. All participants can 'write' or 'draw' on any material displayed, simultaneously if required. Complete audio–video recording with replay is provided. Because of the exigencies of diagramming, the distribution panel has undue visual prominence. In operation it is not a control centre; the participants themselves decide the switching.

retrieval, the equipment achieved, by 1977, an adequate level of refinement and automation to make possible an experimental public service. This consists of linking the facility to a cable TV system in Ottawa so that stored information can be retrieved by the cable TV subscriber on demand through a touchtone telephone. The subscriber calls up the Wired City, asks his question, and receives the reply on his TV screen in alphanumerical form. About one hundred firms in the Ottawa area have deposited information in the computer.

The original proposal for the experimental network was for inter-connecting, by coaxial cable, four locations in Ottawa (Bowen et al, 1971). This was later modified to setting up multistation audio and video transmission and receiving facilities in separate rooms in a building in Carleton University. The rooms simulated users' access to the network— teleconferencing, teaching–learning, interaction with computers, etc (see figure 3.1). The emphasis of the network was therefore for use as a laboratory rather than as a field facility.

By 1972 the objectives were:

" • to design and implement a flexible laboratory for testing and evaluation of broadband communications and information services for business, teaching, research, the community and the home.
• to provide multipoint audio, video and data communications and to have the capability for monitoring the communications processes in a variety of ways.
• to conduct a program of research into the effects on the individual, on groups, and on society at large, of the expanding capabilities of readily available communications and information handling systems.
• the investigation of the technological alternatives that might be used to provide any or all of these widespread information services.
• to create an impetus for technological innovation, product development, and academic research" (Coll et al, 1974, page 9).

The technical research included the design of a data system, exploration of video-based information storage and retrieval, narrow-band image transmission and software systems, and simulation of wired city services. The humanistic research covered user behaviour, effects of the media on communications, study of human communication processes, surveys of user attitudes, design of terminals, etc. Eight major groups of exercises and experiments were conducted up to February 1974: teleconferencing effects, the impacts of different communications systems upon risk-taking in groups, simulated disarmament negotiations, effects of teleconferencing on urban and regional planners' activities, typical human relations concerned with leadership roles, seminars in psychology, use of the switching centre and one node by Bell Northern Research, and the effects of mediated communication on the quality of the solution of problems. User impact assessment studies were also carried out.

By mid-1974 the control policy aimed to:

" • Construct those models of possible future communications facilities
     which can be practically achieved using state-of-the-art technology.
  • Simulate the technology of tomorrow using existing technology to
     demonstrate its potential applications.
  • Animate the services of tomorrow using existing special effects
     technology to demonstrate their potential effect on existing
     services" (Coll et al, 1974, page 19).

The typical individual terminal, or node, equipment consists of a
number of monitors mounted at the back of a desk at which two persons
can sit; two video cameras—one to take the head and shoulders of the
user and one overhead to cover an area of the desk on which graphic

Figure 3.2. Wired City, Carleton University: individual terminal, May 1973. The
camera picking up the head and shoulders of the user is visible just above the
microphone. The overhead camera picks up material displayed on the right-hand end
of the desk. The larger, central monitor can give eyeball-to-eyeball contact. One
monitor gives the outgoing picture of the user. From each incoming node there is a
picture of the user and of whatever he wishes to display. Note that the user has a
continuous view of the faces of all participants, as in a small live meeting. (Photo
courtesy of Wired City, Carleton University.)

material can be placed; a microphone; four speakers; and a control panel. The user of any node can see and hear the users of all the other panels continuously; can command a close-up of any other single user; can display any graphic or written material in such a way that any other user can amend it; can have full audio–video taping and replay; and can see and hear himself and see his own display material on a small monitor. Hence all signals originating from any node can be received by all other nodes and, in the case of visual display material, can be superimposed or blended. Each node generates two TV images (the head and shoulders of the user, and the display material). A terminal, as of May 1973, is shown in figure 3.2. The overhead camera for display is clearly visible; the lens of the camera photographing the user is just to the right of the top of the microphone. A minimum terminal for an office is shown in figure 3.3.

A very important technical aspect of the network is that the video signals are synchronized from a single generator. The switching is by means of a patch panel, giving great flexibility, and easily allowing special effects, and recording, replay, etc. Although the distribution system has surplus capacity it is worth noting that for five nodes the equipment includes fourteen coaxial cables, eight audio cables, and a multipair telephone cable. This is a heavy requirement for connecting links (figure 3.4).

The more recent design of the terminal allows the node to be used for remote teaching, remote learning, group seminars, and teleconferencing. The reorganization of the switching allows simultaneous use for several independent experiments, and permits split-screening and superimposition of data onto the recorded picture. This last allows a teacher to write over a computer-derived image appearing on a monitor (see figure 3.5).

Figure 3.3. Wired City: the office terminal. The illustration shows a minimum terminal for office, or similar use. It incorporates a normal TV set and two small monitors, one of which can display the outgoing video signal. The microphone is on top of the TV set and the video camera, picking up the image of the operator, is below it, in the middle. (Photo courtesy of Wired City, Carleton University.)

Figure 3.4. Wired City: distribution centre. The switching centre of the Wired City is not so much a centre controlling the network as an exchange for giving maximum flexibility to the users of the network. The patch panel is on the right. The monitors are visible above the back of the chair. Note the overhead camera for handling material displayed. All images can be blended. (Photo courtesy of Wired City, Carleton University.)

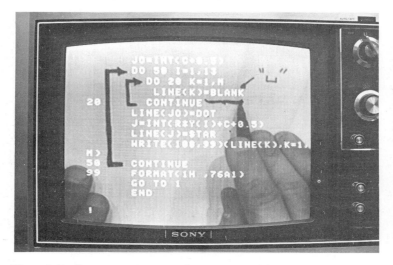

Figure 3.5. Computer printout with superimposed handwritten comment. The Wired City technology allows the superimposition of writing or drawing on top of a live display from a computer. This is extremely valuable for instructional purposes. (Photo courtesy of Wired City, Carleton University.)

As the idea of the Wired City implies considerable human interaction with the computer and other electronic machines (for example, recording devices) the continuing research includes study of human–computer relationships in relation to the network. This interface is being explored with the use of keyboards, light pens, displays, digital technology, language recording, optical character recognition, and includes text-in-speech-out processing. The programme will permit the equipment to read the written text and deliver words by voice, pronounced (87%) and spelled out (13%). Gradually it is expected to achieve spoken sentences.

In 1976–1977 an engineering-sharing project was carried out between Carleton University, Stanford University, the NASA/Ames Research Center in California, and the Ministry of Communications Canada (Ottawa). This used advanced digital techniques in conjunction with the Communications Technology Satellite (joint US–Canada, 1976). The project was oriented toward the development of both the technology and the applications, and included formal and informal interaction. The Stanford end used the facilities of their Instructional Television Fixed Service, which has operated from 1969 and now offers some sixty courses to over one thousand students.

From May 1974 the network was discontinued for general teleconferencing use to allow concentration of effort on educational technology. A full description of the equipment, its uses, and the experiments is in Coll et al (1974).

The Carleton Wired City kind of circuitry has certain very great advantages and a major difficulty. The advantages are its flexibility and its capacity for giving a very close approximation to face-to-face interaction between individuals or groups of individuals located widely apart. The circuitry produces a *common space* in which the individuals on the various nodes can see and hear each other as though in a face-to-face committee. We have already noted that picturephone does not provide the common space either for faces or for document display. Certainly there are differences between the electronic meeting and the flesh-and-blood one. The messages of body language, for example, are somewhat restricted on the network, and the details of the face on a screen are not as precise as in real life. In compensation, however, the network allows the observer to study another's face for any length of time without causing embarrassment. So we may expect some differences in behaviour as between the network and real life, similar, perhaps, to the putting on of a telephone voice. It would be easy to make too much of these differences. Even supposing there is some loss, against that loss we have to place the advantages of spanning distance with a level of verisimilitude in personal interaction far outranging any mode yet devised. To this we must add the great advantage of being able to *superimpose* graphics for display purposes. The value of this is worth illustrating. One node might have the typed text of a legal bill for discussion. The other nodes would have no written material but would receive the image. By superimposing the overhead camera inputs of

C

all nodes, each participant could write in his individual amendments to the text. The end result is a videotape showing the steps by which the final version was reached, the final version itself with amendments, each initialled in the margin, and an audiotape recording the discussion. Such a capability could have very widespread applicability wherever material in document form has to be discussed and answered: medicine, engineering, the law, government, etc.

The major difficulty of the Wired City system concerns general application on an area-wide basis with many subscribers. The desideratum is to be able to provide *random* interconnections on demand as is now available on telephone systems by dialing or digital touchtone. If such circuitry is to be the basis of a general electronic information system the subscriber wants to be able to dial up simultaneously a few other subscribers and then have available the capabilities that have been described. Switching for such a service would be extremely complex and expensive at present. It would be even more difficult to switch the Wired City than to convert cable TV to a two-way system by using the 'hub' technique. The intractability of this problem suggests that it will be a long time before this form of teleconferencing could provide a random-access dial-up service. Its selected-access use is, however, very possible in some form or other—between major nodes as in the Carleton–Stanford example, or between cities or countries. This is particularly so in view of the qualitative improvements being achieved in satellite and other technology.

3.3 Teleconferencing by computer

This technique consists basically of each participant using a computer terminal to type out his contribution to the discussion and to receive the inputs of the other participants. Audio facilities may also be included. The terminal shows on its display screen all material going out, and what is selected for display coming in, in plain language. The computer transfers the material between participants, stores it, retrieves it automatically and on demand. As the signal is digitized, normal telephone transmission can be used. If audio conversion is used, the handset is simply placed in a connecting box and the participant dials up the computer. This method of conferencing can therefore make use of cable, microwave, satellite, and other technologies, including such communications highways as Dataroute and Infodat which already operate across Canada. It is also very suitable for the universal packet-switching networks just coming into existence— Datapac, Cyclades, etc (see chapter 4). The facilities necessary for putting computer teleconferencing into general use are already in place in Europe, North America, and Japan. *The great technical advantage exploited by this technique is that the digital computer and digitized telecommunications match exactly.*

There does not appear to be any difficulty in holding a computer conference of up to one hundred participants. Because of the techniques used, the effectiveness level of discussion can be much higher than in a face-to-face discussion with a similar number. The 5 000 or so hours of experimental conferencing by computer already carried out suggest that the effectiveness level for groups of ten or fifteen and upwards is much higher than in face-to-face discussion. At present it is thought that about only one hundred persons in the world are regularly teleconferencing by computer, but rapid increase is expected. The method has been pioneered by the New Jersey Institute of Technology under the leadership of M Turoff (cf Turoff, 1976).

The computer teleconference breaks out of the limitations of space and time since any participant can join or leave the conference whenever he likes and can take it up on any terminal. The computer automatically indicates any such changes. The printout capability provides a permanent record of all material contributed, and spot retrieval and selected retrieval by key word are possible. Contributions may be in real time in the sense of a conversation (like a telephone conversation written down), simultaneous (that is, contributors can input at the same time), or in delayed time. Typically, a conference begins by somebody putting a statement into the system, and others adding, perhaps over a period of weeks or months. Each contribution is given a number for reference. The participant scans the contributions either as printouts, which could accumulate to be quite a sizeable file, or by retrieval through the computer onto his display screen.

The present costs may be stated as about $20 per hour for computer time. The terminal capital cost is about $1000. By 1980 the computer cost (time-sharing system), may well be down to $1 per hour and the terminal capital cost to $300 to $500. Packet networking already moves toward reducing the costs of the use of the telephone links. Telenet will shortly allow a firm to send about fifty business letters anywhere within the USA for $1.25. When terminals become common equipment for the individual the line costs will be about the same as, or less than, for the use of the telephone.

The advantages of the computerized conference are considerable. It is relatively cheap, or likely to become so. The equipment already exists in easily accessible form and technique since computer and telecommunications are both in common use. The handling of time is extremely flexible. The number of participants can be relatively large. The duration of the conference can be anything the participants wish. Each participant can contribute as much as he wants in his own time; he can enter or withdraw at will without loss of knowledge of what has gone on previously. A contributor can prepare his contribution carefully. There need be no domination by an individual or a group. Anonymity can be used. Any kind of substantive material can be handled, from business discussions to therapy sessions. Private communication can take place within the conference—the equivalent of whispering to one's neighbour in a live conference. The system can do the job of much business correspondence, face-to-face discussion, teaching–learning, management, and playing games and entertainment.

At least five major styles of computer conferencing exist. Examples include: DISCUSS (University of Illinois) which is the addition of computer conferencing to the PLATO computer-assisted instruction project; FORUM for group conferencing, joint writing, planning, etc (Institute for the Future, California); PLANET-1 which is a simpler arrangement of FORUM; and MAILBOX—a commercial development of computer conferencing for technical discussion and exchange of information (Scientific Time Sharing Corporation, Bethesda, Maryland).

A large-scale field experiment is being designed by Turoff (1976; also see *The Futurist*, 1975). Three hundred specialists from a variety of disciplines will form an invisible college subdivided into sets of individuals with common interests. Each participant will be able to put in 30000 words of text material, will have computer space for notebook purposes, capacity for interaction between particular individuals, capability for participating in conferences, and will have access to a directory and a bulletin. The exercise will use the packet-switching services of Telenet at about $3 per hour (see chapter 4). The project will be carefully monitored from a behavioural research point of view (see Hiltz, 1976). An overview of computer conferencing appears in 1CCC (1976, pages 203ff).

3.4 Small-group TV teleconferencing
The principle of these systems is that a group, such as a board of directors, may have their meeting televised by closed circuit to a similar group in another location. Each group receives the image of the other group on a main screen, itself on another screen. Alternatively small individual screens may be used. There may be arrangements for close-up and for the transmission of graphics, etc. Examples of this type are the British Post Office Confravision, the Bell Canada experimental TV Conferencing facility, and the Australian Confravision[2] (see figure 3.6).

This system requires the groups participating in the conference to go to a particular 'studio' in their city and to transmit and receive live. It is relatively expensive at present. As TV monitors are still fairly small and the space to accommodate the group is relatively large, there is a feeling of remoteness. (Large-screen TV—about two metres square—is now available in North America. The retail cost is about $3500. The use of this projection technology could very much improve Confravision.) In the Wired City Facility, by contrast, a sense of the participants being close together can be produced by the use of close-ups and because the screens are only about a metre away from the participant.

---

[2] Confravision was successfully used experimentally between Britain and Australia in 1973, at the beginning of a Confravision service in Australia. The telecommunications link was made by satellite.

The impression one receives from working on this type of system is that it is comparatively formal and rigid. The furniture has to be fixed to keep the cameras in focus, and the chairman needs a fixed place for switching. These arrangements tend to reinforce the corporate hierarchy in a rather formidable way, especially as the chairman may be able to cut a speaker off!

The Bell Canada system has the advantage that, once it is running, no switching operator is necessary. It is therefore possible to offer confidentiality as an advantage of the service.

This kind of teleconferencing is sometimes set up within private firms but there is dependence on a common carrier for transmission between separate locations. The costs are considerable as the TV part of the signal requires a high level of transmission capability. A rough indication of cost is ten times that of audio teleconferencing.

The necessity of going to a special location to carry on the conference is a disadvantage since problems of timing, access to files and other staff obviously arise. The main advantage is that some considerable sense of

Figure 3.6. Confravision allows a group to interact, audio and video, with another group or groups, and to 'display' by audio and video means, or by video only. The transmitted signal may carry the image of the entire group and a close-up of one or two members selected at will, or a mixture of the two alternatives. The present small size of screens makes the faces appear distant from the viewer. Desk monitors, as on the left, can also be used. (Photo courtesy of the British Post Office.)

the presence of the distant group can come through while the costs of intercity movement are eliminated.

An excellent review of TV conferencing systems, mostly experimental and not including the Carleton University Wired City network, is to be found in Post Office Telecommunications (1974a). This issue of the *Long Range Intelligence Bulletin* gives illustrations of the British Confravision, the Bankers' Trust technique, the First National City Bank method, the American Telephone and Telegraph intercity visual conferencing service, the Bell Telephone Laboratories Murray Hill and Holindel link, the New York Telephone Company video conference system, the General Electric Company's conference system, the Bell Canada Conference TV system, and verbally describes some others. The concept is generally the same— one group in a 'studio' interacts with a second group in another studio located at a distance.

3.5 Comment on teleconferencing

Audio teleconferencing, using the telephone system, does not appear to be used as much as its considerable benefits might lead one to expect. Where it has been well organized and publicized—for example, NASA, the UK Scottish Office, the University of Quebec, and the University of Wisconsin— it has been effective, economical, and in some cases has made possible functions not otherwise achievable.

There are various difficulties, both technical and organizational. More-than-two-participant conferencing would be used more if the conference could be more easily and quickly set up than at present. On the technological side voice-switching often results in chopping speakers off, and listeners may have difficulty in quickly recognizing who is speaking.

Audio systems may show some indications of polarizing groups to a greater extent than face-to-face meetings and apparently participants speak less frequently in audio meetings than in face-to-face or audio–video meetings (Canada, Department of Communications, 1976b, volume 1, page 16). Users in different types of employment vary in their degree of acceptance of the mode. In general, research on the effects of the telephone on the locations of, types of, and reasons for transactions is not well developed and this defect has some limiting effect on audio-teleconferencing research.

There appears to be very little information on citizens band radio for teleconferencing use. We appear to have chiefly developed radio as a one-to-many mode and have failed to exploit its potential as a general public facility for short-range two-way communication. As the equipment is cheap and operating costs are virtually negligible there appears to be room for considerable development in this field.

As a general comment audio teleconferencing appears to be an under-developed area of the electronic technology. This observation may be particularly pertinent when combination with other techniques is considered:

the storage of material as record of discussion, etc, the addition of slow-scan video, interaction with material on TV and radio (educational uses), and linkage with computerized material via printout. Present trends toward more varied uses of the telephone equipment—in varying degrees in most of the developed countries—will be likely to increase the use of audio teleconferencing in the immediate future as additional equipment becomes more generally diffused and new capabilities become available. Costs and ways of structuring tariffs, also, in their turn may have effects favouring increased use. Changing ratios of costs between teleconferencing and other modes of transacting will be a further influential factor.

This brings us to the audio–video systems of teleconferencing. The Carleton Wired City kind of technology has the great advantages of live and recorded sound and vision, giving a close approximation to face-to-face interaction. Its chief difficulty in general application is likely to be switching and the high cable or equivalent transmission capacity required. It seems extremely well suited to instructional uses and to cases where regular use between the same nodes is required. The high transmission capacity necessary may be less serious in the future as transmission capability is growing very rapidly.

The Wired City network is essentially a laboratory, although certain exercises of a field nature have taken place on it (see Dakin, 1974). Certain differences have appeared between the results of laboratory experiments and field exercises. The laboratory results showed no increase in aggression, anxiety, fatigue, and concentration for network meetings over face-to-face discussions. The field exercises, however, reported a higher degree of attention necessary and greater fatigue (Canada, Department of Communications, 1976b, volume 2, page 16).

The Carleton system appears to be the only video system seriously attempting to bring several nodes together into a common electronic space. The difference between this and other types of audio–video technology is understood at once when experienced but is difficult to convey in written description. The Carleton system appears to get its highly satisfactory effects by having the monitors near the user and by treating him as an individual, not as a member of a group. The result is not group talking to group, as in the Bell Canada or Confravision systems, but several individuals coming together as though the space in the conference room had been infinitely enlarged. The two concepts are radically different as psycho-technical approaches. Second, where display is required, it is extremely advantageous to be able to superimpose the display space of all nodes. This allows a participant, or several participants, to amend a document together exactly as they might working around a table. This is an immensely valuable capability for many professionals: the ability of distant participants to diagram or write exactly what they wish to amend although their access to the physical document is electronic only.

Third, the interaction of voices on the Wired City network is exactly as in face-to-face meetings. There is no cutoff as in voice-switched audio teleconferencing. One speaker does not electronically cut another speaker out. As nobody is a further distance than anybody else from the chairman— if there is one—no speaker is disadvantaged by his physical position; all voices and images are 'equal'.

Perhaps most important of all, the Wired City is designed as a network in which the technology is determinative of behaviour to an absolute minimum. The aim, in large measure achieved, is to approximate face-to-face interaction as far as possible. (For description of exercises in urban planning and evaluation see Dakin, 1974.)

At present for the purposes of the general public the Wired City type of network is not a likely development. For more special purposes, such as governmental, educational, engineering, and medical, further experiment may well indicate very considerable application, especially in conjunction with computers and packet-switching telecommunications.

Such uses generally require a considerable amount of display. This leads to the question: if display is not needed is the ability to see the faces of the participants worth the cost? Unless the question is placed in a context before any answer is attempted, it is not a very helpful one. Is seeing a singer on TV worth the additional cost over that of hearing the voice on the radio? Much depends on the quality of the picture. Video conferencing is not yet notable for high quality of definition. If, however, it were raised to the level of the best broadcast colour TV, the approximation to face-to-face discussion would be very near indeed[3].

The technology of the small-group audio–video teleconferencing (for example, Bell Canada TV conferencing) is not as effective in giving a sense of face-to-face interaction as the Wired City technology. I am writing here on the basis of personal experience of both systems. The chief reasons are the relative smallness of the screens, their distance from the viewer, and the switching arrangements in the TV small-group conferencing.

Evaluation varies as to the effectiveness of audio–video small-group conferencing. The Bell Canada system is reported as successful "... because it rates high on a number of factors found to determine the acceptability of such systems" (Post Office Telecommunications, 1974a, page 28); on the other hand it is rated "... in spite of being available at no charge today it is seldom used except by Bell Canada employees" (Canada, Department of Communications, 1976b, volume 2, page 8). Evaluation of the British Confravision is on the whole favourable. Evidence of a degree of success is the adopting of the system by the Australian Post Office and the offering of links between the UK and Sweden and Holland. An evaluation by Champness (1974) indicates a higher level of satisfaction for meetings which do not involve conflict, bargaining, or personnel matters, and that

[3] Now done in some TV news broadcasts.

its perceived effectiveness is greater than that of audio-teleconferencing systems. The Australian Post Office anticipates continuing developments which "... may offer new markets to supplement existing telecommunication services" (Australian Telecommunications Commission, 1975, page 107). Small-group video conferencing via private systems appears to be of continuing usefulness to a number of firms. Detailed notes on experience of the Bell system by individuals also experienced on the Wired City network is in Dakin (1974, page 18). Comparative tables of research results as between the Bell system and audio-teleconferencing systems are in Canada, Department of Communications (1976b, volume 2).

In comparing, from direct experience, the effectiveness of the small-group conferencing systems as typified by Confravision and the Wired City network there can be little doubt that the latter is very considerably superior. Its flexibility, its capacity for presenting images of highly detailed visibility, and its sense of giving a close approximation to face-to-face discussion make it an attractive mode. Its relatively high costs in a field in which costs are high in any case is a serious disadvantage. However, costs are closely related to the costs, speeds, and capacities of transmission links—cable, microwave, satellite, etc. Costs relative to capability are falling and speeds are increasing. It is therefore difficult to forecast how these systems will develop. Also the field is very tricky for cost-effectiveness calculations because of the uncertainties in the futures of human costs over a wide range of human activities.

The most flexible, the cheapest, and the easiest to operationalize teleconferencing seems to be the computer conference. It can work over long distances, even globally, without undue cost or complication, by using geostationary satellites. The digital computer, the digitized telecommunications techniques, packet-switching, and the organizational arrangements can be fully exploited in a combined universal mode by using all types of equipment. Its main weakness is that at present interaction is almost exclusively by written word; the participants cannot see or hear each other directly. A computer conference, however, could be amplified by audio conferencing.

This form of conferencing could play an important role in helping to solve the organization–decision difficulties of corporations and other large groups. Because problems change rapidly organizational difficulties arise. One solution to the pressure towards rapidly repeated reorganization is matrix management. This works by asking the best-equipped individuals, wherever they are in the organization, for suggested solutions to a problem. This is difficult if they are geographically far apart or their schedules make face-to-face coming together hard to achieve. The computer conference is excellent for getting over such difficulties. The participant contributes, after time out for careful thought, while still remaining geographically in his position and without disruption of his day-to-day functions. As anonymity can be preserved, the usual difficulties connected with hierarchy can be sidestepped. A great advantage for management is that it allows rationalized use of time and cuts down interruptions. The technique is likely to have a very major impact on the organizational conditions of many activities, from business to education.

The disadvantages are more difficult to assess. The obvious charge of impersonality will be made. The experimenters affirm that this is not as serious as those who have an emotionally negative attitude to the computer would claim. They say that a sense of person does come through. The capacity for anonymity and coolness may, of course, be as much an advantage as a disadvantage.

Much more difficult to grasp is the ambiguity of the ways in which time can be manipulated. The exclusion of spontaneous interruption may be a disadvantage. It may be a disadvantage that the participant is not necessarily 'present' in the sequence in which the contributions are originated. At times it must be a great disadvantage not to be able to see the face of a participant—a requirement very well met by the Wired City type of conferencing technology. It would seem likely that new attitudinal approaches to conferencing will develop if computer conferencing becomes common. We shall have to learn to manipulate time in a way that is different from our present modes of real time and delayed time, as used in the current techniques of the electronic technology (live or recorded material). Also the symbiosis of the human and the artificial intelligence in an ongoing mode is something about which we have little experience, but are on the threshold of exploring. What attitudes and attributes are required for this? Potentially we are envisaging the development of a new kind of collective intelligence different from the collective intelligence we have previously created, such as joint discussion, referring to stored material (books, tapes, etc), and the pooling of expertise.

Although there are good reasons for taking careful account of the disadvantages, the advantages offered in the way of cost and convenience are attractive. Additionally so, when it is remembered various factors will exert their pressure: rising costs of travel and time, falling costs of computer and telecommunications equipment and use, increasing complexity of decisions and knowledge, organizational complexities, the increasingly difficult logistics of mass populations, and the need for increased action at the global level in terms of resources, food, and preservation of the biosphere. Crisis management seems an increasingly likely role that we must play (see Kupperman et al, 1975; and chapter 7). The combination of computer conferencing and computerized models might prove of world significance in terms of war, famine, pestilence, and allocation of resources. The technique opens the possibility of developing synergetic brain nets capable of keeping the best-informed individuals and groups in constant contact for interchange of ideas and developing plans of action (see Dakin, 1973, chapters 3 and 5).

The computer conference, in conjunction with computer modelling techniques and electronic monitoring applications such as the activities of the World Weather Watch (see chapter 7), appears to have great relevance to our concern for the biosphere and its ecosystems (see World Meteorological Organization, 1972). *At the moment when we must learn to observe, consult, and act globally we find ready new indispensable tools to make possible the level of performance required. The distribution of the world food supply, the allocation of nonrenewable resources, the threat of flood or famine, the forecasting of global crops, and many more things could usefully be coped with in new ways by the use of these now available tools and organizational techniques.*

Research in the field of teleconferencing presents considerable difficulties. It is of two kinds: field trials and laboratory experiments. Each has its strengths and weaknesses. The field experiences or exercises have the advantage of being carried out in live situations with individuals who are likely to be knowledgeable in their work areas. On the other hand judgment is likely to be made as in a status quo situation, rather than in a possible future situation. In the latter the mix of factors may be quite different from the present conditions. Costs ratios may be very different. Energy availability and sociocultural evaluations may have changed considerably. What is not acceptable today may have to be accepted tomorrow. The individual offering opinion on the 'usefulness' of teleconferencing may have a position ranging from very conservative to very open, with very wide differences of opinion offered.

The laboratory experiments generally aim at controlled conditions and characteristically use a control-group technique. They concern themselves with trying to establish information about levels of acceptability, effectiveness of communication, and responsiveness to the various modes. They frequently rely on a series of sessions in which the equipment is experienced and questionnaires are administered. The typical product is the attempt at a statistical statement of response to this or that statement. The intentions are not to be faulted but reservations are in order about the way some of these research studies are conducted. The quantity and quality of participant on the networks are very important. Even relatively large researches (for example on Confravision) may involve a universe of only a hundred or two individuals. One has very serious reservations about results based on questionnaires administered to a handful of lackadaisical students induced off the campus by a small payment. Such exercises are likely to be far less effective than market research into TV programming, as anyone who has participated in the latter will confirm. A great deal more behavioural research is required, and one would like to see physiological approaches also extensively included, such as measurements of skin temperature, pulse rate, and eye movement, etc.

The chief research difficulty, however, runs deeper than the matters touched upon above. It is that almost all the research, if it is to be strictly respectable, can be done only within the status quo of the sociocultural conditions of the developed countries. Yet the key interest is obviously future applications in sociocultural not to mention socioeconomical – political conditions which can be expected to change very considerably during the next period of technological application. Further, a difficulty is that the technology itself will have its own major influence on those conditions. A kind of push–pull situation may be rapidly developing between the electronic technology and the conditions of the culture and the society. A purpose of this book is to stimulate enquiry along this line

This research question is one of the reasons it has been necessary to comment at such length on teleconferencing. In other areas of electronic applications we have already acquired more extensive experience. In television, cable television, data networking, computer usage, satellite working, and remote sensing we have a far firmer body of experiential knowledge than in teleconferencing.

Teleconferencing, of whatever kind, should not be viewed simply as a substitute for face-to-face interaction. It has benefits and rules of its own which on occasion may make it superior to face-to-face conferencing. It needs to be experienced to be judged and it needs to be much more extensively explored, by field use, as to its potential. The indications to date are that we have in these various techniques wholly new possibilities for discussion, management, learning, government, and environmental control. It seems likely that the pressures of biological, societal, and cultural conditions will tend to encourage its more widespread use. On communication see Chapanis (1971; 1973; 1975).

There seems to be a considerable possibility that some kind of tele-conferencing will come into common, everyday use. If so, the type or types of technology which are most favoured will be likely to have some major influence in shaping the sensibility of the electrobionic culture. The Wired City type would tend to develop the use of the visual processes of the eye and brain in a gestalt way since the monitors would show the faces of the participants and they would place considerable weight on the facial expression. This could also tend toward face-to-face preferences and would reinforce group working in a near approximation to familiar group dynamics No very great number of individuals could interact simultaneously because the number of monitors that the participant can watch comfortably is obviously limited. Some small expansion of numbers is possible by intermittent calling up of individuals, but a total for full two-way continuou discussion is perhaps ten, with six or seven being a practical limit. Larger groups would have to operate on a classroom basis—one-to-many with only occasional inputs from the many. In general the Wired City type would tend to reinforce the perception style appropriate to the TV—the taking in of many items of information simultaneously in gestalts.

The computer conference, on the other hand, depends heavily on the linear pick-up process of the eye and the mind. It is therefore in the direct line of the preferred perception mode of previous civilizations. The skills and mental biases that we are familiar with in reading books are the ones which again become reinforced. We are making less paper and no doubt moving toward the new paperless office but in doing so by this type of technology we would be *still maintaining and reinforcing the processes of perception and thinking that writing originally imposed and on which all civilizations up to now have been based.* This would suggest a reinforcement of our traditional type of literacy: the word would still be immensely important and would not be in danger of being ousted by pictorial forms of communication. Rather the two—linear and gestalt— might develop symbiotically.

As computer and telecommunications facilities become cheaper and more generally accessible, the computer conference seems likely to become widespread. Electrobionic culture will then be characterized by two dominant perception modes or emphases in relation to material visually presented. TV programming will carry kinds of material that mostly demand gestalt perception of the whole picture at once, a simultaneous taking in of many items. The display screen of the terminal, on the other hand, will show material that the eye must mostly scan line by line in the traditional process of reading. The TV set may be used for both these modes. Electrobionic man will become adept in both kinds of perception and his mental processes will have the characteristics of both modes. His mind will have the possibility of being both 'literary' and 'nonliterary'. This means a potential enhancement of the sensibility of Western culture.

Computer and telecommunications technologies: 2

In this chapter we shall look briefly at key developments in information handling. This will include cable television, which at present is one-way, few-to-many, communication only. The computer is characterized by its capacity for transmitting, processing, storing, and retrieving very large quantities of information. Telecommunications facilities are characterized by being able to provide many channels and several modes for moving very large quantities of information over any distance—across the street or spanning a galaxy. Both the computer and telecommunications operate at the speed of light. For reasons of quantity, speed, and distance the electronic handling of information must be a major focus of attention.

4.1 Community Antenna TV (CATV)

The idea of diffusing information—including entertainment—by land line is not new. Budapest used the telephone lines for this purpose in the 1880s, French and British telephone systems followed a little later. Public radio broadcasting, developing in the 1920s, brought these services to an end. The modern form of the idea is cable TV (CATV).

This service, which essentially consists of an agency receiving broadcast TV signals on a specially sensitive antenna, amplifying them, and rediffusing them locally through a coaxial cable network began, just after the war, as a service to areas in which the signal, when individually picked up, was of poor quality. The early role of cable was therefore developed not to serve metropolitan areas, in which signals are generally of good quality, but rural and later metro-peripheral populations. By the mid-1970s, however, the dominant application of cable was in the cities where the densities of population obviously offer a better ratio between capital outlay for cable, etc and rental revenues than do small low-density rural areas. Also, in the cities it is easy to pick high-quality TV signals off the air. In the USA cable companies were barred from operating inside metropolitan areas until 1972. The purpose of this limitation was to safeguard the interests of the established TV stations. In 1972 there were approximately 2 700 cable systems in the USA with an average subscriber population of 2 000 homes each. Britain, with a history of radio rediffusion from the 1920s, at the end of 1972 had 1300 cable operators reaching nearly 2·2 million homes; France had about 400 systems, Japan about 9 000—some very small indeed. By the middle of the decade the USA had over 3 100 cable systems and approximately 8·5 million subscribers. The average system had 2 600 subscribers and offered twelve VHF channels. Many systems also offered UHF channels. Canada was the most extensively cabled country, with over one-third of all homes served. About 70% of homes in metropolitan Toronto had cable. One estimate for the USA is cable in

30% of TV-equipped homes by 1985 (Arthur D Little). This would allow a considerable amount of channel specialization in programmes offered.

CATV is a matter of concern for governments in all countries, but particularly those with a high level of development in electronic technology, a high per capita income, and the large markets of densely packed populations. Control of cable development generally involves some kind of franchise-granting technique, with varying degrees of definition of requirements by government. In the USA the franchises are granted by the local municipality and requirements are stipulated by Federal government regulation (Federal Communications Commission). In Britain the licence is issued to private companies by the Post Office. In Canada the licence is granted by the Canadian Radio and Television Commission, the licensee being required to abide by the regulations of the Commission (Federal government appointed body).

Within considerably less than a decade cable systems have jumped from obscurity to high priority as a focus of attention for governments, business, education, service agencies, technological development, and entertainment. Their impact, already heavy, is potentially very great, constituting one of the major impetuses for cultural, societal, psychological and spatial change. The reasons supporting this view are many, and in various categories, including:

- The costs of renting a new communication system for the home ($6–$9 per month for up to, say, twenty channels) are easily met by modern mass populations.
- This new access has advantages for the subscriber: more choices of incoming material than is possible directly off the air; additional channels for information, for example, stockmarket quotations, jobs available, reports on commodity prices, aircraft arrivals, weather information, entertainment listings, educational courses, announcements in other languages; services to the home, for example, meter reading, burglar and fire alarm; frequently better signal quality than is possible off the air; more locally originated material than is possible on the main TV networks or even local stations; and eventually some two-way communication, first to the head end of the cable system and later to connections beyond the system, for example to libraries, information centres, schools.
- Cable penetration into homes offers advantages to the cable entrepreneur: he opens up new opportunities for placing information before the public (of significance to government, business, etc); as the technology develops he will be able to offer more services; he can build in excess capacity to ensure future expansion; as the increasing complexity of society enforces more sophisticated access to and use of information, cable TV will be one of the modes increasingly required to cope; and the possibility of two-way services on cable brings a new range of opportunity for the cable companies.

- The technology itself, quite apart from its uses, is advancing very rapidly. The services capable of being offered on cable will increase and improve, thus offering more advantages to both subscriber and entrepreneur.
- The dynamic of the tendency of costs of electronic equipment to fall very rapidly, simultaneously with the tendency for equipment capacity to rise (for example the cassette tape recorder, or the electronic hand calculator) is very powerful; result: wider diffusion of equipment and services.
- The tendency for equipment to become increasingly intercompatible, coupled with the capacity to shift from one region of the electromagnetic spectrum to another (direct visual to TV, film to videotape) and ability to transfer any signal into digitized form for universal handling are very important. CATV can be married with universal public packet-switching to achieve common interworking of all systems.

Cable companies at first usually offered twelve channels in the very-high-frequency wave band. This has now been increased by adding certain channels in the ultrahigh-frequency range, giving in present common use a total of about twenty. The upper limit in practical terms is probably sixty to eighty channels. San Jose, California, has a system with seventy-five-channel capacity. The Toronto area had twenty-four channels working by the end of 1975. Of these, one or two carry the same programme, six are information channels (weather, and news, stockmarket information, programmes available—film titles, etc, supermarket food prices, jobs available, airport arrivals—simply showing the airport monitors), one is 'educational and ethnic', and one is the local community channel provided by all cable companies as a requirement of the Canadian Radio and Television Commission. The channels are switched by a push-button converter of thirty to thirty-five channel capacity. These converters can perhaps be regarded as the first appearance of some kind of terminal in the home.

Because the cable companies of the Toronto area are able to pick United States programmes as easily as domestic programmes off the air, and because of the number of channels offered and the high percentage of homes having the cable, Toronto is an extremely interesting area to watch for developments in cable. At the time of writing, a problem has arisen which indicates something of the capacity for change in thinking and behaviour which cable presages. A cable company, in picking material off the air and rediffusing it, has no difficulty in removing the advertisements and substituting something else. This, of course, hurts the advertising revenues of the station of origin. In 1975 the CRTC announced that Canadian cable companies would be required to remove advertising material from rediffused US programmes. The stations concerned (mostly in Buffalo) applied to the US Federal Communications Commission for permission to jam the pickup operations of the Canadian cable companies. No doubt the argument will rage for some time. What is interesting is the demonstration of how the jurisdictions of all levels of government, including national, are rendered ineffective—the war is technocommercial—and how basic assumptions about jurisdictions and ownership force themselves forward for review. Among other impacts, there is the interesting effect on our ideas of property. If a broadcaster diffuses at large over an area, has he still power over the distributed energy of his diffusion after it has left his antenna? Or is the electrical energy anybody's for the picking up to do with what he will?

One of the important technical capacities of equipment that can be used in conjunction with cable is frame-grabbing. This technique essentially consists of holding a picture on the screen to the individual user's requirements, including printout. The frame to be grabbed can be passed along the cable on a channel being used to carry a programme. Thus, by means of coding, channels may be used for carrying individual messages. For example, the subscriber might want the reference of a book from a library. The question could be asked through the cable system, if operating two-way, or the telephone. The library would send the reply to the cable company, which would forward it to the subscriber using the frame-grabbing technique. The cable system can therefore be used for *individual* communication, at least in a single direction.

When cable companies were admitted to the metropolitan areas of the USA it quickly became apparent that a new epoch in their development was about to open. Nothing of such potential had appeared since the introduction of public radio broadcasting. There would be a scramble to win new empires since clearly the home, from having the two-way telephone and the passive one-way inputs of radio, television, and recorded material, would potentially have a wealth of electronic contacts, including, perhaps, two-way switched video. Simultaneously, the services available through the telephone were going to grow. Consequently, in the early 1970s, there began the first—still far too few—attempts to look at the planning of cable systems as a societal as well as a technological and commercial exercise over the metropolitan area as a whole. Examples are: New York, Los Angeles, The Twin Cities Area (metropolitan regional jurisdiction) of Minnesota, and Washington, DC. We shall look briefly at the last of these since it is probably representative of the best thinking in the field. Figure 4.1 shows the layout.

Washington, the ninth-largest US TV market, was studied as a probe into the general planning of cable for US cities by the Mitre Corporation. The basic question was:

"Can a broadband urban communications system be designed that combines large amounts and varieties of new programming and services, moderate subscriber fees, participation by most households and offices, and system profitability?"

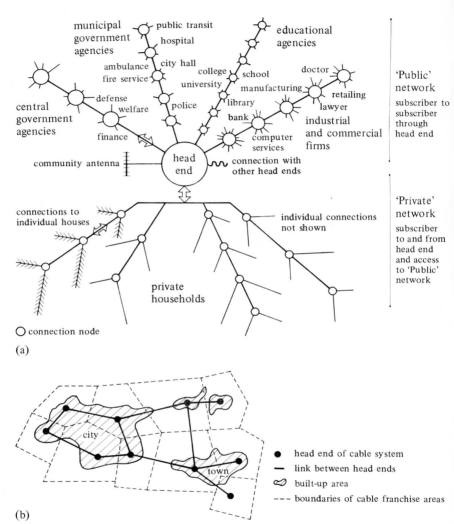

Figure 4.1. (a) *Integrated cable system.* Two network types are combined to be interactive. The upper part of the diagram is for 'public' agencies such as departments of governments, educational agencies such as schools and libraries, and industrial and commercial firms. These have two-way communication on demand with each other through the head end. The lower part shows the network serving the private households. These could have two-way interaction with the head end, but probably not with each other in the present state of the technology. Information could be obtained by the individual household from any of the 'public' agencies. Full audio-video service is technically possible, including access to computer services. (b) *Linked cable systems.* The local systems can be linked through their head ends, by using microwave, coaxial cable, etc. This would allow intercommunication between the various cable franchise areas in a metropolitan region, and would overcome the present limitations which would be seriously restrictive for two-way service in CATV.

The results indicated that profitability can be combined with:

"• a broad range of new programming and services;
• a widespread utilization of these programs and services by many elements in the city;
• a flexibility to meet a wide range of needs of both the public and specialized users;
• moderate subscribers' fees for general programming and services;
• moderate charges for use of the system's transmission facilities for special services; and
• financial support from system revenues for the development of new programming and services" (Mason et al, 1972).

The inputs into the design of the system included studies covering the total community needs, the technology, the costs of producing programmes and services, financial viability, and the economics of building and operating. The exercise showed that success would depend, in large degree, on appreciating the appeal of a sufficient variety of new programming and services. The stress on success in the marketplace is interesting and somewhat different from the assumption of some degree of government financial responsibility traditional in broadcast services in many countries. Equally important is the emphasis that its financial strength would not be chiefly dependent on rediffusion of TV broadcast programmes but would rely heavily on other services for viability.

The system would comprise two networks—one for telecasting (including services) which would be for individual subscribers, and one for point-to-point services which would be in the form of subsystems, one each for connecting Federal government offices, municipal offices, business users, and educational institutions. All networks would be fully interconnected, material originating anywhere being capable of being received anywhere. The US Federal Communications Commission requires all systems in the top one-hundred market areas to provide two-way signal distribution capacity, although two-way terminals and services are not yet actually required. The Washington proposals therefore suggested one-way telecasting services initially, to be followed shortly by two-way subscriber response service (polling, etc). Later still, two-way electronic information-handling services would permit direct individual access to computer output. The range of services is listed (table 4.1).

The Washington unified-system proposal, which would include nine cablecasting studios with appropriate subsystems, contrasts with the usual method of dividing a city into franchise areas, each operated by a separate company. The general area of Toronto, for example, has fourteen companies for a total of 423 330 household subscribers, ranging from about 3 500 to 85 000 for a company. Some political interests strongly favour a fragmented approach on the grounds that the system can be more sensitive to local needs and issues than if it is unitary. The Washington project, however, placed strong emphasis on the point-to-point networks, which would be considerably dependent on a unitary system. Economies of scale, ease of control, and flexibility are also thought advantages inherent in having a single system. Various alternatives are in fact quite workable, on the basis of varying technological, economic, political and societal emphases (see Kalba in Mason et al, 1972, page 81).

The testing of the subscriber response services through the experimental use of home terminals took place in about a dozen different areas across the USA, the best-known project of which was at Reston, Virginia (Volk, 1971). This has been discontinued and an actuality environment substituted in Buffalo in 1975 with handicapped individuals as participants. The principles of the Washington plan have been worked out for Stockton, California. At the time of writing, the allocation of funds for initial implementation has not been made and there is some feeling that to a

Table 4.1. The range of services in the Washington, DC cable plan. The costs (1972) per month were estimated to be: (1) $3.50 for up to thirty channels, (1) and (2) $6.50, (3) $8.50 to $15.50.

(1) *One-way services*	(3) *Electronic information-handling services*
local signals	computer-aided instruction
continuous news, time, weather, FM radio	interactive entertainment
imported signals	social services
movies and sports	video library
local programming	individualized shopping and reservations
educational access	banking and credit
municipal government access	public information services
public information services [a]	pay-TV, professional channels, and private modes
instructional programming	
health services	(4) *Special services*
special interest programming	traffic control
communications for pay-TV, professional channels, and private modes [b]	mobile radio communications and automatic vehicle monitoring
	general purpose digital communications
(2) *Subscriber response services*	local distribution for special common-carrier services
interactive entertainment	
interactive education	(5) *Point-to-point services*
preference polling	municipal government
catalogue shopping	federal government
alarm communications	colleges and universities
communications for utility and maintenance services	business and commerce

[a] Public information services, such as notices of community events, classified ads, etc, could be provided under one-way services, by using mechanical originations, or under electronic information-handling services, using a frame-stopping terminal.

[b] Communications for pay-TV, professional channels and private modes could be provided by one-way leased channels, with the addition of either a scrambler – descrambler system or a nonstandard channel. They could also be provided under subscriber-response services by using an address coder – decoder system.

degree the proposals might be premature in view of rapid developments in universal packet-switching (see section 4.3).

From a regional point of view, the two important elements in the Washington thinking were the point-to-point networks and the concept of total interconnectability. The division of a metropolitan area into many independent franchise areas has obvious difficulties of interconnection if broadband cable systems (includes the use of microwave) are to be used to their maximum potential for general two-way intercommunication. The question of interconnection is therefore of great importance, but it is not yet receiving adequate attention. It can be categorized into various levels: municipal, multimunicipal, counties, regional–metropolitan, provincial, or state. For discussion on this see Schafer (in Hollowell, 1975, page 57). By late 1975 the Toronto cable companies were discussing a proposal for linking their head ends with twenty-channel microwave facilities that would reduce the costs of deleting advertisements and open up a market of up to 600000 homes for pay-TV. In Columbus, Ohio, a system serving 5000 subscribers already computerizes the process of keeping track of the programmes viewers watch and bills them accordingly.

Municipalities in the USA are beginning to look seriously at the question of interconnection between cable systems, for example Detroit and Baltimore, which has an Office of Telecommunications. Intermunicipal coordination has appeared in various areas and many rural counties issue franchises. Regional councils and metropolitan groupings of municipalities are involved in struggling with interconnectability. The greater Detroit area, the Southwest Michigan Council of Governments, the Miami Valley Council of Governments (area of Dayton, Ohio), the Metropolitan Washington Council of Governments, the Metropolitan Regional Council of the New York–New Jersey–Connecticut area, and the Metropolitan Council of the Twin Cities Area, Minnesota are examples (Hollowell, 1975). The last mentioned has undertaken the development of a communications policy chapter for the development guide that will become effectively the legislature's plan for future development. It seeks to integrate the new communications potential with general regional development, in a context in which new needs in health care, education, criminal justice, welfare, government, etc, require new answers which "... greatly increase participation, feedback and accountability, coming close to a self-correcting response loop".

Although the subject is new in its present form, and extremely complex in its dynamics, cable systems—increasingly to incorporate other technological means than coaxial cable—are already producing evidence that they are potentially one of the greatest impacts upon the life of the developed countries. Present literature and action suggest strongly that this new mode of interaction, whether managed by cable companies or by telecommunications undertakers or by computer utility firms, will grow rapidly and have major influence on our patterns of behaviour. It is to be hoped that its services will not remain territorially fragmented, but that interconnection will be vigorously striven for. Existing aspirations give hope that at least metropolitan regional interactivity will be achievable. *The contribution of such flexibility to regional thinking and action would be a strong element, among others, pushing toward a new definition and concept of the region.* This, however, may well bring us back to old sociopolitical difficulties. Schafer has an insight into this perspective:

> "... municipal boundaries do not necessarily coincide with the scope of cable opportunities and problems ... [which] are reflections of society's ... Thus the quest ... becomes the matching of social opportunities and problems with appropriate responses, some of which involve tools of communications technology" (Hollowell, 1975, page 57).

Our present assumptions about, and arrangements of government seem likely to have to cope with yet another set of pressures.

The use of CATV for services other than piping TV broadcast programmes into the home has attracted considerable detailed experimental activity. In some aspects much of this is now beyond the experimental stage. In Britain the Post Office has established a closed-circuit educational CATV service for 1400 schools and colleges in the inner-London area, with about 8400 socket outlets. University departments and teaching hospitals have access to this network, which is probably the largest of its type in the world. Similar, but smaller, systems serve education authorities in Plymouth, Dover, Leeds University, and Heriot Watt University (see Post Office Telecommunications, 1974b). Bell Canada has experimented with providing the teacher in the classroom with the instant retrieval (IRTV) of library material, such as films and tapes, piped into the classroom immediately on demand, from a control centre (Doyle and Goodwill, 1971). The Wired City network in Carleton University, Ottawa, incorporates classrooms as system nodes experimentally (see Coll, 1973, and chapter 3).

An interesting attempt to achieve some measure of subscriber response capability is taking place in Reading, Pennsylvania. Three public information centres are two-way audio–video linked to serve a selected segment of the population of senior citizens. There are daily interactive sessions in which citizens, individuals in various agencies, politicians, officials, etc participate. In their homes the participants use a telephone placed near the TV set to respond or participate in discussion. The centres are linked by coaxial cable. Therefore Reading does constitute an example of CATV working interactively. The underlying community idea is that the operation shall be programmed by the participants themselves, and they will be totally responsible when the research programme ends in 1977. An important aim of the project is to assess how successfully cable TV can be used for delivering certain services to the elderly. So far the evidence appears to indicate that it can be used very successfully. After the initial trial of the project the programming was extended to all 34 500 subscribers of the cable company. Moss (1976) comments: "The experience in Reading indicates that regular teleconferencing between citizens and public officials should be seriously considered as a mode of communication in local political processes". (See also New York University/Reading, Pennsylvania, undated.)

At Milton Keynes, north of London, an open-access communications project is in operation. This is known as *Channel 40*. As in Reading, the key idea is that the programmers are the subscribers themselves. With some professional help and access to the equipment they generate their own programmes. The project is paid for by the central government and is therefore somewhat different in background interest (for example, revenues) from similar community access experiments in Britain (Greenwich, Bristol, Sheffield, Wellingborough, and Swindon), Australia, or Canada where public access to one channel is a federal government requirement.

Cable TV may also be organized to give the subscriber personal choice in accessing stored material. Télécable Vidéotron, Montreal, offers thirty-two channels: thirteen channels for regular telecasting from Canadian and US stations, eight channels offering community events and audio–video documents requested (over 1500 titles), eight channels for information, services and local news, and other channels including programming, community, and catalogue. The subscriber wishing to use the self-programming service first selects what he wants from the catalogue. He then asks for the document by number. If the appropriate channel is free it will be made available. The catalogue is subdivided into various interests. (See Télécable Vidéotron, 1976.)

Two Canadian experimental projects of interest should be mentioned. In Manitoba a rural-exurbanite low-density area near Winnipeg will be used to test the feasibility of using fibre optics technology for simultaneously handling CATV and telephone. The rapidly developing fibre optics technology allows a large number of circuits to be accommodated in a very small space. If successful this could be very important, essentially in merging the two telecommunications systems now in use—the CATV networks and the telephone systems. As already mentioned, thinking in France is strongly in favour of such fusion of the two. Fibre optics and associated technology offer considerable hope of achieving this. The problems of splicing optical cables have been solved; and optical cable technology appears likely to be considerably cheaper than coaxial cable (information from Department of Communications, Canada, concerning field trials of fibre optics technology).

The second project is a telemedicine service on Prince Edward Island. This is a computer-communications-based health information system. Such an information system is perceived as necessary to redress the inequitable distribution of health care services between urban and rural Canada. Primary concentration is on computer processing and interpretations of electrocardiograms. For certain cases computer interpretation is superior to human interpretation. There is interest in using the electronic technology to reduce the overhead costs of health care. After experience has been gained in ECG analysis on the system, additional areas of experiment will be added. These will include: medical computer conferencing, computer-aided peer review, diagnostic and treatment counselling, and epidemiological information. The project has been planned for five years, initially with annual operating costs of $350000, the Prince Edward Island Comprehensive Development Plan being the main financial support (see Canada, Department of Communications, 1976a). At the time of writing this project was in a state of suspension for organizational reasons.

It is difficult at the midpoint of the 1970s to judge whether the "wired city, region and nation" will be essentially a coaxial or fibre optics cable system of the kind sometimes described (for example OECD, 1973). Simultaneously with the growth and elaboration of cable systems, technologies related to the existing transmission facilities are rapidly developing. Among these, digitization is undoubtedly capable of greatly broadening the range of telephone systems and the mixed use of coaxial cable, microwave, and optical-wave techniques is of great potential; especially important are the nationwide universal shared packet-switched services now coming into operation in the developed countries (see section 4.3). Some might see all services becoming parts of the present telephone and telecommunications systems. This is the emphasis in France.

In conjunction with discussion along this line, we have to bear in mind the now serious congestion appearing, particularly in the developed countries, in the allocation of frequencies in those regions of the electro-magnetic spectrum used for communications. Allocation has now become a very difficult planning problem. Further pressure, which is inevitable, will most probably induce an increased reliance on 'piped' techniques (coaxial cable, fibre optical techniques, microwave, wires, etc) and less proportional dependency on broadcast or general propagation modes. It will also very probably be necessary to put a price on the use of frequencies—at the moment the regions of the spectrum are a free resource. This situation is not considered indefinitely viable. This changing pressure raises questions of great complexity with regard to how we should view the development of both urban and rural electronic services. (We should perhaps find new words to describe areas of differing densities, since those in use are no longer adequate.) Fibre optical techniques produce links of high capacity capable of taking telephone services and piped broadcast services simultaneously. In terms of costs this fits a dense urban area rather better than a very-low-density area. It is not, therefore, necessarily to be assumed that the rural emphasis of the Canadian fibre optics project just described, which is related to the general national policy of reducing the disparities between the urban and the rural areas, is necessarily transferable to other contexts. At the same time the emerging changes in growth rates (increase in rural areas, decrease in metropolitan areas in North America) suggests increasing attention to servicing the very-low-density areas will be necessary. In general the technical questions are not difficult; it is the socioeconomic aspects that dominate the context of the debate.

The cable offerings are perceived as capable of: increasing economic growth, giving sociopolitical advantages (control, participation, etc), assisting health and educational services delivery, entertainment, personal convenience, and informational advantages for the individual, together with extensive subscriber response in the future. An interesting omission is the lack of exploration into the role CATV might play in relation to our ecological concern. Can cable television be useful in helping us develop new approaches towards, and action in, ecosystems?

The Office of Technology Assessment of the United States Congress (1976) has completed a preliminary evaluation of cable TV in rural areas. This assessment shows how broadband communications could make a very substantial contribution to overcoming the disadvantages of distance experienced in rural areas. It indicates that telemedical applications are likely to be successful; it points out that fewer experiments have been carried out in teletuition than in telemedicine. The recommendation is for a series of demonstrations rather than a widespread government programme of rural system development. The approach is entirely from the point of view of human convenience and the appropriateness for the processes of human society *as it now exists.* So decentralizing of manufacturing, exurbanite growth, and commercial development receive attention. But the major activity of a great deal of rural America is some kind of farming! Major questions to ask, therefore, are: how can cable TV serve to assist food production, the maintenance or improvement of the health of ecosystems, and—most important of all—help to alleviate the harshness of changes that will be necessary as industrialized agriculture as we know it today encounters mounting difficulties? *The absence of such a focus of attention indicates that the ancient exploitative approaches to the life-support system of the world are as powerful as ever.*

By omission, and quite unwittingly, the US Congress document points up what might be the most important use of CATV in both urban and rural areas of the developed countries. This is the providing of common daily access of millions of individuals to knowledge about the state of the human enterprise, information on how to act (for example, to farmers about new ecological knowledge), opportunity to interact and exchange information at spatial scales hitherto impossible, and possibilities for acquiring an individual and group flexibility necessary for our changing condition. CATV, with its many channel offerings, breaks us out of the rigidity of the restricted, directed programming of the old limited number of one-to-many traditional radio and TV transmissions, and offers the potential of a new era in human relationships.

It is something of a paradox that the potential offered is often more clearly seen in the context of the developing than of the developed countries. Although the developing countries have by no means escaped

Hollywood, they have not suffered the great TV network domination that has characterized the growth of this aspect of telecommunications in the developed countries. The developing countries therefore have the possibility of using the electronic technology to serve developmental ends in the broadest sense. They could use it to disseminate essential know-how to peasant populations so that their life support could be steadily improved; and to permit interchange of information between regions. This role is clearly perceived by Schumacher (1974, page 169) in his plea for intermediate technology. The developed countries may well have to learn from the developing countries in this kind of use of cable TV and other electronic equipment.

4.2 Redistribution of information handling

Although the literature of cable television includes the regionwide and nationwide possibilities, even probabilities, of broadband networks capable of universal service, in common practice the actual development of CATV is at present always relatively local when we think in terms of greater regions. The greater region has at present in fact many cable systems but they are organizationally independent and probably for some time to come territorially separate. Although experimentally signals have been drawn for rediffusion from a thousand miles distant by microwave, there is very little evidence that linkage over regions as entities will emerge in the immediate future. Even the advanced thinking in the direction of planned CATV, such as the planned field experiment in Stockton, California, or the Japanese projects, is local in scope. We must also remember that in the present phase of actual development CATV is one-way and only in its next phase of subscriber response will it begin to offer general but limited two-way capability, such as polling yes–no and some audio participation. In Columbus, Ohio, a cable company now offers multiple-choice answer-back facilities to the home viewer. Called 'Qube', it includes video display. As long as CATV is one-way it cannot give the subscriber access to computer capacity. For this at present he has to use the common telephone facility or a dedicated link. Universal computer access using packet-switching is now appearing. This will influence the future of computer access through CATV. Regional and interregional (that is, 'national') and international levels of advance in telecommunications–computer capacity are therefore taking place, at the moment, largely outside the existing CATV coaxial cable systems. This is notwithstanding experimental projects which combine the two, or the possibility of the use of satellite channels to bring TV programmes from Europe to Canada, as is being investigated by Teleglobe (Canada). It may be added here that although small individual antennae are technically feasible for reception from satellites this technology is not thought likely to be shortly in common use (United States Congress, Office of Technology Assessment, 1976, page D.6). This technology is, however, in operation for global monitoring purposes (chapter 7).

The 'wiring' of the greater region, covering the territorial area of, say, France, aims at ubiquitous access to *all* electronic services. This idea is urged from various directions: to exploit the technological capacity, to overcome the diseconomies of large high-density populations by some degree of dispersal, to promote the arrival of the 'information society', to increase the productivity of information, etc. The advantages that business can obtain from greater regional telecommunications–computer services are such that we probably have to look no further than business initiative for the main dynamic driving toward making high-quality electronic services widely available across regions. As the key opportunity in this field is the combination of the capabilities of the computer with the newer telecommunications capacities we shall look at some of the ways in which new distributions of transactions are proposed or are appearing.

The French are much concerned about the concentration of population, government administration, manufacturing and business activity, and information-handling capacity in the Greater Paris area to the neglect of other parts of the country. They see the planning of information-handling services as one of the tools for redressing this imbalance (see DATAR, 1973). Part of the concept is that Paris would be regarded as the central locus of activity but that data processing would be regionalized outside Paris. This is illustrated in figure 4.2. The regional factories or offices would be able to exchange information with Paris individually or between themselves, but appear to be essentially conceived as operational or managerial in scope, Paris being responsible for policy.

In Britain the Greater London area is the focus of attention in regard to population and transaction location (see Goddard, 1973). Research attention is being paid to the question of further developing the use of the electronic technology for maintaining efficiency in the various arms of government, if further dispersal from London takes place. Study has been extended to the question of general commercial office location under the impact of the technology. Research has included studies sponsored by the Civil Service Department and the Post Office (see Communications Study Group, 1973). These studies have paid a great deal of attention to cost-effectiveness. There has been some limitation in the video field to experiments of the confravision type of technology (1971: between London, Birmingham, Glasgow, Manchester, and Bristol) in which group talks to group (Post Office Telecommunications, 1974a). There has been neglect of experiment with the Carleton (Ottawa) type of system and computer conferencing in which individuals can talk to individuals[1] (Coll et al, 1974). Nevertheless the British research is extremely interesting in showing the difficulties inherent in trying to provide even a part of the

---

[1] The Australian Telecommunications Commission (1975, page 36) appears to favour further development of confravision, while Canadian agencies, on the other hand, do not seem likely to push it.

background for assessing how electronic services are possibly going to develop and therefore what the distributional effects will be. As the researchers point out, cost-effectiveness assessed under present conditions is limited in predictive usefulness because of changes in the various factors (for example, relative inflationary elements in salaries and line costs). Telecommunications and computer costs continue to fall and services continue to improve, while personnel, etc costs rise and probably will continue to do so. Cost-effectiveness approaches are also liable to suffer because of the speed of hardware and software development.

Network thinking in all countries fondly dreams of totally integrated systems. The conceptual goal is a single system for all information processing and transmission. The large capacities and speeds of the newer transmission technologies (coaxial cables, waveguides, microwave, and laser) encourage such aspirations of unity. However, we do not start telecommunications systems *de novo* but already have large amounts of capital committed to the copper pairs of telephone networks, the coaxial cables of CATV local systems, etc, and to equipment designed to specific existing uses. There are vested interests, rivalries, and legal difficulties. In part the drive toward integrated systems arises specifically from the desire to

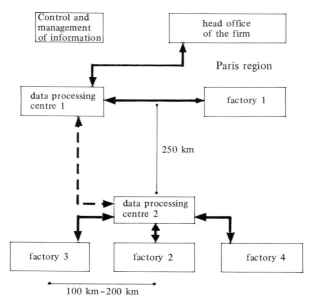

Figure 4.2. Suggested decentralization of industrial firms from Paris by using electronic data processing (EDP) centres. Central control of the firm could remain in the Paris region but some factories could be located elsewhere in France, thus assisting the implementation of the national goal of improving the distribution of economic activity. EDP offers the possibility of new mixes of advantage and disadvantage in the matter of centralization–decentralization. See DATAR (1973).

get rid of such limitations. In the home, for example, it is obviously a less than perfect situation which gives us two-way subscriber-to-subscriber voice communication by telephone but requires us to go to a totally different system for one-way audio–video TV broadcasts. It is clearly a possible aim to join these two modes and thereby enhance the capabilities of both.

Attempts to do this are various. Physically the two cables (telephone and CATV) can be placed in the same conduits and fed together into the buildings. The British call this constructional integration. They have used it in several new towns, for example Milton Keynes, Washington, and Irvine. The British researchers, as in other countries, watch carefully the possibility of both functions being served by a single coaxial cable. This theoretically could give subscriber-to-subscriber video. There are, however, serious obstacles in solving switching problems and at present most transmission facilities would be far below the speed necessary for normal TV. Constructional integration has also been used in North America, for example in residential development in Mississauga, Ontario. At the time of writing, it appears that Bell Canada is moving toward making constructional integration much easier in Canada.

A second approach—this time electronic—is to use the TV set for displaying incoming data fed in through a telephone network or other telecommunications route. The British Viewdata provides such a service. This allows data from a computer to be displayed on a home receiver or standard TV set equipped with a special modifier. A domestic Viewdata service is planned to begin in 1978 or 1979 in Britain. Teletext services, which allow the transmission of textual material, have been developed by the British Broadcasting service and the Independent Broadcasting Authority. One hundred and fifty pages can be transmitted in thirty-six seconds. The Ceefax (BBC) teletext operation keeps up to date a fifty-page magazine of news, etc for ten hours daily. It is technically accessible to about 95% of the population, although at present only a very small number of viewers have the necessary modifying equipment. This costs about $1500. One British firm is building the special equipment into standard TV sets. Teletext and Viewdata techniques appear to be the beginnings not only of joining the capacities of the telephone and the TV but also of the home information centre, eventually to be capable of full two-way operation (see Burkitt, 1975).

Where telephone and cable services are under the administration of different agencies there is a potentially competitive situation as to which will be first to begin a two-way service related to what is displayed on the TV screen. The beginning will most probably be a yes–no balloting capability. An interesting computer-assisted Canadian experiment in this direction took place in January 1976 with the use of the telephone and the Wired City experimental facility of Carleton University Ottawa (described in chapter 3). TV viewers having a touchtone telephone were invited to record their yes–no votes on certain questions arising during a short series of TV programmes. Such voting would be possible to certain subscribers with touchtone phones in the Ottawa and Toronto areas. The results of the ballots were flashed onto the TV screens later during the programme. Viewers polled 1036 votes.

In Japan the drive toward the rationalization of existing information systems includes the emergence of the Living-Visual Information System Development Association. This includes banks, advertising firms, electrical and cable companies, electronic equipment manufacturers, etc. The experiments undertaken at Tama New Town and Higashi–Ikoma are with the collaboration of departments of various levels of government—for example Posts and Telecommunications, Japan Broadcasting Corporation, Public Housing Corporation, and Tokyo Metropolitan Government (see Tama CCIS, 1974).

An important aim of these two experiments is to "... develop a multilateral and integrated cable city information system designed for households" (Tama CCIS, 1974, page 9). The Tama project concentrates on how to develop the multipurpose use of existing CATV, etc services. The Higashi–Ikoma exercise aims to develop an ideal coaxial cable system. Both projects will provide home or personal service and societal information service (economic matters, health, travel, administration). Tama will offer TV retransmission; original TV broadcasts; automatic repetition telecasting services (TV newspaper with audio and still picture); weather; transportation timetables; hospital, city hall, etc announcements; advertisements; pay-TV; facsimile newspaper service; request still-picture service (used for instructional purposes); broadcasting and response service (TV subscriber can respond by voice or data to educational programmes, discussions, etc). These experiments will be watched with interest.

Yet another aspect of the redistribution of transaction or data handling is computer time-sharing. This at first look may seem often to be centralizing in its tendency rather than decentralizing. This appearance, however, should not be taken at its face value. The 'parent' functions can be extensively decentralized although the electronic processing is strongly centralized. The principle of time-sharing allows users in a variety of locations to use the same computer for storing and processing data. For example, government head offices in Ottawa use computer capacity located in Toronto, 350 kilometres distant, taking advantage of cheap line night rates for accessing.

In the early days of computers, firms bought their own machines or hired them. This progressively proved unmanageable. Later developments have been in the direction of time-sharing of computer capacity and shared processing. This makes for both greater efficiency and the possibility for the smaller firms to participate. Some advantages are: disruption of services due to conversions to new equipment is eliminated; the method is pay-as-you-go; and sophisticated resources can be shared.

The organizational arrangements consist of specialized computer utility firms making computer time available to client agencies according to their requirements. The time may be on-line or a package technique may be used. The special software arrangements needed by the client firm are offered by specialized utility firms. These provide and manage the programmes and arrange for the computer time. For example, a department store may do its cash accounting and inventory entries by means of a computer located in a computer service firm, connected by dedicated or common carrier line. The account of the store's customer is automatically debited as a purchase is made. The firm providing the time-sharing computer utility service can manage a number of client firms—perhaps up to a hundred or more. In the Toronto area by 1975 there were about eight such major computer utility firms serving probably about six or seven hundred clients. A very approximate estimate of the 1975 revenues of these firms for their computer utility operations was $140 million. Some clients would be located across the country—as far as Halifax and Vancouver. A few worldwide computer utility firms also existed by the mid-1970s.

Such an arrangement of computer accessing, heavily dependent on dedicated telecommunications links and hirable computer capacity made available when required, could easily be projected to grow rapidly and become common practice. Before this application of the technology had time to diffuse extensively, however, a new development of very great importance arrived on the international scene. This we must now look at.

4.3 Universal shared packet-switching

In the electronics field the dream of a universal data network giving complete compatibility between all computers, terminals, and communications links has been vivid since the time when the close relationships between computers and telecommunications began to be imaginatively grasped. Digitization and the capacity to reconstitute the signal during transmission and overcome the loss of quality inherent in analogue transmission, were a long step toward the realization of this dream. Major difficulties, however, remained: problems of switching circuits, differences in hardware capability and design (for example, cable speeds, nonintelligent terminals), and the incompatibility of different procedures for interfacing and operating. By the early 1970s it began to be clear that the difficulties were surmountable and that universal networking would become operational well before 1980.

The easiest analogy for our present communications and data processing situation is with the early railway age. In the early 1970s each 'system' of computer service and its relevant telecommunications links was a 'railway' with its own gauge, preferred locomotive type, signalling equipment, etc. In the early railway age freight needing to be moved across two railway companies' territories had to be manhandled. Gradually nation states came to see the need for standardization and most countries eventually achieved integrated systems over which freight and human beings could move freely. Complete interchangeability of equipment and organizational arrangements for railways were not, however, always reached quickly; the British did not manage it until the middle of the twentieth century. What is astonishing in the electronics field is that, not merely within the nation state but also between nation states, universality of information handling will be achieved within four decades of the development of the first computer and within about fifteen years of effective interactive computer working, time-sharing, and high-speed, high-volume telecommunications technology being operational. By 1976 the way was clear for universal computerized data communication between Western Europe, Britain, North America, and Japan. Both the technologies and the organizational arrangements were in place.

Let us go back a little. In 1973, as a result of the work of its Computer Communications Group, the Trans-Canada Telephone System set up the world's first commercial nationwide digital transmission network: Dataroute. The Canadian National Railways and Canadian Pacific (CNCP) followed quickly with Infodat. These systems greatly improved the efficiency of transmission by using digitized signals, and reduced costs. Dataroute and Infodat work across Canada and may depend on telephone, telex, or other dedicated link. Their limitation is that they operate essentially by dedicating links with continuous circuit flow between sender and receiver. Switching between a variety of users is not operationally possible. Dedication is expensive because the link is charged to the user whether or not it is actually in use. At the time of writing, the Dataroute technology has shown itself effective and is matched by similar facilities in other countries.

These systems, however, do not totally realize the dream of universality. For this realization, intelligent terminals, packet-switching techniques for the transmission of signals, and virtual circuits (permanent or switched) have to be developed. Solutions incorporating these techniques in operational form began to appear in the mid-1970s: in Canada as Datapac (see Trans-Canada Telephone System, 1976a; 1976b) and Infoswitch (CNCP), in France as Transpac (PTT) and Cyclades (Institut de Recherche d'Informatique et d'Automatique, 1976), in the USA as Telenet (Telenet Communications Corporation, 1976), and also in Japan (see figures 4.3 and 4.4). By 1977 Datapac had Ottawa, Toronto, Montreal, and Calgary as nodes with fifty-four Datapac-serving exchanges. Infoswitch, to have fifty-nine stations, will be operational by autumn 1977 (Montreal, Toronto, Edmonton, and Vancouver are main nodes). Cyclades was operating with computers grouped into geographic zones: Paris, Rennes, Lyon–Grenoble, and Toulouse, the initial participants being mostly universities and research centres. It uses the Cigale facility for transmission. Cyclades also connects with the European Informatics Network (Ispra, Milan, Zurich, the National Physical Laboratory, Teddington, Harwell, etc) and with the European Space Agency with files in Frascati. Transpac is planned to be operational

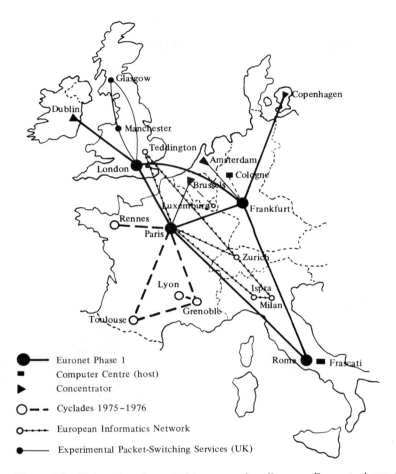

Figure 4.3. *Universal packet-switching networks: Europe.* Euronet, shown here in Phase 1, is a private network funded by the ECC and providing data base access. Cyclades in France began as a pilot operation in 1972, sponsored by the Comité de Recherche en Informatique; it was operational by early 1975 (shown here) under the sponsorship of the Direction Générale à l'Industrie. The participants have mostly been universities and research institutes. The European Informatics Network connects such institutions as Harwell, Teddington, Euratom, ETH (Zurich), and Politechnico (Milan). It can interconnect with Cyclades and with the files of the European Space Agency in Frascati. EPSS is an experimental network being run by the British Post Office. If satisfactory, the system will be expanded into a national public network with nodes probably in London, Edinburgh, Glasgow, Manchester, Birmingham, Reading, Bristol, Leeds. This system would link to continental and North American networks. In the drawing, contributing computers are omitted for clarity. Data from sundry sources including the British Post Office, the EIN Project (1976), l'Institut de Recherche d'Informatique et d'Automatique, and Cigale.

D

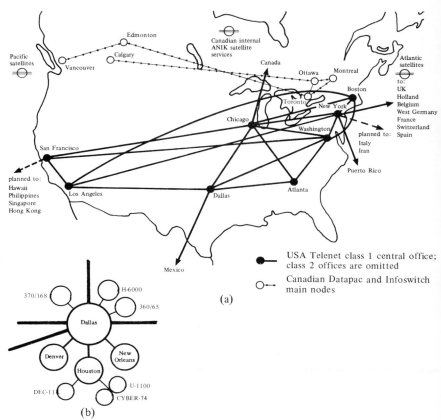

(a)

(b)

Figure 4.4. (a) *Universal packet-switching networks: North America.* The US is
served by Telenet, run by the Telenet Communications Corporation. The service has
eight multiconnected class 1 central offices, thus offering the adaptive routing of the
packets typical of this kind of technology. A network control centre provides constant
monitoring of operations. The error rate is claimed to be approximately one in 10^{11}
to 10^{12} bits between major nodes. Service began in August 1975. Since then the
network has been expanded to its present size shown in the drawing (late 1977) and
further internal expansion is planned for 1978. In Canada, Datapac is a creation of
the Trans-Canada Telephone System. Its 1977 nodes are Montreal, Toronto, Ottawa,
Calgary. Infoswitch has been developed by Canadian National and Canadian Pacific
Telecommunications. Its nodes are Montreal, Toronto, Edmonton, Vancouver. In the
drawing the two networks are shown with a single symbol for clarity. Access is available
to both networks right across the country; additional major nodes will be operational
later. In 1977 Telenet was granted authority by the US Federal Commission to work
to Europe, thus making the first intercontinental linkup for data handling on a routine
basis. The networks of North America combined with those emerging in Europe
(figure 4.3) are the first phase of global data handling on the basis of general accessibility
similar to that provided by the telephone. Material from documents of Telenet,
Datapac, and Infoswitch. (b) *Part of Telenet logical map.* Dallas is a class 1 central
office; Denver, Houston, and New Orleans are class 2 central offices. The computers
available may be linked to either class of node.

by 1978 with twelve nodes, reaching between forty and one hundred exchanges by 1985. The main nodes of the US Telenet were established as Boston, New York, Washington, DC, Chicago, Dallas, San Francisco, and Los Angeles. By mid-1977 about eighty US cities were connected and one hundred and fifty customer computers were linked up. Telenet had also been designated as an international carrier linking with the United Kingdom and points beyond by the Federal Communications Commission. The European Informatics Network covered agreement between ten countries plus Euratom by mid-1976, and had been accepted as the basis for Euronet, which will link terminals and data bases throughout Europe. Also by 1976 operational protocols had been agreed between Europe, North America, and Japan. As will be described later, this will give universality between these areas.

The national and international packet-switching public networks are developing rapidly and by the mid-1980s will cover all parts of the nation states concerned. Circuit time on all these networks is paid for only while data are actually passing and in some the tariffs are independent of geographical location. Speeds are of the order 75 to 50000 bits per second. It is to be noted that speeds in this range are not sufficient for TV, but, of course, graphic material can be carried, and slow-speed video technology can be used.

Very simply stated, packet-switching networks operate as follows. Telecommunications linkages in general may be of several types: point-to-point (direct between terminal and computer), circuit switched (gives the possibility of switching to a variety of destinations), and multipoint and multidrop (several terminals linked but connected with the computer via a single link). The digital Dataroute type of network uses these latter techniques, thereby winning increased speed and economy over the point-to-point linkage. Even this type, however, is limited by problems of traffic flow, of low facility utilization (because the links remain closed to all but their specific users), and of running computers below their capacities. A further difficulty is that these private systems are incompatible with each other. In this form universality cannot be achieved. Packet-switching eliminates these limitations by making possible universal, shared, intelligent networks which can handle many uses, many types of equipment, many computers, and many users. It can give universal access between them exactly as does the telephone but with the addition that all data and all processing are accessible universally.

The key idea is that nodal switching allows the matching of various types of hardware and software having various characteristics. The nodes are interconnected by Dataroute type digital links. These nodes, which are programmable minicomputers, make it possible to divide the material into separate packets for transmission. *This eliminates the need to link the transmitting and receiving ends by a physical continuous-flow circuit.*

The packets are reassembled for reception. They may travel by various routes, automatically allocated according to the traffic on the various links. The material of a complete message may therefore travel over several routes to the point of reassembly. See figure 4.5.

The packet itself consists of (a) the instructions and address, etc, (b) the data to be transmitted, and (c) an error control frame. The packets are fed into the network as soon as they are available from the point of origin, in any order. Link capacity is thus capable of being fully utilized.

It is the packet-switching nodes, virtual terminals, and virtual circuits which make possible compatibility between various kinds and brands of equipment and between various types of software. The mode of operation is transparent, that is, not tied to any particular symbolic logic.

Reaching general compatibility operationally also requires some rules of procedure to be agreed and set up. These are called protocols. The protocols are organized in several levels: client-server (rules for the client to observe in interfacing the equipment), virtual-terminal (standard method for all terminals to access the computer), end-to-end (packetting, transmission, error control), network-interface (between the transmission stations and the packet-switching function). The general acceptance of the details of these protocols is now proceeding rapidly, thus making possible the linking of networks for universal working-compatibility of networks. At the time of writing the only operational internetwork apparently working is the Cyclades–National Physical Laboratory hookup, although sporadic connections occur elsewhere, for example on Cyclades. As, however, the basic protocols for international hookups are already being agreed, the process of linking up will develop fast. This became clear during the deliberations of the International Computer Communications Conference (Toronto, 1976: see ICCC, 1976, page 343). The International Telegraph and Telephone Consultative Committee (UN) has produced a standard protocol for international packet mode operation. This is known internationally as recommendation X.25 (in Canada as SNAP—Standard Network Access Protocol; see Trans-Canada Telephone System, 1976a), ratified in March 1976. At the time of the conference, Japan, the USA, Canada, the UK and certain Western European countries had broadly accepted this protocol. X.25 covers three levels: the 'physical interface', the 'frame-level logical interface', and the 'packet-level logical interface'. Protocol X.25 was developed by Study Group VII of the International Telephone and Telegraph Consultative Committee (CCITT) in 1976.

The very great importance of all this is that the technology and the human organizational agreement necessary to use the technology most effectively have reached the point of potentially universal data communication between all types (terminals, computers, telecommunications links) and all makes of equipment on a worldwide basis. Potentially all hardware and all software are compatible. That this is a very major step in the development

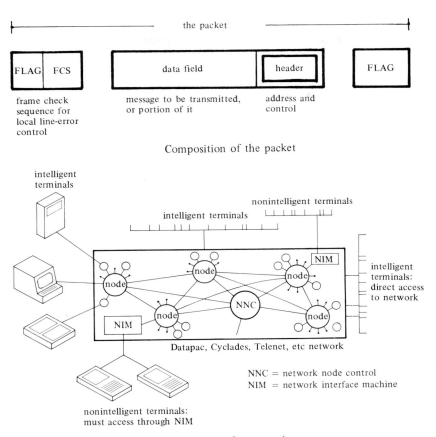

frame check
sequence for
local line-error
control

message to be transmitted,
or portion of it

address and
control

Composition of the packet

Datapac, Cyclades, Telenet, etc network

NNC = network node control
NIM = network interface machine

nonintelligent terminals:
must access through NIM

Logic map of a network

Figure 4.5. *Universal packet-switching networks: operation.* The message is broken down into small packets, transmitted by any route conveniently available, and reassembled at destination. Packets from many messages are interleaved so that high transmission and computational efficiency is achievable. The circuits and the nodes are described as 'virtual' because the message is discontinuously transmitted. Physical links are provided by existing facilities such as Dataroute in Canada and Cigale in France. Terminals incorporating microprocessors (microcomputers) can access the network directly. Nonintelligent terminals must access through special interface equipment (NIM). Each node may be connected to several others, but not necessarily all others on the network, as any node can relay a packet forward. Access points, shown as small circles, connect to the nodes, as do the computers offered for accessing (the small dots). As representing New York, the top right node will therefore extend the service to Buffalo, Rochester, Philadelphia, etc.

*of communications and therefore of human culture can scarcely be
doubted. It perhaps ranks with the jump from hieroglyphics to syllabic
phonetic writing. Computer-stored material and programs will be capable
of being universally accessible on an instantaneous basis.*

Of all the potential international developments made possible by packet-
switching between countries—industrial, commercial, monetary, educational,
cultural and political—none will perhaps be more important than the
opportunities made available for science at a time when the mounting costs
of scientific research become increasingly difficult for nation states to meet
individually. The difficulties and dangers of this situation were pointed out
over a decade ago by Alexander King (in Goldsmith and Mackay, 1966). The
greatest first bulk use of this technology, however, is at present considered
to be for transferring funds—between banks, etc, between firms and their
customers, and between countries. As the universal data network represents
a radical change in direction in the evolution of information-handling
systems the technology will not only serve existing institutions but will
foster the development of new communities of interest.

One such new area of interest will be the development of the technique
of networking between nations for purposes of global decisionmaking.
The need to initiate research in this field was responded to in mid-1977
by the International Institute for Applied Systems Analysis in Austria.
At that time the institute began to organize a series of workshops to be
followed by a formal research programme for investigating internet operating
and developing a structural model for linking national packet-switched
networks. The model would presumably relate to both technology and
protocols. Some such conceptualization will be essential for maximizing
the potential of the electronic technology for the purposes of handling
global issues in ways reflecting our more humane aspirations.

4.4 Data base management

The arrival of universal public packet-switching increases the acuteness of
the difficulties connected with the retrieval of data from computer storage.
The architecture of present computers is such that the user is unavoidably
involved in the details of data storage and manipulation when he attempts
to retrieve data. As the storage capacity of computer memories has
increased, this has led to increasingly complicated and expensive software.
Users frequently need specific programmes to be written for their particular
accessing of the computer files. Unless other approaches to data
management can be found, this will become progressively unwieldy and
computer usage will hit restrictive limits. These difficulties will rapidly
become acute as data stored in a computer is liable to be demanded by
an increasingly heterogeneous group of users through packet-switching.
Research attention is therefore now being directed in computer development
toward alternative models of data storage and accessing. An important
effort in this field is *relational associative processing*. This is being explored

in the University of Toronto where a Relational Associative Processor (RAP) is currently being built [2].

The principle of RAP is to devise ways of eliminating the need for access paths and mappings. This can be done by developing a computer architecture based on having many processors and memories linked in parallel with associative addressing of the data. With this method the data can be split up into more processable segments than at present. It can then be distributed over many processors and memories. These work simultaneously for storing, searching and retrieval, and processing.

The associative analysis on which the system depends is simple. A relation is seen as a table of data listing a set of similar entities, while the whole table represents a function. Thus in a department store, for example, one table shows sales, giving such data as the type and number of items sold and the name of the sales clerk. Another table lists employees— name, salary, department. A third shows location. And so on. Data in two or more tables can be related through common items, for example the sales clerk's name. Such a relational conceptualization of data makes it easy to program for accessing and is complete for computational purposes. Operations based on hierarchical, network, or relational models of data can be performed.

Newly developed capabilities in semiconductor technology provide the means for RAP. Relatively large storage capacity can be achieved in the very small space of silicon chips. This miniaturization allows a large number of cells, each with its microprocessor and memory, to be accommodated economically. The typical number of cells envisaged is one hundred. RAP can be directly connected to a conventional type of computer and accessed through a terminal or can be distributed within the terminals themselves. It can include a statistical arithmetical unit for processing data drawn from the cells.

If on-line planning (Sackman and Citrenbaum, 1972) and crisis management using computerized models and computer conferencing (Kupperman et al, 1975; *The Futurist*, 1975; also chapter 7) are to become realities, equally important with universal access to data is *rapidity* of access. Indeed, it would seem likely that the benefits of these techniques will be severely limited if individual programming for retrieval has to continue to be accepted for the larger proportion of the retrieval operations. RAP appears to offer a possible solution by giving great flexibility of data base and rapidity of search. Without it or something similar, the model-building and conferencing necessary to on-line planning would appear to be slow and likely to fail to capture the full benefit of the computer's capacity for high-speed computation.

[2] I am obliged to Dr K C Smith, University of Toronto, for information on RAP. (See "Data Management by RAP", 1976.)

The reader requiring a fuller access to the material on the forecasts for computer development may wish to consult Turn (1974), which deals with the next fifteen years or so in language manageable for the layman. Some of the major items of the forecast follow.

The range of alternatives in the architecture of computer systems will be widened and rendered more economical by the mass production of large-scale integrated (LSI) and medium-scale integrated (MSI) circuits. This development will increase computing speeds and allow some present software functions to be satisfied by built-in hardware. This will simplify the present proliferating complexities of the software part of accessing.

Solid-state and laser (argon) memories appear likely as an important development. Solid-state (for example magnetic-bubble) is used for mass memories with very large capacity for storage and cheap, but slow access. Such storage techniques are forecast by Turn (1974, page 194) generally to replace the present rotating kinds of storage technologies in the 1980s. Permanent-recording memories based on the laser are already in use. If holographic techniques are combined with the laser (electro-optical processing) a whole page of printed material can be instantaneously recorded and accessed extremely rapidly. This technology may well dominate in high-speed computers in the 1980s.

In general, in the storage capabilities of computers the problems appear to revolve round attempting to raise the storage processing speeds to the high speeds of the logic circuits, the rendering of the access to stored material more flexible, and enlarging the variety of the computer system architecture [3].

---

[3] During the several years that the material in the telecommunications–computer chapters has been built up, it has been noticeable that organizational, policy, legal, etc problems have become steadily more complex and more widely ramifying. For example, Cyclades has undergone a further recent reconstruction, terminology is often uncrystallized, questions surrounding monopoly of systems have arisen, and debates about equality of access to data and the availability of on-line data bases in the context of universal packet-switching have developed as suddenly operationally important. Very important also is the growing status of the infrastructure planning of the telecommunication–computer capability, particularly at national, and now beginning, at international scales. At the present levels of information much of this material is still very difficult to handle in a study of this kind, and must be left undetailed; for example, the focus of attention for international networking is not yet clear (see IIASA, 1977).

I have been unable to include in the text details of computer networks emerging in Eastern Europe. Some information, however, has been obtained; in Poland work proceeds on a network linking scientific establishments in Warsaw, Cracow, Wroclaw, Poznan and Gdansk (Bazewioz and Mika, 1977); also in Hungary, Czechoslovakia, and Latvia (between centres of the Latvian Academy of Science). The International Institute for Applied Systems Analysis, Laxenburg, Austria, is developing networking between institutes in several countries, including Latvia and Poland. I am indebted to Dr A Butrimenko, of the Institute, for the above information.

Breakthrough: understanding the life-support system

5.1 Perspective

We now approach the second area of major knowledge breakthrough. This is our understanding of how life is supported on the earth. Biology and ecosystems theory have been able to provide progressively coherent descriptions of the life systems of the world and how they have evolved. Darwin and Wallace put forward their hypotheses about evolution well over a hundred years ago, but it is since 1900 that ecology has most rapidly developed to become today a firm and rapidly expanding body of knowledge. An understanding of it is basic to the human enterprise because it illuminates for us terms under which our life continues on this planet.

For our present purpose ecology can be viewed as the study of living things, plants and animals, etc, in their interrelationships with each other and with their inanimate surroundings. More generally an ecosystem is a system of associated organisms which interact with each other and with their environment in mutually supportive ways.

Although McCulloch (1965, page 157) could write: "Today no biological process is fully understood in terms of chemistry and physics ... Few chemical properties are yet reduced to physical relations of atomic constituents. The mathematics is too cumbersome", we have discovered in very large measure the details of the ways in which the various living things (biota) relate to each other, to the energy of the sun (photosynthesis) and to the other constituents (abiota) of the physical world, in continuing systems which strive for stability, complexity, and diversity. The aggregate total living material in an ecosystem is called its biomass.

The life sciences, as well as moving downward in scale to very small systems in microbiology, have also tended at the same time to build their knowledge upwards so as to be able to handle ever larger entities. The concern for the larger physical systems supporting life is our interest in this study. The global aggregate of these systems is generally referred to as the biosphere, although ecosphere is equally correct.

Using knowledge provided by physics, the electronic technology has also followed this pattern of upward hierarchical development into ever larger systems, the smaller systems supporting greater systems above them. So we find some natural common order between ecosystems and our technological applications of the capabilities of the various regions of the electromagnetic spectrum.

In looking at ecosystems it is helpful to bear in mind that biological knowledge often emphasizes the living cell as the key small-scale entity, or basic unit. This is larger than the molecule of chemistry or the atom of physics. Biology also achieves a conceptual unity for the variety of life manifestations on the basis of all life on planet earth using nucleic acid

for storing and transmitting hereditary information in all species[1]. Kuhn
(1970, page x) points out that this clarity of form safeguards biology and
the physical sciences against certain difficulties evident in the behavioural
and social disciplines. *This coherence is a very important aid in attempting
to construct conceptualizations which will help us to bring together our
understanding of life processes, our uses of the regions of the electromagnetic spectrum, and certain aspects of human cultures.*
    One further item requires preliminary stressing. An element common to
all three areas is physical global space. All concepts of ecosystem must
take account of space, since an ecosystem always has some kind of physical
spatial expression—ranging from sea to pond, from a colony of microbes
to a continent. The electronic technology interacts with this fact of space
in that it virtually eliminates, or very heavily modifies, the friction of
space in regard to information flows. Human cultures generate relationship
with global space which result in modifications to 'natural' ecosystems,
and through various technologies, to dominating and 'hominizing' them.
Up to recent times, civilizations have also been spatially identifiable in
their occupation of specific parts of the world's surface. Until now no
civilization could claim to be global. Today we have an electronically
based emerging global culture, and to use a concept closely associated with
Teilhard de Chardin, we have a continuous sphere of mind enveloping the
earth, analogous to the biosphere. *This is a new ecological condition.
Locality now means something different from what it meant in the past
because it is comprehended in the context of the total world process, and
potentially all localities are in virtually instantaneous informational contact
with each other. Therefore all ecosystems are more closely related and the
ecological coherence of the entire globe has undergone a major change.*

5.2 Ecosystem theory
While ecology deals with self-perpetuating systems of all dimensions—
laboratory culture, pond, forest, wilderness, and biosphere—we shall
concern ourselves here only with ecosystems at the scale where human
populations can be seen as supported in the context of terrestrial space.
This means that the human sense of space on earth is a kind of common
denominator. As our sense of space is progressively enlarged by our
physical terrestrial movement and our use of the electronic technology,
our need and ability to understand larger ecosystems will increase. We
have already the beginnings of the conceptualization of the biosphere.

[1] Sagan (1975, page 53) points out that biology stands to gain a great deal from
space exploration because of the possibility of finding life based on principles other
than those on which life on planet earth depends. The biologist is constrained by
having only one type of life available for study. Exobiology may become a science
with great influence on earth biology. Physics also has a basic identification for all
matter, but this is universewide: protons, neutrons, and electrons are the same for
all matter, wherever found.

For practical purposes we can think of ecosystems amenable to some degree of human management as subsystems of it.

The sequence used in figure 1.1 is a helpful hierarchy to bear in mind: organisms, populations, communities, ecosystems, and the biosphere. The basic ecological entity at small scale can be regarded as the organism. The ecosystem can survive only if the relationships proper to all supporting organizational levels are adequately maintained. *The concept of levels of organization or integration is therefore of key importance. Yet, although the idea of hierarchy is clearly involved, no one level is to be regarded as dominant or as necessarily more important than any other. In ecology the total range of subsystems, all necessary, is cardinal to the concept of the ongoing system.*

The interrelations of subsystems are synergetic in the sense that the working together of two or more subsystems produces a new symbiosis (that is, upper-level system) whose characteristics are not deducible from the characteristics of the contributing subsystems themselves. A new level with some new and superior qualities or capabilities comes into being and continues to survive. A simple example of the principle of synergy can be found in water. The *atoms* of hydrogen and oxygen constitute separate lower-level systems; when combined in certain proportions they constitute water, which is a higher-level, *molecular* system. The properties and capabilities of water are not deducible from, or inherent in, the properties of hydrogen and oxygen. The same phenomenon of synergy takes place in psychosystems, as we shall see, and possibly in electronic circuits where 'learning' occurs. We are here touching on the theory of integrative levels formalized by Feibleman (1954), and generally accepted in systems theory.

A more detailed, but brief, definition of an ecosystem may be quoted:

"Living organisms and their nonliving (abiotic) environment are inseparably inter-related and interact upon each other. Any unit that includes all of the organisms (i.e. the 'community') in a given area interacting with the physical environment so that a *flow of energy* leads to clearly defined trophic structure, biotic diversity and material cycles (i.e. exchange of materials between living and nonliving parts) within the system is an ecological system or ecosystem" (E P Odum, 1971, page 8; emphasis supplied).

In the ecosystem certain substances such as water and carbon dioxide circulate round the system. These assist in the process of creating new materials, such as the protein and carbohydrate, necessary for the existence of what we conventionally call living entities. Atmospheric conditions also play their part. The system has in it *producers*, which are mostly green plants capable, by means of the sequential process of photosynthesis, of producing living material from nonliving substances. There are *micro-consumers*, mostly bacteria and fungi, which break down dead material thereby releasing inorganic material which can be taken up again by the producers to create new organic material. Thus the cycle is completed. Functionally, an ecosystem involves energy flows, food chains, nutrient cycles, and control processes. It is characterized by spatial and temporal diversity, complexity, cyclicity, the capacity to change, and a striving toward stability. The ecosystem exists in a condition of steady state. The North Sea is an ecosystem and so is the Amazon forest.

In the ecosystem we therefore have a concept which leads to a particul global view of the way in which life has evolved, is maintained, and continues to evolve on the earth as a whole. This is Spaceship Earth (Ward, 1966). Ecosystem theory, however, must be capable of coping with ecosystems containing large numbers of human beings, often in dense packed agglomerations. H T Odum and some other ecologists have taken the concept to be applicable to the city, inferring that the requirements an ecosystem can be satisfied even under conditions of human dominatio over virtually the whole ecosystem.

A key idea in ecosystem thought is wholeness, or the necessity to view the system in its totality. The concept therefore stresses synthesis and is *holistic* in emphasis; the parts must be seen in functional terms in relatic to the whole. Comprehension is not, therefore, simply a matter of understanding relationships between components. No single element can be said to be dominant in relation to the whole. Nor is the presence of system necessarily identified because relationships between components are found. The energy input, which is from the sun, can only occur, however, through the stages of photosynthesis taking place either in real time (contemporary photosynthesis) or in past time (past photosynthate stored as coal, oil, or natural gas).

The process of photosynthesis is very complex. It consists essentially the plant, through the chlorophyll in its leaves, bringing nutrients togeth with water and carbon dioxide to form new organic material. The proce can be diagrammed as follows in a very simplified form, for the daytime part of the cycle:

$$\text{nutrients} + H_2O + CO_2 \cdots\cdots \overset{\overset{\text{light}}{\downarrow}}{\text{plant}} = \frac{\text{new organic}}{\text{material}} + O_2 + \text{heat.}$$

Respecting molecular entities, this may be written:

$$6CO_2 + 6H_2O + \text{light energy} \longrightarrow C_6H_{12}O_6 + 6O_2 \ .$$

Energy originates from the atom fusion process of the sun (hydrogen helium) as radiation. This is absorbed by the plant and transformed into chemical energy, some of which is converted by animals, etc into heat, movement, etc. (For the details of the process see Lehninger, 1965, page 114 ff.)

This process of photosynthesis produces the material that serves for food for all living entities, since obviously the animals that the carnivores eat must originally owe their sustenance to vegetation or other photo-synthesis-dependent entities (for example, algae). The process takes place mostly within the visible region of the electromagnetic spectrum but also in the adjacent marginal areas of the ultraviolet and the infrared. It may be called photobionic as it is also in the same region of the electromagnetic spectrum that human beings have used to make the extension from sound to light (chapter 2)[2].

The stability of ecosystems implies some control process, or self-regulation. The concept to describe this, whether in ecosystems, in electronic circuits, or in biological entities (for example, temperature control) is homeostasis. The system always strives toward achieving and maintaining some plateau level of stability, equilibrium, or steady state. *This is substantially achieved in ecosystems, as in other systems, by positive and negative feedback loops, the operation of which holds critical variables within the limits required for stability of the system as a whole. Positive feedback allows growth; negative feedback prevents overgrowth. The tendency of any component of the system to run wild in overproduction or to fail to produce is thus controlled.* The relationship between cat and mouse populations illustrates: as the mice increase, more kittens can survive, but as the cats increase they press more heavily on the mice as food supply, and the mice then tend to diminish; and so on until a dynamic equilibrium is reached and will be maintained.

Energy and energy flow—the movement of energy through the trophic levels of food chains—are other important concepts related to ecosystem theory. E P Odum (1971, page 37) places the ecosystem within the laws of physics in regard to the first and second laws of thermodynamics, seeing the ecosystem maintaining itself at a low level of entropy by "... the total community respiration which continually 'pumps out disorder' ". Bertalanffy (1968, page 39) has a somewhat different view, maintaining that conventional thermodynamics holds only for closed systems, and that because ecosystems are open or steady-state, a new thermodynamics is required. This view is supported by the observation that life systems have increased in complexity and ability to support quantity of biomass during the process of evolution. For the moment it is enough to note that energy continuously flows through ecosystems, that is, energy is transferred from component to component in the system in controlled processes. Without this transfer there could be no growth, no life itself. The energetics of ecosystems is a study of rising importance (see, for example, Lehninger, 1965; Morovitz, 1970; Phillipson, 1966).

---

[2] Photobionic is used to describe life processes taking place in the visible region and marginal parts of the ultraviolet and infrared regions. In some ways the word lumino-bionic would be preferable but it has the objection of mixing linguistic roots.

5.3 Diagramming ecosystems

Ecosystems are usually elucidated by using diagrams in which certain
conventions are observed. Solar and fossil fuel energy are usually shown
entering the system from the left of the drawing. Niches occupied by
different species are shown with an ascending order of dependency.
Symbols are used to indicate: energy transformation, energy storage,
consumption unit, work gate, heat sink, etc. For full details of this
symbolic language see H T Odum (1971, page 38, and page 257 for
comparison with symbols for electrical circuitry).

As ecosystems are complex, a single diagram is generally only adequate
for showing some particular characteristics and must omit others for
clarity. To illustrate ecosystems in an overview several diagrams, each
with its own emphasis, are given in figures 5.1 to 5.4. Figure 5.1 is
designed to show the connections between producers, consumers, secondary

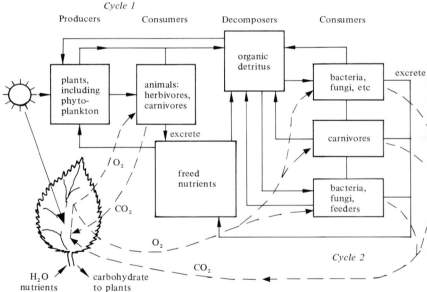

Figure 5.1. The ecosystem is diagrammed here to emphasize the basic relationship of
recycling between the biotic components: producers, consumers, and decomposers.
Through photosynthesis carried out by the light of the sun, primary living material is
generated out of abiotic materials. The nutrients are recirculated in the system by
excretion and through death. The diagram is for a land ecosystem; in marine
ecosystems bacteria play a role that is not yet clearly defined. The circulation flow at
the top left represents direct recycling of certain material. The autolysis pathway from
detritus nutrients is not shown. Carnivores appear twice because they function in both
of the major cycles. In cycle 2 on the right they are small and very small animals that
feed on the detritus feeders (mites, etc) and on the bacteria feeders. The leaf shows
the photosynthesis process taking place in the box representing plants; it permits the
paths of exchanges of gases between various kinds of biota to be shown: plants taking
in carbon dioxide (CO_2) and giving out oxygen (O_2), and animals the reverse.

consumers, decomposers, dead material, excreta, and free nutrients. These
are linked together through two major recycling sequences. First, top left,
plants provide food for animals, whose excreta directly supply the freed-
nutrient pool. Second, extreme top left, their dead bodies, etc become
organic detritus, which is linked to that cycle for freeing nutrients for
reuse through the components on the right side of the drawing. The
whole process begins with the plants, including phytoplankton, which are
capable of producing new living cellular material. This is done by the
plant being able to use the radiation from the sun to convert the freed
materials available to it (through roots, etc) into new organic material
(growth and maintenance of the plant itself and the production of its
seeds). Essential materials for this new production are carbon dioxide
(CO_2), water (H_2O), and minerals. Refer to the formula in section 5.2
above. All cycles recommence with the freed nutrients being converted
into new living material. The herbivores live on the plants and in their
turn provide food for the carnivores. Living material on death, and
excreta are broken down by the decomposers—fungi, bacteria, etc (macro-
decomposers and microdecomposers). The detritus feeders also provide
food for some carnivores. The full details of the microbial process of
decomposition are not yet completely known. The essential idea to
emphasize here is that the entitites—plants, animals, bacteria, etc—exist

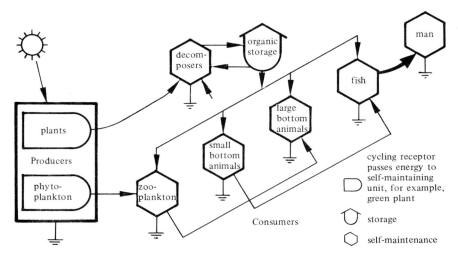

Figure 5.2. In this diagramming of the system the principle of trophic levels is
emphasized: life forms ascend in an order of niching. The chain shown illustrates the
sequence from phytoplankton to fish in an estuary. Organisms exist as systems
themselves by continuous throughput from their environment. The energy flow shown
is by habitats; the sequence of dependency can also be demonstrated by species,
trophic roles, etc. The symbols used are typically those of ecology; see also figure 6.2.
Each energy transformation involves the loss of energy from the system—shown by the
symbol for a heat sink.

because of continuous *throughput* powered as a total process by solar radiation, which is approximately 45% visible light, 45% infrared, and 10% ultraviolet (clear sky).

Figure 5.2 is designed to show how species build on species. The concept is that each species occupies a fixed position in an ascending range or hierarchy of life forms. This emphasis is often described in term of food chains. Each upper level feeds on a level below it. The principle holds throughout ecosystems. As at each level energy is lost in respiration, fewer individual organisms are supported as the hierarchy is ascended. The niching may be illustrated: the chain is driven by several varieties of phytoplankton; these support varieties of zooplankton; on the zooplankton live a range of small consumers—together with larger animals such as crabs the next niche consists of varieties of fish; fish may end as fish meal supporting pigs; pigs in turn support the top niche occupied by human beings. Ecologically speaking, the decomposing of these last is not entirely satisfactory.

Figure 5.3 introduces the process of respiration in ecosystems. This has to do with the interchange of gases. External respiration is the movement

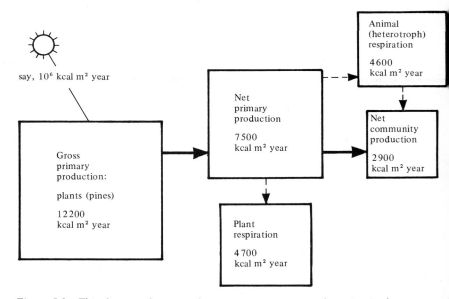

Figure 5.3. This diagram shows production in a young pine plantation in the temperate zone. The plantation is still in its 'young' phase. The squares are drawn so that their areas represent proportionately kilocalories per square metre per year. The bold arrows show the production chain. As the plantation will contain animals there will be a loss as a result of animal respiration which is necessary to maintain all the living material that must have organic inputs for its sustenance. This includes microorganisms fungi, and some bacteria—the heterotrophs. The net community production is what is stored after all plant respiration and heterotrophic respiration has been satisfied.

of air through lungs or water through gills. This involves taking in oxygen (O_2) and exhaling carbon dioxide (CO_2). Respiration also means the chemical reactions from which the organism derives energy at the level of the cell. This is called internal respiration and may be aerobic or anaerobic. The former uses free molecular oxygen but the latter does not. Some organisms use both, but some bacteria live without using free oxygen at all. In the diagram the energy budget of a particular ecosystem dominated by young pine is shown. About half is not used by the system. Of the other half the largest fraction is lost to respiration. This is why, as the food chain is ascended, the number of individuals in any niche diminishes in comparison with the niche below. The top predator in a series may be present in relatively small numbers. Time for growth also enters into the matter. It takes a shorter time for a mouse to grow but it is still the case that it takes a lot of mice to maintain one cat.

In figure 5.4 the presence of human beings in relatively large numbers in the possession of considerable technology is introduced. Our previous diagrams have shown essentially 'natural' ecosystems in which the species are presumed to be mostly other than human. If ecosystem theory is to be fully useful at a regional and global level it will need to account also for the large total population of the species *Homo sapiens* and take account of the special capabilities that this species has developed for influencing the behaviour, stability, diversity, and cyclicity of ecosystems. We are only at the very beginning of tackling this area of knowledge.

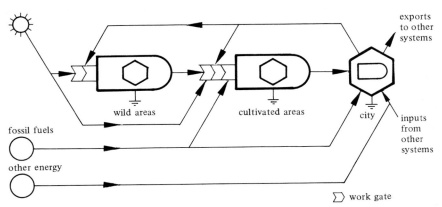

Figure 5.4. Some ecosystems are dominated by large human populations. The ability of human intelligence to 'design' parts of the systems then becomes an important component. Certain areas, however, such as forest and the seas remain wild, that is, in their 'natural' condition. Human-dominated ecosystems frequently import energy other than directly from the sun—from other systems in the form of fossil fuels, electricity, minerals, food, etc. These are 'artificially' stabilized systems dependent on heavy energy and mental inputs from outside themselves. The long-term durability of their stable states in their present organizational forms is dependent on these subsidies. The symbols are simplified for clarity.

Figure 5.4 attempts to show some aspects of preliminary conceptualization. Energy arrives from the sun to drive the 'natural' systems of wilderness (necessary for maintaining pools of genes, etc) and agriculture. The wilderness can fairly be called 'natural', but agriculture, although essentially operating on the base of photosynthesis, is heavily dependent on 'nonnatural' inputs in the developed countries. Energy in the form of food is produced both by the wilderness areas (includes the seas) and from agriculture. Both areas produce some energy in the form of timber, hydroelectrical generation, etc, conventionally classed as renewable resources. A second source of energy is drawn upon in the form of residues from photosynthesis which took place in previous epochs in the evolution of ecosystems—the fossil fuels. Progressively heavy dependency on this relationship with the products of extinct ecosystems has characterized Western societies for two centuries. These are nonrenewable resources.

In this diagram the notion of relationships with other systems becomes very important. The total system is only self-maintaining provided these relationships continue. Inputs of food, manufactured goods, and services come from other systems and in exchange the system itself sends out some of its product. Much energy is likely to be lost to heat, and 'waste' materials are likely to be random matter having no integration with the rest of the ecosystem. This applies to both inorganic and organic 'waste'. A completely efficient ecosystem has no such commodity as 'waste'. The total pressures of city on the 'natural' ecosystem are called the *ecological demand*. The essential purpose of figure 5.4 is to bring out the existence of *the very important question of how we are to make compatible and synthesize this knowledge of 'natural' systems with our embryonic attempts to understand 'human' systems.*

All the ecosystems of the world build up into the single global ecosystem, called the ecosphere or more usually the biosphere. The concept of the biosphere was originated by the Austrian geologist, Eduard Suess. The concept is of an envelope of life completely and continuously surrounding the earth. The biosphere is one of a series of spheres, which includes the lithosphere, the hydrosphere, the troposphere, and the stratosphere. The biosphere ranges between about 11000 metres above sea level, at which height only spores and bacteria can still live, to about 11000 metres below sea level. Very limited marine life can survive down to about 9000 metres. The range from just below sea level to about 3000 metres above contains 95% of all life. At sea level the extent of the biosphere is about 504 million square kilometres. Of this total 145 million square kilometres is land, and 359 million is water.

The biosphere is thus defined by the limits of distances out from the centre of the earth between which what we call life has appeared and evolved. With energy derived mainly from the sun, but also from the earth's geothermal and kinetic sources, life has developed and is sustained within the interactions of atmosphere, hydrosphere, and lithosphere.

It is important to note that the biosphere is quite precise and measurable as a statement of things observed. In one dimension it is the vertical range within which life exists and horizontally it includes the entire surface of the planet. It is therefore a *description* of something finite. But inasmuch as as we choose to describe by certain selected elements—living things, range of height, and range of horizontal extent—it is a *concept*. Concepts are of great importance because they are the building blocks of theory [3].

All areas of the biosphere are accessible to a wide range of the capabilities of the regions of the electromagnetic spectrum. The biosphere in its present stage of evolution is, however, *maintained* through heavy reliance on radiation in the region of visible light and marginal parts of the ultra-violet and the infrared. This dependency is shown in figures 1.1 and 19.1 where the photosynthesis band of the electromagnetic spectrum is fanned out to show the sun as the directly received source of energy at four levels: the biosphere, the ecosystems of the biosphere, the biomass, and the vegetation. We should note the component of conceptualization in all these descriptive words. Even vegetation—very finite—is in fact a conceptualized category, or type, of substance.

5.4 Many ecosystems are 'artificial'

It is very important when looking ecologically at the biosphere in its present state to recognize that many areas which we would describe as ecosystems are no longer in their 'natural' state. Human beings have altered various elements and processes in their effort to persuade ecosystems to deliver more human-usable material than would be possible from the 'natural' ecosystem. This species cuts down forests and plants grain, dams up rivers and dries out wetlands.

Because our numbers are increasing and our technology is advancing we shall inevitably push this process of persuading ecosystems to deliver ever more human-usable biomass to even greater lengths. The problem becomes one of maintaining the 'artificiality' of the ecosystems satisfactorily without degradation and reduction of desired output.

The danger of massive degradation of land and water ecosystems is only just beginning to be recognized. Advanced technology is just as capable of being used in ways that cause degradation as in ways that ensure continuation of existing steady states. Some apparently steady states may not be capable of long-term continuation without subsidy. Ecosystems are therefore vulnerable as never before, and the danger is global in scale.

As a point of departure it is useful to think of the 'artificiality' of ecosystems along two perspectives. The first of these is that the 'natural' ecosystem is induced by the application of human knowledge and

[3] Concepts frequently fuse two or more measures. For example, a hertz combines periodicity and time; watts are amperes × volts. Concepts then allow linkages between themselves, as a number of watts being equivalent to so many horsepower. Such linkages help to make it possible to develop a theory for designing electric motors.

technology to suppress its inbuilt drive toward the climax state and remain in a stage of relatively high productivity. The purpose of holding the ecosystem in this 'young' phase, is of course to obtain a greater output of human-usable biomass—food. This aim is further pursued by injecting additional energy into the ecosystem in various forms—oil for machinery, fertilizers, pesticides, etc. Under the pressure of industrialized agriculture, sometimes called agribusiness, many ecosystems of the world are now in a highly 'artificial' state. If they were to revert to a 'natural' state, in which only the products of contemporary photosynthesis were used, their output of food would fall drastically.

The principle of 'artificiality' is not new, but the present *degree* of it in the developed countries is new. Since human beings transcended gathering wild berries and catching small animals with bare hands they have introduced some degree of interference into the working of ecosystems. This has been done essentially by techniques or technology. The result has been more food and therefore increased populations. Until relatively recently the interference was at a low level and ecosystem stability was only rarely endangered. In some instances, for example, in some parts of ancient China, where horticultural methods of food production prevailed, long-term ecosystem stability was achieved while the ecosystem was sustaining relatively large numbers of human beings.

In the modern world the ecological demand is very high because of population pressures, sophisticated knowledge, and high-grade technologies. Apart from the question of the supplies of nonrenewable resources we do not know to what extent we can further increase the ecological demand or step up the degree of 'artificiality' in ecosystems. There are reasons to believe that there are ecological limits and that once a certain stage is reached very rapid collapse of an ecosystem can follow.

The second perspective is that large masses of human population are urbanized. Frequently urbanization takes the form of very large masses of population being concentrated in relatively small areas. These areas—cities or metropolitan centres—also themselves cluster, as in the eastern seaboard of the US or in northwest Europe. We have come, possibly wrongly, to think of these massed human beings and their physical equipment as entities. Whatever they are and however they may be conceptualized, it is clear they are very major components of ecosystems and that many ecosystems cannot be adequately described without including them. Furthermore they are the physical locations out of which emerge the means for 'artificializing' the ecosystems themselves. That is, looked at holistically, the city has a major component role *in the working of the system itself*. The city is not thus apart from the ecosystem(s) that feed it but is a constituent component.

This unity of human beings, their activities and ecosystems is strongly stressed by E P Odum (1975). He reiterates the need to avoid thinking in terms of man and nature and to conceptualize the systems as inclusive of human beings and their activities, even when the human beings are very strongly dominant by reason of numbers and capability for interfering in the working of the system.

Ecologists attempt to come to grips with the problems that this view entails. Although various researchers tackle segments, probably H T Odum is to be credited with the most persistent effort to be comprehensive. He has attempted the transfer of ecological understanding from the 'natural' world to 'human' systems (H T Odum, 1971) and has attempted some conceptualization of a 'world system'. He does this largely through the concepts of energy and 'work done'. He is thus able to diagram such subsystems as an 'energetic basis for religion', the energy relationships between the city and the food-producing areas, and the internal energetic dynamics of the Roman Empire (H T Odum, 1971, page 232).

A key human question is: How much further can we 'artificialize' ecosystems, and, to what extent is it now necessary to reduce our ecological demand on ecosystems, if we are to maintain human life as hitherto understood? And, what strategies can we develop?

5.5 Spaceship Earth: shakeup

During the 1960s there emerged a growing concern for what is often referred to as the 'environment' and for the possible exhaustion of non-renewable resources, such as oil, certain metals, etc. Such farseeing thinkers as Harrison Brown, MacKaye, and some others, had begun somewhat earlier to look at man's relation to his habitat with a new emphasis and to sound warnings of danger. Parallel with this emerging concern, biology was making great strides and ecological theory was rapidly becoming a rigorous discipline capable of offering a coherent view of the world's life system and of the essential workings of the biosphere.

By the early 1970s the stream of environmental awareness had become much stronger so that knowledge, concern, and ideas that had been confined to a relatively select few in the previous decade now received a general distribution. A feeling that human societies should pay conscious attention to the future well-being of the biosphere became widely diffused. There were certain books which received wide circulation, for example the British *A Blueprint for Survival* (*The Ecologist*, 1972) and *The Limits to Growth* (Meadows et al, 1972) sponsored by the Club of Rome. This latter, a private group of globally concerned individuals from many nations, has supported further research which was popularly recorded in *Mankind at the Turning Point* (Mesarovic and Pestel, 1974) and has sponsored subsequent reports by Laszlo et al (1977) and Tinbergen et al (1976).

By the mid-1970s the concern for the human enterprise on Spaceship Earth had some clearly identifiable major foci of attention[4]:

---

[4] An attempt to identify foci of attention in greater detail and to indicate some of the leading writers associated with each focus is given in Dakin (1973, pages 23–42).

1 Concern for 'overpopulation' of the world, in the sense of food and water supplies becoming grossly inadequate; poor adaptations by particularly urban populations (Dubos, 1965) producing deleterious cultural conditions; monstrously large urban agglomerations (Doxiadis, 1967); and unacceptable toxic levels in water, air, earth, and food.

2 The discovery that exponential growth quite quickly generates very large figures for the demand for resources like oil, metals, electrical energy, etc, and that some of the growth rates in the industrialized countries were already exhibiting exponential characteristics. A general conclusion that this rate of growth could not go on was reached and pervaded the consciousness of the period. Supplies would run out. From this insight there have developed a variety of notions about growth, some of them doubtless erroneous but some of them persuasive. The perception that attention to growth matters is important has reached the public consciousness, and previously assumed but unexamined values about growth, progress, and development have come under scrutiny.

3 There appeared fears for the stability and continuance of a society which had held certain ideas of freedom and liberty as particularly to be valued. The evidence for mounting instability was thought to be visible in rising crime rates, decaying and mutilated central cities particularly in the USA, decline in personal safety, and a strong tendency to rely on personal or local-group private security measures (in hospitals, shops, schools, etc), very serious difficulties in distributing the ever greater wealth produced, problems connected with the variable value of currency units, and a flight of the individual from communal responsibility. In 1975 the City of New York had about ten thousand youths in gangs committing every kind of crime including murder, and faced bankruptcy as a municipality. Some analysts, for example Heilbroner (1974), saw the situation in terms of an impending need for authoritarian rule as the only way of holding vast urban mobs in some disciplinary framework minimally necessary for society to continue. Emotionally charged books on how to survive began to appear (for example Ehrlich and Hariman, 1971).

These foci of concern were very generally acknowledged and by 1975 were receiving considerable attention from the mass media and in popular books. The reader may wish to refer to the considerable literature on 'environmentalism', for example O'Riordan (1976). Several other foci were also receiving some, but less, popular attention. Among these we could identify an important emerging focus that might be roughly called psychological. This ranges in interest from looking at the individual who is in some kind of trouble—for example perceptual, emotional, characterological difficulty—to speculating about the manifestations of difficulties that change causes in society, where the culture and the individual interact closely. A society holds together by the vast majority of its individuals being 'sane'. Rapid cultural change appears to affect the capacity of the individual to behave 'reasonably'. We may be looking here at confusion in society as a cause of the individual's difficulties or as an effect of changes in the underlying assumptions carried in the culture. We might see it as the culture being unable to sustain the society in forms that would be recognizable to us. Maslow (1970), May (1967; 1969), Fromm (1968), Laing and Esterson (1970), and others have worked persistently in this area of concern. These writers have seen it along the perspective of psychology or psychiatry, that is, of the individual's inability to perform in the society as at present constituted. Ecologists, however, have tended to look rather along an ethical perspective: different human behaviour is necessary not because the human being is sick but because the life-support system now requires new patterns of behaviour to ensure continuance.

5.6 Ethical dimension of ecosystem theory

The ethical transformation of contemporary societies has rapidly emerged as a focus of attention in the context of ecological thinking. This ranges from expressed concern about the ethics of business or politics to very serious attempts to generate new ethical postulates. Such postulates would aim to ensure that human behaviour would be appropriate for avoiding serious degradation or destruction of the life system of the world within which the human species must live. They would link behaviour to food supply at a fundamental level. To do this has always been a necessity of human existence in groups.

It would seem that this focus is dependent on the conclusion or insight, or, if we wish, simply emphasis, that many of the things as *individuals* we know very well we could and should do we somehow fail to achieve as *mass populations.* This is sometimes seen as the need to get people to behave 'properly'. The question, of course, is begged, since the whole problem is to decide what is 'proper'. An example of this difficulty is our touchiness over what we call propaganda. This usually has an overtone of brainwashing or influencing by means felt to be illegitimate or immoral (Ellul, 1973). So we regard Goebbels' propaganda as unacceptable, 'improper'. Yet, along the perspective of Heilbroner's (1974) scenario it would be 'proper' for the individual to be willing to accept the action demanded by the state propaganda on the grounds that it would be in the interests of holding the society together, specifically in regard to behaviour connected with the stability of ecosystems.

In practical terms, our scientific comprehension of our life-support system makes the challenge of survival starkly real to us. Part of the challenge is whether we shall have the ethical stamina to do *now*, or refrain from doing *now*, what may be necessary for maintaining the present artificial condition of food-producing ecosystems so that the *future* survival of even more of us will be possible. The relationships in terms of the ecosystems are simple: the systems must be changed by man so as to produce more human-usable biomass. As we do this the danger of system collapse will increase, so that ever greater care is required to counteract mounting vulnerability. The mechanics in terms of human decisionmaking, however, are very complex indeed. Action has to be taken at the level of the group or the society. But no society can act, in the long term, unless its individuals support the society by their individual actions and attitudes. Group life works on cybernetic principles. We therefore must look at the individual. No amount of societal reconstruction can substitute for this. *What emerges as a key idea from ecosystem theory and our discovery of how the life-support system functions is that the nature of the psychic profile of mass man may decide survival or destruction for the human enterprise through its relationship with ecosystems.*

From this linkage of ideas the question of whether a new ethic for a global humanity can be developed out of ecosystem theory emerges as very important. This question is fairly faced by ecologists such as Simpson (1964), H T Odum (1971), E P Odum (1975), as well as by thinkers from other disciplines such as Potter (1971) and Ferkiss (1974). Ecological theory could serve as support for Albert Schweitzer's philosophy of respect for all life. What, however, can be the basis of belief or motivation for behaving in accordance with the requirements of any such ethic? Scarcely, one would think, such weak psychological dynamics as H T Odum's (1971, page 253) suggestion of teaching the young "... the love of the system". It is this part of the cybernetic cluster of feedback loops, holding individual and society in viable symbiosis, which must become a prime focus of attention.

The pressure to develop a new general ethic for human societies seen as globally bound together moves in upon us from several directions. We need an acceptable ethic of survival simply on the basis of human numbers in our present condition, let alone when the earth will have to carry twice the present number of human beings. Second, in our electronic technology we have an enormously powerful tool for damaging or improving and protecting the capacity of the life-support system. It is an ethical question how we use it. Third, the technology is also a tool for forming attitudes and behaviour patterns and therefore for generating and maintaining a relationship between the individual and the society which can make a survival ethic workable. A new ethic mediating human action and the environment appears clearly to be necessary.

In the last analysis, however, human life is grounded in the photobionic processes. We are ourselves part of our own life system. We are not apart from it. It is the great gift of ecosystems theory that it has made clear to us this reflexivity. Humanity is a component of the natural order. The species and its actions are contributing elements in a bioenergetic system of which interdependence of parts relating to each other in a stable steady state is a key factor. Strivings toward a greater social justice and equity will achieve little unless the biological base of human life—now threatened— can be adequately maintained. Our numbers press upon the stability of the world's ecosystems.

5.7 Conclusion

Spaceship Earth quivers under many heavy blows. We have achieved, quite suddenly, a global view of ourselves. This realization has come from many directions more or less simultaneously: from electronics through virtually instantaneous communications (for example McLuhan, 1970); from space exploration looking back at the earth as an entity—the spaceship visible as a total object seen from outer space; from astronomy (for example Sagan, 1975); from biology—all earth life is a unity based on the DNA molecule; from knowledge about world population and resources; from the unity of the regions of the electromagnetic spectrum; from the understanding of ecosystems and the biosphere (for example, E P Odum, 1971), from general system theory (for example Bertalanffy, 1968); and from the unification of thought generated by the scientist as also mystic (for example Teilhard de Chardin, 1970).

This multiplicity of aspects of change, arising from the simultaneous perspectives of many approaches, is the ambience in which we now all have to think and feel. This is the ground of our emerging sensibility. It would be splendid to try to deal with these aspects all together. This is too difficult but must remain an aim. For the present we must adopt a more modest strategy. It will perhaps be productive of some firm outcome if we limit the attack to our immediate focus of interest, namely, the ecosystem and its relationship to our uses of the capabilities of the electromagnetic spectrum, in the context of the behaviour of mass human beings.

A very major difference between our two breakthrough areas is that a great deal of application exists in using the capabilities of the regions of the electromagnetic spectrum, particularly in the telecommunications–computer field, but in the area of application of ecological knowledge our experience is much more restricted and often at very small scale.

In the next chapter we shall look at some of the applications of ecological knowledge that seem important as pointing the way.

Applied knowledge of ecosystems

6.1 Perspective

The recent energy crisis has been attended by increased attention to the detailed linkages involved in our uses of energy, particularly of oil. We have become aware that it is not sufficient, indeed is dangerous, to concentrate only on the few links represented by the search for new sources, processing, marketing, etc, and are now alert to the need to trace out the full implications of our uses of energy. There is now concern to discover how much new energy will have to be expended in obtaining new increments or even maintaining present supplies of energy. Net energy studies will increase in importance.

The question of oil, gas, and electricity supply and consumption in their more immediate and obvious aspects has entered the public debate. This will not be discussed here. The threat of disruption of industrial production, employment, and urban life generally is obvious when it is remembered that manufacturing industry uses about 41% and transportation about 25% of all energy available in the USA, and that rates of increase in consumption threaten future supply (Ford Foundation, 1974).

The public is much less aware of the relationship between energy supplies and our industrialized agriculture. This question is receiving very considerable expert attention but what might be termed the 'agricultural establishment' remains pretty much as it was in its attitudes before the present energy crisis. The contemporary very heavy dependence of agriculture on energy from nonrenewable sources in the developed countries must now be considered a matter of very grave worldwide concern, made even more serious by the transfer of the attitudes and methods of industrialized agriculture to the developing countries, even as manifest in the 'green revolution'.

World stocks of grain have diminished from 105 days world consumption in 1962 to thirty-one days in 1976 (L R Brown, 1975). Only North America and to a much smaller extent Australia can be considered as grain-exporting areas. The capacity of these countries to export is heavily reliant on energy resources which are not indefinitely secure in either the absolute or the cost sense.

Part of the reason for the real situation being obscured is that we have relied on conventional monetary units for counting the costs of food in a period of 'cheap' energy. In monetary terms an item of food on the table may be very inexpensive. When counted in energy units—kilocalories or kilowatts—the cost may be very high indeed. In Europe and North America a single calorie on the table may have cost from five to twenty calories to produce (*Journal of the New Alchemists*, 1974, page 36). Sometimes an item of food may cost far more energy than it represents in itself. Most of the calories will have come from fossil fuels of limited supply and requiring increasing energy to win. Modern industrialized agriculture is therefore energetically unsound, however healthy it seems in conventional economic terms.

Modern industrial agriculture may be unsound also when measured by certain economic measures. The farm debt supervised by the US farm credit bureau was over $21·8 billion in 1973. It requires more and more capital to apply the energy necessary to run our mass-production farms. This capital is required largely for energy, either directly applied or injected along the support processes, such as acquiring the oil from which the fertilizers, pesticides, and herbicides are derived, and the obtaining of energy for the manufacture of equipment.

A third area of weakness in modern food production is that it encourages ecological conditions requiring correction. Uncorrected they may lead to major disaster. Monocultures encourage pests. These have to be suppressed by further applications of energy. They also reduce the number of niches in the ecosystem, so its overall productivity falls. To what extent natural ecosystems can be restructured to produce enhanced outputs of human-usable biomass on a permanent basis appears a very complex matter to determine. It seems clear, however, that areas now farmed under industrialized techniques can remain biologically stable only by continuous massive inputs of energy in various forms. If these inputs cannot be continued, and indeed increased, we cannot expect to maintain the outputs. Reversion to the techniques of 1880 could reduce production to one-tenth of the present food output in developed countries. This means that we are taking more out than can be expected as a continuing process. We are degrading ecosystems, and some suggest we may also be lowering the overall productivity of the ecosphere as a whole in our drive to bring ever more land surface under cultivation. This reduces the world's forest areas and impairs their functioning in the global ecosystem (see E P Odum, 1969).

The energy question is being tackled at various levels ranging from enquiries by governments, through major research projects (for example Ford Foundation, 1974), to individual experiment. Hitherto unexploited sources of energy such as solar, geothermal, wind and wave movement, and atomic fusion are being studied. Some of these are, very interestingly, sources which would not be depleted by being used. Solar heating for houses is an example. Brubaker (1975) thinks that one strategy open to North America, and perhaps the world, is to aim at using the remaining nonrenewable resources to develop new inexhaustible sources of energy. Many others see the development of renewable sources as essential to help eke out the nonrenewable energy supplies.

On the ecological side, experiments are appearing in many countries. These experiments aim at supporting human beings as far as possible within the contemporary working of ecosystems and without inputs from photosynthesis which has taken place in the distant past (oil, gas, coal).

The method consists essentially of respecting the diversity and cyclicity of the local ecosystem so that the system runs itself in a condition of continuing balance or steady state. Fertility of the soil is maintained onl by the products of the system itself. The ancient agriculture of China an other garden cultures indicate that relatively large populations can be continuously maintained in this way. Further, the energy cost may be very small, with variations depending to some extent on climate and soil. Some farmers in Malaysia and New Guinea can produce twenty calories o food for one calorie of energy as input (*Journal of the New Alchemists,* 1974, page 123).

Food and energy are closely connected to each other both as problems facing the world and in nature—since it is on direct solar energy that the production of all carbohydrate depends through photosynthesis. The simultaneous production of both food and energy in human-usable form suggests itself as a field for experiment. Can we capture more of the contemporary energy (for example, radiation, wind, etc) than at present and use it for enhancing the capacity of the ecosystem for producing food? Effectively, this must imply increasingly using the ecosystem's own energy to hold the system in its 'young', highly productive phase. If this can be done it may help us to find ways of living more within our energy income over the long term[1]. To do this it will be necessary to reduce the energ losses of human-dominated ecosystems, and closely integrate biological and renewable energy systems.

Various small-scale experimental attempts to do this are under way. Two examples are selected for description here: the work of the New Alchemy Institute under the direction of John Todd and the Nissan Island proposals in Papua, New Guinea. Todd and his associates have had considerable success in designing and running a miniaturized ecosystem at Cape Cod, Massachusetts. They were recently awarded $354000 by the Canadian federal government to develop their ideas further. They have now built a 'survival ark' at Little Pond on Prince Edward Island in the Gulf of the St Lawrence—officially opened in September 1976—and are further developing the Cape Cod experiment.

6.2 The New Alchemy Arks
The three-year experiment at Cape Cod has shown that an area about the size of a suburban house lot can accommodate a virtually closed-circuit life-support system capable of feeding a family of four or five persons

[1] We normally 'borrow' from ecosystems outside the one(s) we live in. The borrowin concept brings up questions of how we 'pay'. We shall see in chapter 20 that this matter is very important for ecosystems carrying large human populations in dense masses. In some measure such 'home' ecosystems pay 'distant' ecosystems by exportin *mental* activity. A great deal of work appears necessary in ecosystems theory to examine this kind of interchange between systems. Ecologists do not claim that they can yet offer the necessary conceptualizations.

(Todd et al, 1973). The system is based on algae (phytoplankton) production with the subsequent stages producing vegetables and fish. There are no 'artificial' inputs of energy, fertilizers, pesticides, herbicides, etc, but energy for pumping the biologically enriched water round the system is required. This is provided by wind power. Solar heat is

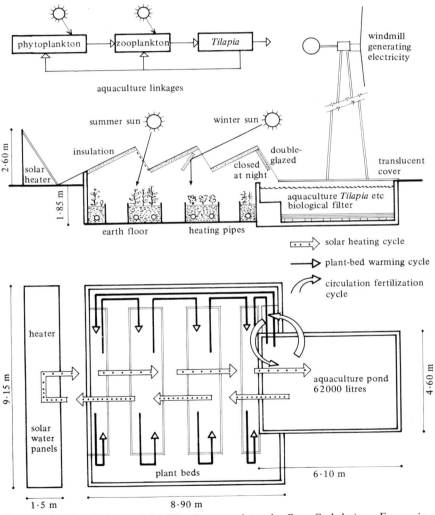

Figure 6.1. New Alchemy Ark. The diagrams show the Cape Cod design. Energy is from renewable sources: wind, solar, and geothermal (pit greenhouse). The system replaces the usual chemical controls with biological ones. Water is pumped through the system to circulate heat and nutrients. In the aquaculture the waste–algae cycle must be maintained at a level productive for the total system. The pond has to be held at about 30 °C. Redrawn from *Journal of the New Alchemists* (1974).

captured for maintaining the necessary temperature, with some reliance on geothermal energy, which is exploited by placing the vegetable growing areas below the frost line. The system is driven by the algae carrying out the processes of photosynthesis. The sequences and niches of the system are shown in figure 6.1 and the ecological analysis is diagrammed in figure 6.2.

A key to the success in obtaining the necessary high level of productivity is persuading the fish that they are living in a river and not in a pond. It is a matter of observation that fish in a small pond or tank are not as prolific and do not grow as large as those in a river, where there will be a better flow of nutrients. Part of the explanation of this difference appear to be that there is some sociobiological control of population by the population of the species itself, on the basis of the availability of food and other inputs. Hence if the food supply is sensed to be plentiful the fish will breed more and grow larger [2]. The mechanics of the experimental technique therefore consist of supplying the fishpond with enriched water as it would be found in a river. This technique has been developed out of Todd's research into the yellow bullhead fish (*Ictalurus natalis*), which he showed sends messages to others of its species by excreting chemicals into the water. These messages have to do with the species population exercising control over its rate of reproduction (Todd et al, 1967).

The 'bioshelter' now in operation on Prince Edward Island, Canada, comprises about the same covered area as a large suburban house (figure 6.3 the site, donated by the Prince Edward Island provincial government, is approximately seventy-three hectares and includes seashore. The island receives about 2000 hours of sunshine annually and has a high wind profile—useful for generating electricity by windmill.

The principle of the ark is that it is an artificial river, water moving through it at about 2000 litres per hour. The pumping operation is powered by a group of specially designed windmills. The 'river' permits the maintenance of a complete food chain. This begins in the first set of tanks where algae (phytoplankton) are grown under sunlight. Reinforcing nutrients are pumped into this set of tanks from the last set of tanks in the chain, where the fish are. The effluents from the fish stimulate the algal growth; the algae in turn can be eaten by the fish. In the second set of tanks algae and zooplankton are grown. The enriched water from this stage is pumped into the third bank of tanks, which contain the fish.

---

[2] Todd's bullhead fish research suggests that he has found the biochemical control linkage between environment and population. The key concept is food-population. In man the control linkage cannot be inferred to be biochemical alone. Later, this book attempts to suggest certain concepts to help deal with this. In principle the key idea is that controls are no longer 'biological' alone both for 'nature' and for 'man-environment' but now depend heavily on 'mind' (or its product, *psychomass*—chapter 19 because of the size and general global distribution of the human population.

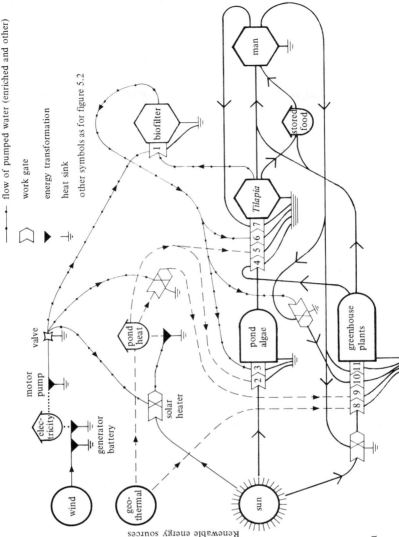

Figure 6.2. Energy flows of the New Alchemy Institute's Massachusetts ark. Although strict self-sufficiency is not necessarily a major goal of the Institute's research, this system is self-sufficient. That part of the system which directly supports the human beings through photosynthesis in plankton and vegetation is shown in heavy line at the bottom of the diagram. The geothermal and wind energy loops are shown lighter for easy reading. The system is, however, to be regarded as a totality. The symbols used are those conventionally employed in ecological energetics. The reader desiring a full explanation of the symbols should consult H T Odum (1971, page 26ff and, for equations, his appendix). The process of the system includes: 1 enriched water from fish pond (*Tilapia*) pumped through biological filter; 2 growing temperature of algae raised by geothermal and solar heat from pond; 3 nutrient fish wastes pass into algae pond; 4 terrestrial plant material fed to fish; 5 geothermal and solar heat passes to fish tank; 6 growth inhibitors removed; 7 fish husbandry by humans; 8 geothermal heating—pit greenhouse; 9 night warming of greenhouse; 10 irrigation by nutrient-rich water; 11 vegetable gardening by humans. Drawing based on diagram in *Journal of the New Alchemists* (1974).

Because the water is enriched, the fish reproduce rapidly and grow up to one kilogram or so in weight. The fish chiefly used, found by experimen to be the most productive, is *Tilapia aurea* (St Peter's fish), which comes from East Africa and lives in freshwater. About ten species of fish, including Israeli carp (*Cyprinus carpio va. Specularis Lacepede*), are used.

The system yields a surplus of aquatic plant material. This can help to support livestock outside the system—chickens, pigs, etc. Also some of the enriched water can be diverted to provide irrigation for the growing o vegetables. Some indoor growing space is included in the project, for

(a)

(b)

Figure 6.3. (a) The south front of the Prince Edward Island Ark. The greenhouse stretches across the front of the building. It is roofed with translucent plastic sheets. The living accommodation is on the left-hand side. The sea—the east end of the island—is behind the camera. (b) Plant beds in the greenhouse and, on the left, the rows of translucent plastic fish ponds.

producing such vegetables as tomatoes, beans, lettuce. In the Prince Edward Island ark the temperature in the tanks is maintained by liquid-type solar heaters and the greenhouses by air-type heating that uses rocks for heat storage (figure 6.4). The basic threshold of climate, however, is provided by the 'river' of tanks holding the phytoplankton, zooplankton, and the fish (up to 20000). Very interestingly, research has shown that the transparent plastic tanks can maintain their own temperature as a result of the life processes going on inside them. They act as solar furnaces [3] (Todd, personal communication).

In addition to aiming at a high degree of self-sufficiency, the Cape Cod ark will be expected to provide an income for those who run it. Todd thinks these arks might become the farms of tomorrow, and talks of 'farming ecologists' and 'biological designers'. The Prince Edward Island ark comprises a variety of basic activities: living space, laboratory, aquaculture, and greenhouse, capturing its own energy, and recycling its wastes. Power from the windmills, when surplus, will be made available to the public supply system of the island. Research findings will also be an 'export'. Produce may be sent to market.

The Institute has had considerable success with its demonstrations but is modest in its claims. The idea is to develop *one* alternative to our present industrialized and energy-hungry agriculture. The proposals would be a way of reducing the energy demand of our present mass processes of food production and would shift the focus of at least some food production back to the small group.

Todd sees the arks as ways of beginning to diversify and therefore render more stable our ways of producing food. He visualizes a new type of farm that is near self-sustaining and could supplement food supplies in our present kind of socioeconomy. In the poorer countries it might provide a vehicle for survival. Further, as the techniques can be applied in very small space even city dwellers might use them. Already a beginning is being made with solar heating for houses in several countries.

The New Alchemists range well beyond the immediacies of their experiments and techniques into questions of worldwide significance. "The trend toward global biological homogeneity must be reversed, with some of the land presently being farmed or intensely forested being

---

[3] The plastic tanks (two thicknesses of transparent plastic with air space between) used in experiments at Cape Cod maintained 5 °C in an outside temperature of −20 °C. The plastic tanks allow a maximum penetration of light. This biological solar furnace effect may be a discovery of a natural fact very important for our manipulation of energy, like the fact that steam expands as the pressure is lowered—a key fact in the design of steam engines. When visited in June 1977 the tanks in the Little Pond ark had not been connected up and it was not entirely clear whether this would be done shortly or the tanks would be kept separate for a new programme of research. The principle described is essentially that which governed the working of the Cape Cod ark. Its effectiveness appears to have been clearly demonstrated.

E

allowed to revert back to nature" (*Journal of the New Alchemists*, 1976, page 63). "In the future the scale of human endeavors should be reduced and regionalized, so that by so doing we shall become more sensitive to the direct effect of our actions" (page 75). "Restructuring agriculture is fundamental to the future" (page 61; also see Todd in Clarke, 1975).

Todd's overall view needs to be given as essential context for his practical applications. It is that science has now become so fragmented into uncoordinated specializations that it is without any vision of the whole. But, he thinks (personal communication), *there is a holism emerging of which biology may be taken as the metaphor.* We are "... at the cutting edge of a scientific revolution which will fundamentally alter our culture" "... the design maps of the twenty-first century must come from the living world". He strongly emphasizes the systems approach to what he is doing

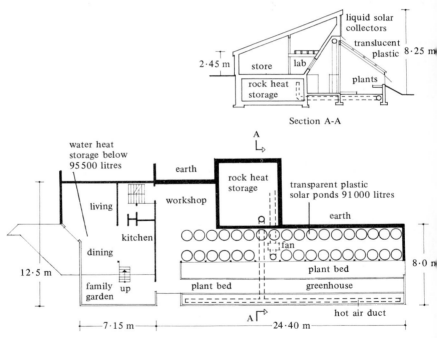

Figure 6.4. New Alchemy Prince Edward Island Ark, Canada. The algae–fish sequence is accommodated in the plastic solar ponds. At present the ponds, designed interconnected to form a solar river, are independent. The air in the greenhouse heats up by day, its heat being retained in the rock storage and drawn upon when necessary through the air ducts. Heat is also collected by the upper-level vertical liquid collectors and stored in the water storage under the family part of the building. The solar ponds make a contribution to heating the building. Experience through the first winter, 1976–1977 suggested that the rock-storage air system together with the solar ponds is substantially capable of meeting the heating need. The architects for the project were Solsearch, Cambridge, Massachusetts.

a most important aspect of the ark being the electronic monitoring of its biological conditions—temperatures, flows of gases, amount of sunlight, etc—to help understanding of the system as a whole.

It is very interesting that the provincial government of Prince Edward Island is giving strong support to the efforts of the New Alchemy Institute. The government is placing great emphasis on the development of renewable energy resources and has withdrawn from a proposed atomic reactor scheme for electricity generation intended to serve Prince Edward Island and New Brunswick.

6.3 Some comments on the arks experience
With full appreciation of what is being achieved, it may be useful to raise some questions and underline some aspects. First, how are the micro-elements, such as phosphorus, copper, etc, lost in the produce exported, to be replaced? These would appear to be steadily drained from the system. Second, what do calculations of net energy show? The buildings and equipment represent energy inputs which have to be paid off before net energy can be credited from solar and wind power. Cement, all metals, especially aluminium, and glass require considerable inputs of energy for their manufacture. So does transportation of material to the site. Solar energy is not 'free' until it has paid off the energy costs of its panels, pipes, plastic, etc. The net energy balance sheet of the arks would therefore be of great interest. In theory at least, the calorie costs of the labour used and the costs of the information brought to bear should also be in the calculation, although these add complications. (It seems that we urgently need to broaden our processes of costing many things to include energy and information costs; energy is measurable in calories or kilowatts, but a measure for information costs seems lacking).

A third comment is that the underlying scientific discovery of Todd's original research on the bullhead fish appears to be yet further evidence that understanding of behaviour can be derived from biological studies. "We found that ... some fishes have evolved *chemical* languages by which they communicate complex and intriguing *social* information" (emphasis supplied; *Journal of the New Alchemists*, 1974, page 81; for detailed paper see Todd et al, 1967). This does not mean that Todd is unaware of other aspects of such relationships for he also comments: "... it may be the animals with intricate social organization that act as the biological regulators and tuners of the ecosystems they inhabit" (*Journal of the New Alchemists*, 1976, page 64). The first part of this two-flow process is represented by the Lamarckian stream in modern thought strengthened today by the work of E O Wilson (1975), J B Calhoun (1970), G Bateson (1972), W S McCulloch (1965) and many other neo-Darwinian thinkers. The key idea of this stream is that life is built up in a hierarchy (mounting levels) of progressively complex systems, each successive system being capable of functions unattainable by the system below it. The second stream—the idea that highly developed societies strongly influence their ecosystems—is more widely diffused, more conventional, and more implicitly assumed. Perhaps because it flatters the human species! What is interesting about Todd is that he acknowledges and combines the two—an achievement of reconciliation quite possible when we think cybernetically.

A further perspective is that of human know-how related to ecosystems. As populations increase, human beings have to learn how to obtain more human-usable biomass from ecosystems. Increasingly we must do this without impairing the ability of those systems to continue the production of food. This means that more knowledge must be continually obtained and applied if population increase is to be sustained and nutritional standards are to be held. So we must drive toward the acquisition and application of more knowledge in order to maintain and improve standards of living, understood in the broadest meaning. This implies that the biology on which we depend must be ever more closely linked with 'mind'. As we shall see in a later part of this book, the notion of *the dependency of the biosphere on the development of mind must now be a very major focus of our attention. The biosphere is no longer to be assumed as automatically capable of repairing the damage it may be sustaining. The experiments and thinking of the New Alchemists appear to point directly to this new requirement.*

An extension of the Institute's line of thinking would be to add the maximum use of the telecommunications and computer technology to the bioshelter. The intention would be to achieve maximum opportunity for interaction between separate bioshelters, with minimum physical movement of human beings. This would make possible a high level of information interaction with a very small expenditure of energy—a small fraction of that provided by the windmills. For this purpose computer communication and conferencing (chapter 4), among other modes, would seem likely to prove practical. The bioshelter or ark would thus be a centre of high biomass production for human use and would maintain a high level of information and interaction. The latter seems increasingly to be as important as the former in the face of global population pressures.

Lastly, thinking on the global scale, the Alchemists' vision of at least a partial reversal of the present dominance of mass production in agriculture as understood in the developed countries would fit very well with the views put forward by Barbara Ward for the 1976 United Nations Conference on Human Settlements (Ward, 1976). As the present rural population of the world (nearly $2 \cdot 5$ billion) will be about $3 \cdot 5$ billion by 2000 AD it will be essential to encourage small farming—thus providing needed jobs—and increase the productivity of the small farm, particularly in the developing countries. She stresses that already in some countries (India, Taiwan, Japan, Brazil) the higher yields come from the smaller rather than the larger farms. The potential outputs are indicated by the national differences in annual grain output in kilograms per hectare: for example, Japan, 841;

Denmark, 708; India, 173; (Ward, 1976, page 176ff). Todd's techniques of combining aquaculture, greenhouse culture, and renewable energy resources within a largely self-sustaining system could be a useful addition to the small farmer both in developed and in developing countries. And also, small may indeed be beautiful, as Schumacher (1974) so cogently argues.

6.4 Ecodevelopment for a community: Nissan Island
There now exist the beginnings of thinking and experiment in planning the development of communities' life-support systems and socioeconomies on an ecological basis. The example we shall examine is the project for Nissan Island, Papua New Guinea, drawn up by Chan and Saini (1975).

The proposal is designed to support development within an eight-point policy framework adopted by the government of Papua New Guinea. These points include: increasing the proportion of economic activity controlled by individuals and groups, distributing income more equally, decentralizing economic activity while emphasizing agriculture, and fostering of a more self-reliant economy.

The diagram of the system—mixed ecological and socioeconomic—is shown in figure 6.5(a). The underlying principle is that all 'wastes' are utilized by being made available to another part of the system. The flow of water through the system is basic; it flows out of the system carrying nothing in the way of 'wastes', nutrients, or minerals. The plan includes water, land, and resources management.

As the proposal is ecosystemic, description can theoretically start with any component in any one of the cycles, but for convenience we may begin with the livestock and the human beings [figure 6.5(b)]. The livestock are pigs, chickens, goats, and cattle. Water is wind-pumped to ensure supply to the whole system. The animals and human beings feed from the products of the system. All excreta are collected in a digester which settles up to 69% of the solids and generates methane gas. This is supplemented by producing hydrogen from the electrolysis of water, electricity being provided by wind turbine. The gas is an energy source which can be used domestically and for powering small industries. Further energy may be provided by damming up water.

The digested effluents from the digester are led into algae tanks to grow animal feed and to supply the tanks in which plankton is grown. The plankton supplies the fish tanks with food; the fish tanks in their turn deliver their outflow of enriched water to the gardens for growing vegetables, etc. There are three levels of photosynthesis: the algae tanks, the plankton tanks, and the fruit and vegetable gardens. The fish ponds help support ducks, geese, and shellfish. The system keeps going essentially because of the very rapid growth of the algae and the plankton. Under favourable conditions weight of the algae can double in twenty-four hours. The sludge from the digester is dried and used as humus. The livestock can be fed with the fish and the produce of the gardens together with the algae, which are rich in vitamins and protein. Where a market is near the settlement, however, it may be profitable to sell the produce and buy animal feed. The human beings can eat the livestock, algae, plankton, fish and garden produce.

The size of the working unit is interesting. A digester of about 1135 litres will serve twenty-five to thirty pigs and an equal number of chickens, and will provide enough fuel for a human family. The piggery would be large enough to shelter ten sows. The algae tanks would total about 112 square metres. The total area of land per family of six individuals would be about one hectare. The families would be aggregated into clusters of eight. This becomes the basic settlement unit capable of sustaining certain communal functions.

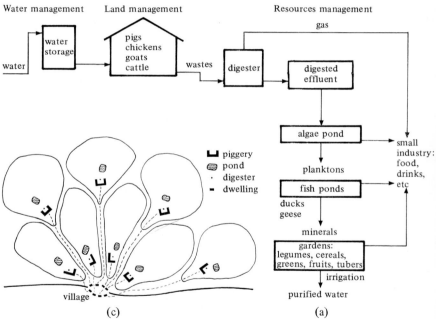

Figure 6.5. Nissan. (a) *Integrated farming system.* This example of a designed short food-chain system for sustaining human beings stresses full use of all organic wastes. The outside of the digester is painted black so as to maximize heat absorption and thus to accelerate the bacteriological action. Theoretically all that remains unused at the end of the sequence is pure water. Redrawn from Chan and Saini (1975).
(b) *Diagram of relationships.* Note that the livestock receive feed from several levels— algae, fish, and gardens. Surplus wind-generated electricity is used to break down water to release hydrogen, which is added to the methane from the digester to provide energy for minor industry, etc. Adapted from Chan and Saini (1975).
(c) *Clustering of farms.* The residential buildings can be clustered so as to form a hamlet capable of providing some basic social interaction between the human beings. Each farm is about one hectare in extent.

It is noteworthy that all animals must be fenced in so that effluents are concentrated and that a daily supply of new material must be fed to the digester. The functions of time and temperature are important to the proper working of the digester.

The plan of the grouped farms allows the houses to be clustered at the focus point of the farming lots [figure 6.5(c)]. This village would have eight houses and perhaps a communal building. Two or three such villages could be located very close to each other to make a sizeable rural settlement capable of serving as a sociopolitical unit.

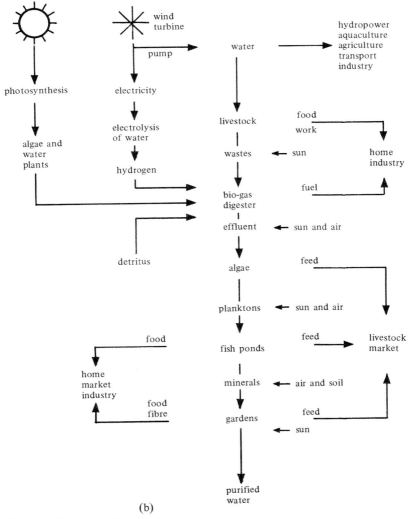

(b)

Figure 6.5 (continued)

6.5 Comment

Among the many experiments in setting up human life-support systems
with a large measure of self-sufficiency, the examples of the arks and the
Nissan proposals stand out for their completeness. The arks concentrate
on the shortest possible chain of linkages—algae, zooplankton, fish. Nissan
exploits a much larger chain and takes off material for human and animal
food at a succession of levels and therefore offers a richer variety than the
arks. The price paid would appear to be greater complexity of system and
heavier demand on management skill.

Both systems depend on wind power and therefore need to have efficient
wind turbines. These are not easy to design and have size limitations.
Todd's use of hydraulic lines to concentrate the power of several mills may
well overcome the size difficulty. An entirely new kind or turbine which
does not have to face into the wind is being developed in Canada and may
provide a breakthrough in this technology.

Perhaps the most important area of comment is that which lies around
the relationship of the nearly self-supporting system to the 'outside'
socioeconomy. This is difficult to think about because we do not appear
to have adequate concepts or a paradigm of theory to help us tackle our
ecology–socioeconomy. Attempts are made (for example H T Odum, 1971)
to do the necessary linking through energy flows. This is essentially the
approach of energetics. This line of thought is clearly pushing well into
the question but leaves out something of the essentially cybernetic nature
of the system examined since informational-flow aspects may be equally
significant. Ecosystems and socioeconomic systems both depend heavily
on information and its movement in the system.

The Nissan proposal is extremely interesting in that it demonstrates in a
practical way the difficulty of bringing different disciplinary areas together.
The proposals show most careful attention to the life-support system but
very little to the socioeconomic aspect except to allow for products—food
energy, etc—moving into some sort of a presumed market economy. What
is omitted is that the workings of that market economy would have their
repercussions on the working of the well-thought-out life-support system.
The need for a paradigm of thinking and acting that will cope with both is
apparent[4].

The problem is difficult to focus. If the socioeconomic system is
successful it will tend to find cheaper (meaning apparently lower-cost)
ways of handling some of the essential sequences of the life-support
system. These sequences, being neglected, will ruin the viability of the
whole. For example, fishing out to sea from the island might be far more

[4] It is to be noted that because the relevant disciplines have not yet been brought
together there is a clumsiness of technology. We have to distinguish life-support
system thinking from socioeconomic thinking, at least until some conceptual joining
can take place. Socioeconomic theory and practice can destroy the life-support system
This has happened in historical examples.

productive of fish than the fish tanks, for the effort expended. Then the system loses the fish effluents which salvage minerals and pass them on as fertilizer for the gardens. We are therefore faced with the need to show against what criteria of assessment the chain of linkages is to be judged. Both systems would presumably need criteria and some of these would be the same. For example, stability of system would seem desirable in both the ecological and the socioeconomic system.

For the moment this matter must be left here. The presence of this difficulty is alone enough to suggest that we are, in a sense, in a prescientific situation and that a new framework within which to think is required. This is essentially Todd's point of view.

6.6 A note on possible national applications
The examples offered to illustrate ecosystemic planning are very small in scale. I have been unable to find any large-scale application of the full principle of ecological knowledge with the exception of the management of wilderness areas. While these latter are of interest, and are of course important as illustration of application to the essential role of wild areas in the total working of the biosphere, they are not very useful for dealing with the problems arising from the activities of human beings in ecosystems.

In considering large human populations in their interrelations with the other components of ecosystems we have to think in terms of relatively wide territorial areas: the eastern side of the US or a country, say, the size of France. Many physically small nation states occupy only portions of the ecosystems of which their populations are components: for example, Belgium or Ghana. It is difficult, if not impossible, for ecosystemic planning to be done in such instances without major collaboration between nations. In the case of the nations with larger territories we can think of them as possibly occupying several different ecosystems and therefore of being theoretically more capable of planning their relationships, particularly in regard to biomass productivity, within ecosystems in ways according with the needs of the systems for stability, diversity, cyclicity, etc.

Does any example of such attempt to plan ecosystemically at national or ecosystem level exist? We have largely to rule out the Western industrialization of agriculture—known as agribusiness—and even approaches such as that used by the (US) National Advisory Commission on Food and Fiber (1967) of a decade ago. These are essentially based on subservience to the supposed needs of the socioeconomy. The key test of the existence of ecosystemic planning might well be the presence of evidence of seeking to plan within the conceptualization of a single system—ecosystem *plus* socioeconomy.

Denmark tries to move in this direction by an overall national zoning of land utilization into areas for urban use, areas for agricultural development, and areas for recreational purposes. This approach, while not necessarily

implying an ecological emphasis, at least recognizes the importance of land
for producing food as a major support of the national socioeconomy.
Denmark's output of food per hectare has long been one of the world's
highest (second in wheat after Holland) and she is also an exporter.
Although the nation state of Denmark does not cover the whole of the
ecosystem of which she can be counted as a component, the inference
may be drawn that, whether by consciously designed policy or not, the
behaviour of the Danish socioeconomy as a component of the ecosystem,
is ecosystemically reasonably viable.

Japan is interesting because of its attempts to restructure various
elements of the socioeconomy in order to produce more food from the
same basic land and sea resources. North Korea and South Korea also
come under this heading (see *Scientific American*, 1976, page 197ff).

Immediately after 1945 very high priority had to be given to maintaining
the basic food supply while at the same time developing industry. Japan
was successful in both these areas, reaching full employment and a high
material standard of living very quickly. But there was a price: serious
environmental pollution and a socioeconomic dependence on a very high
rate of throughput of energy and materials. In 1973 the world energy
difficulty led to a reevaluation of Japanese goals, and new policies were
developed for stabilizing the socioeconomy and controlling the gross
demand. An effect of this change was a slowing down of economic growth,
and there began to emerge an appreciation of the significance of the
relationship between the availability of food and the level of employment.
Employment in agriculture dropped from 16 000 000 in 1955 to 12 000 000
in 1963, decreasing still further since then at about 3% per year. The need
to reassess national goals has been responded to, and new goals are being
developed. The approach, however, is apparently more 'environmental'
than 'ecological' in emphasis. For brief report see Laszlo et al (1977,
page 101ff).

Ancient methods of farming rice in Japan, depending only on rainfall,
produced under one tonne per hectare. The first phase of irrigation raised
the output to two and a half tonnes. The addition of scientific technique
lifted this to four tonnes. Further increase to nearly six tonnes per hectare
has been achieved in the last few decades by structural transformation which
has reorganized the rural economy, and replanned its off-farm support.
Again, the ecological effects of such structural transformations in the socioeconomy are not yet known. Borgstrom (1973) and others have written at
length about such ecologically cumulative processes as the overloading of
water bodies, the building up of toxicants, the elimination of ecologically
useful species and the progressive ineffectiveness of some chemical controls.
The achievement of greater socioeconomical–technological efficiency in
'winning' food is clearly not necessarily synonymous with long-term
capability for continuing at the new level. Japan now has some very
serious environmental difficulties.

A third example of interest is China. There is difficulty in getting reliable information about the relationship in China between government policies for agriculture, the fact of Chinese self-sufficiency (or near so) in food, and the extent to which emphasis is given to an understanding of the relationship between the ecological rules of food production and other major activities in the socioeconomy, such as industry. Although China is indicated as a food deficit country on the world map (*Scientific American*, 1976, page 32), in 1975–1976 it showed only a relatively small and falling import of grain—very small in comparison with the grain imports of the USSR and Eastern Europe, Western Europe, Japan, the rest of Asia, and Africa. China can be counted as virtually self-sufficient in food.

Chinese agriculture, whether because of government policy or not, in fact very heavily emphasizes reliance on the first trophic level (autotrophs) of the food chain. That is to say, the food grown is mostly eaten by the human population as direct intake and without greatly involving the second trophic level (heterotrophs) where human beings eat animals that are themselves fed on the first product of photosynthesis. The most efficient human relationship with the biomass would be for human beings to be entirely herbivorous. If gross ecological efficiency is counted of the order of 1% to 2% at the first trophic level, we have a rough measure of the significance of a vegetarian diet when we remember that cattle raised on cropland products are about 10% efficient. Vegetarian intake of food is therefore ten times more efficient in calories than animal food sources. Of all intake only a percentage is, of course, used and absorbed. These figures are very approximate indeed; the reader wishing to obtain an idea of the complexities of the measures should consult Phillipson (1966, chapter 5) or H T Odum (1971, chapter 3). In the seas, where the food chains may be much longer than on land, the proportion of energy available to humans may be much less. It takes five hundred kilograms of phytoplankton (autotroph) to make one gram of cod (heterotroph). The Chinese emphasis on the first trophic level of production appears ecologically sounder than the Western high reliance on the second trophic level, especially where the human population is large in relation to the area of land available for growing food. Is it, then, a specific policy of the Chinese government to maintain the population on a virtually vegetarian diet? If so, modern China is an ecologically based project of giant proportions. China has a tradition of heavy reliance on the first trophic level, but also has suffered ecological catastrophe—particularly about three millenia ago—comparable with the ecosystem degradation which took place in the Mediterranean basin at the beginning of the Christian period.

Laszlo et al (1977) reviews the present goals of the eight major areas of the world. In his examination of the key policies of the People's Republic of China he does not throw any direct light on the question of whether the holding of the Chinese population to a virtually vegetarian diet is a matter of consciously enunciated policy or not. In effect it does ensure as

high a level of food intake as possible for everybody by minimizing the
energy inefficiency of major reliance on animals for food and by keeping
agricultural activity within the long-term carrying capability of the
ecosystems. Laszlo's analysis, however, while not specifically mentioning
this matter, does point to some relevant items of existing Chinese policy.

The first of these is the de-emphasizing of the technical efficiency of
growth, and the strong emphasis on indicators for showing the direction of
the society's general development. The essential measure is the degree of
benefit for the people, who are themselves making the necessary guiding
judgments.

Second, the policy of 'standing on two legs'—agriculture and industry,
high and intermediate technology, centralized and decentralized leadership
etc—means that the human being will transform himself as he transforms
his natural environment. This is a totally different approach from that
which is usually understood by the term 'modernization', with its reliance
on high technology, high-level expertise, central planning, and intensive use
of capital. It may turn out in the end that Japan will be seen to have
taken the modernization route and China to have avoided its pitfalls.
Present lack of answers to the questions raised above about Chinese
policies being based on ecological principles seems to suggest that a
distinction between the approaches of the two countries cannot yet be
properly made. In China the increased accumulation and use of capital
for applying higher levels of technology and energy to food production
might still lead to the very same ecological problems that have been
generated by Western agribusiness. China's traditional agricultural practice
would, however, appear something of a deterrent to this possibility.

Third, the Chinese approach does not heavily rely on the view that it is
the nature of the economic base which determines the structure of society
and the ideas which its members hold. Laszlo comments that in Chinese
ideology emphasis on such determination is considered to lead away from
the nonexploitative and cooperative societal development which is the aim
of Chinese effort.

A final question has to be raised. What contribution is the Chinese
approach making to the achievement of a *total* system having the inbuilt
self-regulatory processes necessary for the long-term survival of large masses
of human beings? The self-regulation may be conceived as unself-conscious
as in the 'natural' ecosystem, having no single specific control mechanism,
or as self-conscious, as in the application of our knowledge of systems
[for example the attempt of Beer (1974a) in Chile; see section 7.4]. It is
possible that the Chinese approach, with its emphasis on the essential
participation and contribution of the peasant to the total socioeconomic
process, may be developing a multiplicity of elements of control at the
grassroots level that in effect aggregate into a self-regulating system. If
so, the component of unself-conscious self-regulation within an agreed
framework of values or goals, absent from Beer's operations research

approach, may be being generated in China. Or alternatively, we might see in the Chinese way a mixture of unself-conscious and conscious control[5].

It will be useful to bear these matters in mind side by side with Ryan's sociofeedback approach to human beings developing ecologically viable behaviour through planned use of the electronic technology (see chapter 11).

Very important to this whole question is the future development of agriculture in the tropical and subtropical regions of the world. These regions at present are usually low in overall productivity, but there is general agreement that we now possess the technology for increasing yields in tropical areas considerably. It is precisely in such areas, however, that ecosystems are liable to serious degradation, and at a much more rapid rate of deterioration than in the temperate zones.

A final point needs to be made. Neither of our specific examples (Todd and Nissan) concerns itself very seriously with a socioeconomy heavily involved in cash-wages transactions. That is to say, they do not particularly address themselves to the fact that for very large areas of the world the relationship between the ecosystem and the human populations is mediated by transactions which depend on flows of cash. Later in the book we shall refer to this as the production–job–wages–consumption nexus. Heavy reliance on this nexus has so far been workable for giving large populations access to food. But it relies for its operation on the availability of jobs. That availability in its turn depends on many factors not normally regarded as ecosystemic and frequently occurring outside the ecosystem in which the population is maintained, for example automation, import–export of manufactures, etc. Further, as the world population increases, the syndrome production–job–wages–consumption may be progressively unworkable for an increasing fraction of the world's population. Ward (1976) attaches great importance to this facet of the global population–food problem. Already many impoverished urban populations are in the position that their sole access to food is through money. They have no money because they have no jobs. Hence they cannot eat. This does not necessarily mean that the territory they occupy is insufficient in extent and fertility for producing enough food.

What emerges as of key importance is that to be really useful in the human enterprise, the designing of ecosystems for productivity and viability must be done in conjunction with full understanding of the role of other components in the socioeconomy. This suggests that many countries will need to base their planning on the securing of the food supply. This leads to very different approaches and results from those arising from taking manufacturing industry or the introduction of advanced technology in this

[5] For a compact conventional description of the Chinese economy see Bhagwati (1974, pages 321–353). There is no mention of the ecological context of agriculture in China but the 'food problem' is treated in some detail. There is also a clear recognition of the likely role of agriculture in coping with unemployment and under-employment.

or that sector as the point of departure. This shift in emphasis may shortly be just as necessary for the developed as for the developing countries, since serious difficulties in providing jobs are already appearing in the developed nations.

The importance of our two main examples is that they provide experienc of operationalizing our ecological knowledge to obtain the highest level o efficiency for sustaining human life on a long-term stable basis. We urgently need detailed working knowledge of such an approach. At the same time this has to be quickly related to the actual operations of existing socioeconomies, developed and developing. For the moment, judgment apparently has to be suspended on the structural transformation in Japan and the working of the Chinese system since we do not know whether these are genuinely viable ecological solutions.

Electronic technology and knowledge of ecosystems

The telecommunications and computer technologies are becoming rapidly involved with ecological interests and concerns. The interrelations fall into two main categories: *information* about the condition, performance, or future state of ecosystems, and taking *action* with regard to their condition, performance, or future state. It is inevitable that the electronic technology will have an increasingly important role to play in the future management of ecosystems. Especially is this crucial in the light of growing global population pressures. In this chapter we shall illustrate both the information relationship and the action relationship.

7.1 Global environmental monitoring

Among the many areas of interlock between our two bodies of breakthrough knowledge and practice, the activity of environmental monitoring has a very important place. Monitoring consists of making routine, regular reports on some aspect of the environment. It normally involves detecting the presence of substances significant for estimating quality of an environmental component such as air or water, and then determining the quantity of the substance present by means of some standard measure. For example, carbon monoxide in the air is identified and measured as being present by stating its presence as so many parts per million. Monitoring can give early warning of environmental changes important for human well-being, and can show a shift in a significant trend. Early detection is therefore an aim stressed by agencies involved in environmental monitoring. The basic motivation for instituting monitoring services is to protect the present and future health and safety of human populations by understanding, and therefore attempting to cope with, environmental conditions before they become unmanageable. Monitoring and management of the environment are therefore very closely related.

Monitoring is in principle applicable to, and desirable in regard to, aspects of the physical environment in detail (for example, urban air pollution) and at large (for example, ocean pollution); also to the socioeconomic condition of society, and the cultural and psychic conditions of communities and individuals.

Monitoring of the ecosystems and the biosphere on a global basis is being greatly facilitated by the electronic technology using satellites, computers, and telecommunications facilities. The capacity to monitor up to the global scale by automated techniques has become effective at the very moment when human pressure on the biosphere demands the development of agencies capable of providing continuous flows of information about the states of the various environments and the statuses of many kinds of resources—nonrenewable, renewable, and human.

7.1.1 The World Weather Watch

The World Meteorological Organization approved the idea of continuous monitoring of the world's weather in 1963. The first plan ran from 1968 to 1971; the second was 1971 to 1975, and the third will be for 1976 to 1979. This is the basic programme of WMO.

The main purpose of the Watch is to provide each member with meteorological and related environmental information "... required to enjoy the most efficient and effective meteorological and other related environmental services possible"; a further aim is to facilitate the research necessary to "... extend the useful range of weather and related environmental forecasts and to enable the possibilities and consequences o weather and climate modification to be more accurately assessed" (World Meteorological Organization, 1972). The Watch is an integrated global system viewed as consisting of three levels: global, regional, and national. It provides observational data and processed material to its members.

The World Weather Watch consists of three systems: first, the Global Observing System, which makes observations on land and sea, and from aircraft, satellites, etc; second there is the Global Data-processing System, which consists of centres for processing the observational data for real-time and nonreal-time uses; and third, the Global Telecommunications System, which collects and distributes the observational data and the processed information. It is planned that these three systems will become fully operational in the 1976 to 1979 period. They will include taking full advantage of the developments in electronic technology, including geostationary satellites, high-speed data transmission and coded digital facsimile techniques, and improved trunk circuit arrangements. It will also be possible to benefit from the use of the universal public packet-switching networks.

The observational data consist of material originating from measurements by instruments, and compiled descriptive information (form of clouds, etc) The networks are organized globally, regionally, and nationally. The information is provided at scales ranging from planetary to small-scale (100 kilometres). The observational system is subdivided into a surface-based subsystem and a space-based subsystem operating in various mixes. Both subsystems are vitally dependent on the electronic technology, with considerable reliance being placed on automation and radiometric measurement. Five geostationary satellites are needed to provide full global coverage. All five are expected to be operational by the end of the 1976 to 1979 plan.

Satellites provide the following information: vertical profiles of temperature and humidity; temperatures of sea, land, and top surfaces of clouds; wind field derived from cloud displacements; amount of cloud; type and height of cloud top surfaces; snow and ice cover; and radiance balance data—making it possible to infer the radiation balance of the whole earth system. Experimental satellite data may include, soil moisture distribution; ice definition; sea state; cloud composition; distribution of particulate matter in the atmosphere; and marine pollution. The space-based part of the programme is expected to improve rapidly in its technical efficiency.

The Global Data-processing System provides quality control, decoding, etc; analyses of the structure of the atmosphere; prognoses of the structure of the atmosphere; storage and retrieval; classification and cataloguing

World Meteorological Centres are in Melbourne, Moscow, and Washington, DC. These provide global material. Examples are: upper-air meteorological analysis; sea surface temperature twice a day; prognoses; alerts; storage and retrieval of data; development of research; and testing new technology. There are twenty-four Regional Meteorological Centres around the world. Their function is to provide material "... for ready use by Members as aids for providing services to users". The National Meteorological Centres provide upper-air analyses and prognoses to meet national needs for all users, alerts and warnings, quality control, storage and retrieval, and research.

The Global Telecommunication System (GTS) at world level has the main trunk circuit and its branches, regional telecommunications networks, and national telecommunications networks. At each level the GTS is responsible for collecting and transmitting the observational data, ensuring effective distribution, checking, establishing radio broadcasts, etc (see figure 7.1).

As the data provided by the World Weather Watch are of importance to many interests, the Watch will relate closely to other emerging world

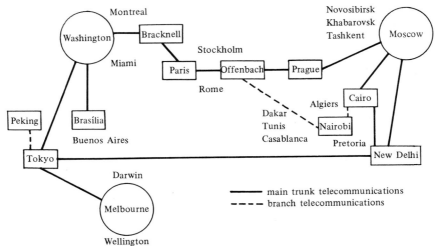

Figure 7.1. The World Weather Watch. The World Meteorological Centres are shown in circles. The regional telecommunications hubs are shown in boxes. The location in the boxes and the free-standing names comprise the Regional Meteorological Centres around the world. These have real-time and nonreal-time functions such as surface and upper-air analyses, and storage and access of observational data.

monitoring activities such as the Global Atmospheric Research Programme, the Integrated Global Ocean Station System, the Intergovernmental Oceanographic Commission, the Earthwatch programme of the UN Environmental Programme, and Comsat's marine communications network (MARASAT). Such activities are made increasingly possible by ever more efficient communications technologies and their organizations, such as Teleglobe, Intelsat, etc[1].

The World Meteorological Organization seems likely to become increasingly concerned with monitoring various kinds of pollution, the mathematical modelling of water quality, studies of environmental impacts of man's activities, and studies of changes in saltwater–freshwater balances.

The World Weather Watch is a very important contributor to the organizational effort necessary for global monitoring in a hierarchically arranged system as a prerequisite for the management of world ecosystems. It makes vigorous use of the capabilities of the electromagnetic spectrum in the context of major ecological concern. It demonstrates the increasing integration of these two areas of knowledge and organizationally is of great interest as an example of potential cooperation on a global scale. It is to be hoped that the initial operational difficulties it has encountered will be quickly overcome. Such global pioneering efforts are extremely complex and subject to many accidental elements.

7.1.2 LANDSAT: remote sensing

Remote sensing is the group of techniques used to study the surface environment of the earth or other heavenly bodies, by means of sensing devices using various regions of the electromagnetic spectrum, including the infrared, the microwave, and the radiowave. It includes processing, analysis, and application of data. The techniques often require backup support from information collected at surface level and in the laboratory. The technology includes sensors, satellites, space and airborne craft, data processing, and telecommunications, etc. The principle exploited by the technology is that the sensors pick up reflected energy from objects scanned.

The organizational origin of LANDSAT lies in the 1969 NASA proposal for the Earth Resources Technology Satellite programme (ERTS). This has now become the LANDSAT programme. The Canadian contribution was commenced in 1970 with programme aims:

1 initiate an experimental high-altitude airborne remote-sensing operation;
2 carry out research and development on sensors;
3 study the incidence of cloud-free areas;
4 study appropriate data processing and reproduction systems for resource satellite data.

---

[1] The substantive interests use the general world communications networks. These are developing very rapidly. Comsat, for example, in 1976 completed its ship-to-shore services global coverage, using three satellites. It is anticipated that this service will be effective for navigation.

It was considered that a national effort to develop remote sensing was necessary because the new tools for exploiting the environment need to be matched by new tools for monitoring its condition, and to ensure that Canada will be capable of developing the equipment necessary for her particular requirements (see Harper, 1976).

The major uses of the research satellite facilities being employed include: forest fire mapping; monitoring of forestry activities in logging etc; water area mapping; separation of land-use classes; northern ecosystem mapping and mapping of surface geology; water-mix studies of large rivers, lakes and oceans; and monitoring of snow melt. The technique is also capable of providing good-quality records of urban areas at large-view scale. The output includes well-registered composite images in colour.

The satellite LANDSAT I was launched in 1972 and is still operating. The spatial coverage of the imagery is 100 × 100 nautical miles on an eighteen-day cycle. LANDSAT II is in orbit opposite LANDSAT I so that the effective world cycle of the two satellites is nine days, every spot on earth being covered at that interval.

The project maintains a technical information service which provides the output to interested parties and advises on the best uses, etc. A browse facility is available, and printouts, microfiches, etc can be provided. An on-line retrieval system includes computerized documentation, thus providing easy access.

An important application of remote sensing is the mapping of large areas of tropical land surface which cannot be normally photographed by using the visible region of the electromagnetic spectrum because of heavy interference from cloud cover.

Remote sensing can be used for the mapping of urban and rural areas. It is capable of making distinction between various densities and different uses. The technology seems likely to prove exceptionally useful for dealing with large areas in which there are many urban centres, such as the Great Lakes or the industrialized area of northwest Europe.

The original ERTS programme was devised as a research–development tool for exploring the usefulness of remote sensing for assisting in the resource management of the globe. It has proved very successful, the first satellite continuing to work long after its planned life. A third satellite will be launched in 1978. The future of the programme will be closely related to NASA's Earth Observatory Satellites. After 1980, satellite launchings are likely to be dependent on the development of the space shuttle programme, which will make a space platform available.

7.1.3 Comment on monitoring technology

From these two examples, and others (for example, ocean and ionosphere programmes), it is clear that capabilities of the electronic technology are very rapidly being exploited for monitoring the earth on a global organizational basis. The information provided by such activities, whether day-to-day as by the World Weather Watch or less ephemerally as by the LANDSAT programme and other 'observational' projects, will build up a body of systematic knowledge of immense value for the purposes of resource and environmental management. It seems impossible to doubt that the very presence of this knowledge will have a profound impact on how we look at and act upon our environment. On the basis of improved understanding of global processes we can expect a rapid growth of our knowledge of the biosphere and its ecosystems. The two areas— the knowledge of ecosystems and the technologies based on the capabilities of the electromagnetic spectrum—are now indissolubly bound together in their future development. They will grow by reciprocal stimulation. Most probably they will grow faster than we shall be able to conceptualize the significance of their interrelation. It seems impossible to overemphasize the capacity for stimulus which lies in the global organizational use of the electronic technology for such purposes.

7.2 Organizing global monitoring

Global organizational approaches are already appearing. As an example we can cite the Global Environmental Monitoring System (GEMS). The concept is a "... world-wide linkage of national and environmental monitoring networks" (Munn, 1973). This idea originated in the Scientific Committee on Problems of the Environment (SCOPE) set up by the International Council of Scientific Unions. It was approved by the 1972 UN Conference on the Human Environment in Stockholm. The immediate goal of SCOPE is the "... improvement of scientific procedures for assessment over the long term of changes in environment". The components of GEMS include monitoring the atmosphere, oceans, rivers, lakes, groundwater, soils, vegetation and forests, drinking water and foods. The Stockholm conference accepted as objectives for GEMS:

"To provide the information necessary to ensure the present and future protection of human health and safety and the world management of the environment and its resources by:
a) (i) increasing quantitative knowledge of natural and man-made changes in the environment and of the impact of these on man's health and welfare;
(ii) increasing understanding of the environment, and, in particular, of *how dynamic balance is maintained in ecosystems, as a basis for managing resources* (emphasis supplied);
b) providing early warning of significant environmental changes (including natural disasters) in order that protective measures may be considered;
c) making it possible to check the effectiveness of established regulatory mechanisms and to plan optimal technological development" (Munn, 1973, page 15).

The intention of this project is to serve the ultimate end of protecting the biosphere and its ecosystems as our global life support. It is a manifestation of our understanding of ecosystems and our need to protect and manage them as a necessity of survival. Clearly such a global project will be heavily dependent on the electronic technology in the same way as the World Weather Watch. Again, we are seeing the emergence of the close knitting together of ecological concern and understanding, the uses of the regions of the electromagnetic spectrum, and global organizational arrangements.

7.3 Crisis management and planning

On the action side, the electronic technology offers the possibility of greatly speeding up the policymaking process. This includes: generation and arraying of alternatives, simulation of outcomes, evaluation, and reaching agreement. Implementation would also be accelerated. The speeding up of the processes of planning and follow-up action would be generally beneficial, but is likely to be especially useful in disaster and crisis situations. A great deal of time can be saved by combining various electronic technologies and techniques in modes which suggest that societies may be able to reach higher levels of reliability of action than previously.

7.3.1 Computerized life-support crisis management

The ideas of Kupperman et al (1975) provide a very provocative lead. They are concerned chiefly with crisis management at the international level and include, as background, experience of approaching global military affairs through modelling techniques. This latter is a field in which the electronic technology now plays an important role, including diplomatic links via satellites, computerized gaming activities, etc. Kupperman's proposals in the international sphere would appear equally applicable to the emerging greater metropolitan region, not only on a crisis level but as a normal ongoing process for planning and management.

The basic idea is that computer conferencing and computerized modelling of the entity about which decisions have to be taken (planning, crisis avoidance, management, etc) can be combined into a much more effective approach than anything we have at present. In operational terms he suggests that a beginning could be made by trying the technique on an area commonly agreed to be in need of concerted action—famine in the Sahel region of North Africa where the interests of several nations are implicated.

The technique consists of mounting a computer conference (in the way already described in chapter 3) and embedding within it dynamic computerized models simulating the entity, or aspects of it, to be planned or managed. The model or models are descriptive (mathematical or verbal) and are not conceived as at any time complete, but are intended to grow continuously and to approximate more closely the reality modelled while the conference proceeds. Several models may be embedded in the conference. In a conflict situation the contending parties might each have a somewhat different model, and a contender might have a model of both his own and the adversary's view of the situation.

Embedding the models in the conference means that the model material would be in the computer, accessible to all parties, and would be capable of being drawn upon for inclusion into the process of the conference at any time. Further, the conference would modify the models as the proceedings might suggest. In this way the model building becomes an integral part of the conferencing discussion process. The conference constructs a progressively realistic model. It is noteworthy how well the asynchronous nature of the computer conferencing technique fits with the time needed for modifying and rerunning a model on the computer to make the new results available back into the conference.

The technique is interesting for its likely capacity to make values visible. Kupperman comments that it would be helpful in that most difficult area in planning, the measurement of utility. This matter is particularly intractable when it is a question of comparison between different and perhaps competing value systems. He sees the technique as capable of constructing bridges between different values areas, ultimately computer models being "... expanded until they become accepted surrogates of an unattainable reality" (Kupperman et al, 1975). That is to say, we admit we cannot understand the whole reality, but we can agree, working through the development of dynamic models, to accept the model as the best in fact that we can do. The important point is the agreement on a working basis. He illustrates how this process does already take place: "Military leaders in the United States have often ended up adopting the results of models they have severely criticized initially .... They do so for a very simple reason: there appear to be no better alternatives for justifying their specific weapons and budgetary requests". This may prove to be a very significant lead for other kinds of planning and management, for example of metropolitan areas or greater regions, when one acknowledges the very real problems now facing decisionmakers in such areas.

In the context of the greater region we have at present very little experience of planning as a whole. We are limited to considering special subsystems such as the generation and supply of electrical energy, physical communications, or industrial development. The electronic technology has been almost totally ignored. Kupperman's technique of computer conferencing and computerized modelling, bringing together scientists, technical applications experts, resource managers, political and other decisionmakers, might provide a new operational approach to the planning and management of greater metroplitan regions in their combined urban and nonurban aspects on the fundamental basis of using the most advanced technology to bring differences in values out into the open and of using creative discussion as a continuous process. *What would be hoped for would be the progressive development of the models as agreed best statements of how reality is perceived.*

7.3.2 On-line planning

Harold Sackman (1971, particularly part IV; Sackman and Citrenbaum, 1972) has made an important contribution to the idea of on-line planning and thereby to the methodology of planning. He sees the mass use of computer information utilities revolutionizing the ways in which society makes its decisions as it moves into the future. *He stresses that plans must become evolving hypotheses which are continuously generated, tested, and verified. For this, information must be continuously drawn from real world situations and used in the decisionmaking process.* Values, attitudes, goals, and expectations would be an important component of such information. Obviously the electronic services are well suited both to the process of tapping information and to discussing the action to be taken. Sackman proposes, in effect, nothing less than the almost total reconstruction of the planning process. If this challenge is not willingly taken up it is arguable that we may well find it forced upon us later under much tougher conditions than the present[2].

Using the on-line time-sharing technique for greater regional planning would require the modelling of a region's ecosystem(s) together with continuous monitoring of their states. It would also imply that the operating of the technique would be much involved with the question of how to relate socioeconomic modelling to ecosystem modelling. At present there is a large gap between these two, although the ecologist is moving into the field of human-dominated ecosystems and biologists, such as Wilson (1975), clearly seek to construct models of communities and their activities out of the concepts of the life sciences. (It might be added that this area of research might be very considerably helped by the application of the on-line idea to greater regional planning and management.)

The on-line technique inevitably means the overt and specific bringing together of our two breakthrough areas in both an operational and a conceptual–theoretical sense. It might well be that the problem of how to bring the knowledge developed by science into closer and more intelligent relationship with our socioeconomic processes of making decisions will be significantly probed by the electronic technology and our knowledge of ecosystems (on which life depends) being brought together through a combination of computer conferencing and computerized modelling. Already we may identify some adumbrations: for example,

---

[2] Sackman (1971, page 43) emphasizes the new social research possibilities offered by the on-line use of the computer: "The real-time computing system has not been recognized as a massive breakthrough in experimental method that makes it possible, for the first time, to study real-world social behavior in a well-defined, operationally specified system setting".

the use of ERTS imagery to map ecosystems in a greater region (see map
NASA, 1974, page 13); electronic monitoring of water quality in a river
basin; attempts at modelling human-dominated subsystems, such as
socioeconomic and transportation models; the operational feasibility of
electronic conferencing of various kinds; and the probably imminent major
diffusion of individual two-way electronic capability. These techniques
and their technologies almost certainly will be stimulated to develop by
the mounting cultural and societal difficulties we shall encounter as our
global limitations of physical space, food, and energy are progressively
forced upon our notice.

Already there are some plans afoot. In 1975 the Swedish Board for
Technical Development established a working team to promote regional
development with the aid of telecommunications techniques. The approach
is to concentrate on the services perceived as needed by the region—
decentralization of certain functions, getting information to those who are
at present information-poor, developing manpower, etc. The technology
to be used is narrow-band transmission, considerable resources for data
banking and processing, decentralized neighbourhood communication
centres, and simple (nonintelligent?) terminals. Computer teleconferencing
techniques will be developed in the ongoing conference of three hundred
expert participants being mounted by Turoff (1976) in the New Jersey
Institute of Technology.

The rapid development of universal shared packet-switching potentially
making all terminals and computers interactive (chapter 4—Datapac,
Cyclades, etc) will interlock very well with the on-line management and
planning proposals described above. The conceptualization of the techniques
emerges at the very moment when a gigantic step forward by the technology
will make them easily and universally possible in the developed countries.

7.4 On-line systemic national development: Allende's Chile
Although theoretical work exists to suggest the potential of on-line planning
after the style of Sackman and Citrenbaum (1972) and Kupperman et al
(1975), it is very hard to find examples of application of the principles
relating to the 'transparent' operation of organizations. Transparency
refers to the ability of the electronic technology to provide information
of a level of currentness that is virtually exactly contemporary with the
moment of action over a relatively wide physical territory, a large number
of entities (for example, firms, or concentrations of populations), or both.
With such immediacy, both information and action are contemporaneous,
and the total process of information handling plus decisionmaking is said
to be transparent.

In the attempt of President Salvador Allende to reorganize the Chilean
socioeconomy along on-line planning principles we have a unique example
of the attempted operationalization of the concept at state level. The
experiment was cut short by the violent change of government which took

place only two years after the beginning of the project. The chief scientific adviser and designer was Stafford Beer (see Beer, 1974a; 1975). The first reference contains a compact description of the way in which the Chilean socioeconomy was in the process of being reconstructed when the end came; the second reference explains Beer's overall approach in greater detail. The procedure here will be first to describe the project and subsequently to underscore some of the major ideas. Although in its brief life the Chilean project concentrated on the industrial sector of the socioeconomy, it would in principle include ecosystem regulation. Hence it is included in our present class of examples.

The point of departure was that of society as a self-regulating system which is continuously evolving. This is not a description of all societies: some are not systems in this sense. The key idea is that the system (society) is self-managing: it does not have government imposed upon it. The concept is therefore very near to that of the 'natural' ecosystem, which has no specific 'management' component, but has regulation of the total system inherent in all its processes. The Chilean system was conceived as "devolutionary, popular and pluralistic" (Beer, 1974a).

A second point of departure was that information is the essence of regulation or management, and that patterns for regulating the socio-economy of a modern society are, however, not adequately correlated and suffer from a considerable lag in currentness. Beer sees consumerism in the developed countries as a manifestation of this lag—one having disastrous effects. A key focus of attention would therefore be the establishment of a regulatory process in which this lag would be reduced to an absolute minimum.

These two ideas put together resulted in the Project Cybersyn which "... aimed to acquire the benefits of cybernetic synergy for the whole of industry, while devolving power to the workers at the same time" (Beer, 1974a, page 6).

The first item to be tackled for conceptualizing the new system was to set up clear concepts related to centralization and decentralization. This was done by defining the decentralized condition as horizontal and the centralized condition as vertical. The horizontal elements could have as much variety as they liked except for that subtracted by the vertical centralizing function. The systemic principle to relate the two was to define autonomy as the minimum subtraction of horizontal variety necessary for ensuring the cohesion of the total system. This would apply at every level of recursion and would be regarded as a computable function. The horizontal–vertical relation was admitted as present right through the system, starting with the single human being in his section of the workshop and moving up to the top recursive level of the economic system as a component, or subsystem, of the state. The overall picture, then, is of any subsystem at any level having maximum autonomy or variety within the requirements of its next subsystem upwards imposing vertical restriction in the interest of the total system. This conceptualization meant that the same model could be used at each recursive level. The model was the basis of a generalized computer programme capable of being applied at each level. The same model was therefore usable for every act of evaluation of whatever situation.

The next step required a standardized descriptive mode of showing the operations of the various industries, plants, workshops, etc. This was done by devising flow charts, all drawn to the same conventions so that they could be quickly compared. Parallel with the generation of these charts, data were required about critical variables such as condition of stocks, bottlenecks, absenteeism, output, etc.

Getting the information in the flow charts and the data of the critical variables to the switching centre in Santiago presented a difficulty because Chile had no sophisticated electronic infrastructure. The problem was solved by using telex, arranging access for every firm so that the required information could be moved daily. In Santiago the material was handled by computers. This organization, using telex, would have eventually served the whole country and acted as a kind of nervous system carrying day-to-day information about the state of every firm.

The computer programme for rendering all this information in a form suitable for making decisions used the following logic. In the firms, each critical variable was reported as to its *capability* and its *potentiality*. Capability relates to how the variable should perform when the whole system is running at its best (actual or envisaged), and potentiality means how much better the variable could perform if some addition were made (for example, add another machine) over and above its level of capability. The ratio between capability and potentiality is called *latency*. The level of performance coming daily over the telex is the *actuality*. The ratio actuality/capability is what is normally called productivity, and actuality/potentiality is the performance index.

The daily processing procedure was designed as follows. The actuality figure is examined and, if it is accepted, the capability and potentiality figures belonging to the variable under consideration are processed with it for comparisons to be made. The basic time period used for establishing mean levels of productivity and latency was to be one hundred days. These levels were then to be applied to the flow charts of the next upward recursive level, right through the entire system. This builds up a picture of the productivity, latency, and performance for all industry.

As the computed figures show variations from day to day there is the important matter of estimating the significance of variations. This was done by calculating by means of short-term forecasting techniques four probabilities, of which two would be considered indicators of significant change. Whenever these latter appeared the firm or industry concerned would be immediately informed. The effect of this was that the firm's management would be immediately alerted to the emergence of change in output quantity and quality, morale of workers, etc. Effectively this provided all firms with the benefit of computer assistance for quickly identifying new shifts, and therefore of taking early the necessary decisions.

The key experience in Chile with this technique was that it changed the approach with which both government and industry viewed the problems: "... the use of the (new) tools imparts new dimensions to the management process" (Beer, 1974a, page 13). This ought to be obvious, but apparently it is not properly appreciated that new tools and new methods change our perception of what we are doing, and can do.

In addition to organizing the generation of the flow charts and selecting the critical variables it was necessary to have weightings assigned, since variables are not all of equal significance. The setting up of these matters was done by operational research teams in the factories. These teams also had the function of assessing how long it would take to restore productivity to normal if a falling-off occurred. The time required would be weighted according to the weighting of the variable and incorporated into the computer programme as "a kind of clock". If the clock time ran out before correction took place, an indication would be passed up to the next highest level to the effect that action was needed. This Beer called the algedonic system, suggesting that it carries the cry of pain from a part of the system to the system's upper regulatory areas.

Beer also extended the algedonic idea to register the general feeling of satisfaction, or otherwise, of groups at all levels. He devised a simple meter which could be set to show visibly the degree of satisfaction expressed by relatively small groups. The readings of these located round a factory could be summed in one or two conspicuous positions. Each group could then compare its setting with the aggregated reading. The perceived differences operate systemically to induce changes in effort, response, morale, etc. *It is seeing the differences that makes the difference. This is information acting as regulator.* Extended to the nation it becomes a form of socio-feedback, operating much as biofeedback does for the individual.

A very important part of the concept of the project was the Santiago operations room. This was conceived to serve as the chief nerve centre for the whole socioeconomy. It was built and was operational, although it never actually functioned fully in its proper role. The idea was that it would be a place where creative thinking could be done about the socio-economy on a running basis with immediate availability of the necessary current information supplied through the processes described.

One wall carries the neurocybernetic model of the system. It is animated and its context can be changed to match the recursive level being dealt with. The productivity and latency rates are displayed for the level concerned. Flow lines move and can be regulated to three different speeds. An algedonic signal can also be flashed. The second wall has screens showing the day's output figures from the computer programme and algedonic signals from the recursive level below the level under consideration.

The third wall is occupied by *datafeed*, which can be called upon to provide additional information on request. This information is visual in form, consisting of slides showing graphic material such as flow charts and photographs of the recursive level in hand.

The room contains seven chairs. This number is considered the largest size at which a creative group can effectively operate. Each chair has a control panel on the arm so that its occupant can call up material he wishes on the various wall equipment.

The room also contains an animated model simulating the working of the whole economy. The use of this model would allow the group to try out various alternative actions and judge their effects in simulation. This process would make possible projections up to ten years ahead.

The last item in the central operations room is the national algedonic meter. This would display the aggregated total of all meters across the nation in real time. The meter would be used to give instantaneous monitoring of responses as policies were being explained to the nation. The information would be disseminated by TV in the villages, etc, and the response, expressed as a degree of satisfaction on the local algedonic meter would be transmitted electronically to the operations room. Thus, in theory, even as a speech is being made, the nature of the response could be seen, and judged, by the speaker. This capability would be available a all recursive levels.

There are several items of great interest about Beer's approach and the 'Chilean process'. At the strictly operational level it is important to take full notice that a highly sophisticated electronic infrastructure is not absolutely essential for the operationalizing of concepts to render the workings of the national socioeconomy transparent. A relatively crude infrastructure can be made to serve in spite of very slow transmission speeds and sometimes actual physical gaps in the communications network This suggests that the developing countries need not feel that their lack of equipment must exclude them from attempting to approach the regulation of their socioeconomies by these concepts and techniques.

Second, extremely impressive is the fusing of conceptualizations of the socioeconomy, the necessary logic of system, and the human questions relating to the sense of freedom, or satisfaction, etc. In the socioeconomy the centralization–decentralization issue is precisely conceptualized so tha its variations become computable on the basis of a logic acceptable in human subjective experiential terms—the individual, group, etc enjoying a maximum freedom in making decisions that affect itself and its work. *The necessary logic of system has to satisfy the posed problem of reconciling the micro and macro scales so that the total system works.* As the project was brought to an untimely end before it was fully operational, it cannot be demonstrated just to what extent the logic of system was adequate, but the indications suggest that it would have proved a very workable point of departure, and that it would have been capable of being refined as experience of working with it was gained.

Beer's approach to the human questions is to emphasize in the workings of the socioeconomy the satisfaction of the individual human being not as an economic unit but as a person who operates on the measure of eudemony rather than of money or material goods. The concept of eudemony (εὐδαιμονία) might be described as a sense of well-being (Beer, 1975, page 163ff). To Beer, the goings-on of the socioeconomy are decided more by the desire for eudemony than for monetary profit. Thus a metasystem whose goal is to maximize eudemony underlies the overt system we roughly call the economy. Hence Beer, like Boulding, Masuda, and others, is not much impressed by the use of the GNP as a measure of the condition of the socioeconomy. To this we must add Beer's democratic emphasis: that eudemony is not for a few, but for all.

On the side of the techniques of simulation it is noteworthy that modelling may be now considered to have advanced beyond a descriptive role into an operational function in the real world. The Chilean process used a model based on J W Forrester's (1968) work and Dynamo II language. One may comment that the usefulness of such models can now be most effectively developed further by operationalization in such experiments as the Chilean. Actual operations, however, cannot be better than the models; and the models can be no better than the conceptualizations that underpin them. A poor conceptualization of what the human being is— for example, say he is an automaton—can lead only to a model limited by this conceptualization, however technically good the model may be. The operationalization of such a model could not facilitate the working of a society in which the individual would be more than an automaton. *The conceptualizations of the modeller are perhaps the biggest limiting factor in the operational use of the model.*

Beer's overall conceptualization is of a system—let us say 'human' system for the moment—which regulates its processes through a multiplicity of self-acting controls operating at all levels in the total system. This implies that there is no specialized single control component in the system. There is certainly no dictator, but also there is no single homeostat, but many. This is precisely the ecologist's concept of the 'natural' ecosystem.

A question to be raised is the extent to which such a conceptualization is suitable for imaging human societies. We can observe that ecosystems, at any rate in the world's temperate zones, are no longer entirely 'natural'. They are now largely controlled by a specialized regulator—human beings, who so order their processes that the systems are held in their 'young' phases and produce a maximum amount of human-usable biomass. The world's ecosystems have thus been hominized, have had a special form of control imposed upon them. We do not know to what long-term extent this imposition, in the forms at present applied, is viable.

Equally, we do not for certain know what is the long-term viable mode or conceptualization we should use for acting on and within human societie Our age has its preferences. Beer's model is perceived as humane and therefore attractive: it aims for human well-being from the grass roots Yet there is a question unanswered in *systemically* placing the opportuni for decision in the hands of all the population in a transparent fashion. This concept can work safely only on the supposition that the *perceived* eudemony is indeed compatible with the viability of the total system. What if the eudemony, perceived by the individual, is in fact a running wild of a component or linkage of the system? In short, there is a built-optimism about the nature of the response of the individual that may no be justified.

This raises the very important question of what is likely to be the natur of the mass individual's concept of eudemony, particularly in the large mass populations of the developed countries? And is this particular kind of eudemony destructive or reinforcing of the system's viability, stability, and variety? This eventually leads to questions probing for the regulatory processes that control the profile of the mass individual. If regulation is inherent in all parts of the system where is it in the mass individual?

This is one of the chains of reasoning which leads us to the need to examine the character profile and sensibility of the mass individual (chapters 16 and 17). Our epochal tendency, in this area of thinking, is to focus on society. This has its dangers, and requires compensating for by giving closer attention to the nature of the mass individual.

The overall body of thought comprising Stafford Beer's approach is of great interest; for a comprehensive statement see Beer (1975). For reason of its complexity and space it cannot be recorded here. The reader, howeve may obtain some general idea from figure 7.2. A cardinal idea is the shif from a society preoccupied with making things to a society which would give a great deal of attention to guidance and self-regulation. His diagnos of *Homo faber* society includes the concept of undecidability. Proliferatin variety produces an inability of the system to cope with new situations through its existing organizations. The system must learn to match the new variety with increased variety of its own. New structures or institution will therefore have to be developed. Undecidability can be coped with by developing a metalanguage and metasystems, since present stereotypes of thinking are destructive of the new thinking we need to have.

Beer's general background view is that we now have enough scientific knowledge for application to human societies. He thinks a 'corpus of theory' can now be synthesized by drawing on Shannon's communication theory (for example Shannon and Weaver, 1949), Ashby's laws of variety (for example Ashby, 1960), McCulloch's research in logic and neurology (for example McCulloch, 1965), Pask's principles of self-organization (for example Pask, 1975), and Walter's automata (for exampl

Walter, 1963). To these areas of knowledge we can add considerable experience of modelling (see Beer, 1975, page 135).

A key idea of Beer's in diagnosing our present condition is that it is characterized by perturbations occurring with a frequency too high for effective control by regulatory means devised by ourselves. The system is too complex and too unstable for such a solution. Hence government

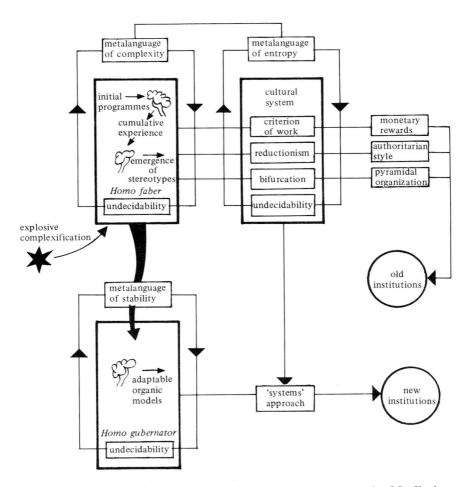

Figure 7.2. A concept of cultural change. This diagram expresses much of Stafford Beer's systemic thinking. It stresses his very important emphasis on the change from 'making' to 'guiding'—from *Homo faber* to *Homo gubernator*. It shows the role of metalanguages and implied metasystems relating to the inability of the overt system to provide an adequate context in which decision can be reached, and it suggests the emergence of new institutions capable of self-regulating behaviour. Redrawn from Beer (1975), by permission of John Wiley and Sons, Inc.

action, for example, becomes progressively less effective. The generation
of a metasystem is therefore necessary and can be created through meta-
discussion of the systemic structure.

7.5 Computer-assisted regional development and environmental control
In the Hyogo prefecture of Japan (about 5 million population and 8373
square kilometres, with a central city, Kobe, of about 1·35 million
population) an attempt to integrate regional and environmental planning
by using the electronic technology very extensively has been under way
since 1972.

The approach is instigated by appreciation of the serious environmental
difficulties that have accompanied Japan's recent economic growth;
particularly, various kinds of pollution have become a health hazard. The
basic idea is to use the capability of the computer for rapid modelling of
possibly adverse environmental effects under the conditions of hypothesize
locations for new industry, residential areas, etc proposed as components
of future development. Multilevel assessment of impacts is integrated wit
the planning and development process. The method is essentially a system
approach.

The impact assessment side of the total process aims at the resolution
of conflict by building in the principle of assessment at all levels. This is
done by using computer graphics to display the known data and the new
proposals, for discussion by managers and policymakers up through the
various organizational and spatial levels. The material stored in the
computer is carefully structured in the best way for giving maximum
flexibility between the machine and the human beings interacting with it.

The two main parts of the system are: (1) the Regional Development
Project Impact Assessment System (PIAS), and (2) the Computer-Assisted
Regional Development Planning System (CARPS). PIAS is the operating
system and CARPS is instrumental to it (see figure 7.3). CARPS has the
following capabilities: geo-data handling and display; processing of geo-dat
on a time-period basis for operating the predictive functions; generating,
operating, and cross-relating the models; assisting the organic linkages
within the total regional development planning system as required by the
users of CARPS and PIAS. The subsystems for regional management are:
basic management (information about the region—land uses, environmental
quality, etc); impact prediction (estimates based on regional dynamics and
referring to national socioeconomic conditions); assessment of impact
(multidimensionally); societal coordination (conflict resolution,
participation by firms, public, etc).

On the plan-generation side the target is for a comprehensive plan for
the area by 1985. This will include a basic plan and a regional developmen
plan. The method of generating the plan includes presenting to the publi
the output of a series of simulations at various levels of the society
through symposia. The analytical material is under three headings—land

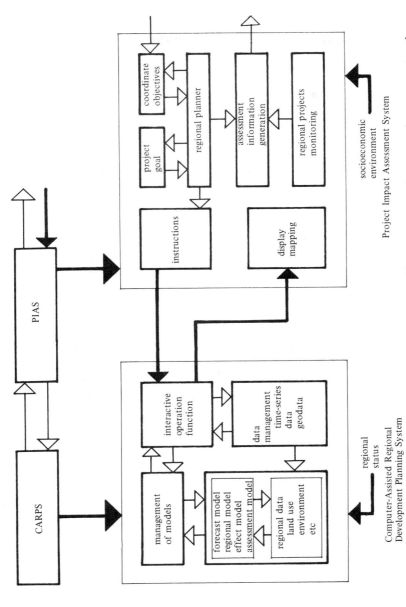

Figure 7.3. Hyogo, Japan: computer-assisted planning system. The concept comprises two major components: the planning–development function and the environmental impact assessment role. The aim is to allow the active fostering of development and growth within a context of environmental awareness. Adapted from Shiina (in Laconte, 1976).

F

development (sprawl, highways and traffic, deterioration of natural environment); urbanization (overpopulation, traffic congestion, pollution, damage to health); and industrial development (GNP-oriented production pollution, water shortage, energy shortage).

This example of a systems approach heavily reliant on the electronic technology for relating planning and environmental control was presented to the Conference on *The Environment of Human Settlements,* Brussels, 1976 (see Laconte, 1976, volume 2, page 103ff).

A comparison with this example of the Hyogo region of Japan with Todd's approach and the Nissan experiment (see chapter 6) brings out an important distinction. Both Todd and Nissan are based on the need to concern ourselves with the ecological processes of the systems in which, and by which, we must live. The Hyogo project on the other hand places emphasis on avoiding the possible undesirable results of developmental action—on land, water, and pollution particularly. This is a fairly limited approach to the question of human action in relation to the physical environment. It is possible to avoid pollution successfully yet seriously damage the life-support system. Monoculture is a frequently cited exampl of such damage; monoculture does not present itself as pollution, but, particularly in the tropics, its application may drastically reduce ecosystem viability.

With these thoughts in mind, we should be wise to distinguish between a concern for the environment—often referred to as environmentalism, *an a concern for the preservation of the long-term viability of ecosystems. The two approaches are not by any means to be considered identical. Th former may, of course, be an important component of the latter.*

Part 2

New visions

The applications of the two areas of knowledge—of the full range of the electromagnetic spectrum and of the functioning of ecosystems—lead to probing the future and to generating suggestions for various paths of development which society may wish or be under some compulsion to follow. Examples of efforts to visualize a new society selected from the two areas of application are described and given a preliminary assessment.

Electronic and ecological futures: as continuation of certain present trends

8.1 Perspective

Our progress in mastering the capabilities of the electromagnetic spectrum and in understanding the interdependencies of the life-support components of the world system has naturally led to a focus of attention on the future. On the ecological side this focus has been sharpened by our awareness of the dangers inherent in human population growth rates and realization that certain nonrenewable resources are being consumed at increasing rates which are not capable of being indefinitely maintained.

We have identified two breakthrough areas of modern knowledge of basic importance to the human enterprise—knowledge of the full range of the electromagnetic spectrum and of the functioning of ecosystems or the life-support system of the world; and we have selected and described key contemporary examples from these fields of knowledge and expertise. We must now briefly look at examples of how the literature of our two breakthrough areas looks at the future.

Writers dealing with futures essentially and often implicitly move along two perspectives:
1 If things go on as they are, we may expect this and that to happen by such and such date.
2 Given certain particular conditions and certain technologies we could *plan* to achieve certain changes in values, behaviour, material equipment, etc by such and such a time.
Very frequently these approaches are combined.

In this chapter we shall look at estimates of how the computer–telecommunications technology is expected to develop and how some observers view the future of our life-support system under the first of these approaches. In the three following chapters we shall describe examples under the second heading.

8.2 Some computer developments

In computer development large-scale integration (LSI) and increasing miniaturization are most likely to become very general. LSI refers to the fact that elements with large numbers of circuits can be manufactured together. This allows easy mass production with attendant fall in cost. This will result in microcomputers of considerable capacity. This development may be expected to modify the present technique of time-sharing based on the capacity of large centralized computers and will change also the role of firms now providing the programmes, the computing power, and the memory facilities to clients needing computer service. This aspect is additional to the changes implied in universal packet-switching. Martin

(1971, page 263) thinks that the role of the larger, more centralized, computer will change to an emphasis of storing data rather than computing. This would mean that the functions of present computers would be split up and distributed spatially in new ways. There seems little doubt that the on-line storage capacity of computers will be enormously increased in the future, probably to the extent that its low cost will make other forms of storage relatively expensive. If this condition reached a certain threshold, economic pressures would rapidly accelerate the rise of computerized storage of all kinds of information and knowledge with attendant decline of storage using paper or electronic off-line storage such as tapes. If relational associative processing became workable for the architecture of data storage, as described in section 4.4, accessing of material would be greatly improved and usage increased.

A microcomputer of modest cost, requiring no special terminal and incurring no costs of line to link with a centralized computer service, would handle all the recording and much of the routine computing of a department of a firm or an individual. Further, the microcomputer would serve as accessor to other computers of larger capacity. This kind of technique is already in use for packet-switching where the microcomputer acts as a virtual terminal.

The implications are also suggestive of major change in our use of books. It is not difficult to envisage that membership of a library will mean being given permission to access a battery of centralized computers. The book desired could be transferred by line to the member's microcomputer to be read when he wishes, discarded or retained according to need. This is now possible. This concept is far in advance of, and basically much more useful than, the emerging techniques which allow electronic browsing through a catalogue, useful though that is. Greatly enlarged memory capacity, especially in conjunction with fibre optics technology, could provide the book itself, page by page, to be read, flipped over, and conceivably scored, just as its physical counterpart. The approximate figures for a book of one hundred and fifty pages might be:

150 pages at 1500 bits per page	225 000 bits
transmit by copper pair (telephone) at 1 000 000 bits per second	$\sim 0 \cdot 25$ seconds
cost 1970	$\sim$ \$2.00
cost 1980	\$0.02 perhaps.

In addition there would be the advantage of interlibrary accessing by means of data packet-switching transmission between distant points on a network. So we see the possibility of virtually instantaneous access to any book or document wherever it is physically located. News of the early demise of the book is, however, probably grossly exaggerated by some observers.

Since Martin (1971, page 256) wrote, events, particularly in the development of universal packet-switching, have confirmed his expectations. The emergence of virtual terminals and virtual circuits is dependent on microcomputers, and with packet-switching, together with the necessary telecommunications facilities and techniques (for example, Dataroute, etc), they indicate new emphases in the use of the various sizes of computer. It already seems clear that the future of firms providing computer service by dedicated line is not as rosy as appeared five years ago. With Datapac, Transpac, etc techniques any terminal can access any computer. It is difficult to hazard an opinion of how this will affect the uses of computers. Martin may well prove to be right: the large-capacity computers will be used mostly for data storage, and smaller, more widely distributed computers will be chiefly used for processing, although they also will have limited memory capacity.

Certainly on the side of the capacity of the technology the picture becomes clearer. The individual terminal will, in terms of the technology, be able to have universal access to all data and all software (programmes for processing data, etc). The organizational and cost aspects at present are very much less foreseeable and are more fluid. Clearly, willingness to allow data to be accessed becomes an important question.

Early in this decade Martin (1971, page 263) had foreseen this development: "The technological trends foreseeable are rapidly pushing the economics further in favor of digital transmission and time-division multiplexing. As these trends develop, the telephone networks will become, in some aspects, like a vast digital computer". He foresaw that large-scale integration circuiting would be joined with pulse code modulation (PCM) to produce area-wide integration of computer capacity and data transmission. PCM uses digital transmission (pulses) in which each pulse transmits a bit. By manipulating the frequencies it is possible to send many signals over the same line, without interference, at high speed. The bits may represent voice, visual material, quantified data, etc. We thus have a standard electronic form, so to speak, in which to transmit anything and everything. This allows existing telephone channels to carry more traffic of wider variety and at a lower cost than is generally possible at present. As Martin stresses, this alters the nature of the telecommunications networks so that we must envisage them as functioning like a worldwide digital computer. The Trans-Canada Dataroute and Infodat systems may be seen as early manifestations of this concept (Trans-Canada Telephone System, 1976a; 1976b).

The digital bit rates are interesting as indicating the capacities being thought about. Voice (telephone) requires 56000 bits per second, picturephone takes 6 million, and colour television 96 million. Ordinary copper wires can be made to carry 1·5 million, as in the present Bell T1 system, introduced in 1962. This Martin thinks to be the basic building block of our future telecommunications systems (Martin, 1971, page 263). Bell's T2 carries 6·3 million bits per second, capable of handling dial-up picturephone. Other T-type carriers are in their initial stages of application. Dataroute and Infodat operate by cable and microwave, at telephone-voice speed and T1 speed according to facility capacity.

In 1975 the transmission speeds of cable in North America were:

T1	1 554 000 bits per second
T2	6 300 000 bits per second
T3	46 000 000 bits per second
T4	281 000 000 bits per second.

T1 is used up to 250 miles and T4 will be used for transmission up to 4000 miles. The latter is already in use between Montreal and Ottawa and between Montreal and Toronto. This is the equivalent of being able to send the contents of 1000 medium-sized books per second. T2 is in use for experimental picturephone in the USA (Chicago area).

Another developing area of potentially great importance is optical information processing. In this technique, which would use the laser extensively, transmission is by light beam. An advantage over digital processing is that the whole image can be handled as a single entity. This means that operations which would be cumbersome by digital techniques can be handled easily, for example, complex-pattern recognition and the correlation of different data—recognition of objects, photo interpretation, radar processing, voice recognition, improvement of visual material transmitted by other means such as video pictures from satellites. These techniques would greatly enlarge the capacity of the computer for handling visual material, and for increasing its capacity for simulating the human eye–brain function of recognition. It would be a major breakthrough in the problem of computerizing large quantities of written material, such as library collections.

8.3 Telecommunications and computer possible futures

At this point it will be useful to give, in highly compressed form, what the technical experts see as potentially available in the future. The literature is extensive. One way of making a brief statement is to attempt to select agreed key items. A second way is to recognize the advantage of the material being filtered through a single mind versed in the field, and later to add material from other sources. The latter technique will be used here and a compression of James Martin's (1971) assessment will be attempted. He ends his *Future Developments in Telecommunications* by offering statements of what the technology could potentially do by target dates up to the late 1990s.

Late 1970s

Dial-up picturephone is available in many urban centres.

Picturephone lines are used for very high-speed data transmission.

Video-conference facilities develop (for example of the type experimentally operated now by Bell Canada between certain cities, the British and Australian Post Offices' Confravision, and others).

Up to 65% of American homes have cable TV.

TV becomes more local in origination of programmes, but also much of it becomes international, using satellites.

Hi-fi music is piped extensively into homes.

TV wall screens receive attention.

Cartridge films are in common use.

Domestic geostationary satellites are used in North America as part of the common carrier systems (for example, Canadian ANIK satellites), including the use of direct rooftop pickup.

Satellite broadcasts to the developing nations increase, where TV is used mostly for education and propaganda. TV comes to many parts of the world for the first time.

Touchtone phones with twelve keys are almost universal in North America. This allows easy interaction with computers.

Data processing continues to spread rapidly. Computer costs fall still lower and computers "... promise to invade almost every aspect of life". The fastest growing area will be that of communications-based systems. Terminals spread.

Dial-up data networks spread, and cheap transmission costs allow corporations to maintain nationwide data banks.

Picturephone capacity lines allow many peripheral computer functions to be carried: colour picture, video recording, graphics reproduction, etc.

Digital transmission is standard. Bit rates are T1 and T2 and faster.

Computer-assisted instruction (CAI) is used widely. "The style and technique for developing good teaching programmes becomes understood."

Many well-educated families have home terminals in conjunction with the touchtone phone and the use of the domestic TV set.

An increasing amount of work is done in the home.

Because of the great increase in crime, homes are connected to police computers and pedestrians begin to carry radio alarm sets.

Use of car radiotelephones increases greatly.

Early 1980s

Cost of long-distance communication has fallen, with easy worldwide access. This affects the organizational arrangements of national and transnational corporations. Data banks are used intercontinentally.

Data banks carrying 10^{14} bits of on-line stored material are fairly common (equals about $0 \cdot 5$ billion paperback books of 2×10^5 bits per book).

There is recognition of the importance of the human element in transactions.

Business uses 'war rooms' extensively.

Cash transfers take place inside the electronic systems (electronic payments systems).

The technology is used extensively in medicine, with automatic monitoring. remote diagnosis, etc.

Picturephone spreads rapidly and falls in cost.

Direct voice interaction with the computer begins; the computer gives a spoken reply.

First public laser channel appears, and fibre optics are in use (useful for TV wall-screen circuits).

Hi-fi TV service begins, via cable.

The use of millimetre-wave radio frequencies in some cities begins. This gives high channel capacity and low noise. Also infrared and optical links are in use. The advantage is that many links can use identical wavelengths without interference. This would mean a much more varied use of the wave bands—personal links, etc. This fits very well with the characteristics of geostationary satellites if unobstructed path is necessary for effective operation.

Early 1990s

Direct access data banks contain up to 10^{18} bits.

TV wall screens are common.

Laser channels are installed in homes, giving many hi-fi TV channels.

Dial-up TV channels appear.

Office and apartment blocks have computers for controlling screen fragmenting and concentrating—allowing several images simultaneously at will.

Wall screens are used for education, with individual students in various locations, with two-way audio–video.

Printed newspapers end.

Telecommunications directories are in general use.

Shopping is done on the home screen.

Almost 10% of the GNP of the USA is spent on communications services.

As the date under review moves further into the future the precision of the technological material becomes less, as might be expected, and the literature exhibits a tendency to make good with statements of behavioural change. Detailed changes in society are not a focus of the present study and will not be pursued here as the literature on that subject is large. The general reader may obtain an overall idea from James Martin's writings.

It will be helpful to glance at other technological opinion, in addition to Martin. From Olaf Helmer (1966) we could add:

implantation of plastic and electronic organs	by 1984
automated libraries	by 1984
universal satellite relay system	by 1984
automatic translation machines	by 1984
dominant role of automation	by 1984
a universal language through automated communication	by 2000
man–machine symbiosis—electromechanical relating of brain to computer	by 2100
direct education into the brain	by 2600

The dates, which should not always be taken too seriously, are generally the medians of Delphi exercises.

Martin's early 1970s expectations for picturephone are not being borne out, since for the benefits it offers there appears to be only an extremely limited market at the likely cost. Bell Canada does not appear to have any intention of offering picturephone, and at present has no T2 cable in use—the minimum cable capacity required for it. Rather than picturephone it is possible that the conference TV developed by Bell, the British Confravision, the kind of facility represented by the Wired City, and computer conferencing as previously described, will have greater likelihood of acceptance provided the user–technology interface can be improved, and in the case of the Wired City type, switching can be automated. Martin is also a little early for touchtone phones being in universal use. Their general use domestically in North America is perhaps 1985 to 1990 rather than 1980. Businesses get them earlier than residences under present priorities. Martin underestimates, probably, the importance of the optical modes of transmission. Apart from these comments Martin's expectations have held up well to 1977, although some institutional elements, for example education, have proved more conservative and slower than he anticipated.

In looking at the future applications of the computer–telecommunications technology it should be constantly borne in mind that the technology has enormous capabilities, which grow exponentially. It is therefore not so much a question of whether or not the technology can do so-and-so, as it is a matter of cost, established values, already committed equipment and its organization (for example the telephone system), timing, levels of income, etc. Picturephone is an example of the area of debate. Technically it presents no difficulty, but because of some of the nontechnical reasons just listed, its common use is now generally accepted to be unlikely. Because of this condition, predictions which rely too heavily and too narrowly on the technology and on technological forecasting are of only limited value and require caution.

8.4 Fears for future global ecological stability

The emerging awareness of possible worldwide difficulties in the life-support system received considerable popular stimulus in the early seventies when there appeared *A Blueprint for Survival* (*The Ecologist*, 1972) and *The Limits to Growth* (Meadows et al, 1972). Concern for the quality of the environment, for our use of nonrenewable resources, and for the condition of the world's land and water ecosystems has grown since then, and many governments are now committed to research and action directed toward safeguarding the environment.

Whereas the approaches to futures in the electronics field are relatively uncomplicated, ecological futures are approached through a number of complex routes, which interconnect. In general the telecommunications and computer futurists are content with technological forecasting,

estimating the dates for various degrees of application for particular piece
of technology, and with attempting to foresee impacts on present society
The ecological writers, on the other hand, are observing changes and
threats of change in the world of living things and emphasize the need to
question whether society can survive if certain present trends in human
behaviour continue. The electronics writers are optimistic; the ecologists
are not. Their pessimism about the future of the world's life-support
system is an unavoidable component in our contemporary thinking about
ourselves and Spaceship Earth. It serves in some measure to conceal the
very major but obscure question of whether or not the human enterprise
totters on the edge of disaster.

The threats to, and therefore the future of, the biosphere and its
ecosystems have received a great deal of attention. The literature is vast.
One way of coping with it is to identify foci of attention and then
examine the material to see which writers have addressed themselves to
particular foci (see Dakin, 1973, page 23 ff). Such questions of interest
are, for example: concern for the use of natural resources; paying
attention to the condition of the regional ecosystem; and controlling
populations. Very many well-known names can be drawn upon: Bates
(1960), Simpson (1964), Dubos (1965), Caldwell (1964; 1972), Julian
Huxley (1961), E P Odum (1971), H T Odum (1971), Commoner (1972),
and Ward (1966) to list a few. This approach is useful for our present
purpose but the brush strokes will have to be broad. It will be necessary
to separate the identifications of the condition, or future likely or possibl
condition, from suggested action for controlling the trends perceived as
dangerous.

The areas of concern for the future condition of the life-support system
reflected in the literature include:
1 short supply or exhaustion of certain key nonrenewable resources—
   fuels, metals, potable water;
2 continuance of increasing rates or even present rates of demand and
   consumption for certain commodities;
3 the rate of the world human population growth coupled with the
   absolute numbers of human beings predictable for the middle future;
4 pressures of certain present technological applications upon the stability
   diversity, cyclicity, and productivity of ecosystems—monocultures,
   industrialized agriculture, so-called pollution, etc;
5 loss of, or heavy reduction in the populations of, certain species;
6 increase in interrelationships between ecosystems on a global scale;
7 the effects of reducing the world's wilderness and forest areas below th
   level necessary for global ecological stability at present levels;
8 interference with the composition of the atmosphere—the oxygen
   supply, the ozone layer, increase in ultraviolet penetration;

9 the destructive capacity of nuclear fission—vitally and genetically harmful radiation caused by accident, war, civil misdemeanour, or radioactive waste from nuclear power plants (all reactors discard fuel material containing plutonium);

10 the reaching of critical conditions, going beyond which means passing a point of no return in ecosystems or even the biosphere;

11 the failure of certain feedback loops in human societies to ensure that human populations make the responsive corrective actions necessary to ensure ecosystem safety; this includes the danger of mass populations losing sight of their natural physical base;

12 certain conditions, demands, trends, and difficulties now manifest specifically in the world's large agglomerations of human beings—not confined to Western or developed societies;

13 the population–food–energy syndrome.

The above foci of attention in the ecological perspective are diagnostic in nature. They claim to identify areas in which the continuance either of present trends or of the present condition signifies present or potential ecological danger and therefore danger to the human enterprise, local or global. We should note here that the concern for ecological safety can rest entirely honourably upon the desire to ensure the continuance of human life on a planetary scale. It is not necessary to become involved in arguments about the desirability of acting for the benefit of the world's ecosystems independently of human interest. Evaluation of the worth of this green globe at solar system scale is not possible, since we do not yet think in value terms at that systemic level.

The essential futures emphasis of the ecologists tends to be of the order of warning that unless human beings change their present behaviour to patterns more capable of being safely accommodated by the biosphere the capacity of the world to produce the human-usable biomass necessary for our survival will be seriously reduced. Some, for example Maddox (1972), think this view exaggerated, and some engineers and others, for example Fuller (1969), think that the application of knowledge can keep the biosphere's processes within the desired limits. The body of expert opinion issuing serious warning is, however, both weighty and large, and already we sense the general diffusion of the idea that we cannot continue in our present socioeconomic ways but must change direction.

Proposals for change range from the highly technical in the biological field to the development of an ecological ethic. At the biological end of this spectrum we have looked at the projects of Todd (chapter 6). At the other end we have mentioned the ethical emphases of H T Odum (1971) and Potter (1971), and shall record in detail the efforts of Ryan to develop new feedbacks in society so that appropriate ecological individual and group behaviour may be ensured (chapter 11). As preventive and remedial action is future oriented, it is now necessary to indicate briefly some of the areas of proposed action that lie intermediately along this range.

On the side of action suggested for future coping with the ecological questions listed above, and therefore from the 'human' systems perspective it will suffice to mention the major approaches found in the literature of the ecologists. Well-known names associated with each emphasis are added

1 Safeguard and improve the *regional* ecosystem (Boulding, 1971b; Caldwell, 1972; E P Odum, 1971; H T Odum, 1971; Ward and Dubos 1972).

2 Plan the use of nonrenewable natural resources (*The Ecologist*, 1972; Ehrlich and Ehrlich, 1970; Meadows et al, 1972; Mesarovic and Pestel 1974; Ward and Dubos, 1972).

3 Develop policies related to energy (Brubaker, 1972; *The Ecologist*, 1972; Ward and Dubos, 1972).

4 Recycle used physical material (*The Ecologist*, 1972; McHale, 1971; Meadows et al, 1972).

5 Develop land and agricultural policies (Bates, 1960; *The Ecologist*, 1972 Ward, 1976).

6 Develop policies for physical and electronic communication (*The Ecologist*, 1972; Galbraith, 1973; an outstanding writer linking telecommunications to ecological perspectives at the policy level appears to be lacking).

7 Move from an economy of flow to a socioeconomy of stock (*The Ecologist*, 1972; Fromm, 1968; Meadows et al, 1972; Theobald 1972).

8 Modify land tenure traditions and determinations of land uses (Brubaker 1972; Galbraith, 1973; Theobald, 1972).

9 Decentralize from present metropolitan areas (Dubos, 1965; *The Ecologist*, 1972; Ward and Dubos, 1972; Ward, 1976).

10 Develop a new world view and ethic (Caldwell, 1964; *The Ecologist*, 1972; J Huxley, 1961; Laszlo et al, 1977; H T Odum, 1971; Potter, 1971; Simpson, 1964).

11 Develop a consciously organized knowledge system directed toward society's interests, rather than group or individual interests (Caldwell, 1964; Fuller, 1969; Theobald, 1972).

In addition to the above we should record concern for the well-being of the world's oceans, covering questions such as pollution, overfishing, and the extraction of natural resources—oil, metals, etc.

A major preoccupation with the threat posed by the increasing numbers of human beings runs through all the items listed above. Most ecological writers accept that this increase will continue at a high global rate until the end of the century despite some probable recent slackening in the rate of increase. The attempts to deal with this additional load include both efforts to meet it as it is and proposals to reduce it by policies of population control initiated by governments, as recently in the Punjab.

Unlike the electronic technology futurists, the ecologists tend not to give dates by which a condition may appear. There is an exception, however, and that is in the area of nonrenewable resources. Here, dates for the 'exhaustion' of a metal or a fuel are frequently estimated. Careful examination of the available estimates usually uncovers considerable discrepancies. The energy question, for example, is presented with a wide range of opinion stretching from 'techfix' to major upheavals in society. As for ecosystems, ecologists rarely give likely dates for reaching a deteriorated condition.

This difficulty of dating a future adverse condition relates to certain variations in the outlooks of the ecologists and the analysts of the world system. Meadows et al take the view that emphasis should be given to the world as a single system. They give a general date for collapse of this total system as about the middle of the twenty-first century, assuming the continuance of the present trends. They urge "... a controlled, orderly transition from growth to global equilibrium" (Meadows et al, 1972, page 188). Mesarovic and Pestel, on the other hand, place the major emphasis on seeing the world as a system of interacting regions, and see collapse at a regional level as possible long before the middle of the twenty-first century (Mesarovic and Pestel, 1974, page 55). The recommendation offered is for differentiated or organic growth rather than undifferentiated growth.

The Mesarovic summing up would probably achieve a large measure of general agreement, even from those who claim that the alleged dangers to the planet's life-support system are exaggerated. The overall ideas are:

the present difficulties are not temporary;
solutions must be developed in a global context;
traditional methods will not produce adequate solutions;
the difficulties can be overcome by cooperation rather than confrontation (Mesarovic and Pestel, 1974, page 163).

We should note here how the approaches of the ecologists have encouraged the first attempts at conceptualizing total world systems. This is the important contribution of Meadows et al and Mesarovic and Pestel. Ecologists, however, criticize these efforts as not being adequately based in biological reality. Others object that such models of the total world system are naive in human terms. Whatever the shortcomings, whether on the narrow technical side of model construction or on the side of adequate generalized basis of thinking, the outcome of the thinking of the ecologists and of the global modelling of the world systems analysts has been to alert us to the need to think about the future in terms of the global picture. It is impossible to go back on that breakthrough.

8.5 Comment on electronic and ecological futures

With the possible exception of Paul Ehrlich, who is essentially a population expert, Toffler's (1972) *The Futurists* does not include an ecologist. This is clearly not because he is unaware of the ecological perspective on world futures since he has written about this elsewhere (Toffler, 1975). A conclusion to be drawn from the absence of ecologists from the list of futurists is that they have not yet made their mark in what is counted as futures thinking. We shall see, however, in chapter 10 that at least one group of ecologists has come forward with proposals for action by society to deal with impending difficulties. Such proposals are clearly different from the essentially technical approaches suggested in the stricter ecological context, such as Todd's or the Papuan experiments.

This distinction draws our attention to the need for closer scrutiny of the differences in relationships between ecological knowledge and society and the electronic technology and society.

On the side of the telecommunications and computer technology we find a heavy reliance on estimating new developments in the technology itself, and from these trying to envisage how society will use the potential and what kinds of changes in behaviour will be likely to result. The underlying assumption is that somehow or other a new piece of technology appears and that this inevitably generates a certain kind of response in our behaviour. We accepted this notion of strong technological determinism for a long time without noticing that the context in which new technology or improvement in existing technology appears has changed. Further, we are capable of consciously changing the context, and indeed already frequently exert considerable influence in this direction. Governmental action, the allocation of research funds, the pressures of changing market conditions, war, and public opinion all have considerable influence on what areas of technology shall be developed and what will not. The arbitrary and haphazard earlier mode of growth in technology appears to have been curtailed in recent decades, partly no doubt because of the greatly increased costs of developing new technology or introducing innovation. *We may now be considerably in the position that society, through its various institutions and associations, influences the development of the technology rather more than the technology decides the organization and functioning of society. This possible change of dynamic now requires much closer attention than it receives at present.*

Major evidence is to be found in the way in which state or other agency control of technology has grown in recent decades. For example, quasi-state agencies allocate the essential resource of the frequencies of the electromagnetic spectrum. Special bodies, such as the International Telecommunication Union, arrange the use of this resource between nation states. National agencies such as the US Federal Communications Commission stipulate what shall be required of TV cable companies.

National undertakers such as the telecommunications agencies of various countries decide which telephone technologies shall be developed and which potentials shall be ignored. Computer technology drives toward greater capacity, not arbitrarily but because there is money to be made out of providing it. Research resources are consciously allocated toward the development of a piece of technology that can be seen as a good fit to the present and emerging condition of society. So, if we are going shortly to have general access to data stored in computers through universal packet-switching we 'need' to develop computer storage technology giving much faster access than at present. This 'need' will attract the necessary resources—scientists, equipment, money—and eventually the required technology will be developed. The process is consciously societal, orderly, and carefully examined as to risk and probability of success. All this is vastly different from the context of the growth of technology in, say, George Stephenson's day or even during the initial period of radio broadcasting. We are now a purposefully technological society. In this role we undoubtedly have various options open to us.

The obverse of this new situation is that in probing the future from the perspective of technology we are developing the concept of *impact prediction*. So we examine the effect on personal privacy of electronic payments systems, or the changes which universal accessing of data will bring in our notions of property related to knowledge—copyright, reproduction rights, etc. At this point there emerges a direct connection with preferred values held by the society. In the West we therefore find concern for the preservation of our traditional views about personal security, freedom, and privacy. In this context of technology these values tend to be regarded as somewhat fixed and static. By contrast, in the nontechnological literature they are frequently seen as undergoing or needing to undergo considerable change. Looked at from this perspective the studies of technological impact would be seen as in a condition of cultural lag.

On the ecological side of futures the most impressive features as far as action or operations go is the widespread and consistent call for a new ethic which will restore human behaviour to patterns compatible with long-term ecosystem viability. The ecologists repeatedly warn that the behaviour of the human race is progressively undermining the life-support system on which it is based. The problem does not seem to them so much a question of knowing what to do as to getting human beings to agree to do it. Ecologists tend to see the obtaining of the necessary change in human behaviour as a matter of ethics, and specifically in terms of an ethic specially to be developed to ensure the necessary feedback loops in human societies. Specific proposals take the form of ecological 'commandments', such as those suggested by H T Odum (1971, page 244) and Potter (1971).

These commandments are addressed to the individual. They enjoin him to behave so that the viability of ecosystems will be safeguarded. The underlying notion is that ethics, starting with the regulation of behaviour between individuals and advancing to the regulation of the behaviour between the individual and the group, must now advance to the regulation of the behaviour between the individual/group and the global life-support system. Current efforts to increase our awareness of the details of behaviour in this area are seen as the beginning of the emergence of this third area of ethics. Conservation, respect for the processes of life, and adequate control loops between 'natural' and 'human' systems are the keynotes.

The ecologists, however, do not and indeed cannot tell us how to ensure that human beings will obey the new ethic. Yet this is an all-important aspect of the whole matter, especially as we have to deal with the behaviour and perceived 'needs' of very large mass populations. It is in these that the feedback control loops traditionally operative have been destroyed. The individual, whether as himself or in a group, has come to behave in ways which result in *aggregated* behaviour which cannot now be certainly continued. It is the perception of these connections which will lead us to the need to look at the nature of the mass individual in chapter 16 and 17. We shall see in chapter 11 how one area of research—that of Ryan—makes a frontal attack on this basic aspect of the whole problem.

For purposes of understanding, it is, I think, useful to separate the two attitudes to society outlined above from those approaches which claim the need to reform society's behaviour because of its internal contradictions, injustices, inequalities, and inefficiencies. Such latter approaches have been the most preferred ones of our time and the aspirations which they embody have a common human appeal. They do not, however, generally go the technocratic way nor do they give any particular emphasis to the need to ensure the adequate continuance of the life-support system. Such approaches may therefore have a dangerous bias which consciously directed change in society may unwittingly build into a new system. *A major point to which attention should be paid seems to be that we must avoid the concept of two systems—one 'natural' and one 'human'. We have to conceptualize a single world system.*

These matters will be probed further in chapter 12. But first we shall look at three examples of attempts to envision our future fairly holistically as large human groups, along our two perspectives. The first starts from the electronic technology as the point of departure; the second is ecological in approach; and the third tackles the development of viable human behaviour *within* the ecosystem.

The information society as seen for Japan

9.1 An emerging approach

In this chapter I shall describe the most comprehensive proposals for basing the major future growth of an entire society substantially on the electronic technology. The country is Japan. The context and motivation for the effort are in part the realization that maintenance of the recent growth rate of the economy, based essentially on industrial production of physical commodities, is unlikely to be possible indefinitely. There is also the imaginative perception that the computer and telecommunications technology offers human beings such great new capabilities as to imply major changes in our culture and societies. There is perhaps also a competitive consideration: massive rewards may well be won by the nation which 'informationalizes' first.

At the outset of looking at concepts for 'information-based societies' it is necessary to remove some possible areas of misunderstanding. First, the emphasis on information does not imply that present industrial bases are abandoned. Indeed, it does not necessarily mean that they are even modified, except perhaps in their growth rate. In the example which we are going to look at, the physical life support of the society would apparently remain much as at present, the concept essentially being one of continuing growth in the total socioeconomy, but with the sector of growth being shifted from physical goods and services to information and the areas associated with it. Second, stabilization in some aspects of the life of a society is quite compatible with very rapid growth in other areas. It is possible for societies, just as individuals, to live at an adequate but stabilized level of physical well-being and yet enjoy a rapidly expanding intellectual, aesthetic, and creative life. There is no reason to suppose that a continuously expanding access to physical goods and services is essential to attaining and maintaining a viable life balance between the individual and the group. This aspect later becomes very important, and is approached in chapters 21 and 22. Third, we should not assume that the concepts and foci of attention that are at present associated with those disciplines which study the socioeconomy will necessarily serve us at the new level at which we have to think. Boulding, himself an economist, pointed this difficulty out twenty years ago (Boulding, 1956). Conventional economics, concerned with the production and consumption of physical goods and services and, as Boulding stresses, confined to a low level of systemic conceptualization, will need to be amplified on the one hand to cope with "the information society" and on the other hand to allow biological and socioeconomic knowledge to be reconciled. Fortunately, there is already substantial work going on along both avenues of exploration (for example Parker, 1976a; H T Odum, 1971; at a still more basic biological level, Wilson, 1975).

9.2 An informationalization plan for Japan

The idea that the electronic technology is leading to a worldwide human society in which information or knowledge is the mainspring is commonly found in the literature (for example Drucker, 1968). To date there have been very few attempts to look at this as a planned goal for a nation state. Very interesting exploration in this direction is being done by the Japan Computer Usage Development Institute (1972). The name chiefly associated with this work is that of Y Masuda, whose books *The Computopia* and *The Computocracy* have been best-sellers in Japan. His plan for the information society (Japan Computer Usage Development Institute, 1972) is of great interest because it goes far beyond the obvious applications of the technology in the piecemeal style so prevalent both in real world developments and in research approaches, and boldly moves toward facing the need for new disciplinary modes of thought.

The context of the proposed plan to achieve the information society was the realization of difficulties likely to be experienced in the further development of Japan's successful postwar industrialization: serious shortage of intellectual manpower, widening information gaps, pollution and traffic difficulties, and other problems connected with urbanization. The aim is to realize a "... society that brings about a general flourishing state of human intellectual creativity". This is seen as being in contrast with the past concentration of industrial society on the production of material goods, which must now undergo modification because of the perceived limits in natural resources. The plan targets for 1985 and assumes that the transformation to an information society will be a major development programme of the Japanese state. The estimate of cost in national funds investment is about $68 billion (1971) to cover the period up to 1985. The financing of the plan has been carefully worked out, the final version being considered probably realizable.

The plan is nothing less than a restructuring of the culture: "The plan should be intended to prepare the background to enable establishment of computer mind, and to prepare measures that will compensate for the drawbacks arising from computerization" (Japan Computer Usage Development Institute, 1972, page 3). The plan would be jointly carried out by the public and private sectors, including the development of a 'third sector' which would combine the other two in nonprofit activity (for example, databanks, hospital services, think-tank centre, new-town development corporations, etc).

The technical basis of the revolution is computerization, but Masuda goes on from that to make proposals about the fundamental socioeconomic and value-system changes that will be necessary. There is also concern for safeguards against tyranny (issuing in proposals for a national congress for the development of the information society), a review system, arrangements for citizen participation, and a computerization policy council with representations from all strata of society. The plan therefore includes the proposals necessary to cope with the changes that the plan itself will engender.

The main goals, in the context of the need to shift from a cultural base excessively concerned with material goods and services to one substantially reliant on 'informationalization', are:

"To promote the knowledge industry in Japan,
To solve social problems such as medical, transportation, pollution and distribution problems,
To hasten the change from industrialization to informationalization smoothly" (page 6).

The main characteristics of the plan are:

a medium-term impact plan and a long-range basic plan;
attention is focussed on information, rather than on the extension of present industrialization;
the plan is oriented toward software rather than hardware. *This plan is to reorganize the systems in various fields of our society, and to improve the quality of society instead of expanding the quantity of materials in our society*" (page 7, emphasis supplied);
the plan is multiphased and includes many subplans.

Table 9.1. Computerization development periods. (Source: "Problems on Japan's Computerization from International Viewpoint" compiled by the computerization committee's survey team report on Europe's computerization.)

	First period 1945-1970 (big-science base)	Second period 1955-1980 (management base)	Third period 1970-1990 (society base)	Fourth period 1980-2000 (private-person base)
Objective	defense, space development	GNP	GNW [a]	GNS [b]
Value system	national prestige	economic growth	social welfare	self-realization
Subject	country	enterprise	people	private person
Object	nature	organization	society	human being
Basic science	natural science	management science	social science	behavioural science
Information pattern	attaining the goal	pursuing efficiency	solving problems	intellectual creation

[a] Gross National Welfare.
[b] Gross National Satisfaction.

The plan does, however, assume the continued sustained growth of the GNP, and indeed the GNP is required to become several times larger to support the information society. The conceptualized phases are conveniently shown in table 9.1.

A key econo-technological factor is the achieving of a considerable distribution of computer terminals in private homes. The plan anticipates this will be achievable to a workable level by 1985—terminals in 250000 homes. This is covered by a progressively increased percentage of the GNP being invested in computerization, reaching 15% of the GNP in 1985. Meantime the GNP is assumed to grow at 11% per annum. The main problems are not seen as technical or financial but as lag in government attitudes and policy, and the present relatively high cost of information. (It is interesting that ecologists see their difficulties in operationalizing in much the same light.)

The first five years (intermediate impact plan) will include nine projects:

"Administration data bank.
Computopolis plan.
Medical systems that cover broad areas and remote localities.
Computer oriented education experimental school district.
Pollution prevention systems covering broad areas.
Think-tank center.
Introduction of MIS (Management Information System) into small and medium-sized enterprises [this is modernization, including improvements in tax, data, consulting matters].
Labour force development center.
Computer peace corps [foreign aid to developing countries]" (Japan Computer Usage Development Institute, 1972, page 20).

The total cost of the impact plan is shown as $3247 million (1971), of which the largest items are for computopolis ($1169 million), pollution prevention ($584 million), think tank ($386 million), and education ($266 million).

Computopolis consists of building a new town as a demonstration, comparable with Tama new town, near Tokyo. It would feature CATV, a computerized transportation network, automated supermarket, regionalized health control including automated hospitals, regionalized cooking and heating, computer-oriented education, a research centre, integrated pollution prevention and monitoring, a think-tank centre, a labour development centre, etc.

The main plan would include:

"Formation of the Nation-wide Information Network.
Rationalization of Administration.
Upgrading MIS.
Computer-oriented Education.

Modernization of Health Care.
Pollution Prevention System.
Modernization of Distribution Channels.
Computerization of Traffic System.
Diffusion of Home Terminals.
International Cooperation in Computerization.
Measures to Eliminate Demerits of Computerization" (page 30).

At first, telephone lines will be used for the information networks but at the time of the plan being worked out it was anticipated that a new broadband system using coaxial cable and microwave would be required. The total network would comprise the two systems (see chapters 3 and 4 for technical description). The broadband system was to be operational by 1985, but the very rapid development of packet-switching may modify this (see chapter 4; Nippon Telegraph and Telephone, 1974).

Considerable emphasis is placed on education. The aim is a computer-oriented education for all Japanese children. The plan requires every school from kindergarten upwards to have a classroom equipped with terminals for individual student use by 1985. The educational emphasis will be on developing the child's potential, encouraging problemsolving and creativity, and developing a new ethical outlook based on "self-control and democracy". Within twenty years it is expected about 30% of the population will be proud possessors of "the computer mind". If this sounds utopian we might remember that a public utility computer network seemed utopian only five years ago. It is now an accomplished fact in several countries, and capable of intercontinental operation; transoceanic working across the Atlantic and Pacific has been shown operationally feasible.

The report goes on to examine the merits and demerits of the proposals, concluding that in spite of the enormous monetary costs the merits outweigh the demerits. A detailed analysis of evaluation is given. The merits of the proposal are stated as:

the foundation of the information industry will be secured;
there will be rapid improvement in societal well-being;
renovation of social and economic systems will occur;
intellectual creativity will blossom.

Some demerits are thought to be:

fear of creating a controlled society;
increase in the gap between the intellectual elite and the general public;
danger of loss of the sense of humanity and damage to ethical standards.

The report argues that steps must be taken to deal with the likely disadvantages. The main ethical emphasis appears to be on strengthening the stoic attitude to life. One can readily believe that such a philosophy would indeed be necessary to the sanity of the individual, not to mention the safety of the state!

The "probable plan" gives $35 938 million for education; $7 792 million for modernization of medical care; $3 503 million for the national networks; and $5 636 for management information systems.

Masuda points to certain socioeconomic difficulties into which the Japanese will be running in the 1970s. Other industrial, or 'postindustrial' countries are likely to share them. First, there will be a shortage of intellectual manpower. Second, the application of the information processing technology at present is only weakly directed toward socio-economic development; information needs to be integrated. At present there is a wide gap between the amount of knowledge—growing very rapidly—and the *application* of processing technology; more and better information exists than we are able to bring easily into use. Third, there are serious environmental problems, which we are only just beginning to acknowledge. If industrialization proceeds as in the recent past these problems will be severely aggravated. The 'informationalization' of society is seen as hopeful in assisting the meeting of these difficulties.

"The target of computer mind is to make computer general knowledge instead of specialist's knowledge. We can see a blue print of a new society where people use computer in everyday living in business, government, university, school and home. Our ultimate goal is to present you a vision of a new society where people create ideas and new thoughts with the assistance of computers" (JCUDI, 1972, page 124).

These proposals strongly imply the broadening of the base of economics. Masuda (1975) has not turned away from facing this difficulty, as many writers do, but has offered certain new concepts which are developed out of our new capacity for handling information.

9.3 Masuda's 'information economics'

The problem is not easy to formulate briefly, but it can at least be pointed to in the following way. We have seen our increase in wealth over the last two centuries along an economic perspective which strongly emphasizes our increasing capacity to produce material goods and services. The division and specialization of labour and later the mass production of goods are viewed as among the key causes of the growth of our production capacity. Hence we have come to develop a certain kind of mental discipline, called economics, to assist our understanding of the process. *When, however, we come to look at knowledge (or information) as wealth we find we have few concepts with which to handle it. This leads to the question of whether we can enlarge our thinking to describe a system that has appropriate emphasis on knowledge as a kind of superior 'economic good'.*

As we have said, such a socioeconomics would not imply that the production of material goods will cease to be very important and require continued effort, but would recognize that there are limits to the present growth in physical production. The invitation is to try to visualize a kind of upper level of production, concentrating on knowledge or information.

In developing his economic concepts Masuda (1975) starts by emphasizing that economics as an academic discipline has been unduly culture bound. He points out, for example, that the *Wealth of Nations* appeared at a time when new wealth was about to result from increased productivity arising from the division and specialization of labour and from the new technologies which were beginning to appear. Smith's theory very largely arose out of a situation existing in the ongoing world of action. Thus Masuda accepts— as is increasingly being borne in on us in these days of inflation—that economic theory in any age to a large extent is a product of that epoch's socioeconomic conditions and preoccupations. He subscribes to the view that the mode of productivity largely decides what the theory will be, and diagnoses our present global condition as:

we are on the threshold of an age of new style productivity;
this productivity is information productivity and it is different from the industrial productivity which concentrates on providing material goods.

His 'information economics' has three basic concepts:

1 *Globalism is the spirit of the time.* This provides the ideological support for an information economics just as the spirit of the Renaissance did for classical and neoclassical economics. Globalism is characterized by the spaceship idea, and although Masuda does not go in detail into the ecology of the biosphere, he stresses that we must come to terms with our global limitations—coexistence of man and nature. This, he thinks. must override liberalism and individualism. A new ethical viewpoint will be necessary, and more emphasis will have to be placed on human than on material values. This implies the end of the spirit of the Renaissance.
2 *Information productivity is the core of information economics.* The view prescribed is that the productivity of information is entering a period of enormously heightened growth: information will very rapidly become highly productive. This is due to the development in the telecommunications and computer technologies and their widening diffusion. The coming enhancement of productivity in information is incomparably larger than the magnification of productivity in material goods typical of the industrial revolution.
3 *Time-value is a new concept of human value* (Masuda, 1975). Time-value is a new concept in the area of values. It is: "... the value that is created by man when he spends his free time in a purposeful way ... if man uses his time for the satisfaction of his wants, time produces time-value". The computer increases our effectiveness, "... largely removes

limitations on the scale and time of our purposeful action", and gives
man greater time free from material production (automation of physical
production). Time-value development is dependent on the field of
information space, for the first time now provided by the electronic
technology. Time-value is essentially concerned with the satisfaction of
"... human and intellectual wants, in contrast to the fact that material
value corresponds to the satisfaction of physiological and material wants".
Only increased productivity in knowledge–information can directly
generate time-value.

The essential chain of Masuda's reasoning is that the jump in information
productivity:

"promotes automation of goods and services, and
this in turn results in shortening working hours and increasing free time,
and at the same time
mass production of normative and compound information and its public
utilization will become general,
which will help raise the probability of people's objective-oriented acts
being accomplished" (Masuda, 1975).

An emphasis on forward thinking pervades Masuda's theory. This
includes the need to develop feedforward techniques to keep both the
individual and the society heading in the right direction. He uses the
phrase "self-actualization for future time"—the electronic technology will
"... *greatly amplify and enlarge man's future time*". In a later paper
(ICCC, 1976, page 165) he probes still further into the enigma (for
economics) that information or knowledge is used but not consumed, and
notes the analogy between this fact and von Neumann's (1958) theory of
the self-multiplicative production of machinery—also enigmatic. *The key
problem for Masuda is that the information technology expands the time
available for human beings. How do we conceptualize a system which
describes this?*

9.4 Comment
In good humour one may comment that in targeting his first phase of the
computerized society for 1985 Masuda missed Orwell by one year! In his
enthusiasm is Masuda unwittingly bringing us 1984? Sometimes he sounds
utopian; at other times the vision, perhaps unwittingly, suggests the
regimentation of the mass society par excellence. At the present time this
is difficult intellectual and emotional terrain. It is useful perhaps to
remember George Steiner's (1971, page 59) question of whether any
thinking into the future can be done without some ingredient of utopianism:
if we wish to move coherently into the future we must tolerate some
utopianism, despite ourselves. In justification of his ideas Masuda could
well point out that many of the expectations of his earlier writings have

already materialized. The development of packet-switching and the organizational agreements necessary to make it work have at a single stroke made Masuda's vision of the common public use of the computer a potential fact of existence in the developed countries. Even his date of 1985 will be about right for widespread use of common public data-processing networks.

There are certain items of general importance raised by Masuda's thinking:

1 While in the industrialized countries productivity in agriculture and manufacturing industry has risen spectacularly during the latter part of the last century and this century, productivity in the tertiary sector has grown only very modestly. French thinking on the decentralization of information handling gives strong emphasis to this discrepancy (see DATAR, 1973). This lag in the tertiary sector may provide part of the socioeconomic space into which the electronic technology will move.

2 Masuda is strongly supported by Parker's analysis of US employment. For about twenty-five years the number of workers in the area of physical production has been steeply in decline and the number in information or knowledge work has risen very steeply and is now dominant in the US labour force (Parker, 1976a). Masuda draws our attention to the fact that our conventional measures are now failing as indicators of key changes in the socioeconomics of the developed countries.

3 In socioeconomic terms the differences between goods and services on the one hand and information or knowledge on the other need much more attention than they have been given. Goods are consumed by use: information is not. *Again, a kind of socioeconomic space looms into view.* What are the socioeconomics of an unconsumable wealth, and what will be the nature of a society very considerably based on this?

4 There is general agreement that a new ethic is necessary and suggestions for its precepts are not lacking. The electronic technology, perhaps just as much as our new ecological knowledge, points to this need. At the moment we only fumble.

5 In probing for fundamentals along the perspective of the electronic technology it is startling to discover how close relationships with similar probes in other fields emerge. In asking questions about the nature of information in society Masuda's thought moves out toward the new epistemology developed since 1950 or so (see for example Bateson, 1972; McCulloch, 1965). In thinking about problems of a new ethic he touches the similar conclusions of ecologists (see for example H T Odum, 1971; Simpson, 1964). *These mergings or overlaps suggest we are moving toward some new synthesis or overview. They are very exciting to discover.*

6 Masuda, as others who are deeply involved in technologies, will be accused of being a techfixer as far as curing society's troubles goes.

A useful restraint on making judgments at this superficial level is to remember the four billion that we now are on Spaceship Earth and the six billion we soon shall be. Masuda's viewpoint is that Japan must soon see the limits to continuing her present sociotechnical condition.

7 It is very important not to confuse the characteristics of energy with those of information [a "difference which makes a difference", as Bateson (1972, page 271) defines it]. Our socioeconomic thought is largely based on energy flow. Information flow is not the same. Realization of this difference and study of its implications has already had major effect in many disciplines (figure 9.1).

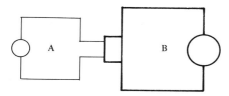

Figure 9.1. Information: the difference that makes a difference. A change in loop A instigates a change in loop B. The circle in loop A signifies a cause of change in the flow round loop A. As a result, change is triggered in loop B, whose function (the circle) undergoes change. Note that the energy flowing round A does not pass into B it only activates an element in B which generates change in the flow of energy in B.

Masuda's thought is reaching for fundamentals. He raises questions which must be tackled by thinkers in a variety of fields. His viewpoint is supported by a growing opinion. We may cite as examples: Parker (1976a; 1976b); Spence (1974); Arrow (1974); Hirschleifer (1973); and the forthcoming major research project being set up by the Organization for Economic Co-operation and Development. Chapter 22 probes further in this direction.

Toward the stable state

10.1 Stable state as an ecological concept

In this chapter we shall look specifically at certain proposals, supported by thirty-eight British scientists, for reaching socioeconomic conditions which could continue for a very long period. The key principle is that of living within the capabilities of the world's ecosystems to meet the ecological demands made upon them by the human socioeconomies.

The basic idea is derived from ecology and it is the notion of dynamic system. The system is conceived of as normally capable of striving toward restoration of an established position of stability. If, however, it is pushed too far off this position, the capacity for restoration may be impaired. For stability the flows of energy and materials through the system must be sufficient for, but not in excess of, the flows necessary to maintain the particular position of stability.

This understanding of life-support systems is coupled with the observed fact that the throughputs of energy and certain materials in developed socioeconomies are in excess of the requirements of the systems for stability. Consequently the ecological demand made upon the ecosystems is such that the present level of 'stability' is not maintainable. This is seen in terms both of what is 'taken out' of the ecosystem as human-usable biomass and of what is 'put back' as energy and as 'wastes'.

With this knowledge available to us we can reach the idea of planning our socioeconomies so that their ecological demands are kept below the level at which appropriate ecosystem stability becomes uncertain. This will mean modifying our present exponential growth rates in energy and materials consumption and living more nearly within the renewal limits of the system.

One or two comments need to be made before the proposals are described. First, the general idea is common knowledge: it is widely held that we have to change our socioeconomies so that they 'live' much more nearly within their means. This idea now has a large measure of attention given to it. Second, most proposals for conscious change, or planning, implicitly conceive of two systems: the ecosystem and the 'human' or socioeconomic system. The proposals we are going to look at bring the two together. They envisage the need for socioeconomies to be reconciled with ecosystems but with an emphasis on stability for both systems. The message of ecology is one of unity. Therefore ecosystems should properly include 'human' systems. Socioeconomies may not indefinitely be able to dominate ecosystems; indeed they can exist *only* within the continuing viability of ecosystems. Third, the idea of the stable state does not rule out growth any more than the stability of the ecosystem precludes the system from evolving, that is, changing, into a condition where it sustains an increasing quantity of biomass. Stability is not stagnation.

It should also be mentioned that the stable state has also been seen as the present sense of cultural and societal continuity with the past. Schon (1973) uses this emphasis. The idea here is that we are leaving, or have already left, the stable state. Schon is not concerned with ecosystems, and in this chapter we shall not deal with his viewpoint.

10.2 Present socioeconomies already stabilizing

Boulding (1972) makes the case that the 'stationary state' is already in sight anyway for the developed countries. The growth rate of the GNP of the US has declined sharply since 1967, and over the longer period, economic growth in the US has taken thirty years to raise the real per capita disposable income 50%. He also comments that 'productivity-stagnant' activities (education, government, personal services) have heavily increased in proportion to all gainful activities. Therefore the areas over which productivity is likely to be capable of increase diminish. His conclusion is "... a substantial decline in the rate of increase in gross productivity in the next few decades" (Boulding, 1972, page 20). On the population side he notes that the US is very near a net reproduction rate of one, that is, zero population growth. This is confirmed by recent census figures.

These two major indicators lead Boulding to envisage the stationary state as Zero Population and Productivity Growth (ZPPG). This would be characterized, he thinks, by conservationism—Canadian governments are already talking about the 'conserver society'—and by a conservatism necessary for holding things together.

He develops some interesting implications, of which the most important might be that system stability rather than social justice might be the support for equality between individuals. This would be because of the need to minimize conflict so that the system can be kept workable within the limits of stability.

It therefore becomes clear that Boulding has added to the debate the question of whether the stationary state can be stable, but in the context of seeing the ZPPG as a distinct and not distant possibility for the developed countries. The horns of a dilemma begin to surface. If we reach or promote the stationary state, shall we find acceptable stability eludes us? If we do not, do we continue to increase the ecological demand on the ecosystems so that the global life-support system is seriously impaired, even to the point of breakdown?

What must be underlined at our present juncture is the ambiguity in the uses of words and concepts in this area. Perhaps we most importantly need patient work at the conceptual level.

In the meantime we have to cope with action, or proposals for action, from the perspective of ecology. For the example we shall look at the efforts of a group of British scientists.

10.3 Argument for moving toward the stable state

Early in 1972 the editors of *The Ecologist* produced *A Blueprint for Survival* in book form. Concern was focussed on the mounting disruption of ecosystems and the depletion of resources on a global scale. Our present interest lies in the strategy proposed for changing from socioeconomies of growth to stable societies capable of being sustained for a very long period.

The first part of the book states the need for change. The essential dynamic is seen as the relationship of growing human populations to ecosystems. As populations increase their impacts on the environment the ecological demand on the biosphere increases, possibly to unacceptable levels. The concept of ecological demand was developed in *Man's Impact on the Global Environment* (1970), and uses the United Nations' *Gross Domestic Product* (less services) index (page 117). The GDP, which is population multiplied by the material standard of living, has been increasing at over 5% per annum since 1950. On the supposition that this rate will continue, the total ecological demand would multiply by over five in the period required for the human population to double (page 119). Ecological demand is increasing exponentially. The practical meaning of this is seen in the figures for food production. From 1951 to 1966 world food production increased 34%. To achieve this we increased investments in nitrogenous fertilizers 146% and boosted investment in pesticides 300% (*The Ecologist*, 1972, page 20).

Second, ecological demand as at present constituted includes exponential growth rates in energy consumption and the use of nonrenewable resources. Sixteen major metals in common use are listed as subject to depletion within fifty years at present increasing rates of extraction, with the exception of iron and chromium, which would last a further forty years (*The Ecologist*, 1972, page 129). The fossil fuels, with the exception of coal, are seen as in no better shape. Because, however, nuclear power, especially that produced by breeder reactors and eventually nuclear fusion, appears capable of producing very large amounts of energy, the authors did not see energy as clearly a limiting factor for growth (page 132). Emission of radionuclides and their buildup in living material may limit the extent to which fission may be used. For details on nuclear reactors the reader may wish to consult Patterson (1976).

Third, ecological demand includes the impacts of 'wastes' on the stability of ecosystems. These impacts, which have to be absorbed by systems, come from organic and inorganic materials, heat, pollutants, radioactivity, and accidents which are imposed on the ecosystem and which the ecosystem must absorb or shift its position of stability in the hierarchy of complexity. Many impacts come from our efforts to increase agricultural output by means of chemical fertilizers, pesticides, etc. Increasingly our ecosystems are observed to be carrying larger amounts of waste matter, that is, matter which is random in that it is outside the organizational arrangements of the ecosystems.

From observing the disruption of ecosystems with its concomitant failure of food supply under population pressure and exhaustion of nonrenewable resources *The Ecologist* moves on to express concern for the possible collapse of human society.

The basis of the authors' approach to human societies is that they are subject to the same rules as any other kind of society we know. Human societies are not seen as unique and therefore "... their functions cannot be understood apart from that of other natural systems, such as ecosystems and biological organisms, i.e. in the light of a general theory of behaviour" (*The Ecologist*, 1972, page 95). The study of human society is seen in principle as a branch of the natural sciences: our societies are examples of *natural* systems. This view is holistic and systemic; it is the approach of sociobiology, represented by E O Wilson[1].

The 'collapse of society' is seen as essentially a systemic failure in that the conditions produced by the factors listed above will result, if pushed much further, in the loss of the self-regulatory behaviour which is essential to the continuance of any society. This loss can happen before suitable alternatives can be developed. Signs of the systemic failure are stated as including: disproportionate consumption of protein, fuels, and nonrenewable resources between the developed and the developing countries; drift of population toward urban centres; the potential of massive unemployment; increasing and even prohibitive costs of urban life; insidious physical weakening of urban populations through pollution; damage to self-regulation through increasing asystemic controls; violence; etc.

The key conclusion reached is that society must be continuously in a condition of self-regulation. If not, it will be unable to adapt to its environment. As all societies are based on the life-support system of the world and are capable of damaging it, self-regulation is imperative for survival. If self-regulation is the key requirement, then society must be goal-directed (*The Ecologist*, 1972, page 103).

10.4 Proposals for moving toward the stable state

The chief requirements for the stable society are listed as: ecological processes shall be subject to a minimum of disruption, energy and materials shall be conserved to a maximum, population shall be numerically stable,

[1] Wilson (1975) in his *Sociobiology* has put forward the case that societal arrangements and behaviour arise considerably out of biological conditions. This is strong support for the view that human societies can be approached in the same way as other societies. Identical or similar rules may be expected to operate in both human and nonhuman societies. This approach emphasizes the need to see human societies in their context of the life-support system of the world rather than as isolates. The bias of the disciplines dealing with human society is at present to neglect this context of natural phenomena by grace of which alone human societies exist. Wilson is naturally attacked by those who do not wish to face the possibility that some components of human behaviour are genetically determined.

and the social system shall be such that the "... individual can enjoy, rather than feel restricted by, the first three conditions" (*The Ecologist*, 1972, page 2).

The authors anticipated that reaching this state would require changes through the following operations:

1 control of ecological disruption by technical means;
2 halting of certain present trends;
3 most dangerous components of certain trends to be substituted by technological applications; these are asystemic substitutions;
4 systemic substitutions—present technological processes are replaced by 'natural' or self-regulating ones;
5 production and application of new technologies which conserve energy and materials, and which cause minimum ecological disruption;
6 decentralization of socioeconomic and political activity into communities "... small enough to be reasonably self-regulating and self-supporting";
7 education appropriate for this kind of community.

At the very outset the two chief bogies of any aspiration toward massive change in society are faced: the possibility of massive unemployment and the need for greatly increased expenditure by the society. The view is taken that the shift from an expansionist society—for example an organization of society which depends on continuous expansion for holding itself together—and a stable society can be achieved without coming aground on either of these two reefs. Avoidance of catastrophe is to be assured through a carefully constructed and implemented "totally integrated programme" and an "open style of government". Details of the proposals under the headings given above will give an indication of the scope of the programme.

10.4.1 Minimization of ecological disruption

Reduce the use of chemical pesticides. Achievement of reduction will require freezing at present levels and asystemic and systemic substitution. Freezing is not difficult for the developed countries but is expensive for the developing countries; they would require larger subsidies from the developed countries. Next comes progressive substitution of persistent by nonpersistent pesticides. The systemic phase consists of using national controls to a large but not total extent, for keeping pests at acceptable levels. Before integration of the three stages can be reached, however, considerable research will be required. Agrochemical interests should be encouraged to invest in such an integrated programme.

Fertilizers that are inorganic in origin are dangerous to ecosystem stability because of overuse. In the area of fertilizers the freezing operation consists simply in not increasing the use of inorganic materials and therefore in withdrawing their present subsidies. This would be fairly easy for the developed countries but very difficult for the developing countries because the new high-yield grains need massive inputs of fertilizer. The population–

food–energy syndrome is apparent here: emergency efforts to assist the developing countries with food supply would have to be made by the major grain producers while the developing countries build up the quality of their soils. The asystemic stage would consist of the gradual substitution of organic fertilizers and the use of crop rotation. The final stage is the achievement of cyclical fertility in which the nutrients in the soil are continuously cycled in a nearly closed system. This provides long-term stability and maintains the fertility of the soil. This ties in with the question of disposal of domestic sewage. At present the nutrients in this waste are not returned usefully to the soil in developed countries, partly because of mixture with industrial wastes and the relatively high treatment and transportation costs. The proposal is for separation of human and industrial waste and the decentralization of population to achieve a better mixture of urban and rural activities than occurs at present in the developed countries. Sewage processing should produce ecologically usable sludge. As for the industrial waste, processes that conserve energy and materials should be used, with a maximum of recycling.

10.4.2 Conserving—from economy of flow to economy of stock
Resource management
The basic idea is to reduce the demand for new material, thereby reducing pollution. For inducing the shift from the present high rates of consumption of new materials a raw-materials tax and an amortization tax are proposed. The first tax would penalize resource-intensive industries and would encourage employment-intensive industries. Short-life products would also be penalized. The second tax would be tied to the life of the product, penalizing the ephemeral and rewarding the durable. Recycling requires energy. Therefore a power tax penalizing power-intensive industrial processes will be required. Industrial pollution would be reduced by shifting away from synthetic products, such as detergents, and synthetic resins, to 'natural' or genetic materials. This, it is suggested, would reduce the consumption of energy.

Stress is laid on maintaining variety in the genetic resources. Gene pools of certain species of plants and animals are being seriously diminished. The programme includes proposals that certain wilderness areas in the world must be protected, and suggests how this might be done. Among other dangers are those posed by the widespread use of the new highly productive grains (the so-called green revolution) which could quickly reduce drastically the present global variety of grains. The chief requirement, however, is the conservation of relatively large areas of still-natural habitat. Human populations would not be excluded from these but they would be left to continue their food gathering and hunting within the ecological limits of stability.

Social accounting

A social accounting technique appropriate to the goal will be required; it will need to be more informative of the full costs and benefits to the society than are present methods. Such accounting will include procedures for showing what development society wants or does not want. The principle that the polluter must pay is suggested, and the value that emphasis must be placed on "... distribution, quality and variety of the stock" rather than on throughput as at present is stressed. The present measure of GNP is a throughput index, not a stock index. Boulding (1971b) suggests that the GNP should be regarded as an index of gross national *cost*. Standard of living should be measured by the quality of various aspects—purity of air, nutritional value of food, etc—and not by the quantitative measures solely. This leads to a distinction between conventionally accepted and 'real' costs. Our simplification of ecosystems, for example, is ultimately a real cost but does not appear, under present accounting methods, even as an accepted cost. Economics and ecology must be united: "... ecology should provide the approach, the framework for an understanding of the interrelationships of social and environmental systems; and economics should provide the means of quantifying those interrelationships in the light of such understanding" (*The Ecologist*, 1972, page 45).

10.4.3 Stabilization of the human population

In thinking about this a major difficulty is to know how to decide upon the optimum size of population. This may be impossible, and consequently it may be necessary to concentrate on the largest size of population sustainable according to certain standards. Such measures can be defined as capacity for acquiring adequate food supply and capability available to the individual for satisfying emotional needs and to the society for satisfying group aspirations. The ultimate measure, however, is the food supply, which depends on ecosystem capacity for producing human-usable biomass. The authors next relate this question to the present condition of Britain and conclude that it must become self-supporting in food. As no significant increase of output per acre can be expected they deduce that the UK population must be reduced before it can be held at a stable level— a possible thirty million. Some countries would be able to stabilize at near present population levels, for example the US, whose population appears rapidly to be approaching the stable state. The argument rests considerably on fair distribution of food, since although inequality of distribution may allow some of the population adequate nutrition a considerable fraction may be deprived, especially of protein. Shortage of protein stunts mental development and therefore truncates intellectual and societal growth. Optimum population must therefore be measured in terms of the optimization of the emotional, etc values of the total population.

The authors recommended national population services be established to:

1 Give wide publicity to the connections between population size, food supply, resource exhaustion, and the quality of life, and to urge that couples do not exceed two children (their own replacement). Certain present values will need changing to produce a responsible attitude toward reproduction.

2 Provide free advice on conception control.

3 Provide a free 'domiciliary service' which would make available contraceptives, sterilization, and abortion.

4 Commission appropriate research. This is very important because we know extremely little about the dynamics of populations. The hope is for an understanding of how to handle socioeconomic restraints.

The first three items are considered to be possibly effective controls for the next twenty years. The fourth item is the second phase and is envisaged as likely to provide the means for the third-stage control in which couples would be encouraged to have families slightly less than the replacement size. This would reduce the total population. At $0 \cdot 5\%$ per annum this would achieve reduction without adversely affecting the population balance.

10.4.4 A new social system

The major change seen as necessary is the decentralization of our present centralized activities and locational arrangements. The reasons for taking up this position are:

1 The pressures which will have to be supported will require great restraint and moral courage. *This may in part be imposed from outside the individual, but greater effectiveness is achieved by control internal to the individual.* Therefore full public participation in public decisionmaking is very desirable. This is more easily achievable in small communities than in large, where control from outside himself appears as coercion to the individual. The reaching of a condition in which population is in small communities is seen as implying decentralization.

2 Integrated, ecologically based agriculture—as opposed to agribusiness— calls for small farms run on a team basis with the use of various specialists. The aim is high diversity and keeping the ecological demand within the capacity of the ecosystem. As sewage will have to be returned as nutrients to the land, a closer urban–rural relationship will be required. Similar arguments are advanced for the decentralization of industry: closer relation between producer and consumer, integration of jobs with communities, increased responsiveness by industry to community needs and wishes.

3 The dynamic of the smaller community is a source of satisfaction to the individual, who is denied this in the large agglomeration where he feels atomized. Satisfaction through community participation could assist the reduction of consumerism and therefore the pressure on resources.

4 Reduction of the ecological impact of the human population can be assisted by decentralization. The per capita costs of running urban settlements increase as the size increases. Self-sufficiency is more possible in small than in large communities, and, the authors think, "... self-sufficiency is vital if we are to minimize the burden of social systems on the ecosystems that support them" (*The Ecologist*, 1972, page 53). Each community should be as self-supporting and self-regulating as possible. But it is also vital that adequate discussion takes place at regional level, for relevance upwards as much as downwards. The authors are tentative about sizes of communities but suggest 500 persons for neighbourhoods, 5000 for communities, and 500000 for regions. The purpose here is to foster "... *community feeling* and *global awareness*" (page 53).

The first stage toward a stable society is seen as the alteration in the direction of growth: for example, shift considerable movement from road to rail, from private to public mode. The second stage would be to redirect industry toward the conservation of materials and energy: "... flexible, non-polluting and durable, employment-intensive and favouring craftsmanship" (page 56). The method would include lowering the ratio between capital and labour. The belief is that population will decentralize as industry decentralizes. This will be assisted by the redistribution of government, which should be decentralized to a large extent. The educational system will be required to implant the values of the stable society.

10.4.5 Orchestration and implementation
Very careful timing and integration are stressed as essential for Britain to become stable. A kind of critical-path diagram is given in which specific dates up to 2075 AD are indicated for the twenty-six major items.

Thirteen major items are shown as initiated by 1974, including in detail: national population service; raw-materials, amortization, and power taxes; legislation for disamenity; air, land, and water quality; recycling grants; social accounting; subsidy for inorganic fertilizers discontinued; grants for organic fertilizers; emergency food programme for developing countries; integrated-control research; end of road building; clearance of derelict land; renewal programme; restrictions on private transport; research for materials substitution; redistribution of government; education research. Most of the remaining thirteen items are to be introduced before 1985. Examples are: the first phase of the decentralization of industry by 1985; introduction of diversified farming by the late 1970s; experimental community by 1980; development of rapid mass transit, research into materials substitution and alternative technologies before 1985; the second decentralization of industry by 2010. By 1995 diversified farming and integrated control will produce an agriculture appropriate for small, fairly self-sufficient communities, and the development of alternative technologies and redirected industry will be interlocking. Maximum redistribution of government will be achievable by 2030, a target to be reached by linking with educational development. By 2050 diversified agriculture, redistribution of government, and education for the stable society should be adequate for the setting up of self-sufficient, self-regulating communities.

Final target date for the full operation is 2075. An experimental or model community of about 500 population is suggested as a continuing research operation beginning in the early 1980s.

The final part of the main text of *A Blueprint for Survival* reiterates the goal: the replacement of the present industrial society by a stable society living within the limits of manageable ecological demand. The role of a varied environment is stressed, and the importance of realizing that 'economic cost' and 'economic value' do not correspond with 'real cost' and 'real value' is underscored—the market is not an index of ecological viability. The stable society means the bringing of these concepts to reconciliation. Finally, the emphasis is on unity between 'nature' and human life: all is a single system.

10.5 Comment

Since the document was published in 1972 in the form of a book many governments have begun to show interest in taking the 'conserver society' seriously. Certain events, notably the oil crisis and what is loosely called the environmental lobby, have helped. The present situation is that governments are sponsoring research into many of the items required for the stable state as conceived by the authors of *A Blueprint for Survival*: diversified ecology-based farming, ways of conserving energy, development of energy sources which are renewable, attention to the energy costs of buildings, reduction of travel through electronic data processing, increased use of public transit, recycling and the use of alternative materials, and demonstrations of alternative human settlement arrangements. In addition to the interest shown by governments there is ample evidence of a rising scientific and intellectual interest in such items and related matters. In general it can now scarcely be doubted that the broad line of approach formulated by the British scientists represents a very major component of our contemporary forward thinking, not merely in terms of the practical matters of planning but also in terms of helping to develop a philosophical viewpoint appropriate to our emerging condition.

The three new visions looked at in this part of this book will be commented upon in some detail together in chapter 12. It will be useful here, however, to offer some general comments on the approach and proposals of *The Ecologist* (1972):

1 Both approach and proposals may be felt too utopian to be useful. Utopia is not only out of fashion but if George Steiner (1971, page 59ff) is right the West will be unable to respond to the call to make the necessary effort (also see chapter 17).

2 We cannot actually be sure of how great the ecological demand on ecosystems can be before collapse or the reaching of a point of no return. How do we answer the question: Can, or cannot the world be turned into a very extensively hominized ecosphere?

3 No account has been taken of our changed socioeconomic structure with regard to production. A very large number of jobs now are concerned with handling knowledge and information, while a still heavy decline in manufacturing employment is going on (see chapter 22). If the stable state is to be a target, our knowledge of the real nature of the socioeconomy will need to be much more sophisticated than that used by the authors.

4 *The proposals acknowledge that restraint and control that come from within the individual are essential and superior to control imposed from outside. To obtain the required behaviour, reliance is placed on education. Nothing is offered by way of support for the idea that education can be successfully used to generate the required behaviour. We are pointing here to the importance of the interior dynamics of the individual for plotting any kind of course for society into the future.*
    In the next chapter we shall look at an attempt to tackle this last question precisely within the assumption of the need for ecological viability.

11

Integration of human individual and group with ecosystem the project *Earthscore*

11.1 The problem perceived

We saw in chapter 5 how characteristically ecologists have raised the question of human behaviour toward the processes of the 'natural' world. The danger they warn us against is that human societies will behave or continue to behave in ways which will eventually weaken or destroy the capacity of the earth to support them, at any rate at their present levels of well-being. Nobody would now quarrel about this general statement as at least a possibility to be considered. At regional, but not global, level this kind of collapse of the life-support system has already happened in recorded history.

Many ecologists, and others, are able to go further to observe that one way of approaching the debate on how to ensure the appropriate response is to think along the perspective of the relationship between the behaviour of the group and the behaviour patterns of the individual. As we have seen, the notion that a new ethic is required has gained currency (for example, Simpson, 1964; Potter, 1971). This includes injunctions for both the group and the individual. Seen in this way, the crucial area of the relationship between the two behaviours might be expressed in the following sequence: the group is necessary to ensure the protection, safety, and ultimately, especially in mass urban societies, the sustenance of the individual; to achieve these basics the society, in sum total, must act within the limits of the life-support system; to achieve this, individual behaviour must be appropriately directed, either from outside or from inside the individual; *but* the individual may not *see* what is necessary or may be *unwilling* to comply; failure of individual behaviour may aggregate to failure of the society to stay within the limits of the life-support system; if so, drastic changes in behaviour will be likely to be forced upon both society and individual and a new symbiosis will have to be developed.

This set of linkages is the commonly found underpinning of the ethical interest recently developed by ecologists. Although it intersects with many notions for the reconstruction of society, so dear to the heart of the twentieth century, it is fundamentally different from most of them. The difference essentially is that the ecologically based vision of the need for a new ethic rests on concern for the continuance of the life-support system itself and not narrowly on preoccupation with its products. The ecologist' call for a new ethic is therefore not primarily motivated by the perception of inequalities and injustices within society and the desire to right them, but by a perception of the necessity for society to right its relationship with the global life-support system. The ecologist would see this relationship as the more fundamental in a condition in which the basic support of life is threatened.

A further important aspect of this question is that during our century there has been a worldwide rise of the state. We have progressively come to rely on the state—governments, laws, and bureacracies—to take a large amount of responsibility for an increasing number of areas of group and individual living. No doubt, on very good evidence such as mounting complexity and costs, it has seemed reasonable to demand that the state undertake these growing responsibilities[1].

Among these responsibilities we are now beginning to number taking steps to protect our environment in the sense that we are increasingly casting the onus for the long-term ecological viability of the human enterprise upon the state. Hence come our 'departments of the environment' with their environmental assessments, legislative instruments, and exhortations. We have dimly perceived a danger and immediately have made the state responsible for coping, without any serious consideration of the question of its capability for such a task.

The state, although not entirely, is predominantly an authority external to the individual. It tells the individual what to do or what not to do; it threatens, persuades, compels, assists, protects, and punishes. The state must work on the assumption that its requirements are justified and must therefore assume that the individual believes they are. Quite obviously, however, the individual may well have other views. This difference leads us back to the set of linkages described a few paragraphs above. In disagreeing with, or questioning, the state's requirements the individual is using other references of justification than those used by the state itself.

However, "we have seen the enemy and he is us". This Gilbertian witticism very nicely illustrates the cybernetic nature of the relationship between the group and the individual. The state, in considerable degree and especially in the Western countries, is what the aggregated mass of the individuals wish it to be. If the state insists on free education for all children it is largely because the mass of the population feel it to be reasonable that children have it at the public expense. Here we begin to see an important significance of the linkage mentioned above: the individual's demands on the state may be unrealistic in terms of the working of the 'human' system. The costs in money may be too high, motivation to behave as necessary may be impaired, or exaggeration in some area may occur (for example, excessive materialism). Even though unrealistic, the demands may still be pressed.

[1] Just what should be counted as constituting the state becomes progressively more obscure. While the state now undertakes many functions hitherto not performed by the state, it becomes clear that bodies, such as large commercial corporations and unions, which were not hitherto to be counted as parts of the state, now in fact are. For my purpose, the state can easily include these since the key aspect to be extracted is that of 'external' authority, contrasted with the authority within the human being himself.

A difficulty with authority external to the individual and wielded by the state is that when the group aspect of the society gets into rough wate progressively tough measures have to be imposed upon the crew. Diocletia has to enact that every son must follow his father's trade or profession: Western democracy is seized of the need to apply wages and prices control Such impositions are inevitably felt as restrictions by the individual and ultimately must lead to the authority wielded being questioned.

There is still a further stage. At some point the exercising of external authority may become incrementally less effective. Each new enactment or administrative fiat must be more severe, to achieve ever less. At this stage certain feedback loops between society and individual have become weak or nonexistent, and the 'human' system has lost and cannot regain its previous stability. This is dissolution, chaos, revolution in traditional perspectives. The old accommodations will no longer work. Many differen readings of the manifestations become possible; such as allocating blame from, say, the class struggle to loss of moral fibre. Although possibly correct, such allocations may do the disservice of deflecting attention fror more fundamental questions connected with ecosystem viability.

An underlying debate—and it may soon erupt—is about authority: its nature, its justification, who wields it, and how it is wielded. Already thi becomes apparent from looking at those countries in which the state has become, or has been forced to become, a tyrant. The very strong moral emphasis of a Solzhenitsyn tells us something in this context. Perhaps we begin to look timidly round the blinkers that have confined our thought in this area for most of this century.

This awareness of the authority debate has, however, scarcely begun to penetrate the area of relationship between 'natural' systems and large, mass 'human' systems. In this perspective the struggles about the reconstruction of society look very like fights amongst the crew while the sea gets rougher. The whole question of authority looks differently according to whether it is seen from the point of view of the seamen's union or in relation to the violence of the storm.

Along this perspective a major danger looms in the conventional separation of 'human' and 'natural' systems. Both are in fact conceivable as parts of a single global system which must now be acknowledged and understood. This implies that the authority debate must take place in a new context. The message of the ecologists is that if we insist on the separation, the 'natural' systems will exert their own authority (see E P Odum, 1975).

With this all too brief contextual statement of some very difficult questions we have some background for looking at an ongoing experiment which uses the electronic technology to explore ways that human groups might use for relating themselves ecologically to the life-support system through new perceptions of authority.

11.2 "The earth and I are of the same mind"

We now come to the most difficult to understand of all the examples we are examining. The project is called *Earthscore*; its intention is to reach the condition described in the quotation above. The documents serving as source are Ryan (1974; 1975). Ryan's approach may be very succinctly stated as follows:

1 Human behaviour is now substantially counter-life in many of the ways it relates to the earth's life-support system. It is necessary to find ways of bringing behaviour into accord with our life-support to ensure long-term continuance.

2 The essential question is to find out *how* to do this. The question of authority is identified as crucial and *new ways of deriving authority are seen to be needed in the relationships between the individual and the group (society).*

3 The electronic technology, particularly that using feedback techniques in a self-processing way, offers the means for the human species to achieve a new level of self-awareness or enhanced reflexivity. At this level it may be possible to develop a new concept and operationalization of authority.

4 The mind, or mental processes, are perceived as essentially cybernetic in their operations and capable of being changed by self-processing, or self-metaprogramming, so that new behaviour patterns can be generated that are in accord with the ecological imperative. *The outcome desired is the emergence of an appropriate internal authority.*

5 The interrelations between individuals and groups are illustrated by certain concepts from topology (the study of relationships of position and inclusion, independent of measurement).

6 Field exercises essentially based on feedback by the use of videotape can be devised.

Under the heading of the ecological necessity Ryan's thinking is: "We are now an endangered species. We are in the process of destroying our own ecosystem. As Bateson (1972) says, the species that destroys its environment destroys itself. In Bateson's estimation this process has gone so far that we cannot trust nature not to overcorrect and wipe us out. It seems that only by self-correcting our behaviour on this planet can we preclude such an overcorrection by nature" (Ryan, 1974, page 92).

The key idea is that there are certain restraints by which we must abide if we are to survive. The problem is: What are these restraints, and how do we find them? Ryan at this point uses the concepts of C H Waddington (1968), particularly his concept of the *chreod*. This idea, derived from observation of biological processes, is that a living system on seeking to return to equilibrium after disturbance will tend to follow a set path or route. The word is composed of Greek χρή ('it is necessary') and ὁδός (a 'way' or 'road). The chreods of a system are conceived as very largely

responsible for its morphology or structure. Ryan then applied the concep
"There exists an identifiable ensemble of evolutionary processes before
which our species must restrain its behaviour if we are to maintain life.
To destroy these chreods is to destroy our life. Such chreods are to be
taken as sacred" (Ryan, 1974, page 93). This is essentially his idea of wha
the sacred is, and hence the title of his book: *Cybernetics of the Sacred.*

Waddington's approach—and Ryan follows it—is that respecting the
chreods produces the species behaviour by way of information transmissio
In the human species words have played a very major role in developing
the symbols used for maintaining the chreods. This bias, says Waddingto
has resulted in "interorganismic authority structures", which have now—
especially recently—resulted in ethical subsystems no longer capable of
holding the human species viable within the ecosystem. Ryan amplifies
this and interestingly notes that the role of the theory of logical types ha
dominated Western thought and that it is very closely related to the habi
and thought modes connected with writing. These thought modes and
habits, he suggests, are the origin of present hierarchical authority structur
in society. The very word hierarchy is itself revealing by its origin. Rya
is trying to find a way to "... a self-corrective *heterarchic* society with no
class and no interorganic authority structure" (Ryan, 1974, page 95). Th
is his idea of *how* the Marxian classless society might be achievable. He
sees this as being possible: "It seems to me that by using such media as
videotape, holograms, electric sensing devices, and perhaps computers, we
can model the morphogenetic field that supports our life. By patterning
these chreods in a system of triadic relations there would result ... in wha
Waddington sees as a desirable alternative ..." (page 93).

A note is necessary here on the theory of logical types because the
authoritarian nature of this mode of thinking has forced Ryan to search
for another mode, and to find it in certain aspects of topological theory.
Hence his development of *kleinform*; which will be described shortly.

The theory of logical types embodies these statements:

1 No *class* can be a *member* of itself.

2 If we define a *class*; next indicate that everything else outside it is in
   another class, the original *class* cannot be a *member* of the second *class*
The usefulness of this theory of logical typing to Ryan's thinking can be
deduced from his reliance on Bateson. In this context Bateson points out
that logic and observed phenomena do not necessarily agree, in part because
time is absent from logic but present in phenomena, but adds that there i
an important analogy (Bateson, 1972, page 280ff). Bateson concludes:
"The whole matter turns on whether the distinction between a *class* and it
members is an ordering principle in the behavioral phenomena which we
study" (page 282). From this he goes on to classify the types of learning
with regard to items and classes. We need not follow him further but shoul
turn to another source of thinking along this line on which Ryan relies.

This second area of reliance is on the research of McCulloch (1965). He devoted a lifetime to enquiring into the way in which 'thought' processes in the brain and nervous system identify the rule under which information must be classified by the organism so that it can act. How does the central nervous net of the animal, processing sensory inputs, classify the information and instruct all cells of the body to cooperate in standing and fighting, or running away, or eating, etc? Logics of classes, propositions, and relationships are needed. McCulloch indicates that the mental–physical mechanism dealing with logics has not itself evolved through evolution but has remained much the same while other structural elements have changed. There is at present no theory to explain the circuit action. "The problem remains the central one in all command and control systems. Of necessity the system must enjoy a redundancy of potential command in which the possession of the necessary urgent information constitutes authority in that part possessing the information. The problem is clearly one of triadic or n-adic relations ... we lack a triadic logic" (McCulloch, 1965, page 397)[2].

This complex set of ideas may be simplified as follows. Logical structuring, the processes of the brain and nervous system, and action by the organism are interdependent: logic gets translated into action. The processes by which this happens are, however, not simply of a yes–no kind but are such that sometimes they will also alternate and sometimes synchronize according to the logic to be handled. McCulloch diagrams the 'switches' in the neural system as including triodes: three connections are made. This is in contrast to a diode which has two and represents yes–no or on–off. A very crude analogy might be the ordinary switch turning on a light. This is dyadic logic. But it is possible to have two switches in the same circuit so arranged that the light may be turned on or off at each switch. We now have a kind of triode. Although this is not a strictly correct analogy, it demonstrates the two and the three in terms of circuitry by counting spatial discontinuity as the third component: there are three components—lamp, switch, and switch. *The two switches must work symbiotically.* [The reader interested in this may wish to pursue it further in F H George (1961, chapter 5). The principle which is interesting for our understanding of the triad is the 'flipflop' switch when it is used several times in the same circuit.]

The particularly difficult logical type to develop a circuit theory for is abduction. In abduction thinking we begin with the rule and conclude on examination of the evidence that the case under consideration is *probably*

[2] Modern epistemology has been very much influenced by systems theory and cybernetics. It also relies heavily on ongoing research on the brain and the nervous system. The discovery of the very wide application of feedback appears a major discovery of recent years.

an example[3]. This is different from both induction and deduction as a logical process. Medical diagnosis is very frequently abductive.

With these ideas in mind we can now return to the theory of logical types with its classes and members. The defining of a class *includes* members and *excludes* the rest. We have therefore: an element which defines, elements which are defined, and elements which are excluded. If we wish to relate these we need a calculus of *triadic* relations. The concepts of 'firstness', 'secondness', and 'thirdness' belong to the field of phenomenology, and are particularly associated with Peirce's efforts to eliminate in phenomenology the previous bias attaching to the traditional vocabulary of the subject: 'phenomenon' (associated with nature), 'idea', 'reality', etc. Peirce coined *phaneron* to stand for "... the collective total of all that is in any way or in any sense present in the mind, quite regardless of whether it corresponds to any real thing or not" (Hartshorne and Weiss, 1960, page 141). Nor did he differentiate as to the when of the occurrence or in whose mind it took place. Both the 'inner' world and the 'outer' world experienced by human beings are therefore included by Peirce. There is no separation of 'material' and 'mental'.

Peirce put forward the proposition that, phenomenologically speaking, relationships can be only monadic, dyadic, or triadic in an undecomposable form, and that anything more complicated is simply a compound of triads. This conclusion comes basically from mathematical logic (see Goudge, 1950, page 79ff). This ties in with McCulloch's need for a logic of triadic and subsequently *n*-adic, relationships. Following Peirce, *n*-adic would simply be compunds of triads. If this argument is correct, Ryan has good support for basing his experimental work in human relationships on the fundamental cell of three individuals.

Peirce concentrates on the three categories of experience as firstness, secondness, and thirdness, without denying that there may be others. These represent the three basic logics of relationship, in his view. *Firstness* "is most predominant ... in being something peculiar and idiosyncratic" (Hartshorne and Weiss, 1960, page 149). It is dominant in feeling, rather than in discursive reason or will. My firstness is my inner sense of myself. This is essentially monadic.
Secondness involves mutual action between two elements and is dyadic. Hence it has the characteristic, says Peirce, of struggle. "A sense of

[3] Peirce (Hartshorne and Weiss, 1960) differentiates reasoning into three types:
1 *Deduction*. States the rule; observes a case, and proceeds to deduce a fact. All motorcars run on wheels; this is a motorcar; therefore it must have wheels.
2 *Induction*. States the cases; guesses what the rule is. These and these and these move people about; they all have wheels; therefore all motorcars run on wheels.
3 *Abduction*. States the rule; observes the fact; guesses that the fact is an example of the rule. All cars run on wheels; that object carrying those people runs on wheels; therefore it is *possibly* a motorcar.
Out of these three types of logic the brain and nervous system provide authority for the organism to act.

commotion, our action and reaction, between our soul and the stimulus" (page 161). Cause and effect. The real impinging upon our firstness. Existence is dyadic—the inner and the outer.

Thirdness is the connecting link between the first and the second. It is means, mediation, continuity, conduct, law, sympathy for another individual, generality, infinity, diffusion, growth, intelligence (page 172). Concepts and classes are thirds. Even my concept (as distinct from my feeling) of myself is a third. Thirdness is the most complex of all three categories. For example, a symbol involves: itself, its meaning, and the reading of it. Thirdness is essentially triadic. It can only appear when reflection on what is perceived is present. This is synthetic consciousness. It is the learning mode.

These are Peirce's three modes of consciousness. He concludes that the nervous system must have some threefold quality to relate to them or explain their origin (Hartshorne and Weiss, 1960, page 204ff). This again relates to McCulloch's research. Peirce applies his principles of firstness, secondness, and thirdness to phenomenology, psychology, physiology, biology, and physics. In biology, firstness is exemplified by fortuitous variations; secondness by hereditary transmission of traits; and thirdness by elimination of unfavourable traits. In physics, firstness is indeterminacy; secondness is force; thirdness is statistical regularity. (See Goudge, 1950, page 109.)

In order to assist thinking along this line Ryan has developed certain ideas found in topology. He starts with the simplest example, the Klein bottle. The German mathematician, Felix Klein, was the originator of this physical form. It has a single continuous surface, a kind of three-dimensional Moebius strip. Imagine a trumpet-like tube; take the narrower end and bend it up to the side of the tube; carry this narrow end into the 'inside' of the bottle, passing it through the side; broaden out the narrow end and join it to the wide end. Ryan's point is that this is the nearest metaphor to his sociofeedback insight. Biofeedback gives conscious control over some of the automatic nervous processes—heartbeat, etc. Might the same be done for the societal processes?

Ryan goes on to observe that a distinction must be made between the Klein bottle and other possible kleinformations. The bottle has *part contained* passing directly into *part containing* but with no involvement with *part uncontained.* The idea of kleinformation, developed by Ryan, is precisely that all three parts are present and participating in the total process. In this way triadic metaphors can be generated. The difference between the Klein bottle and Ryan's kleinformation is that while the former does not interpose the uncontained between the contained and the containing, a kleinform always does this. There are therefore *three*, not *two*, self-differentiating parts. The principle is "never less than three", interacting in such a way that "... a recurring variable three-fold relationship between *part contained*, *part uncontained*, and *part containing*" is generated

(Ryan, 1974, page 50). Thus the relationship is triadic and what Ryan suggests here is a conceptualization that could perhaps satisfy McCulloch's required calculus of intention. (See figure 11.1.)

With these preliminaries held in mind we can now look at Ryan's New England field project in which he attempts to operationalize these ideas.

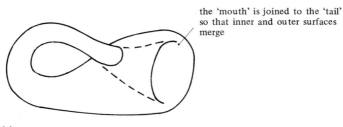

the 'mouth' is joined to the 'tail' so that inner and outer surfaces merge

(a) Klein bottle

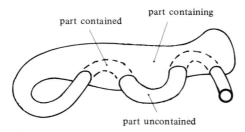

part contained   part containing

part uncontained

(b) Kleinform

Figure 11.1. Ryan's development of Klein's bottle. The Klein bottle is the basic form of topological description. The surfaces are continuous, a kind of Moebius strip in three dimensions. Ryan has developed the concept so that it may serve as metaphor for the three basic modalities of human personality expressed by C S Peirce as firstness, secondness, and thirdness. Ryan relates this conceptualization to our contemporary task of learning how to develop in the individual and the group the control loops necessary for the long-term stability of ecosystems. Redrawn from Ryan (1974).

11.3 *Earthscore*

The underlying aim of *Earthscore* (Ryan, 1974) is to develop new modes of generating authority and operationalizing it in society by using the basic unit of three instead of two. (Note the meaning of authority in McCulloch the authority of some cells to tell the rest what to do.) The means used is the principle of feedback made available by the electronic technology, thus giving a new possibility for awareness of self and of others' firstness, or uniqueness. The context of the aim is that much of human activity is seriously out of harmony with the life-support system. To get into harmony we must develop new ways of interacting within our own species

Ryan describes it thus:

"Competing authority systems within the human species render our species increasingly unable to behave coherently in the face of the current crisis in our ecosystem. *Earthscore* is a formal composition for an information transmission system that is not dependent on intraspecies authority. The actual production of such an information system involves the formation of an on-going community that is non-authoritarian in structure. *Earthscore* includes both the design of the information system and the self-correcting community whose *raison d'être* would be the production of *Earthscore*" (Ryan, 1974, page 67).

Ryan's technique is related to biofeedback and when applied to groups can be thought of as a kind of sociofeedback, provided it is remembered that basically it is the cybernetic loop at the individual level which is the source of new possibilities in society. He uses audio–video playback *for the individual to be present at his own performance*: the individual hears and sees himself instantaneously—sees himself 'objectively' while actually making his movements 'subjectively' (or in slightly delayed time). Thus watching himself, the individual can correct or modify his action in its ongoing process, for example in a public discussion on a community issue. This infolding produces a new knowledge of the self, a new self-awareness. In group feedback the anticipation is that there will be developed "... a mode of thinking structured in shared perception and concurrent self-corrective behavior patterns". In order to assist this Ryan makes an important distinction between orientation and nonorientation, the latter being a "... habit of mind in which the assigning of direction makes no difference in determining relative position". The meaning here is that the flow of information round the cybernetic circuit can move in any direction, without necessary assignment specific for making it work. This means that circuits, or systems, can be developed without assignment of direction from antecedents. See Ryan (1974) and chapter 19 for this occurring in the conceptual sequence from biosphere to noosphere.

The operational basis is that videotape is used to record an individual's firstness (unique personality quality), record the way of his firstness (how he organizes it), in order to allow him to enhance his way and learn the ways of others, to open up the patterns of differentiation of "... many natural and man-made forms in such a manner as they can be understood structurally by man", and to permit triadic relationships that are self-corrective and stable (Ryan, 1974, page 109). The significance of the last is that such relationships are the basis of community.

Using the "Canon of Self-correction" ("Never Less Than Three"), Ryan sets up injunctions, among which is the notion of each individual being a member of three different cells: *chreche* (sic) (function is the care of its members), *chreod* (Waddington; function is the decoding of ecological processes), and *work* (function is all other processes necessary for maintaining community). Decoding would be secondness and work would be thirdness.

The chreche cells start up the process by generating audio–video tapes of firstness (uniqueness of the individual). These are made triadically: Red makes a tape of himself and gives it to Yellow; Yellow makes a tape of himself and gives it and Red's tape to Blue; Blue makes tape of himself and gives it and Yellow's tape to Red; Red passes Blue's tape to Yellow; Yellow, Red, and Blue make three tapes together. Cells proliferate from each other to form families. Families make up communities using the same technique of self-corrective tape interchange.

The thirty-six community members form twelve chreod cells whose members do not coincide with those of the chreche cells. Each cell is to make one tape a month to decode its ecological context, the chreche tapes acting as models of understanding. These decoding tapes are exchanged with other chreod cells. Ryan quotes Bateson (1972) on how the decoding of the environment might be started by the chreod cells. They can examine:

"non-living form: earth, water, air
 living plant: three plants characteristic of the region
 animal: three animals characteristic of the region
 man: three technological extensions of man used in the
                      region" (Ryan, 1974, page 114).

Each community will form twelve work cells. Their activity is to conform with the restraints decoded in the ecosystems by the chreod cells. The work, chreod, and chreche cells are not to coincide in membership. Work cells use taping for stabilizing activity. Specialization is to be reduced as much as possible.

The chreod cells (those looking to understand and be continuously aware of the ecological context in which life must be sustained) are assembled into groups of four. These are also self-correcting. The grouped cells do tapes to stabilize themselves before addressing themselves to the task of decoding the workings of their ecosystem. Ryan describes the decoding:

"In the decoding of ecological continuum let the chreod cell members realize that their most treasured resource is in the varied firstness of the members of the community. This forms a kind of 'vocabulary' of differentiation, the understanding of which will make easier the decoding of the different chreods of the ecological process. Conversely, let chreche cell members realize that care of firstness is part with decoding the ecology in which the community lives. The wisdom of the ways in which members learn to relate to each other provides wisdom for understanding the larger systems of which the community is only part" (Ryan, 1974, page 118).

The work cells are formed into three self-correcting groups of four cells each. Maximum community flexibility in action is aimed at here. Whatever work the cells and groups do must be within the restraints that the chreod groups and cells identify in the ecosystem. Specialization should be moderated by rotating the different kinds of work. The work cells and groups constitute the organization of the world of work.

After describing the structure of *Earthscore* Ryan suggests that certain regulatory 'chapters' will be necessary to cope with various matters, such as how to acknowledge death, handle the chreod of the relationship between the sexes, educate children, arrange ad hoc cells for dealing with special difficulties, and deal with departure from firstness.

Some further details are given by Ryan, but they need not concern us here. By early June 1975 he was running his first cell of three males attempting to build up a data base. About sixty-five hours of ecological decoding had been done and thirty hours of inventing triadic behaviour. By September 1977 the project had several cells and had got well under way.

11.4 Comment
There are several aspects of Ryan's complex web of thought which it will be useful to examine.

First, his argument and experiment rest considerably on certain similarities between the working of the computer and human mental processes. Not all such processes can be mimicked by the computer, but there are a large number of researchers whose work shows that important similarities exist and that this is useful knowledge for exploring our thought processes. The basic link, of similarity, is of course in the area of logic. The computer and the brain–nervous system have common areas of logic. The brain, receiving information through the senses, must process it according to logical propositions if the organism is to act for survival. Another link is to be found in the process of feedback: both human and 'artificial' brains depend very heavily on the working of cybernetic loops.

Some of the researchers in this field whom the reader may wish to consult are: McCulloch (1965), Bateson (1972; and particularly 1971 for the notion of the mind as a self-preserving system), Lilly (1969; and particularly 1974), and F H George (1961). Along Ryan's perspective we may take Lilly's research on metaprogramming as illuminating because Ryan's essential emphasis is on the problem of how to reprogramme the attitudes, values, and therefore the actions, of individual human beings and their groups.

Lilly (1974) views our thinking apparatus as a 'human biocomputer'. The key idea is that the human mind is similar to a computer in its workings in that it is programmable: "The human brain is assumed to be an immense biocomputer ... [which] operates continuously throughout all its parts and does literally millions of computations in parallel simultaneously.

It has approximately two million visual inputs and one hundred thousand acoustic inputs" (page 3; note the preponderance of reliance on the visible region of the electromagnetic spectrum). Control and coordination are achieved in a programmed fashion, and some programmes are built-in. Some programmes can be modified—a process Lilly calls metaprogramming. Metaprogramming means that the human biocomputer is different from that of the ant: through experience, conditioning, education, etc the human biocomputer can accommodate the addition of new programmes and have existing ones changed. These new programmes or changes will result in changed behaviour. Most important for our present purpose is Lilly's concept that the human biocomputer can not only metaprogramme other biocomputers but can self-metaprogramme. The mind is itself able to rewrite some of its own programmes. This means that it can learn new behaviour better-suited to survival. In this context we might also note Bateson's three levels of learning, which also include self-metaprogramming (Bateson, 1972, page 283ff). Lilly (1974) defines mind as "... the sum of the programmes and metaprogrammes, e.g., the software of the human computer".

Ryan's approach is essentially the metaprogramming and self-meta-programming of the individual human biocomputer so that 'mind' will achieve an improved relationship with the life-support system. Here we can link up again with McCulloch in that Ryan is emphasizing the need to metaprogramme and self-metaprogramme triadically as a superimposition on dyadic programming.

The essential technique used by Ryan is feedback relying heavily on the electronic technology. The underlying discovery is biofeedback, which can permit the individual to self-metaprogramme with regard to certain inbuilt programmes which operate below the level of consciousness. The pulse rate, not normally subject to conscious manipulation, can be brought under a degree of conscious control by creating a new cybernetic loop which works through sensory perception (say, an eye watching a fluctuating needle on a gauge) and through some mental processes connected with intention. That biofeedback constitutes the creation of new feedback loops in the 'mind' is well established, although not very much appears to be known about their durability.

Ryan uses biofeedback for self-metaprogramming. There is good reason to hold as a hypothesis that it is workable. By seeing and hearing himself perform—by being present at his own performance—the individual will see himself differently from his view of himself 'from within'. We know this works; ballet dancers, for example, use the technique. The individual can infold his experience of himself. Ryan's tapes of 'firstness' perform this function. Anyone who has used audio–video tape in this way can confirm that this is a viable technique of self-metaprogramming. We have hardly begun to use it. Videotape is still relatively expensive and the equipment much more cumbersome than the equivalent for audio-only tape.

His next stage is less well based. It is that self-metaprogramming by the individual can be shared with two other individuals so as to achieve an interchange of self-knowledge leading to mutual knowledge. This in turn modifies the self-metaprogramming iteratively. There is no proof yet that this can work, but Ryan's experiments may tell us something in due time.

The last level of Ryan's effort is to probe the possibilities of systematized self-metaprogramming for the community or society. Can we learn new ways of sociobiofeedback: biofeedback applied not only to the individual but to the group? Can a group learn to self-metaprogramme by these same techniques by which the individual may be able to learn to generate new control loops? Because we have institutionalized the use of the electronic technology for communication of one-to-many (radio, TV, records, commercial tapes) we have no widely diffused experience of using the equipment for group infolding techniques. For one-to-one with vision the video camera will have to attain much wider diffusion than at present. Again, Ryan's efforts in trying to build community on the assumption of the total diffusion of the necessary electronic equipment may eventually show some very interesting results. The expectation is that video cameras will become relatively inexpensive. (The key benefit of the video camera over a movie camera is that it gives instant replay.)

On this first area of comment we can therefore say that Ryan's work is based on certain firm evidence from a variety of sources: the brain as computer, the workability of biofeedback as capable of producing new consciously controlled physico-mental loops, and the idea of self-meta-programming as a result of using the technology. Whether this latter can be spread to a mutualization process between individuals and ultimately into operations of society is more speculative, but if proved workable would be very important, and is therefore worth pursuing operationally. Intellectually speaking, there is no excuse for not making the operational effort, even though there might be great practical difficulties in translating the findings into the requirements of mass societies.

In conclusion, Ryan has taken a known technique newly made possible by developments in electronics and has generated an imaginative extension of it to new areas of the human enterprise.

Second, we come to the chreods. Since Waddington (1968) developed this concept scientific opinion has somewhat changed, and reference to this idea is now rare. The more recent emphasis is that the route of restoration for a system that has lost its position of steady state is not as tightly determined as previously thought; greater emphasis is now given to chance, randomness, and unpredictability, but the notion of genetic drift is not excluded. The principle of equifinality states that an identical result may be reached by several different routes. Such plurality is not necessarily destructive of Waddington's chreod, but it does suggest that identifying those ecological factors which absolutely must be respected is more complicated than might be envisaged by expecting to find a set of fixed items.

The major question raised essentially by this matter is fundamental to the whole debate about human behaviour with regard to our life support. It is the question of how far we can 'distort' the 'natural' ecosystems to serve human purposes without those systems becoming degraded so that their support function is seriously impaired. In other words, on the assumption that the idea of chreods is workable, *how far can we depart from, or modify, some of the chreods of the ecosystems in their present states without incurring degradation, or can we substitute an existing chreod for a new one? Equifinality suggests flexibility.*

This problem is, of course, not confined to Ryan's thought, but is general to the whole human–ecological discussion. That human beings live within a finite system as components of that system is now known; that the system has in it linkages that make its steady functioning possible is now known; and that components and linkages can be damaged or run wild is also now known. What are not properly known are the limits of flexibility, to what extent some of those limits are now being approached, and the degree to which substitutions are likely to be viable. Does the human species have to live within a certain fixed frame of life support or can it substantially redesign the frame? The first belief is piety; the second is Faust. Ryan might say that his approach could accommodate both. Yet his use of *sacred* suggests a certain piety, a respecting of the essential. The sacred, however, has historically demonstrated itself amenable to change, especially under the impact of science and technology. Could we perhaps hold tentatively the view that in any system in its status quo at any time, and discounting its evolutionary capability, there are certain items which must not be negated if degradation is to be avoided?

This seems likely a priori but it does not get rid of operational problems. For example, the physical delimitation or definition of the region or ecosystem is very often likely to be difficult. Failure to cope properly with problems such as this might lead to lapsing into a kind of static sentimental approach toward 'nature'.

Third, we have to deal with the triadic relationship. In a sense all feedback is triadic: the initial impulse, the recording of its effect, and the resultant correction. I make a statement verbally, listen to the playback of myself, and reformulate my original statement. In this sense Ryan's heavy reliance on feedback techniques is triadic.

It is much more difficult to come to terms with the triad or the *n*-adic at the level of logic and the cerebral–nervous processes with which it is allied. The interesting fact in this context is that the organism both generates logic and uses it in order to act. *McCulloch's argument that the biological arrangements for doing this have not changed for a very long time appears to support Waddington's idea that at least in part our authority structures rest on our biology.* The emerging field of sociobiology seems likely to add considerably to our knowledge of this question. Among other things, it appears to be saying that in part our arrangements in society arise from the way we have evolved biologically and the biological stage in which we are now (see Wilson, 1975). Certainly it is clear that we have to explore what biological origins authority in the human species may have. It is a relatively new idea that authority in human society may have some origin in the genetically transmitted arrangement of groups of nerve cells.

Ryan's contribution—as yet speculative—is that new feedback loops can be generated by using the electronic technology to produce new neural patterns or paths. These in turn might give the possibility for new authority structures to emerge. If self-awareness is a very important, not to say the most important, characteristic of our species then we can expect further development through enhanced self-awareness. Ryan is deducing that there are ways of using the electronic technology to achieve a very powerful enhancement of our self-awareness. That the technology can be and is at present extensively used for discouraging the growth of self-awareness is, of course, obvious.

Fourth, and most important of all, Ryan is daring to tackle the problems of the human enterprise from an approach which has been progressively neglected during this century. Relying on theories of society formulated in the primitive and early industrial age we have naively tended to see our task as the operationalization of these theories into our existing societies. In the developed countries, especially those in North America, society has changed radically since as recently as 1950 when the USA achieved its maximum employment in manufacturing industry. Concurrently with this decline the 'information age' has very rapidly developed, making its contribution to changing society (see chapters 1 and 22). While these developments have been going on, the rise of the power of the state has occurred on a worldwide scale. The state, as it has developed in this century, both is, and is perceived as, an authority 'external' to the individual. *It has seemed that the state has been progressively necessary to operationalize the theories of society we inherited.*

An important matter concerning the nature of all societies has tended to slip from view. It is that two kinds of authority need to be in viable relationship if society and its individuals are to endure. For certain purposes the group must speak with the voice of authority and be obeyed (the state). But not for all purposes, and this authority must not bear upon the individual beyond a certain point. If the symbiosis of group and individual is to work properly the individual must also support *willingly* the necessary authority in the group. In order to be able to do this the individual must have an 'inner' authority. Without this he will eventually feel oppressed by the group. But in another way he must develop a logic within himself which matches as well as measures the logic by which the group operates. The problem is: How does such a logic get generated and keep nurtured in the individual? In very crude terms: How is the individual to be *willingly* responsible enough to support the external authority?

It is precisely to this crucial question that Ryan addresses himself. Further, he is not only saying that the authority question demands new solutions to the relationship between the human individual and group but also emphasizes that these solutions are equally as necessary as, or more necessary than, the solutions between the individual and/or group and the life-support system of the planet. While attempting to find ways of reconstituting the group authority, he nevertheless puts his weight on the need to begin with the development of a new 'inner' authority, first in the individual. Grasping the capability of the electronic technology for enhancing self-awareness, other-awareness, and ecological awareness, he aims at the development of authority structures to reduce our inherited oscillations between group and individual. He hopes that new interpersonal knowledge and new human–ecosystem knowledge can be generated.

A great difficulty with Ryan's approach is that we now have to deal with very large mass populations in which the individual has certain characteristics which do not at all jibe with the direction of Ryan's efforts. We shall look at these characteristics in chapters 16 and 17.

The great merit of Ryan's thinking is that he appreciates the dangers of predominantly external authority and the deficiencies of the dynamic–weak exhortations of the ecologists to embrace a new ethic, and suggests a new way of trying to achieve the right tension between group and individual and between them and the life-support necessities.

In the next chapter I shall comment comparatively on the various examples I have described.

Perspectives on the examples

12.1 Preliminary comment

It is the purpose of this chapter to indicate certain major items of assessment of the examples. These comments will be made from a variety of approaches in order to reduce the dangers of the oversimplification inherent in taking a single perspective. We already have single-perspective approaches in which considerable critical material is accumulating. We have studies of the impacts of the telecommunications–computer technology on society and a wealth of literature on our ecological condition. These developing bodies of knowledge are extremely important and need to be developed rapidly. They are, however, mostly highly specialized, even when they involve interdisciplinary research. They are unable, and do not necessarily pretend, to look simultaneously from several different directions.

Perhaps the most significant of all are likely to be foci of attention which may emerge not in a single but in several examples, or may be seen to underlie the direction of an example's approach. Such matters might offer themselves as centres round which initiatives for thinking might cluster later. The motivation for saying this is in part the observation that new conditions—for example, population pressures, diffusion of the electronic technology, and ecological difficulties—will demand not merely new solutions to problems but new imaginative effort in envisaging options and opportunities. Such effort is difficult to make. It is heavily dependent on an ability to develop synthesis and synergy.

Most of our attention will be directed to the last three examples, although the examples which have preceded them will be drawn upon because they are inevitably implicated in any working out of these last three. The last three are all essentially addressing themselves to the whole society, or are at least purporting to do so. Masuda sees the potential of the electronic technology in the context of the need to sustain an industrialized population in a possible situation of the serious weakening of the present industrial base. The British ecologists fear for our continued ability to support present populations through continued increase of demands on ecosystems, and call for stabilization of economies and heavy reduction of ecological demand through governmental or societal action. Ryan also fears for the survival of human societies but sees as basic the necessity for completely restructuring the relationships individual–group–ecosystem, and uses the electronic technology to begin by reflexively developing the self-awareness of the individual, and thereby achieving a self-modification of behaviour.

12.2 Perspective on employment—role of the job

Almost completely in the developed countries but also progressively in the developing countries the socioeconomy depends for its ability to feed, shelter and clothe the population on the linkage: production–job–wages–

consumption. Although in the developed countries certain considerable groups in the population are not directly dependent on this linkage they are reliant on it at one stage removed. Children, adolescents, many young adults, pensioners, and those supported by unemployment and welfare payments, are not in the work force and are not dependent therefore on job-wages for their ability to consume. They are dependent, either directly or through the mediation of the state, on those in the society who keep the production-job-wages-consumption system in being. These must produce enough to carry both themselves and the others.

Until a few decades ago production was predominantly concerned with output of physical goods and services connected with physical, concrete things. Even as late as the mid-1940s planners, such as Abercrombie who was responsible for the plan for London at the time, thought of employment with this emphasis. Work meant going to factories. Not until the mid-1960s did British planning administration begin to apply equal control to office location as to factory location through the use of the Industrial Development Certificate. During that period in the developed countries employment in service activities, particularly 'knowledge' activities, grew very rapidly. In the USA the apogee of employment in manufacturing industry was reached as early as 1950. A result is that, although the linkage production-job-wages-consumption has not changed, the *kinds* of production and the *ratio* between the quantity of output and the numbers of workers required for the various kinds of production have altered radically.

Second, the production of physical goods and services requires ever larger inputs of energy and raw materials. This increasing demand on resources is now perceived as having limits. Therefore the concept of a continuously expanding industrial output cannot serve as the long-term basis for supporting our very large populations. The syndrome production-job-wages-consumption with emphasis on physical goods and services must undergo modification in some or all its elements and/or in some or all of their relationships. For example, we might develop new connections between production and consumption, or we might very much increase the production (and consumption) of 'commodities' other than physical goods and services.

Masuda places this understanding as basic to his proposals for the computerization of Japanese society:

He appreciates the vulnerable position of Japan in relying heavily on growth in manufacturing industry to keep the population fed, etc through the linkage production-job-wages-consumption; he thinks such growth cannot go on indefinitely.

He acknowledges the inherent differences between the production of physical goods and the production of information or knowledge; he therefore examines our conventional economics and concludes that an extension of the discipline of economics will be necessary to cope with the special characteristics of information production, etc.

For this he develops the concept of time-value, which would be superimposed on the traditional notion of use-value.

He generates a national plan for moving toward a society in which the viability of the production–job–wages–consumption linkage to support the population would depend on a 'lower' level of production of physical goods and services and a 'higher' level of production of information or knowledge.

First of all we must note that although the syndrome production–job–wages–consumption is the dominant linkage of the developed socio-economies it is far from being the only one which is capable of sustaining human life. Subsistence farming operates as work-production-consumption. Those who live by being part of the running of the state—the armed forces, the bureaucracy, etc—depend on the linkage production–expropriation–consumption. Expropriation is used in its basic sense of taking away from others by taxation, force, etc. These syndromes are generated from the consumption end because the problem, in the condition of a very large and increasing world population, may be seen as how to make it possible for the individual to be able to consume what is required for sustaining life. In mass populations the entitlement to consume is possession of money. Where populations are now concentrated in very large urban centres some syndromes or linkages are ruled out. Subsistence farming is scarcely a solution for the hordes of Calcutta or New York. Ward (1976) sees it, however, as an increasingly important type of syndrome for the world's next billion or so population.

In this context we have to ask of the Masuda proposals if the syndrome will have to change in order to accommodate the proposed superstructure based on information. To get at this, Masuda finds it essential to go down to the fundamentals of the discipline of economics. The fundamental he thinks most important is that of value. The key idea is that when our 'necessities' are satisfied, another kind of value emphasis can take precedence. This idea is not new. Ivor Richards (1928) and R B Perry (1967) in the 1920s worked on the notion that an appetite—Richards used the word *appetencies*—when satisfied releases its energy for an appetite further up the hierarchy of values. What is new is Masuda's joining together this idea with the insight that in socioeconomic terms there are differences between the way the system will work in the area of producing physical goods for basic subsistence and the way the system will work for the superimposed levels where production will not be physical, but essentially mental. He then attempts the next stage of applying this idea to an existing mass society, hoping thereby to get it off the hook of perpetually having to expand physical production.

Second, in the writings of Masuda that I have been able to read (not all are translated from the Japanese) there does not appear to be much attention given to controlling or directing the production of physical goods and services. Control would be necessary because by implication his thinking demands a considerable degree of stabilization in that part of the socioeconomy. Increasingly production must come to mean production of information, etc when seen in the syndrome production–job–wages–consumption. There are two reasons for this. First, the socioeconomy cannot continue indefinitely relying on ever-increasing physical output. At some point the effort to get more will cost too much. Control will be required to preclude running right up into such a situation. Also, the growth of information production necessitates the growth of new values (for example, time-value) which will have to be consciously fostered. Specifically the *operationalization* of new values will have to be accelerated. This is already tacitly recognized in our attempts to insert the new capabilities of the telecommunications–computer technology into the workings of the status quo of the developed socioeconomies: for example how to use excess cable TV capacity; how to obtain payment for access to ideas and information; how to use surplus satellite channel capacity; how to use more fully our enormous electronic computational capability. These attempts at insertion are a kind of reciprocal support of Masuda's thesis; we are already trying to do this but have not as yet the necessary theoretical base to give us major entry. The history of the last two hundred years suggests that major technological capability does eventually become fairly fully exploited.

Very essential to Masuda's proposal, therefore, would appear to be plans for the stabilization of the physical production side of the socioeconomy to be implemented *pari passu* with the planned development of the informational side. Presumably, arrangements would have to be made for the switching of resources from the one to the other. Also it would be necessary to familiarize the public with the idea that there is a limit to the acquisition of physical goods and services. After a certain point, demand would have to be discouraged. A way of looking at this is to see it in the perspective of our present market orientation. Conventionally the expansion of markets is seen as an unassailable way to prosperity. This traditional market orientation would either have to be reduced in its general importance or at least have to be extensively modified as to the 'commodities' marketed, for example by a greater emphasis on marketing information, etc. We touch here on the role of the market in society and its important place in classical economics.

This deficiency of planning of the physical production of the socio-economy that we have suggested is apparent in Masuda's thinking can be contrasted with the stabilization emphasis so important in the British ecologists' proposals presented in *A Blueprint for Survival*.

Here the key idea is precisely the progressive control of the use of physical resources, the slowing and eventually the halting of rates of growth, and the stabilization of the socioeconomy. The key idea is that the physical life-support base can be—must be—stabilized at a level which will give the expectation of long-term ability of the socioeconomy to live within the capability of the supporting ecosystem(s). The ecologists' assessment of this requirement with regard to Britain is that it must become self-sufficient in food. Their solution is quite ruthless—reduce the population from its present fifty-five million or so to about thirty million.

The British ecologists are aware of the importance of the production-job–wages–consumption linkage, and see the danger of many individuals not being in this linkage manifest as massive unemployment. Their proposals, however, are made with the claim that the shift to a stabilized socioeconomy can be made without serious loss of jobs. The key idea is that this will be arranged by achieving a better urban–rural mix through the progressive decentralization of industry from the present urban centres. This, it is anticipated, will reduce urban costs: transportation, waste disposal, administration, medical, etc costs.

Although the British ecologists look at how the production–job–wages–consumption linkage is to be maintained in the stabilized condition and therefore are more realistic than Masuda with regard to the physical subsistence underpinnings of the socioeconomy, some questions have to be raised. Perhaps chief among these is the possibility that the general policies recommended are precisely policies which will tend to reduce jobs. Hitherto it has been the cities and towns which have encouraged the growth of tertiary and quaternary sectors of the socioeconomy at the same time that secondary industry has declined as a source of jobs. These are super-structures on the basic subsistence economic activity. Savings or reductions in administration, transportation, certain kinds of entertainment, etc will reduce the jobs in those fields. In some sense our ability to maintain our large *national* populations is built on our *local* urban concentrations of population being capable of considerable tertiary and quaternary job growth. It is known that greater concentration of population costs more in equipment and administration than does distribution of population in smaller urban centres. This extra cost may, however, be very well more than carried by the tertiary and quaternary 'superstructure' benefits which accrue to the socioeconomy through large population concentrations. We raise ourselves up by taking in each other's washing. Hitherto this has necessitated high physical concentration. The British ecologists' proposals do not offer any replacement for this in terms of the production–job–wages–consumption syndrome.

A second observation is that the ecologists do not acknowledge, or perhaps understand, the socioeconomic significance of the electronic technology with regard to its role both in manufacturing industry and in the 'knowledge' industry. In the former it makes possible extensive automation. This tends to reduce the jobs required for achieving a given output. Theoretically, in a socioeconomy of stabilized output of goods made from recycled materials and designed to last as long as possible, we can imagine only a relatively small labour force being required to maintain the equipment. This seems hard for us to grasp; we still think of

manufacturing industry as fairly labour-intensive. But many industries
now cannot be so regarded when viewed against their capital demands or
their physical output. Further, there is a built-in inducement to become
ever less labour-intensive as labour unions' demands and public expectation
become oppressive. Thus it seems reasonable to conclude that the
progressive application of electronic controls to manufacturing industry
would tend to reinforce any other tendencies in the proposals toward
reducing the jobs generated by manufacturing industry.

On the side of the 'knowledge' or information industry extensive
decentralization would be expected, given certain conditions, to increase
the number of jobs. Chief of the conditions would be that the total numb
of transactions within the society would not be permitted to decline as a
result of decentralization. Granted this, many transactions now done in
other ways would have to be done electronically under a decentralized
pattern of settlement. This might tend to create new jobs in manufacturing
and maintaining new equipment by requiring new organizational elements
and employing more people working on the equipment. These areas coul
obviously be planned for growth to compensate for the job losses likely i
manufacturing industry. However, automation is also being applied very
rapidly to the tertiary and quaternary jobs, which are white-collar. The
lag which has existed in the processing of paperwork is being reduced and
the demand for workers in this field, characteristic of the last two or thre
decades, may level off. The increase caused by decentralization might we
be considerably offset by the inroads of automation into the sector of
'paper-pushing' jobs. It is a somewhat rough-and-ready statement, but
gives some measure of the recent change, that computers in the USA now
'occupy' as many jobs as the entire American labour force in 1950.

The stage beyond this would be the consciously forced development
of the 'knowledge' industry as superstructure of major dimensions on top o
the subsistence sector. This could provide a large expansion of jobs, as it
already has done in North America, and could be developed under
governmental stimulus to account for a very major part of the total
production–job–wages–consumption requirement. It is this potential whic
Masuda sees quite clearly, and which the British ecologists have missed.

The omission is perhaps in part due to the different rates of developme
in this field in various countries and the degrees of awareness that this
implies. Not very much is known about the differences between the
developed countries. The forthcoming research project on this subject
now being mounted by the Organization for Economic Co-operation and
Development should provide some answers[1]. As general comment, it
seems clear that the development of the knowledge–information sector o

[1] The project is entitled: "Macro-economic Analysis of Information Activities". It
will aim to find out how far certain trends already documented for the US are presen
in other member countries of OECD, and in what degrees (from correspondence with
H P Gassmann, OECD).

the socioeconomy is most advanced in the USA, where there is now a relatively high level of awareness of its potential.

Looking simultaneously at Masuda's proposals and those of the British ecologists one is struck by their complementarity. If, indeed, a developed country perceives a limit to its continued reliance on an ever-increasing consumption of resources and output of physical goods then some stabilization has to be accepted. At least one analyst—Boulding (1972)—thinks that the most highly developed countries are already fast approaching such a condition of stabilization. This means, as the ecologists stress, a reduction of throughput in the socioeconomy and a greater reliance on stock, recycling, and use of renewable resources. This change, however, threatens further weakening of the production–job–wages–consumption linkage and a possible reduction in physical well-being. If therefore such a change is decided upon, a complementary set of proposals aimed at compensating for this in other areas of life would appear to be necessary. Such proposals would have to be for growth in the 'mental' sphere and avoid growth in physical output. This is the aim of Masuda's 'information society'. The conclusion is that even a 'stabilized' society must have a growth sector since it has to survive in an existing world by maintaining itself through transactions.

Ryan's approach in the matter of work is quite different from those of the other two examples. For him, work is 'thirdness'. It comes after the sense of oneself as an individual and after the incursion of the outside world upon that 'firstness'. To him work is essentially the thirdness activity necessary to maintain human life in the context of the ecosystem. As thirdness arises from antecedent manifestations of firstness and secondness, Ryan's approach to work is primarily seeking to integrate all three logics of the human personality.

It is this assumption of the responsibility for integration which makes his approach interesting, despite its sketchiness. Herein he tackles a key problem which the other two hardly acknowledge to exist, let alone solve. Both Masuda and the British ecologists implicitly proceed on the belief that the perceived difficulties must be attacked by an 'external' and essentially analytically based reconstruction of society. In doing this they may very well be grossly underplaying the role of the 'internal' controls of the individual which need no external coercion to make them function beneficially for the group.

What Ryan sees is that work can be internally controlled in its relation to the stability of the ecosystem and holds that this must now be done in the human species because that species has learned how to circumvent the natural external controls. Consider the lions, who like ourselves, are top predators. Lions are 'successful' at catching and eating their prey only for about a third of the 'work' they do; two animals out of every three the lion chases either escape or are eaten by other animals after capture. This 'control' keeps down the lion population. It is external to the lion.

Supposing we modify the control by giving the lions shotguns. For a tim
the lions do very well, but soon the stocks of zebra, wildebeests, etc are
so heavily depleted that the lions are themselves endangered by lack of food
At this point either another external control must be applied or a control
internal to the lions themselves must be developed; that is, the lions must
understand their problem and act voluntarily within themselves to reduce
the use of their shotguns. We have raised the question in section 6.6
whether China has found its way to some such form of internal control.

This is the whole point of Ryan's emphasis: there is little expectation
of an external control for the human species except disaster. We are
therefore left with the need to develop the necessary internal control, or
logic. This directly relates to work because that is what we do to the
ecosystem in order to win and maintain the niche of our species in it.
The mechanics of this last are taken care of by the study of ecosystem
energetics but that study does not, and cannot, go into the *motivation* of
the species to follow a certain pattern of behaviour with regard to energy
flows through the system.

All three examples see work as the winning of sustenance. Masuda see
it as the winning being essentially within the 'human' system, although he
acknowledges the problem of progressive shortage of resources. The British
ecologists see it as the human *society* winning sustenance within the viab
workings of the ecosystem. Ryan is saying that we cannot achieve the
changes in behaviour necessary for the other two unless we can find out how
to *motivate the human individual* to the required new patterns of behaviou
This, he thinks, may be possible by developing a new understanding of
each others' firstness—a hope offered by the reflexive capabilities of th
electronic technology—and building on this new knowledge.

12.3 Technology

The changes our examples propose as necessary in the socioeconomy
require changes in various technologies. For example, recycling and wast
technology, alternative sources of energy, agricultural technology, building
technology, and the development of alternative uses of physical resources

It is not the intention to examine here the significances of the changes
in these areas. But it is very useful to observe how varied are the exampl
in their degrees of emphasis on such matters, and to draw a conclusion.
As for the degrees of attention paid to such technologies, we might cite:
Todd's survival arks give primary emphasis to developing a certain kind o
technological approach to physical support (food and energy); Masuda
pays no attention to such matters but assumes the continued security of
the physical base and its capacity to support an elaborate informational
superstructure; the electronic–technological experts proceed largely on
the assumption of a continued free market for technological development
and the British ecologists call for socially directed technological advance
such areas as recycling, energy, waste use, and agriculture. The examples

Todd and the Papuan experimenters base their food production on carefully thought out agricultural technologies which depend on precise design of food chains, but the British ecologists do not give a very great emphasis to this, although they might imply it. As for the telecommunications technology, the examples dealing in detail with the technology assume society to revolve round the technology, or society is seen as passive and the technology acts upon it. Todd and the British ecologists ignore the electronic technology except that Todd will run a sophisticated monitoring operation in the Prince Edward Island ark. Only Masuda sees the vision of the possibility of consciously planning society's future through the systematic development of the potential of the telecommunications and computer technology.

A very important conclusion to be drawn is that in the present state of the art we are doing little more than viewing not only our supposed problems, technologies, etc but also our concerns for society and the individual from somewhat specialist and unintegrated perspectives. The result is proposals for change which may be technically very sophisticated from one viewpoint but simplistic from another, and if applied may prove as damaging as beneficial to society. For example, the extensive application of Ryan's approach to the use of the technology by itself and not complemented by the careful use of other sophisticated technologies might lead to regression in society's institutions. Similarly the British ecologists' decentralization of present large urban populations could reduce the transactions possible to individuals and thereby fail to maintain the general socioeconomic level and greatly reduce the opportunity for informational, intellectual, and aesthetic interchange.

A difficulty in the way of integrating approaches, knowledge, and proposals lies in the specialist nature of our bodies of knowledge. Many of these are now so large and so complex that their practitioners can spare very little effort for exploring outside their own fields. The ecologists know little about the rapid development of electronics and its impacts and potentials. The electronic technologists on the other hand do not know enough about ecology to give it the emphasis it demands. *There is no central, common body of values and knowledge into which new knowledge and its significance can be drawn and assimilated.*

A result of this deficiency of integrative capability is that technologies generally develop without cultural and social direction. There are, of course, exceptions. Medicine and war frequently receive the stimulus of public resources to speed up technological development. But, in general, technological development, including that of the electronic technology, is largely without benefit of any great attention to its likely overall societal–cultural usefulness.

The suggestion of the need for guidance in the development of technology implies a possible parallel requirement for the direction of the development of knowledge. Again, whilst there is some directing of the development of knowledge for purposes of medical treatment, war, and industry, the growth of knowledge is often largely haphazard. It is subject to the erratic availability of various resources, the vagaries of mental processes, and the prevailing cultural climate and condition of society. A question which raises its head in these matters is: What would be the most appropriate perspective for approaching the development of knowledge and technology? What is the key context?

We may tentatively suggest that a lesson to be learned in this area is that groups of technologies have to be looked at together if planned development of society is to be taken seriously. We are remarkably slow at this in some fields. For example, the technologies connected with transportation have to be looked at in conjunction with the other technologies which make large, high-density centres of population possible— sanitation and water supply technology, telecommunications, building technology, etc. We have learned some measure of integration of some of these on a largely fortuitous basis. But in practical terms the relationship between the technologies of physical movement and those handling data movement have been mostly ignored. Only in the last few years has exploration begun (see for example Harkness, 1973). But the telephone is over one hundred years old! What now seems most likely to be significant is the interaction between certain very influential technologies. It is a task of integrative research to find out which are the most significant for future development and to discover how to relate them to each other. Perhaps for this we might learn to think about knowledge–technology–technique as a basic syndrome.

12.4 Information
Like the word *environment* the word *information* is used with a variety of meanings or emphases. The way these meanings are classified depends on the intentions of the classifier to some extent. Information theory—a branch of cybernetics—is an attempt to define the information required to *control* processes of given complexity. This is a kind of operational definition since it concentrates on the end result of controlling the system. In cybernetics the principle of feedback has a strong influence on the meaning which information is perceived to have.

In economics, information may be seen as very closely connected with uncertainty of present and future markets, market signals, incentives, falseness or otherwise of information, monopolistic elements in information markets, and the role of information in the socioeconomy. Information is gaining an important place in economics both as an 'industry' in itself and as seen in the pervasive effects of its products through all sectors of the socioeconomy (see Spence, 1974).

In biology information plays a very important role as coded instructions carried by the DNA molecule, which is common to all terrestrial life. Each species preserves its own coding and thereby ensures its continuance.

In ecology the emphasis is on interspecies relationships and relationships between the species and other system components such as nutrients, temperature cycles, radiation, etc. An ecosystem has no equivalent to the fixed coding that the organism has in its DNA molecule. Information is therefore seen in ecology in terms of complexity of organization, uncertainty, possibilities of combinations, and alternative pathways of energy flows. A system which has many possibilities of combination and energy flow is seen as information-rich. These characteristics may be approached quantitatively—for example by counting the alternative pathways of energy flow available—and therefore may be measured. H T Odum follows Shannon: $I = \log_2 C$, where I is information and C is the number of possible combinations (Shannon and Weaver, 1949; H T Odum, 1971, page 169). A pathway opportunity is accepted or rejected; uncertainty (availability of information) arises as a single decision has to be taken between the two options offered by the opportunity. Margalef (1968) has developed techniques for examining information content in relation to species composition. Concentration of information can be measured in ecology. Information availability is related to the degree of order in a system and to the ability of the system to remain negentropic. Rather more attention is paid in ecology to the concept of energy than to that of information. As in electronic control systems, information in ecosystems may act as 'a difference that makes a difference'. A small amount of energy may trigger a very much larger energy flow than itself. This function is informational. It is the key characteristic of feedback. For this reason a minute energy flow may thwart massive disorder in a system (see figure 9.1).

In diagramming ecosystems with strong emphasis on the 'natural' system it is not common to include information as a specific component. Energy and nutrient flows are usually shown as subsuming information. In applying ecological theory to 'human' systems it is not sufficient to do this because of the special nature of information developed by human beings and also because of its vast accumulation in our present stage of cultural evolution. In 'human' systems H T Odum includes as a component the storing and processing of information [H T Odum, 1971, for example figure 7.2(d)]. A 'natural–human' system can be seen as regulating its energy flows by using its stored information. The storage is partly biological and partly cultural. The 'human' component of such a conceptualized system is now evolving very rapidly under the impetus provided by massive use of fossil fuels and our very rapidly growing capacity to produce, process, and store information. *The way in which information is dealt with and the place it is given is therefore an extremely important measure of any proposals for planning the future culture and society.*

For our purposes some distinctions can be usefully made as to ways of looking at information. These may emphasize:

1 Knowledge about the *organization* and *working* of 'natural' (for example, organisms), 'human' (for example, societies), and man-made (for example, motorcars) systems.

   This is basic information about how things are put together and how they function, and is generally considered essential knowledge for any kind of purposeful action. The better the information, the more successful the purposeful action is likely to be.

2 Knowledge about the *state* of the systems, in the past, the present, or the future.

   This has very much to do with the 'health' of the system, what it will be needing next, what it has in excess now, etc. Any proposed change must, realistically, be envisaged in the light of understanding the state of the system. Industrial and commercial operations rely very heavily on information in this category, from today's prices for hogs' bellies to copper futures.

3 Knowledge about the intentions of those components in systems that can be counted as purposeful.

   In particular, 'human' systems have such components. Many kinds of action are dependent on the knowledge available about the intentions of individuals or groups[2]. Information of this kind is often of overriding importance.

4 Knowledge about the environment in which the system is sustained. A motorcar must exist in an environment composed of air temperatures and humidity levels which vary, other motor vehicles, roads, varieties of drivers, etc. A 'human' system—a socioeconomy—must exist in an environment capable of providing food, allowing the perpetuation of its societal structure and functioning, and the safeguarding of its culture. This kind of information is essential for any proposals for injecting change into a system. Changes have to be made with due respect to the danger of upsetting the viability of the relationship between the system and its environment.

5 Changing the taxonomy, we may differentiate between information provided from outside the organism and that which is generated by the organism itself. Of the first kind is the information I obtain from an advertisement about a product. Of the second, is the information I acquire by using the object advertised. The two sets of information about the same object do not necessarily agree!

[2] This raises questions of finality. For discussion see Bertalanffy (1968, page 77ff). The following distinctions from Locker and Coulter (1975) are also useful: *teleonomic* indicates the design of a system with single (or several) fixed goal(s); *teleozetic* indicates the capability of the system to choose a goal as may be required from a group of predesigned goals; *teleogenic* means the system is capable of generating new goals when the predesigned goals are no longer viable.

Sometimes experiential knowledge is not available. On the other hand, many aspects of 'human' and man-made systems are heavily dependent on it. Experiential knowledge is often hard to codify and transmit, and also to process by machine.

6 Knowledge or message of change of state, which triggers action. This is the 'difference that makes a difference'. I read the statistical statement of the link between cigarettes and lung cancer (new message—the difference), and stop smoking (resultant difference).

This emphasis in information is the very essence of all control technology and technique. A low-power circuit is used to effect a difference in a much higher-power process—for example electronic control of smelting operations or cycle changes in dishwashers. Feedback technology, including biofeedback, is of this type[3].

In the light of these descriptions we can enlarge our understanding of the examples. Ryan starts out with the premise that information is the key to changing our habituation to certain kinds of action. He proposes to generate and use information in new ways at each level of his conceptualization of how a new world view must be structured for survival: chreche, chreod, and work cell. For action to be ecologically satisfactory the individual must improve his knowledge of his own firstness and the firstness of two others. This improved firstness information will make a difference in the way action affecting the ecosystem is perceived. This is information under the fifth heading above plus something from the sixth. Ryan's proposals are also specific for items one, two, and four: information about how the systems work and their states must also be obtained as a primary task. Item three—intention—in Ryan's thinking is dominated by the perception of the need to maintain the ecosystem viable.

Masuda's thought is also pervaded by a strong sense of the primal place of information but his emphasis is quite different from Ryan's. Although he is sensitive to the realization of our century that the globe is finite and that limits, whether identified in detail or not, must inevitably exist, he sees the development of information as a means of maintaining 'human' systems viable particularly in their production–job–wages–consumption perspective. Hence for Masuda the important thing will be to increase the quantity, quality, accessibility, and handling of information as a mass 'good'. He inevitably must believe strongly in the importance of the *productivity* of information. Productivity is in item six above: the difference can be read as an enhancement of *productivity* of information— 'better' information improves output. Masuda's proposals also rely heavily

[3] At this stage of the discussion I have followed the conventional distinction between 'natural' and 'human' systems, as a matter of convenience rather than precision. The distinction raises monist–dualist questions. My own preference, as is that of the British ecologists, is for the monist view: 'human' systems should be regarded as examples of natural systems. Some ecologists, however, retain the distinction at least in part.

on items one and two—knowledge of the workings of systems and especially of 'human' and man-made systems and the states of those systems.   The purpose here is ever more sophisticated human manipulation of those systems.   Underlying Masuda's thought, one senses the continued influence of the older world-view assumption that the globe is infinite in its capacity to sustain human expansion, although intellectually his thesis is based on the admission of finite limits to human production of physical goods and services.   Masuda, as an economist, essentially directs our attention, with urgency, to the need to explore and exploit information as an economic 'good'.   *His urgency is the threat of collapse in 'human' systems because of their internal dynamics, while Ryan's urgency is the threat of collapse of the 'human' system because of its failure to behave within the rules of the ecosystem.   But both begin with information.*

The British ecologists on the other hand pay almost no attention to information although the *raison d'être* of the proposals is, of course, information from items one, two, and four.   In the case of knowledge of the working of the system and the state of the system they are relying on our relatively recently discovered understanding of ecosystems and are warning of dangers.   In the case of item four, which is information about the environment of the system, the viewpoint is taken from that of the 'human' system.   The socioeconomy is seen to sit, so to speak, in an environment consisting of the ecosystem.   That this view is of dubious validity need not concern us here as our focus is the approach to information.   The ecologists therefore give high priority to information describing how 'it all holds together' and to the states of systems.   Their view has to be seen under item three—intention—as the aim of bringing the 'natural' system and the 'human' system into long-term viable accord. The ecologists do not appreciate the role of information in such a reconciliation and therefore make no mention of the need to develop information as a key operational factor in making their proposals realizable.   Under their proposal for the decentralization of large human populations massive change in the present roles of information would appear indispensable.

As information leads to action it is closely connected with ethics.   The emphases of the three examples in the area of ethical demand vary somewhat.   All three acknowledge the ethical question as an important component of their proposals.   This they cannot avoid since they are calling for changes in behaviour in the face of newly perceived threats. Ryan alone goes to the root of the matter and therefore logically starts at that level and not at the level of items one, two, or four—knowledge of the systems and their states in the 'natural' world and the 'human' world. His *belief* is that the human species, like all other species, can learn, or relearn, the rules of ecosystems and can discover or rediscover how to keep behaviour within them.   This is a kind of natural ethic.   This belief may eventually, as a result of experiment, be justified, but in the present speculative condition of the matter it is at least necessary to face the fact that the development of self-consciousness in the human species might lead to quite other assumptions. One of these would be the notion that a high level of self-consciousness implies that a new ethic must be *consciously* generated and made operational. The reason for suggesting this is that the relationship of the human being to the environment is to a large degree already mediated by self-consciously held values: notions of liberty and justice, and sentiments of humanitarianism and aspiration. Part of the price paid for such values and the achievement they have permitted the human species may well be the loss of the unself-conscious operating of the kinds of cybernetic loops which hold the action of the individual lion and zebra within the limits of the stability of their ecosystem. Having said that, it is necessary to stress that Ryan's approach appears uncertain as to the degree to which his ethical loops would be unself-conscious or self-conscious in their operation—as distinct from their formation or fabrication.

Masuda and the British ecologists have a more or less common approach and one which is already beginning to find favour in our present societies in the developed countries. This is the idea that behaviour can become more appropriate for achieving viability if individuals and groups participate in the making of those decisions which affect them. This is often described as public participation, but the concept is operational in many areas of our society: firms, schools and universities, the activities of bureaucracies, citizen groups concerned with the urban environment, etc. A good deal of institutionalization has already taken place in the belief that if individuals and groups understand why certain action is necessary and have helped to formulate it they will agree to, and respect it. The ecologists and Masuda rely on this characteristic of human psychology to achieve behaviour appropriate for arriving at their visions of a new society and for sustaining it in being.

Confidence in the efficacy of this approach in part rests on the idea that if the individual has the relevant information, or is educated enough to grasp the meaning of what is going on, he will know how to behave. This is essentially the belief of the *philosophes* in the value of education: adequate information and appropriate education will produce right action. Unfortunately there is no proof that this connection exists and much evidence to suggest that at best it is unreliable and erratic. Translated into our present interest, the belief becomes the notion that knowledge of the ecosystem and its current state together with knowledge of the 'human' system and its state will lead to appropriate behaviour, so that we shall ultimately, through knowledge, learn to safeguard the workings of our life support. There is very little reason to suppose that this belief is justified, especially in our postidealistic age. The dynamic of liberal, scientific humanism has already sadly waned.

The motivation for the proffered solution of public participation and improved informational levels is more interesting than the solution itself.

Governments, managements of firms, and governing bodies of universities have not become involved in having the governed participate in governmer and management out of simple goodness of heart. Participation has appeare as partly a demand from the governed and, no doubt, partly a response tc avoid conflict by those who have the responsibility for governing or simply for getting necessary things done. Particularly in countries with liberal democratic traditions governments, but not particularly business managements, are sensitive to public disapproval or outcry. Attempts to make the necessary changes in society to ensure the viability of ecosystem to manage nonrenewable resources more responsibly, and to accelerate th progress toward a stable state and the 'information' society will inevitably meet plenty of resistance, disapproval, outcry, and sabotage. Hence the motivation for participation of those attempting to restructure society arises from anxieties about the very nature of the relationship between th individual and the group.

In cybernetic terms the matter may be usefully viewed as the problem of generating new control loops or revitalizing certain ineffectual ones anc weakening or stopping off certain existing ones. The new loops to be created have to do with linking human action ecologically with the life-support system—this is expressed as the need for a new ethic—and with the linking of the individual's action with the community's action so that these together aggregate to what is required ecologically. The loops which have to be removed or weakened are those which lead to action contradicting or countermanding the new controls that have to be created. For example modification is needed in the loop: increased population–increased demand for food–increased inputs of chemicals into the soil–depletion of soil fertility. This loop now produces the situation in which the rate of increase of the input of chemicals increases. Another example is: improvec availability of information to the public about the intentions of government increased opportunity for opposition to these intentions–increased articulat opposition by minorities–increased attention given to minority opposition by governments–increased complexity of decisionmaking–diminished capacity to act–public dissatisfaction–governmental appeasement. The linkages between the elements in these loops are, of course, formed by information and its availability.

12.5 Some tentative conclusions
It is now possible to extract certain major areas of attention about which it seems likely we shall need to think in greater detail. These include:
1 There has emerged an underlying preoccupation with our newly acquirec understanding that Spaceship Earth is a finite system and that its finiteness is particularly relevant to the present and immediately future quantity of the human species to be carried. We are leaving behind the age-old assumption that the globe and its resources for sustaining the species could be regarded as unlimited.

2 This realization is forcing us to look at the way we behave toward the life-support system and, looking, we conclude that dangers exist in our present behaviour.

3 The need is perceived to change behaviour. This means visualizing new patterns of behaviour capable of meeting the new needs. This appears as the call for a new ethic linking the human species to the ecosystem. This in turn is perceived as calling for a new ethic dealing with intra-species relationships (that is, between human beings).

4 New behaviour patterns are perceived as requiring new socioeconomic concepts and arrangements. The connection between behaviour and the socioeconomy therefore is perceived as very important.

5 Stabilization of the socioeconomy with regard to growth in physical output is rated as very important.

6 Proposals and programmes for doing this are coming from several directions, ranging from biological experiments with nearly closed mini-ecosystems to fostering planned growth in the nonphysical—information and knowledge—sectors of the socioeconomy.

7 Development and growth in the electronic technology and its applications proceeds largely in a socially undirected way. But the direction of this development and growth could interlock with the need for stabilization.

8 New relationships appear to be necessary between the individual and the group. This in turn brings into prominence the attitudes, values, and sensibility of the individual.

9 Questions are raised about the nature and meaning of production and productivity because of the characteristics of information. This raises questions about how to enlarge our knowledge of the workings of the socioeconomy.

In the next section we shall look in more detail at some of these matters.

Part 3

Expanding our understanding

The new visions at present have little benefit of contextual relationship to other areas of knowledge and aspiration. Several contexts are offered here as necessary for expanding our understanding of how to approach the changes in society and culture inherent in the application of our two new areas of knowledge. One very important area of context common to both the electronic technology and our ecological knowledge is the character and sensibility of the mass individual. His attitudes, beliefs, and behaviour are daily moulded through the agency of the technology. His behaviour, aggregated in millions, will decide the future viability of the world's ecosystems.

Conquest of the limitations of space and time

In this chapter I shall try to put our present electronic capability in
communication into the perspective of our most important traditional way
of breaking the bonds of time and space. Historically in the development
of civilization this has been writing and reading, with the later elaborations
made possible by printing and photography, etc. A backward glance at
the way in which writing first emerged and the context of its emergence
will be helpful.

13.1 The first extension of communication capability: historic glyph civilizations

Up to the present, most civilizations, but not all urban settlements, have
used writing and its variations. Many civilizations have been very heavily
dependent on it. It has been the chief method of recording and
accumulating useful information, of breaking the 'natural' bonds of space
and time, and of developing language. The word 'glyph' can be used here
in acknowledgement of the earliest systematized writing being 'scooped
out' on wood, stone, or clay. The sense is present in 'hieroglyph'. Glyph
is a technical word associated with studies in indigenous American cultures,
but is useful for wider application.

The glyph was a very great invention. Basically it transferred sound,
which is very severely limited in its space and time ranges, into a light-
sensitive medium. That is, it extended speech from being solely dependent
on generating waves in air to capturing the benefits of the visible band of
the electromagnetic spectrum for passing information. By doing this, vast
new areas of human development were made possible. The restricting
effects of space and time were extensively loosened. Written messages
could now move across distances infinitely greater than those achievable
by shouting, drums, using a runner with a verbal message, or sending
smoke signals. Similarly the handicap of required instantaneity inherent
in speech could be overcome: the written record could be read at any time
in the future, and knowledge could therefore be amassed systematically[1].

Looking along our present perspective we can say that the glyph
civilizations learned how to become photobionic. Their effectiveness in
large measure consisted of bringing their communicative capability into
the same region of the electromagnetic spectrum as that which sustained
their food supply and indeed the entire biosphere. *Light became the*

[1] Some archaic societies attempted to extend the range of sound by special means,
for example the drum 'languages' of the Congo. Others transferred to light, using
smoke signals, etc. Quite late glyph civilizations used refinements, for example
Napoleonic France and the British Admiralty of the same date used a system of
semaphore relays. Light signalling is still useful at sea. None of these attempts, however,
was capable of major development within itself or of originating any cultural leap.

means of extended communication as well as the key input of energy for food production. Although civilizations other than our own have not understood the working of the ecosystems of which they have been parts they have learned by experience how to increase and sustain the growth the biomass to ensure a stable food supply. This has made possible increased numbers and concentrations of human beings. This steadily growing capability has been progressively dependent on the use of the ey to register abstract markings made visible by light—writing. The marking have become more and more capable of conveying refinement of meaning and, using them, human beings have cumulatively increased their knowledg of the nature of things. The history of the saga societies of the Norseme and the Oceanic peoples suggests that the human species would not have developed very far culturally without being able to accumulate and constantly use the large bodies of information made possible through writing. The building of writing on speech, or the jump from sound to light, opened the gates to the enormous development of knowledge which has characterized the species for the last five millenia.

Childe (1951) supports the view that civilization was first manifest in cities. The 'urban revolution', although based on a food-getting revolutio was its beginning. It seems quickly to have become typically associated with a favourable geographic area in which a group of cities could flourisl partly on the basis of some reciprocal surrender of economic independenc This meant specialization of activities and the abandonment of autarky fc each settlement, and demanded improved communication. One city migh have access to copper ore but have no timber; another might need stone but have a pool of highly skilled goldsmiths able to export some of their product. Childe summarizes the development before the advent of writin

> "Between 6000 and 3000 B.C. man has learnt to harness the force of oxen and of winds, he invents the plow, the wheeled cart, and the sailboat, he discovers the chemical processes involved in smelting coppe ores and the physical properties of metals, and he begins to work out accurate solar calendar. He has thereby equipped himself for urban lif and prepares the way for a civilization which shall require writing, processes of reckoning, and standards of measurement—*instruments of new way of transmitting knowledge and of exact sciences*" (Childe, 1951, page 87; emphasis supplied).

Around 3000 BC there appeared early written material. From examinir this, something of the socioeconomic workings of Sumer and Akkad can be deduced. Childe gives very careful attention to the revolution in human knowledge associated with the invention, elaboration and diffusio of writing:

> "The revolution inaugurated a new method of transmitting experience, fresh ways of organizing knowledge, and more exact sciences. The

science requisite for the revolution has been transmitted in the form of craft lore by oral precept and example. The beginnings of writing and of mathematics and the standardization of weights and measures coincide in time with the revolution. The synchronism is not accidental. The practical needs of the new economy had, in fact, evoked the innovations" (Childe, 1951, page 143).

The evidence from Sumer shows clearly how writing developed. At first it was used for generally practical needs, such as trade records. Later, a little after 3000 BC, come religious texts, spells, legal codes, treaties. It took a long time, however, to reach the understanding that writing would "revolutionize human knowledge", and to see it as "... the first step to raising science above the limits of space and time" (Childe, 1951, page 148). A perhaps comparable instance of man hitting on an idea for a limited practical purpose and later discovering that he has invented something of much greater importance was the invention of the thermionic valve by J A Fleming in 1904. For a long time the valve was used strictly for radio purposes; only later was it realized that it (and the transistor later) had generally useful properties, particularly for electronic control systems. Such control systems have now come to underpin almost all our activities much as the written record did in the Near East onwards from the third millenium BC.

13.2 The second extension of communication capability: electronic modes
Having learned to extend the communication of information from sound (air) into light (radiation) and having built up vast accumulations of knowledge thereby, the human species stands today in the position that it has very recently achieved a further new extension of its information capabilities. The first extension involved only the visible band of the electromagnetic spectrum. The new extension—extensions of the original extension—now spreads the capability of information communication and processing (a mindlike function) into several other regions of the electro-magnetic spectrum.

The original extension and the contemporary or second extension are shown in figures 13.1 and 13.2, respectively. In these diagrams speech as spoken, dependent on waves generated in air, is at the bottom of the drawing. The meaning of the words spoken in figure 13.1 may be extended into various kinds of visible modes dependent on radiation, not air. These are indicated by the continuous band in the middle of the drawing, linking directly the two eyes of the sender and the receiver. At its most basic level this represents eyeball-to-eyeball transfer of information. In more complicated modes it includes a variety of visual signals (semaphores, smoke signals, signs of all kinds). Characteristically these can only work provided sender and receiver are operating simultaneously and are within direct visible range. In these modes the signal frequently disappears, once passed, and is not permanent. (It is worth noting that animals as well as human beings use sense organs, developed essentially for receiving, to transmit information. The eye, for example, issues information–signals.)

The next stage is to eliminate the distance limitation. This is done by making the signal permanent in some way so that it can be physically transported: the book, clay tablet, newspaper, painting, etc. This mode is represented by the narrow horizontal lines shown discontinuous in figure 13.1. Now the 'natural' limitations of time and space have been considerably overcome. The book can be read at any time in any place.

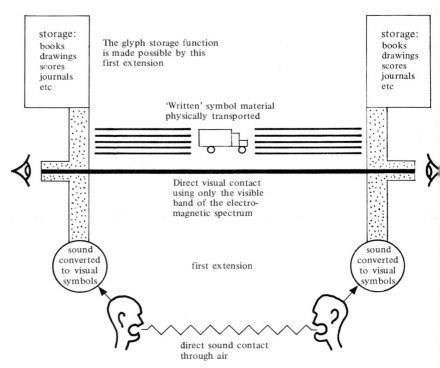

Figure 13.1. Conversion between sound and light in cultures using only the visible band of the electromagnetic spectrum. Without visual symbol, communication is largely restricted to how far the human being can project language as sound through air. With the extension of sound into visual symbol—signs, writing, etc—communication achieved its first extension, breaking the bonds of time and space. In the diagram the wide black line between the eyes indicates direct, instantaneous communication. This can use symbols basically built on language; distance is traditionally very limited although modern technology has improved performance. The effective extension in common use is shown by the conversion to portable written material. The close parallel lines indicate the role of the physical movement of the written material. The written symbol breaks the bond of time; its capability for being territorially moved (for example, as book) breaks that of space.

Its movement over distance does, however, consume time. Communication has now been very much improved but the actuality of the living being has been considerably sacrificed. All civilizations previous to our own have been based on this first extension of our information communication capability. These are the glyph civilizations dominant up to, say, 1900 AD.

The second extension, which is an extension of the first extension, is shown in figure 13.2. This extension handles both the spoken word and the written sign or signal—everything receivable by the eye. Direct sound is shown at the bottom of the drawing as before. The extension of this, still in the spoken form, by transfer to the radio wave band of the electromagnetic spectrum is shown by the microphone. Impulses, or waves, in air are transferred to the electromagnetic spectrum, transmitted, and then transferred back to sound (waves in air). This is live radio.

As in the previous drawing the spoken sound can be extended to the sign or symbol (book, etc). This is shown by the stippled channels, which indicate the first extension—from sound to light—to the visible portion of the electromagnetic spectrum. Once in this form the second extension, consisting of moving to other bands of the spectrum, can take place [2]. We now shift within the spectrum itself to obtain the benefits of electromagnetic transfer over distance. We now can move the contents of the book, data, pictures, drawings, etc over global and solar system distances virtually instantaneously. This capability is shown by the wavy lines. There is yet a further mode we have discovered. The continuous line joining the eyes in figure 13.1 can also be extended so that direct vision can be used over infinite distance. This, as before, is the heavy black line within the stippled channels.

Storage of material is shown in both diagrams. In figure 13.1 there is only glyph storage—books, scores, drawings, even notches on sticks and knotted strings. In figure 13.2 electronic storage is added: electronic information storage capability based on discs, tapes, etc. A further enrichment of this second extension is that the two kinds of storage reinforce each other. Books can be placed in electronic storage and electronic storage makes possible new and better ways of setting up and printing books. Further, electronically stored material can be duplicated in mass quantity just as can the material of traditional glyph storage.

The diagrams require a little time for absorbing their significance. They are not without their difficulties because of the need to combine the several processes. It is necessary to bring the processes together in as unified a way as possible because of the unification that has in fact taken place electronically. *This unification, based on the digitization of the electronic signal, seems likely to be a major step in human culture.*

---

[2] The visible band is relatively narrow, its upper end being at a frequency of 10^{15} cycles per second. The communications band is relatively wide—exceeding 10^4 to 10^{11} cycles per second. See also figure 1.1.

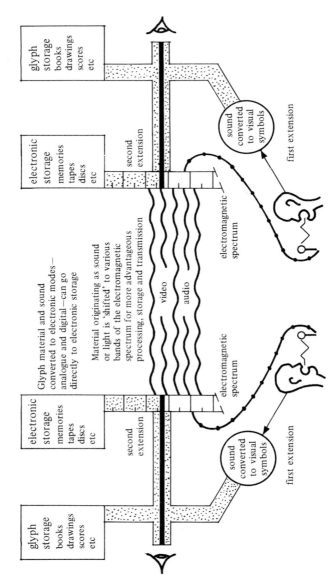

Figure 13.2. Conversion of sound and light to other bands of the electromagnetic spectrum: electrobionic culture. In this second extension, use for communication is extended beyond the 'window' of visible light to many other wave bands of the electromagnetic spectrum. These other wave bands make possible transmission over distances of the scale of the solar system and our galaxy, and beyond. To glyph storage (books, etc) electronic storage is now added, giving complete mastery over time and space. Electronic storage is also able to handle glyph storage, thereby greatly extending the flexibility of the earlier storage modes based only on the visible-light band. This extension allows all signals, audio and video originated, to be universalized into a single digitized electronic pulse sequence. Certain variants of the second extension, such as the use of x-rays and gamma rays for penetrating matter to achieve visibility, are omitted from the diagram for simplicity. It is noteworthy that eyeball-to-eyeball contact is possible in the second extension; hence the black line plus the radiation lines indicate instantaneous visual contact over infinite distance.

The two modes for handling material electronically—and probably mentally—are the analogical and the digital. If I stretch out my arms fully to indicate the length of the fish I have caught, that is an analogue. If I keep my hands in my pockets and say the fish was big, that is a digitally based mode. Whether taken as sound or as written signs, 'big' represents the process of transferring the information by assembling recognizable symbols which build up into a message or item of information. Language is essentially digital although a number of words in probably all languages are also analogues—their sequences of sounds suggest the things themselves. These are called onomatopoeic words: cough, tintinnabulation, howl, rasp, etc. It has been suggested that the evolution of the human mind has been from the analogical to the predominant use of the digital modes[3].

The extremely important point from our present perspective is that visual as well as audio material is electronically digitized. That is to say, the same mode is used for transferring information whether it originates and arrives at its destination as sound or as light. A kind of common sensory mode has now been achieved. Computer can talk to computer without 'translating' from the digital mode. Further, as we have seen, any brand of computer or terminal can talk to any other, potentially anywhere in the world through the new technology and organizational techniques of universal packet-switching (section 4.3). We have therefore created a universalized, standardized system for handling both audio and video sensory material and the mental products (bodies of knowledge) we generate with that material. The direction of development is toward universal digitization, although broadcast TV will remain analogue for a considerable time.

It will take a long time to absorb the significance of this second extension of our communication capability both in its aspect of adding the use of other regions of the electromagnetic spectrum and in the technique of sensory unification achieved by digitization. We already have, however, some inkling that a new phase in human cultural evolution is opening. As a speaker at the 1976 ICCC conference said in the context of universal packet-switching: "We have hardly yet finished writing the preface".

13.3 Study of the sociocultural significance of the second extension is prescientific

Considerable research is being carried on in detailed endeavours to examine the effects of the second extension of our communication capability directly on the individual or group. We are familiar with such studies as

[3] Writing when phonetic is essentially digital. The letters of our alphabet, however, very interestingly appear frequently to have been analogues in their original forms. For example, our M in its Phoenician version clearly represents ripples on water. In Hebrew water is *Mem*. The sign first stood for water (analogical) and later came to stand for the initial sound of the word *Mem* (digital). Similarly, the Greek Δ: in Hebrew *Daleth* meaning a tent door, of which it is obviously a pictogram. Chinese is also interesting for its analogical and digital mix.

those examining the effects of violence shown on television, differences in responses to information received electronically, and changes in behaviour patterns arising from the habitual use of electronic media. We are also familiar with the kinds of experiments associated with these studies. These experiments and studies are often well controlled, but the idea is frequently expressed that our best way of moving toward understanding is first to accumulate practical experience of using the facilities offered by the technology. This suggests that we have serious difficulty in generating the image or paradigm—to use Kuhn's (1970) approach—for scientific study at the larger scale of the culture and the society. If Kuhn's view is correct— that in the prescientific stage all sorts of approaches are tried more or less indiscriminately—then it would appear that our present attempts to grasp the cultural meaning of our new capability must be classed as prescientific. It has at present a typically somewhat random nature.

We have, as yet, no effective conceptualization of the audio–video medium constituted jointly by radio and TV diffusion, cable, telephone, telecommunications, the computer, feedback/playback, and control techniques. That these constitute some kind of a whole seems clear but we have no word for it. This is probably an indication that we have so far been unable to see it as a concept, like mass or energy in physics. The word 'medium' is unsatisfactory and liable to confusion with the mass media. It is important to note here that it is frequently the radio and TV which are touted as the key cultural entity. Our examination of the whole electromagnetic spectrum indicates that this approach is likely to restrict thinking. Perhaps the nearest we have to a holistic view is that of those, like Norbert Wiener (1967) and E T Hall (1973), who hold that cultures and societies are essentially their messages or communications. For these thinkers the communication *is* the culture. However, another emphasis can be given to this perspective: perhaps it is the dominant *mode* of communication which is the key to a culture since the degree of flexibility and ease or frequency of communication may be more significant than what is communicated. This may be particularly true for change in the culture and society.

The idea that the freedom of expression conferred by a method of communication may be much more important than the message conveyed is not at all new. The British Navy put this insight into practice in the 1780s as a result of the work of Kempenfelt and Howe[4]. In flag signalling the flag as indicator of a preset instruction was superseded at that time by a signalling system which allowed the naval commander to say more or less anything he wished to other ships. Under the old system a particular flag

---

[4] The French were the pioneers of separating the instruction from the signal for naval communication. The new British system was numerary. If necessary an admiral could spell out any word. Speeding up was achieved by making certain numbers stand for commonly useful words and sentences. (See Lewis, 1948, chapter 6.)

could convey only a rigid instruction such as: "proceed in line ahead" or "take up battle stations". By 'digitizing', the eighteenth-century admirals made it possible for an infinite variety of messages to be conveyed by the sequential placing of flags, each one of which comprised only a part of the message. So Nelson was able to compose and signal his famous order of the day at Trafalgar—a signal he could not have made fifty years earlier.

Today we have achieved a similar breakthrough, but on a gigantic scale. The imaginative understanding of it has not, however, properly emerged. But we are not without some probing.

One of the best known of these is McLuhan's (1964) condensation that the "medium is the message". The latter part of this book attempts to develop concepts which may contribute to the imaginative process of generating the necessary conceptualizations.

13.4 Possible key ideas emerging from the extensions
Our brief backward glance at the glyph phases of human development in the context of our need to understand the meaning of the second extension of our communicative powers suggests some key foci of attention. We may hope that such foci will help us discover when new concepts are required or where old ones need to be linked.

The following appear worthy of identification:

1 The first extension—enlarging the transactional and the mental capabilities by extending speech into writing—has been a very major factor in the recent (say, five millenia) quantitative and qualitative advances made by the human species. The second extension—spreading the first extension from the visible band of the electromagnetic spectrum into several other regions—must provisionally be held to be of similar magnitude of importance for the human enterprise. We do not yet have the concepts necessary for saying precisely what this new level will make possible for us.

2 In more detailed terms, writing has played a key role in enabling human beings to extract increased amounts of human-usable biomass from ecosystems. Even coal and oil are to be included here since they are the biomass of extinct ecosystems. This growing capacity of human beings to attract increasing energy to their own use has allowed them to create increasingly large and more numerous socioeconomies. The second extension seems likely to increase yet again this capacity. This enlarged capability comes at a time when we anticipate a considerable increase in human numbers and increased demands being made on the world's ecosystems. We might see the two circumstances as interlocking. Further, we may suspect that a qualitative change in socioeconomies may be emerging in the form of societies that are predominantly 'informational', although still resting on the physical base made possible by the first extension.

3 Because it gave the capacity for accurate storage of information, writing increased the mental capability of our species. Memory was vastly enlarged and relationships could be traced in reliable ways. A special symbiosis was developed between human beings and bodies of knowledge; they grew together. The second extension has provided an entirely new order of storage, computational ability, and information or knowledge transfer. Again, it would seem reasonable to hold the provisional view that the new extension will have major influence on our mental development.

4 The nature of the technology of the second extension is such that it can be used as much to reinforce the characteristics of glyph cultures and societies as for developing the new. The very means which are used to transcend old attitudes, values, technologies, organizational arrangements, and controls are paradoxically capable of, and being actually used for, reinforcing these elements. Electronics makes quite feasible the elimination of the printed book even as it makes cheaper its production and widens its diffusion. We are worse off than the starfish whose legs severally try to propel it in different directions. For us, a single leg simultaneously moves us toward reinforcing the past and generating the future.

Globalism as emerging world view

14.1 Rapid change in our sense of the world

In a previous section I identified the relatively recent understanding of the world as a finite system to be characteristic of our time. Emphasis on this view is imaginatively expressed by seeing ourselves as passengers on Spaceship Earth. Boulding has described it: "We are now in a long transitional period in which our image of man's relationship to his environment is changing. We are ridding ourselves of the notion that we live on a physical frontier" (Boulding, 1971b). Another way of saying it is that we have come to realize that there remain on earth no more physical frontiers beyond which lie inexhaustible quantities of resources; our frontiers have been shifted to elsewhere in the solar system. This shift inevitably forces us to develop a new sense of this planet and of ourselves. The limits by which we must define have changed.

Forty or so years ago when Tansley (1935), bringing together the ideas of his predecessors, was laying the foundations of modern ecosystem theory, and before the appearance of computers and highly sophisticated telecommunications, we looked out upon the world very differently from the way we do now. In those days Africa, Australia, the Orient, and even America were places remote from Europe, distant from the centrality of Western culture. The geographic cultural centre was still essentially Europe. The rest of the world was known in an intellectual way to exist as parts of the spherical earth, but was unknown as experience, even as the vicarious experience provided today through the electronic mass media. Shortwave radio did not span the Atlantic for popular purposes, and there was no TV or efficient electronic storage (tapes, etc). English school children still unconsciously learned to 'think' around the world by going east through Suez, although Americans already looked around the world both ways—Atlantic and Pacific. With the exception of a handful of specialists nobody thought of the world as an ecosphere, and Spaceship Earth did not exist as a concept.

Today our view is very different. Our understanding of how the life-support system of the world works, our enormous capacity for instantaneous computation and communication, our very rapid physical communication, and our exploration of space beyond the earth are forcing us to see ourselves, our planet, and the nature of things holistically. Together with these impacts there have appeared certain understandings, and fears, about the continuing support of human life. This we have referred to as the world population–food–energy syndrome, but we could also add anxieties about resources, pollution, and the degradation of ecosystems. This emerging consciousness may conveniently be called globalism. Some have also called it planetism. We must presume ourselves to be at the very beginning of understanding what this new consciousness is and what it signifies.

As the life-support system is the basis of the whole global enterprise we should perhaps regard it as the most fundamental aspect about which to ask questions concerning the concept of globalism. In this chapter we shall look at the idea of globalism from the point of view of our areas of interest. The reader requiring a more general statement may like to consult O'Riordan (1976).

14.2 Seeing ourselves in ecosystems

A major feature of our globalism is that we have arrived at the idea of ourselves—human beings—as components of ecosystems. We are learning to think not of human beings *and* nature, or ourselves *and* the environment but of our species *in* nature and as a component of the total system. This changing viewpoint is a direct result of our having reached an understanding of how the life-support system of the world functions along the perspective of knowledge of 'natural' systems.

Grossly simplified, this understanding consists of the following major realizations. The world is built up from a small number of basic components. All matter is essentially composed only of a very few constituent parts such as protons, neutrons, electrons, and subatomic particles. The nature of all living material is controlled by the DNA molecule. On these two extreme economies of key components the intricate complexity of the world is raised. In this sense the world is a manifestation of progressive complexity. As we have seen in figure 1.1, this complexity can be conceptualized as mounting in a hierarchy from atom to biosphere. Each succeeding system is perceived as more complex than the one below it, as capable of performance not achievable lower in the hierarchy, and as having qualities not present in systems located 'below' it. The upper system in any position in the ascending range exists only because of the presence of the lower systems supporting it.

This hierarchy of systems with ascending complexity is seen as the result of change over time—evolution. It has taken a period of time for each system to develop and diffuse its existence around the world. This process is continuing, although change in species (organisms) is extremely slow when measured by the scale of human community history.

It is important to stress the evolution of systems because the development of a system to a present steady state may have taken a very long time. Further, its poise or stability may be comparatively delicate, easy to upset and difficult to reestablish. Loss of steady state might well imply that a very long period of time would have to elapse before the system could again achieve stability or even existence. The Arctic and the Amazon forest are examples of ecosystems in this condition of fragile stability. It is from this emphasis of systems thinking that arise our contemporary fears of what damage we may be doing to the ecosystems of the world and therefore ultimately to the ecosphere itself.

To these understandings has been added the concept of the biosphere. This, as we have seen, is the concept of the envelope of life continuously surrounding the earth. In depth, it is effectively commensurate with the zones or spheres in which oxygen is available.

If we hold these ideas simultaneously in mind we have as an image of the world the picture of a total system (ecosphere or biosphere) existing in a stable but dynamic condition of perpetual decay and renewal. This is Spaceship Earth—a concept which stresses the totality and integrity of the highest system in the hierarchy. The system is driven by the input of energy from the sun, past and contemporary. Supporting the ecosphere are ecosystems which in their turn are basically supported by organisms. Of these organisms human beings have now reached a position of dominance by their ability to reach some understanding of how components of ecosystems are linked and thereby to manipulate them—food production, technology, etc.

Such is our emerging globalism along the perspective of our knowledge of the 'natural' life-support system of the world. It raises certain questions which must now be mentioned.

14.3 Do ecosystems exist?
There is a considerable body of system theory, the approach being common in many disciplines. The validity of the concept of system can be fairly easily confirmed for systems low in the hierarchy. Atoms can be 'sensed' by the electron microscope, and the processes of the living cell can easily be observed. If we move upwards in complexity to the mammal or human body we find subsystems as an almost universal and operationalized concept: respiratory, circulatory, alimentary subsystems are identified. Yet questions put to a variety of medical experts very interestingly showed no unanimity of concept for the system as a whole, for the organism *human being.* Although we may not have a scientific conceptualization of the total individual human system we recognize that it exists because the human individual stands there as an entity before us. When we look at the shadowy concepts conventionally used to describe human groups— society, community, etc—higher in the hierarchy of systems than the individual human being there are even greater difficulties about describing the system, although again definitions of subsystems may be more manageable. This problem of defining the elements of systems is well handled by Krebs (1972, page 556).

Can we apprehend the ecosystem and confirm its existence as easily as we can admit the system 'human being'? The answer is not simple. Some ecosystems, such as a pond or lake, or a laboratory culture, can sustain demonstrations that give effective proof we are dealing with a well-enough-defined entity. The fish in the pond can be changed experimentally and the adjustments of the system measured. Such an experiment is repeatable and will produce the same results if the same conditions are maintained.

Further, we have no difficulty in showing that such small-scale systems can be broken down and their recuperative powers destroyed.

The large-scale ecosystems, such as regions or extensive areas of land or water, which human societies have to manage and of which they are themselves components, are frequently more difficult to define precisely. Experiments in which the totality can be observed are very difficult to mount. Can we say that the ecosystem really exists at this level? The answer is affirmative if we accept the ecologist's own view that the test of the presence of a higher level of integration is that two or more subsystems integrating at a lower level develop an activity or have characteristics which none of the lower-level subsystems could produce alone (Feibleman, 1954: first law of levels of integration). In the case of the human being this is obvious: all the subsystems, working in very close harmony, are required to run a mile. Similarly in large ecosystems we can judge the presence of higher and lower levels of activity by such indicators as the quantity and kinds of biomass produced and sustained, and by the energy flows. If higher levels of integration were not capable of being derived from lower levels, the biomass of the world could not increase and the evolutionary process could never have taken place. System builds on system. Therefore we have support for affirming that large-scale ecosystems, regional in extent, can be viewed as existing entities just as can a cell or a macromolecule, although at times we may have great difficulty in physically delimiting them spatially in detail at the planetary scale of earth[1]. Mapping of the earth's ecosystems in practice proceeds apace, assisted by satellite technology.

In spite of this difficulty of delimitation we can clearly move to the global level and conceptualize the biosphere as a system capable of certain activities, such as ensuring the distribution of the world supply of oxygen, or maintaining the water balance of the world, or controlling the amount of ultraviolet light reaching its surface. These functions would not be achievable at lower levels of system. The behaviour of the component ecosystems functioning in unison is the only way these activities can be performed. We thus have a concept of the biosphere as a total dynamic system capable of producing, maintaining, and increasing a level of global biomass.

A systems approach also appears justified along the perspective of hierarchy within ecosystems themselves. Ecosystems are in varying conditions of maturity. The more mature a system the longer are the

[1] An important criterion of system existence used in science is the level of bond strengths between the entities that hold together the system elements. The strength of the energy bond lessens as the size of the element increases. Thus atoms hold together more strongly than molecules; macromolecules are bonded still more weakly. This may be a very important fact for looking at the relationships between ecosystems (see Pattee, 1973, page 9ff). Some edges of ecosystems can be easily defined, for example the southern limit of the Canadian Shield is an edge.

food chains. The less mature, the shorter are the circuits of circulation of minerals, gases, water, etc. The more mature an ecosystem, the lower its net productivity of new biomass but the higher its consumption of energy for maintaining the level of steady state it has attained. The relationships between productivity, energy consumption, and level of steady state provide evidence of analysis based on systemic concepts being a credible reflection of the reality. (It may be added that the important principle of this paragraph—that net productivity falls and energy consumption increases as maturity or the length of food chains increases—is of great importance for the production of biomass circuited to the human species: food and other living material used by human beings.)

For a long time in history human beings lived in such small concentrations and had so weak a power to deflect the energy flows of ecosystems permanently that there was no threat to the global life-support system as a whole. By Roman times the species had spread so considerably and had developed such powerful techniques that in several parts of the world its numbers and activities were causing localized damage. Changes were induced in some ecosystems that have not even yet been reversed and may be forever irreversible. The basin of the Mediterranean is a frequently cited example. Its flora and fauna underwent permanent and massive change between the time Achilles and Agamemnon burnt the seventh city of Troy (1184 BC) and Constantine declared Christianity the official religion of the empire (313 AD). The chief material cause was the large increase in the number of human beings with concomitant increase in energy drawn off for human use as food and fuel. The improvement and application of technique and technology were doubtless a secondary but very closely related cause since increase in numbers tends to force human populations to improve their techniques for winning ever more human-usable biomass. At this stage, however, ecosystemically speaking the damage to the global system was only local and not very dangerous.

It is a giant step to our own time. We now are four billion in numbers and possess knowledge that gives us use even of the basic stuff of the universe. Further, we have accumulated enormous wealth so that we can finance many activities at scales hitherto unimagined. Today the effluents from about four hundred million population flow into the Mediterranean—a little less than the estimated population of the entire world in Shakespeare's time.

By our numbers and activities we may therefore be a potentially serious threat to the continuation of the biosphere at its present level of stability and productivity. If so, we are a potential threat to ourselves. Such an image of ourselves has become common intellectual property in the last few years, and is now slowly beginning to influence action. It is not yet, however, lodged deeply in our consciousness.

The biosphere and its constituent ecosystems are now known to rely on energy flows. The energy input is essentially the radiation which daily falls on to earth from the sun through the visible region and adjacent frequencies of the electromagnetic spectrum. In the temperate zone this energy is between 3000 and 4000 kilocalories per square metre per day. We also draw on the results of past photosynthesis to supplement this daily flow—oil, coal, natural gas. Energy circulates, thus producing change in systems and their constituent parts. Some energy escapes as heat and cannot be recaptured. We can therefore comprehend the globe and the ecosystems in terms of energetics—the transfer of energy circulating around systems and through organisms much as money does in the socio-economy. Energy is provided from outside and the world does 'work' with it (see Phillipson, 1966).

Incomplete as our knowledge is about many of the details of the life system of planet Earth, there seems reasonable evidence to support the view that systemic conceptualizations are effective for delivering knowledge of the processes of life, and may very likely provide a working view of the reality—of the 'logic' or 'rationality' that holds the whole together.

14.4 Global stability threatened by human numbers and activities
Biologists consider 'nature' to be self-regenerating. If 'damaging' effects cease there occurs a process of return to the predamage status provided there has not been a too great departure from the condition of stability. Thus a lake polluted by mercury may clean itself, if no more pollutant is added, by seepage, evaporation, and flow of water through it. Ecosystems may, however, be pushed too far off their positions of stable state and may not be able to recuperate. Or, the 'damaging' effects may be continuous so that the process of degradation is reinforced. When such a situation is perceived we have now learned that purposeful action to slow or halt the process of decline is required, and can be effective.

Realization of this is a component of the notion that human beings are able consciously to shape the future. Contemporary preoccupation with this idea takes a variety of forms. We have quickly generated many kinds of planning. We find cultural diagnostic statements such as McLuhan's: "We must invent a new metaphor, restructure our thoughts and feelings" (McLuhan, 1970, page 14). There are historical interpretations of our cultural development, such as Childe's (1951) *Man Makes Himself*, which fit this perspective. There is the concept of the individual being largely responsible for creating his own personality (for example, May, 1967). Existentialism stresses this assumed freedom of human beings to shape themselves and their future. And there are the familiar plans for physical and socioeconomic development typical of our century. Perhaps most significant of all are those 'planning' efforts which are directed at structuring ecosystems for human benefit, such as we have looked at in chapter 6. These attempt to design the system specifically to sustain the human species, but they keep within the rules of ecosystem stability. Intermediate are those like *Blueprint for Survival* (*The Ecologist*, 1972) that imply an ecological global assumption.

Out of this way of perceiving our human situation a moral or ethical issue of our future emerges. How do we learn to behave as individuals, as communities, and as a single global community so that we preserve the life-support system which is the basis of life for all? Whatever cut we choose between the purveyors of gloom and doom and the more optimistic others (danger-not-proved, will-last-my-time, we-are-beginning-to-change attitudes and the techfixers) the ethical or moral issue still confronts us, because, like Adam and Eve, we now *know*. We have learned how the biosphere works and that it can be irreparably damaged. Knowing how it works, we have to learn to intervene in its processes with the hope of obtaining predictably benign results. We are forced to intervene by the need to eat. *Thus we are in a new moral situation in regard to how we act toward the earth. While no longer able to see ourselves as the centre of things in the old way, we now do have the opportunity to perceive ourselves in the key role of saving ourselves. This implies the need to generate a new morality, basically a new behaviour toward the globe but also inevitably one that involves changes in the relationships between human beings.*

Realization of this need for new rules governing action toward ecosystems is very widely diffused through the literature of ecology. Many ecologists have expressed their strong ethical concern. Simpson (1964), Potter (1971), H T Odum (1971), Hardin (1968), Falk (1972), and Commoner (1972) are well-known examples. Some writers, such as H T Odum and Potter, devote attention to developing the details of the required rules. Governments increasingly attempt to regulate behaviour through the coercive powers of the state in efforts to control pollution, conserve energy, etc. These are direct responses to our understanding of our dependency on the life processes of Spaceship Earth—a kind of globalism of life itself.

Our globalism along the ecologic perspective is also inclusive of our perception of the population–food problem. Particularly during the early years of this decade sensitivity to the effects of the growth of world population and the condition of the food supply came to have a global dimension. By now we have a clear perception of the trends in food supply and demand, and of the relationship between them and the condition of the world's ecosystems. A global condition of food scarcity is emerging at the same time that ecosystem degradation (for example in the Sahel region of Africa) makes itself visible. Realization of the two factors is simultaneously forced upon us, compelling a globalization of our thinking. Lester Brown uses the phrase "ecological undermining of food systems" to express this fact (L R Brown and Eckholm, 1974). We have the most urgent of reasons for learning how to act so that our life-support system is maintained adequately stable at the global level—the threat of hunger and the degradation of community that this produces. Such approach as we have to this challenge at present is comprised in the idea of planning.

14.5 Globalism of the telecommunications-computer technology
The virtual instantaneity of electronic communication around the globe,
the enormous range of the equipment—out beyond the limits of our sola
system and even its galaxy—and the universalization of the mode of
transmission by digitization have contributed a special sense of the
oneness or unity of the globe as a subsystem of a yet greater system.

Along one perspective the perception is that the 'great globe' of Prospero
has been shrunk down to McLuhan's 'global village' (McLuhan, 1969).
The sense is of a telescoping of terrestrial space and of a loosening of the
bonds of time as we have previously known it. We are aware that our
technology has reduced the apparent size of the world because all parts c
it are in immediate informational contact. This awareness is, however, at
present probably predominantly intellectual rather than emotional in
emphasis. It is reinforced by the space technology which allows us to
view our world from 'out there'. This technology is heavily dependent o
the electronic technology.

Business, governments, news media, and entertainment interests have
quickly seized upon and developed certain of the global capabilities of th
electronic technology for their own purposes. Transnational firms are
largely dependent on it; governments have hot lines connecting them;
audio-video intercontinental interviews have become standard news items
in telecasts; the entertainment industry is able to move material in real c
delayed time across the world with great ease. This image of being one
world, electronically held together, is further enhanced by the video
material obtained by satellites and spacecraft showing our globe, seen fro
'outside', as it moves through space. Certain technical developments, suc
as the extensive operationalizing of universal shared public packet-switchin
networks already described, will give a further massive stimulus to this
practical side of globalization.

So far, we have substantially only these two approaches—the
imaginative and somewhat literary appreciation of the meaning of the ne\
communications capability in terms of our sensibility, and the practical
day-to-day exploitation of the capabilities for obvious purposes. A third
line of thinking does exist but as yet it is in no way global in emphasis.
This is that body of writing which examines the immediate effects of
applying the technology to present society, and speculates about the
future in that context. A good example of this approach is the work of
Martin (1969; 1971). As we have seen, he, and many others, proceed by
examining how a part of the technology is likely to develop and then
suggesting how a particular society will change its behaviour and institutio
as it makes use of the new opportunities, both by adapting and by exploitin

A global aspect of the technology does, however, appear in the working
of those international bodies which act as vehicles for regulatory agreemen
between nations. The agreements basically have to do with such matters
as allocating the available spectrum resources and developing protocols fo

using the technology. Examples are the World Administrative Telephone and Telegraph Conference, the International Telecommunication Union, and the United Nations. Such organizations enforce a kind of global thinking with regard to resource sharing and the behaviour of nations and individuals in the interest of obtaining the best performance for everyone. The field of electronic communications has a history of quiet success in fostering this kind of global responsibility. We have already seen the speed and efficiency with which the X.25 protocol for packet-switching was agreed to in March 1976 (see section 4.3).

Electronic globalism, perhaps because it is based on a very rapidly expanding and robust technology, has not yet produced any awareness of danger as has the globalism of ecology, except perhaps with regard to such things as space platforms from which to launch attack. Yet we might be justified in suspecting that comparable dangers may be emergent, particularly as universal packet-switching networks will be fully operational in the developed countries by the end of the 1970s. Transnational corporations will obviously be able to outwit national governments. Electronic capability can be used as easily by the criminal, whether individual or national, as by the law-abiding. The emergence of new power relations is inevitable. Obviously the threat of electronic control of armaments together with the exploitation of atomic technology is a global matter.

Such possibilities have received some attention, but generally along the perspective of power play or of scenarios of the coming world (for example Heilbroner, 1974). The literature of the technology itself does not exhibit very much interest in developing new standards of behaviour or a new ethic, as does the literature of ecology. Rather, the ethical question at the global level has been left to peace movements and individual thinkers such as Russell (for example 1968), and has been substantially confined to focussing attention on the destructive capability of atomic armaments. The ethical questions that may be emerging at the global level because of our greatly enhanced informational capability have hardly yet been probed.

Light may be shed on this matter by posing a question inherent in the material of some of our examples. What kind of global behaviour will be nececessary in a world in which the rich and well-developed nations reach a new level of wealth as they become 'informational societies', and the less-developed nations still have to struggle for bare physical existence? The likely importance of this question is already emerging. The rich nations appear to be getting richer and the poor, poorer. The ethical requirement needed to deal with this is connected with the ethical requirement put forward by the ecologists but would not appear to be identical.

14.6 Information and ecosystems

The globalism which depends on the ecological perspective and that which is arrived at through our telecommunications–computer technology appear only fortuitously linked. What linkage exists is at present observable in

the use of the technology for providing information about ecosystem
conditions. As we have seen, examples are to be found in techniques
using satellites—the World Weather Watch, LANDSAT, the Worldwatch
Institute, etc. Such agencies, however, merely employ the technology to
perform their functions of monitoring weather, crops, shoals of fish, etc
and gathering surface and subsurface information about the earth. They
do not attempt to explore the relationship between ecosystems and
information in any sophisticated way. Perhaps the nearest we have to a
unified approach are operational proposals such as Kupperman's use of th
technology for handling ecological crisis conditions coupled with comput
conferencing (see Kupperman et al, 1975; Beer, 1974b; and *The Futuris*
1975; also chapter 7).

Perhaps a reason for the two areas of knowledge and practice not
having been brought together formally is that ecological knowledge is not
yet widely applied while electronic applications are universal, at least in
the developed countries. Fairly recently ecologists have begun to look at
cities in terms of energetics (H T Odum, 1971; Jamison and Friedman,
1974). This is the beginning of understanding cities as ecosystems in
which human beings are heavily the dominant species. We may look
forward to great improvement in our knowledge of cities along this
perspective. As urbanization is now a globally distributed phenomenon
and all urban places around the world are in virtually instantaneous
electronic contact with each other, this improvement in our knowledge is
urgently required.

Important as energy flows are as a key to understanding the processes
of mass populations, it is obvious that human settlements hold together
also through their reliance on information. It is information which make
prediction and successful action possible, particularly for self-conscious
human beings who must now rely heavily on the power of the discursive
reason. We have exchanged the unreflecting and instant operation of our
human biocomputers for the capacity to discover and amass very large
quantities of information by highly organized self-conscious techniques.
The result is a staggeringly successful control over certain aspects of the
world. This mass of information, stored in libraries, etc, is now potentiall
universally available, virtually instantaneously on demand. Knowledge ha
become global.

The notion of looking at the human settlement as information handler
was broached, well over a decade ago, by R L Meier (1962). We still,
however, have only fragmented knowledge of information in the city and
although some of this knowledge is detailed, it is not consolidated. Further
most of it remains raw data revealing next to nothing about relationships.
We know little about urban information flows. Urban and regional
information systems (URIS; see DRCG, 1970; 1971) are being set up, but
until extensive data are banked, processed, and analyzed these systems wi
deliver nothing more than information useful only for ad hoc purposes.

There are differences between information as handled by the electronic technology and as functioning in the ecosystem. As we have suggested in the previous chapter, these differences need study. In the ecosystem, information appears much closer to the concept of energy than in the 'human' system. The 'difference that makes a difference' may be satisfactory at a basic level of conceptualization but may require different developments of thinking in detail. This may be very important if we stabilize socioeconomies, because stabilization will involve quantitative stabilization, if not reduction, of energy flows through socioeconomies. Quantitative energy flow in an ecosystem is a measure of productivity. This is not necessarily true of 'human' systems. *Therefore very careful conceptualization will be necessary and caution will be in order with regard to the transfer of concepts from one system to another.* In 'human' systems, or subsystems of the ecosphere, energy flows and information flows are very clearly connected at global level—we move oil across the world in response to market information—but they must be kept clearly identified as separate entities, at least until we have a better understanding of just what information is in both 'natural' and 'human' systems.

The electronic technology operating instantaneously and at global scale, together with other technologies, certainly brings an entirely new level of information or knowledge to the working of ecosystems. The application of new information into an ecosystem may initiate changes in the system just as much as may an alteration in the energy flows. Specifically, human information can be passed very quickly from one ecosystem to another or within an ecosystem. One type of crop may be abandoned and another concentrated upon. Human information about energy resources from the past working of ecosystems (coal, oil, gas) is very important because of its application to the contemporary working of ecosystems. By means of such information an ecosystem can be held at a level of development most efficient for producing food for human beings. This growth of information and its effects now ramify through all the ecosystems of the world, even the polar regions, and into the biosphere as a whole. Here we can glimpse some notion of the now close relationship between information and the global life-support system.

A tentative suggestion of why there is only a poor linkage between ecological research and information studies is that ecologists and others have not paid any great attention to the role of 'mind' in connection with ecosystems. Bateson (1972) and McCulloch (1965) are examples of researchers who have extensively explored the ecological concept of 'mind' and have conceived it in systemic terms. 'Mind' is a product of, and component of, ecosystems, however it may be defined. Much is now known about the brain and nervous system as a result of the development of cybernetics. On this modern epistemology considerably depends. Whatever 'mind' is, because of the global distribution of human beings, the accumulation of information to present levels, and our computational–

communicational capabilities, it is to be seen as global in scope. This new
realization is conceptualized in the word *noosphere*. This signifies the
continuous envelope of 'mind' around the world, a concept closely
associated with the thinking of Teilhard de Chardin. To this I shall return
later, and offer some suggestions for further conceptualization (chapter 19

A further important feature of informational globalism is in the general
diffusion of current 'information', such as news, entertainment items,
attitudes, values, fears. The electronic technology has enormously increased
the quantity, quality, and speed and extent of diffusion of this kind of
knowledge. An effect is a tendency toward universalization of something
we might call the global cultural background. This diffusion must
contribute considerably to creating the foundations of a worldwide cultur
consisting of universally distributed values, assumptions, attitudes of mind
etc. No doubt other technologies do this also—a Chinese air pilot and an
American ground-control officer must think the same in relation to the
task of landing an aircraft. Nevertheless the electronic technology is
particularly significant in this question of generating a kind of global base
culture because universality is implied not only in using the technology
but also in the material it carries. This points to something again connected
with behaviour and therefore reinforces the indications which stress the
importance of the individual's behaviour patterns. Although this links up
with the concern for an ecological ethic it also suggests that the possibilit
of the development of such an ethic can hardly be considered without regar
to the base culture being universalized through the electronic technology.

In the next part of this book I shall attempt to develop some concepts
which may help to being the ecosystemic and informational studies closer
together.

14.7 Relation to socioeconomies
One further facet must be acknowledged in relation to ecological and
informational globalism. This is the socioeconomic–political perspective.
In these aspects it is generally observed that the world has become smaller
and the nations more closely involved with each other. Our concern here
is not so much this shrinking of the earth in human relationships as the
fact that our ecological, informational, and socioeconomic–political
perspectives are not in accord. That we cannot comprehend the natural
world through our present socioeconomic–political perspectives should be
obvious, although the view is still often held that all we have to do is to
reconstruct society. If our ecological understanding of the world life-
support system is correct, then our socioeconomic–political thought and
action will have to be brought to a minimum condition of at least not
contradicting it. At the global level it is not very difficult to see that suc
a concept needs to be reached imaginatively. Operationally, however, at
lower levels—ecosystems and communities—it is much harder to visualize
and harder still to arrive at in right action.

We are, however, witnessing some reflection of the environmental concern into the pronouncements and decisions of governments. Legislation dealing with pollution is becoming more common and bureaucracies are being restructured to acknowledge the environment as a recognized focus of governmental attention. The emerging governmental departments frequently have no executive resources or powers. Their function is usually to coordinate, advise, monitor, etc. They concern themselves with policy formation, environmental impact assessment, information gathering, and conceptual matters.

At about the same time government departments of energy or energy and resources, technology, culture and technology have made their appearance. This emergence may be an indication of changing emphases and may be some recognition of the importance of interrelatedness between the traditional institutionalized foci of attention conventionally allocated to departments of government.

A global socioeconomy of humankind which degrades the ecosphere through damaging individual ecosystems can be seen only as a global menace. It is no use pretending that at present we understand the problem of how to relate the human activity of socioeconomies to the stability and productivity requirements of the biosphere. We can only stress the potential global danger of the processes of socioeconomies being of such a kind that they may seriously impair this basic stability and productivity.

As a general observation, it appears that the telecommunications–computer technology operates more within the workings of the world's socioeconomies than within the workings of the ecosystems. Quantitatively, the great preponderance of the use of the technology is commercial–industrial–financial. The effect is that short-term ecosystem productive capacity can easily be exploited at the price of long-term stability. Here we see starkly the friction between the interest of the socioeconomies as at present functioning and the life-support interest of the ecosystems. This brings us back again to the matter of behaviour. *How to ensure that our vastly improved informational capabilities do not accelerate the process of degradation in ecosystems becomes a very major question.* We shall return to the problem of how to ensure that the individual behaves as a component—as individual and in aggregate—of the ecosystem as well as of the socioeconomic system. This we must do in ways that will ensure the adequate continuance of the life-support processes of the world. *This is nothing less than the age-old problem of reconciling the actions of the individual with the continuity needs of the community. But now it is raised to a global scale.*

As here we are concerned with socioeconomies in relation to the telecommunications–computer technology and ecological knowledge, we need to raise a question implied in the previous paragraph. It is to ask whether existing socioeconomies, of whatever political colour, use the electronic technology in ways which accelerate the progress toward instability and degradation in global ecosystems. *Mostly controlled and used by governments, industrial–commercial, and military establishments having national and transnational interests, is the technology being applied to conserve an outdated and no longer viable world view in the minds and behaviour patterns of mass populations? We have to consider whether this constitutes a major flaw in our emerging globalism.*

Some analysts, for example Beer (1974b), think that it clearly does. Beer, in common with Wiener (1967), Vickers (1970), F H George (1970b) and many others, holds that society is viewed most illuminatingly in systemic terms with the help of cybernetics. He stresses that we need much better models of the socioeconomy than those we currently use and emphasizes that they must be dynamic and not static simulations. This means working on a basis of continuous change, much after the method suggested by Kupperman et al (1975). The essence is dynamic variety. Beer's view is that far from developing the use of technology to create new institutions to meet our new situation we are using it to reinforce the old (Beer, 1974b, page 35ff). *If correct, this means that far from moving toward a more realistic coping with our emerging global situation through the application of the electronic technology we are simply tending to strengthen through our present socioeconomic behaviour the very processes we need to modify or eliminate.*

Beer's solution—the 'right' use of science—has in the end the same deficiency as solutions by ecologists and others. As we have noted, this is the omission of consideration of the *motivation* to behave 'as appropriate' for the health of the system. Beer's last words are exhortation: "And let us use that acquired and ordered knowledge: science" (page 100). As we shall see, his fellow Massey lecturer, George Steiner (1974), shows that exhortation is not enough.

14.8 Conceptualizing the global system

Since an awareness of the finiteness of our life-support system began to penetrate our consciousness during the postwar period there has appeared a lively interest in looking scientifically at what is usually described as the world or global system. Observation of certain trends which are cause for alarm, availability of certain data at global scales, and increasing sensitivity to the whole question of futures are among the motivators of this kind of global approach. The 'shrinking' of the globe through rapid physical communications and virtually instantaneous electronic communications has played its part. The electronic computational capacity that we now command has also been a stimulus because it has allowed hitherto unmanageable calculations to be done with ease, and great speed, thus making mathematical models simulating global activities feasible and useful.

Work on global models has increased since the early 1970s when *The Limits to Growth* (Meadows et al, 1972) made the initial impact.

It was followed by Mesarovic and Pestel (1974). Since then the field has broadened and comparative studies of global models have become possible (for example Clark and Cole, 1975). Such models seek to know the world and to influence policies of management. Among other results, they help to structure discussion and do themselves contribute to our consciousness of the globe as a single system, whether in emphasis they are ecological (and biospherical), technological, socioeconomic–political, normative, cultural, or mixtures of these approaches. Their very emergence is an indication of our realization of a need to think globally.

The Limits to Growth model simulated a single global system whose projections could be varied by changing inputs. The standard run, which assumed the continuance of present trends, showed that world resources would be virtually used up by 2100 AD. The Mesarovic model divided the world into ten large regions interacting with each other. This simulation led also to final breakdown plus increasing tension between the haves and the have-nots—the North–South conflict. These models do not predict the future. They do, however, allow the interaction of certain variables, within certain predetermined contexts, to be examined. The degrees of their approximation to reality are not known and indeed may never be known. The capacity of the human brain is finite; a maximum of about 10^{10} neurons prescribes a limit to what can be comprehended. We do not know to what degree the comprehension of the total world system may be beyond our understanding.

The development of models of the global system naturally leads to incipient global planning. For example, consideration of the global significance of the socioeconomic difference between the developed and the developing nations is becoming more detailed and specific. Tinbergen suggests the creation of a world treasury, global agencies to manage supplies of resources, food, etc, and an oceans management body (Tinbergen et al, 1976). Leontief thinks that our global limitations are not so much physical as institutional, especially in the developing countries (Leontief et al, 1977). He calls for major change in the world economic order. Like Beer, he appears to advocate that the technology be used to make the informational base of decisionmaking more up-to-date. The aim of Leontief's proposals is to halve the gap between the developed and the developing countries by 2000 AD. The technique is to double and treble land productivity. Leontief is a good deal more optimistic than many analysts and planners would care to be, and reservations have to be made about whether his approach is not precisely the preservation and reinforcement of the old order that Beer deplores.

As Leontief's is the most recent of the world-system models, it will be useful to look a little more closely at it. Sponsored by the United Nations, it attempts to produce results which will agree with the UN major resolutions and policies on future global development, generally encompassed under the International Development Strategy (United Nations, 1970).

This strategy aims at arresting deterioration in the environment while vigorously pursuing economic and social development, particularly in the developing countires. The basic problem addressed is whether growth has to be modified for reasons of environmental pollution. The concept is that of finding out how growth can be increased while still keeping the costs of 'pollution abatement' at acceptable levels.

On the basis of this perception of the task, an input–output model of the international order is constructed to show the world economy as in 1980, 1990, and 2000 in comparison with the base year 1970. The world economy is described in fifteen regions and forty-five economic sectors. The model allows interrelationships to be worked through for imports– exports, capital flows, aid transfer and foreign interest payments, changes in technologies, costs of production and prices, environmental pollution abatement policies, constraints on minerals, and the production of food.

After discarding other scenarios for development to the year 2000, the goal selected was "... to reduce, roughly by half, the income gap between the developing and the developed countries by the year 2000, with a view towards closing the income gap completely by the middle of the next century" (Leontief et al, 1977, page 3). Assuming a declining growth rate in the developed countries, the model showed an increase in average per capita gross product, ranging from two and one-half times to four times in the developing countries would be required from 1970 to 2000. These figures assume a world population increase of 60% in the period.

The conditions required to meet the overall goal are considered to include a very substantial increase in food production, especially by the developing countries, assurance of supplies of minerals, ability to meet the costs of pollution abatement, heavy increase in investment and industrialization, and development of world trade with substantial increase in the share of the developing nations. The changes required are seen as amounting to a "new world economic order".

The expectation of being able to increase very considerably the world food supply is based on the statement that further "fairly large reserves" of arable land can be brought under cultivation. Supposing that to be a reasonable statement—it is by no means clear that it is—the productivity of agriculture in the developing countries would also have to be trebled to achieve the required 5% annual increase in output by 2000. After claiming the technical feasibility of his food production statements Leontief has to stress that "social and institutional" reform will, to a large extent, be the basis of success.

The only other condition of growth to be mentioned in any detail here will be that of 'pollution abatement'. Under this condition comes the whole approach to the relationship between the behaviour of socioeconomies and the life-support system. The idea of the study in this regard is restricted to the perception of increased human activity causing increased environmental pollution. However, by spending money this can be cleaned up.

The question of importance is seen as: at what cost? Some regions (those with under $700 per capita gross product) will not require any abatement. Where abatement in developing countries is necessary, it is estimated as not likely to exceed 1% of the gross product. Pollution is concluded to be a "technologically manageable problem", and therefore does not "... pose an unsurmountable barrier for accelerated development along the lines considered in the study".

In summary the Leontief analysis accepts the need for accelerated growth and therefore sees as necessary: (1) "... far-reaching internal changes of a social, political and institutional character in the developing countries", and (2) "... significant changes in the world economic order" (Leontief et al, 1977, page 11).

This study demonstrates neatly part of the gap that exists between economic global thinking and modelling and ecological globalism with its fundamental concept of the biosphere as a living system. To the ecologist many activities not considered polluting may be ecosystemically dangerous (for example, monoculture, intensification of chemical energy throughput). Viability of ecosystems, especially when they are held in their highly productive phases, for producing human-usable biomass, is by no means guaranteed by simply paying to 'clean up' pollution. Ecologically speaking, such an approach is so wide of the reality as to be ludicrous.

We now appear to be entering a phase in which we struggle first to make the models simulate reality more exactly, and second to criticize them and their outputs more stringently, with a view to understanding better how the global system operates and to formulating more realistic proposals. The thinking of Laszlo (Laszlo et al, 1977) belongs to this new phase.

His attention is given not so much to socioeconomic matters—although these are not neglected—but to the values and the cultural conditions of populations which underpin the socioeconomies. The concern is to study the goals that global society needs to develop. He criticizes some of the proposals I have mentioned as unrealistic; he thinks populations would not bear with them. Why should the economic order agree to stabilization? Why should individuals limit the number of their children? What, asks Laszlo, can we conceive as motivations for behaving for the global good? He mentions that Meadows et al found missing any long-term global goal for mankind and the will to reach it; and that Mesarovic calls for a new ethic with regard to the use of resources. Laszlo concludes that in order to achieve the necessary motivation we need a new concept of human freedom, a new concept of national purpose, and a sense of the nation being a component of the global system of human societies. We further need a new concept of personal happiness which allows the individual to experience the satisfaction of his own needs without impairing that same ability for others. Such changes, he thinks, would constitute a "transmutation of present cultures".

He hopes that such transmutation could be achieved by: extension of
the sense of brotherhood to the whole human family, the harmonizing of
present or potentially conflicting values as between the various nations,
and the promotion of humanism as a philosophical stance. The basic idea
is that cultures are mutable and that therefore we need to foster "desirable
mutations". Operationally this is seen as calling for: detailed study of
the operational effects of present cultures, identification of elements
favouring and disfavouring the desired mutations, and broad popular
discussion on needs and potentials for transmutations in cultures. Laszlo
agrees with Beer that, at present, counterfunctional elements dominate
most cultures. Future cultures must be indigenous, must spring from the
people, but they must be globally responsible. Their values must come
from within themselves, and not be imposed from outside[2].

It needs to be added that the present thrust of thinking towards a new
world order appears to come most strongly from those areas of thought
which deal with the socioeconomic–political aspects of the human
enterprise, for example Tinbergen et al (1976) and Laszlo et al (1977).
Characteristically these approaches pay only the most sketchy attention to
the all important matter of maintaining the viability of the life-support
system, even though they may go into detail about the need to increase
food production and improve its distribution. They miss the two key
items of the emerging globalism represented by our ecological knowledge
and the operational fact of our electronic capability.

In looking at these three major perspectives of globalism—as in
ecosystem thought and practice, in the practice and application of the
telecommunications technology, and in the relationships of these to socioeconomies—there repeatedly emerges an element of fear connected with
human behaviour. The cybernetic concept of socioeconomies implies that
a major role is played by the values and attitudes held by the individuals
comprising our mass populations. Right action by our species with regard
to the life-support system will be extensively dependent on the values and
attitudes entertained by the individual. I shall examine various views of
the values and attitudes of the mass individual in chapters 16 and 17.

----

[2] For analysis of world models see Clark and Cole (1975). Laszlo estimates that
there are now about a dozen useful quantitative world models and normative futures
scenarios. These include the work of the Institute for World Order, the Fundacion
Bariloche, the Policy Research Center of the Stanford Research Institute, the Hudson
Institute, the International Labour Office, as well as studies sponsored by the Club of
Rome (Meadows et al, 1972; Mesarovic and Pestel, 1974, Tinbergen et al, 1976;
Laszlo et al, 1977). It also ought to be mentioned that operationally and organizationally
we are at the stage where research may be internationally organized. The Stockholm-
based International Federation of Institutes of Advanced Study would appear capable
of this role, as would the International Institute for Applied Systems Analysis in Austria.

15

Technologists and fellow travellers

15.1 Technology and technique
The great material success of technology over the last two hundred or so years has endowed it with a justification appearing self-evident. Our high level of physical well-being in the Western world is dependent on it. It is therefore a major perspective along which to look at our two foci of attention. Some, for example Ellul (1964), think that technology and the techniques of all kinds which it spawns are the dominants of our culture. Others would see the technological manifestation as essentially a product of capitalism. For our present purpose there is little need to attribute dependency. In any case this is very difficult to do with precision since over the last two centuries the relationships between science, technology, and entrepreneurial effort have changed radically. What concerns us here is simply to point out some of the ways in which technology is useful as a context for thinking about our electronic capability and our ecological situation.

Following Ellul, I will consider technology to include technique. Such techniques as the organization of labour in primitive agriculture or the working out of electronic network protocols in our own day are therefore essentially seen as technology. It must also be added, however, that the strict hardware of our time—the actual pieces of equipment—play an enormously important role in society simply because of the magnitude of their capabilities. The computer—the hardware—is clearly more basic than the techniques for using it. This emphasis was not always dominant. Some technological offerings, for example the wheel, have been simple and their techniques of use more important than the hardware.

15.2 Approaches of the technologists and entrepreneurs
In general the approaches of those with the technical and promotional knowledge and expertise are more direct than those who write from the standpoint of the humanities. A reason for this is perhaps that the technologists are chiefly concerned with practical action. The technologist must make something work as a reliable piece of equipment. He frequently has to translate an item of scientific knowledge into an item of practical use. The usefulness is generally perceived as self-evident; the new application will either do something better than before, or allow something new to be done. As these two possibilities most likely offer opportunities for profit, they will attract entrepreneurial attention in our culture and will be only very cursorily examined from any other standpoint. We have a cultural willingness toward technological development, which is a kind of bias or favoured condition of our time. Such appears to be the nature of capitalism. The failure of Hellenistic society to generate a technology based on its considerable scientific knowledge serves as a useful contrast

to our 'successful' tying together of science, technology, and entrepreneuria
initiative.

Like the scientist, the technologist must think in terms of mastery. Th
scientist masters, usually in part only, some unknown. The technologist
must master the unknowns of actual performance. Thus, the scientist
Hertz demonstrated that radio waves were of the same nature as light, bu
it took the technological application of the earthed antenna as a guess by
Marconi to make radio waves accessible in practical use for sending messages
over long distances. Such mastery breeds confidence since success is highly
visible. The technologist therefore must look out upon the world with a
perspective of confidence based on mastery-success. Although Leonardo
da Vinci may fear that human beings will put his invention to evil uses
and decline to make it known, this mastery-success has its own dynamic,
usually driving toward general diffusion of the capability developed.

A questioning along this perspective is beginning to appear, but perhaps
more obviously in science itself than in technology. We are beginning to
debate whether there are explorations from which science should refrain,
particularly in biology, for fear that experiment might get out of hand an
do irreversible damage in the world. In C P Snow's (1954) *The New Men*
it was the scientists who raised the moral question of whether the new
atomic knowledge should be technologized to make the bomb. The
engineers got on with the job.

It is obvious that from a certain perspective the technologists have a
background of sustained and enormous success as far as their inventions
and applications are concerned. The technologist also appears to have
support for a confident future as long as Western culture can maintain an
ongoing process of scientific exploration on which new technology can be
raised. Without such a continuously growing base of science, technology
would stagnate—a future which, it has been suggested, might be America's

The sense of confidence of the technologists is felt best as an underlying
tone in their writings rather than as specific detail of statement. Martin
(1971, page 13) writes: "Although he might possibly have realized that
they were conceivable in theory, a reasonable forecaster in 1940 would
not have predicted the computer; in 1945 he would not have predicted th
transistor; in 1950 he would not have predicted the laser; in 1955 he would
not have predicted the use of pulse code modulation, large-scale integration
solid state switching, computer time-sharing, on-line real-time systems in
commerce, direct-access data banks or synchronous communication
satellites; in 1960 he would not have predicted holography ... . Today's
computers would have been quite inconceivable in 1940. The idea would
have been laughed at as the wildest fantasy. Yet within two decades the
data processing industry in the United States is likely to exceed the Gross
National Product of 1940. The rate of developing new technology is
increasing constantly. We can expect the number of technological surprise

in the two decades ahead to be greater than the number in the past two decades". The underlying confidence is unmistakable.

Nothing succeeds like past success for moving confidently into the future. The tone of confidence often appears justified. But it is fully justified only within technology itself. It is now guessed that it is a mistake, and very possibly dangerous, to carry this sense of justification, unexamined, out into the society and the culture. This is the message of the humanities writers. We are no longer Victorians. No longer can we see technological progress and improvement in human well-being and behaviour necessarily as the same thing. And yet we have the mounting pressure of human numbers. How else can very large human populations be maintained than by the further application of knowledge, that is, by yet more technology?

The importance of the entrepreneur to the development of technology does not appear to have received adequate attention. Yet an examination of the dynamics suggests that the energy with which we exploit a piece of technology for the market is an indispensable component of our use of science. Marconi is an example of the two functions in the one individual. He made technological improvements while simultaneously floating companies which, of course, aimed at commercial success. The operations of companies such as Bell Canada have shown the same mix over several decades. Examples of entrepreneurs taking up independently produced inventions must be myriad. The thrust of the technology and the drive of the entrepreneurial activity towards commercial success fit well together, and both are strongly entrenched in our society and culture.

The full component is, however, perhaps most usefully seen as essentially tripartite: science, technology, and entrepreneurial initiative. All three are confident, with a confidence based on past success. They move into the future hopefully. They do not waste psychic energy regretting a lost civility or expulsion from Eden. Instead, they tend still to see the golden age in front of them. They are often as millenial as Marx, and—a claim not unjustified—they point to their success in providing *now* some of the hardware of paradise.

15.3 Fellow travellers of the technologists

Purest-of-the-pure technologists are now perhaps comparatively rare, or are anyway somewhat quietened by the spirit of the times. Certainly the techfixers are not now accepted as unquestioningly as once they were. We therefore find a body of thought, writing, and action which, while it is within the ambience of technology–entrepreneurship, is also looking closely at technology in the context of society. The phrases 'social impact', 'environmental impact', and 'technological impact' are common in this context. In this group we find very considerable attention paid both to the direct exploiting of technologies for sociocultural improvement and to trying to visualize what kind of a society we may be moving into.

Both types are supported by the futures thinking of the technological forecasters (for example Wills et al, 1972).

Of the first type we might instance the experiments in the application: of the telecommunications and computer technology proposed by the (American) National Academy of Engineering (1971). The idea was very simple: all sorts of functions of society could be performed more effective than at present by applying the technology: education, law enforcement city management, air pollution monitoring, transit information service, public housing and institution security, automatic vehicle monitoring, etc Therefore all that is basically necessary is to find out in detail how to proceed to apply the new technology immediately to the existing condition

This approach is very important because of the inbuilt tendency of the society to exploit the potential of all technology: a present function can be performed more efficiently, or more effectively, or a new function can be introduced. *This may appear to be entirely satisfactory until it is realized that the effects of applying the technology may totally revolution the function.*

The developed societies of the world steadily move all the time in the direction of applying new knowledge and technology to their existing conditions and functions without any very careful prior investigation of the full effects. The strong entrepreneurial thrust within our society is a major cause of this. The entrepreneur sees that the educator, or the polic officer, or the city manager has a problem. Application of a newly availab piece of equipment suggests the solution to the problem. So a market is generated and expanded but the effects are left to look after themselves. For example, equipping a police cruiser with means for instantaneous referral back to files in the police data bank is an obvious step forward i catching a criminal on the street. It is also potentially an enormous step in the direction of the police keeping tabs on everybody, criminal or not Similarly the solutions to problems connected with computerized banking involve the storing of information about individuals, and therefore give new power over them to anyone, legally or not, who has the capability c adding data to the system or removing it or of accessing it. The new function here already has a name—electronic payments system, by which the merchandizing firm directly debits the customer's account. In short, powerful new technology very likely leads to a functional shift which ma well change a locus of power. Therefore the application of a technology capable of producing extensive change in human transactions is neither as simple nor as innocent as it may appear at the straight entrepreneurial level. Those who see matters chiefly in the light of direct applications to existing functions must, therefore, clearly be classed as technological fellow travellers.

Also within the ambience of technology are those who see society in the future having characteristics based on certain technologies strongly pervading the culture and the society. As an example of this type we might cite Drucker (1968) who, with others, takes his stand on the idea that we are moving into a society in which the dominant kind of work consists of handling knowledge and not of directly producing physical goods and services. This is a deduction from observing the growth of the telecommunications and computer technology and the way in which the advanced countries have undergone a massive employment shift from manufacturing industry to tertiary and quaternary activities—'servicing' of all sorts. In the USA about 50% of all employment is now 'knowledge industry' or 'knowledge-related industry'.

> "The greatest of the discontinuities around us is in the changed position and power of knowledge .... The discovery of skill created civilization. Now we are about to make another major move. We are beginning to apply knowledge to work ... even the first faltering steps we have taken have shown that applying knowledge to work is a big idea and an exciting one. Its potential may be as great as was the potential of skill when first discovered. The development may take as long. But the impacts already are very great—and the changes they imply are tremendous indeed .... Above all the shift to knowledge as the foundation of work and performance imposes responsibility on the man of knowledge" (Drucker, 1968, pages 379, 380).

And again Drucker:

> "The 'knowledge industries' [a phrase coined by F Machlup] which produce and distribute ideas and information rather than goods and services, accounted in 1955 for one-quarter of the U.S. gross national product .... Yet by 1965, ten years later, the knowledge sector was taking one-third of a much bigger national product. In the late 1970's it will account for one-half of the total national product. Every other dollar earned and spent in the American economy will be earned by producing and distributing ideas and information, and will be spent on producing ideas and information. From an economy of goods, which America was as recently as World War II, we have changed into a knowledge economy" (Drucker, 1968, page 263).

Although Drucker should not be classed as a futurist and is claiming only to examine our present discontinuities with the past, he has much to say about what we must tackle now "to make tomorrow". Like others of similar preferences he relies much on new technologies and assumes that our present heavy involvement with technology will continue and even get stronger. Essentially he graces the technological group, though without using such a forthright phrase as Ferkiss's 'technological civilization' (Ferkiss, 1974).

Next we should mention those who study the effects or impacts of technology, particularly future applications and developments. From these are excluded for the present purpose those who are opposed to, or doubtful

about, the societal or cultural effects of a technology. Included are those
who accept the technology but wish to have a firmer base of knowledge
for applying it. So, an organization supplying telephone services for
example, fully committed to developing the use of its lines for data
transmission, will wish to investigate likely effects before it embarks on a
major programme of development. Such desires may lead to far-reaching
studies of widely different subjects, from voice prints to patterns of
metropolitan planning. The studies will be likely to die off very quickly,
however, if they stray outside the primacy of the technological assumption

Last among the fellow travellers of the technologists we come to those
who come out fair and square for a future which is heavily technological.
Whether philosophers or futurists, this type believes strongly that we can
only survive through accepting further technological support, a major
argument being the problem of looking after an enlarged human world
population. Ferkiss (1974) is an example of this kind of approach. Whil
not himself a technologist, he nevertheless thinks the power of technology
unassailable and its growth inevitable. He thinks in terms of technologica
civilization:

> "How the people of the future eat, sleep, breathe, shelter themselves,
> interact socially and culturally, and order their societies will depend on
> their techniques" (Ferkiss, 1974, page 16).

> "Men and women of the future will not be able to escape from the all-
> pervading influence of technology—whether of the work-performing or
> communicating variety—for the simple reason that by the twenty-first
> century the world will be incapable of supporting the vast population
> which is already inevitable (barring world-wide catastrophe) without the
> use of highly advanced technology .... Even to provide the untechnical
> amenities of life—clean air and water, wilderness and access to nature,
> maximization of the option to choose simpler and more natural
> lifestyles—will paradoxically require more technologically based
> knowledge, controls and management. The problem of the twenty-first
> century will not be whether to accept or reject technological civilizatio
> but how to order it to truly human ends" (Ferkiss, 1974, page 17).

For our purpose it is the assumption of the inevitability of the
technological base which is important at this stage. Having assumed the
necessity of technology (and therefore he is a fellow traveller) Ferkiss
moves in the direction of trying to suggest a frame of reference for
controlling it. This frame he calls 'ecological humanism'.

Our fellow travellers of the technologists therefore range in approach
from those who somewhat simplistically apply specific technologies to the
'improvement' of the accepted way of accomplishing an existing function
in society, like education or police surveillance, to those who seek to
conceptualize the essentials of an emergent technological civilization.

15.4 Ecosystems and technology

Our present concern for the quality of the environment implies a close relationship between technologies and ecosystems. The literature relating the two, however, is largely limited to specific questions, such as radioactive fallout, accidents in atomic power installations, and agricultural technology related to pesticides and herbicides or the techniques of monocultures. We do not appear to have very much work based on the notion that technology progressively invades ecosystems as the global population–food–energy syndrome presses ever more heavily on the available resources.

Perhaps the most basic perspective in which to view this matter is to remind ourselves of our species' earlier condition. Once we were a few scattered bands having nothing comparable with modern technology, but only a few simple techniques for obtaining what food the ecosystem offered for the easy taking. At that stage we occupied in any ecosystem a strictly defined niche from which we had no power to escape. Consequently the species did not threaten or impair the stability of the system. We were not of great consequence as a portion of the world's total biomass.

But there came a time when the species developed physical, and especially mental, capabilities which resulted in its being able to expand its niche. First technique and later hardware technology were the means. We learned to deflect more of the biomass and the energy of the ecosystem to our own use. This tended to alter the stability and productivity of the 'natural' ecosystem. The soil became less fertile; fewer types of living material could flourish. But for a time the application of the new knowledge would enlarge the available food supply and human numbers would increase.

This population increase in its turn would induce a steady demand for more food, perhaps even as the ability of the ecosystem to provide it was already diminishing. Hence further applications of knowledge–technology would be required and would tend to be forthcoming since technology grows cumulatively. This process has continued to our own time and still goes on. Because of our 'success' in deflecting ever more of the world's biomass and energy to our species its numbers have increased to the present four billion. We do not know whether the ecosphere can carry this quantity and, if so, for how long and at what levels of biomass and energy consumption. One calculation suggests that the biosphere's maximum population at present US agricultural and industrial levels is about one billion only (Hulett in Anderson, 1971). It is also clear that the present load is carried by means of assistance from the workings of ecosystems in the past (fossil fuels). We do not live on the products of our contemporary process of photosynthesis. We do not know whether we could do so, at our present global numbers.

The role of technology in general is twofold. First, it must keep developing so that ever more biomass and energy can be captured for our direct use. Second, it must ensure that the ecological conditions are maintained so that the first requirement can continue to be met.

As we have seen in chapter 6, there are the beginnings of a quest for alternatives to our heavily industrialized—technologized—agriculture. The thought motivating the experiments is that we should develop such alternatives against the day when further increases of inputs of energy into the food-growing process will produce no increase in output and may even be unavoidable simply for maintaining the level of output already achieved. Such alternatives would very probably require population distributions different from those existing now in both developed and developing countries. They would also be likely to require the modification or reversal of present global trends of urbanization.

Such shifts would require changes in the technologies obviously connected with food production and also in some of those further along the chain of support. Again, we already have evidence of attempts to explore what this may imply. An example is the attention paid to the so-called intermediate technology concept. The idea is that more success may be achieved in increasing the productivity of ecosystems by making relatively simple technologies a little more sophisticated and efficient rather than by introducing more complex technology into a situation where the backup of skill and supplies cannot be relied upon. The advocacy of Schumacher is notable in this area (see Schumacher, 1974).

In the end technology is based on knowledge and know-how. Any changes in the application of technology to food production will therefore be closely related to the generation, processing, and diffusion of knowledge. The electronic technology has a rapidly increasing capacity for allowing the carrying out of these knowledge functions at a global scale. *We therefore are in possession of one particular and very powerful technology which can serve the application of other technologies to ecosystems. On the one hand the electronic technology is able to diffuse information, leading to increased production of human-usable biomass, and on the other it is able to monitor the effects of this increased pressure on the ecosystems and give warning that remedial action is necessary. We* could *learn how to get more human-usable biomass without increasing the risks to the global life-support system as a whole.*

This aspect of technological shift and the role of the electronic technology appears to need the development of new concepts. I shall attempt some suggestions later.

15.5 Technology facing in two directions

Technology may be utilized with two basic orientations. First, as we have already mentioned, applications of technology may be made directly to the existing functions or transactions of society. The expectation of such applications is that improvement or greater efficiency will result. The future assumed here will be much like the present, but with less inefficiency. Applications in urban planning, in such functions as business, education, and government have been and still generally are of this type. Second, facing the other way, we find attempts to use the technology for functions which do not yet exist but are simultaneously developed by the very applications themselves. These new functions are conceived as at least in part coming out of the applications themselves. Biofeedback, psychofeedback, sociofeedback, computer modelling, automation, TV and radio for entertainment and space exploration, the playback of the tape recorder or the videotape, and experiments in setting up self-contained physical environments are examples of this more open type of application of technology.

The more powerful the technology and the wider its diffusion, the greater will be the likelihood that out of it will come new functions and transactions. For example, rocketry plus electronics has made possible the entirely new function of global monitoring. The bringing of unconscious bodily processes such as the beating of the heart into the sphere of conscious observation opens up new types of preventive as well as therapeutic procedures.

This potential of technology either for reinforcing the present functions of society in their existing modes or for developing new functions appears complicated by another factor. The innocent application of a new technology to an existing function may well have such an impact on that function that it undergoes massive and explosive change. The electronic technology, for example, has already reconstituted banking and is about to create entirely new institutional arrangements linking banking and commerce through electronic payments systems using packet-switching (see chapter 4). Medical services, law enforcement, and education are other examples already changing into something other than we have previously known. The process is one of largely unquestioning application of the technology with perhaps pressure from several directions—economic squeeze, new demands by the public, and new threats of collapse. The institutional clusters of behaviour patterns previously associated with such functions are disrupted and come to require reformulation. Thus we are forced to admit the need for the reconsideration of existing functions in society and for their redefinition[1]. *The important observation is that the drive for greater efficiency or even continuance of the function, powered by the application of new technology, may tend to destroy the very function whose greater efficiency is sought and to move toward the creation of a new function or the redefinition of an existing one.*

[1] I am using here the idea of clustering of activities simply as a way of conceptualizing the material. Institutions are therefore clusters of behaviour patterns. Skill in conceptualizing consists in grouping these patterns into clusters that can be fruitfully handled. As the culture shifts, some of the old clusters become virtually useless for thinking and new ones have to be generated. These are working concepts, subject themselves to change. They may also be called rubrics, although there is danger in using this word because of the connotation given by psychologists to rubricization. The sociological concept of institutions may now be no more useful than the obsolete anthropological idea of a fixed and universal human nature.

This facing in two directions—the Janus nature of technology—sheds some light on an apparent paradox in contemporary society. On the one hand it seems clear that exposure to the cinema and television has produced in mass populations a facility for taking in information through other channels than the written or printed word. McLuhan has familiarized us with the idea of a new sensory emphasis or preferred mode of communication. The book and the lecture, he affirms, are finished. On the other hand, however, there has been a sharp increase in the number of new books appearing and of old ones republished. Quite obviously the book is far from finished and is indeed enjoying a popularity greater than ever before.

This situation is not internally self-contradictory if we remember that the electronic technology is simultaneously both able to render the book obsolete by providing alternative modes, and to make the book more widely accessible through a variety of new techniques. As a mode of learning, the series of televison interpretations of Bronowski's (1973) *Ascent of Man* was an example of a new mode of accessing knowledge. It was superior to the book because of the movement of the images, the physical presence of the author himself, and the multiplicity of sensory inputs. Rich as was the book the television presentation was richer still. It was also faster. The electronic mode surpasses the printed mode. This is the new. But simultaneously the computer and the telecommunications capabilities allow cheaper and more widespread access to the book. An existing mode is reinforced in the very act of being surpassed! The rapidly developing optical technology makes possible the electronic storage and accessing of whole libraries, page by page. The electronic technology has revolutionized the process of book printing and the accessing of books.

Perhaps we are witnessing the consolidation and increased accessibility of our past and present capabilities and accumulated cultural material—the efflorescence of all glyph civilizations—while at the same time we are very rapidly developing the potentials of the new.

This facing in both directions simultaneously is also noticeable in our use of ecological knowledge. Improved knowledge of how to intervene in biological processes allows us both to obtain more productivity from traditional agricultural approaches and to think out entirely new ways of handling food chains. Direct application to traditional methods is represented by the use of chemical fertilizers, herbicides, pesticides, and monocultures, together with the extensive use of energy derived from outside the contemporary ecosystem. As examples of how the new knowledge can make possible new systems which include the production of food we have looked at ecological arks and specifically designed multi-niche systems (chapter 6). The two faces are by no means incompatible and are as likely to exist side by side, as in the applications of the electronic technology.

Of the two attitudes the first is liable to be fairly narrowly technological. The second may be rather more firmly based on science. The first is apt to be obvious in its applications and sometimes in its results. The second may often seem far out and remote from general applicability. The first will get financial support without difficulty if profit seems likely. The second has less likelihood of resource backing, although in some quarters there is appearing a realization that narrow approaches are not enough: for example, the governmental support of Todd's ark on Prince Edward Island.

Finally, we should bear in mind these two attitudes while thinking about alternative futures. Science and technology could, paradoxically enough, be effective for a time in holding culture and society in a more or less static and frozen condition. While both are prime causes of change it is also to be observed that they are considerably under the control of elements, such as business, industry, government, and education, which may have very major reasons for suppressing change. The first attitude described above might easily be the dominant one for sometime to come, since our large organizations in certain respects need a degree of societal and cultural stasis for their self-perpetuation.

15.6 Technology is knowledge

In considering ecosystems and technology in their relationships a useful perspective is to start with an understanding of technology as basically knowledge or information. In the ultimate analysis it is the winning of knowledge and the ability to apply it at the right time and place which make it possible for us to modify the 'natural' life-support system so that more biomass and energy are deflected to the use of human beings. The hominization of ecosystems therefore depends on knowledge, and a continuation and extension of the process must depend on acquiring and applying ever more knowledge. The significant fact about human beings in ecosystems is that they increase the quantity, improve the quality, and enhance the accessibility of information in ecosystems. The jump from pulling up naturally growing roots to devising and using a digging stick is a jump in information. The result of the jump is an increased human-usable output and the diffusion of the knowledge of the invention of the stick. We see in this linkage the importance of connecting the electronic technology with the ongoing processes of ecosystems, whether 'natural' or hominized. Diffusion of information is made extremely easy through the technology. Also the technology is able to enhance the capacity for the production of human-usable biomass and at the same time to monitor the condition of ecosystems in relation to their stability and capacity to bear new demands placed on them by the increase in human numbers.

Information is moved electronically between ecosystems. Technologies connected with agriculture, for example, are rapidly diffused around the world. Technologies such as the use of pesticides and herbicides very quickly achieve global application. Again what is essentially diffused is information.

This global movement of information as a substratum of interaction between ecosystems is to be regarded as a new phenomenon because of its sophistication and the instantaneous nature of information transfer. New ways of thinking about this are now clearly required. I shall attempt later to provide some suggestions.

Profile of the mass-individual character

16.1 An ecological view of human populations

The most obvious approach is purely quantitative. Our human numbers increase very rapidly, raising questions about the limits to the carrying capacity of the world. We know that species 'in nature' do not increase in numbers indefinitely. We do not know whether we shall be clever enough to avoid major episodes of cutback in our own numbers.

I suggested in a previous chapter that increased quantity of human beings is made possible by the development of information and knowledge and their application to the life-support system. By improving technology (including technique) we manage to sustain ever more human beings. This process has reached dizzy heights, particularly in the areas of those ecosystems which accomodate very large populations, such as the eastern seaboard of the United States. We have seen also that our knowledge of how the life-support system works and our electronic technology are key factors in maintaining these large populations at their present levels of physical well-being.

The relationships between ecosystem production, technology, and human numbers are not, however, to be left at the mechanistic level. Human beings are not simply components of ecosystems as are trees or molecules of water. With the evolution of animals, including humans, ecosystems have developed advanced mental capabilities. These capabilities, when exercised by human beings, turn back upon the workings of the ecosystems of which the humans are a part. Thus changes are imposed both by conscious purpose and unintentionally.

When human populations were very sparse this turning back upon the ecosystem by this peculiar component called 'mind' was not able to have any great influence on the whole system. Ecosystems either achieved permanent new positions of steady state or they quickly made good the damage done. In our own time the situation is quite different. The human numbers are comparatively very large and the capabilities of 'mind' are very highly developed indeed. The turning back of 'mind' into the working of world ecosystems is now potentially of great power for changing the stability, productivity, and diversity of ecosystems.

This leads to questions about the ways in which such capabilities are used, can be used, and ought to be used. We are now beginning to familiarize ourselves with such problems, and a considerable literature already exists. A key in debating such questions is very clearly the attitudes and values of the human populations which make demands on the ecosystems. The mental characteristics of the populations are an important component in any society's capacity to act. *The ability of governments to mediate successfully between the demands implied by the mental characteristics and the physical limitations of food supply, etc is of crucial importance for the continuance of any society.*

We have a special interest in this set of relationships because the electronic technology is particularly well suited for influencing the mental characteristics of large massed populations, very quickly in some regards. In other regards, however, the technology may generate resistance to necessary changes or make it impossible for change to be brought about. We therefore need to look at the nature of the mental characteristics of our contemporary large massed populations.

16.2 The mass individual
In trying to find worthwhile descriptions of the mental profile of contemporary human beings, particularly the urbanized variety, we have to be careful to avoid ephemeral and trendy emphases. We may do this with some degree of success by choosing writers who have recorded their views some time ago. The test of time can be applied by putting what they wrote against our present impressions. Many names come readily to mind: Ortega y Gasset, Fromm, May, Zolla, and Rogers—to suggest a few who have made this kind of attempt. We shall first look at José Ortega y Gasset and Elémire Zolla. They wrote over forty-five and twenty years ago respectively.

Ortega y Gasset, writing *The Revolt of the Masses* in 1930, used the phrase "mass-man" to describe the profile of the contemporary Western human being. For simplicity the phrase will be retained here, although fashions in the uses of words have changed since he wrote. Ortega y Gasset's basic description of mass man is that he has:

> "(1) An inborn, root-impression that life is easy, plentiful, without any grave limitations; consequently each average man finds within himself a sensation of power and triumph which, (2) invites him to stand up for himself as he is, to look upon his moral and intellectual endowment as excellent, complete. This contentment with himself leads him to shut himself off from any external court of appeal; not to listen, not to submit his opinions to judgment, not to consider others' existence. His intimate feeling of power urges him always to exercise predominance. He will act then as if he and his life were the only beings existing in the world; and, consequently, (3) will intervene in all matters, imposing his own vulgar views without respect or regard for others, without limit or reserve, that is to say, in accordance with a system of 'direct action'" (Ortega y Gasset, 1957, page 97).

No doubt with an eye on the individual but also on the mass manifestations of Bolshevism, Fascism, and Nazism in the 1920s and 1930s he wrote: "The actual mass-man is, in fact, a primitive who has slipped through the wings on to the age-old stage of civilization" (page 82).

If one may dare to make a condensation of so rich a book, the characteristics Ortega y Gasset describes might be compressed as follows:

1 The masses have achieved "complete social power".
2 "The sovereignty of the unqualified individual of the human being as such, generically, has now passed from being a judicial idea or ideal to be a psychological state inherent in the average man" (page 23).
3 "He feels lost amid his own abundance" (page 44).
4 Government is in the hands of the masses and exists from hand to mouth; it drifts just as mass man does.
5 The soul of the contemporary European mass man is much simpler than that of his predecessor: he is a primitive whom it has been impossible to educate. "... they have been hurriedly inoculated with the pride and power of modern instruments, but not with their spirit" (page 51).
6 Mass man has come about through, and is supported by, liberal democracy and technical knowledge. By these he lives, but he places their continuance in imminent danger. (Ortega y Gasset notes that Hermann Weyl, coworker of Einstein, commented that the death of ten or twelve scientists simultaneously would cause the loss of physics for ever.)
7 During the nineteenth century and the first part of the twentieth, for the bourgeois and later for the workers, life came to be felt as secure, orderly, exempt from restrictions. This was a new condition for man: millions were relatively free from poverty, difficulty, and danger.
8 Therefore mass man does not feel any obligation to limit himself. His appetite is incited. Tomorrow will be even richer.
9 He believes that all these technical marvels come, as it were, by nature and forgets they are based on the ability of a few highly endowed individuals. He forgets that continuance of this condition requires the support of "certain difficult human virtues".
10 He has two fundamental psychological traits: "... the free expansion of his vital desires, and therefore, of his personality; and his radical ingratitude towards all that has made possible the ease of his existence" (page 58). He is the spoilt child. Everything is permitted; he has no obligations.
11 "My thesis, therefore, is this: the very perfection with which the XIXth century gave an organization to certain orders of existence has caused the masses benefited thereby to consider it, not as an organized, but as a natural system. Thus is explained and defined the absurd state of mind revealed by the masses; they are only concerned with their own well-being, and at the same time they remain alien to the cause of that well-being. As they do not see, behind the benefits of civilization, marvels of invention and construction which can only be maintained by great effort and foresight, they imagine that their role is limited to demanding these benefits peremptorily, as if they were natural rights" (page 59).

12 In the past man felt himself limited. Today he feels: "To live is to meet with no limitation whatever, and, consequently, to abandon oneself calmly to one's self. Practically nothing is impossible, nothing is dangerous, and, in principle, nobody is superior to anybody" (page 61). He appeals to no authority outside himself and is "... satisfied with himself exactly as he is". Why not, since nobody tells him he is a second-class man? He is "lord of himself". He is inert. Not active, merely reactive. His soul's texture is "wrought of hermetism and indocility".

13 Mass man will not be able to control the process of civilization because it is too complex for him. He knows how to work the machinery but he is ignorant of the principles.

14 Mass man is cleverer than his predecessors but cannot effectively use his cleverness.

15 "Barbarism is the absence of standards to which appeal can be made" (page 72). Mass man acknowledges no such standards since he is the measure of himself.

16 "This is the new thing: the right not to be reasonable", the "... reason of unreason ... . He wishes to have opinions, but is unwilling to accept the conditions and presuppositions that underlie all opinion" (page 73). This leads to "direct action", namely violence, taking the law into his own hands, force as the *ultima ratio.*

17 Mass man, here including technicians like doctors and engineers, disregards science. But it is on science that all is built. Politics, law, art, morals, and religion are "... at least temporarily bankrupt. Science alone is not bankrupt" (page 87).

18 "If you want to make use of the advantages of civilization, but are not prepared to concern yourself with the upholding of civilization—you are done" (page 88). *Mass man thinks civilization is like nature. By this belief he becomes a primitive.* The classical world died because of lack of technique to support increasing numbers. "But today it is man who is the failure, because he is unable to keep pace with the progress of his own civilization" (page 91). Life gets better but also more complicated.

19 Unbalanced specialization is also an origin of mass man's mentality. The specialist may be narrow and shut up within himself. He also assumes civilization to be there by nature.

20 The modern state is dangerous: the whole of life is bureaucratized. It is the state that provides the security that mass man is born into.

21 "This is the terrible spiritual situation in which the best youth of the world finds itself today. By dint of feeling itself free, exempt from restrictions, it feels itself empty" (page 136).

The Revolt of the Masses is astounding for its clarity of vision. Forty-five years have only served to enhance its ability to chill the spine. How will this mass man react to further injections of technology, particularly that of the telecommunications and computer applications, and to the knowledge that his numbers and behaviour threaten the continuance of the ecosystems that are his life support? As far as mass man's reaction to the ecosystem question is concerned we have, as yet, very little information. But we do have some studies of how mass man is responding to the electronic technology. For this we shall now turn to Elémire Zolla's *Eclipse of the Intellectual*, published originally in 1956.

Zolla first reviews what observant minds thought of the industrial revolution while it was taking place. He does this specifically focussing on the kind of mentality that was brought into being by it, rather than by pointing up the socioeconomic and physical manifestations. Particularly in Melville, Poe, Engels, and Dostoevsky he concludes that the character of the industrial mass of human beings was perfectly understood: "... it sways between hysteria and gloom, for among these coerced worshippers of Baal the emotions are formless" (Zolla, 1968, page 19). The essential concept is that the mass has suffered some kind of psychic trauma: atomization, abolition of the ability to contemplate, an absence of vital motives, the emotional response of the warrior being superseded by that of the gambler, being walled within himself, bored, a new sensibility with a taste for the morbid, the macabre, novelty, and brutality. And a new phenomenon appears: the culture industry.

Zolla quotes from a letter written by Goethe to Schiller in 1797 already noting that: "All the pleasures, even the theatre, must simply distract" (page 32). Distraction as an indispensable component of mass man's boredom has been examined by many writers. Zolla notes that the newspaper was a very early form of this manifestation. "Formalistic writing had to be rapid and sensational" (page 33). This was the beginning of the culture industry which has grown to huge proportions in our own time. Madame Bovary herself is the classic example of the victim of distraction in an earlier phase, and the book is an early product of the culture industry.

But it was the motion picture, thinks Zolla, that really put the culture industry on its feet. The dream that the movies offer inhibits the development of man's inner self since the real persona of the actor is not present. "Cinema as a form of art rapes reality instead of representing it, nor could its technique sustain a high level above the average of the society in which it exists" (page 40).

Toward the end of the nineteenth century came advertising and sport as part of the industry. Thus had arisen powerful means for blunting and debasing mass man's sensibility still further, pushing him into a "fake duplication of reality". In the twentieth century Zolla diagnoses that preoccupation with these pseudorealities has become obsessive, and industrial literature has become ever cruder, catering to a "... morbid need of repetitions and stereotypes". The purpose is to get rid of boredom but the cure produces even more boredom. The result is the development of a

"... culture industry even more oppressive than the industry conditioned by the laws of the market" (page 49).

One of the reasons for stressing the importance of the culture industry, which in Zolla's view must include the Futurism of the 1920s, Dadaism, and Cubism, is that mass man is entirely at its mercy. It grabs at him in the press, radio, television, advertising, film, record, the fiction of industrial writing, and even a good deal of so-called serious art. The inclusion of the last is particularly interesting; it implies that art has also become subservient to the culture industry and therefore to the omnivorous appetite of the culture as a whole. So, to accept the cultural reality of industrialism is to become its servant.

Can we return to the old values and forms of preindustrial society? Of this possibility Zolla says that this means:

"... harbouring the illusion that by sheer will one can convert the mass into a real community, individualistic selfishness into heroism, the monotony of time divided into work and entertainment into a perpetual celebration. Of course, all one can really do is cover the reality determined by industry with dreadful advertising tinsel, cultivate the hysteria of the masses in accordance with the methods developed by the commercial specialists in mass psychology" (page 57).

This is to say that return can only be a masquerade: a dead end. But he goes on to say: "He can save himself who travels the other road, who does not want to restore anything yet does not renounce the past which survives in the principle of style and form" (page 59).

Zolla next expounds his reasons for saying that mass man has had forced upon him the role of the gambler in replacement of that of the warrior and the farmer. He must submit himself to an anonymous objective world. "The gambler's emotional substratum is therefore composed of boredom and an irresistible association of images" (page 69). The gambler is infantile. The individual gambler has also now become the group gambler: "In a modern firm, the employees are taught to play their positions as on a football team. And playing this way means that those who win lose against themselves as persons .... Sometimes he finds himself out of the game: when he meets a living person, when he contemplates a beautiful spectacle, when he concentrates on a personal work. But he cannot give up the attitude of the gambler unless there is a preliminary act of understanding with that person, the spirit of that spectacle, and with himself, an understanding that the game should end and the spontaneity of life return, so that the civilization that imposes the archetype of the gambler be condemned without appeal" (page 80).

Next, bourgeois man is shown to be the predecessor of present mass man. The bourgeois owned, rather than enjoyed, his enjoyments, and was forced to consider everything a commodity. Because they are useful he supports patriotism, religion, and community—not because they are

intrinsically valuable. He therefore becomes a split personality with a
false consciousness or bad faith. He playacts. The bourgeois is regarded
as killed in 1914. From then on it is mass man with whom we have to deal.

While bourgeois man was somewhat inefficient in his split personality,
mass man has "... learned to dodge the dangers of emotion. The mass man
has divided his life into separate sectors—work and leisure—and has
entrusted them to forces outside himself that control him by removing the
burden of decision and choice ... . For his part, he approaches both work
and leisure in the same spirit: the spirit of sport, humor, and repression"
(page 88).

Mass man has an exceptional memory which selects to obliterate
"... everything that can speak to him of man, his emotions and thoughts".
His taste is certain: he opts for the fake rather than the real. He is
"... boundlessly presumptuous and modest to the point of self-annihilation".
He knows what he is but intentionally devaluates awareness. "Reason
remains impotent." He thinks intensely but to no good purpose. He is
poetic. He multiplies language, making new ones for various activities or
interest. "Traditional language decays." This means that mass man does
not wish to communicate: "He loves small talk and avoids conversation".
He avoids communication by self-contradiction, for example: "That which
is boring is amusing and vice versa". He is deaf, blind, crippled, and a
slave. "To suffer the consequences of the errors of others seems to him
less of a burden than to suffer the consequences of his own errors"
(page 105).

Zolla goes on to say that mass man knows how to differentiate himself
but not how to defend himself against the evils of massification. He deals
with mass eroticism; the message here is that the emotion has become a
commodity similar in significance to the desire for a car or other offering
of the market. It must not be taken too seriously, for there is danger of
"getting out of control". "While the bourgeois devalued love with a
rhetoric of excitation, the mass-man depreciates it with excitation taken as
a joke" (page 123). Like beauty it becomes *kitsch.*

"Mass-man's reflexes are as conditioned as Pavlov's dogs. And since this
is a general repressive system, the system of mass society, which is divided
into sectors with different laws, it is basically unitary since the constituent
standards are identical in all sectors and the principles of repression are
unfailing" (page 134).

Zolla (1968) has some interesting comments in a chapter on the
decadence of persuasion. How is it possible to communicate with mass
man? "The new means such as the telegraph, the telephone, television,
radio, taperecordings, and stereophonic projections introduce us into a
universe where the private sphere is destroyed, where syntax is no longer
the structure of discourse and we return to an oral culture: the objects of
attention are presented simultaneously ... . The literary and linear vision
of reality was pernicious in that it pushed analysis to extremes, as Blake

saw, and it had need of myths to give it substance. But the new era, which supplies an integrating image of the world that is oral and auditory lacks any unifying myth other than a feeling of reverence for the unifying means themselves—the mass media. McLuhan observes how the young people exposed to the television image receive an orientation in space that makes the linear language of the press remote and alien .... It seems useless to try to evaluate the change, since the evaluations are those of linear culture and of space in perspective, which have now been condemne by technique" (Zolla, 1968, pages 146–147)[1].

And further: "... the new oral and stereophonic universe which we have entered does not return to a mythical syntax after having abandoned the analytical one, but flings us into a state of social atomism in which the sphere of the private has disappeared and man, for lack of syntax of communication, remains alone in the crowd" (page 148). We might remember Pasternak's (1959) insistence, in *Dr. Zhivago*, that the revolution had annihilated private feeling.

On the eclipse of the intellectual Zolla says: "So we live in society that can easily do without the intellectual, a society that asks the well-adjusted to confine themselves strictly to their particular work and makes certain, if by some chance some of them escape the orbit of work, to crush them by means of the culture industry. The intellectual becomes the true enemy of the society .... Society's tendency is now directed toward depriving the intellectual of all authority" (Zolla, 1968, pages 167–168)[2]

---

[1] Also changes in the eye muscles occur. When the eye scans lines of type (reads) regularly the muscular arrangements of the eye are habituated to a linear movement and when they are in tone reading is easy. When, however, the eye is not used for reading very much but is used more for looking at TV the linear movement muscles lose tone and consequently reading quickly tires the eyes. Clearly, therefore, literacy of the type based on reading is dependent on the habitual use of the eyes' linear movements. If this habituation is extensively lost then we risk the loss of that kind o literacy. It may be that the eye scanning line by line was never a very effective form for picking up information, but it has clearly been the dominant form of our culture for some time. Its eclipse as dominant may already have taken place. It receives littl attention that we have two kinds of illiterate—those who never learned to read at all, and those who once could read but have lost the ability because their absorption of information is mostly through the changing patterns of the TV screen. This scanning or nonscanning question may prove extremely important for our future cultural pattern

[2] Zolla has a fairly strong emphasis on the determination of the individual's profile by the historical processes of the society. This emphasis is part of our heritage from the thought of the nineteenth century. Perhaps because of our better understanding o biological processes, much of the best thinking of our time is far less deterministic. The profile of the individual is clearly to be recognized as helping to shape 'history', whether we think of the mass or of the outstanding individual. I prefer to think of the relationships between the individual, the group, and 'history' as reciprocal and to keep an open mind for the particulars of emphasis that may vary from circumstance t circumstance.

Enough has been given to put over the general idea—that mass man is a fake but that the technologies connected with communication (Zolla makes no mention of the computer) are already producing a new mode of mental process. Of course, mass man could himself reply: "How do we know that all this represents the facts? This is not how I feel myself within myself". Even in the Dark Ages the individual saw the sun shine day by day.

The view that the modern mass individual has a certain typical and recognizable character structure has been strongly supported in the postwar period by many distinguished practitioners in psychology and psychiatry. The names of Fromm, May, and Rogers are associated with the idea that this typical character is immature. This conclusion of these thinkers is particularly useful as it comes out of lifetimes of clinical experience—a quite different route from that of Ortega y Gasset's and Zolla's thought.

The general conclusion of Fromm will be familiar to many readers. His diagnosis—quite distinct from his proposals for treatment, which are traditional–humanist—is that the mass individual of our time characteristically lives out his life as a personality unable to mature fully as a human being. Freedom is denied to him by elements both external and internal to himself. Fromm (1968) conceptualizes the personality or 'mind' as structured in a cybernetic whole. This means that components are seen as systemically linked or clustered to form various types of structure, much as in the conceptualizations of Bateson (1972) and McCulloch (1965). For example, the structure in which freedom is denied will be found inevitably to contain resignation, aggression, and loss of vitality; or, if there is long-lasting boredom, passiveness and indifference will be concomitants.

He therefore considers that character structures have fixed parts, some of which always come together. This concept is very important because it means that we cannot pick and choose; we cannot hope to encourage the 'good' and inhibit the 'bad'. The structure has its own fixed rules, set in part by its experience of the world outside it. What choice we have is therefore only between various whole structures: there are no composites possible.

Fromm's message is clear: grow or be enslaved. But the mass individual has great difficulty in growing beyond a certain point very generally identified by many analysts as short of the level required for full maturity as a human being.

From our understanding of humankind as major component, when aggregated in huge populations, of the ecosystems of the biosphere we can now perceive that enslavement will not necessarily guarantee continuance of the life-support system. *Socioeconomies may fail ecologically because of the character structure of their mass individuals. Our ecological knowledge therefore supports the analysts' view that the evolutionary development now required lies in the area of character or personality structure.*

16.3 The message of mass man

Ortega y Gasset and Zolla have been left to speak for themselves. In this field—the humanities—the quotations are the evidence or data we have to handle. Essentially they are saying that the mental profile of mass man is not suitable for ensuring adequate continued support for the science and technology which make his present level of life possible. This could also be stated by saying that government, the state, or the bureaucracies will be inhibited in their efforts at effective deployment of society's resources by the attitudes and values of the electorate.

Neither Ortega y Gasset nor Zolla said anything about mass man in the context of ecosystems. Whatever other perspectives we now may use to look at the human condition we certainly cannot omit to see mass man as a component of ecosystems. *He is a component of his own life-support systems in ways hitherto unsuspected. If he does not understand this but regards the high level of human performance that keeps him alive as nothing other than part of 'nature', he will not be able to behave in ways essential for maintaining the stability of his life-support system. The necessary feedback loops for controlling the system will not work.*

In considering human beings in ecosystems it is therefore hopelessly inadequate to think only in terms of physical head counting, food supply and availability of resources. We have to include human beings as ecosystem components capable of various behaviour patterns. Some patterns are reinforcers of the life-support system; some are not. Behaviour is the product of the mental profile. *Hence the mental profile of mass populations is a key component of ecosystems.*

Without being particularly ecological in emphasis, a report just being made available by the United Nations indicates appreciation of this general emphasis. Approaching the question of world resources up to the year 2000, Leontief et al (1977) concluded that the resource and pollution problems of the world *can* find acceptable solutions. The really difficult problems are seen as political, social, and institutional. Another study, headed by Tinbergen (Tinbergen et al, 1976) and published by its sponsor the Club of Rome, has this same emphasis on the need to change world power and socioeconomic structures, and to reconstruct the international order. To say that socioeconomic reconstruction is necessary at the global level is not perhaps very original. It should be obvious by now that we should be suspicious of 'solutions' to supposed 'problems' along economic or any other lines. What is difficult is to discover how to proceed in order to identify perspectives capable of producing effective action. One of these may well be to emphasize 'mind', and particularly mass human mental profiles, as key components of ecosystems. For this new concept are required. Some will be suggested in the next part of this book[3].

[3] Although such reports as Leontief's and Tinbergen's very interestingly stress the need for change in attitudes and institutions, they possibly do something of a disservice in failing to emphasize adequately the essentially ecological context of the support of

Ortega y Gasset and Zolla imply a gloomy future. The electronic technologists and their fellow travellers on the whole are optimistic. We can bring the two views into fruitful relationship by seeing the electronic technology as a major instrument for helping to shape mental profiles so that the role they play in ecosystems will be benign. Doubtless this means coming to terms with propaganda, revising some views about the role of the state, and questioning what we really mean by the socialization of the individual through education. All caveats aside, it is obvious that the telecommunications–computer technology is capable of being an extremely potent element in the management of ecosystems via action on the mental profiles of mass populations [4]. It seems likely also that at present we are influencing the formation of the mental profile in directions which are not benign for the continuance of the life-support system. We saw in chapter 11 how the experiments of Ryan are attempting to break into this field.

In the next chapter we shall look at how the mass individual feels about himself and of what his sensibility is composed.

all life, human life included. Socioeconomies, in the last analysis, can exist only within the viability of ecosystems. The needed institutional changes must satisfy the ecological requirements equally with those belonging strictly to the socioeconomies. This comment is notwithstanding the fact that Leontief and others do have an ecological concern. What counts is the *attitude* to that concern. Ecosystem stability is not necessarily capable of being ensured by approaching it through policies of 'pollution abatement'.

[4] I am sharply aware of the objections to using a categorization such as Ortega y Gasset's "mass-man". The objections seem to me less important than the insights delivered by the use of the categorization. Nearly fifty years after Ortega y Gasset wrote we can test for validity against other sources, and, very practically, by looking at the people we know, and, if we dare do it, at ourselves. We have to own up to certain common characteristics of personality.

Approach to contemporary sensibility

17.1 Difficulty of articulating current feeling

In thinking about human beings as key components both existing within ecosystems and acting upon them, it is not sufficient only to develop a profile of the character of mass man as has been provided by Ortega y Gasset and Zolla in the last chapter. It is also necessary to have some appreciation of contemporary sensibility. Sensibility may be thought of as the substratum of feeling which supports the attitudes and values of the individual. It includes also the underpinning of belief and motivation, and in some measure provides explanations for elements in the profile.

Historians are very properly cautious in coming to conclusions about their own time. It is notoriously difficult to get contemporary material into a focus that will endure. The same applies to looking at current sensibility; we find it hard to separate the ephemeral from the lasting. We cannot here have the benefit of the lapse of time which has conferred an increased credibility on the conclusions of our two analysts of mass man. We must not, therefore, be surprised that the most penetrating enquirers disavow any possibility of presenting anything like a complete statement and content themselves with trying to get certain things into focus.

17.2 A view of recent sensibility

For our purpose reliance will be placed largely on two volumes of lectures by George Steiner: *In Bluebeard's Castle: Some Notes Towards the Re-definition of Culture* (Steiner, 1971) and *Nostalgia for the Absolute* (Steiner, 1974)[1].

Steiner's overall view, if we may presume to attempt to condense it, seems to be that a major historic cause of the present collapse of Western high culture is the persistent drive toward perfection or utopia which has been typical of it. We can no longer sustain the effort necessary to continue the hypocrisy of living up to the traditional standards required of us by our culture. Exhortations to do better, to strive for the millenium, no longer work. We cannot take it anymore:

> "Monotheism at Sinai, primitive Christianity, messianic socialism: these are the three supreme moments in which Western culture is presented with what Ibsen termed 'the claims of the ideal'. These are the three

---

[1] George Steiner, not to be confused with Rudolph Steiner, is a humanities scholar in the University of Geneva. He has a very wide knowledge of European languages and literatures, past and present. I have chosen to use his writings because direct experience of past sensibility is virtually indispensable for bringing the essentials of present sensibility to the threshold of consciousness—at best a difficult and uncertain process. Steiner knows from personal experience the sensibility of prewar Europe, and is able to draw on the records of the sensibility of Europe's long past. See also Eliot (1948).

stages, profoundly interrelated, through which Western consciousness is forced to experience the blackmail of transcendence ... . Unceasingly, the blackmail of perfection has hammered at the confused, mundane, egotistical fabric of common, instinctual behaviour ... . But the insistence of the ideal continued, with a terrible, tactless force" (Steiner, 1971, page 40).

Steiner begins *In Bluebeard's Castle* by describing our present sensibility— that is, the way we feel about our own cultural state—as dominated by a feeling of how poor our time is compared with "the imagined garden of liberal culture" located (in England and Western Europe) from the 1820s to 1915: from Waterloo to the battle of the Somme. Nineteenth-century culture is now looked back upon as orderly and civilized: "There are still a good many alive today for whom that famous cloudless summer of 1914 extends backward, a long way, into a world more civil, more confident, more humanely articulate than any we have known since. It is against their remembrance of that great summer and our own symbolic knowledge of it that we test the present cold" (Steiner, 1971, page 15), "... a great garden of civility now ravaged".

He goes on to emphasize that our *image* of lost coherence, of "a centre that held", is more powerful for us than the historical truth, and argues that this fact must match some "psychological and moral need" that we now feel. He suggests that this need originated in that "summer of 1815–1915".

We have inherited an ennui which accumulated during the nineteenth century. During the Revolutionary and Napoleonic period life very rapidly accelerated, consciousness sharpened, and personal expectations rose rapidly. "Hegel could argue, with vigorous logic of feeling, that history itself was passing into a new state of being, that ancient time was at an end" (page 21). This was followed by reaction and a drop in tension. "The past drove rat's teeth into the grey pulp of the present; it exasperated, it sowed wild dreams" (page 22). A reservoir of unlived life began to fill up. This was being felt at the same time that the industrial city was in the making, with all its dehumanization and unorganized growth. From this mix grew the response of romanticism.

In his second lecture Steiner (1971) approaches the question of whether it is "... realistic to perceive in humanistic culture express solicitations of authoritarian rule and cruelty?" He asks this in the context of noting that high culture continued in close proximity to the barbarism of the First World War. He looks at this in the context of the psychology of religion and it is here that appears the argument of the first quotation given above.

He affirms the commonly accepted link between mass manufacture and the dehumanization of modern man, but says that the sources of the barbarism must be looked for at a deeper level. He thinks the huge increase in population, particularly in the industrial cities, is considerably responsible: individual worth is reduced; a feeling for destructiveness appears.

K

The aggression of the twentieth century may be "... an attempt to get air ... even at the price of ruin" (page 46).

Perhaps yet more crucial than this Steiner thinks that: "It is to the ambiguous after-life of religious feeling in Western culture that we must look, to the malignant energies released by the decay of natural religious forms" (page 46). For six hundred years the Western mind was preoccupie with Hell. At last it acted it out (the wars): "In our current barbarism an extinct theology is at work, a body of transcendent reference whose slow, incomplete death has produced surrogate, parodistic forms. The epilogue to belief, the passage of religious belief into hollow convention, seems to be a more dangerous process than the *philosophes* anticipated. The structures of decay are toxic. Needing Hell, we learned how to build and run it on earth ... . In locating Hell, above ground, we have passed out of the major order and symmetries of Western civilization" (page 48). We are now in a *postculture*.

The geographical centrality of Western culture—Europe—remained unself-consciously accepted until the 1920s and 1930s. Today that has been lost and "... there can be no natural return to the lost centrality. For the great majority of thinking beings, certainly for the young, the image of Western culture as self-evidently superior, as embodying within itself almost the sum total of intellectual and moral power, is either a racially-tinged absurdity or a museum piece" (page 53). But this posture of self-indictment is a typically Western characteristic. Steiner thinks this centrality cannot be recaptured.

Also lost is the sense that Western history is ever ascendant; the assumption of inevitable progress is irreparably damaged. "The Kierkegaardian concept of 'total possibility', of a fabric of reality open at all points to the rift of absurdity and disaster, has become a commonplace We are back in a politics of torture and of hostages. Public and private violence laps at the foundations of the city ... Our threshold of apprehensio has been formidably lowered" (page 57).

At the same time, advance in science and technology is immense. But "... we now know, as Adam Smith and Macaulay did not, that material progress is implicated in a dialectic of concomitant damage, that it destroy irreparable equilibria between society and nature" (page 58). Ecosystems come under threat and may be destroyed.

And then Steiner states the most terrifying insight of all:

> "*It is not certain, moreover, that one can devise a model of culture, a heuristic programme for further advance without a utopian core*" (page 59).

It is terrifying because we have the understanding of our position and we have the technology with which to act, but we can no longer bear the burden of the utopian effort. If Steiner is right we cannot tolerate anothe trumpet call to make yet another moral effort toward perfection. And, he asks, if we cannot assume historical progress, what good is knowledge?

Steiner's next major point is that we can no longer correlate humanism with humane social behaviour, in the real world. The fact that individuals are educated does not mean that they will automatically behave in civilized ways. The eighteenth and nineteenth centuries assumed the validity of this correlation, that 'the humanities humanize'. Such minds as those of Voltaire, Jefferson, Marx, and Arnold assumed this was so.

Steiner (1971) is therefore suggesting that we now suffer from three "irreparables":

the loss of cultural centrality,

abandonment of the assumption of historical progress,

failure to be able to continue to believe that knowledge and humanism inevitably guarantee civilized behaviour.

"All these signify the end of an agreed hierarchic value-structure" (page 65). "If the gamble on transcendence no longer seems worth the odds and we are moving into a utopia of the immediate, the value-structure of our civilization will alter, after at least three millenia, in ways almost unforeseeable" (page 73). Elsewhere he refers to these as the collapse of eighteenth-century rationalism and of the liberal–humanist expectation.

The last lecture of *In Bluebeard's Castle* deals with "Tomorrow". He takes the view that whether or not our sense of doom is justified is not the debate. We have to acknowledge the fact that this is interwoven in the texture of our sensibility. It is with this we have to live. As return to the old is not possible, he addresses the question of whether there is a new literacy, since classic literacy is finished, its 'felt life' at an end. We now have academy and populism. The first is the preservation of the old literacy in the 'museum culture'—the maintenance of that logic which is dependent on the word, especially the printed word. This would essentially correspond with our notion of glyph cultures (chapter 13).

As the 'word' declines in its importance as a carrier of meaning, more and more information is transmitted in picture form, or in the notations of mathematics and symbolic logic. Steiner strongly affirms the view that Western civilization and its societies have been grounded in the logic of the word; the syntax and the psychology are so closely related that to lose the primacy of the language is to "... demolish the hierarchies and transcendence-values of a classic civilization. Even death can be made mute" (Steiner, 1971, page 88). A new phase in human development is opening.

He asks whether popular music can be a new literacy, pointing out its global instantaneity, its power to heed new fashions and life-styles, new private and public sociologies: "... the vocabularies, the contextual behaviour-patterns of pop and rock, constitute a genuine *lingua franca*, a 'universal dialect' of youth. Everywhere a sound-culture seems to be driving back the old authority of verbal order" (page 91). The word gives place to the musical phrase. He goes on to add that classical music also is to be included in the "presence of sound". New reproduction techniques allow it to reach a growing audience, which can listen at will. But the effects are ambiguous since the most profoundly emotive music may be used as background to some other activity. "A Muzak of the sublime envelopes us."

Steiner speculates whether this musicalization of our culture has to do with "... new ideals of shared inner life, of participatory emotion and leisure". Reading is an isolatory process whereas listening to music is shared, gregarious activity. "... the search for human contact, for states of being that are intense but do not shut out others, is real. It is a part of the collapse of classical egoism. Often music 'speaks' to that search as printed speech does not" (page 93). "In the absence or recession of religious belief, close-linked as it was to the classic primacy of language, music seems to gather, to harvest us to ourselves" (page 94). He compares the effects of using the capabilities of the electromagnetic spectrum with the spreading of written literacy by cheap books and the newspapers in a previous age. A new "culture outside the word" is being propagated.

He then looks at mathematics as another nonword language, pointing out that in any future culture the mathematical and natural sciences will be decisive. Science and technology progress at a fantastic pace. "The revolutions of awareness that will result from full-scale computerization and electronic data-processing can only be crudely guessed at." At some point in 1969, the information-handling capacity of computers "... passed that of the $3 \cdot 5$ billion brains belonging to the human race. It is probable that this electronic cortex [telecommunications plus the computer] will simultaneously reduce the singularity of the individual and immensely enlarge his referential and operational scope" (page 97). Since Steiner wrote, the development of universal packet-switching that is described in chapter 4 has made this enlargement fact from Tokyo to Zurich.

He mentions the ecological concern of our time but not in any detail.

In concluding *In Bluebeard's Castle* Steiner arrives at the view that we must incorporate science in the "field of common reference". For doing this "... the true motives ought to be those of delight, of intellectual energy, of moral venture. To have some *rapport* with the sciences is, very probably, to be in contact with that which has most force of life and comeliness in our reduced condition" (page 98). But this is easier said than done without a knowledge of mathematics.

This leads him to look at our drive to seek the truth, which, he thinks, has led modern man to worship fact to the detriment of ideas. But, in his view we shall persist and open the last door in Bluebeard's castle even though we perceive the possibility of self-destruction, so strong is our desire to acquire knowledge and our belief that science does this.

Nostalgia for the Absolute was given as a series of five talks for the Canadian Broadcasting Corporation in 1974. Here Steiner develops the idea that the erosion of European theology during the last hundred and fifty years has resulted in an "immense emptiness", and has left in disorder "... essential perceptions of social justice, of the meaning of human history, of the relations between mind and body, of the place of knowledge in our moral conduct" (Steiner, 1974, page 2). In using a theological perspective to think about our contemporary sensibility Steiner is depending on part of the mainstream of the tradition of the West. It is a part which might seem, especially to superficial observation, to have been progressively in recession since the Enlightenment. This appearance is precisely a major point of Steiner's argument.

Steiner believes that it is through myths that human beings make sense of the world. This is the way in which they come to reach a coherent world view. "Man is a primate capable of manufacturing, creating myths, and through these enduring the contradictory, insoluble tenor of his fate" (page 26). He sees religion as having been the great mythmaker in the past, and in its present collapse thinks that the contemporary Western world has sought to use the thought of certain recent thinkers to fill the void. He sees contemporary sensibility as trying, or having tried, to make new myth out of Marx, Freud, and Lévi-Strauss (1968). As an aside it should be noted that this view is not a critique of the scientific achievements of these writers. That is not the focus of attention. The emphasis is on the way in which contemporary human beings use, or have used, the knowledge developed by these thinkers as tenets of belief. For Steiner, this has occurred because of the contemporary vacuum at the very core of our present culture. There is nothing derogatory in suggesting that a body of thought has become the basis of a myth.

Steiner sees Marxism and Freudian psychoanalysis as already receding into history. But Lévi-Strauss, building on the other two, he sees aiming for a total mythology—*la science de l'homme*. Lévi-Strauss sees a binary world in which the most important pair is Nature and Culture: "It is the interplay between biological constraints on the one hand, and social–cultural variables on the other, which determines our condition" (Steiner, 1974, page 27). The interplay is dynamic but ambiguous, and the transition "... from a natural to a culture state was also a destructive step". "Man is in an unnatural power-relation to his environment and his own animal origins" (page 29). We clearly have here the assimilation of ecological thought but the placing of it in a traditional religious perspective. Human beings have misbehaved toward the life-support system; driven forth from Eden humankind must now learn what it means to experience the Fall.

Lévi-Strauss examined in detail about eight hundred American Indian myths. Steiner thinks him mythmaker par excellence: "If I do not mistake his meaning, Lévi-Strauss has been voicing a prophetic vision of apocalypse as vengeful, as persuasive, as any conceived since the Book of Revelation and the millenarian panics of the tenth century" (page 31). He concludes that Lévi-Strauss is providing a "... great postreligious, pseudo-theological explanation of man". In this mental condition man has ravaged the earth and must now turn on himself. Our attempts to repair the damage to the biosphere come much too late according to Lévi-Strauss: all will end in extinction. Man has failed to "... observe his contractual responsibilities to creation" (Steiner, 1974, page 37).

Lévi-Strauss thus joins hands with the ecologists. We might usefully recall here that writers in the field of ecology characteristically reach the notion of the need for a new world ethic whereby human beings will be able to guide their behaviour to respect the necessities of the biosphere. Not a few ecologists go in detail into the specific ethical formulations that will be required (for example, commandments: H T Odum, 1971, page 244).

To sum up Steiner's view on contemporary mythmaking the following quotation is appropriate: "Here are three great mythologies devised to explain the history of man, the nature of man, and our future. That of Marx ends in the promise of redemption; that of Freud in a vision of homecoming to death; that of Lévi-Strauss in an apocalypse brought on by human evil and human waste" (Steiner, 1974, page 37).

The fourth lecture in *Nostalgia for the Absolute* deals with some rather more obvious evidences of decline: "... ours is the psychological and social climate most infected by superstition, by irrationalism, of any since the decline of the Middle Ages, and, perhaps, even since the time of the crisis in the Hellenistic world". He instances the growth of belief in astrology, unidentified flying objects, 'extra-terrestrial callers', clairvoyance, magic, the occult. He says the externals do not matter. What is important is: "... the implicit idealization of values eccentric or contrary to the Western tradition. Passivity against will; a theosophy of stasis or eternal return against a theodicy of historical progress ..." (page 45). These changes are indication that the Western psyche has been severely damaged by the failure of the secular reason of the Enlightenment and the destruction of the liberal–humanist contract. The collapse of these two main supports of recent Western culture has been catastrophic and has led to a flight into unreason. But, says Steiner, this is a symptom; the underlying feeling is a "nostalgia for the absolute"[2].

Steiner thinks that out of the wreckage of these disasters one area of confidence, of felt solidity, is salvageable: "The foundation of personal existence on the pursuit of the objective scientific truth: the way of the philosophic and exact sciences. But has it a future?" (page 49).

Western man has believed, since the Greeks, that the disinterested pursuit of the truth is morally valuable. By the end of the nineteenth century, progress was assumed to be dependent on finding the truth, albeit provisional. In the twentieth century this comfortable assumption has been challenged; the attempt has been made to explain the pursuit of the

---

[2] It is not entirely clear how Steiner views the absolute. Perhaps, in the long tradition of Western man, his meaning is essentially religious. Science is not very sympathetic to any concept of absolute truth, viewing all truth as only provisionally held.

truth as a cultural phenomenon characteristic of the bourgeois society of the West. Truth becomes political. "The enshrinement of scientific laws, whether Newtonian, Darwinian, or Malthusian, reflects a conscious investment in intellectual and technological control over society" (page 54). So the attack against science is "... mythical, religious, political–dialectical". Steiner tackles another aspect: that the pursuit of the truth and our ideas of social justice do not necessarily coincide. Our science, or the fruits of it, may destroy us. War, interference in genetic processes, even the emotional absorption of the supposed heat-death of the world may bring us to our end [3]. Can we backtrack to a simpler state? Steiner does not think so— at least he finds no precedent. He concludes that the pursuit of the truth (knowledge) is "fatally imprinted" in our cortex. Therefore we shall keep asking questions and looking for answers even though the answers may destroy us. Traditionally, from the Greeks, we have held the view that "... the truth was somehow a friend to man, that whatever you discovered would finally benefit the species" (page 60). Is this "our greatest romantic illusion"? In spite of this question he thinks the pursuit of the truth does have a future. He is not sure whether man has.

17.3 Composite image

The three analysts of the inner condition of contemporary human beings— Ortega y Gasset, Zolla, and George Steiner—have been allowed to speak for themselves, without other than marginal comment and no attempt at refutation. Their views, obviously pessimistic about both the present and the future, can easily be matched by the opinions of a host of lesser critics. If we say the picture is painted unduly dark and that the future will show this, we have to remember that Ortega y Gasset's future is our present now—he described what we now have nearly fifty years ago—and Zolla put his views down over twenty years ago. Steiner represents a more strictly contemporary view that cannot yet be tested by the lapse of time.

The three humanities writers have been quoted from at length to give the reader the opportunity of staying with them for a considerable time, exactly in the same way that it has been necessary to stay with the electronic technological and ecological writers. Unless a reasonable time is devoted to key areas, in very roughly equal proportions, new linkages will not be generated in the mind, and new perspectives will not emerge. In the next chapter I shall attempt to bring together the various foci of attention developed in this section of the book. In the meantime the more immediate task is to create a composite picture from the material

[3] The notion of the inevitable heat-death of the world is modified by those who call, like Bertalanffy, for a new theory of thermodynamics which would allow for the upward movement of creation; by being joined together in the sun, atoms of hydrogen die but in the process they give birth to helium. So while it is true to say, as in physics, that some energy descends into 'sinks' from which it cannot be retrieved, this is not correct for all energy.

offered by the three humanities analysts. What follows is not therefore an exercise in evaluation so much as in discrimination and synthesis.

The following highlights stand out in the profile of the contemporary Western human being, according to our analysts:

1 He is the measure of himself: he recognizes outside himself no authority superior to himself, whose right to weigh him is acknowledged.
2 He is weak in will and has become passive. He gives pride of place to subjectivity, but longs to have his emptiness filled.
3 Because he feels himself free and without restrictions he suffers a sense of feeling empty.
4 He attempts to fill this emptiness by using stereotypes and flights into unreason, and relies on the offerings of the culture industry. Boredom results.
5 He does not believe in any unifying myth.
6 He assumes the right to the offerings of high technology as though they were the gifts of nature and not the result of hard-won discipline and accumulated application. Ever more is demanded, irrespective of the availability of supply.
7 He has a sense of power and wishes to intervene in the running of affairs.
8 He adopts this profile as a defence against the collapse of reason and liberal humanism.
9 He cannot respond to yet another call to make the effort toward utopia. Instant gratification is demanded.
10 He has a sense of living in a time which comes after an age of confidence and security. The image he has is of a lost coherence that cannot be regained. He has a sense of a major break with the past, connected with a disintegration of belief in the primacy of Western thought and feeling.
11 He worships fact to the detriment of ideas, and compulsively pursues the truth although it may destroy him.

The above description attempts to suggest the key elements of the human being in contemporary mass society as seen by certain humanities analysts. This is a portrait of modern, urban Western man, heir to and product of industrialism, massive population growth, science with its fostering of scepticism, and philosophical–political revolt against older systems of thought and feeling. The portrait is not attractive, and, even allowing for bias in the analysts, the sitter may well be no better than the picture. This is a far cry from Rousseau's image of the human being. The dynamic of the Enlightenment, in this regard and along the perspective of the humanities, appears spent. Yet the implications of the attitudes of the technologists and their fellow travellers suggest a more sanguine view, although in general they rarely make excursions explicitly into this field.

In the simplified portrait just given, all sociocultural effects and implications have been eliminated. These will be looked at in the next chapter in conjunction with our two major foci of attention—the telecommunications and computer technology and our ecological knowledge.

18

Comments on some emerging areas of attention

18.1 Preliminary

In this brief chapter I shall point up certain emerging areas in which thinking appears necessary as we progressively sense the presence of the new context in which we are already living.

The process of identifying areas of thought to which special attention may need to be given has a great deal to do with the generating of a world view, with integrating knowledge from various areas, or, in common parlance, attempting to make some sort of working sense of what we know. I take this making of sense to be the process of the individual truly assimilating selected new incoming information so that a certain coherence of 'mind' is maintained even as the content of 'mind' is expanded. This is the meaning of the observation that knowledge is personal (Polanyi, 1958), and of the concept of 'mind' as a kind of ecological system and having as essential characteristics diversity, stability, productivity, feedback, and capability for protecting its own integrity (Bateson, 1972; McCulloch, 1965).

The drive to make sense to ourselves of what we know as conscious individuals is manifest in the existential *angst* of our time, and the period immediately preceding our own. If knowledge cannot be felt to have meaning in our ongoing processes of experiencing ourselves we shall have difficulty maintaining the motivation to pursue the development of knowledge, or its application to the necessary management of our situation in the present stage of evolution of the total world system. This need for existential meaning is certainly a major, and perhaps the dominant, fact of our contemporary sensibility. In any thinking about how the present will move into the future it must have an important role. Seeing this helps us to place in perspective any predominantly technical solution or attempts to think and act about societal matters on narrow technologically modelled modes of thought (Ellul, 1964). What follows in this chapter is intended as support for this view and as point of departure for looking at detailed areas in the next part of the book. This chapter will include a brief description of one attempt to build a necessary framework of thinking (Harman, 1977).

18.2 Concept needs related to electrobionic culture and the new globalism

I have suggested that the emerging culture—electrobionic in description because of the two major components of the electronic technology and our ecological understanding of the world system—is a superimposition upon the glyph culture of previous civilizations, and as such it will both reinforce some characteristics of those earlier cultures and supersede some other characteristics through the generation of new ones. This is the Janus nature of the situation in which we are. I have also concluded that a new kind of globalism, or planetism, is a concomitant of this new cultural development.

These two emerging areas of awareness are potentially productive of very powerful new mental images, if we are to judge from similar situations in the past. The great age of physical exploration of the 'world' in modern times imaged a new world in the mind of the sixteenth and seventeenth centuries. The eighteenth century produced a further new image of the globe by coupling global physical exploration with the pursuit of science and technology. The nineteenth century added the notion of the physical and biological evolution of the world. We are less well informed about the change brought into human cultures by writing, whether of pictogram or of syllabic form, but it is hard to believe that the intellectual efflorescence of classical Greece was not a direct product of the access to new mental powers specifically conferred by the assimilation of writing.

As this book is not a study of previous cultural development but is essentially an attempt to think forwards, we need not pursue possible parallels any further. What is important for our purpose is that such massive changes as we are at present experiencing will inevitably call into being new conceptualizations and concepts, and that these can, in some measure, be consciously fostered in their growth. Appreciation of our ecological situation suggests that such conscious fostering is not an option but a necessity.

A conceptualization I take to be an overall assembly of ideas, wishes, and ideals which can be held together in adequate interaction with each other to allow exploratory thought to be developed. So our emerging sense that the total world system can be purposefully influenced in its evolutionary processes is a conceptualization, arising out of our understanding of ecosystems, population–food–energy pressures, and the knowledge that we have means at our disposal—the electronic technology and other—for realistically aspiring to operate consciously at the global scale.

A concept is somewhat narrower and more precise. Energy flow in ecosystems is an example. It consists of transfer of energy into the system from the sun, its metamorphosis, and its transfer round the system. Note that we cannot conceptualize without having some concepts to begin with, but at the same time we cannot discover the ways in which an area conceptualized functions in detail without developing specific concepts and relating them to each other. New conceptualizations possibly both emerge from concepts and at the same time generate concepts. A systemic relationship exists. Detailed theory, theory in the sense of generating working hypotheses, cannot be developed without adequate concepts being first available. Hence their importance.

Perhaps the most complex conceptualization with which we have to deal is the emerging notion of a total world system. This is appearing mainly, but not exclusively, out of ecosystem knowledge. Yet a total world system conceptualization must be more inclusive than the conceptualized ecosystem. It must clearly give a very major place to the fact that some ecosystems are strongly human-dominated and carry human populations in greatly disproportionate numbers to other populations. Second, a total world system conceptualization must give a very important place to human 'mind' and the now highly sophisticated electronic means for handling its products and bringing 'mind' to bear on the physical life support. Ecological theory, as at present developed, cannot adequately cope with these two major items. Contemporary attempts at framing world systems, whether ecological or other in approach, are at present lacking in their underpinnings of conceptualization and concepts (see, for example, Meadows et al, 1972; Mesarovic and Pestel, 1974; H T Odum, 1971). Even the most elaborately worked out model can be no better than the quality of its initial conceptualization and its designed concepts. If, therefore, we wish to find ways of thinking about the 'world' (physical, mental, societal, and cultural) we first have to make an imaginative effort to generate a conceptualization of quality good enough to sustain our efforts to use it exploratively. That process must include the search for concepts that will help do the detailed work. An example is to be found in the underpinnings of the physical sciences. Their basic conceptualization is a physical world that can be understood in its relationships by the human mind; the physical world is not seen as a lawless, unpredictable, capricious chaos of unintegrated material, but as a coherent working whole in which all parts are connected by consistent linkages. This is a conceptualization that has proved itself of adequate quality, or 'truth', to sustain much detailed exploration, which in its turn has made possible the development of large numbers of working concepts. These in their turn have made possible further detailed elaboration of the original conceptualization.

Our emerging task, therefore, in the presence of a new major conceptualization so to speak condensing, is to identify and explore its key areas as they now begin to appear, and to generate new working concepts. This will mean that we shall need to probe such questions as how to relate global concepts connected with 'mind' (such as noosphere) with our ecological knowledge so as to obtain continuity between those two major areas of enquiry. Similarly we need to try to link society–individual with its life support so as to be able to pass in our thinking from 'natural' to 'human' systems and back again with coherence. In the next part of this book I shall offer some suggestions for generating the necessary links. In the final part I shall explore ways of using these suggestions and offer some possible guides for operationalizing.

At this juncture it will be useful to give an example of how efforts of this kind are already beginning to be generated and made available for discussion.

18.3 Example of an attempt to conceptualize current incompatibility of socioeconomies with the life-support system

An interesting example is provided by the work of W W Harman and his associates in the Stanford Research Institute (Harman, 1976; 1977). As analysts of the developed socioeconomies, particularly the US, they have used a variety of techniques for thinking about the future.

These include: projections of existing broad trends in society, identification of the manifest problems of advanced industrial society, search for the metaproblems, the writing of alternative histories of the future, and the subdivision of the metaproblems which are the generics of the particular problems, the writing of alternative detailed scenarios, and the subdivision of the metaproblems into those that are technologicall solvable, those that are intractable because they are part of a 'cultural malaise', and those that will require major change in the institutions of society.

With these approaches attack is made on the key characteristics of our advanced industrial society. These are given as:

science – technology,

industrialization—labour replaced by machines,

acquisitive materialism—growth,

manipulative rationality—control of 'nature',

pragmatic values—emphasis on the individual.

The attack produces evidence that we face four major dilemmas, and that some difficulties are unlikely to be capable of solution within the frame (our present society. Even more serious, the dilemmas cannot be resolved collectively within the paradigm of industrial society because they are inherent in it and are requirements for or concomitants of its success. The difficulties are termed 'systemic dilemmas' to indicate that systemic transformations are judged necessary for their resolution. The dilemmas are identified as: growth, control, distribution, and work role.

The growth difficulty is that our growth rates in economic and resourc terms are seen as of only limited continuance. The costs of reducing the growth rate include accepting some economic decline. This is seen as meaning societal stresses of very serious magnitude. This is the familiar limits-to-growth argument and the deductions to be made from it.

The control dilemma is around the question of directing technological development so that it is humanly safe. Yet we decline centralized contr(of it because of fear of damage to the free-enterprise system.

The distribution problem is seen globally as the need to achieve a more equitable distribution of the world's resources. If the developed countrie: do not attend to this matter, global social stability comes under serious threat. The industrialized advanced societies, however, as a system, have no mechanism for achieving redistribution on a global scale between themselves and the developing countries. [See, however, Tinbergen et al (1976) for systematic thinking in this direction.]

The work-role question is essentially that the advanced industrialized socioeconomies are progressively unable to provide enough jobs of humanly meaningful kinds to match the 'needs' of their populations. In addition to the failing job-producing capability these socioeconomies are faced with a present 25% to 35% of the total potential work force being squeezed out in various ways. This failing situation is also important as work is a cultural and psychological function as well as a more narrowly economic one. Harman concludes that the work-role dilemma may be the most difficult problem of all to handle.

Harman puts the four dilemmas together to identify the "world macro-problem". This is seen as the often made observation that microdecisions, which are individually satisfactory, aggregate into unsatisfactory results at the macroscale. Abbreviated, the logic sequence offered is:

"The basic system goals that have dominated the industrial era ...
and that have been approached through a set of fundamental subgoals ...
have resulted in processes and states
which end up counteracting human ends ... .
The result is a massive and growing challenge to the legitimacy of the basic goals and institutions of the present industrial system" (Harman, 1977, page 9).

He concludes that failure to resolve the basic dilemma will produce ever greater stress in society. But resolving it will need "... fundamental systemic change and there is no very orderly way for such change to be accomplished" (page 9). Two main responses are concluded as possible. One, the present collective trend can be continued, or, two, the collectivist trend can be reversed. The catch in the former is that it depends heavily on centralized control, and the difficulty with the latter is its need for some form of coercion. Harman appears to come back to the idea of reeducation as a possible way.

18.4 Comment on "The coming transformation"

Harman's approach and findings have considerable common ground with the contents of this book, but also there are certain very important differences. His point of departure appears to have been the socioeconomy as a whole. My point of departure has been to take two major dynamics— the uses of the regions of the electromagnetic spectrum for communicating and computing, and our ecosystemic knowledge of our life support—and work outwards from them, but without specifically aiming to be all-inclusive, or particularly focussing on the socioeconomy.

This difference in approach leads to somewhat different emphases. For example, I reach the conclusion that, since the behaviour of mass populations is of key importance, it is vital to give very great attention to the values, attitudes, etc of the mass individual. Hence I move from the technology

and knowledge areas very quickly to the question of the mass individual's
character profile and sensibility, to make a trio of key areas of attention.
This involves certain socioeconomic foci of attention *but they follow as a
result, and are not set up a priori.* This produces a different picture of
the work role from Harman's.

In common with Harman I have found the notion of trying to identify
key areas of difficulty to be very useful. On the grounds, however, that
we do not yet have the conceptualizations and concepts necessary for
handling the matter they involve I have moved in the direction of probing
for the necessary intellectual tools rather than rushing head-on to attack
the dilemmas. I therefore move from formulation of the key areas of
difficulty to two levels of directions of action. It is by no means the case
that the formulation of the dilemmas, reached by whatever process, can be
considered firm at this stage. I have tried to hedge as much as possible
against this uncertainty by relying heavily on the firm, experimentally
supported knowledge of the telecommunications–computer technology
and ecology, and, on the side of the character of the mass individual,
drawing on well-respected contemporary and older sources, chiefly from
the humanities.

18.5 Some areas requiring major attention

At this stage some key areas can be identified. Although these can be
separated to some extent, we have to remember that the interrelationships
between them are of great importance in assessing where to direct our
efforts in the new situation. Some foci emerging are:
Globalism implies interrelationships *between* ecosystems. Their interdependence now becomes an important area of study. This is the perceived
unity and finiteness of the physical world through appreciation of the
life-support system. Not only do natural materials, such as oxygen and
water, flow between ecosystems but also human-generated commodities
and human-extracted elements circulate in ever-increasing quantities.
Globalism is being formed by the 'shrinking' of the world through the
electronic technology. This implies greatly increased interaction between
ecosystems of the biosphere. Information is the substance of this
interaction. As information is essentially mental, not physical, this aspect
of globalism will require the linking of our concepts about 'mind' to our
concepts of the life-support system.
The simplistic technological approach to matters considerably involved
with human beings in their society–individual aspects is dangerous because
of threat to ecosystemic stability. The global management that is now
becoming necessary is not amenable to such an approach. Ways have to
be found of 'ecologizing' or 'humanizing' our approaches to technology.
This requires an entirely new examination of technology.
A requirement of the above is that ways need to be found for including
the individual human being in the society–technology–ecosystem debate.

Because the character and sensibility of the mass individual exist as a widely distributed phenomenon (irrespective of whether we have the details exactly understood) the mass individual's profile is a key component in the management of the life-support system. This has to be investigated through the linkage mass individual–socioeconomy–life-support system. *The danger is that the behaviour appropriate for dealing with our life support at the socioeconomic level may be rendered unachievable because of the unsuitability of the profile of the mass individual. The role of the electronic technology here is strongly instrumental both toward the working of the socioeconomy and toward the formation and maintenance of the mass individual's inner profile. We can no longer think chiefly in terms of reconstructing socioeconomies; that is now insufficient.* Very important for the above is examination of the way the mass individual is supported within the socioeconomy (Harman's work role or what I have identified as the production–job–wages–consumption linkage in order to separate the physical supporting function from the psychological and other functions of work). What seems crucial here is to reach an understanding of the emerging nature of the developed socioeconomies in terms of job availability. The notion of the information society turns out to be very important, here, together with Masuda's attempts to plan for it.

Also very significant for the mass-individual question in the linkage which runs from the individual through society to the maintenance of ecosystems, is the support that has to be given to the development and application of knowledge. The mass individual has to have enough motivation to sustain this effort from the very core of his being—willingly. If not, the only other way is an unacceptable coercion. *This implies that the question of whether the mass individual can relate objective knowledge to his existential experience of himself becomes crucial.* In order to approach such questions new conceptualizations and concepts will be needed.

In the next part of this book I shall try to offer some ways of assisting our understanding of these major areas of attention. The approach will not be head-on, but somewhat oblique since the overarching sense is that acknowledgement of interconnectedness is a first priority—"whole system emphasis" to use Harman's phrase. Superficial logics with simplistic categorizations need to be avoided. The really major areas of importance can, perhaps, be built up only by, as it were, marginal accrual resulting from close attention to specifics.

Part 4

Generating concepts

For thinking in this area new concepts will be required, as will new relationships between concepts. New conceptualizations will be the building blocks of future theory. Some new concepts are suggested, some linkages between concepts are attempted, and some conceptual difficulties are raised.

Suggested concepts for linking ecological and mental approaches

19.1 Need for such linkage

In order to minimize the risk of confusion by appearing to become involved in grand theory this chapter is pragmatically structured to put forward, first, certain suggested concepts. Indications of selected theoretical considerations follow later. As a preliminary perspective, however, it will be useful to list briefly some of the reasons why we are faced with the need to generate conceptual links between our understanding of how the life-support system of the world works and our understanding of mental processes, or 'mind', not forgetting the products of those processes—information, knowledge, and know-how. These primary *products* give rise to secondary products, which in their turn also generate. And so on. Some of the reasons, then, can be stated:

1 The role of 'mind' is not adequately accounted for in ecological theory describing the life-support system[1]. The products of 'mind' tend to be seen as work, or presented in energetic terms. Clearly the specialized emphases given to the concept energy by the physicist and the biologist are not alone sufficient to describe the manifestations we call mental, that is, those emanating from the 'mind' functioning consciously and subconsciously.

2 'Mind' and its products now play a critically important role in the ongoing processes of the world's ecosystems. This role is being rapidly magnified in its significance because of the accelerating rate of the development of knowledge and its application, and the need to apply ever more knowledge to ecosystems so that they can sustain ever larger populations.

3 The extremely rapid growth rate of our information handling capability is the chief accelerator of our growth rate in knowledge and application. We thus have a rapidly increasing knowledge production capability as well as a rapid increase in actual production of mental output—greater *ability* to make and apply new knowledge as well as a rapidly growing stock of knowledge.

4 The capacity for the instantaneous presence of new knowledge in an ecosystem must now be a potential condition for all ecosystems. New knowledge can be very rapidly applied anywhere in the world.

---

[1] One at once thinks of the approaches of Bateson (1972) and McCulloch (1965). But they are essentially applying ecological thinking to the *study* of mind. They are not much concerned with the role of mind in the working of ecosystems. Calhoun (1962a; 1970), von Foerster et al (1960), and Wilson (1975), on the other hand, are concerned with how ecosystems produce mind in an evolutionary sense. They also only concern themselves with 'mind' as ecosystem component secondarily.

5 It is only by the application of knowledge to ecosystems that the global
   population–food–energy situation can be responded to within the
   limitations imposed by the need to maintain the stability and productivity
   of ecosystems in their world context.

To sum it up, the role of 'mind', its products, and supporting technologies
are destined to become ever more important to the maintenance of our
life-support system. In chapter 5 we saw our knowledge of the life-support
system to be firm and rapidly increasing. We understand the systems in
their various levels and can accurately quantify such processes as the
movements of nutrients, the flows of energy, the amounts of respiration
and radiation, and the molecular changes of decomposition. In chapter 2
we saw the extent of the growth of our knowledge and information
handling capability. This also is very firm knowledge and know-how, tested
continuously in the real world of application. Thus far, however, we have
not looked at what we have developed as a concept of knowledge at a
global or ecosystem level. This we must now do before attempting to
suggest our linking concepts.

19.2 The idea of the noosphere

Our conceptualization of the activities of mind in their manifestations in
the world—our knowledge of knowledge—is not as coherent as our
biological understanding of the life-support system. We know only
specialized items about how knowledge is generated, diffused, updated,
and handled in a global sense. In short, we have little by way of systemic
conceptualization of what we are handling. There are some attempts to
fill some of these gaps, for example Machlup's (1962) review of knowledge
in the US. But we have no ecology of knowledge, although Bateson (1972),
McCulloch (1965), and others have devoted attention to the ecology of
'mind'—a concern very closely related. And although cybernetics has
revolutionized epistemology since 1950 (see for example F H George, 1970a)
it does not appear to have offered much in the area of conceptualizing
knowledge globally so that it can be related to our ecological understanding
of the life-support system.

   The need is for a group of concepts to handle knowledge and 'mind' as
a globally distributed phenomenon comparable with the concept *biosphere*
used to describe the global distribution of the phenomenon we call life.
The word *noosphere* has achieved fairly general currency to meet this
need. Noosphere is used as an observation-concept to indicate that human
mental activity now stretches round the world as a continuous sphere, an
achievement made possible by the mechanics of our numbers and our
technical ability to create global and other networks that diffuse and make
readily accessible information and other products of 'mind'. Since birds
and fish may be said to have mind, the noosphere could be considered
roughly coterminous with the biosphere. In practical terms, however, it is
the human mental manifestations with which we are chiefly concerned.

Therefore the noosphere can effectively be conceived as coinciding only with that vertical range of the biosphere in which humans normally exist.

The concept of the noosphere (Greek νοῦς, mind), though not originated by Teilhard de Chardin, is strongly associated with his name. In the *Phenomenon of Man* he wrote of the noosphere: "Much more coherent and just as extensive as any preceding layer, it is really a new layer, the 'thinking layer', which, since its germination at the end of the Tertiary era, has spread over and above the world of plants and animals" (Teilhard de Chardin, 1970, page 202). He conceived the noosphere as having originated with the emergence of man's self-consciousness: "Psychogenesis has led to man. Now it effaces itself, relieved or absolved by another and a higher function—the engendering and subsequent development of mind, in one word noogenesis. When for the first time in a living creature instinct perceived itself in its own mirror, the whole world took a pace forward" (page 201)[2]. This ability for mental activity has now spread in a continuous membrane around the earth.

If the noosphere can be thought of as analogous to the biosphere, and as a kind of twin but at the mental level, we might anticipate the possibility of conceptualizing lower-order systems and develop concepts useful for handling the products of mental activity. We should note in passing, and will examine later, the fact that life—thought of generally as biological with a physical emphasis—and 'mind' do not inherently require the dualism that has for long been characteristic of Western thought. *On the contrary, the details of our conceptualizations drive hard toward a monist view. They strongly suggest that it is not useful to emphasize the separation of 'mind' from body but that it is more helpful to envisage a single continuum.*

If we follow up the idea of lower-order systems making up the noosphere we at once see that certain areas of the noosphere are characterized by very intensive and varied activity while other areas have low levels of activity. The eastern seaboard of North America is intensive; the Sahara is very low-level. For looking at any such zone, but especially at the very intensive areas, we can identify as useful some of the concepts used in studying ecosystems. Products of mental activity circulate; they are

[2] Teilhard de Chardin stresses consciousness as the essential characteristic of the noosphere. I do not think this is necessary and it is not desirable to do so. It used to be said that it was consciousness which differentiated the human being from the other biota which could be acknowledged to have 'mind'. This distinction is very possibly not valid and certainly is outdated. Although we are conscious—self-aware—of some of our mental processes, we do not 'know' them all. Indeed, we very possibly have access to a very small portion. For the present, therefore, I take the liberty of extending the noosphere to include what we call both conscious and subconscious 'mind'. Biology must describe man according to kingdom, phylum, class, order, and family, genus and species. He is phylum Chordata, class Mammalia, order Primates, suborder Anthropoidea, and family Hominidae, genus *Homo*, species *Homo sapiens*. We should note that 'biosphere' is as much a concept as the description of a physical fact. It is an observation-concept or description-concept.

stored; they are assembled to generate new material; some old material decays; the systems have stability but they must also withstand pressures from inside and outside themselves which tend to move them from their positions of steady state; and great diversity is present. Some characteristics of ecosystems are not present necessarily in the constituent lower-order systems of the noosphere. Most important among these, as we shall see later, is the limitation placed on the productivity of ecosystems through the finiteness—the quantitative limit—of radiation falling on the earth through the visible window of the electromagnetic spectrum. This difference will prove very important. In general the transfer of concepts from biosphere to noosphere looks as though it might be rewarding.

From this position we see the need to find ways of joining the conceptualizations already in common use for studying the biosphere with the concept noosphere. In this way we may hope to weld our ecology of the physical world and our ecology of the noosphere into a single ecology able to handle material in both areas by the use of similar types of concepts. To do this we need to find bridging concepts. If we cannot find a way of bridging that is acceptable, the two ecologies will remain fragmented and the perpetuation of the traditional dualism will continue to inhibit our thinking.

19.3 Neuromass and psychomass as bridging concepts
What might seem to be required would be evidence which would firmly show 'mind' to be describable in biological terms. This, at present, is not available although some, like McCulloch (1965), appear to think it possible to uncover such evidence. Even if it were available, however, it would now meet difficulties which arise from classifying the human being as the occupant of a rather inconspicuous niche in the taxonomy of biology. Such an approach, which biology can hardly avoid, has the objection of perpetuating a bias which is already considered to inhibit our ability properly to conceptualize ecosystems containing large masses of human beings. We shall look at these difficulties in the critique which follows the bridging proposal.

With this in mind I shall now tentatively put forward a possible way we may develop a three-stage conceptual bridge. The first stage is to identify the biological locus of mind as being the *neuromass*. This consists of those specialized cells of the brain and the nervous system that we believe to be the seat of key mental processes. We can identify these as clusters of cells, specialized as are the cells of other parts of the bodies of animals, insects, and plants, without necessarily having to enquire at this stage about how they achieve the mental process we call 'mind'. These specialized cells are physical and are accounted for by biology although their functioning may not be as fully understood as that of some other specialized cells.

We can next identify (figure 19.1) all the cells connected with mental processes in all the living creatures of an ecosystem in aggregate as part of the system's biomass. They are living physical material. This could be called the econeuromass, consisting of the total neuromasses of all animals and human beings of an ecosystem. The neuromass of the animals is not significant for our purpose as it does not contribute to the noosphere, only man's mental output being presumed to envelope the globe. We are therefore left with the neuromass of man himself. *For convenience, it is simplest to use neuromass to denote the total aggregate mass or weight of all the human brains and nervous systems in an ecosystem or the biosphere.* Neuromass, then, is our first-stage concept. It is readily assimilable by ecological theory.

The second stage is to conceptualize what it is that the neuromass does and what it produces. First, it directs the life functions of the organisms: it ensures survival by responding to sensory inputs, by promoting action, or more accurately by rendering decisions, storing and processing information, and building knowledge–know-how. Second, in human beings the activity of the neuromass goes far beyond what is needed for survival and has developed a unique growth dynamic of its own. For the moment let us say it produces, organizes, and uses knowledge, imagination, and feeling. Again, we need not for the moment pursue the question of *how* it does this.

This output of the neuromass we could call the *psychomass*. This is not process but strictly product. It is not how we think and feel but *what*. Like the neuromass it is therefore, in theory, measurable and 'concrete'. Its existence is not theory or speculation since it can actually be pointed out in the form of knowledge, etc. We shall see that it is important to keep this concreteness in mind when we come to look, later, at the concept of psychosystem.

Like neuromass, psychomass should strictly be used to describe the totality. It could be used to describe all knowledge, etc generated by all insects, animals, and human beings in an ecosystem[3]. Since our present interest is only in that part of the psychomass which belongs to man, the word will be used with that meaning.

19.4 Nature of psychomass
The nature of neuromass need not greatly concern us since we are involved only with its product. Impairment of the neuromass functioning (produced for example by prolonged stress) would, of course, have adverse effects on the psychomass, for example what we call 'madness' or 'insane' acts might be produced. We must, however, indicate the elements which constitute

---

[3] There would presumably be little difficulty in accepting the presence of 'mind' throughout the kingdom Animalia. Logically, my position would have to be that the possibility of 'mind' in the rest of the biota must not be excluded.

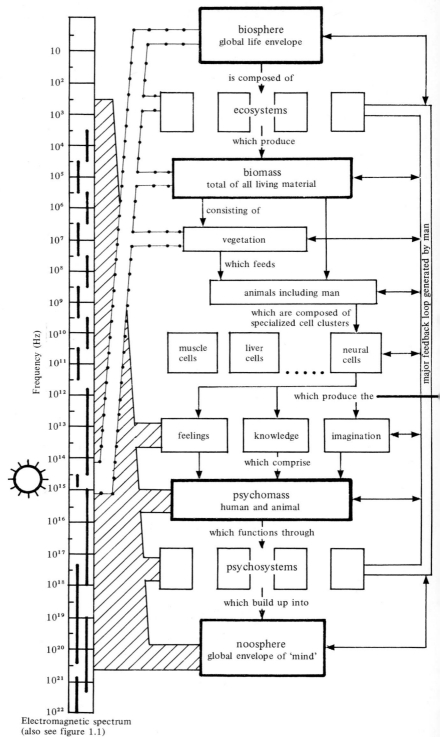

Electromagnetic spectrum
(also see figure 1.1)

systems

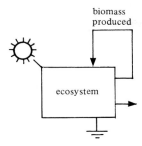

biomass
produced

ecosystem

Each ecosystem reaches
a climax condition.
There is a limit to growth.
Application of psychomass
may push back this limit
but cannot eliminate it

the type of system changes

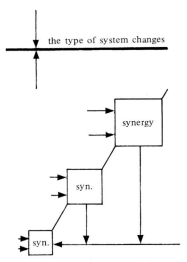

synergy

syn.

syn.

Psychomass production proceeds by
synergy. There is no known limit to
psychosystem production of
knowledge inherent in the total
system of the noosphere. This is
partly because psychomass is not
consumed by being used.

Figure 19.1. Linking biosphere and noosphere. By introducing the concepts of neuromass (neural cells) and psychomass it is possible to make a continuous linkage between the physical living systems and 'mind'. The noosphere and the psychomass which it produces and maintains are now major evolutionary elements. In the diagram the upper part is the ecosystemic area, fed by solar radiation and shown by the dotted paths; the lower part is the psychosystemic area, shown by using the regions of the electromagnetic spectrum (the hatched area). Glyph cultures used only the solar radiation band to serve the psychosystemic area. The diagram therefore demonstrates the magnitude of the increase in communicative capability that electrobionic culture has achieved. Note that the type of system changes. Shown on the right, the ecosystem has limited productivity. Psychosystems have no limits either to the levels capable of being reached or to productivity, since human mental capability is self-reinforcing in many ways, including the production and use of 'artificial intelligences'.

psychomass. A series of points may do this best:

1 Psychomass is defined as the products of neuromass seen as concrete 'objects'—items of knowledge, etc. It does not involve description of *how* production takes place, and therefore does not contain intervening concepts such as psyche or subconscious. The neuromass is physical and the psychomass concrete.

2 It includes all *products* of the 'mind' for which we have descriptive terms, therefore:

3 It includes all scientific knowledge.

4 It includes all experiential knowledge.

5 It includes all skills.

6 It includes all information.

7 It includes all value hierarchies capable of being stated.

8 It includes all emotions, that is, not the process of generating the feeling but the emotion produced—anger, fear, etc.

9 It includes the products of imagination, for example new 'ideas', concepts, states of being, the material of the arts, and wishes.

Psychomass is analogous to biomass; it is the aggregate of products. Biomass represents the aggregation of all living material sustained in an ecosystem; psychomass represents a similar aggregation of the products developed by the neuromass (which is itself part of the biomass). Biomass has been carefully studied in all its forms, from the virus through to the human beings as components. A score of highly developed disciplines continually expand our knowledge, systematize it, and apply it. The psychomass, however—itself the disciplines—is not at all well studied. Some psychomass, such as the emotions, values, attitudes, we know very little about, except experientially. There is, therefore, an imbalance between our knowledge of the biomass and our knowledge of the psychomass of the world. We know in detail the cycle of events represented by the tree. But we know little about the birth, diffusion, influence, decay and disappearance of an item of knowledge. We know how the Amazon forest works in its production of biomass but little of how the area of London generates, relates, and uses its psychomass. We ought to take this deficiency seriously into account when we consider the productivity of modern nation states. To do precisely this is the thrust of Masuda's argument summarized in chapter 9.

The characteristics of psychomass in which it is similar to biomass are:

1 Psychomass is classifiable as of different kinds, or species.

2 It is both product and producer, and therefore is systemically describable

3 It is dynamic and not inert. Some concept of energy appears relevant.

4 It can build upon itself, higher levels being successively attainable; it is aggregative and may be cumulative [4].

[4] In ecological description this is the notion of niches, each upper niche being made possible by the sequence of niches below it. Psychomass shows a similar sequential structure in many regards. Physics depends on the availability of mathematics. Over

5 It is variable in its density across global space, sometimes being scarce,
   sometimes being highly concentrated.
6 Cyclicity—the circulation of material—is typical and now global.
7 It is concrete, identifiable, even measurable.
8 It is characterized by symbiosis of species, or kinds.
But there are some very great differences between biomass and psychomass:
(a) Psychomass is not consumed or lost by being 'used'.
(b) It is not necessarily fixed in space but is often easily transferrable,
    frequently instantaneously in some of its forms, over great distances.
(c) There are no apparent limits to the amount that can be produced.
(d) It can be stored indefinitely.
(e) It is reflexive, that is, self-conscious, and can turn its own processes on
    itself.

19.5 Noosystem or psychosystem

The third and last part of the bridging that has to be generated is the
conceptualization necessary for dealing with psychomass in its aspect of
being an output component of the noosphere. Just as the biomass is
produced within the systems of the biosphere, so psychomass is capable of
being seen as product of the ongoing processes of the noosphere. This is
not incompatible with its also being product of the neuromass, as indicated
above. The trees of the biosphere have also this double relationship, as do
all other components which go to make up the world's total biomass. The
living material of the tree can only make more living material because of
the operation of all the processes of the ecosystem of which the tree is
itself a part. At the same time the detailed production of new leaves, sap,
and fibrous material is carried out by the entity or organism *tree*, specifically
by using radiation through photosynthesis to produce the new material.
The detailed production is done by the entity; the wherewithal is
provided by the larger system at the appropriate time and place and in the
appropriate forms and quantities. Essentially the process is one of *assembly*.
Psychomass is produced similarly. The larger system provides the materials
but it is the individual concentration of neuromass (the human brain,
nervous system, etc) which makes possible the assembly of the materials
into new product—new psychomass.

  The level of system which provides the materials may be called the
noosystem or the psychosystem. The latter is perhaps preferable as it is
more obviously comprehensible. Julian Huxley, who was much impressed
with Teilhard de Chardin's thought and was instrumental in seeing that his
later work was published, suggested in 1961 the word noosystem might be
coined to indicate dominant idea-systems. He does not appear to have

time, science is cumulative although the additions may come sporadically and some
additions may not be permanently admitted. Psychomass developed experientially may
be characterized by sequential buildup. But other psychomass may not be so clearly
cumulative although it may remain aggregative.

developed the concept[5]. The use suggested here is that the product of mental activity should be called psychomass, the system of which it is a component being the psychosystem. The psychosystem would include various species of psychomass in their spatial, temporal, cultural aspects and would mediate such characteristics as cyclicity, diversity, and steady state in the psychomass. There is also the very important feature that a psychosystem can be identified as relevant to an individual, a small group of human beings, a larger group, and finally to the total population of th world. As with biomass, psychomass is amenable to subsystemic analysis. The tree is a portion of the total product of the ecosystem, but it is itsel a lower-order system.

Research on psychosystems by no means matches that which has been devoted to ecosystems. As we have seen, knowledge of ecosystems is precise at certain levels. We can measure respiration, the flow of nutrients the weight of biomass, etc. In psychosystems we find isolated forays into the field from many different approaches. At the micro level we have Bateson (1972) looking at the psychomass of the alcoholic and identifyin what he is seeing as a cybernetic system. At the other end of the scale w have recorded Ortega y Gasset and Zolla describing what is essentially the psychosystem of the mass human being in the Western world in this century (chapter 16).

For ecosystems we have criteria which have to be satisfied, and generall acknowledged identifications: pond, forest, lagoon islands, the broad ecological areas of the North American continent, seas, mountain areas, etc. Equivalent criteria and identifications do not exist for psychosystems. We d not have any list even of broad classifications. At this stage we might sugges that psychosystems should be studied as similar in type to ecosystems so that evidence of *level* of complexity of system may be gathered. Here we should go back to chapter 1, where the problem of matching the ascending ladder of systems (atom to biosphere, figure 1.1) with some range of system types (static, dynamic, cybernetic, etc) was mentioned.

In the absence of any commonality of approach to studying psycho-systems the following characteristics of perspective may be suggested:
1 A range of psychosystems might be developed to match the upper part of the biological range in figure 1.1. This would imply seeing an equivalent range to organism (for example the individual human being), population, community, subglobal entity, and global entity.

[5] In a footnote (Huxley, 1961, page 13), appears the suggestion that noosystem might be used to indicate "dominant idea-systems". He did not, to my knowledge, adopt the word but did use idea-system to include "... beliefs, attitudes and symbols a well as intellectual concepts and ideas". My use of psychosystem is not identical sinc it refers to the *processes–structures* which handle the ideas, etc. For the ideas, etc I use psychomass—parallel to biomass. Von Foerster et al (1960) has used ideo-mass to cover information only but did not, to my knowledge, follow the suggestion up with any detailed study.

2 It needs to be questioned whether all psychosystems, of whatever level, are to be regarded as essentially ecological in their processes. Some researchers, such as McCulloch and Bateson, clearly think so.
3 Where psychosystems are not seen as ecosystemic in type are they of a 'lower' order? For example, is the psychosystem of an entire culture capable of being held in a steady state by its own internal processes or is it to be regarded as inherently nonstable? This relates to the phenomenon of succession to maturity in ecosystems and the problem of decline from the maturity condition—a common notion in the study of cultures.
4 Does a psychosystem have the equivalent of a climax condition? It is necessary to know whether a psychosystem can reach only so far because of its particular condition. For example, we shall see later that biology cannot go beyond a certain point because of the basic approach with which it starts out. This may be similar to an ecosystem at its climax having a relatively low rate of production of new biomass and a relatively high rate of consumption of energy to maintain existing biomass (for example the Amazon forest).
5 As psychosystems are essentially human their development is dominated by human beings. Like technological systems they are essentially human-created, and human-manipulated, although they are dependent on 'natural' neuromass. This leads to a focus of attention on system characteristics. Are they similar to those of the ecosystem?
6 As in our present age the bringing together of knowledge from different disciplines has proved so productive of new knowledge and applications, we have to enquire about the role of diversity and cyclicity in psychosystems.

The above foci of attention are not in any way comprehensive but are only indicative of certain areas of research necessary to examine the concept, psychosystem. In addition to identifying and examining such foci of attention having to do with the possible parallels between present ecological knowledge and knowledge to be discovered about the noosphere, there are certain assessments which need to be made about psychosystems and psychomass. These will now be attempted in as brief a form as possible.

19.6 'Mind' and its products now a global dominant

During the time that our knowledge of the workings of the biosphere and the applications of our electronic technology have been developing their own particular globalisms (chapter 14) psychomass has been accumulating on a world scale at a very rapid rate. Very substantially this now vast accumulation of knowledge is represented by the outputs of science and technology, although the growth of the total quantity of simple stored information must now be included in a conceptualization of the aggregated knowledge–information that we have amassed. The important fact here,

then, is that the human species has generated and stored very rapidly a ver
large quantity of psychomass around the world. This is a new condition.
There is now a large aggregation of a new substance in the world.

The second key fact is that the electronic technology has provided
entirely new capabilities for handling our global psychomass. It can be
stored, processed, and retrieved at new levels of quantity, speed, and
spatial dimension. Packet-switching, as we saw in chapter 4, means
literally universal access to information on a global scale. Further, the
electronic technology is now the main support of almost all processes for
producing new psychomass; there is hardly any discipline which does no
rely on the computer, and to an increasing degree the telecommunication
technology, for doing its leading-edge research, not to mention the refinii
and application of its knowledge at more routine levels. Also, this
production of psychomass is a global process.

If we put these two facts together and place them within the broad
context of thinking about the world as a whole, it is immediately apparei
that we are looking at a total global condition vastly different from that
which existed as recently as eighty years ago when our capacity to shift
from the exclusive containment of information handling in the visible
band of the electromagnetic spectrum into other regions of the spectrum
was just beginning to be developed. The total global system now has to
be seen as including a very large amount of information and knowledge
which is freely accessible and still expanding extremely rapidly. We
cannot, therefore, view the total world system as simply a 'natural'—that
is, a nonhuman—system in which psychomass is held either not to exist (
to exist only in very small quantity. Psychomass must now be seen as a
very major component of the total global system.

This, then, is the first and very basic reason why we have to begin to
think about developing concepts such as psychosystem and psychomass.
Some such concepts are urgently required to allow us to think about the
total system of the world in a condition in which the components of the
system have recently changed their weightings and relationships radically.

19.7 Limitations of ecological theory
As claimant to the position of overall body of theory for describing the
total world system, ecology evinces some weaknesses. Among these
are difficulties bound up with exactly the ecosystem component of
information–knowledge that we have just considered.

Ecosystem theory, in its very fruitful insistence on a monist or unitary
view of the world—it sees the world as a whole and not dualistically with
man and nature separate—emphasizes that the human species is one amor
the many elements of the biomass. This, of course, it is. We are part of
the natural world as are the trees and the other animals. But we are muc
more than an organism through which water and minerals are cycled. To
see ourselves chiefly with this emphasis is a severe limitation when we

come to look at ecosystems in which human beings are the dominant component, as in the cities of the glyph civilizations, or when the quantity and quality of psychomass may be of very great importance, as in our emerging electrobionic global culture. The limitation specifically takes the form of seriously underestimating, or relegating to a very minor position, the role played by what for the moment we may call 'mind'. This can be held to stand conveniently for both the mental process and the product, the psychomass and the psychosystem in this part of the discussion.

   This limitation in ecological theory can be viewed as unavoidably self-imposed by the exponents of the discipline. This is because the understandings provided by ecology in large measure stem from adopting the classifications of biology. *Homo sapiens* has to be allocated his position in the descriptive totality of all living material. In order to be biology at all, the discipline must accept this self-imposed mode of definition, classifying the human species as one among many. In classificatory terms the biologist may note that the human being has attributes not possessed by the amoeba, but he cannot therefore accord him a special importance. We are hitting here a limitation inherent in all Aristotelean classifications and characteristic of all the sciences.

   Looked at biologically, *Homo sapiens* is one among the animals. But he is the most highly evolved, and the gap between him and even the most highly developed of the primates or the insects is enormous. The most significant difference is in the area of 'mind'. We are a very special element of the biosphere, or of any ecosystem in which we are present, because of our mental development. In some ecosystems, for example in those having very large numbers of human beings, we are the most powerful living component, able to influence almost all other components, including the air temperature, the water cycle, the biota, the earth's surface. Teilhard de Chardin's name is closely associated with the identification of the need for a taxonomy which would acknowledge this emphasis. "Man, who has appeared as a simple species, has gradually come to form a specifically new layer enveloping the earth by a process of ethnicosocial unification" (Grenet, 1965, page 158). Teilhard de Chardin's own comment appears as a note to the effect that the current taxonomy in biology will not fully serve his purpose (Teilhard de Chardin, 1971, page 80). Bronowski (1973, chapter 13) makes the same point: human beings cannot be adequately described as a species in a biological series. They are that but much more also. The thrust of the present argument is that in the 'ethnicosocial unification' it is the role of information–knowledge that now dominates.

   This biological classification of the human being may be partly the reason why ecologists have dealt much less penetratingly with the city than with nonurban ecosystems. They have hardly gone further than treating the phenomenon of large numbers of human beings living in close proximity as a 'natural' (nonhuman dominated) ecosystem. This approach sees the city as having inputs of energy (food and fossil fuels), doing work, producing goods and services, having losses and wastes[6]. This is a way of describing what we call a city but it is approximately equivalent to describing a horse as something that eats oats and draws a cart. This does indeed describe a horse, but only in a certain context and for certain purposes; the rest is omitted.

Some ecologists are aware of the limitation which this matter of classification imposes on them and try to circumvent it. For example, E P Odum (1975, page vi), attempting to show how ecology may form the link between many disciplines, emphasizes the avoidance of the 'man and nature' dichotomy. He stresses the integrative role of ecology in bringing together the "... physical, biological and social sciences". The principle underlying this viewpoint is that of integrative levels of organization (see Feibleman, 1954). A difficulty with this approach is that the disciplines which deal with human society, in focussing on human beings in their interrelations, underestimate that perspective of the human being in nature which is the very core of the ecological approach. The problem raised by Teilhard de Chardin may well not be amenable to solution by integration at this level.

It is necessary, however, to stress how far some ecologists have moved in probing the difficulty. Again E P Odum's thinking is illuminating. He thinks about 'human ecology', and points out that in the last twenty or so years there has been strong interest by a wide variety of disciplines in coming together to develop such an ecology. This awareness has been reflected in the appearance of academic interdisciplinary research institutes dedicated to studying 'the environment'. Fairly rapidly a focus of attention has come to be the relationship between human cultures and the 'natural' ecosystems to which they relate. So we find E P Odum writing, as a reflection of one view of the city: "It is the ultimate creation of human civilization where want and strife are unknown and life, leisure and culture can be enjoyed in comfort by men shielded from the harsh elements of the physical environment". Odum comments that this will only come "... when the city functions as an integral part of the *total biospheric ecosystem*" (E P Odum, 1975, page 512; emphasis supplied).

Here we may have an Achilles' heel of present ecological thinking when applied to ecosystems in which man predominates. Without being clearly aware of it, the ecologists suddenly seem to abandon their basic idea of the unity or totality of the system. They now talk of human cultures *and* nature, of the need for cities to become integral parts of the biospherical system, as though human beings have somehow become something outside the biosphere. This is not so. We are just as much a component and product of the biosphere as the trees, *even when we misbehave ecologically*.

---

[6] The best representative of this line of enquiry is perhaps H T Odum (1971). He does incorporate the role of information in his chapter 5 but not at the level of importance I am suggesting for psychomass (chapter 20).

We may be reducing the stability of ecosystems, but if ecological theory means anything, it cannot deny that we are integrally bound up with the life processes of the ecosystems in which we here and now exist and with those other ecosystems with which we have relationships by way of trade, investment, and dependence for resources such as water, oil, and oxygen. Human populations cannot be counted as outside the world system if ecology is to be claimed as the discipline which is the integrator of all disciplines.

We must ask whether the ecologist has fallen into this self-contradiction or denial of his ultimate principle because he has failed to account in his systems thinking for that element in human beings and other animals we call 'mind'. And, further, whether the reason for this inability or unwillingness to account for 'mind' is that he must see human beings as a species and as a marginal subdivision of the biota. The mechanics of the failure is that this 'wretched' (Teilhard de Chardin) view of the human being discourages the search for concepts that might make possible, first, the perception of the weakness and, second, its correction.

A little while back the phrase 'total global system' was used. By this it was intended to suggest that we can envisage a totality of the world, including the physical and the nonphysical, without necessarily being compelled to do so by adopting the approach of any single particular discipline. If we then put against this E P Odum's phrase—*the total biospheric ecosystem*—we obtain another highlight on our problem. Odum seems clearly to be thinking of ingesting the human manifestation into the concept of the biospherical ecosystem. This, I have tried to suggest, cannot be done because of the emphasis inherently and unavoidably present in the biological classification *Homo sapiens. Hence ecology, as it stands, cannot* alone *be the body of knowledge that will provide the guidelines within which large human populations must act and live.*

However, there is no other comparably reliable body of knowledge which is capable of describing for us how our life-support system functions. Biology–ecology is firm in this regard and if we fail to act within the basic rules governing ecosystems we shall run serious risks. A wise approach, then, would be to search for ways of extending our knowledge of the life-support system into areas not yet properly accounted for, while simultaneously fostering the growth of our present approaches to the study of the life-support system and governing our actions by what we already know and further learn. Nothing much can be gained and a great deal might be lost by focussing attention on narrowly human processes to the neglect of ecosystem processes.

This, then, is the logic of the attempt of this chapter to suggest a way of extending our ecological knowledge of the life-support system so that the limitation we have identified might be circumvented. As the key characteristic of the human being is our high level of mental development, we have to extend our ecology so that the total global system can be conceptualized with an adequate role for 'mind'. *Hence we have developed*

L

from the concepts of ecosystem theory to concepts of neuromass, psychomass, and psychosystem, which make possible a continuous chain between the existing concepts of biosphere and noosphere. This must inevitably lead us to a critique of the validity of such a process of concept formation and comparison.

19.8 Transfer of ecological concepts

Biological–ecological concepts and theory have been so effective in discovering the working of the life-support system of the world that it is not surprising that attempts are made to transfer them to other fields. For example, such a transfer is attractive for the study of cities (for example Newman, 1975). These attempts often consist of the shifting over of such concepts as system, productivity, energy, stability, entropy, without examining differences between the originating field of ecology and the receiving field. Some studies try to keep the meanings of the concepts constant during transfer. So H T Odum (1971), for example, traces energy flows through cities using the same concepts and measures as are used in 'natural' ecosystem studies. Difficulties arise, however, when mental 'energy' has to be admitted (other than as a somatic output) and information has to be included.

It is justifiable to be wary of such transfers particularly when it is remembered that many of the processes of the life-support system are very complex. The elucidation of a relatively small part of the biological energy-flow sequence, the Krebs cycle, can be enough to win its discoverer a Nobel prize. Leaving aside such simple questions as how the input of oil is divided up amongst the various users, it may be that the flows of energy in human masses are also very complex, especially as 'mind' enters into relationship with commodity. A city does not use oil in the rigid physical sense that a tree uses carbon dioxide.

Neuromass is the least difficult to justify. This is physical—the aggregation of all brain and nerve cells. This mass is clearly a subdivision of the biomass of any ecosystem or of the total biosphere. It is conceptually as identifiable as all the tree-mass or elephant-mass. The concept of neuromass is therefore acceptable to present ecological thinking. It does have a difficulty, however, in that we do not know whether the neuromass is exclusively responsible for mental products. It has been suggested that every cell of the organism may have a memory function—that memory is holographic. If true, however, this would not vitiate the biological support which underpins neuromass since it would simply be a matter of moving upward in the hierarchy of systems from the organ (brain and nerves) to the organism (the human being a defined physical body). The neuromass would still remain concrete and physically identifiable and would not extend outside the human being. Artificial extensions do, of course, exist and with computers and telecommunications networks we do arrive at joint human and nonhuman neuromass. But of that later.

Psychomass is the product of the neuromass and of the psychosystem of which any particular neuromass is a part. Production—the generation of more than already exists—is a key concept of ecology. By assembling components into concentrations and holding them in being, ecosystems permit additional production to occur. This happens in a process of succession up to a climax condition. The system condition evolves and eventually stabilizes. The period of evolving is characterized by the production of new material—new biomass. Production is therefore essential. Thus there is no difficulty in the acceptance biologically of the fact that the neuromass produces.

Production in a psychosystem has at least one major characteristic which differentiates it from production in an ecosystem. In an ecosystem production is limited at the climax stage so as to be only enough to satisfy replacement needs. The aggregate biomass does not increase. Any given ecosystem therefore has an upper limit of production. This is not true of the psychosystem. All psychosystems appear capable of unlimited production of psychomass, whether or not they are producing at any given time. If, for example, we consider a group of physicists, the aggregation of psychomass called physics, and the equipment (laboratory, computer, etc) to be a psychosystem, then there is no reason to suggest that there is any limitation on the quantity of psychomass which could be produced. There may be qualitative upper limits, but that is another matter which might open a useful line of enquiry. This systemic difference is diagrammed, very simplistically, in figure 19.1 (right-hand portion).

In addition to allowing that the notion of producing is common to ecosystems and psychosystems in the perspective of psychomass, we can observe a major difference between the nature of biomass and that of psychomass. Biomass is always physical, by definition. It is mass, as in physics. If 'used', it is consumed or metamorphosed. Once broken down it can only be recreated by the processes of the ecosystem. This is not true of psychomass. Information or knowledge may be used repeatedly, simultaneously by many users and is not consumed or broken down. It can, however, disappear through inadequate storage or because superseded by psychomass of superior quality—new discoveries render existing 'knowledge' obsolete.

The question of storage presents no difficulty in the conceptual sense. Both biomass and psychomass are stored by their systems for short or long periods. The aggregated individuals of species constitute the 'reservoir' of stored biomass. The forest is stored biomass in the form of trees and animals. Psychomass is stored in human memories, in the visible-band storage modes of glyph cultures—books, scores, etc—and in the electronic storage modes made available through the use of other regions of the electromagnetic spectrum. Climax ecosystems have a limit to the amount they can store. We cannot assume that a given psychosystem necessarily has an upper limit.

Looking now at the psychosystem as concept we can try to find characteristics that we already know exist in ecosystems. One which appears very important is the inbuilt tendency of a system to respond to change in ways that will ensure its continuance. This is the same as saying that there is a capability of return to a condition of steady state if the system is disturbed—a kind of drive toward self-preservation. This characteristic is well authenticated in ecosystems. Even organisms will behave in the same way. Group psychosystems may be argued to show this characteristic. An academic discipline tends to protect and perpetuate itself. There is also evidence that the psychosystem of the individual is based on this principle; Bateson (1971) argues cogently that it is precisely this characteristic of the psychosystem of the alcoholic that makes it so difficult to cure him. Bateson demonstrated very convincingly the ecology of the alcoholic's mental processes.

Perhaps enough has been indicated to suggest that the three concepts— neuromass, psychomass, and psychosystem are useful and are likely to be capable of responding to comparison with ecosystem concepts. It seems probable, however, that the ways of diagramming the two types of systems will show differences as well as similarities because of the differences in characteristics that we have indicated. So psychosystems, while not identical with ecosystems, may perhaps prove to be characterized by certain ecological principles. If so, our hopes for a conceptual continuum from biosphere to noosphere will not be in vain. The benefit would be the command of a framework capable of holding together the image of a total global system.

19.9 Other avenues and issues

The attempt to generate a conceptual continuum from biosphere to noosphere suggests several other areas of justification, development, and application additional to those discussed above. Among these others we can include: the matter of pressures exerted by the growth of our telecommunications and computing capacity and the global population–food–energy syndrome; profound disturbances in our received ways of looking out upon the world; the workings of the processes that have already forced, and still continue to force, the development of human mental activity; and the very important fact that certain kinds of mental activity are being progressively carried out by artificial or human-made neuromass—*the capacity of the global human neuromass for generating and handling psychomass has been enormously increased by the reflexive application of the neuromass's own products.*

The task of looking at such other matters cannot be addressed here, although some will be tackled later. We must now consider certain likely key areas in which our conceptual continuum biosphere–noosphere may prove useful.

Relationships between ecosystems and psychosystems

20.1 Interrelations between global ecosystems

In their 'natural' state, before human beings existed in appreciable numbers or the noosphere had been generated, the ecosystems at global level were linked only through movements of air, water, animals, and the nutrients, seeds, debris, etc that those components would carry. Human beings have interfered with these linkages just as they have changed the internal workings of the ecosystems themselves, especially in the temperate zones. The world has now reached a stage where this interference must be counted a major factor in the ongoing ecological processes. The interrelationships between ecosystems have therefore moved a long way from their earlier condition and we must conclude that we have a new ecology of the ecosystems themselves as, in their continuing evolution, their ongoing processes maintain viable the global ecosphere. (See figures 20.1 and 20.2.)

Perhaps the most basic perspective along which to look at these interrelationships is that of the symbiosis between heavily human-populated ecosystems and ecosystems which are extensively controlled in their succession processes to produce large quantities of human-usable biomass—food. As an example of the heavily human-populated ecosystem we may

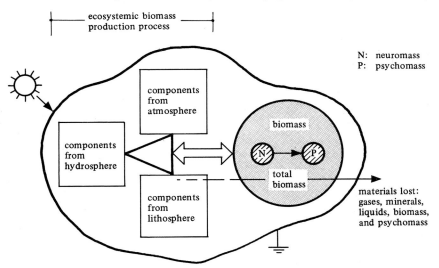

Figure 20.1. Ecosystem self-sufficient in biomass. As indicated by the size of the neuromass the human population is relatively small and is supported entirely within the life process of the ecosystem. There is no export of biomass and no necessity to export psychomass or its products in exchange for edible biomass. This type is exemplified by a rural area of 'self-sufficient' farmers. Minor modifications can include some export in exchange for farm equipment, etc, and some minor winning of fossil fuel within the system itself for heating. Natural inflows of materials are not shown.

take the eastern-seaboard ecosystem of North America, stretching from the edge of the Canadian Shield to the northern end of Florida, and bounded westward by the Appalachian Mountains. This carries fifty or so million human beings very expensively maintained in terms of energy at a high level of calorie intake of biomass. This biomass itself is expensive to produce when costed in calories[1]. This ecosystem could not support this population at its present level unaided. The human-usable biomass has to be obtained from other ecosystems—grains from the prairies, produce from the southeast and southwest, fish from the Atlantic, etc. For this to be possible to the extent necessary, the land ecosystems have to be held in a permanently arrested state in their evolutionary succession. This requires inputs of energy from outside the producing system, and these inputs have to be 'paid' for. We conventionally account for the 'paying' in terms of the exchange of goods and services. So the megalopolis of the eastern seaboard pays the Middle West with manufactured goods and services.

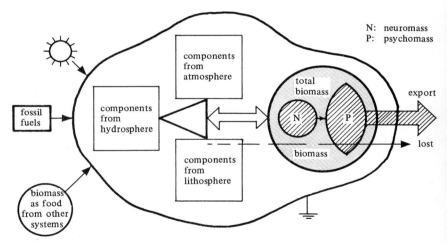

Figure 20.2. Ecosystem not self-sufficient in biomass. The relatively large proportion of human beings is indicated by the enlarged neuromass area. The total biomass area is shown as before. Food (biomass) from another system must now be imported. This will be 'paid for' by exporting materials, manufactures, or psychomass itself. All export is, however, eventually traceable to psychomass—a product of neuromass activity. The psychomass will therefore be considerably enlarged. Natural inflows of materials are not shown, but fossil fuels are shown as imported from other ecosystems.

[1] Costing by means of only the monetary measure may be entirely misleading. The ability to pay in dollars and solvency in energy are not the same. Energy measures remain constant—calories or kilowatts. Much energy is lost in conversion processes which are not essential for life support. For example, the feeding of grain to animals to produce protein has approximately 10% of the efficiency of direct human consumption of the grain. The process of photosynthesis has an even lower level of efficiency.

The boundaries of 'natural' ecosystems are determined by biotic and abiotic components. A hot, desert area will be differentiated from a temperate zone ecosystem having abundant vegetation by the differences in quantities and types of biomass, in the quantities of the flows of water, gases, and nutrients, and by differences in capacity for capturing solar radiation and holding material in the system. Human beings are also held in being in this sense. They are assemblies of nutrients and their aggregate physical mass in an ecosystem is maintained only so long as those nutrients remain 'fixed' in the part of the biomass represented by human beings. In 'natural' ecological theory the amount of the biomass so being maintained in the ecosystem is strictly limited by the capacity of the whole system to support the populations in its hierarchies of niches. In our present global situation of four billion human beings many ecosystems are carrying human biomass far in excess of their 'natural' capacity. The condition appears likely to continue with ever greater need for still further areas of biomass-producing ecosystems to be permanently held in the highly productive 'young' phase of ecosystem succession and the inhibiting of the system's movement toward maturity (figure 20.3).

Ecologists, particularly E P Odum, have pointed out that there are limits to the amount of the total global land surface that can be inhibited in this way. It is considered that a sizable fraction of the total must be always permitted to reach and maintain the succession climax. Among other

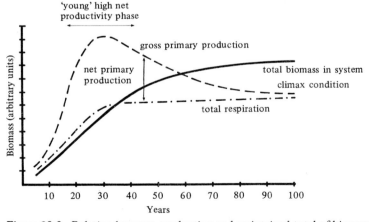

Figure 20.3. Relation between production and maintained total of biomass in a natural ecosystem. The example shows growth from algae to climax forest. The total biomass of the system steadily increases over time from a start, theoretically of zero, to a stable climax condition. In the earlier phases the system produces new material at a relatively rapid rate. In the later phases this rate slows down as ever-increasing energy must go to maintain the stock of biomass until a steady state is reached and sustained. No further new net production then takes place. Human intervention, in hominized ecosystems, is directed toward keeping the system in its relatively 'young' and highly productive phase so that human-usable biomass (food, lumber, etc) can be continuously drawn off for human purposes. (Adapted from E P Odum, 1971.)

things, Odum also notes that the oceans of the world should be left in thei climax state, it being considered that this is a stabilizing requirement of the biospherical ecosystem. Extensive interference with the oceans, pushing large areas back into the 'young' phase, might cause very serious climatic changes and hence degradation of land ecosystems (E P Odum, 1969).

On top of this problem of keeping some ecosystems or parts of some ecosystems permanently in the 'young' productive phase of the sequence of system development without risking regression or collapse—remember the dustbowl regression of the 1930s—there is the question of where the energy is to be obtained to do this. *It requires large inputs of energy from outside to hold an ecosystem in the 'young' phase at the levels of production necessary to support our present mass populations at existing nutritional and caloric intakes. Without these inputs, food intake would have to be reduced—porridge and potatoes might be the highest dietary level obtainable.*

Our typical source for this additional energy input is the fossil fuels, particularly oil. Oil not only makes large-scale mechanization of agricultur possible, it is also the base material for fertilizers, herbicides, etc. The fertilizers foster the better growth of the desired crop and the herbicides inhibit the growth of nonusable biomass. In bringing heavy reliance on oi into the processes of industrialized agriculture we are introducing yet another type of relationship between ecosystems.

Our first type of relationship between ecosystems is characterized by strictly contemporary photosynthesis. The human biomass of the dense megalopolis is maintained biologically by the products of photosynthesis, roughly on an annual turnover basis. Some crops, of course, are harvestec several times in a year but for the most part the staples can be countec as annual for purposes of discussion. Enough prairie grain is grown in the annual growing season to sustain a population for twelve months. Contemporary photosynthesis can therefore be taken to mean the process lasting over one year. An ecosystem containing large numbers of human beings therefore may be seen as symbiotically existing with other ecosystem which are artificially held in their 'young' phase, within the context of th *contemporary* processes of photosynthesis. This is shown in figure 20.4 a two ecosystems interrelated[2].

The food-producing ecosystems have, however, long since ceased to be in a 'natural' ecological state. They do not produce simply on the basis o contemporary photosynthesis. We rely on the second type of relationship

[2] Some food producers take several years to reach the mature phase of the organism itself and then produce annually. Examples are fruit trees. Other human-usable biomass, such as trees for lumber, take several decades to come to maturity and then provide only a single cropping. In spite of these variations it is useful to think of annual cropping of biomass for human uses, since human intervention arranges to take off available biomass at relatively short intervals. Forest management, for example, effectively is a way of phasing growth so that the produce may be drawn off within the range of time of contemporary photosynthesis.

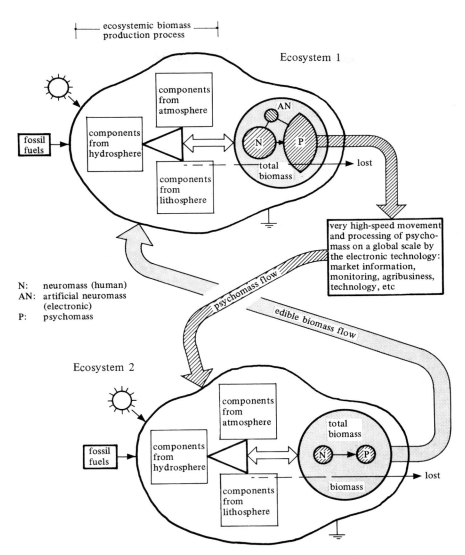

Figure 20.4. Symbiosis of two ecosystems. Ecosystem 1 has a larger human population than it can feed. Biomass must therefore be obtained from other system(s). Its larger population can, however, generate and use psychomass more effectively than can ecosystem 2. Interchange of psychomass for biomass is therefore possible. The application of psychomass from ecosystem 1 maintains production in ecosystem 2 in its 'young', highly productive phase. This diagram is a way of conceptualizing the interrelationship between biosphere and noosphere since it demonstrates the basic interchange. The artificial neuromass enters into a very close working relationship with the natural neuromass of human beings. It is increasingly important for helping to produce very sophisticated psychomass, which in its turn makes possible enhanced biomass production. The global operation of the electronic technology brings a new level of interdependence between the ecosystems that comprise the biosphere.

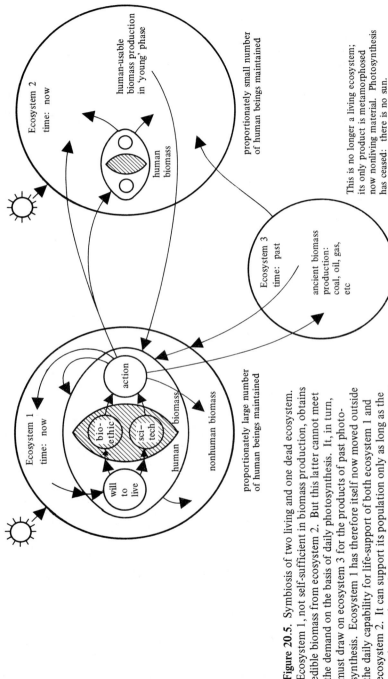

Figure 20.5. Symbiosis of two living and one dead ecosystem.
Ecosystem 1, not self-sufficient in biomass production, obtains
edible biomass from ecosystem 2. But this latter cannot meet
the demand on the basis of daily photosynthesis. It, in turn,
must draw on ecosystem 3 for the products of past photosynthesis. Ecosystem 1 has therefore itself now moved outside
the daily capability for life-support of both ecosystem 1 and
ecosystem 2. It can support its population only as long as the
past photosynthate of ecosystem 3 lasts. In this diagram strictly
human and other biomass are separated, and 'will' and 'action'
are added as representing the link between psychomass and
its application. They are not themselves psychomass.

Labels within the figure:

Ecosystem 2
time: now

human-usable
biomass production
in 'young' phase

human
biomass

proportionately small number
of human beings maintained

Ecosystem 3
time: past

ancient biomass
production:
coal, oil, gas,
etc

This is no longer a living ecosystem;
its only product is metamorphosed
now nonliving material. Photosynthesis
has ceased: there is no sun.

Ecosystem 1   time: now

will
to
live

bio-
ethic

sci-
tech

action

human biomass

nonhuman biomass

proportionately large number
of human beings maintained

in which the food-producing ecosystem must call on past periods of photosynthesis for oil and other inputs. This type of relationship connects present with long-departed ecosystems, using metamorphosed products of the past ecosystem. Such past ecosystems have functioned as a kind of storage of the daily solar energy which has previously fallen on the earth's surface. Human beings have thus learned to live extensively outside the limitations of the processes of contemporary photosynthesis. Anyway as long as the fossil fuels last! Other ways of tapping the energy of solar radiation than by photosynthesis exist, but so far, with the exception of limited hydroelectrical techniques, we have not succeeded in exploiting them on a major scale. (Sources are wind, tidal action, wave action, temperature differentials, solar energy techniques applied terrestrially and in outer space.) Brubaker (1975) and others urge that we use the time still remaining for the fossil fuels to concentrate on developing these other ways of capturing the energy of contemporary radiation, as well as pushing on with the exploitation of atomic fission and striving to master atomic fusion.

Along the perspective of biomass production and maintenance our ecosystems can therefore be seen as tripolar in their relationships. We can conceptualize the situation as two symbiotically related contemporary ecosystems dependent on a past or dead ecosystem for continuous inputs of additional energy. The heavily human-populated ecosystem is, of course, just as dependent on fossil fuels as the industrialized agricultural ecosystem. Indeed, much of the fossil fuel which ultimately reaches the food-producing ecosystem passes first through the other by way of manufacturing processes. We can therefore diagram our three ecosystems as shown in figure 20.5. Oil, etc are taken from the lower (past) ecosystem by the two upper (contemporary) systems. Some of this energy is interchanged between the two systems as oil, etc plus human 'energy' and some moves across as oil, etc plus the product of contemporary photosynthesis together with some human 'energy'. It is this human 'energy' which is the interesting element since it alone makes the symbiosis of the dead ecosystem and the two contemporary ecosystems possible. This 'energy' is our psychomass.

20.2 Symbiosis of ecosystems dependent on psychomass

For the more routine purposes of socioeconomic acting and thinking, the exchange of food for goods and services may be sufficiently satisfactory. For our present purpose, however, we have to ask questions about the light in which we should view the creation of these goods and services. In doing this we should also remember that holding an ecosystem in a 'young' stage of productivity also needs the injection of psychomass. 'Natural' ecosystems do not so inhibit their development toward maturity of their own accord.

In looking at the meaning of the creation of goods and services we must first ask whether we can find a lead as to how to conceptualize production by drawing on our knowledge of ecosystems. The first answer to this question is affirmative. The process of ecological production is that the system at each level, coinciding with the entity (macromolecule, cell, organism, etc) *assembles* disaggregated components into an assemblage which has capabilities not possessed by the individual components. This is, in part, accounted for by the notion of the integrative levels of system (Boulding, 1956; Feibleman, 1954). It is first the ability to *assemble* and second the ability to *hold the assembly together* that characterize the process of the production of biomass. The tree, at the systemic level of organism, 'knows' how to bring together the components it can take up from the ground and the air, and the energy of solar radiation in order to increase its size, up to a limit, and to continue maintaining itself for a 'programmed' duration of time.

Our manufacturing of goods and generation of services can also be conceptualized in this way. Any 'manufacture' is an assembly. In this sense a very simple operation such as picking up a stick and making a hole in the ground is a manufacture. Putting a seed in the hole would be a further manufacture. Stick, hand, soil, hole, etc constitute an assembly. At the other end of the line we have such assemblies as space vehicles, which are very complex. Similarly, services can be seen as assemblies. The more physical ones imply the bringing together of some 'manufactured' assembly with the skill, etc needed to use it. Changing the wheel on a car is an assembly of this order—the jack, the machine for tightening the nuts and the know-how (psychomass) of the mechanic. Professional services are not different, but are simply assemblies of specialized psychomass. Again the key function is that of bringing components together, assembly.

We do not understand how the tree 'knows' how to assemble the components, although we have discovered the processes of assembly. That is to say, although we have found out how the chain of photosynthesis works we do not know *why* the tree can do this. About the human being's processes for assembling components we know a good deal, although we cannot yet answer certain basic questions. Indeed, we cannot be certain of asking the right questions. In terms of our suggested concepts, however, it is clear that we do not know why it is that the neuromass can generate psychomass—essentially, no doubt, a process of assembly.

Such difficulties do not prevent us from thinking fruitfully about the role of psychomass and psychosystems in the total global conceptualization of the world. We may note, for example, that what we call consciousness as developed by human beings, may be directed toward fostering the growth of the capacity to assemble[3]. This may be applicable to fostering

---

[3] This does not rule out the action of subconscious thought in this role. Animals also 'assemble' data in this sense. Bertrand Russell and some other mathematicians have written about the role of their subconscious activity in solving problems. We should not insist that consciousness, or even self-consciousness, belongs only to *Homo sapiens*

the capacity of rice to increase its yield, or reflexively to the capacity of psychosystems to produce more psychomass. Knowledge can be used to produce ever more knowledge equally as well as it can be used to make more sophisticated assemblies for producing more biomass.

We may also note as very important that the human capacity to assemble is now worldwide. This is the meaning of the concept noosphere. 'Mind' is now an envelope encompassing the entire globe, exactly as is the biosphere. *This extension and fusion of psychosystems to comprise the noosphere is very recent, representing a new evolutionary phase in the development of the total global system of the world. Obviously this new phase will evolve rapidly under the stimulus of the growing world population—there is simply more neuromass—and the greatly enhanced human capability for interconnecting psychosystems and developing and assembling psychomass generated by the electronic technology. An enormous jump has been made here, which simultaneously both overleaps the limits of the glyph cultures and greatly enhances their potential.*

This increase in the human capacity for assembly of all kinds of components in both ecosystems and psychosystems means the possibility of increased flows of psychomass into ecosystems essentially producing biomass. This raises the question of whether the total global system can develop to a stable steady state on the basis of a symbiosis of ecosystems and psychosystems. This symbiosis would be seen as moving toward stability within the limits of contemporary photosynthesis, or contemporary photosynthesis assisted by some virtually inexhaustible energy supply such as that provided by atomic fission or fusion. The latter possibility is quite conceivable in terms of fission since the estimates of the reserves of uranium indicate a plentiful supply (Ford Foundation, 1974). Atomic fusion would rely on even larger basic resources. Such developments would depend on the production of special psychomass (for example, fusion technology) and some kind of global management of the ecosystems producing human-usable biomass. Such a possibility would, however, have to be viewed within the frame of other limitations such as that imposed by the absolute global amount of minerals required to maintain human beings (phosphorus, magnesium, etc).

From this mode of thinking we begin to comprehend the need to integrate some such concepts as psychomass and psychosystem into our study of the life-support system of the world as major components. That system is no longer to be safely seen with as heavy a biological emphasis as was possible even a few decades ago. The very rapid development of psychosystems and the very rapid accretion of psychomass have made the biosphere and the noosphere twin concepts. *Ecosystems depend on psychosystems as much as on their own processes or on the products of past photosynthesis.*

A second major thought must be the need to entertain reserve about the world being a finite or limited system when viewed operationally.

Ecologists appear to be saying that the world cannot carry an unlimited human population. Clearly there are physical limits spatially, but we are obviously nowhere near them. Similarly there are component limitations such as of air, water, or minerals. But again the limits are very far in the future in absolute terms, although perhaps not within present socioeconomi capabilities. If it boils down essentially to increasing the energy available to the human species, then the resources of matter—the net energy extractable from the atom—together with the development of psychosystems may prove to be capable of reaching and sustaining a total global system whicl need not be held at the present level of ecological conceptualization.

A third avenue of thought is that these ideas imply the systematic development of psychosystems and psychomass. Just as we hold an ecosystem in a highly productive 'young' phase so we may need to find ways of maintaining the psychosystems of groups and individuals at high levels of productivity. *Just as we manage ecosystems, so we shall have to plan the structure and development of psychosystems.* At present such development takes place largely in a process of random growth. We do indeed look for and find more sophisticated ways of assembling but this i done in an uncoordinated fashion. *Clearly the electronic technology, witl its capacity for interrelating components located anywhere in the noospher is an enormously powerful vehicle for coordination in this field. It unifie the noosphere as oxygen unifies the biosphere.*

20.3 Key ecological role of psychomass
The development of psychomass of all kinds—experiential and scientific knowledge, know-how, and what we generally include as artistic or aestheti knowledge—is not to be regarded as a kind of nonessential bonanza developed by the human species outside the necessities of the life-support system. On the contrary, it is an integral component even in its apparently more biologically useless manifestations such as philosophy or religion. It is now an integral component because of the evolved relationship between the biological drive toward increase of population, what Ivor Richards (1928) called the appetencies of the human being, and aggregations of psychomass in the form of human cultures.

It is likely that psychomass has its own laws of development. Not unreasonably we may suspect that it was not fortuitous that early flowering of philosophical thought appeared more or less simultaneously in Greece, India, and China. The growth of psychomass into cultural systems in the historic period of human development is studied by a variety of disciplines and a few writers, for example Reiser (1958), have tried to offer integrated views of the whole human enterprise. Such is not the intention of the present comments. It will be enough for present purposes to look at psychomass in the perspective of population growth and the enlargement of the scope of the appetencies.

In the most profound sense the pressure to generate and apply psychomass—that is, to learn how to assemble components—is underpinned by the drive to reproduce. In 'natural' ecosystems this drive operates in a context which is strictly cybernetic. The population and the food supply oscillate across a position of stability. If the food supply increases, the population increases until the food supply again stabilizes. If the population increases further, the available food per capita of the population diminishes and thus slows the growth of the population. In both population and food there is an inbuilt runaway ability. Symbiotic existence, however, means mutual control of growth. In 'natural' systems those individuals which cannot cope competitively for food die. Hence the runaway growth tendency in both population and food supply is held in check.

Somehow human neuromass has discovered how to provide alternative cybernetic loops to those operating in 'natural' ecosystems. Under pressure of numbers of human beings in excess of the capacity of the human niche in ecosystems, human beings have been stimulated to develop psychomass for diverting energy in ecosystems to themselves in quantities greater than their niche commands by 'nature'. As we have seen, this essentially consists of holding the ecosystem, or part of it, in the highly productive 'young' phase.

This process of providing alternative loops is a comparatively recent development. In its worldwide application it is very recent indeed—two centuries or so. World population and the global psychomass have increased together, simultaneously, until we have now reached the situation where population at the global scale is already larger than the capacity of the psychomass to make sufficient food available. This present operating of a cybernetic loop may not work so much through the quantity of human-usable biomass produced as through psychomass defects or deficiencies connected with distribution.

We can therefore reach the view that the global psychomass has its growth forced by the demand for human-usable biomass and that the workings of ecosystems must be extensively dependent on psychosystems. The world has moved from being a 'natural' biosphere to a biosphere which is progressively forced to depend on the continued development of one of its own products. The biosphere has in it the drive toward life. In the human species this has exerted pressures calling into being ways of circumventing the basic cybernetic biological controls on reproduction and survival. The result is a new situation which cannot be viewed simply along the biological perspective. *Neuromass, a once comparatively insignificant component of the ecosystem, has become the producer of a new type of product and system which together now form a special control component in the ecosystem.*

In addition to the biological relationship between human beings, their food supply, and psychomass there is a secondary drive which must be considered in the individual and group psychosystem. This is the observed fact that the satisfying of a human need does not necessarily destroy or even diminish the generalized drive to seek satisfaction. As Ivor Richards and others have pointed out, a characteristic quality of the human being is that the satisfaction of one appetency, as he called it, usually leads to the formulation of another. This tendency must therefore be considered inherent in those psychosystems in which human beings are counted as a major component.

In the operational sense this intensifies the pressure toward what we have called assembly, far beyond the level required to keep ecosystems in their 'young' phase simply to satisfy the need for food. When that is reasonably satisfied, other appetencies are generated by the psychosystems. These frequently involve quite different modifications of the ecosystems. In our present evolutionary phase of biosphere–noosphere development we may see our megalopolitan areas in this light. Whole ecosystems, such as the eastern seaboard of the USA, northwest Europe, and the lowlands area encircled by the Blue Mountains in New South Wales, are already in the condition that they are casualties of the hierarchy of appetencies that human beings have somehow built in as psychomass has been generated and psychosystems have gradually coalesced to form the present noosphere.

20.4 Evolution of psychosystems

As a hypothesis, the growth of psychosystems could be accounted for as a product of the pressures raised within ecosystems as human beings have found ways of making the ecosystems support them in ever larger numbers. As we have suggested, this demands the generation of ever more psychomass. This demand could be the stimulator of psychosystem evolution. In the earlier evolutionary phases the pressure could be in the direction of psychomass which would be particularly relevant for assembling components useful for mastery over the physical world.

Interactions or transactions between individuals or groups would seem to be essential to the process of stimulating psychosystems to increase their output of psychomass. New information comes to the individual and group from outside. This information may be capable of being assembled so that either existing activity is improved or new activity is made possible. As human numbers increase, transactions increase and diffusion speeds up. Both the creation and the dissemination of psychomass may be accelerated simply by the increase in the number of human beings. Further, psychomass builds more psychomass exactly as biomass is self-increasing. Psychosystems may be visualized as having their detritus and decomposers as do ecosystems, thus releasing components for reassembly.

New transactions relate to new psychomass, which in turn modifies the psychosystem's concepts or understanding of the world. This is dependent on the fact that human beings have psychosystems which function reflexively—they are self-aware or self-conscious. The modifications progressively make the assembly process more sophisticated so that more subtle manipulations of ecosystems are possible, resulting in ever larger populations being carried. Reference to historical examples, however, suggests that psychosystems may also lose their evolutionary trends for a time and be unable to produce the new psychomass necessary for maintaining the ecosystem in an ever more enhanced 'young' condition. *When this occurs populations decline in numbers, not inevitably because of ecosystem overload but because of psychosystem inability to provide the required new psychomass.* The new psychomass might be of any kind from a new energy technology to discovering how to generate a new balance in the group/individual behaviour patterns.

The idea of the upward evolutionary movement of human cultures has been interestingly exploited by Calhoun (1970) and applied to our present situation in which instantaneous communication and computation play such a large role. Using calculations and ideas from von Foerster, Calhoun describes an historical sequence of conceptual revolutions, each requiring a major reorientation of our perception of the world and of ourselves. He arrives at the *communication–electronic* phase as based on 1988 AD, and a succeeding phase, called the *compassionate-systems revolution*, based on 2018 AD (Calhoun, 1970, page 431)[4]. His argument for our present situation is:

"Use of the term 'systems' to designate the new means for coping also reflects the new perspective. As an outgrowth of information theory relating to the transfer of information over networks, in conjunction with the related development of the field of cybernetics, there arose a body of concepts designated as 'general systems theory'. This theory views all of nature and all of human activity as a hierarchically arranged structure of levels of interlocked subset systems in which the process of any particular subset system affects and is affected by other subset systems at its own level, as well as below or above it. *We are now moving into an area when this perspective (involving the related techniques and strategies for designing and guiding interrelationships, and for permitting self-organization of subsystems) has become imperative*" (emphasis supplied).

Without going into von Foerster's doomsday analysis and stabilization of human planetary population between nine and thirteen and one-half billion, by which level no further conceptualization growth is supposed to be able to take place (von Foerster et al, 1960), we can use his, and Calhoun's, notion that increase of population pressure forces the generation

---

[4] For technical reasons of calculation the compassionate-systems phase commencement is shifted from 2018 to 2027, with possible continuation to 2400. The communication-electronic phase he adjusts as beginning 1984 and extending to 2027 AD: in this latter period increased capacity to cope will depend essentially on condensing information, according to his view. We already begin, possibly, to sense this. *The key idea is the enlargement of conceptual space.* (See also Calhoun in Attinger, 1970, page 36.)

of larger conceptual space. With this in mind we can raise the question of whether at some point this hitherto automatic process must be given conscious guidance. Such a shift from jumps of a largely uncoordinated kind to guided overall advance in the development of psychomass may be compared to the revolution made by early man when he moved from living off the biomass without altering its unhominized processes to beginning to 'assist' the ecosystem to produce more of certain kinds of human-usable biomass (agriculture). Analogously we can reach the concept of psychomass culture. This would mean the coordinated systematic organizing of the growth of psychomass, perhaps of all kinds, in the emerging and succeeding phase of the enlargement in von Foerster's total human conceptual space. The key hypothesis suggested is that the growth of the psychomass and the pressure of human numbers on the biosphere have reached a stage where the increased growth will induce a need and a capacity for overall conscious guidance.

Our conceptualization of psychosystem would fit well to the growth dynamic suggested by von Foerster and Calhoun. They do not, however, allow for regression in the level of system operation, although some thoughts along this line might be inspired by Calhoun's own experiments with rodents. In these he removed the control loops connecting population and food supply. 'Too much' population in the physical space available resulted in 'too many' transactions, which in turn led to 'unnatural' behaviour. In our terms, new psychomass was produced but proved unacceptable for coping with the situation. Human beings are not Norway rats, but similar linkages may obtain between ecosystems and psychosystems whether we are talking about ourselves or about other members of the Kingdom Animalia. The key suggestion is that density of transaction has much to do with psychosystem development and change.

The concept of psychosystem would therefore modify the von Foerster–Calhoun description of the evolution of 'mind' to allow for the regressed condition in the system. Looking at history, this would seem essential. *Looking at the future, it would safeguard against a facile optimism that population pressure and increased density of transaction must inevitably produce psychosystemic responses adequate to meet the new challenges. On the contrary, it is necessary to face the possibility of serious regression in our contemporary psychosystems.*

It might be advantageous here to apply the notion of climax maturity to psychosystems. We might consider whether we face the problem of holding certain of our psychosystems in a 'young' stage in order to ensure continued high productivity. It might be argued that some psychosystems in which academic components play major roles are no longer productive of new psychomass. This would raise the question of how a psychosystem is pushed back and held in the 'young' phase. In ecosystems it is easy to clear the ground and tip in fertilizer. The equivalent for psychosystems is by no means simple. We are perhaps forced to hold the view, provisionally, that psychosystems, unlike ecosystems, evolve not steadily with an inevitable upward sweep to a stable maturity but follow an undulating pattern of rise and regression. The noosphere, however, may perhaps be conceived in its long-term development as in a steady upward climb. It is possible to hold this view without necessarily having to subscribe to Teilhard de Chardin's religiophilosophic standpoint. The very wide distribution and careful storage of knowledge now achieved by modern technology gives reasonable grounds to hope that loss of key psychomass, as happened in the Dark Ages, can be avoided.

20.5 Artificial neuromass
Because of their capacity to reflect, human beings have been able to develop additional neuromass capability outside their own brains and nervous systems. The glyph cultures did this mostly in the form of extending the human memory and increasing the computational capacity. The increase in storage ability was the result of writing, as information could now be stored in infinitely large quantity and for very long periods. This allowed various metaprocesses to be developed. Among these were the metamemory, which does not remember the specific piece of information but remembers where the information is to be found and how to retrieve it, and the process of generating new information by synthesis and synergy. Hence relationships which are not self-evident can be extracted.

The electronic technology is building very rapidly on the glyph enlargement of the natural neuromass capability. As we have seen, the technology both enhances the diffusion and accessibility of glyph-handled material and enormously extends the sensory, memory, and computational capability of the human being so that a global level of common operation can now be seen to be coming into existence. In previous chapters we have looked at the globalization process of these enhanced capabilities—intercontinental TV, global interlinking of national public universal packet-switching networks, global monitoring by satellites, and universal electronic storage and processing of information. In this aspect our electronic communications have been thought of as an artificial global cerebral cortex intricately interconnected with our human neural processes. This may prove a useful image in helping us to develop a conceptualization of the world which can cope with the enormous step that we have taken in moving our cerebral processes into the several regions of the electromagnetic spectrum. If our blasé attitudes take the edge off our appreciation of this we should recall that as recently as Captain Cook's time we were still struggling to complete the physical exploration of the world and that a hundred years ago we had just achieved some reasonable approaches to explaining how living systems have come to be the way they are.

There is a considerable literature on artificial intelligences. It is not necessary, however, to use such an exalted concept to make the point that the symbiosis of the electronic technology and human mental processes is

producing a new order of psychosystems. Glyph psychosystems were
relatively slow-acting and restricted in their computational scope by the
relationship between time and neuromass capability. Many calculations
now made routinely in science and applied science could not be done by
human neuromass alone because they would take too long or tie up too
many individuals. They must be done by artificial neuromass. *Per contra*,
this means that we can efficiently perform many calculations previously
beyond our reach. In its turn, this means new firmness of prediction, the
development of sophisticated simulation, and entirely new possibilities for
psychosystems to produce new assemblies of components.

We must conclude that the concept of psychosystem will progressively
be required to incorporate the activity of artificial neuromass which
functions in close relationship with human beings, although the modes of
storage, processing, and retrieval may not be the same. Indeed, without
getting into science fiction, we have to envisage psychosystems which may
be dominated by artificial rather than human neuromass. We already
programme computers to design electronic circuitry, and are working to
achieve new kinds of artificial storage of information such as relational
associative processing (chapter 4).

20.6 Conceptualizing linkages between various ecosystems and psycho-systems

A task to be tackled, then, is examining how we are to study the
relationships between the various elements we have described so that a sense
of the greater whole may be reached. It will be useful to list the key ideas:

1 Some ecosystems carry human beings, as biomass, in numbers far in
   excess of the systems' capacity to do so within the limits of self-
   sufficiency. They 'pay' by 'exporting' psychomass and its products.
2 The edible biomass required to sustain them physically is produced in
   part by other ecosystems. A symbiotic relation therefore exists between
   ecosystems having large numbers of human beings and other ecosystems
   concentrating on the production of human-usable biomass and having
   relatively few human beings.
3 In order to concentrate on food production the producing ecosystems
   have to be held in their 'young', highly productive phase.
4 This cannot be done without bringing in additional energy. This
   additional energy is predominantly supplied in our current situation,
   from the proceeds of photosynthesis in long-departed ecosystems.
5 We therefore have at this stage relationships between ecosystems in
   contemporary photosynthesis and relationships between them and past
   ecosystems. Such groups of systems, however, are not viable in 'nature',
   since the energy of past ecosystems can be captured by contemporary
   ecosystems only by the intervention of human beings and because it is
   only they who can circumvent the cybernetic controls built into
   'natural' systems.

6 It is the development of psychosystems and the resultant psychomass which makes possible these interventions and therefore these 'artificial' relationships between present and past ecosystems.

7 We must therefore bring psychosystems into our conceptualization of how the life-support system now works, in such a way that the significance of their role is given proper importance.

8 We have, then, to accommodate: contemporary ecosystem with large human population, contemporary ecosystem producing human-usable biomass held in the 'young' phase, past ecosystem from the produce of which is extracted fossil fuel, and present and past psychosystems which make available new and existing psychomass.

In figure 20.4 an attempt is made to diagram the concepts to be handled. There are various difficulties. The contemporary ecosystems, where held in the 'young' phase to produce food, fit with ecological theory. The human-dominated ecosystem, however, must for the moment be considered unknown in its maturity aspects. Some conceptualization of culture is required here, of a sort we may not yet be able to develop. Another problem is to know how to diagram the psychosystems since they may be of many forms and of several epochal stages. Yet another area of difficulty is that of the representation of space. Ecosystems are space–time definable. But psychosystems are only sometimes space–time definable. They often escape the limitations of physical space and utilize very extensive manipulation of time.

In spite of the difficulties it seems fruitful and necessary to learn to think in some way such as this, if we are to escape our present shackles. These become ever more restrictive as new thought and practice become dominant. Hence we do have to try new ways of thinking and generate new concepts, preliminary to searching for new empirical avenues of effort.

Mass individual and life balance

21.1 Mass individual in the range of systems

In the previous chapter I tried to conceptualize how contemporary and past ecosystems and psychosystems may be thought of in their interrelations. I suggested the idea of psychomass as a twin to biomass and developed the notion that the one is interchanged for the other to permit the high spatial concentrations of large masses of human beings. Essentially food is bought by mental product, since it is ultimately the activity of 'mind' which makes possible all 'production' or, as we have said, assembles components, just as the tree assembles nutrients and radiation to generate and maintain its entity.

It is important to reemphasize this ultimate origin of 'production' or assembly. Curiously, this is rarely stressed in attempted descriptions of how 'human' systems come into being and sustain themselves. Occasionally a writer with a socioeconomic habit of mind remembers to make this basic emphasis. Schumacher, for example, reminds us that "... it is man, not nature, who provides the primary resource; that the key factor of all economic development comes out of the mind of man" (Schumacher, 1974, page 64). Even he, however, quickly leaves this fundamental insight to speculate about our contemporary "metaphysical disease".

It is this capability of the psychosystem for assembly, analogous to the capability of the organism or the ecosystem for assembly, that must be the very basis of those systems which we think of as essentially 'human'. The fact that we think in terms of groups of human beings, human cultures, and socioeconomies reinforces the anthropocentricity of our thinking about 'human' systems and leads us to undervalue and neglect in this context the basic life-support system on which all 'human' systems are raised. We might counteract this tendency to some extent by using the botanist's word *consociation* as an additional perspective for describing our 'human' systems. This term means domination by a single species in a system. We could therefore argue that large and densely concentrated mass human populations are not so much communities as examples of consociation. As such, they have common and perhaps uniform characteristics with regard to their capability for assembly, and something in common with ecosystems in their climax condition.

Let us now turn back to figure 1.1. This shows the conventional range of systems used by the biologist and others, from macromolecule through organisms, communities, and ecosystems to the biosphere. We now sense an ambiguity at the level of community. In ecological terms this word means the living together of groups of different kinds of organisms or species, inhabiting a common environment and related through food chains. So the mud worm is eaten by the bottom fish, which is eaten by the top fish in the pond, which is pulled out of the water and eaten by the bear. This is not what human community is at all, and only confusion arises from the common use of the word. Consociation, however, is a manifestation occurring right through the whole order of living things, from beech or maple forest to London or New York, and it could be used with consistent meaning.

We can view the ecosystem which carries a large mass of human beings, as described in the previous chapter, in the light of an ecosystem dominated by a consociation of human beings. This is a kind of climax condition. The human organisms aggregate to a special kind of biomass having the special ability to assemble components through what we suppose to be its unique capability. This is its ability to generate psychomass, which is itself an assembly. We therefore find ourselves with a concept which we might call *consociation–assembly*. On the consociation side this is different from the product or assembly of community, which is vitally dependent on diversity of species. On the assembly side it is different from the assembly processes of 'nature' because there is no inherent limitation on the amount of psychomass that can be produced. Psychosystems can continue producing, assembling, indefinitely as their chief characteristic is synergy[1].

This way of looking at large human populations offers some liberation from the narrow transfer of ecological knowledge from 'natural' systems to so-called 'human' systems. Such transfers, although not without their uses, have serious limitations. These already may be constraining the development of the kind of thinking we need for conceptualizing a general world system. Succession, for example, in urban land uses undoubtedly occurs under conditions of change; the various kinds of jobs in a nation may be viewed as analogous to the niches in a 'natural' ecosystem; energy (defined somehow) can be said to flow through human populations. Yet these and similar direct transfers from ecology to 'human' systems have not offered us very much insight into the workings of the human enterprise when manifest *en masse*. Liberation from this narowness may well consist of declining to emphasize the polarity implied by the words 'natural' and 'human'. Indeed the assumption of the rightness or usefulness of this polarity may now be a very serious handicap to assimilating and applying our new knowledge. 'Human' systems are perhaps most fruitfully seen as outgrowths and continuations of 'natural' systems, and as a development which has been slow and difficult and which is characterized by fragility in the system itself. The drive of conceptualization should be toward envisaging a single system.

If we wish to retain the concept community we should use it to describe the relationships between various species, of which one would be ourselves.

---

[1] Psychosystems are perhaps ultimately limited in their productive capability by underlying basic ideas. Also it is clear that basic ideas lose steam over time. Nevertheless, when a body of knowledge has reached a certain stage it may continue to produce by synergizing—putting together existing components to form a new component of a higher systemic order. A great deal of science and technology today fits this description.

The community would consist of human beings and the species which
comprise the ecosystems producing our food supply—plants and animals.
The consociations of our urban populations are therefore in a relationship
of community with the populations of other species in their own ecosystem
producing human-usable biomass and with the populations of species of
other ecosystems. Where large human populations are concerned we
therefore have to think of community as describing the symbiotic
relationships of various species between different ecosystems, as well as
the 'home' ecosystem within which the mass human population is located.
Thinking in this way we may begin to break down the notion that we
have ecosystems on the one hand and socioeconomies on the other.

Another approach to breaking down our stereotypes in this area of
thinking is to dismantle the developed–developing distinction. We are in
the habit of separating the developed countries from the developing
countries mostly by reference to the differences in their socioeconomies o
'human' systems, and differences in their levels of development. This may
be a misleading trail since we do not know whether the 'human' systems o
the developed countries have any long-term viability and to what extent the
may be a model for the developing countries. The exercise of looking at the
developing countries without our conventional socioeconomic approaches to
'human' systems might help us to see ourselves as consociational component
of a single systemic whole.

21.2 Human consociation

Human consociation—the dominance of the species in a geographic area—is
a modification of the ecological principle of diversity. Somehow the
system has come to a climax situation in which the population of a single
species dominates and yet a high quantity of biomass can be successfully
and continuously ensured for maintaining it. The consociate population,
however, can continue only if there is symbiosis between itself and
populations of other species in other parts of its own ecosystem or in
other ecosystems.

A consociation of oaks or maple trees survives on a competitive basis.
That individual tree flourishes best which most efficiently assembles
nutrients and pushes out the largest area of leaves to capture the radiation
of the sun. The individual tree maximizes the opportunities offered to it.
By some it has been supposed, perhaps for reasons of convenience rather
than from observation, that consociations of human beings functioned best
in the same way. This was laissez faire. Most human societies have,
however, been at considerable pains to soften the asperities of competition
They can hardly survive if they do not do so.

Today we certainly do not tend to give the biological characteristic of
competition pride of place when we are considering human consociations.
We might describe our present image of the key set of linkages now
holding—or failing to hold—human consociations in being as focussing on

the relationship between the individual and the mass. This relationship might be characterized as composed of two basic needs, or necessities. On the part of the consociation as a whole there is a necessity, or requirement, that its behaviour shall be such that its symbiotic relationships with its own and other ecosystems will remain viable. If this is not achieved at adequate levels of performance, the necessary interchange of biomass and psychomass will not continue, and the amount of available human-usable biomass will diminish.

In large masses of human individuals, we are talking in this context of aggregate behaviour, namely the sum total of the behaviour and behavioural effects of the total population. This aggregate is, of course, composed of the behaviour and behavioural effects of the individuals. Individuals have their necessities too, just as do whole consociations. *These necessities, however, can be of a different kind because they are not seen to relate directly and obviously to the ecosystems. The individual is therefore in the situation that he can act in total disregard of ecological linkages, and without feeling under obligation to respect the necessities imposed upon the consociation as a whole. Indeed, he can flout such necessities, without retribution apparent to himself.*

The necessities under which the individual operates in mass society are in part necessities of basic survival, as for any species, and in part of another kind. The human individual may obtain his requirements for survival by means which aggregate to behaviour at the consociational level not appropriate for the survival of the whole. In a primitive farming society the individuals who eat their seed grain are acting in this way. In complex Western mass societies there is difficulty in tracing all the cases but examples are not difficult to identify: the workers who take so much out of the firm in wages that they 'eat' the equipment; the civilization which uses as income a nonrenewable resource such as oil, which is really capital, to 'survive' at a certain level of material well-being; the individual who 'plays' the welfare services, seeing himself as having no alternative but to do so. The aggregation of these and similar short-circuitings can result in the inability of the consociation to continue in its status quo, and may jeopardize its entire life-support system.

The other kind of necessity which presses upon the individual in a modern mass society is an interior one. This we looked at in chapters 16 and 17 when we examined the views of Ortega y Gasset, Zolla, George Steiner, and others on the inner profile and sensibility of the contemporary Western individual. This mass man, as Ortega y Gasset called him, is compelled to see himself in a certain way. He feels himself as powerful yet powerless; as himself the only measure of himself; as entitled by right to the fruits of science and technology; as a solitary individual yet craving interaction with his fellows; and as having lost an earlier coherence and centrality. In addition to the behavioural necessities which arise from these characteristics he has a driving necessity to pursue the truth through science, and to apply what he discovers. Capability in these areas is now very great and has conferred on mass man, as individuals or small groups, enormous powers for interfering with the processes of the life-support system of the biosphere. This disproportionate development of a certain kind of psychomass has not only made possible the great human consociations of our world but has, simultaneously with bringing them into being, made imaginable and possible their later disaggregation, dispersal, or even extinction.

If we think in terms of systems about the relationships between the human individual, the consociation of human beings, and the community of species (including *Homo sapiens*) by which both individual and group must survive, we can say that there now appear in mass populations weaknesses in, or absences of, certain cybernetic feedback loops. The necessities under which the individual feels and acts do not necessarily aggregate to a respecting of the necessities under which the consociation must operate. *If, however, the consociation fails, the pressure of the necessities under which the individual must live will increase. But as those increase, the divergence between the behaviour of the individual that seems necessary for his survival and the behaviour necessary to support the consociation will increase. There is no corrective feedback. The key idea is increased divergence of the two levels of behaviour without adequate feedback loops. The increasing divergence will make appropriateness for survival ever more difficult to maintain or attain. In contemporary societies this condition manifests itself, among other ways, in ungovernability.*

21.3 Balance of life
In terms of densely packed modern mass populations we might now see the components which have to be kept in viable relationship with each other as: consociation (the large mass of human beings), community (the symbiosis of the populations of the various species—human beings and their food, etc), psychomass (output of 'mind', which is exchanged for food), and the human individual seen as sentient, self-aware being and basic behavioural organism of the consociation.

Although the workable relationship of these components must have long been the ingredients of the mix of human societies, however primitive, the particular characteristics of the components themselves have been subject to wide ranges of variability. For examples we may cite: consociations have ranged from a very small number of individuals to the present very large mass populations, and may well go to gigantic dimensions if we are to believe Doxiadis (1967) and others; community of existence between human beings and other species has ranged from picking berries and catching small animals to the massive ecological control of monocultures; psychomass began small in quantity with a very slow growth rate to become in modern times very large in quantity, highly refined in quality, and very fast-growing; and, from being closely tied into the ecosystem in direct awareness of certain 'natural' processes, the individual has developed a sense of self which divorces him *en masse* from the realities of the life-support system which alone can sustain him.

The differences in the components between our own and previous periods of the world's development are very important because previously workable solutions to the problems of getting all to hold together cannot be assumed to be still viable in the changed nature of the components. However, the balance between the group and the individual behaviour may remain a constant in the sense of being the relationship most difficult to maintain in proper condition. Failure to achieve this results in dominance of the one to the detriment of the other. Either the consociational behaviour deprives the individual of too much of the 'freedom' felt necessary for satisfying himself and eventually the individual 'revolts' against the 'system'; or the individual concedes too little to the consociation's behavioural requirements with the result that the individual cannot obtain from the group enough food, protection, etc to keep himself viable because the group is too weak.

Previous attempts at solutions have frequently taken the form of developing organs in society which could operate on the individual from within and without, although the implied sharpness of distinction between those two words is not always evident in the reality of the interaction between human individuals and their groups. Church and state have nevertheless been very common manifestations of the attempt by human beings to achieve a balance of life. The history of the Dark and Middle Ages is the story of attempts, on the one hand, to coerce the individual externally into behaving as was necessary to ensure the food supply, shelter, defence, etc of the group and, on the other hand, to make him act from interior compulsion in ways that avoided short-circuiting the system. Both church and state coerced and cajoled. Both, however, had also to make considerable concessions to the individual in order to 'keep him at it'. On feast days—their number steadily increased through the Middle Ages—the lid was temporarily lifted off. But this would not work for ever. The new views of the state that we associate with the Renaissance and the new interior demands within the individual that we call the Reformation finally blew the lid off for ever and Western civilization had to search for new ways of balancing the basic components.

On the ecological side the Dark and Middle Ages did not encounter any great difficulty and, in Europe anyway, their agricultural methods did not endanger the stability of ecosystems. The amount of biomass diverted to human beings was easily within the capacity of the ecosystems of northern and central Europe and, in general, parts of the systems were maintained in a relatively 'young' stage of high net productivity successfully without inputs of additional energy from outside. This would be possible as long as the individual human being continued to carry out the seasonal agricultural chores, being constrained by the pressures of the group–individual balancing process described above. Hence the church calendar was essentially an agricultural calendar—instructions when to do what to the land. Also the control loops were strengthened by the peasant being constantly reminded of the biological context in which he must live. Failure to plant cabbage meant that no cabbages could be eaten later. Some of the cybernetic loops linking food supply, the group, and the individual worked very well But there was the weakness that something inside the individual was being denied its proper scope. This, in due course, would be claimed.

The medieval situation with regard to psychomass was also very different from our own. Information and knowledge were limited in quantity, frequently very defective in quality—all sorts of false ideas about the nature of the physical world were commonly held—and the rate of production of new psychomass was extremely low. Indeed, many psycho systems produced nothing at all, at best only maintaining the stock they had inherited. This weakness, however, at least prevented medieval human beings from damaging ecosystems or even very much changing the natural relationships between them, as modern mass populations have been able to do.

21.4 Contemporary imbalance

Our own situation may be seen as characterized by gross, even grotesque exaggerations in the four components:

1 At the level of population—the consociation—the present global pattern of population distribution typically stresses urbanized masses and a continuing process of urbanization with its move away from the land. *This emphasizes consociation and weakens community.* Further, the absolute quantity of human beings being carried by Spaceship Earth is of an entirely different magnitude from what it was as recently as 1900 The problem of consociational behaviour is therefore also of a different order.

2 The community between the human populations and the populations o other species, which provide food, has been enormously extended in space and time. Mass human populations in the developed countries draw food from ecosystems all over the world. In the dimension of time human-usable biomass is preserved and stored sufficiently long to even out supply over the annual cycle. Further, this spatially extended community of species is largely dependent on the past product of photosynthesis in extinct ecosystems. The immediacy of community of species—the essential symbiosis of human beings and all the other contemporaneously living things—has been radically changed and its ancient lines blurred. Our sense of community is in the process of becoming global, even as it remains backyard. This is an enormous and perilous jump.

3 Our information and knowledge have very rapidly increased in quantity quality, and availability. The electronic technologies which make possible

their enhanced availability also stimulate increase in quantity and
improvement in quality. This relationship causes still greater acceleration
in the rate at which we create new psychomass and apply both the
existing and the new. This is now the fastest growing element in the
socioeconomies of the developed nations. It is the great growth of our
knowledge capability which has brought about the conditions outlined
in the previous item. This is the essential cause of the changes brought
about in the world's communities of species. It may also not be an
exaggeration to think of our electronic equipment, aggregated over the
world, as a new addition to the numbers of those species since
computational capacity of the world's computers is perhaps already
greater than that of the aggregated brains of the world's human
population. Our electronic capability has globalized our ability to
manipulate the world's ecosystems.

4 The exaggeration in the interior profile of mass man as an individual lies
in the separation, or detachment, from an awareness and comprehension
of the three foregoing components. Because of his particular self-
consciousness he has lost the capacity to give much of himself up to the
consociational component, by whose continued efficient operations, in
fact, he eats. Worse, he even exploits for supposed personal gain some
of the efforts—health, educational, welfare services for example—made
on his very behalf at the consociational level. Second, he has lost track
of his place in the community of species. He thinks only of dominating
the populations of the other species so that they will deliver up to him
what he conceives to be his right. There results an exaggerated and
entirely unreal relationship between him and 'nature'. He also has a
detachment from the knowledge and technology which has made
possible the detachment just mentioned. *Thus he remains ignorant of
both the substance and the significance of the knowledge in the very act
of using its products.* In this way he greatly encourages the growth of
exaggeration in the other components. The characteristic psychomass
of which mass man is in possession is therefore severely limited in its
usefulness for assisting the achievement and maintenance of a workable
balance between the four components, especially when their condition
of exaggeration is taken into account.

Our century has been a period in which the relationship between the
consociation and the mass individual has been a burning issue. Some
attempted 'balances', for example those developed as Fascism and Nazism,
have disintegrated after a brief life. Others, which have endured longer
and have seemed more successful, may not, however, be of lasting viability.

Of whatever political ethos, the quest for a new balance has typically
been accompanied by the rapid growth of the state all over the world.
Governments have both undertaken to do more for the mass individual
and, together with the institution of work, increased their demands on the
mass individual. It is a reasonable hypothesis worth examining that the

state emerges strong when the control loops keeping the behaviour of the society as a whole and the behaviour of the individual in viable symbiosis are weakened or broken. It would be satisfying to believe that when such weakness occurs the state waxes strong to restore things to a long-term workable balance as a kind of automatic or reflex manifestation. Unfortunately, the grounds for holding such an optimistic view are anything but firm. The state, abstraction that it is, is just as likely to exacerbate one or more of the exaggerations we have mentioned in the four components as to make the effort to move toward a workable balance. Frequently the state has turned out to be the voice of mass man himself, or the imposed domination of a junta of oligarchs having no real intention of trying to achieve a balance of life.

It is not the present purpose to explore the nature, function, or origin of the state. Much ink and blood have been already spilled in this terrible century. The purpose is to point out that new major factors are now entering the debate. It will therefore take on a very different tone from that to which we have become familiarized up to the present. Our response to this change is very slow at present.

21.5 Aspects of the imbalance

If the identification or diagnosis of the bedrock problem of human existence given above is correct we must presume it to be a constant. The identification is that balance must be found between the behaviour of the individual that he wishes for himself and behaviour which he must follow so that he may benefit from the actions of the group. All societies must act appropriately to ensure the food supply, etc and to maintain group cohesion. The dilemma is that the group and individual needs cannot both be totally satisfied yet are inextricably bound up together. At least the requirement to reconcile them stays firm, whatever variations there may be in context and solutions.

Our century has expended great effort on generating and applying solutions, but very little on examining the context in which reconciliation must take place. It is precisely this context which is the focus of attention here. As the context changes not only will new solutions to the necessary compromises be required, but it will also be possible for new solutions to emerge from the changes in the contextual components of the bedrock problem.

The two most massively changed and changing areas of the context are provided by our new knowledge of the ecological workings of Spaceship Earth and our enormously enhanced capacity for handling psychomass. What the first of these breakthroughs does in terms of the basic human problem is to bring us up sharp against the finiteness of our life-support system. What the second does is to make available entirely new possibilities for negotiating this finiteness.

On the consociational side—whether we think by nations or by groups of nations—the behavioural requirement is that the consociation shall behave so that reasonably long-term stability is achievable. It is fairly clear that this is not the condition of most Western nations at the present moment since growth rates in energy consumption and acceleration in the output of industrialized agriculture cannot be for certain maintained even as long as to the end of the century. *Consociationally, Western societies have to face an entirely new contextual situation for finding the balance between the group and the individual. This aspect of the new situation is biological in the sense of being lodged firmly in the processes of contemporary and past photosynthesis. Both of these are limited in output; they are not infinitely capable of being expanded. Our recent consociational behaviour has been based on their being infinitely expandable.* Solutions that do not start with an understanding of this change in the context of the bedrock human problem will be liable to gross failure because of the human population pressure and our psychomass capacity to upset permanently the stability and diversity of the world's ecosystems. The massive application of more 'agribusiness' in the developed nations would almost certainly be self-defeating because of the likelihood of falling into a condition of substantial net energy loss. Therefore solutions for the bedrock problem that rely on increased 'agribusiness' will have only a poor chance of success. In the developing countries of the Third World widespread industrialized agriculture simply cannot be reached. World energy resources are insufficient. Hence in the developing countries 'agribusiness' cannot be the basis on which to achieve the consociation–individual balance.

Still on the consociational side, the other major element of context— the electronic technology and the psychomass handling that it makes possible—offers entirely new means for coping with the biological context and for assisting in achieving a new, workable, and long-term balance. As we have seen, the technology is already producing entirely new levels of information about the physical condition of the globe. Such information is absolutely essential for action at the consociational level. In principle it allows us to understand how far management may change ecosystems without damage. It allows us to keep parts of them in the highly productive 'young' phase within safe limits. As it will be increasingly necessary to do this to more and more of the earth's land surface, the function of electronically monitoring what goes on will become increasingly important and helpful in providing guidance for consociational behaviour. On the action side more quantity and enhanced quality of psychomass specific to this aspect of things will be required. A continuous output of new psychomass will be needed as well as greatly improved availability of what is already known. The electronic technology, now organized and operating globally in many of its aspects, is a means commensurate with the need.

In this sense the human species is indeed fortunate in that at the moment when it requires a much increased supply of human-usable biomass it has developed a global psychomass system (knowledge plus the technology for handling it) capable of finding ways of meeting the need. Previous civilizations have foundered at this point.

The technology is also of great potential importance in helping the consociational level 'deal with' the mass individual in terms of 'persuading' him to behave as will be appropriate for the whole group. The words have to be placed in quotation marks to suggest the perspective along which the group representatives may perceive the mass individual's behavioural tendencies.

We do not like to think of ourselves as being propagandized. We do not relish the thought that government manipulates us, even if to achieve a legitimate behaviour on our part for the benefit of all. Yet, obviously, the capability of the electronic technology for manipulation is very great, and already the mass individual in the developed countries is strongly under its influence. We hate to face it, but one way of achieving the desired balance is to manipulate mass man appropriately through the mass media. As Nazi Germany demonstrated, the power of the media when firmly grasped by those purporting to act for the consociation can be devastating. It has been said that the Russian governmental propaganda machine could rouse the population to a holy war against anyone within twenty-four hours. In authoritarian states the electronic technology has been a key instrument in achieving and maintaining a supposed viable balance between the behaviour of the mass individual and that of the consociation in the twentieth century.

21.6 Contemporary mass individuals generate the mass group

Ellul (1973) has probed the propaganda question in relation to the mass individual in aggregate becoming the effective group or consociation. This is a different emphasis from that of Ortega y Gasset or Zolla. Now what has to be faced is that the approaches and attitudes of the subgroups within the consociation have largely become the same as the interior profile of the individual. The balancing or corrective differences between the behaviour of the consociation and that of the individual have disappeared. This is a new twist of the screw, which we have felt but not yet looked at carefully.

The contemporary subgroup acts and reacts as the mass individual. These subgroups are corporations, unions, etc in industry, commerce, business, service delivery agencies such as health and education, entertainment, and government. These mass groups do not necessarily behave in the interests of the whole society but only in those of their particular group. This is exactly the mentality of Ortega y Gasset's mass man. He is the *only* measure of himself. The group becomes the only judge of its own behaviour.

The mass individual is weak in resources and can only be effective at the consociational level by a process of aggregation of the behaviour of many millions. Not so these group mass men. Small in numbers, they command huge resources. The assets of Ford are about $14 billion. The oligarchs of the great unions in any country exercise an influence on the behavioural balance between the consociation and the mass individual which is totally disproportionate to their numbers. Such groups are mass man plus huge powers to affect the life balance of contemporary societies.

Certain mass groups have virtually captured the media and become the sole possessors of the electronic technology in its propaganda-capacity aspects. They are able to maintain or alter the interior profile of the mass individual and inhibit or enhance the ability of that profile to entertain and strive for the behaviour necessary to maintain the whole society.

With this present arrangement of the consociation—the group mass men and the mass individual—there appears a failure of a key controlling feedback loop in the system. Firms producing goods and services strive to increase their share of the market. Even a saturated market must be persuaded to absorb ever more output. To achieve the necessary demand, intensive advertising is resorted to. This set of linkages reinforces the already uncontrolled activity of the whole process. It is as though the growth drive of the population of a species in an ecosystem were to run wild. The same applies to unions and governments. The essential control loops become defective.

Changes made by governments may be seen in the light of attempts to reinforce existing control loops or establish new ones. However, in the Western world, governments are by no means the only ones who take decisions at the consociational level. It is obvious that big business and big unions have a big say. It is for this reason that we need to be cautious about expectations that the 'state'—what is it?—will be able to ensure the balance of life, or that favoured solutions supposedly emanating from it are necessarily workable because that is their origin.

The danger of looking to the state for salvation lies in part in the inclination to separate 'natural' systems from 'human' systems. The perilous situation is that we may overhaul and reconstitute the 'human' system in this or that way only to discover that the 'natural' system is unable to support the 'solution'. Reconstruction at the socioeconomic level is no guarantee at all of viability at the life-support system level. If it were, the USSR, with the largest area of good grain-growing land in the world, would not have to import grain from North America.

We can relate this thinking to ecosystems as follows. Not only have we the situation in which the mass individual has become unable to maintain an awareness of the need for him to behave in consociationally appropriate ways, but group mass men are able to apply vast resources to behaving in ways which not only ignore the consociational requirement but also work contrary to it in a powerfully positive manner. The mass market for food

M

encourages, indeed demands *now*, behaviour by the individual agricultural group that cannot be fitted to the *longer-term* consociational necessities. Our situation in trying to find a stable set of relationships required to balance the needs of the consociation with those of the individual is therefore much worse than that of the Middle Ages or even, perhaps, the Dark Ages. In those periods the stability of the ecosystems was outside the debate and was ensured largely independently of human activities. There was a similar situation with essential resources; the nonrenewable resources were then mostly in plentiful supply—stone, water, clay, iron, etc—relative to the demand. The key emergent factor now is that the relationship between the behaviour required at the level of society and that required at the level of the individual is massively involved with the great changes wrought by the aggregated mass individuals. At this stage we could oversimplify it and say that the mix is now consociational behaviour–mass-individual behaviour–ecosystems resources. This places the small-group mass men in an instrumental category, in which indeed they are

This is not all; there is a further instrumental element of great importance. This is the new global role of the electronic technology. On the one hand it makes it possible to increase rapidly the dominion of the group mass men over ecosystems and nonrenewable resources. This could result in a still further loss of control, bearing in mind the dynamic of ever more mouths to feed and the resultant reinforcement of an uncontrolled approach to industrial agriculture and the production of physical goods. On the other hand the same technology permits global monitoring of ecosystems' conditions and allows rapid acting and innovative techniques for countermeasures to be developed and applied.

Examination of the new global capability for information production and handling suggests, however, that there may be more in it than the instrumentality of making industrial production more efficient, allowing more human-usable biomass to be squeezed out of ecosystems, promoting the growth and use of psychomass, and propagandizing the mass individual to 'keep him at it' within the confines of the present synthesis or life-balance arrangements. We have to be open to the possibility that our electronic control systems, CATV, computer capability, telecommunication capacity, and perhaps above all our universal packet-switching when added to our existing level of industrial and agricultural production imply that an entirely new kind of human transactional ability is being developed; and that this new ability means the human enterprise is entering a phase, hardly yet recognized, in which the individual will be able to reach hitherto unachievable levels of personal development. There is already a considerable number of substantial thinkers who take this view. We have already looked in detail at Masuda's work (chapter 9) and have referred to Parker (1976a) and others. We must now look more fully at this matter, but before doing so a tabloid statement of where the argument now stand will be useful.

21.7 Telegrammic statement of the components

To have something for contrast we may recapitulate the medieval synthesis or life-balance solution, as I have preferred to call it.

Church and state were the authorities in society for ensuring that the individual behaved as was necessary to ensure the food, etc supply, safety, and protection of that same individual. This was the chief cybernetic aspect of the system. In principle the state controlled from 'outside' the individual; the church worked from 'inside'. In practice each both cajoled and compelled in order to ensure appropriate behaviour by the individual. Agricultural techniques and technology and the groups in society were at such a level that no action could seriously jeopardize the stability of the ecosystems of Europe. In communications, technology was so poorly developed that transfer of biomass from one ecosystem to another was virtually impossible. Their interrelations therefore remained stable. The growth and accessing of knowledge was also slow and posed no threat. The result of all this was stability of the system for a relatively long period, achieved, however, at a cost to the individual which he would not bear, from an interior point of view, for ever.

Now let us look, in telegrammic form and much simplified, at the components we have acquired and which we have to hold simultaneously in mind as we struggle to consider our stage in the human enterprise.

1 The basic necessity for finding a life balance between the behaviour of the individual and the aggregation of that behaviour into the behaviour of the group remains a constant, not eliminated by affluence or high technology.

2 Science and technology have made it possible, and population numbers have made it necessary, for the human species to dominate many ecosystems and to bring past and present ecosystems into symbiotic relationship with each other. The continuing viability of the relationship: large populations–high technology–domination of ecosystems is now dependent on nonrenewable fossil fuels.

3 The relationships between the behaviours of the nation group, the mass group (small groups of special interests), and the mass individual are such that the capacity of ecosystems for producing food can be seriously reduced by the pressures of those three interacting levels of behaviour. The behaviours of the mass group and the individual are not such that the nation state can necessarily ensure the continuance of the food supply.

4 The key behaviour is that of the mass individual since his behaviour becomes that of the mass group and of the society at large. This behaviour has now escaped from the restraining influence of previously operating control feedback loops.

5 The electronic technology is now the indispensable support of almost all other technology. In addition it is a very strong influence on the behaviour of the mass individual. Further, it is very closely integrated in the process of generating new knowledge and technology, and in

making all information cheaply available. It now enables mass groups to press ever more heavily on ecosystems. But it also offers the possibility of managing ecosystems so that they continue productive for human beings without losing their stability; it further potentially affects all relationships through its capacity for being the vehicle through which the behaviour of the mass individual could be remoulded.

6 In conjunction with other components, the electronic technology has already caused great changes in our socioeconomy and will cause still more relatively rapidly. *The basic change is that North America, followed by Western Europe, Japan, and Australia, no longer is a socioeconomy characterized by the predominance of agriculture or manufacturing. These countries now are socioeconomies very heavily involved in, and reliant upon, information. These are new kinds of socioeconomies.*

7 These new socioeconomies interact with ecosystems differently from the ways in which the manufacturing socioeconomies did. The physical base of manufacture will need to be maintained, although doubtless modified. *What comes over the horizon are new relationships between the life-support system and socioeconomies having intricate superstructures of information constructed to rules quite different from those which we suppose to apply to our traditional patterns of behaviour.*

In the next chapter I shall look at this new transactional situation in Western society.

Socioeconomies with information superstructures

22.1 Adumbrations of change

Serious imaginative and productive insight that the electronic technology would mean major shifts in the nature of the developed socioeconomies may conveniently be said to have begun with Wiener's *Human Use of Human Beings*. First published in 1954, this book marked the effective civil emergence of the computer and electronic control technology. In essence, Wiener saw what he called *automatization* as the keynote of the second industrial revolution (Wiener, 1967, page 205), the core of its processes being what we subsume under the concept *information*. Wiener also applied his insights to the workings of human groups, in the same book formulating a cybernetic view of society which has had a strong pervasive influence throughout the disciplines studying the relationships between the individual and the group. Others in the same period, notably W R Ashby (1963), simultaneously developed the discipline of cybernetics and applied its principles to many other fields. Most important among these principles was the discovery of the very wide application of the feedback loop in relation to the state of any system, biological or man-made.

In the 1960s we began to hear about the 'information' or 'knowledge' society. The insight here was that those socioeconomic activities which handle information or knowledge were rapidly rising in their importance proportionally to other activities. Hitherto 'work'—'productive' socio-economic activity—had been seen almost exclusively as meaning the production of physical goods, and more recently as including physical and some other services. Now it came to be sensed, rather than measured, that a new sector which would be called information–knowledge was already playing a major role. This realization led to such concepts as 'the information society' and 'knowledge-work'. The phrase 'postindustrial' was often used to describe the emergent socioeconomy and culture. Drucker, who had been writing in this area since the 1940s, expressed the insight very vividly in his *The Age of Discontinuity* (Drucker, 1968), while others, notably Masuda (Japan Computer Usage Development Institute, 1972), were going a step further and thinking about how to plan for the coming informational society. Along this perspective the emerging underlying concept was of a kind of informational socioeconomic superstructure which might be raised on a 'stabilized' base of production of physical goods and services.

In the late 1960s and the 1970s these insights have been followed up by search for firm corroborative evidence that the information society is already with us. Such evidence is now beginning to accumulate and some quantitative statements can be tentatively made for US society. I have not been able to find equivalent detailed material for other developed countries. It seems likely, judging by figures for expenditures on electronic hardware, that the other developed countries are following the informational socioeconomic developments in the US with varying degrees of lag, but following nevertheless. The project at present being mounted by the Organization for Economic Co-operation and Development to investigate this very question should tell us something shortly.

The firm evidence emerging is of the kind provided by Parker (1976a), who disaggregates employment and GNP figures and reaggregates them to produce an information classification, and OECD (1973), which gives information about capital investment in telecommunications–computer equipment, present expenditures, and future projection for various countries. We may also look at the proportional status of expenditures on such items as education, radio and TV, and communications made by the public and by governments. Also, although comparatively small, research expenditure by governments and other agencies is a significant indicator. Such research investment includes important exploration into the socio-economic significance of having a large information sector and of the kinds of changes likely—for example the substitution of electronic for physical commuting (for example Day, 1973).

22.2 Work-force evidence of the informational society
Statistical evidence of the rise in importance of activities related to information has been concealed by the conventions followed for aggregating socioeconomic activities and transactions into certain major classes for easy manipulation. One of these classes has long been known as 'service activities'. Under this heading many kinds of employment have been lumped together without our paying close attention to changes going on in the mix during the last three decades. We have noticed the rise in 'service' activities and it has been a common observation that the growth area in the socioeconomies of many Western metropolitan areas is increasingly represented by them and no longer by manufacturing industry. But we have been very slow to look carefully at just what it is in the service sector that accounts for its growth. A certain amount of analysis of the service sector data directed at extracting informational activities is now beginning to appear.

Parker (1976a, page 8) states the basic underlying change: "US society is in the midst of a transition from an industrial society to an information society ... the trend is unmistakable". With Porat (1976; 1977), Parker arrives at the new curves for US employment shown in figure 1.2. The proportion of the US labour force conventionally classified as in industry reached its apogee around 1950. In 1950 it was 62% of the total work force. In 1900 it was 36%, and projections for 1980 give 38%. The numbers under the conventional classification (US Bureau of Labor Statistics) for 'service activities' were 26% in 1950 and 37% in 1960; and projected to 1980—60%. Agriculture shows a decline from 35% in 1900 to a projected 2% of the labour force in 1980.

Parker and Porat have disaggregated these classifications and have devised a different breakdown of the work-force figures so that a new sector called simply information can be identifiable. This makes it possible to compare the numbers in the information sector with those in all other occupations and in the new revised sectors of service, industry, and agriculture. In reading figures and graphs care therefore needs to be exercised when comparing the new figures with the Bureau's figures; the information sector has been created largely at the expense of the old service sector. It should also be noted in looking at figure 1.2 that the curve showing the information sector is an average between conservative and liberal interpretations of what should be included in the information sector. If all jobs in which the main activity is information processing are classified into a sector called 'information' then we have an indication of growth in information employment (expressed as percentage of all US employment—approximate median figure):

Date	1900	1950	1960	1970
Percentage	12	31	44	48

The projection for 1980 is for only a slight increase over 1970. If jobs are divided into 'information' and 'noninformation' the figures are even more interesting. In 1950 only 31% were in information, with 69% representing all other jobs. In 1960 the percentage in information was 44, with 56% for the rest. A decade later 48% and 52% represented a slower change in the ten years. The further change to 1980 indicates a much slower rate of increase in the information sector, which is by this date estimated to be clearly the dominant activity of the labour force. The year 1975 can be counted as a possible crossover year for the US, depending on definitions and variations in predictions. If a more conservative method is used it might be 1980. The variation is, however, quite small—a few percentage points over a decade. *We can take it for all practical purposes that half the US labour force is now employed in activities classifiable as predominantly informational, and that the number is about twice that of those employed in industry.*

An earlier paper by Parker listed in detail the occupations which are shifted from the conventional classifications to generate the new 'information sector'. Managers (over four million), bookkeepers, secretaries (well over two million), many of whom would conventionally be included in 'industry' are now placed in 'information', as are those manual workers who service the hardware of information (for example, telephone linesmen and data processing machine repairmen), together with the more obvious information workers such as the two and a half million schoolteachers.

As a second area in which to look for measures of the growth of the emphasis on information, Parker takes the GNP and the annual National Income. He quotes Machlup (1962) as estimating that 30% of the US national income was dependent on information in 1958. A third area is that of expenditures by the public on the consumption of information.

From 1950 to 1971 the amount of personal income allocated to information increased 39% in the US. By 1967, 53% of all employee compensation was derived from the information sector.

A few comments will be useful at this point.

1 Parker and Porat have found a valuable statistical approach for supporting the insight that information is now a very major activity (measured by three criteria) of the socioeconomy in the US, with the high probability that it will clearly be the dominant activity in the next decade.

2 Jobs do not account for all human activities. Although the measure of expenditures of personal income on information covers to some degree the information-based activity of the individual occurring outside the job, it seems reasonable to suggest that a time-budget approach might show an even greater preponderance of information in the sum total of all activities. A great deal of nonjob time is now spent on activities rich in information and using heavily the equipment for handling information We might bear in mind Masuda's time-value concept here.

3 The US category of industrial activity for 1970 included about three million 'operatives' (machine minders, etc). Many of these jobs are potentially capable of being automated by means of electronic controls. Socioeconomic pressures in the developed countries push firms in the direction of eliminating jobs whenever possible. Increased automation and consequent reduction in the numbers of industrial workers appear likely. This would give a still greater preponderance of employment to information.

4 Parker does not appear to include in the information sector those in manufacturing industry who make equipment predominantly used for handling information. This is now an important function of all industry and could usefully be put beside the information sector as a subsector. Almost all electronic, though not all electrical, equipment has an informational component.

5 If the Parker and Porat analysis is correct in its expectations, the great period of fast growth in the information sector took place between 1940 and 1960 and we are now in a period of a slower and falling growth rate. It is possible that the absolute numbers in information jobs may increase only slowly in the 1980s, while those in manufacturing industry and agriculture may continue their present decline. The information sector has provided new jobs roughly to match those lost in manufacturing industry since about 1945. This must have been a major stabilizer in the US job market. There is no guarantee that this role will be continued. The very rapid development of microprocessing and its great potential for very wide use already suggest that the rate of its diffusion will be limited by serious shortage of trained personnel. Filling this need may give another respite, but it may well be that to win it we have to make a very major societal effort to achieve the numbers of trained workers required—national policies of computerization such as

those suggested by Masuda for Japan. The whole question throws a vivid light on our deep ignorance of how socioeconomies actually work and even what their key elements are[1]. As one category of job declines in numbers although the physical output of the class increases, is there any inevitability that another category will increase in its demand for workers, so that the syndrome production–job–wages–consumption is maintained as the chief distribution linkage?

6 The nature of information presents, once more, various definitional problems. Since Parker's and Porat's emphasis is on jobs in the information sector we might stress here one question along that perspective. It is that information can be 'frozen' in a piece of equipment. Even the simplest machine—say a can opener—is frozen information; the human being with bare hands does not have enough information to know how to open the can. This freezing becomes an enormously important characteristic of information when applied to any kind of goods, whether physical or mental. Frozen information reduces the human labour necessary to achieve anything and therefore, in this perspective, is a reducer of jobs. In another perspective it may, of course, equally generate jobs. What is production? And what is 'mind' in relation to it? Further, supposing we can find a satisfactory definition for productivity of information, how is it to be measured?

7 Increase in the numbers of those using information and working in the areas classified as information, and increased expenditures on information and associated equipment will mean increased production of information. The production and use of information will be mutually self-reinforcing. We can therefore anticipate a burst of growth in information itself, even though the numbers working in the information sector may level off, or even fall. We have a precedent for this relationship in manufacturing industry, which for a time has had a rising rate of increased output with a steadily and rapidly falling number of workers being required[2].

[1] As agriculture in Europe became more efficient during the eighteenth century, producing more food with fewer workers, early manufacturing grew rapidly to provide jobs for the 'surplus' population driven from the land. The two processes—decrease of jobs on the farms and increase in jobs in the factories—interlocked during the nineteenth century. A similar interlocking appears to have occurred in this century. As employment in the factory has declined, jobs in the office, school, university, entertainment industry, etc have increased. The question to be raised is whether this interlocking has occurred twice fortuitously or whether our sociocultural characteristics make its occurrence a probability. The sequence is: agriculture–manufacturing; manufacturing–information; information–what?

[2] The actual process of manufacturing is now often farmed out by US manufacturers to agencies in countries with lower wages than American workers, for example Japan, Korea, European countries. An apparently US radio or TV set may be manufactured in Japan; a New York published book may be printed in Amsterdam. Manufacturing emigrates from the countries where labour costs are high. Those countries appear to be 'compensating' for the loss of industrial jobs by concentrating on information sector employment.

Increase in the production and use of information will have effects, as yet unprobed, on the life-support system and will enormously enhance the capability of human beings for what I have called the 'assembly' function in ecosystems. Information is now the source both of new technology and of its applications. Also information can be folded in upon itself: information can automate the processes of its own production and application. It is already doing this by way of computers that design circuits and computers that issue instructions to other computers (as in the virtual terminals of universal packet-switching).

8 Increased availability, diffusion, and use of information will relate closely to the character profile and sensibility of the mass individual. Even granting that the organizational arrangements for originating material on TV or radio are changed radically it still appears most probable that a good deal of broadcasting will continue in the mode of one-to-many. This means that through his day-to-day casual attention to the information diffusers—quite apart from his specific quest for particular information—the mass individual is going to continue to be subject to the selection of information accessed through the operation of the media. This will be reinforced by an increasing public awareness of information. An obvious result is the formation of a certain similarity of mind in large masses of individuals simply because of the uniformity of the information accessed. Propaganda and advertising might find a place even greater than their present one in the culture and society.

22.3 Aspects of information in a market context

In some degree in contrast with Parker's thinking, but also reinforcing the concept of the information society, there is appearing a literature having as focus of attention information seen as a major component of the concept of the market-oriented socioeconomy. Here emphasis is on the production and consumption of information as a commodity of the market and the informational assumptions underlying the market concept. We find under this heading studies in the 'economics of information', 'informational economics', and such special areas as 'market information', 'technological information', and the 'informational structure of markets'.

The overall emphasis of interest along this perspective appears to be the search for ways of estimating the effect of information on the performance of the market (see Spence, 1974). Study of the informational structure of markets therefore becomes very important. The context is general equilibrium theory, in which a considerable role is played by the existence of uncertainty and variations in the amount and quality of information available as preliminary to initiating a transaction.

In the workings of the market, asymmetry in the availability and distribution of information plays an important role. Generally sellers have better information than buyers. Asymmetries cause limitations on what transactions can be performed. The reduction in asymmetries is presumed to be capable of improving market performance. Spence refers to these asymmetries as 'informational gaps' in various markets, for example in jobs and insurance, medical, and other services. These gaps stimulate search activities, attention to signals, and methods of moving information in markets, advertising, the production and dissemination of information connected with research and development, patents, consumer information handling, etc. Spence's evaluation of current economic thinking is: "I think it fair to say that a large part of recent economic theory is either directly about or related to information problems" (Spence, 1974, page 60).

For our purpose an important distinction can be made between the private and the community return on the possession and use of information. The possessor of certain information may be able to use it to his personal benefit while simultaneously causing public disbenefit. The process of urban development sometimes involves the conscious exploitation of this possibility. For example, the developer can devise ways of putting certain costs on to the public charge, himself recouping as a private agent. Land values may be manipulated in this way. Agribusiness may deplete soil fertility, leaving the resultant problems to be solved by publicly financed action. Fisheries may be overfished to the benefit of the private fishing interests and the ultimate public disbenefit in the decline in the quantity of seafood available. This is familiar matter in the perspective of ecological knowledge, where we have seen it cause ecologists to call for a new ethic in our handling of ecosystems. We are now seeing the same observation made by economists looking along the perspective of information–private benefit–public disbenefit. There appears a relatively visible link between the thinking of the two disciplines in this area. Given the present systemic linkages which hold human societies together it is information which makes possible the deflection to the private agent of benefits derived from certain capabilities of both the ecosystem and the 'human' system. The economist may see the ethical question in a somewhat different light from the ecologist, but both are basically thinking about the need for regulation of some kind.

To a certain extent the market tries to handle information like any other commodity. In some regards it is similar to bananas or bricks. It can be produced, bought and sold, and used to some specific purpose. In other regards it is different. It does not disappear or become vitiated if used. If bought it may also remain the property of the seller (for example, a lawyer's advice, which may be sold many times to different clients). It is very difficult to measure, and often hard to assign a precisely determined economic value to information. We have looked at some of these difficulties in the perspective of psychomass in chapter 19. In spite of such problems, information has in fact been considerably integrated into the workings of our kind of market economy, as is evidenced by the job classifications which Parker has reassembled into the information sector of the socioeconomy. This present, and rapid, integration draws our attention to several matters of likely future importance.

22.4 Integration of information into socioeconomies

Perhaps the most provocative question to raise is the possibility of further massive integration of information into our market-oriented socioeconomies. This matter has many facets, of which it will be possible to mention only a few.

First, it is clear that information has only so far been integrated in those respects that are easily assimilable by a market socioeconomy of the kind with which we are so familiar. Substantially this assimilability is limited to a commodity-in-the-market concept. The market economy has not been able, indeed has not tried, to assimilate great storage processes of information such as public or university libraries, and it has captured only a fraction of the information capability of the free electronic diffusion of information by radio and TV. There, advertising must leave unused by the market vast areas of information to serve as pegs on which to hang its own assimilative capability.

The very important questions to which the identification of this unintegrated component leads have to do with its present and possible future size and the possibility of either greater integration or the creation of a superstructure to our economy of a type other than a market economy. For convenience I have called this last a superstructure to suggest that it may have some different rules from those governing the market economy.

As knowledge and information of all kinds are growing very fast in quantity we can expect the size of the unassimilable component to increase, probably very rapidly. Furthermore, access to this growing psychomass will become easier, cheaper, and more generally diffused on a global scale. Some of this additional material will doubtless prove capable of being assimilated, but on balance it seems that we may shortly find ourselves in a situation in which this is less and less possible unless we can find ways of making a new transactional framework for information.

If I understand Masuda correctly, his recommendations for the 'information society' concentrate on increasing the component of information assimilable into the market economy by making information of various kinds more accessible, more widely diffused, and of progressively better quality. As for the component which is now and in the future not assimilable, he develops his new economic concept of 'time-value' as part of the basis on which to raise what I have called the superstructure (see Masuda, 1975; and chapter 9). Others have perceived something of the problem and have expressed the need for the better integration of information as an economic good.

A second question concerns the GNP. Spence points out that our notion of growth being limited by the availability of resources must already need some considerable modification if the information sector is as large as indicated by Parker's research. The reason for requiring modification is that the production of information is not itself limited, but new information has a bearing on how expendable and limited resources can be used. Therefore, supposed limits to growth may not be what they appear to be because of reliance on methods of measurement such as the GNP. *As already suggested, it is the productivity of information with regard to the productivity of other socioeconomic processes (for example, manufacturing industry) which is important in this area.* Without doubt a chief socioeconomic characteristic of information is its multiplier effect. This is parallel with its infolding capacity socioculturally speaking.

Third, questions arise about the currentness of information within the workings of the market socioeconomy. Lag in up-to-dateness is a major cause of asymmetry in transactional information. The electronic technology has already improved currentness, and especially currentness linked with degree of geographic separateness between those carrying out transactions. This improvement will continue. The questions appear around the problem of the change implied in taking advantage of such improvement in currentness (see Arrow, 1974). Individual firms make effort in this direction, but as yet there appears very little response at the level of the nation or the city. Kupperman's proposals for crisis management incorporate the idea as we saw in chapter 7, and Beer's contribution to the restructuring of Chilean society was a large-scale proposal exploiting the currentness possible with the electronic technology (Beer, 1974a; 1975; and chapter 4). We have also noted Turoff's computer conferencing project (Turoff, 1976). The difficulties of operationalizing suggest that we suffer from a lag between the information generated and available and our capacity to bring it to bear in the world of action. This may be due to problems in the assimilation of information into our present socioeconomies or to difficulties connected with our slowness in developing the informational superstructure. Or both.

A fourth area of concern appears around the idea of the stabilization of the growth rates of outputs of physical goods and services in the socioeconomies. We have noted this notion of stabilization as a goal for the British ecologists' proposals (*The Ecologist*, 1972; and chapter 10), and as an actual emerging condition diagnosed for US society by Boulding (1972). If Boulding is correct, several of the socioeconomies of the developed countries may already be in the incipient phase of the stabilization of output of physical goods and services. This, Boulding points out, relates to the stabilization of population numbers. The USA is now virtually stable in population (1977).

A socioeconomy in Boulding's condition of zero population and production growth (ZPPG) may be heavily reliant on certain kinds of information for maintaining itself in a satisfactory condition of material well-being. *Problems, which in a growth situation may disappear or be solved simply because of growth, are no longer solvable by the fortuitousness*

of the growth process if the socioeconomy is stabilized. This feature may
be particularly marked in the matter of employment opportunities. During
the last few decades many industrial jobs have disappeared in the Western
nations. But new jobs have been generated through the appearance of
whole new industries (for example, manufacture of plastics and electronic
calculators) and, as we have seen, the area of job expansion has essentially
been information.

*It seems likely that the stabilized socioeconomy will have to explore the
conscious development of the information sector to compensate for the
job losses likely to result from stabilization.* That is one way to go. It
implies that if stabilization is a planned goal, as the British ecologists and
others propose, then the development and growth of the information
sector must also be planned. Planning means here conscious action being
taken by society as a whole through those agencies responsible for the
common weal. This would not, of course, preclude planning by private
groups, such as firms, provided such planning were in the framework of
public planning.

Another way to go is to modify, amplify, or add to the production–
job–wages–consumption syndrome. This approach implies a modification
of our insistence that the right to consume is virtually exclusively dependent
on being in possession of money or at least credit. It is predominantly
the job which provides the money in our society. Hence the basic
importance of jobs. As we have seen, the growth rate in jobs in the
information sector is already slowing up and manufacturing jobs continue
to decline in the US. We could reach the situation where we have, first, a
pile of goods which we cannot access properly because of failure of the
'job' component in the production–job–wages–consumption sequence, and
later an unused production capability since production without consumption
is a nonviable condition. An inference is that for some purposes we could
think about relinquishing our insistence on the wages–consumption link
and promote consumption on the basis of some other concept. Does
'payment' have to be in money?

If planned development of the information sector were to be adopted a
policy for the stabilized society, it would imply the planned development
of new information and knowledge (psychomass). This would raise
questions of priority in the allocation of resources. Society, through its
appropriate agencies, would have to weigh very carefully the relative
merits of investment in such areas as science, literature, the performing
arts, technology, etc. Further, there would be the need to decide which
areas of, say, science and technology, should receive favoured treatment.
The beginnings of this kind of activity are already visible in national arts
councils, subsidies to broadcasting agencies, and the scientific research to
which public funds are funnelled. Presumably such agencies would become
much more important and new ones would be created.

The specific and purposeful development of knowledge is already well formalized in both the public and the private sector of the socioeconomy. A possible explanation, in part, of the appearance of this condition is that efficiency in the production of goods and services is not now sufficient. It is also necessary to be efficient with regard to the use of available knowledge for production and for prediction in regard to the future market (see Arrow, 1974). This loops us back to the likely enhanced role of information in the stabilized socioeconomy.

It is difficult to get clearly at the nub of the problem, and perhaps at this stage the best we can hope for is to achieve glimpses of it from several perspectives. One might, however, hazard that a key idea is that along either the economic or the ecological perspective there is no free lunch. The worm in the pond appears a free lunch for the bottom fish, but is not in reality because the bottom fish is itself a free lunch for a bigger fish. So the bottom fish wins his worm by making strenuous effort to avoid being the bigger fish's lunch a little later. In economies everything has to be paid for. The key is perhaps the making of effort. The real cost paid for the opportunity to consume is met by the consumer making some kind of effort. In our socioeconomies the effort is conventionally recognized as of certain kinds. The question we have to ask in connection with the information sector is whether there are other kinds of effort which might be used and whether the emphasis on present different efforts can be altered in their relative proportions.

22.5 The 'information society' and ecosystems

There is a considerable literature linking our socioeconomic thought with our ecological understanding. Loosely, it goes under the title of environmentalism. To date it has identified various areas of difficulty, for example the ethical question, problems concerning our socioeconomic assumptions about values, alternative institutional arrangements, uncertainties about measuring pollution, environmental damage, and allocating costs. We also now have compendiums which bring together these identifications and offer critiques of them: for example, O'Riordan (1976).

There is, however, very little existing material on the relationship between information in economic systems and information in ecosystems. Some observations can be offered.

First, if socioeconomies decide to accelerate the growth and use of information consciously—that is, if they actively promote the 'information society'—more and better information will be available for acting upon ecosystems. This in itself cannot be counted as one of Boulding's 'bads', but it cannot be assumed that such additional information would be used always with such restraint that no further degradation of ecosystems would occur. The 'human' part of the total global system would have to find controls for individual and group behaviour even more effective than those already—and overoptimistically—proposed by those who agree to the necessity for restoring or generating effective cybernetic loops in the socioeconomies.

Further, the direction by society of the development of information, suggested as a likely major feature of the 'information society', would probably emphasize the growth of precisely the kind of information necessary for deflecting still more energy, especially in the form of food, as throughput of the socioeconomies. This could simply be a function of increasing world population, inevitable globally even though ZPG is achieved in the developed countries. Given the present value systems of the socioeconomies, the whole process would appear to have the danger of possibly encouraging exactly those trends that appear undesirable from the point of view of ensuring the viability of the total life-support system.

Information is a product of the developed countries rather than of the developing. The developed would therefore tend to increase their exports of information so that information pressure would increase on the ecosystems in which the developing countries have to exist. The notorious groundnuts scheme in Africa and many examples of the application of agribusiness to tropical and subtropical ecosystems indicate that this process has already begun. Aggressive development and export of information by the developed countries would further encourage this trend, particularly as the developed countries with their swollen urban populations would be forced to extract more food from ecosystems other than their own because of the high costs of energy and the stabilizing of the socioeconomies.

The extensive pushing of 'Northern' agribusiness into 'Southern' ecosystems and their socioeconomies is not only particularly dangerous because of likely ecological degradation, but is precisely the opposite of what appears necessary for sustaining Southern populations within socioeconomies that can provide them with at least the minimum requirements for life. These populations have probably only a modest capability for running societies essentially on the production–job–wages–consumption linkage. As Ward (1976) convincingly argues, these societies must maintain very large numbers directly on the land. They must depend on the syndrome work–production–consumption, without intermediary link of job or wages. Agribusiness makes this impossible by its mass application of high-grade and expensive technology. It simply preempts the land in large tracts. This in turn means that in the developing countries both some of the present and most of the additional population to come must go to the cities, there to be forced into the already overloaded production–job–wages–consumption linkage. There are scores of major cities in the developing nations where this has already happened and the process is also known in the developed countries.

This scenario, then, suggests that if, in a condition of either 'naturally occurring' or planned stabilization of the production of physical goods and services, the developed countries force the planned growth of information to maintain their present socioeconomies, the effects on the 'Southern' countries may well be opposite of what may be necessary for solving their problems of population–food–energy. The result could only be a further tragic widening of the gap between the developed and the developing.

Let us turn to more cheerful possibilities. If, in consciously developing information, emphasis were placed on the production, diffusion, and application of information especially useful for increasing the human-usable biomass of ecosystems without endangering their stability, we could see a way to carrying larger populations at perhaps even higher physical levels of well-being than at present. This possibility could be further reinforced by using the electronic technology to modify the recent and still continuing tendency toward massification of populations into gigantic clots almost wholly dependent on the production–job–wages–consumption linkage.

With regard to the emphasis on ecosystem information and its application we already have some leads in such efforts as I have described in chapter 6. Such experiments attempt to move human activity toward maintaining the productivity of ecosystems while still ensuring their indefinite continuance. This offers new opportunities for sustaining segments of populations in the developed countries at relatively low densities and at least partly reliant on the direct linkage production–consumption. Todd's arks could serve an entirely new kind of 'farmer' or 'homesteader'.

For him the electronic technology would have several very important functions:
1 providing him with up-to-date information about running his micro-ecosystem: such information would be generated by research laboratories, market analysts, etc and would be disseminated as soon as available;
2 permitting 'urban' transactions, such as tapping sources of information and advice, school, higher and adult education, entertainment, interaction with other families, getting access to data processing equipment, and services such as telemedical centres;
3 monitoring his system and exchanging monitored information with his 'neighbours'—who might include families hundreds of kilometres distant;
4 permitting participation in the development of the 'ecological-information society' through access to electronic meetings, computer conferences, and two-way radio and TV.

It is not necessary in visualizing what it would be like to live in such conditions to assume that a cocoon-like existence would be inevitable. Not at all. The delights of the country might indeed be combined with many of the advantages of city living—an ancient dream familiar to us from Theocritus to Louis XV and Madame de Pompadour playing at shepherds in the forest at Versailles.

Such a scenario would mesh with the urge for a return to a simpler way of living without abandoning all sophistication. G R Taylor (1974) uses the term 'paraprimitive' to describe his view of such a society. This is no Tolstoyan return to the simple life, but rather some simplification of the very complex. The electronic technology would play a vital role, but it is difficult to imagine the feel of it until we have actual experience of the next stage of the technology in daily use. The extended use of the telephone systems and the cable systems, in some of the ways we have described, now need to be experienced and absorbed by mass populations before we shall be able to sense how we shall decide to use the new capabilities. The next decade or so will give us, fairly commonly: home terminals, video storage, computer conferencing, access to data processing, extended use of cable. It will also give us further breakdown in the syndrome production–job–wages–consumption and therefore increased unemployment. This will mean a push to try new possibilities.

Here perhaps is a dynamic, not particularly in the direction of a more ecological *ethic* but in the direction of a different set of *behaviour patterns* which might be more appropriate than the present patterns for ensuring the continuance of the life-support system.

23

The humanist operational difficulty

23.1 A preliminary contrast

In the previous chapter we looked at evidence indicating that the advanced developed countries now have socioeconomies which are heavily emphasizing information–knowledge. We saw that this is not just a matter of the explosion of knowledge—that has indeed occurred—but of the very considerable integration of information as a major component of existing socioeconomies as testified by the figures for work activities and expenditures. Because this change has not been identified until very recently as a major shift in our culture and society it has received minimal attention or direction by society, although it has enjoyed energetic promotion by group interests in business, industry, and research. Only very belatedly has the notion begun to emerge that, if society needs a degree of direction, then this area of growth also is important in its implications for our future. Even now sociotechnical decisions in the field of the electronic technology receive only very poor coverage by the mass media, and hardly rate as news.

This approach of attempting to understand the change that has occurred and is continuing, together with the incipient notion of directing the further development of the technologies for the benefit of society as a whole, is in some degree of contrast with much of the conscious change which has been introduced in many countries in this century. Much of this change has been inspired, not so much by a clear understanding of the condition or potential of the resources available to society but by a desire to change certain of its elements for human or humane reasons. Ideals of justice, equality, security, health, personal worth, etc have had a strong influence in justifying and actually bringing about change in many societies. Manifestations in the last hundred years have included free education, universal suffrage, pensions, health services, public housing, democratization of society, etc.

These changes have not greatly relied on an understanding of how society has been evolving or on the potential for change inherent in science and technology but have emphasized human aspiration or vision of what society and the life of the individual in it *could* be. Perhaps they are to be seen not so much as reconstructions of society, which is how we have been familiarized to view them, but rather as superimpositions of desire or wish imposed upon society without any very great understanding of its ability to sustain the new developments.

This approach to change in society—one might almost say the very idea that society can evolve—is closely connected with the movement in Western sensibility that we call humanism. Into this we must now probe a little because it has vital links with the demand for a new ethic made by ecologists, with our cybernetic concepts of the workings of society, with the psychic characteristics of the mass individual, and with all attempts to plan.

23.2 Certain relevant aspects of humanism

Humanism as a world view stems from the Renaissance, when its most distinguished exponent was Erasmus. Its heyday was the Enlightenment. Modern humanism is different in emphasis from that of either the earlier period or the eighteenth century. At first, after the long medieval centuries of looking inward, the delights of directing the gaze outward toward the marvellous variety of the natural world were a dominant fascination. After several centuries of progressively successful science this fixation is waning. Indeed, we may already be seeing a turning inward again as suggested by rising anti-intellectualism and apathy toward new scientific discovery. That first rapture of humanism has long since generally departed, although the individual may sometimes still retain his sense of wonder.

A second distinction may be drawn between the feeling of the Enlightenment and that of ourselves. Eighteenth-century humanists strongly held that understanding and rational explanation would automatically beget reasonable, humane conduct. Belief in the power of human reason to open the secrets of nature as well as to order and run society justly and efficiently was held with passion. The rags and tatters of that conviction are still with us in the underlying assumptions we continue to hold in such institutionalized activities as education, social planning, urban planning, some of our political 'philosophies', and often quite strongly in our thinking about the applications of technology. Two world wars separate us from the hope which inspired the *philosophes.* We have seen from looking at George Steiner's diagnosis of our contemporary sensibility that there is strong evidence for thinking that the liberal humanist contract as a basis for society is dead (chapter 17).

A third distinction is that a variation called scientific humanism has had a great deal of influence in our century. This view, very well exemplified by the thought of Julian Huxley, has placed great emphasis on human beings consciously directing their cultural and societal evolution through the use of knowledge made available by science. The collection of essays by twenty-six humanists which Huxley (1961) published under the title of *The Humanist Frame* remains an excellent statement of this approach. By this date the contribution of evolutionary theory was clearly recognized and new ethical questions that were connected with human behaviour related to ecosystem viability on a global scale had been raised.

Writing of evolution as a progressive process, Waddington saw humanism as "... man's duty, not only to mankind but to the living world as a whole, to use his special faculties of reason and social organization to ensure that his own future evolution carries forward the same general trend" (Huxley, 1961, page 73). He called for the development of a "supra-ethical criterion" which would serve as a measure against which to assess ethical principles with regard to their efficiency for promoting human evolutionary development. Note the emphasis on duty. The humanist is not a hedonist, but must stress ethical obligation and responsibility. Waddington described the human being as an "ethicizing animal"—a view supported by Julian Huxley, Simpson, and many others. The view put forward is that, as human evolution now takes place predominantly in what Huxley called the 'psychosocial' sphere—anyway until biological and electronic components become fused—ethics perform the function of mediating the behaviour of human beings in an evolutionary context. They are cybernetically generated, that is, the evolutionary process itself produces the ethical imperatives. Ethics is thus seen as a product of the natural world: there is no need of any supposed supernatural base. Simpson acknowledges Waddington's very important contribution in bringing out the "evolutionary origins and function of ethicizing" (Simpson, 1964, page 143), but does not fully agree with Waddington's view of authority mentioned in chapter 11.

Simpson himself has devoted a good deal of attention to the ethical aspects of biology and ecology. He is perhaps best described as an evolutionary humanist. He declines to fall into the trap of thinking about the question on the basis of conceptualizing society as a kind of supra-organism above the individual (Simpson, 1964, page 147). He prefers to take as analogy the operation of natural selection. This allows him to see ethical decisions as often compromises between evolutionary drives toward individualization, and socialization. He makes a second point that a standard or universal set of ethical requirements applied to all human societies would be *unethical* in the greater context of human psychosocial evolution. Ethical systems must remain functional—in a systemic sense— and, to ensure this, change must be possible.

Above all, Simpson underlines that it is in the nature of the human condition (many choices of action, choices of goals, varieties of modes of adaption) that behavioural controls are not exclusively imposed on human beings but are voluntarily applied, at least in considerable part. Human societies cannot expect that ethical controls will automatically develop and be automatically applied. *The penalty for having become an ethicizing animal is the free acceptance of the responsibility it implies*[1].

We now come to see that, although the ethical capability of the human species has its roots in biological evolution, it is necessary to stress that it is no longer there that we must look for solutions to the problem of how to balance the behaviour of the individual and the group within the

---

[1] It is interesting that Simpson, essentially starting out from the concept of evolution in biology arrives at the same conclusion in this area as Fromm (see chapter 16). Fromm's humanism (for example Fromm, 1968), like that of others described in this chapter, fails to raise properly the question of motivation to 'right' action. Fromm insists that the individual must stop relying on the mass; but how is he to be motivated to do this?

context of the ecological viability of Spaceship Earth. The emphasis of Simpson and many others is essentially humanistic: we—unaided human beings—have the obligation to make the effort, and some success may be hoped for through the application of our knowledge.

23.3 Ethical formulations in ecology

The question of human behaviour, and therefore of ethics, arises in ecological studies because of impacts of human beings on the viability of ecosystems. Understanding of this is an entirely new development in human sensibility. It presents us with the challenge of transcending all those attitudes with which we have been able comfortably to ignore consideration of the life-support system. This separates our time sharply from the humanism of the Enlightenment.

It also introduces a new and highly disruptive element into the humanism of the first half of our century that stressed those humane values we have mentioned, through vigorous, consciously planned societal reconstruction. *Like its predecessors, this humanism ignored the question of the continued viability of the life-support system. It seemed necessary to worry only about ensuring the individual gets fair shares and opportunity for his personal development. Into this wholly human, but now demonstrably limited, set of assumptions dropped the bomb of our understanding of the ecological support of life and the indeed terrible news that the globe is finite in resources and capabilities.*

First, the ecologists came to see the importance of human collective behaviour toward the life-support system. The dangers of pollutants, of soil exhaustion, of system instability, of loss of system productivity and ability to retrieve a position of equilibrium, and of extinction of species began clearly to be attributable to specific elements of human behaviour. This is substantially the origin of what we sometimes call *environmentalism*.

Second, the ecologists together with others in various fields have come to see the matter very much in the light of a triadic relationship: the individual, the group (society, nation-state, etc), and the biological arrangements by which life continues. This last is no longer seen only in its aspect of how to 'win' subsistence from 'nature', as all civilizations had previously perceived it, but also in its aspect of how to do this within the rules that maintain natural systems continuously viable.

This understanding led to a sharpening of attention to the relationship between the individual and the group. This, as we have suggested, is really not two but four elements: the individual, the small group, and the society or nation-state, being the first three. Logically, we must also add the total human world population, for its actions also must be subject to the rules, although no genuine global societal group can yet be said to exist.

The concern for the ethical relationship between human beings and the life-support system is sometimes referred to as *bioethics* (see for example Potter, 1971; H T Odum, 1971; but none has a firmer idea of what it is than Simpson, 1964). In general, ecologists call for a change in human behaviour toward the world's ecosystems. Some, like H T Odum and Potter actually attempt the formulation of ethical precepts to guide the new behaviour. Ecologists have also generally perceived the importance of the relation between the individual and the group for ensuring the necessary behaviour toward the life-support system.

H T Odum, for example, suggests that we need a new ten commandments to guide our use of energy so that it will be held within limits defined by our ecological understanding. This is necessary to his thinking as his emphasis in ecology is on energy flows, etc. His ten commandments, however, also place great emphasis on the concept of system, and the obligation to understand system (H T Odum, 1971, page 244). The commandments enjoin us not to waste energy, to use observation of energy flows as indicators of how to act, to respect the natural system (life-support) as one's own, to measure value by energy not money, not to take from man or nature without return of equal value, to preserve the heritage of information, to favour stability over growth and "survival process over individual peace". The whole passage (pages 242–253) is worth reading as indicating how far some of these ideas can be pushed. It is necessary not to be put off by Odum's bogus archaic language.

Potter (1971) produces a bioethical creed for individuals. This is based on the idea that if correct beliefs are held they will lead to appropriate action. Potter does not, perhaps more wisely than Odum, suggest specific 'dos' and 'don'ts'. Each element of his creed is, however, related to a specific commitment (page 196). The creed requires belief in the need to provide prompt action in the context of world crises, realization that the future of the human species depends in large measure on what is done now, understanding of the uniqueness of the individual with his need to contribute to the greater whole in ways compatible with long-term societal requirements, acceptance that some human suffering is necessary but rejection of human beings' inhumanity to each other, and acceptance of death and veneration for life.

Ferkiss (1974) develops a philosophy of *ecological humanism* as the way forward, after dismissing as "roads to nowhere" the "-isms" with which our century is familiar. Ferkiss sees our ecological future implying strongly the need to get control of technology. He subordinates economics to politics (understood in the broadest sense) in the interest of balance in society taking precedence over growth. His ethic is based on the need to make effort to achieve the transition to the humanist ecological society. He calls for "... socially mandated and supported changes in the laws and life styles of the whole community" (Ferkiss, 1974, page 269). The transition is seen as an "open conspiracy" and an "unstructured, unorganized movement for reform". The reformers will, it is hoped, be dedicated and unified by common perceptions.

Enough has been mentioned from a variety of writers with an ecological interest—not all of equal quality by any means—to indicate the general idea. This is that the need for new behaviour toward the life-support system having been perceived, the next step is to discover how to achieve the new behaviour patterns. This has been attempted by specific formulation (for example H T Odum), by belief formation through a creed (for example Potter), by development of a supposed new philosophy (for example Ferkiss), and, most importantly, by simply exploring the evolutionary and biological bases of the matter and going no further than suggesting that, as we alone are aware of our sociobiological evolution, we should "... deliberately work for the desirable" (Simpson, 1964, page 146).

All these approaches have a common Achilles' heel which we must now look at.

23.4 The leap to operationalizing an ecological ethic

We may admit that our understanding of the finiteness of our human habitat will require new values and new behaviour patterns by human beings both individually and in groups. Let us admit the case has been made for the need. We can also agree that, if this is allowed, then it is not unreasonable to explore the possibilities of trying to formulate what the new patterns may be.

The justification for the logic of this stage is that the need for the conscious formulation of a new ethic is inherent in the fact of the human species being responsible for its further development in a self-conscious way. Therefore it can be argued that it is not merely reasonable but unavoidable that we develop the new ethic consciously, at least in part. Simpson makes the case for this, as we have seen.

The problem is that the price for consciously developing an ethic is erosion of the motivation to obey its commands. Ethics are not simply a matter of intellect but are also very much concerned with feeling and will. We may formulate the details of a new ethic, as our examples have done, but we have not faced the question of how to motivate vast mass populations to obey. I have not been able to find any ecological writer with any worthwhile suggestion of how to cope with this difficulty. Exhortation is present in quantity, but it is not likely to be enough. Understanding of how the system works is impressive and can be generally diffused quite easily through the electronic technology, but we now know—as the *philosophes* did not—that knowledge and appropriate action are not necessarily connected. Fear is also offered [for example Heilbroner (1974) and all those who compose scenarios of a totalitarian future] but, as a control, this frustrates the very intelligence we must use to do our best to follow the path of our sociobiological evolution. A last possibility, already tried for other purposes in this century, is saturation propagandizing, but this offends our entirely legitimate expectation that our awareness shall not be falsified.

Some idea of the failure to find a way to motivate the individual to the ecological behaviour deemed necessary can be gleaned from the end of H T Odum's chapter on this question. He states that the essential survival requirement is a "... subsystem of *religious* teaching which follows the laws of the energy ethic ... . We can teach the energy truths through general science in the schools and *teach the love of system* and its requirements of us in the changing churches" (H T Odum, 1971, page 253; emphasis supplied). What Odum's diagrams cannot show is any psychological dynamic which will lead the individual to love the system and therefore behave within its requirements. We have some evidence that for human beings God, political creed, family, and even that unlovely thing the nation-state can inspire love, devotion, and sacrifice. But the system? We may be 'persuaded' to avoid action which may damage the system but that is the dynamic of fear, not of love.

Fear is the coercive way. Any kind of compulsion is based on fear of the sanctions which follow if the necessary behaviour is not forthcoming. So we may seek to compel the necessary behaviour by passing laws and issuing administrative fiats. Punishment follows noncompliance. This is much the route Western countries have elected to take for the moment. Legislation is enacted to prevent the more obvious affronts to ecosystems, such as leaving opencast coal mines unrestored or tipping radioactive waste into lakes. Love of the system is not required; only compliance with the regulations. That this approach can do a great deal of good is obvious, but it is equally obvious that it can only bring change within severely restricted limits, and relatively slowly. There are also various dangers and problems inherent in the method. It may overreach itself, producing extensive evasion. It may reduce the individual's motivation to responsible action, since mere compliance is enough. It will go no further than a democratic society will agree to let it go, and that may not be enough. In short, as a control loop it is useful, but in itself is likely to be insufficient. The psychic level of motivation required is very probably deeper than that which can be touched by the operation of law and administration.

Fear can also be used by instituting such harsh sanctions for non-compliance that obedience to authority becomes near total. An authoritarian government could stipulate very tough requirements for both individual and group behaviour towards the ecosystem, meting out very heavy punishment for failure to comply. Some ecological writers see this as our fate. As ecological demand increases, ecosystems will deteriorate, food and energy will be more difficult to win, and therefore ever tougher planning and control will be necessary. This will bear progressively heavily on the individual, who will have to be progressively coerced to be kept in line. The society will have to ask more and more of the individual to keep the whole ('natural' and 'human' system together) viable. This is essentially Heilbroner's (1974) scenario.

It is in this context that arises the contemporary discussion about freedom inasmuch as it is inspired by our ecological knowledge. The question is raised whether the liberal understanding of freedom that we have inherited will not have to be modified in the new situation of understanding the finiteness of the world and its resources. H T Odum (1971, page 216ff) sees this as a juxtaposition between freedom of the individual and organization. Potter (1971, page 62) sees it in mental terms, as our minds having a kind of creative disorganization juxtaposed to organization. Ferkiss defines freedom as "... the ability to achieve a desired future state" and thereby hopes that he has disentangled it from its liberal bourgeois meaning (Ferkiss, 1974, page 156ff). Moving slightly away from the strictly ecological field, but still very much adjacent to it, we find examples of concern for a necessarily changing view of freedom appearing in such apparently widely separated writers as Vickers (1970), Jantsch (1975), Skinner (1971), Marcuse (1969), and G R Taylor (1974). Many of those whose views are worth hearing along this line are explicitly or implicitly pointing to the weaknesses of humanism. Heilbroner emphasizes that it is necessary to "... examine the 'nature' of man in ways much more courageous and much less pietistic than those it (radicalism) uses in the name of 'humanism' (Heilbroner, 1974, page 124)[2].

We have instanced an operational attempt to deal with this question of the freedom, or autonomy of the individual or group within the greater society when we looked at Beer's chain of reasoning for the 'Chilean process' (section 7.4). There, autonomy was specifically defined as a 'horizontal' or decentralized capability for maximum freedom for making decisions within minimum limits imposed by the 'vertical' or centralized necessities of the greater whole. Beer in his general theory also pays considerable attention to the ethical question in society, viewing it operationally. His view is "a meta-argument for change" (Beer, 1975, page 345ff). He sees our present behaviour as an "ethic with a busted gut": it makes impossible the proper expression of the solutions required for solving our societal problems. His solution is along the line that we now have the science and technology to develop the "relevant ethic" for the society of *Homo gubernator*. But he also leaves untouched the difficulty of how to generate the motivation necessary for the mass individual to practice the ethic.

Another attempt at operationalizing a new ethic may perhaps be found in the relationship between the individual and the group in modern China.

[2] Wagar (1963, page 171) comments that the basics of ethics appear to be agreed by all world thinkers: reverence for life, freedom, and integrity of the individual, the quest for transcendence by the existential self, and the spiritual resources inherent in the power of unconditional love. Our ecological knowledge gives us a new perspective on the first two of these in global terms. Wagar's thinking at that stage did not include ecological insights. In that he was typical of the period.

There, the debate on whether economic growth or social change is the first objective, or both together, appears essentially to have an ethical base. As does also the image of the human being transforming himself as he transforms 'nature'. And so also based is the concept of continuous two-way interaction flowing up and down the social system. The theory seems to be that the peasant is motivated to behave as is necessary for the continuance of the greater society because he is participating in deciding and guiding its direction of development. See Laszlo et al (1977, page 88ff). The underlying image of the human being is presumably that he is inherently good—a proposition that other ages have denied.

Out of all the discussion on freedom and authority perhaps we can most usefully extract the possibly key notion that in the long period of time before ecosystems and the finiteness of the world were understood, freedom as a concept could be of a kind which it could not continue to be after those understandings had been realized. The world being finite, freedom for the individual as one of four billion cannot be the same as for the individual as one of four hundred million. Hence has come the realization that freedom must be rethought. It cannot yet be said that we have made much progress in doing that. But it may be reasonably hoped that our ecological knowledge will force the pace of the enquiry.

The last way is saturation propagandizing. Ellul (1973) reminds us of the psychological characteristic of persistent heavy propaganda: that it results in the victim acting as required without any critical thought about the action. The propaganda tells him what to do, and he does it, *tout court*. Intellectual objections and moral scruples are equally rendered ineffective provided only that the individual is subjected to continuous strong pressure from the propaganda source. In this scenario therefore we imagine a government, convinced of the need, first, for massive change in popular behaviour and, second, for the continuing of the new behaviour to ensure the viability of the life-support system, instituting massive propaganda directed at individuals and groups. This is brainwashing. Irreconcilable with our traditional view of freedom, affronting to our sense of individual awareness and self-worth, and destructive of the value we hold as truth, it is a solution which will scarcely commend itself to Western societies in their present condition of considerable affluence.

Certain feedback loops in our societies in fact make such saturation propaganda impossible to attain. In democratic countries of the Western type the electorate has some say in how its tax money is spent. Propaganda, being of necessity public, cannot avoid being visible as a public expenditure. The high visibility and overt cost of saturation propaganda might therefore work against its continuing for very long.

Propaganda considerably short of saturation is, however, another matter. In the environmental field it is used considerably by governments; with what effect is not much known. It seems likely that in conjunction with dedicated minority groups it might be much more effective than it is at present without offending our sensibilities and therefore losing its effectiveness. The electronic technology is very well fitted to such a purpose. Governments and minority groups together could develop new feedback loops in society by intelligent exploitation of the technology through propaganda techniques without running the risk of brainwashing.

Consideration of motivation is of only very limited usefulness unless there is also regard for the kind of individual to be motivated, since we have to start from where we are in terms of values, attitudes, and other springs of behaviour. We must therefore now bring motivation into relation with the characteristics that we have indicated belong to the mass individual.

23.5 Motivation and the character of the mass individual

In chapters 16 and 17 I recorded the views of Ortega y Gasset, Zolla, and George Steiner on the mental and emotional profiles and sensibility of the contemporary, essentially urban, Western mass individual. In chapter 21 I had something to say about his character in relation to the problem of the planetary balance of life, and suggested that four elements now have to be brought into a stable relationship: the *consociation* of human populations, the *community* of these populations with other species (particularly those species connected with providing food), the *psychomass* (the organized global body of information and knowledge now possessed by human beings), and the *human mass individual*. At the end of that chapter I also listed in telegrammic form certain key ideas, including the observation that mass-individual and mass-group behaviour had now escaped from the restraining influence of previously operating control feedback loops. We are now looking at some of the key elements in such loops. In previous sections of this chapter we have looked at ways of motivating. We now must attend to the character to be motivated.

Of the assessments of the qualities of the mass individual to which we have referred, perhaps one particularly might be considered to dominate all others in the matter of motivating the individual. This is the overriding characteristic that he considers himself to be the sole measure of himself. This needs some elaboration.

In any culture and society the individual may be offered, and accept, an aspirational model of values and behaviour for approximation toward which he may strive, and be encouraged to strive, by various agencies in society. Institutionalized religion has been a major agency for this function for several millenia in Western and other civilizations. The method has been to give strong institutional approval to the individual's efforts to modify his own inclinations in favour of emulating the exemplar offered. It makes no difference whether the details are arranged through the intermediary of a priestly caste or through the individual having direct access to, and the right to interpret, the precise meaning of the exemplar's teachings. *In all cases the dynamic of aspiration in the individual to transcend his own immediate preferences is the motive force. In other words, he has a measure of his own values, attitudes, and behaviour, which is outside himself. He is self-evaluative, self-critical.*

This capacity for self-criticism can be part of a feedback loop relating individual to group behaviour. Food production in medieval Europe was in part safeguarded by this loop being maintained by the Church. Religion may or may not have been 'opium of the people' but it certainly helped ensure the food supply. The loop also allowed the individual to develop a sense of the good of the whole society, and to see his own conduct in the light of it. This was manifest in much eighteenth-century behaviour. Edmund Burke, for example, understood this matter very well (see quotation in the front of this book). The social philanthropic movement of the nineteenth century also owed much to this ability and willingness of the individual to think for the whole. In the twentieth century, political beliefs have performed something of the same function.

If Ortega y Gasset, Zolla, Steiner, and indeed many other observers are right, this capacity for self-evaluation and self-criticism has largely disappeared from or is in severe erosion in contemporary Western culture. The measure of the individual has now become his own wishes and desires— in short, himself. Consequently there is a much weakened aspiration to behave as may be necessary to benefit the whole. The last remnant of this may have been the secularized manifestation of the exemplar in modern Western socialism in the prewar and immediate postwar period[3].

If, for the modern Western mass individual, the main reference for action is now his own wishes and his own existing values and attitudes, and if what he is and what he does are entirely satisfactory to him, it is very difficult to see how exhortations to change his behaviour as may be necessary for survival will be successful. The position is that he is required to change voluntarily—as an act of insight or aspiration—*before* the difficulties connected with the population–food–energy syndrome actually cut down or even cut off his living capability. It is *before* that is the key word both psychically and materially. Psychically because this is very hard for the mass-individual personality to do, and materially, of course, in the sense that the psychic failure can only be made good by demonstrated failure in the continued supply of material things, especially food. But such a demonstration may well spell disaster in that permanent ecological damage may be done in driving the lesson home.

It looks very much, therefore, as though the mass individual is unlikely to give ear to any appeal to understand and follow any new ethic. He sees no particular reason for not pleasing himself and as he sees the immediate possibility of satisfying himself why should he worry about tomorrow? It is hardly necessary to instance the obvious examples that we now have around us: the unalienable right to 'do our own thing', the

[3] Even global thinkers such as Laszlo (1975) underplay the motivational difficulty. He, for example, simply *affirms* that "... the inner limits, if properly focussed, can motivate behavior that respects the outer limits". But what is the evidence for this hope?

deteriorating motivation of the young in academic education, the demand
for instant gratification—"I want it now", the deterioration in the
individual's sense of responsibility for public safety, the erosion of honest
in all sorts of dealings, and even the increase in falsification of experiments
scientific work. All these, and some more, are related to the contemporar
basic perception of the individual as he sees himself: "I am the measure
of myself". Ortega y Gasset called him a primitive.

Maybe. *The operational problem, however, is to know how to motivate*
this primitive to the behaviour necessary to match our understanding of
our highly sophisticated total life-support system. The ecologists see that
freedom, as we have known it, can only be maintained in conjunction
with our ecological necessities through a new ethic. And, logically, they
proceed to formulate the ethic. But they do not comprehend that the
defectiveness of their humanism in its dependence on the behaviour of a
mass individual also has no motivation to follow the ethic. An essential
link in the feedback loop is therefore missed.

Although mass man experiences himself strongly as an individual, he
also feels lonely and isolated. He longs to be one of the group and,
paradoxically, relies for his experience of himself on the opinion that the
group holds of him. This mixture of independence and dependence
renders him very susceptible to propaganda. As the electronic technology
has equipped us with the most powerful means for propagandizing, this
characteristic of the mass individual raises further ethical questions.

23.6 Ethics and the electronic technology

Certain obvious questions related to ethical issues in the applications of
telecommunications and computer technology are now commonly debated
Examples are to be found in the area of the use of information about the
individual. Privacy of information has received a good deal of attention,
as have the right of the individual to know what others hold as informatio
about him and the legitimacy of confidentiality of information gathered a
the public expense (for example, reports on urban planning issues and
atomic energy uses). Such matters belong essentially to the area of
relationship between the society and the individual. They have been well
aired and will not be considered further here.

More to the point in the present interest is the question of how far can
government, knowing the mass individual's susceptibility to it, go in using
propaganda and still remain within the limits of an acceptable ethic. This
question is the more difficult because mass individuals in a modern state
having well-developed electronic services exhibit a homogeneity of values,
attitudes, and behaviour patterns probably unparallelled in history.
Certainly never have so many thought and felt so alike as today. It is not
uncommon for a TV programme to number its regular watchers in tens
and even scores of millions. All are acted upon by the same material,
often during the precisely same period of time.

In the modern world the nation-state can readily command means for immediate, on-line, and massive propagandizing. It can intervene in a situation with extreme rapidity. We are beginning to see the value of this immediacy in the use of data and running models for planning, as we saw in chapter 4, but we have failed to notice that in the area of propaganda such immediacy is already extensively exploited (broadcasts of news, political speeches, advertising). During this century several countries have developed this capability of the nation-state extensively and all use it to some extent. We have had clear demonstrations that the mass individual can be fed, and will accept as truth, material which is false; and that he will pattern his behaviour as directed without enquiring into the validity of the 'persuasion'.

Western civilization has always placed a high value on truth. To argue that the technology is neutral and that the ethical question lies simply in our use of it is to fail to appreciate that the new scale of information handling gives a new perspective to old problems, enormously magnifying the opportunities for falsification and the results that flow from falsification. It also fails to take properly into account the character profile of the mass individual in this context. Humanism, particularly scientific humanism in part based on the very demanding ethics of science in pursuing the truth, has incorporated the traditional Western reliance on the ability of the truth to set human beings free. This would seem irreconcilable with the 'truth' of propaganda, which is directed to obtaining a particular behavioural result. The knot is this:

we shall pursue the truth in trying to understand how the life-support system works;

this understanding will need to be applied toward the humane end of ensuring that the behaviour of the individual is such that the system which must support all is safeguarded;

but the mass individual will not necessarily so behave voluntarily;

therefore we can propagandize him into the appropriate behaviour;

but in order to propagandize, truth must be selected, and if this is to be maximally successful dissidents must be suppressed; *a false consciousness, a denial of truth, must be created.*

The end of this sequence denies the beginning. If we wish to keep the humanistic values, it looks as though we cannot use the heavy propaganda technique for inducing the required behaviour. If we conclude that the propagandizing is the only way, short of violence, that the mass individual and the group can be brought into life-support symbiosis, then we seem to have to forego something of our scientific humanism. As by definition the phrase means belief in the value of knowledge to maintain the human enterprise any such foregoing would appear self-contradictory.

23.7 Conclusion

The ecologists have identified as important for the safeguarding of
ecosystem viability the behaviour of human beings toward the life-support
system and have stressed the need for a new ethical approach superseding
that which has characterized our attitude to a previous world of unlimited
space and resources. They have arrived at the insight that the human
species is now consciously responsible for its own evolutionary development,
which now takes place culturally–socially, and that this development is
achieved through the 'ethicizing' capabilities of the human being. They
have further reached down to reemphasize the key societal fact of the
human enterprise—the need to balance the behaviour of the individual and
that of the group (subnational, national, and global).

But, although they have offered commandments, creeds, and philosophies,
they have not attended to three vital matters essential for action:
1 Why should the individual adhere to the creeds and obey the
  commandments? This is the problem of motivation.
2 The kind of mass individual who has to be motivated affects the
  motivation possible.
3 What are the problems of using the means (the electronic technology)
  available and likely to be effective for motivating this mass individual?

We have suggested that there is no particular reason why we may expect
the mass individual to behave as may be ecologically necessary, and that
heavy propagandizing, as the method most ready to hand for motivating
to new patterns of behaviour, exhibits an inherent contradiction of the
underpinnings of the means for maintaining the life-support system itself
viable.

In the next chapter I shall suggest some areas of thought and action to
which it may be worthwhile to begin to pay attention.

Part 5

Directions of integration

In our new efforts to think about and plan for the global human enterprise
we shall need to bring into conscious relationship our telecommunications–
computer knowledge and our life-support system knowledge in a present
context of mass society in which the mass individual's character and
behaviour are a chief component. In this part the attempt is made to
relate the derived concepts and their images to the mass individual's
character and sensibility profile. Areas of thinking toward which effort
will need to be directed are suggested.

Integration: concepts and images

24.1 Developing an image

It would be pleasant at this stage to be able to proceed toward synthesis of the material in the three major areas of attention, the telecommunications–computer technology, our knowledge of ecosystems, and the character profile and sensibility of the mass individual. As we have seen, expanding understanding in the ecological and electronic fields has forced attention by specialists in these areas to matters well beyond the limits of their expert interests. Ecologists have been compelled to probe the role of human behaviour in ecological processes and have tried some measure of integration between biology, ethics, and the structures and processes of societies, human and other. Electronics engineers have carried what they have discovered in their own field into the study of the workings of the brain, the processes of society, and the nature, production, and handling of knowledge.

These attempts have had the great advantage of starting from firm, well-established bodies of rigorous science. Although both ecology and cybernetics are recently developed sciences they have quickly achieved general recognition. This has been done chiefly on the evidence of performance, particularly in electronics. Other areas of knowledge towards which they move for purposes of integration are not all equally well based. For example, our knowledge of the workings of society is far less exact, reliable, and well organized than is our knowledge of the ecology of the pond or the electronics of the computer.

Characteristically therefore such integration as we have mentioned above tends to move from firm knowledge in a well-proved science toward attempted formulation in a less well-developed area. So W R Ashby or von Foerster can move from the *precision* of feedback in electronic circuitry to the *speculation* of feedback in societal processes. This is very probably an acceptable and fruitful transfer, but in the first we have the full details; in the second the details are liable to be debatable, although the general process may be clearly visible.

With due deference to the knowledge and skill of all concerned, it has to be stressed that sallying forth from firm bodies of science does not solve all our problems. In many matters we still have to act without very precise knowledge; and often our knowledge is grossly inadequate. This is unavoidable to a greater extent than we are sometimes prepared to admit. It is a relatively firm and straightforward matter to develop a technology; it is a much more complex matter to know how to use it so that its benefits can be maximized for the individual and the group. For example, it is *ethically* simple to develop video electronics, however technically complex. But to achieve an ethical use of TV is of a different order of effort. How do we cope with the ethical and cultural implications of general broadcast diffusion which places the diffuser in an enormously influential position and the audience in an almost totally passive situation?

It has been an essential purpose of this book to juxtapose these two poles: that of firm scientific knowledge and its application (the electronic technology together with our ecological knowledge) and that pole which can be identified most easily with the character and sensibility of the human mass individual. For this latter pole we have some scientific knowledge but not yet very much. We have relied here therefore on descriptions derived from sources in the humanities.

To attempt to integrate these two is perhaps best approached as an art rather than a science at the present juncture of our scientific knowledge of the physical world and our predominantly experiential knowledge of the human world. In the end the only condition which will satisfy is that these two fuse. The purpose of this part of the book is to assist the fusion process. In the present state of the art what appears necessary as a base from which to work is the creation, identification and clarification of the new images which will shape the future world. Only within the framework of these images, and perhaps eventually of a single unifying image, will integration be possible.

An image may be thought of in various ways. It may be seen as a unifying myth. In this sense a myth is a foundation of inner mental coherence which permits the ordering of outward-directed mental activities. It allows sense to be made of the world. *In theory the sense made need not accord entirely with the knowledge provided by science, but science and technology are now so vital to our survival that a myth which flouts those findings of science essential for supporting our four billion, and rising, world population would present serious dangers.*

Second, an image might be thought of as a number of 'understandings' or concepts which have caught our imagination in relation to what we know of the world and how we feel about it. Methodologically this is helpful because, although the effort is toward synthesis and integration, it allows us to identify and handle manageable pieces. For example, the concept of digitization or of the virtual circuit is as much a highly imaginative creation as it is a technological operation. To see or use the operations but to fail to appreciate the mental achievement of the concept is to fail in making the image. The concept can be pedestrian, but the image takes wing. To change the metaphor, the image is seminal: it generates, and therefore makes integration possible.

In yet a third sense the image may be a new way of seeing something familiar. Human beings have known knowledge for several millenia. They have developed it in glyph civilizations, stored it, and thought about it in certain fixed ways. But to discover that knowledge can be seen as an envelope surrounding the world, as psychomass, the product of the noosphere, is not merely a new concept. It is a new image which allows linking with another new concept and image—that of the globe as a finite

living system. Some measure of integration begins to appear: knowledge
is a physical product, similar but not identical with biomass, yet, strangely,
growing out of it.

Images are not a kind of extra luxury far removed from practical
affairs. As the image may appear before the concept, concepts may
emerge from images. Images change, and in changing allow us to see new
possibilities and dangers. Our changing image of the physical world is
clearly doing this now. The image may therefore play the very important
role of telling us that certain concepts are changing in their relative
importance. Or, we may be warned that a new and important concept has
appeared and that it implies many difficult changes in present thinking[1].
This function to society has been called the "concept alerting" role by
Calhoun (1970; Calhoun and Wheeler, 1972). As conditions (population,
food and resources availability, etc) change, concept alerting becomes
very important as a way of avoiding the undesirable consequences of
proceeding as before. Concept alerting will, however, be largely dependent
on the ability for generating images and allowing them to be fertile of
new concepts.

The purpose of this part of the book, then, is to try to form a composite
image of our three areas of attention[2]. This unification of the image is
necessary because of their interaction and interdependence. The aim is to
create a gestalt which will be fertile for further integration. The underlying
desire for the integration would have to be acknowledged as the quest for
knowledge of how to act in the emerging phase of the human enterprise.

We shall follow the general gradient of the book—moving from the
experimentally provable knowledge of the natural world to the complexity
of human psychosocial evolution. This chapter and the following chapters
represent upper sections of the gradient. The underlying emphasis will be
on the fact that living, by the individual or by the group, demands action.
We have a progressively urgent need to know how to act. Our images
eventually become our actions.

In this chapter we shall see that scientific and technological knowledge
in the fields of electronics and ecology offer new important concepts, as

[1] In physical studies images and concepts have sometimes been very fruitfully
transferred from one area of knowledge to another. For example, the understanding
of the solar system developed by Copernicus, Galileo, and Newton provided Rutherford
with his image of the atom (1911). The image of the central importance of the sun
through the perspective of the whole electromagnetic spectrum (photosynthesis and
information) of this study is an extension of the original Copernican image of the sun's
centrality. Somewhere, Bronowski has commented that science is as much image-
making as is poetry; science makes images about the world and proceeds to test them.

[2] The matter of image is related to the objective–subjective discussion. This is well
dealt with by Cassirer: "we must set before ourselves in 'images' something not yet
an existing thing, in order, then, to proceed from this 'possibility' to the 'reality', from
potency to act" (Cassirer, 1960, page 75; the whole chapter, page 41ff is excellent
background for what I am trying to bring out).

well as provide new applications for running the human enterprise. The overall image emerging from these areas of knowledge is still largely Faustian. In a later chapter we shall suggest that this image needs modification.

24.2 Key concepts of the telecommunications–computer technology

Basic to this set of concepts is the breaking of the bonds of time and space in audio and video communication. This allows movement backward and forward in time and, although world communications cannot yet provide total global coverage in video as they can for audio, this universality of global accessibility for all audio and video material is only a matter of putting the technology into place. (The major oceans—Atlantic, Pacific, and Indian—are now spannable, thus round-the-world video is operational.) This concept extends everyone's sensory perception beyond the here and now—the immediately present—but also beyond the capabilities of the first (glyph) extension of sense in time and space achieved by writing, drawing, photography, and their multiplier, printing. Audio and video material is now conceived as infinitely manipulable in spatial and temporal dimensions. In accessing information the human species has escaped potentially completely from a major limitation imposed on all other living species.

The second most important concept is the storage and processing of information. Both functions, for handling both audio and video material, are performed by a common electronic technique. Whether this is the same as that by which the same material would be handled by the natural processes of brain and nervous system does not matter here, although the question is of very great interest. What is important is the universality of the process, the reduction to a single type: electrical pulses, flows of electrons round circuits designed through human comprehension of natural characteristics, are consciously assembled. The first concept of breaking the bonds of time and place would not be possible without the storage function. The processing function allows new combinations of the stored material to be developed.

The third major concept conventionally concerns transmission although it ramifies through the previously mentioned concepts. This is the reduction of all signals, whether carrying audio or video material, to a common digital mode. Digitization reduces the electrical impulse to a single type which can be universally handled. This is analogous to the jump from pictogram to alphabetic writing. This universalization makes possible universal packet-switching of original audio and video information; that is, the message can be divided into discrete packets to be transferred from sender to receiver by any link convenient and in a single type of signal. This is achieved by the concept of the virtual circuit and the virtual terminal. *The combination of digitization and virtuality of circuits (as discontinuous circuit) is a very powerful concept, and may eventually rank as one of the most fertile developed by the human species.* All data in whatever original form may be sent anywhere in a single mode by any

kind of transmission link (radio, cable, microwave, laser, etc). This means
that machine can communicate with machine, handling material that was
originally audio or video, without transfer back into the original form.
All information has been universalized and is processable in a unique mode.

These concepts are not easy to grasp. Particularly the last one is difficult.
A reason is that we are not necessarily handling single concepts but complex
groups of concepts. Perhaps they should be called conceptualizations.
Another reason is that we live by means of our senses of hearing and sight.
Their modes are deeply entrenched in the way we think, and not only in
the way we actually perform the sensory processes. Light and sound are
quite different for us. To conceptualize their unification into a single
'vehicle' is not easy for us. It may be, however, that to the human
biocomputer (brain, nervous system, and possibly other components for
memory) they are the same, and that in the combination of digitization
and packet-switching we have a mechanism at least analogous to that
which handles information in our own organisms. And if in us, it is
likely that this principle will relate also to everything else which may be
considered to show evidence of 'mind'.

At this level the concepts become vaguer. They have to do with the
relationship of 'human' and 'artificial' brains. The clearest concept is
probably that of symbiosis between the two, or amplification of the
human capacity by means of electronic capability. At its most exotic, but
not at all inconceivable, is the direct input of information into the human
'mind'. Helmer (1966) quotes this capability as achievable in the twenty-
first century. Digitization would allow a kind of entry into the human
system for input data at a level more basic than that of entry through the
ports of the senses. Digitized signals carrying video material would
presumably produce the picture in the mind's eye or actually in the retina,
optic nerve, or elsewhere, such that the image appears exactly as seen in
normal vision. This is difficult to visualize but it is not so difficult to
imagine how music could be fed digitally straight into the 'mind's' ear.

24.3 Key concepts of ecology
The most important concept of ecology is that of a system which has the
capacity to remain in steady state and yet change. The system is maintained
in some degree by throughput, as in the organism, and in some degree by
recirculation of the components that constitute it. Throughput implies
input and output. Recirculation implies a tendency toward self-sufficiency
and therefore a limited reliance on input from outside the system.

This overall concept is more difficult both to describe and to grasp than
superficially appears. To grasp and hold in the mind a firm idea of what the
concept is requires considerable familiarity with the material. A difficulty
is that the ecosystem is a different kind of system from the man-made
systems with which we daily live—motorcars, human organisations, bodies
of knowledge. In these latter we have a certain acquired pragmatic facility

of understanding and manipulation. We do not have the equivalent, as yet, as far as ecosystems are concerned. Ecosystemic thought is not a mode of thinking that has yet any very wide diffusion. Hence this primary concept needs a special effort of comprehension and assimilation.

The second concept is that system builds on system. This may be said in a variety of ways. We may call it hierarchy, or synergy, or even organization. Along whatever perspective it is examined, the concept is essentially the result of observing that two systems in combination may achieve capabilities not possible for either singly. Strictly speaking, this is an observation-concept. This characteristic, which is an essential of ecosystem theory, makes possible the development of the varieties of species, and orders their numbers of individuals relative to each other. It is not a difficult concept to acknowledge, as we are familiar with it in human organizations and in man-made systems. Explaining why and how it occurs in 'natural' systems is very much more complex and requires different kinds of explanation for different levels of system. It is simple at the level of water and complex to explain at the level of photosynthesis in the leaf. The concept can, however, easily be accepted without requiring a full range of detailed explanation.

Living systems plus hierarchy lead to the third concept—the biosphere, or more correctly the ecosphere. On the principle of hierarchy the ecosystems of the world build up into the next level of system, which coincides spatially with the surface of the globe itself. It is not clear that this is a throughput system, but it is driven, as a global system incorporating abiota and biota, by past and present inputs from the sun. With this concept, usually under the term biosphere, we have now some general familiarity. We can grasp something of the concept in its imaginative embodiment as Spaceship Earth.

Ecosystem theory is also rich in concepts relating to particular aspects of systems rather than to systems themselves. Examples are the following diversity of species, respiration, cyclicity, steady state, energy flow, information, etc. This category of dependent concepts is important for their significance in helping us grasp the major concepts and for their usefulness in transferring to other systems, for example to systems heavily dominated by human beings, or machines.

Amongst these there is one which must be specially emphasized. It is the concept of the assembly of physical material into systemic entities. Radiation from the sun assembles nutrients first into new beings or organisms and second into physical material for maintaining them. This is the concept not only of making new material but of generating out of random stocks of material self-sustaining, self-propagating ordered entities. This is the concept of ordering, of bringing order out of chaos. We have been familiar with this concept of life for a long time, but imaginatively rather than scientifically, and have only recently acquired scientific precision in it.

24.4 Certain concepts common to electronics and ecology

The idea of system belongs to both areas of knowledge. They share particularly aspects of systems relating to homeostasis and feedback. The basic common concept is that the system has inbuilt capability for control of its own processes. Temperature in a building and temperature in an organism are controlled by mechanisms of similar conceptualization. The yes–no, on–off by which the computer works its way through a programme is similar to the closed–open of the synapse of the nervous system and the firing of the neuron. Electronic and ecological systems are both programmed to maintain a steady state and, if pushed from it, to strive to regain it at the previous level or at a new position.

Control aiming at homeostasis, or stable state, is very much dependent in all systems on feedback. Essentially, feedback takes information from later in a process and feeds it in earlier in the process to ensure consistency in the output, or it 'reads' a present condition, compares it with instructions, and sets change in motion if the two do not agree. The product is used as monitor and corrector of the process. The discovery that this concept is of very wide application is one of the great illuminations of our century. Its use in a wide variety of disciplines has been very productive.

Next we should note the common concept of flow of energy or information. In electronic systems the flow of energy is electrical and is not confined to a single direction. It makes possible whatever 'work' the system does. In ecosystems energy flow is recorded in calories which move from organism to organism. The original source of the energy is radiation, which is converted by photosynthesis into chemical energy (carbohydrates). Energy flows in a single direction—producers to consumers to decomposers. Radiation, as energy, links the two systems, since electronic equipment can generate, diffuse, and use energy. There is a difference in that only a relatively narrow band of the electromagnetic spectrum is available to ecosystems and a relatively large span of wavelengths is available for electronic systems. The common concept is flow of energy in the form of radiation.

Flow of information is conceptually very close to flow of energy. Indeed, information may be conceptualized as one energy flow in relation to another. This is the 'difference that makes a difference' and is the conceptual basis of all servomechanisms. It is analogous to the multiplier effect in economics. The principle is that a flow of energy in one circuit will trigger the flow of energy in another. The second circuit has received 'information'. A key characteristic of the concept is that the first circuit has a very low energy flow, and the second a much larger quantity of energy. Hence a low-energy impulse can be an activator of much larger energetic change. Control is thus achieved by relatively low energy flow. Information in this sense is common as a concept for operational purposes to both kinds of system, from the familiar light sensor for calling the elevator to the relationship between the input of protein and the mental development of the child. (See figure 9.1.)

24.5 Images related to the concepts

The current dominant image in both fields is Faustian: human beings have the power to exert their will upon the natural world. This image is essentially dualistic in that it rests on a stance of the human being against 'nature' and suppresses the fact that he is also a component of it. The electronic technology is enormously successful on the basis of this dualistic assumption. The successful application of ecological knowledge, for example in monocultures, in very limited and specialized ways is of the same order. This of course suppresses the main message of ecology: interdependence.

The overall image offered by ecology is monist. Human beings are not apart from natural systems but are integral components of them and cannot escape this fact although they may have specially developed capabilities for modifying the interspecies and abiota–biota relationships. *This image is new and in sharp contrast with the image of the place of human beings in the order of things inherited from the long past of Western culture. That image has been strongly dualist in emphasis.* We have differed in this from the Chinese, whose traditional attitude has leaned toward the monist view, although without benefit of modern ecological knowledge.

The most graphic presentation of this new monist image is the idea that we are passengers and crew on Spaceship Earth—in the ultimate analysis a heavenly body now consciously responsible for managing its unitary system. The image is embellished, in the literature, by referring to its greenness and blueness as it voyages through the blackness of space. Such emotivations help to sharpen certain aspects of the image but do little to enhance the emotive process where it is needed most—on the implications of the realization that human beings have to survive as components of a unitary system.

How potent is this monist systemic image that ecology has given us? This question cannot yet be answered with any precision, but certain observations can be offered. First, it is intellectually highly stimulating in that for the first time we have a coherent body of knowledge of how the life-support system works in overall terms. That many details are still missing does not invalidate the significance of this gigantic step forward in human knowledge. *No such overall understanding of the nature of things has ever before been offered to the human intellect. We have reached a conceptualization of the physical world far more encompassing, far more firmly based, and far more intellectually coherent than any achieved by our own or any other civilization previously. Who cannot be intellectually moved by this must indeed be dead.*

Second, the monist systemic image is emotionally lowering, if not frightening, to us as feeling beings. It speaks to us of possible personal disaster if societies continue as previously, and of the need to change not only behaviour but also cherished and entrenched habits of thinking, values, beliefs, and attitudes. Now the blue and green of the image— colours perceived as benign perhaps because of our sensory habituation to the colours of vegetation (the seat of the life-giving photosynthesis) and the sky—have faded and become mixed with the red and yellow of the desert and the dark of a turbulent void.

Emotionally this image is more likely to make our teeth chatter than to comfort us. The great difference between it and the dualist Faustian image we have inherited, and which we all carry as a major component of our psychic makeup, is that it offers little consolation to us as individuals, but images preferentially the welfare of the human species. *The dualist image offered individual salvation in a world of uncomprehended process; the monist ecological image offers survival for the race within a comprehended world system. The realization of this is part of George Steiner's 'present cold' that we all feel.*

This image belongs in this area of categorization precisely because of its distance from the emotional core of the human being. *Of itself it cannot solve the problems which it raises.* But the image is very important and has very important linkages to other images we shall look at later.

The overall image of the electronic technology is more difficult to describe. There is no short phrase evocatively equivalent to Spaceship Earth. The image is of universalized information, with information being in the psychomass form rather than in the form of energy relationships just mentioned. This brings in the image of the noosphere, so that we have a mental picture of an unbroken envelope of 'mind' encompassing the world, producing and processing psychomass. The best image is perhaps that of a global cerebral cortex. Through the technology the processing is done with near complete mastery of the limitations imposed on other living processes by the facts of time and space. Psychomass is not physically equally distributed but is concentrated in certain global locations. However, again through the technology, these locations are progressively brought closer to each other. Thus far the image is of a global informational membrane, invisible but instantly accessible anywhere. The signals do not, however, remain bound to earth. As they have broken the bonds of time so they have escaped from the limitations of terrestrial space. Our image therefore extends to include the solar system, which now comes into our consciousness in a quite different way from that of the long tradition of astronomy. We do not only look *at* the other planets. We send messages from them to ourselves. The image then becomes a universalized informational plenum rather than a terrestrial enveloping membrane. Our informational capability stretches across and pervades the universe because it is based on some ubiquitous characteristic of the universe. Into this plenum the human species has learned how to transfer its experience. It has hereby transcended the limitations of the highly specialized ambience of the minute pinpoint in space on which it has evolved. Our daily and thoughtless use of the telephone, radio, TV, and computer probably inhibits the growth of our ability to sharpen this astounding image.

The most important image generated by our study is that of the unity or merging of the two overall images just described. The image of Spaceship Earth and the informational universal plenum join first at the level of the common energy base. Both arise from developments, natural and human, made possible by radiation. The living processes of the spaceship derive their origin, evolution, and continuance from solar energy transmitted by radiation. The same radiation, but of different wavelengths, makes possible the informational plenum. Both are elaborations of the inherent characteristics of universal energy.

Second, at the level of earth the two images concur spatially: the globe has a biosphere and a noosphere. The latter is a product of the former. Biomass has eventually learned how to produce and process psychomass, which can therefore be viewed as part of the total process. This lays the foundation for the image of a total world system, as distinct from the ecosystem or the Spaceship Earth image, which has as limitation a biological colouration.

Third, psychomass operates on the physical arrangements of Spaceship Earth, including the biomass. As psychomass application is heavily dependent on the electronic technology the image of the informational plenum impinges on the spaceship image, particularly in relation to conscious action. Effectively the management of the spaceship is not now possible without the further development of the noosphere and psychomass.

The imaginative effort that has to be made is the generation of an image which brings these other images together in a relationship which will correspond with their relationships in the actuality of things as far as possible and will be fertile for the generation of further concepts required for our continuing psychosocial evolution. The pressure to pursue this evolution is provided by the image of the finiteness of Spaceship Earth. The means to do so is provided by the noosphere and its psychomass as image of information. The vehicle is provided by the image of the informational capability of the electronic technology in the plenum.

24.6 Current operations

In this section I shall relate the concepts and images to current operations in the field of telecommunications–computer technology and ecological applications.

In the electronic technology the concepts are very fully exploited in practical application and are unified by the image of present and anticipated future success. The practitioners are optimistic and strongly motivated by this image of their successful relation with the society in which they operate.

The extension of the mastery over the limitation of space in communications continues very rapidly. The application of this concept has been steadily pressed ever since the invention and rapid popularization of radio. Its conceivable limits of application are not by any means within sight of being reached. Further developments spatially might be illustrated by the extension of packet-switching to the southern hemisphere and the use of satellites for carrying radio and TV programmes from continent to continent, thus giving an enormous spatial amplification to the present local cable TV systems.

An important aspect of the dynamic of the spatial concept lies in the extent to which populations can access equipment. In the developed countries, for example, radio is at virtually total saturation and TV nearly so. Everyone has access to these media. The telephone is less well diffused. And so on down a scale: tape recorder, telex, computer, etc, down to certain technologies, such as Confravision and Ceefax, which are in the incipient phase of diffusion. The general diffusion of the equipment is, of course, essential to the process of breaking the limitations of space in a mass population.

Part of the dynamic for driving to annihilate space as a friction of communicating lies in the financial attractions. There's money in fast communication of information. This, however, is far from a total explanation. In some countries public radio and TV developed without any financial reward to anyone. We must assume the working of some kind of dynamic of image. This is supported by applying the test of obvious utility. As they have been developed in our society, what *use* are radio and TV? The question leads to further questions about the real nature of use, utility, and productivity. These questions have now begun to be raised directly as a result of observing the dynamics of information (for example, Masuda). It seems likely that at some level above subsistence we develop our cultural and societal elements on the basis of wish and not necessity. This does not mean that we escape from the rules which presumably govern socioeconomies but it does suggest that we have available, and do select, some options rather than others. This is the message of Masuda's theorizing.

Another facet of this matter can be seen in the concept of mastering the limitations of time. These limitations have been virtually totally broken. All audio–video material can be treated with nearly total flexibility. Once recorded it can be reproduced at any time in the future into infinite time, provided there is no deterioration in the storage process. This total realization of the concept again raises the question of whether we need it or can use it. At this point the thrust of the market economy makes itself felt. Equipment capable of storing sound and vision, but especially sound, can be manufactured very cheaply, offering an attractive market. The question of the precise uses of the capability come *after* consideration of the possible market opportunity. We proceed to manufacture cheap tape recorders and leave the buyers to develop their use. This is a cultural dynamic. Thus we see a powerful concept—the domination of time—in becoming successfully realized produces a new cultural growth out of the societal conditions which allow the manufacture and wide diffusion of the hardware. It is to be stressed that the various elements go along together: concept, image, societal opportunity, and the cultural innovation.

The second major concept—the storing and processing of information— is operationally well developed in certain regards but not others. Storage of material for straight reproduction in its original form is very well developed and diffused in audio but not so far advanced in video. No doubt this will arrive at a level of common diffusion fairly soon (for example by disc and laser).

With regard to the aspect of the concept which visualizes the general accessing and processing of all kinds of stored material, however, operationalization is only in the incipient phase. The full concept is that material stored anywhere may be accessed and processed for the purposes of the user. In terms of the telecommunications links required for this, packet-switching provides the means and can be counted as already operational. The design of computers does not, however, yet offer the necessary capability, although attempts, such as relational associative processing (RAP), are being made to overcome the problems. There is every expectation that progress will be made in this direction, so that, by linking the various concepts, we have an image of a global electronic cerebral cortex consisting of all the computers in the world linked by various kinds of telecommunications highways so that any user may access and process as he wishes any information stored anywhere. This is a powerful and fertile image and set of concepts when combined with the concepts of the noosphere and psychomass. Its operationalization is, however, at present only incipient. Packet-switching—which would be essential for general operationalization—is only just getting going, and the first large-scale computer conference—also a necessary technique—is only just being mounted. We know, however, that both of these have a strong probability of success in their incipient phase.

The third major concept, digitization, has already proved its operational value and is being progressively applied. The digital computer and digitized transmission form a unity which universalizes the handling of all signals. All transmission links will eventually transmit in digital form, and already telephone companies have moved strongly in this direction. Our universal electronic cortex, whether handling audio or video material, will use, both internally to the equipment and for transmission, a single mode—digital.

This will be so even where by optical techniques the first stage of the process of conversion from the visible-light band to another band of the electromagnetic spectrum is a gestalt process, that is, the whole picture or page is taken in as a signal without line-by-line scanning.

The concept of the 'artificial' brain cannot clearly be differentiated for present operational purposes. In practice, however, human brains and computers do work together. The human brain initiates what shall be computed and the computer does the work. This concept will remain hazy until we know how the human brain (or should we say 'mind'?) works. Progressively we shall undoubtedly use this concept to drive toward simulation of further functions of human mental processes. The image here is the fascinating possibility that the brain and the computer are basically the same in their processes, and that in generating the computer we have unwittingly cracked the basic secret of 'mind'.

The image here is clearer than the operationalizing of the concept. The image is of 'artificial minds' which are able to carry out certain processes better than humans, operating in conjunction with human 'minds'. This conjunction is imaged in a range from benign to malign. The man-made 'minds' might dominate our species because of their superiority in speed and multiplicity of computational process and their unforgetting storage, processing, and retrieving capability. At the benign end of the range of the image, the human and machine 'minds' are visualized as working in harmony for the benefit of our species. *In extremis* we have the thought that we may be the authors of the destruction of our species by producing its more biologically successful successor.

Whatever position on the range we pick we have to add this image to our cerebral cortex image. We now have, then, an image of a universal electronic digitized cerebral cortex, a composite human–machine 'brain' which envelopes the globe in the same relation to the noosphere as the human brain is to human 'mind'. This image is not yet widely diffused. We can only speculate on its dynamic as diffusion proceeds under the impetus of the technological, societal, and cultural pressures that drive it.

Our ecological knowledge is not at present anything near as extensively operationalized as is our electronic knowledge. The large-scale operations based on it are usually negative in the sense that they are not directed toward maintaining the viability of the whole system over a long period of time but are directed at enhanced production of some particular output such as grain or sugar or lumber. The system is maintained in a 'young' phase by special inputs in order to ensure the desired level of production. This does constitute the operationalization of ecological knowledge, but on a short-term basis and without responsibility for all the effects on the long-term viability of the system.

The only large-scale applications of our full ecological knowledge appear to be the management of wildlife areas where attention is paid to the state of the system as a whole and the role of each species is understood and respected. So the bald eagle is not treated as a bird of prey but as an essential controller of the populations of certain other species. These applications, however, do not much concern the human endeavour for finding subsistence although wildlife areas are probably vital for the stability of the ecosphere.

Ecological applications or operationalizations of knowledge of ecosystems, other than in wildlife areas, that show appreciation of their essentially systemic nature are at present entirely small-scale experiments. These are usually exercises in applying ecological knowledge to designing ecological systems for specific purposes or with particular aims in mind. Frequently the aims include self-sufficiency or near self-sufficiency of the designed system, short food chains for simplicity, maximization of human-usable biomass production, efficiency of cycling, and permanency of the ongoing process. Also, a frequent practice is to reduce external inputs of chemicals, etc to zero or near-zero.

Interesting and increasing in number as these experimental applications are, their operationalizing on any larger scale is hardly within sight. They require specialist skills, and large-scale application would certainly require the massive assistance of government and, behind that, public support. At present there appears only a very low-pressure inducement for societies to contemplate large-scale application. In present socioeconomic terms there is no comparable dynamic with that which drives the application of the tele-communications–computer technology. Perhaps only some demonstration by disaster is capable of providing an equivalent dynamic.

Attempts, however, to operationalize our ecological knowledge are made along the perspective of mitigating possible ecological damage and reducing ecological demand. The physical urban pressure on ecosystems can be reduced by "designing with nature" (McHarg, 1969). The use of chemical fertilizers can be reduced and pollution of water bodies, air, soil, and foodstuffs by heavy metals, toxic gases, etc can be controlled. Again, however, it has to be stressed that these attempts are operationalizations of a negative kind; the aim is simply to avoid adverse effects on human beings, and is some distance from the systemic interest of ecologists.

Operationally, then, our ecological knowledge would not appear to have got very far in spite of our formalization of a focus of attention identifiable as *environmentalism* (O'Riordan, 1976). This is a possible crucial area for future attention in view of the population–food–energy syndrome of the world situation. I shall take that question up in a later chapter, as here I am dealing only with the perspective of current operations.

Moving on to relate the relationship of the ecological knowledge and the electronic technology in joint operations, I have been able to report very little activity except the beginnings of electronic monitoring of aspects of ecosystems. The global electronic monitoring of the conditions of ecosystems is only in the incipient phase. For certain purposes global coverage exists and data are accessible, but the organizations are only just getting going. It also seems likely that we have not yet learned how to make proper use of the data being made available.

In terms of operationalization on the side of taking action jointly, there is virtually nothing. There do exist, however, the paper proposals for the electronic technology to be used to bring ecosystem knowledge to bear in the ecologically deteriorating Sahel area of Africa (Kupperman et al, 1975). This cannot, however, be strictly counted as operational and really belongs to our later consideration of what could or should be done in joint operations. Urban and regional information systems (URIS) are coming into being, but their impacts to date on ecosystem management are miniscule.

24.7 Space exploration and the concepts and images
Space exploration is entirely dependent on the electronic technology for control, telemetering, and information passing and processing. A rocket can be held in stable flight only by electronic technology.

Our concepts related to the image of Spaceship Earth have been sharpened by the availability of pictures of the actual spaceship seen as a globe from outside itself. These pictures enhance greatly the potency of that image—an image made visible to millions on the TV screen in real time through shots of Earth from the moon. Further reinforcing of this image will inevitably occur when the space shuttle *Enterprise*, now being tested in California, begins regular return trips into space.

Second, space exploration has begun to enlarge the concept of the noosphere. This must now be imagined as potentially extending into space. Although it is much more confined than the information plenum which is already extended at least to the solar system, we also have to think of the biosphere being extended to space stations. This biospherical extension will be entirely dependent on the electronic technology.

Third, the closed systems of life support developed for space exploration (figure 24.1) have reinforced the concept of the ecosystems of the globe [3]. These closed systems have brought the cyclicity of life systems into sharp focus, and stimulate the image of closed-cycle systems being used on this planet as a planned way of life. *As these closed life-support systems will be progressively developed for activities in space we may expect the concept, and the image of system which goes with it, to become more influential in organizing life support on this spaceship.*

[3] The basic sequences of figure 24.1 are as developed by the Grumman Ecosystems Corporation. I have added the use of radiant energy from the sun to energize the greenhouse and the fish tank, with the intention of eliminating the reliance on electric lamps. The Corporation's tests were for a two to three man crew for up to four weeks. Buildup of trace contaminants in the circulated water eventually killed the fish. Applying sunlight to the fish tank might have the same effect. K S Feindler, technical director of the Corporation, is confident of the eventual viability of such closed systems.

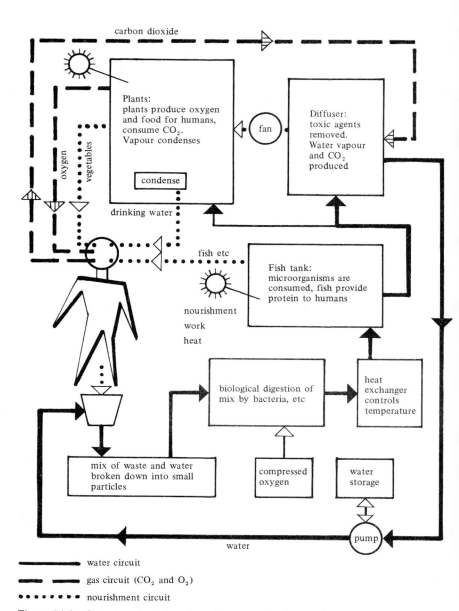

Figure 24.1. Closed ecological system for supporting human beings. The system requires some external input of oxygen to assist in the breaking down of wastes, and some input of energy for photosynthesis. The latter requirement could be provided by sunlight or electrical energy in the form of light. With Todd's techniques the fish tank could also be used for growing plankton by the application of external energy. The external energy sources are indicated by the suns. The system is based on material from Grumman Aircraft Engineering Corporation, Bethpage and the New Alchemy Institute research.

Can we now try to amplify our previous images? We have Spaceship Earth imaged as a finite system supporting biospherical life as an evolutionary process according to the rules of the system. We have the development of 'mind' as a global envelope operating by means of the global electronic cerebral cortex, itself produced through the evolutionary process by 'mind'. To this we must now add the impacting images resulting from an enlargement of the informational plenum considerably into the solar system (by data-collecting automata) and some enlargement of the biosphere. Not only physically but mentally also we have succeeded in getting *off* the spaceship. That component of the total image forever alters many matters *on* Spaceship Earth.

In the following chapter I shall move to the next level of complexity. This will attempt to relate the foregoing to what I have recorded about the mass individual's character and sensibility.

Relating the concepts and images to the mass individual

25.1 Some limitations
In the last chapter I tried to identify the major concepts of the electronic technology and our ecological knowledge, to relate them to each other, and to say something about the images associated with them. I eventually attempted to produce a kind of compound overall image generated by the quest for integration. Concepts and images were limited to remaining within the bodies of knowledge themselves. We were, so to speak, standing within the areas of knowledge and looking at the interrelations of the concepts and images within the confines of their own areas, intentionally cutting off perspectives leading into cultural and societal applications and effects.

In this chapter I shall look at limited features concerned with certain societal aspects of these concepts and images. Limitation of approach is essential because of their very wide ramifications in our contemporary Western societies. The particular area which will be looked at will be certain relationships between the concepts and images and the character and sensibility of the mass individual, for, if the identifications I have already made in chapters 16 and 17 are correct, that should be a key area of our present and future concern.

It is useful here to limit also the scope of the relationship for present purposes. It is essentially confined to the context of society understood to mean predominantly the interactions of individuals and groups with each other—the associational characteristics, the bundles of behaviour patterns we call institutions, and the status-role aspects of human relations. This limited definition, covered by the word *societal*, has the merit of removing from the confusion many items which are more appropriately labelled *cultural*. These latter include values, attitudes, bodies of knowledge, technologies, artistic activities in their intellectual and aesthetic not their societal sense, world views, etc, and their interrelationships. The next chapter will attempt to look at our foci of interest in relation to some of these. The use of the now imprecise word *social*, to include both societal and cultural matters would be best discontinued.

25.2 Transfers of the concepts and images toward society
Certain direct transfers of concepts and images into our thinking about the organization and working of society are already taking place. The concepts become operational, particularly, as we have seen, in the field of the electronic technology, because the applications pay off in obvious ways. In being applied, images are generated which become part of our general thinking about society. On the side of the telecommunications and computer technology the two phrases representing this working out of the images from the field of the knowledge itself are the 'wired city' and

the 'information society'. On the ecological side the carry-over of image is expressed as the 'no-growth society', the 'self-contained society' or 'zero population and production growth' society (ZPPG). These ideas must now be given emphases necessary for our purpose.

The 'wired city or region' was greatly stimulated as an image of the future society by the development of coaxial cable with its enormous increase in circuit capacity in relation to size, compared with cables of copper wire. Instead of only two wires being the basic link between subscribers in any telecommunications system, links of many circuits suddenly became practical and cheap. Very quickly cable TV companies came into existence and many subscribers today use twenty-five or so channels. This represents only about one-third of the inbuilt capacity already installed through a cable only six millimetres in diameter.

The sudden realization of this greatly increased capacity came at a time when the technology of the computer was developing very fast. Capacity, speed, and capability were increasing and size and weight were diminishing rapidly. Telecommunications and computer technologies were coming together with great rapidity to form today's very close association. The imaginative leap stimulated by this cataract of new electronic technology and its application was the vision of a world in which everyone could be in electronic audio and video communication at will. Meantime in practice the technology in certain of its aspects—TV, CATV, telex, computers, shared computer capacity—did in fact diffuse very rapidly. Firms computerized accounting and inventory recording; banking and the credit system became computerized; governments computerized taxation documentation, personnel and other data; in general almost everything became data-banked; and many control functions, such as law enforcement and traffic regulation, became 'electronified'. Urban life came to be envisioned as being run very substantially by the electronic technology. This is the vision of the *city electronic* in which much physical movement would be exchanged for data transference and in which the individual would have greatly enhanced and immediate access to information, knowledge, entertainment, and aesthetic satisfaction. As this was the age of assumed ever-increasing affluence for everyone for the rest of time, the picture included a large place for leisure and avocational activities, many appropriately electronified.

The 'wired city' euphoria calmed down as certain of the realities of the technology made themselves felt. First, random access (like the telephone) of subscriber systems having many circuits proved very difficult in the matter of switching. Second, great technical attention was devoted to finding ways of developing the existing telephone systems so that they would allow the realization of many of the ideas embodied in the image of the 'wired city'. Third, the technology in some regards has overtaken the image. Particularly packet-switching is potentially universal electronic communication for everyone, although at present it cannot cope with the problem of fusing the telecommunications and the public broadcasting systems. Packet-switching plus the actuality and the potential of cable TV, in conjunction with computer development, are bringing the 'wired city' rapidly into being. It therefore progressively ceases to be a vision.

The vision of the 'information society' is somewhat different from that of the 'wired city'. The image is less a vision dominated by the application of a technology and more one of the societally promoted use and development of the technology to help achieve a society having an emphasis substantially different from that which we still conceive our society to be.

The emphasis in the 'information society' is on the socioeconomy being driven by information to a very considerable degree. The manufacture of physical goods is seen as much reduced in the role it would play in the socioeconomy as a producer of wealth and the role of information as a producer would be greatly enhanced. This would be achieved by the massive forced development and diffusion of the electronic technology, as urged by Masuda.

Attempts at investigating the operationalization of this image have brought to light the need to modify or rethink our economics. Pursuit of this thought is only just beginning but it already suggests that our economic knowledge has developed with a very heavy dependency on the accidents of Western socioeconomic history over the last few centuries. This may now exert some inhibiting effect on our approach to the new socioeconomic problems emerging.

Precisely because of this questioning of the nature of an information socioeconomy, the thinking which belongs to the 'information society' image is of a more sophisticated kind than is that of the 'wired city'. However, the intellectually seductive capacity of this appeal to greater depth must not cause us to underestimate the enormously powerful influence and effects of the actual applications of the technology as they in fact drive toward the realization of the image of the 'wired city'.

Both the 'wired city' and the 'information society' are well on the way to being with us. At present the mass individual does not have great personal choice of *outward*-directed informational capability. That is substantially still limited to the conventional use of the telephone. But his *incoming* capability, as a function of the 'wired city', has been very considerably expanded by broadcast and cable TV in recent years. In conjunction with institutional innovations, such as the open university, the private individual's electronic access has been increased, and in the next decade will be much more extended. As a worker, however, the mass individual has already experienced a considerable extension of his capacity for 'knowledge-work' through the electronic technology. Many workers are now routinely using the technology in their daily work. If, therefore, we take the mass individual as private person and as worker we find that he has already a considerable sense and experience of the emergence of the 'wired city'.

As we have seen, the 'information society' can be said to have already arrived by reference to the statistical evidence of the number of workers engaged in 'knowledge-work' and the money spent on information in the USA. With 50% of the workers so employed and with continuing declining numbers in agriculture and manufacturing and nearly static numbers in the noninformational service activities, the information sector can already be shown to be the dominant. This change has provided our urban populations with some experience of the 'information society'.

At the moment the key factor of the information-dominated socio-economy in America is that the dominant sector, in the present conditions, is already over its period of very fast growth when measured by employment figures. This leaves the new emergent socioeconomy in a weak situation immediately after its incipient phase. The socioeconomy of North America, in terms of employment, is faced with increasing production *capacity* but declining job opportunity. For example, supposing the present approximately 300000 vacant jobs in Canada were now to be filled from the ranks of the unemployed, there is still need of about a further 600000 jobs to accommodate the remaining jobless. This is precisely the condition that Masuda has perceived for Japan and this is why his efforts for the conscious development of the 'information society' are so important for all the mature industrialized countries. It is now the information sector which may respond to inducements to grow and therefore produce the new jobs necessary for keeping going the production–job–wages–consumption linkage. The only alternative envisageable to conscious development along this line of thinking would have to be modification of the syndrome. For example, there might be some considerable distribution by direct linkage production–consumption (growing your own cabbages) or introducing new entitlements to consumption independent of the wages–job–production linkage.

It is clear that the concepts out of which emerge the 'information society' and the image generated have a great deal of relevance to our immediate future in the developed countries. It should also be noted that 'wired city' and the 'information society' go together. The 'information society' has to presuppose the existence of the 'wired city', but at the same time it is the 'wired city' which makes the 'information society' the current emergent reality.

We turn now to the image of society derived from our ecological knowledge. At the global level of image this is Spaceship Earth, but as we have no recognizable human society at that level—only groupings such as the UN and exploratory thinking such as Tinbergen et al (1976) and Laszlo et al (1977)—the phrase will not serve our present purpose. The popular form of what we want is the 'no-growth society'. This description, however, is not satisfactory as it carries connotations of stagnation and an end to development. No doubt this association is undeserved, but 'no-growth' is nevertheless misleading. Perhaps the nearest description might be the 'self-sustaining society'. This does not preclude growth in the mental area and suggests care in using resources and maintaining essential relationships.

This image is now leading to the development of policies concerning conservation of ecosystemic components and relationships by attention to wildlife preservation and agricultural techniques, conservation of energy by having regard to use and waste, the development of renewable sources of energy, the reuse of wastes and recycling, examination of energy consumption in total processes—net energy costs, and the development of environmental monitoring systems.

In the next category of activity we find the development of the image in considerable detail. For example, *A Blueprint for Survival* (*The Ecologist*, 1972) goes into the whole question of how to reduce industrial growth rates, reduce the national population, and safeguard employment, and prescribes changes to be made in energy consumption and industrial production for the 'self-sustaining society'. This is carried into the programme phase, and dates are suggested at which the British version would be able to reach the various stages necessary to achieve the ultimate condition of stability and permanence. The general idea is to use renewable resources as much as possible (this means behaving ecosystemically), recycle nonrenewable material, conserve energy, and produce modestly in a socio-economy of stock rather than flow. The image is the modification of human societies so that they do not eat out the future but order themselves for long-term viability within the rules provided by Spaceship Earth.

The image has some appeal, perhaps especially to a pietistic feeling that is probably quite widespread. The astounding achievements of modern technology have a whiff of the impious about them; the thought of living more 'in accord with nature' has its dynamic. However, there is here none of the heady euphoria of the 'wired city' technology or the solid optimism of the 'information society'. No-growth is not very appetizing to us, especially to North America, and particularly as in most Western countries since the war the situation of the nation-state has generally been perceived as requiring the boosting of the effort to increase industrial productivity and output. Furthermore, having learned to emphasize throughput in our socioeconomies we sense very practical difficulties in moving to an essentially stock society in which a major emphasis would be given to the durability of goods.

Boulding (1972) argues, on the basis of the declining rate of increase in productivity and the near ZPG, that the US is approaching the stabilized state. However, it is possible to have stabilization demonstrated by one set of indicators and yet simultaneously have throughput of dimensions horrendous in consumption of energy, and even at an increasing rate of consumption. It is difficult to visualize just what this combination means, but it is certainly far from what was in the minds of the British scientists when they generated *A Blueprint for Survival*. It is also quite clear that the quantity of throughput is directly related to energy consumption and that it is a key matter in looking at socioeconomies in their ecological contexts.

Under these conditions and along this perspective it seems hardly reasonable to say that we are well on the way to the 'self-sustaining society' as it can be said that we are already living in the 'wired city' and are already adjusting to the 'information society'.

25.3 The imaged societies and our existing mass society

We now need to look at the character profile and sensibility of the mass individual in relation to the three images and their societal manifestations: 'the wired city', 'the information society', and 'the self-sustaining society'. The reason for bringing the mass individual into relation with these is that his behaviour will undoubtedly be a major factor, and very possibly *the* major factor, in the realization of these images into the working socio-economies of the future. *A further reason is that during this century the efforts we have made toward reorganizing society have been predominantly from a societal or group approach which has tended to leave out the subjective, individual component of any proposed societal arrangement. The individual's attention has been directed toward societal reorganization rather than toward inducing the individual to examine, and possibly change, his own behaviour in a time of great general change. Perhaps that trend has already died as far as ready acceptance by the Western mass individual is concerned. George Steiner thinks we cannot be induced to make further effort for society. Certainly the behaviour of the last decade tends to suggest that the mass individual is not indisposed to be articulate as to how he feels about continued superimpositions of solutions at the societal level, even though strenuous effort is made to raise his enthusiasm for further reconstruction.*

The great overall factor which has to be included in the images of future socioeconomies is that of very large numbers of individuals. These masses have to be serviced. Above all they have to be fed. At present this is achieved only by enormous inputs of energy, in various forms, into ecosystems whose stability is thereby now clearly under some threat and which will require ever increasing inputs to produce any further increments of output. Ability to face this situation is a measure of our images, and we must first look at them in this light.

The 'self-sustaining' image tries to arrest this slide by reducing demand by the consumer and lowering the ecological demand. This would reduce the throughput of all physical systems. It would probably also require, as the British ecologists admit, a reduction in some populations, for example that of Britain. Unfortunately the populations are already alive, if not altogether well, and effective decline will certainly not come before the next century. Meantime maintenance of this human biomass has to be ensured. The 'self-sustaining' society will have to have growth somewhere in it until such time as its population numbers accord with the capacity of the overall system to sustain it on a continuing basis at the level considered satisfactory. The proposals do not offer anything. Our socioeconomies have, so to speak, long since gone above the self-sustenance level and will strive to stay in that condition until either the numbers are reduced, the levels of physical well-being are pitched lower, or new system relationships can be forged. Therefore although the 'self-sufficient' image seems possible, as *a component* of our emerging socioeconomic image, it does not seem likely or hopeful as the essential conceptual *framework* of it.

The 'information society', anyway after the style of Masuda, tackles the very question which the 'self-sustaining' image misses. Here, the realization, in common with the ecologists, is that the present physical growth, output, and throughput rates cannot continue on their present scale. Therefore, the argument goes, it is necessary to find a new growth area in our socio-economies. This can be provided by the information sector, but to make this really effective will require a new concept of what a socioeconomy is, particularly with regard to how productivity and utility in information are to be viewed.

This image—one cannot yet say model—of a possible future socioeconomy at least has the merit of acting on the identification of limits to growth in physical output and throughput, of searching for a growth area of a different kind, and of attempting the identification of the possible new area. The problem lies in knowing how to force rapidly the development of this informational superstructure. The coming stasis in employment may spur our thinking. As employment in the information sector may tend to plateau in the 1980s we may progressively be deprived of our only growth sector. The resultant progressive breakdown in the production-job-wages-consumption linkage may well force the development of the information superstructure and we may start to enter an entirely new phase in the human enterprise. Or it may not, and a kind of subsistence industrial socioeconomy may emerge as a form of stagnation (we already have a new phenomenon in *stagflation*) or even regression.

Being a vision of fairly straight technological application, the 'wired city' image offers nothing about these matters. It becomes very important, however, if we view it as the means to reaching or at least accelerating the fuller realization of the 'information society'. If what we have to go for is a socioeconomy with a relatively static base of goods and services (measured by various quantitative and qualitative measures) on which is to be raised a dynamic and relatively large growth superstructure of information, the 'wired city' needs urgently to be promoted. *The sooner the electronic capability of the population is enlarged the better. This means giving the mass individual two-way access to data processing facilities and generally upgrading his capacity for handling and using information.* This appears to be precisely the approach in Japan.

A further important linkage needs to be made. Those who generate the 'self-sustaining' image do not appear to be generally conversant with the thinking of those who are developing the thinking connected with the 'information society' and the 'wired city'. *It does not appear to have been observed that the images are complementary in that the two last may well be capable of providing the growth dynamic which will be essential to the operationalization of the 'self-sustaining' image, while at the same time helping to reduce the relative energy costs required to maintain the transactions connected with the running of the stabilized physical base.*

We should also remember here the distinction between applying information to the working of the socioeconomy as at present operating— the incorporation of more information into the system as a kind of commodity—and the idea of information being capable of providing a new economic good, whether Masuda's time-value or some other. Any model of the socioeconomy to be developed would probably have to include both because of our impending production–job–wages–consumption difficulties.

The composite image developed thus far is something as follows. Physical bases will have to be 'stabilized' but socioeconomies will have to have a growth sector to continue at present levels of well-being. The *'self-sustaining' society could find its growth sector in the purposeful development of the 'information society'. This would require the popular diffusion of the technology offered by the 'wired city'. Sophisticated planning would be necessary for using the electronic technology both to accelerate the achievement of 'stabilization' in the physical base and to develop the informational superstructure of the socioeconomy.* As human responses and behaviour will be of paramount importance, we must now look at aspects of the characteristics of the mass individual in the context of this composite image of mass society.

25.4 The composite image and the mass individual

The feasibility of developing any such images or composite image into a model for a future socioeconomy will be very much influenced by the character profile and sensibility of the mass individual who now exists. He is already with us. Indeed none is exempt: we are all mass individuals, living in mass societies and moulded by mass media.

First, how will our mass individual take to the stabilizing of the physical base? Particularly since the war he has been led to expect a steadily rising standard of physical well-being. He has been more than willing to do this because of the nature of his character, but the willingness has been encouraged by the production and distribution agencies in the society. They in turn have possibly been forced into stimulating the mass individual's appetite for goods by the declining viability of the production–job–wages– consumption linkage. We 'need' the jobs as much as the goods. Hence featherbedding, built-in obsolescence, etc. In stabilizing, it is difficult to see how a decline in the access to goods and the availability of jobs is to be avoided for the mass individual. He cannot be expected to respond very favourably to either of these and will undoubtedly object, particularly to the decline in job opportunities. Hence governments will prefer to go very gently on stabilization, and, taking the obvious path, will tend to favour the continued increase in the consumption of energy if it helps the availability of employment opportunity. The cost of energy, however, is rising and ratios between it and other costs are changing. Such changes as this implies may perhaps force some measure of stabilization on socio-economies, as Boulding (1972) already thinks is happening. The mass individual, who neither knows nor cares where all these goods come from so long as he can get them and who regards the products of high technology as his effortless right, is very ill-prepared at present for the change in his thinking and habits that this will require. He will have to restrain his demands, pay more for goods made to last longer, pay more for less energy, waste less, learn to conserve, and accommodate himself to the stabilized state of physical conditions unchanging for long periods of time. At present the desire for variety, change, and novelty is clearly a strong and perhaps unavoidable element in his psychic makeup.

We have to remember here the dual role of the mass individual. He is certainly consumer but he is also a worker at the producing end of the linkage. In the latter role he is conditioned to seek success that is largely quantitatively measured by sales volume, profits, size of organization, and aggressive policies in the market. The two roles at present fit quite well. To stabilize the consumer side will upset this comfortable symbiosis, and will be resisted because seen in this perspective.

Some of this argument appears to be belied by certain current manifestations of the environmental interest. In many countries groups of citizens raise protest against proposed public works on the grounds of potential environmental damage. Expressways, airports, nuclear power stations are among the typical foci of attention. Such projects may even reach the construction stage before being challenged. Many challenges have been successful, for example, against expressways and atomic power stations in the US. The confrontations appear also within governments, where environmental and energy departments or jurisdictions may clash, for example in the emerging battle between the federal and the state governments of the US about the states' rights to forbid supertankers in their harbours. Such prohibition could seriously affect the discharging of Washington's energy responsibilities.

Recent successes at stopping certain public capital works may well have later effects in such things as the restriction of available energy because the 'necessary' expansion has been thwarted. In the winter of 1976–1977 a demonstration of how serious shortage of energy can be was given in the Buffalo, New York area. Prolonged unusually cold weather and heavy snow made the demand on natural gas much heavier than normal. An immediate result was that priority had to be given to home heating. This meant closing factories and laying off workers where gas was used as industrial fuel. The economic life of the region was seriously disrupted.

This produced the double bind of greater costs for home heating and less money to pay for it.

It is not, however, only a question of stabilizing energy demands with which we are dealing, but also a matter of establishing long-term planning to find new sources *even* for maintaining a stabilized demand.

Some sources of energy will become diminished in the next few decades. The future life of natural gas in North America, for example, is probably not long. It is entirely characteristic of the mass individual that there will be difficulty in his seeing such a limitation in its proper perspective. The preservation and conservation of environmental quality is humanely perceived but to press this without due perception of the energy problem is to be exercising a kind of initiative which runs without the necessary feedback controls. The crunch may come long after the crusading success, and when it arrives it bites hard on the mass individual in the form of restriction on home heating and power, high cost of transportation, and reduction in employment. These hardships the mass individual is not equipped to take. *It can be argued, therefore, that the activities of minority environmental groups—intelligent, humane, public spirited, and necessary as they are—do not invalidate the argument that in the end the mass individual as at present psychically constituted will opt for the energy, and suggests that environmental enthusiasms and activities are in fact entirely characteristic of the mass individual and are not evidence of his reformation*[1]. *They may be precisely the opposite of what they seem.*

In conclusion, then, the character profile seems very ill suited to the stabilization of the physical base of society, and we should be wary of manifestations of apparent change in that profile that have not yet undergone the test of the privation inevitably inherent in stabilization.

Second in the matter of ecological behaviour, because of contemporary rapid response links between governments and their electorates, governments will be unable to act responsibly to ensure ecosystem viability unless the electorate gives firm support. This is the ethical emphasis which we have recorded as typical of ecological thought and writing. A new ethic which will respect the integrity of the life-support process is correctly seen as essential if we are going to continue to eat. How capable is the mass individual of understanding this need, of perceiving the significance of a new ethic, and of living according to its precepts?

The ethical recommendations of the ecologists, as guides for behaviour, depend heavily on an understanding of ecological processes. These are not

[1] An example of what may be a characteristic response in this area occurred recently in Toronto. The construction industry in the metropolitan area has an unemployment rate of 40%. This comes after a period of political discouragement of growth, particularly of downtown growth. The press comment was that if this is what no-growth means it would be better to have the employment rather than the no-growth, in spite of the penalties for growth—congestion, pollution, etc. This response may well be a straw in the wind.

easy to grasp and unfortunately salutary demonstrations of trouble are typically likely to appear only in delayed time. The mass individual has neither the intellectual equipment nor the opportunity, at present, to acquire the understanding necessary for seeing the necessity for change in his behaviour patterns. Further, if the knowledge were available, there is no certainty that he would be convinced. Has not human ingenuity beaten such problems before? It is a complex matter to perceive the new elements in the human condition and to admit them to serious thought. It is still more difficult to translate conclusions into mass behaviour

We have seen that, even though the need for a new ethic may be intellectually agreed, there is a lack of motivation in the mass individual to comply with its requirements. The mass individual has no overall myth to which the motivational chariot can be hitched. His world view is fragmented. Also, as we have suggested, the body of ecological thought is not capable of providing any such overarching myth because it speaks not to the individual but to the species. *Any new myth, in order to produce motivation, must address itself to the mass individual as he feels himself in his uniqueness and essential isolation. The hoped-for dynamic of addressing the myth to the mass individual through community or state action can now be felt to be fading. Along that line perhaps now lies only the option of coercion.* The mass individual is required to do what is necessary to ensure his own well-being through the action of the group, to restrain himself in the interest of his own survival by way of the group's aggregated capacity to grant him this. However, he does not wish to do what is necessary now, but responds to the apparent opportunity to take the immediate personal benefits for himself.

Perhaps the ecologists overestimate the importance of the ethical question, or perhaps stressing this matter is inherent in the importance of the taxonomy of biology to ecological thought. There is another possible way in which the behaviour of the mass individual may come more into line with the need to ensure the viability of the life-support system. Could various pressures within the socioeconomy, combining together, instigate the mass individual to change his behaviour patterns as a result of seeing that his individual benefit lies in a new direction? This is a kind of system coercion, but not overtly originating from governments. For example, decentralization of residence from large cities could be motivated, for those who have the ability to move, by such 'pushes' as changing ratios in costs, declining personal safety in cities, and the attraction of a nonurban life-style. Changing cost ratios already relate significantly to costs of shelter, commuting, energy, and food. The mass individual may conclude that he would benefit from leaving the large metropolitan area. If he did so, he might grow some proportion of his own food, rediscover community, and moderate his consumerist appetites. Various technologies make it possible increasingly to combine what we assess as the urban benefits with the advantages of not actually residing in the physical urban concentration

G R Taylor (1974) has suggested a model of this kind in his 'paraprimitive society', and the idea is present in *A Blueprint for Survival* (*The Ecologist*, 1972). The addition made here is that the changes in cost ratios may have much the same effect as the new ethic of the ecologists, without the motivational complications inherent in the idea of consciously generating a new ethic [2].

Having said, however, that the desires of the mass individual may coincide with the behaviour that may be required of him in a new socio-economic situation, it is necessary to underline the important fact that the call for a new ethic, generated by the ecologists, coincides with our need for a world view which must incorporate our new ecological knowledge. Seen in this light, the call for the ethic is a manifestation of the idea that the human species is now responsible for its evolution—now psychosocial, to use Julian Huxley's term—in a conscious way. The ethical preoccupations of the ecologists may therefore be very important as product of the need for a new world view and simultaneously as conscious contribution to it. There are various ways in which this idea may be expressed. The important thing, perhaps, is to avoid being confined to looking along only a single perspective.

We turn now to the relationship between the mass individual and the electronic technology in the context of the images. In this area perhaps the chief characteristic of the mass individual's profile is his susceptibility to propaganda.

This susceptibility stems basically from the mass individual's sense of being alone, an isolate, and his corresponding need to feel himself one with the many. This need predisposes him to an uncritical acceptance of what may be offered to him and renders him open to the effects of saturation propaganda. Under its influence he will act as suggested by the propaganda without seriously questioning its appropriateness or moral implications. When eventually acting uniformly with all the others he can obtain some sense of being one of them, of alleviation of his loneliness.

[2] There is evidence of a new population trend in North America. In the period 1970-1974 US nonmetropolitan area growth was 6·6% and metropolitan area growth was 4·1%. In Canada the percentage of the total population in metropolitan areas peaked around 1972 and the fraction of the total Canadian population in metropolitan areas has been falling since then. There is therefore a corresponding steady enlargement of the portion of the population in nonmetropolitan areas. This may already be a manifestation of the information society. It is also necessary in this context to note that in general in the growth of cities in the postwar period the physical expansion of the urban areas has exceeded the rate of increase in population growth. For details of this in northwest Europe see Robert in Laconte (1976, volume 2, page 157ff). We should further note that the rate for broadcast demand increases more rapidly than the population rate, although I have been unable to find any detailed study of this subject, in spite of its being a matter of great concern to regulatory bodies. All the above need also to be seen in the context of very rapidly increasing pressure on the regions of the electromagnetic spectrum used for communications and the acute problems of allocation which this pressure now causes.

There seems little doubt that this sense of relief from his persistent interior discomfort is spurious and merely exacerbates the suffering, but the appearance of relief is evidently vivid. About that I shall have something to say later.

The 'wired city' and the 'information society' are very well equipped both physically and psychologically for providing propaganda, and especially saturation propaganda when required. The saturation process consists of flooding the mass individual with the necessary statements at all possible times and in all possible places. Radio and TV are obviously well suited to the techniques of propaganda—mass audiences, iteration, cheap reproduction, etc. It is not so obvious, but *any* interchange of information may have a propaganda effect. The reason for this is that the rapid and general diffusion of opinion results in a uniformity of attitude which can have much the same behavioural effects as a specific propaganda drive. The key idea is the uniformity of the supposed opinion held, not the way in which it was reached. This can be authenticated in any area of thought or action. The individuals 'in the business" may be in such close mental contact over a period of time that they tend to think and feel in the same way.

For this reason it is by no means clear that the use of CATV or other technology with a two-way emphasis will inevitably produce greater independence of thought than that fostered by the present one-to-many mode of radio and TV. Participation in discussion does not of itself produce independence of mind. It may equally produce a consensus which *appears* to result in better thinking but merely, under that shelter, confines thought to stereotypes, and generates and perpetuates sterile attitudes. The extension of the parish pump to a national level or a global scale does not necessarily correlate with improvement in the quality of thought.

This is an extremely complex matter on which we have little knowledge. Already, however, we have an inkling that particularly the TV has a strong formative influence on the mass child. His 'mind' is in considerable part being formed by what he is exposed to in the offerings of the media, even while we as adults fuss about the collapse of the formal arrangements for educating and socializing him. The 'mind' being formed is common to all; all are being socialized into a common set of values and the vehicle—for that too has its influence—is also a commonly experienced mode, the electronic.

After allowing for the difficulties and our ignorance of the subject, we can begin dimly to see that in the electronic technology we have a means for socializing the child and possibly the adult more effectively and more rapidly than ever before into a chosen set of values and attitudes. It seems equally clear that the values and attitudes at present inherent in the process of socialization by way of the electronic technology are often not consciously selected, not evaluated or controlled by the society, and are indeed the values of small private groups not, in this matter, generally answerable to anybody but themselves. To date, there is very little awareness of the new modes through which the socialization process is already substantially being carried out. Traditional education and the extended, and more recently the nuclear, family, which have hitherto shared the responsibility for the socialization and acculturation of the young individual, have now lost a great deal of their influence to the electronic mass media. In large measure the young mass individual is now reared by exposure to the values and behaviour patterns experienced vicariously on public television programmes.

This method of socializing and acculturizing the young would seem to reinforce the susceptibility of the mass individual to a thoughtless acceptance of whatever is offered. In terms of our concern for the control loops that hold the mass individual and his society in viable symbiosis within the context of the global life-support requirements, this susceptibility may work to assist the generation of new control loops and the strengthening of existing useful ones or it may work to accelerate the running wild of the system. Left to itself the system may have a very good chance of running wild fairly quickly. If, however, we hypothesize control of the control loops themselves we have the dilemma surrounding authority that Ryan hopes to resolve by sociofeedback. Clearly, the combination of high-level electronic technology with virtually universal diffusion throughout the population and the socialization of the mass young through this mode is extremely powerful as a potential means for creating new societal control loops. It is certain that new loops are being formed, but it is not at all clear yet what they are in terms of necessary societal control functions.

Closely connected with the foregoing we should bear in mind Zolla's 'culture industry' (Zolla, 1968). This is seen as supplying, literally in a consumer sense, the mass individual with the 'cultural' material on which his emasculated imagination must feed. This provision of pseudoculture is made cheap and ubiquitous by the great efficiency of the electronic technology, and it does not essentially depend on the traditional literacy of the written word. The human communication vehicles are the gestalt of the picture, the spoken word, and music. This also is a further weakening of the traditional socialization process by education, since that mode depended heavily on the book.

Zolla's evaluation of the culture industry is that it stunts the inner growth of the mass individual by offering him *ersatz* material. This may well be so, but there is another way in which it may be considered. This is that it provides a way of bringing information further into the workings of the socioeconomy. Bearing in mind the analyses of Porat and Parker that our activities are now one-half information and that we are about to face a period in which a fast-growth area cannot be expected for Western economies, we can see the mass individual's compulsive consumption of the products of the culture industry as an area that could be stimulated. The mass individual may be increasingly persuaded to pay more and more for the only satisfaction left—that of being totally mass man! This is not

o

pleasant as a possible part-solution to the emerging difficulties in the production–job–wages–consumption linkage but it will probably have to be thought about as a matter of specific planning and promotion.

Certain other characteristics of the mass individual that have been identified by our analysts also require brief mention in their relationship to the concepts and images.

Ortega y Gasset's (1957) identification of individual sovereignty now having become a psychological condition of the mass individual is the more dangerous as electronification advances and general participation in all kinds of decisionmaking becomes possible. The characteristic of image sovereignty will make the mass individual convinced of his rightness in intervening in all decision processes, since he has achieved "complete soci power". The widely held view that increased participation in decision-making will render the mass individual more responsible and the decisions more soundly based is not compatible with the mass individual's combine sense of dominance and ignorance of how things work. Looked at in this light, the extension of the electronic technology to general two-way participation is not the happy solution that some think. On the other hand in theory at least, better information should mean better decisions. However, will the mass individual seriously attempt to obtain and apply better information? There is a case to be made that the processes of civilization are now too complex for him to control.

This suggests that if we want to make the best of what is known it will be vitally necessary for the mass individual to become informed about the basic principles underlying several areas of knowledge—ecology, the physical sciences and their application, and the disciplines dealing with society, culture, and behaviour. Far from moving toward this level of better information, the mass individual appears to be harbouring a growing anti-science and anti-intellectual attitude, and to be disvaluing the role of highly endowed individuals. Just at the moment when there is the need to incorporate the specific findings of science into our general world view the mass individual plunges deeper into superstition than he has done for thousand years. *Therefore the image of the good, well-informed, striving and moral citizen, who hovers in the background of our three images ready to be called on stage, is something of an illusion. Nor can he be generated by the application of the images to real life. Our mass individu simply is not like that.* If our images, ecological or technological, do indeed require a moral, public-spirited, amateur scientist to make them workable, we are unlikely to see them realized.

The mass individual no longer feels progress to be inevitable. He therefore not only sometimes questions whether scientific and technologic advance is useful, but has only a languid attitude toward making the effo to promote or apply it. This constitutes a difficulty for the implementatic of the images, particularly the 'wired city' and the 'information society', which demand a degree of enthusiasm for their realization.

25.5 The meaning of the images

All images or models for a proposed societal reorganization must face the fact that the individuals who will constitute the new society will probably have some such character profile and sensibility as we have looked at; this is our existing condition. A test of viability will be compatibility between the image and the character of the mass individual.

In terms of the 'self-sufficient' society our mass individual appears unsuitable except on the basis of coercion or heavy propaganda. The probability that the balance between the individual and the group behaviour required for a 'self-sufficient' condition can be achieved by what we have hitherto known as education seems remote. It will be far outdistanced by the culture industry.

In theory some of the major difficulties of the 'self-sufficient' image might be solved by the intensive application of the electronic technology if the present mass individual did not have to be the user and a different character profile already existed. It does not, and a new character would have to be specifically generated in the actual present context of attitudes and behaviour belonging to our existing mass individual.

Our present mass individual and the image of 'wired city' and 'information society' appear to fit together much better. The mass individual needs the products of the culture industry and these the electronic technology is very well suited for delivering. The mass aspects of the technology correspond with the mass individual's sensibility of emotional noninvolvement—dodging of genuine emotion—and willingness to be propagandized. By means of the technology the mass individual might very easily be governed.

However, the mass individual has become the government in the sense that he has won the social power that makes government possible. Hence the operational possibility: that, *as at present organized in our society, the intensification of the use of the electronic technology may very probably serve chiefly to enhance those characteristics of the mass individual that already tend to destroy the controls necessary for good government, rather than to assist in the development of the new required control loops.*

In the next chapter I shall look at areas of thinking that now seem to need attention in the light of my conclusions.

Thinking through toward action

26.1 Need for a chain of reasoning and dependencies

If we believe, as Julian Huxley and others have concluded, that the new emerging phase in human evolution is psychosocial—our understanding that development must now be consciously undertaken by the human species itself—it can be argued that our first need is to generate examples—models if we wish—of how to perceive, first, the situation we are in and, second, ways to deal with it. Any attempt at such overall conceptualizations is awe-inspiring in its demands and is inevitably likely to shelter misjudgments and partialities. For this reason we need many attempts at this stage, and these should preferably be arrived at from widely different perspectives.

If such attempts are not made, either because of the difficulties they present or because we do not see the need, much of what we initiate in action will run the risk of being useless or perhaps positively damaging. A reason for this danger is that we do not live in a condition of cultural or societal homogeneity but in a situation of rapid, unequal, and often violent change. Action taken on unexamined premises will therefore be particularly liable to be irrelevant. Some other ages have been more fortunate than ours in that the cultural base has been more stable and therefore its reliability could be assumed, thus allowing satisfactory decisions to be taken at a more superficial level than is possible for us. This difference may provide a perspective on the question of why much of our contemporary planning appears minimal in effect, whether we look at its results in cities or in socioeconomies. It also offers some explanation of why those planning efforts that are heavily concerned with technology are usually successful—for example, the space programme and the development of telecommunications. In activities of these kinds the stability of the cultural base may not be of great relative importance, so powerful is the technology and so manifest its success in performance when judged simply by the criteria of technical mastery.

The purpose of this chapter is to offer a sequence of reasoning as assistance for our emergent global thinking. The items will be given in their order of dependency and will latterly bring us to tentative indications for action. This chapter is therefore an attempt to suggest directions of operationalization arising out of all the matters we have considered in the book. Although the way of thinking about these matters is kept as near the perceived reality as possible, the sequence of items which follows is essentially to be seen as a tool for thinking and acting rather than as a rigid prescription. However, that having been said, it is necessary to add that any attempt to generate such an ordering comes very near to the making of a myth, for we do not properly understand how it is we come to act or what the role of myth is in relation to action. At this stage I am not *consciously* trying to generate a myth and to inspire the reader's belief in it.

Therefore, to counteract whatever the author may be trying to do *subconsciously*, the reader would be well advised to regard the attempt which follows as only one among many possibles or futuribles, to use de Jouvenel's word, and to broaden the field of discussion by generating a similar 'base of operations' of his own. What follows will best serve its purpose if it assists in stimulating precisely that activity. In what follows, the context of approach is the assumption that knowledge scientifically obtained can be successfully followed through into action in human affairs— the general assumption of our time.

26.2 A suggested operational chain of reasoning
In this section I shall try to set out a way of ranging certain items to be taken into consideration for action. They will be organized hierarchically as far as possible so that each upper item will have its dependent items below it, although not necessarily always the one immediately below it. The first purpose is to show justification or the reason for an item being where it is in the sequence on account of its dependency on previous items. The second purpose is to use these items to provide a logic for the choice of the items selected later as the foci of attention for action. The third purpose is to suggest some major areas in which action appears to be necessary within the context of the continuing human enterprise. The areas of action are thus derived directly from attempts to understand our present and emerging condition. The range of items is to be regarded as dynamic, the underlying notion being one of systemic linkages. The items are conceived as bound together by many cross-connections which cannot be fully known at this stage or indicated in the sequence. Frequently linkages are multiple and often dependencies have a degree of reciprocity.

26.3 Some instigating dynamics
26.3.1 Population-food-energy
Increasing world population and increasing demand for food, under present conditions, require increasing inputs of energy in a present situation of increasing difficulties of world energy supply and a cultural–societal condition of heavy dependency on nonrenewable sources of energy. This dynamic operates in global ecosystemic contexts known to have limitations in energy throughputs and in other aspects, although some uncertainty may exist at times as to the precise measurement of the limitations. This dynamic is seen as belonging more to the concept of biosphere than noosphere. It is essentially a global dynamic of physical logistics. In spite of some difficulties, the degree of objectivity in diagnosing this dynamic is high: the quantitative measures are reasonably satisfactory.

26.3.2 Socioeconomies
The global distribution of population, food, and energy consumption and the relations between these are at present in a certain condition which

cannot be considered stable but which is the starting point for future action. Access to the basic requirements of food and energy for survival is not available according to national or individual need. Although this is partly a result of the varying natural endowments of the world's ecosystems, it is very considerably also a product of human organizations. This inequality is a global socioeconomic dynamic, manifest especially in the North–South confrontation of the developed and developing socioeconomies, but is also present inside developed and developing socioeconomies.

The 'information society' is a new kind of socioeconomy, at present only in its emergent phase in the developed countries and not existing at all in the developing countries. It may, however, be expected to spread outwards from the developed countries. At present the dynamic of the information society's emergence appears physically as a solid block of countries ranging from Japan to Europe and covering about one-seventh of the four billion world total population. Because of the very rapid progress of the electronic technology this dynamic is very vigorous and will be likely to continue so. Through effects on ecosystems it has heavy impacts on the developing countries.

The production–job–wages–consumption linkage as hitherto operating in developed countries is already under heavy pressure from the information society. Very considerable shifts have occurred since 1950 and the pressures for change in the linkage will be a progressively powerful dynamic in the developed countries as information plays an ever more important role, both in creating change and in providing accommodations to it. In the developing countries this linkage may not be capable of general applicability because of its dependency on an industrial base which is very difficult for many developing countries to achieve. Such a base depends on nonrenewable sources of energy. These do not exist in large enough quantities, with present technologies, to offer any possibility of widespread global applicability to the developing countries. Therefore, in the latter a new dynamic will possibly appear. In both developed and developing countries the operation of this linkage is closely related to many kinds of technology including the so-called intermediate technology. In the developed countries the discipline of the need for money obtainable through the job may be the main control holding the behaviour of the mass individual within a workable society–individual nexus. As job availability declines, excluding more and more individuals from this discipline, the nexus in its present form will be progressively impaired.

The mass-individual character profile is a socioeconomic dynamic because of the relationship between individual and group behaviour and because the typical mass individual in the developed countries is conditioned to high consumption of goods, including food. This pattern of consumption requires heavy throughput of energy in ecosystems. In the developed countries this throughput has grown in recent decades much faster than their populations. This produces a demand dynamic of its own, but also helps to maintain and perpetuate the production–job–wages–consumption linkage in its present form. The mass-individual character profile, being built into the present developed socioeconomies, provides a kind of negative dynamic inasmuch as it can be an inhibitor of necessary change. This dynamic in the present conditions runs wild—an improperly integrated system component.

26.3.3 Psychomass and noosphere growth

As our scientific and technological knowledge increases, the total psychomass possessed by the human species becomes larger and its detail more refined. As the psychomass grows and the electronic technology makes it progressively easier to access and manipulate the psychomass on a global scale, the noosphere becomes denser and its species (disciplines of bodies of knowledge, etc) ever more differentiated. This growth dynamic is powered by our steady search for knowledge and its application and by the intensification of consciousness caused on the one hand by our increased human numbers and on the other by our now highly sophisticated means of breaking the bonds of time and space in communicating with each other, especially by the electronic means. This dynamic is also driven by the new necessities which are emerging in the socioeconomies of both developed and developing countries. It is also part of the dynamic driving toward the creation of a new world view or overall myth and a basic world culture. Two very powerful psychomass areas are our knowledge of the life-support system (not yet well operationalized) and our uses of the regions of the electromagnetic spectrum (very well and extensively operationalized). Both of these are likely to have strong future thrusts, and they are likely to become more closely interactive. In the psychomass we can identify the emergence of new values. Of these, potentially very influential is the concept of our responsibility for the further psychosocial evolution of our species. This implies taking conscious thought for planning the human place in the overall life-support system, and therefore the development of an appropriate ethical approach to human existence and activity. This has already produced some dynamic toward the stabilization of certain aspects of the developed socioeconomics. This implication also drives toward the conceptualization of a world system comprising present 'natural' and 'human' system conceptualizations. Much technological psychomass, in conjunction with present socioeconomic arrangements, drives toward increasing ecological demand, often beyond safe limits. In this sense some psychomass in some degree runs wild in the system, and implies questions of control of psychomass development and use.

26.4 Note on motivations for action

With these three main areas of dynamic in mind we can move on to search for more detailed specifics where action appears necessary. In addressing our attention to this level we need to ask a question about approach because undertaking action raises problems of justification. What is to be the attitude which shall serve as the general support for proceeding toward action? First, we can recognize that there is much to recommend a base of sound knowledge of the material on which we propose to act. In the present stage of human development, in which a great deal of firm information is known about the physical world, there appears little alternative but to seek out and use the best knowledge available as an essential preliminary to acting, particularly with regard to physical matter Acting on this premise, we have been enormously successful in science and technology, our present level of mastery over the physical world having been achieved very rapidly. We could call this the approach of *technologica rationality*. In spite of some appearance to the contrary, this approach is not yet upset by the plethora of its own psychomass. Technological knowledge is still handleable, despite its variety and quantity, and can be applied very successfully, judged only on its own and not on societal term *This is a powerful and still developing approach and must be used to the full, since it is knowledge and technology which allow us to increase the number of human beings sustainable by the biosphere.*

When we come to consider matters of less dominant technological emphasis this approach of technological rationality rapidly declines in effectiveness because it becomes apparent that it does not carry within itself the evaluative means for guiding its own development. Direction of growth and decisions about application have to be provided from outside i This is seen clearly enough if we think about trying to develop an area of psychomass on the socioeconomy exclusively by the way of technologica rationality. This would mean, for example, developing knowledge about how to improve computers for no other reason than to be able to make smaller, brighter, and better computers without relevance to the fact that they are used by human beings for human purposes. In socioeconomic terms it would mean organizing society to run smoothly as a machine, treating human beings mechanistically. Let us hope that we are substantiall outgrowing the techfix approach this kind of thinking generates.

A second approach is to act within the confines of some 'philosophy or 'theory' of the nature of things. Such guidance may be based on conceptualizations of 'how the world works', interpretations of how human societies have come to be the way they are, or aspirations about the way things *should* be. A theory embraced, action is then decided by reference to the preestablished set of tenets, beliefs, etc. Religions, socia philosophies (the two may have much in common especially in the recent past), interpretations of history, and socioeconomic macrotheory operate in this role, although they may also claim, and indeed may have, a ration base. Such bases for action often manifest deterministic emphases, supposedly identified cause–effect linkages playing an important part.

The third approach is experimental and pragmatic. This proceeds on the *suggestion* that something may be worth trying in the real world.

After trial it is judged, and if successful, accepted. If not, it is modified or abandoned and something else is tried. This is very much the way in which we now conceive the biological evolutionary process to work, and in 'human' systems the great example is America. Sociobiology, which attempts to show the specifics of how society (the living together of more than a single organism) is an outgrowth of biological evolutionary processes, might be useful as an intellectual base for combining 'natural' and 'human' systems in a single conceptualization with a common experimental–pragmatic dynamic.

In practice much action is normally carried out with varying mixes of all three underpinnings, and very frequently we do not think out the mix but leave it to chance and circumstances. Perhaps we are now entering a phase where we may be forced to differentiate more clearly the amounts of each approach in a particular mix and give reasons to justify the proposed ratios. In the foci of attention for action which now follow, all three approaches can be taken to be operative in varying degrees of emphasis, as in both practice and mental process they are indeed interdependent.

26.5 Foci of attention for action

26.5.1 Population–food–energy

Strictly considered, no action can be taken directly under this category because these are essentially elements acted upon. Action in relation to them therefore comes through other categories. For example, to increase or redistribute the world's available food is a socioeconomic–technical matter. This area essentially provides the 'external' reasons or justification for acting, and is a generator of certain aspects of goals.

26.5.2 Ensure viability of ecosystems globally

If ecosystems are already in some danger, and are likely to be more endangered, and if we wish to ensure that the present and future world population eats, this safeguarding of ecosystems is the first priority of action. The action required is: positively, that ecosystems shall be organized to sustain more human beings at rather better nutritional and calorific values than at present and, negatively, that the action taken in attempting to do that shall not cause ecosystemic deterioration. This highest-priority line of action primarily requires appropriate development of the necessary psychomass and the formulation of converging group and individual behaviour patterns, especially in socioeconomic contexts.

26.5.3 Generate feedback control loops in human behaviour

This includes regenerating existing useful loops, modifying or destroying damaging ones, and generating new loops to serve as a controlling mechanism for ensuring that human activity does indeed result in safeguarding the viability of its own life-support system. This is a key *means* for the reestablishment of the viability of the human species within ecosystems and of the systems themselves. Although these loops will be *within* the human socioeconomic system, their function will be to regulate both the relationships between the individual and the group inside the socioeconomic and the relationship between the evolutionary development of the socio-economic system on the one hand and the life support over which it has only partial, not total control, on the other. These loops will be required to cover such widely separated matters as population changes, energy use, food distribution, and psychomass development.

26.5.4 Develop psychomass and strengthen the noosphere
The conscious development of certain areas of science, knowledge, technology, and expertise (all components of psychomass) appears to be a corollary of the concept of the human species being now consciously responsible for its psychosocial development. We particularly need to develop psychomass connected with understanding the behaviour and limit of long-term tolerance in the human being, psychomass connected with certain areas of technology (for example, ecosystem design, intermediate technology, energy), and psychomass related to techniques for handling human relationships. Especially important also will be knowledge related to coping with the North–South gap in global human well-being. New conceptualizations and concepts will have to be developed, including methods for alerting to the need for developing them.

The noosphere is very variable in its global intensity, and links between the intensively developed areas also have varying degrees of strength. The intensity which binds together the North Atlantic countries is greater than anywhere else in the world. The linkages between the Northern and the Southern countries appear particularly weak and will require rapid strengthening, as will the intensity of the noosphere in the Southern countries. New psychomass will be required to handle the changing interchange of biomass between the developed and the developing countries and between the ecosystems with very numerous human populations and those which have relatively small populations but which feed the mass populations. In the developed countries new psychomass will have to be developed in connection with the next stage of the development of the information society, particularly with regard to its socioeconomics.

26.5.5 Reconstruct the production–job–wages–consumption linkage
We already have some of the evidence to show that this will increasingly require major attention in developing as well as developed socioeconomies. In the developed countries the inherent drive toward the achievement or elaboration of the information society (say, as measure, 50% of workers in information) is the signal for the emergence of serious difficulties in making physical products (manumass) accessible to consumers because of declining job opportunity in a stable population. In the developing countries the problem is more likely to be the inability to produce enough job opportunity for an increasing population. New linkages between production and consumption will have to be devised and factors

in and surrounding the present production–job–wages–consumption linkage will need modification. We should note that this focus of attention for action is considerably independent of the question of absolute global shortfalls of food and energy.

26.5.6 Reconstruct the mass individual's character profile

This includes the sensibility of the mass individual. The rationale for this reconstruction as needed action is twofold. First, the present profile is deficient in control components capable of keeping behaviour viable in ecosystems and, second, the new ecosystemic conditions together with the new socioeconomic situation (the information society) in the developed countries will require the development of systemic controls heavily dependent on the mass individual's behaviour for their effectiveness. A reason for this latter dependency is that in an information-rich society coercion is bound to be limited in the extent to which it can be applied, whether in physical or in mental form, since by definition the individual has good access to many kinds of information and can expose lies and ignorance. The new profile will essentially include a vigorous concern for fostering an awareness toward the public good and a willingness to modify individual demands in the interest of the whole.

26.5.7 Reduce energy throughput in heavily urbanized populations

Under this heading comes reduction and/or stabilization of the production of physical goods and services in the developed urbanized socioeconomies, so that global nonrenewable resources can be husbanded and ecological demand reduced. This stabilization also is required in the energy throughput applied directly to vital processes in ecosystems in order to maintain the system in a 'young' phase for food production. Reduction in energy throughput will be heavily dependent on the progressively intensive use of the telecommunications–computer technology both to maintain and to increase transactions in a growth-reduced or stabilized situation and to save energy by moving information instead of people to a much greater extent than at present.

26.5.8 Increase transactions—particularly information transactions

The rationale here is that transactions are a major base of productivity and therefore of wealth. As stabilization means reduction in transactions involving physical goods and services, the growth in transactions—part of it compensatory for the transactions lost—will have to be in the area of transactions involving information. This means both the development of psychomass and its transfer from one person or place to another. This has a great deal to do with the *availability* of psychomass. In order to increase transactions, there will need to be improved availability of information. This implies application to the development both of the electronic technology and of the socioeconomic arrangements for handling it.

26.5.9 Reallocate resources with changing ratios

As the ratios between the costs and other factors of resources change, reallocation of resources becomes necessary. For example, as the cost of oil relative to car-use habits changes, resources devoted to making cars an providing public travel facilities need to be reallocated. Increasingly reallocation of a resource has to be seen in conjunction with other resources—their uses, pressures on them, etc. So, for example, the changes in our energy situation induce the desire for changes in commuting patterns, urban densities, working hours, etc. An example of the interrelations of resource allocations is illustrated by the currently popular idea of planning considerable substitution of movement by the worker for movement of the data material he handles. Technically this i relatively easy. However, the proposal to increase the electronically performed transactions comes at the moment when the availability of frequency space in the electromagnetic spectrum is diminishing. Frequenc space is now a scarce resource—a fact apparently not known to those wh would take some cars off the road by putting the transactions on the air. There is yet a second ramification. Urban areas, particularly large ones, have been growing in their physical spread faster than their populations. This produces a disproportionately large pressure on the nonurban land round them, pressing on the viability of their ecosystems. Increased electronification of transactions will increase the opportunity of the urba dwellers to emigrate to the rural areas of the regions, thus accelerating a trend already present in North America, and causing yet further ecologic pressure. The four resources primarily involved in such a nexus—energy, electromagnetic spectrum frequencies, physical land space, and ecosystem viability (that is a very major resource)—can clearly be reallocated only a an integrated operation. Single and isolated resource allocation will run the risk of inducing new and unanticipated conditions in the relationship between these resources, likely chain reactions of unacceptable kinds.

26.6 Some suggested specifics of action

With these nine major foci of attention for action in mind we may proce to look at areas of action in more detail. As these are lower in the scale their linkages are more numerous and it is therefore more difficult to present them in an order of dependency, as has been attempted in the tw previous lists. However, some ordering is possible because particular acti in the real world cannot be taken until some mental or conceptual actio has already taken place. Hence we cannot, in real world action, be very effective in ensuring the necessary long-term symbiosis between 'natural' and 'human' systems until we have done the work necessary for producir some conceptualization of a combined total system. At present this conceptualization does not exist. In our context this implies the need f some activity for alerting that new conceptualizations and concepts have to be generated before action in the real world can even be approached. We shall therefore begin with this kind of conceptualizing action.

(Our time is notable for its detailed proposals for action. Many of these are of little value because of their poor conceptual base. Action is likely to be only as good as the conceptual foundation on which it rests. It is on concepts that 'theories' of action must rest.)

26.6.1 Concept alerting

This action consists of a kind of monitoring function which continuously scans the sciences, technologies, socioeconomies, and human sensibilities for evidence that new conceptualizations and concepts will need to be developed or already are in the process of being shaped. A concept is a specific, such as *energy* or *information.* A conceptualization is a broader area and suggests an overall image or percept, such as *globalism* or *information society.* Because we live in a time when change is pervasive and rapid, previous conceptualizations tend to diminish in their usefulness for action, rendering the action taken progressively less relevant to the real situation. We therefore have to sense when and in what areas we need to generate new conceptualizations and concepts well before the time for needed action. This will require the setting up of special activities—the study of the future is one of these—and the establishing of new organizational arrangements for doing this work. The Canadian Institute for Research on Public Policy is an organization established with some such role in mind. The attempted aim of this book is essentially that of alerting that new conceptualizations and concepts are emerging and are in need of clarification and elaboration.

26.6.2 Conceptual unification of 'natural' and 'human' systems

The need for action here emerges out of the alerting process and the study of approaches used in ecology, consideration of socioeconomic attitudes and practices, and appreciation of the dynamics we have listed. Ecologists often tend to think their discipline is suitable, conceptually, to provide the conceptualization for the overall world system. We have adduced reasons for doubting this claim. Socioeconomists, whilst recently increasingly acknowledging the importance of the ecological approach, have subscribed, and substantially still do subscribe, to now obsolescent conceptualizations that fail to take properly into account the fragility of the global life-support system under its present pressures. Some hope for unification may exist in sociobiology, but at present this emerging discipline has only a minimum to say about human societies. Further hope comes from ecologists who make specific attempts to apply ecological concepts and findings in detail to human societies (for example H T Odum). But, in the present state of knowledge, we are left with an awareness that a new conceptualization is necessary, and that as yet not very much specific work has been done. A very tentative conceptualization joining the 'natural', the 'socioeconomic', and the noospheric systems is offered in

figure 26.1 (page 422). As the production of psychomass is a key link
between ecosystem and socioeconomic processes in the future guidance o
our psychosocial evolution I have given it major emphasis.

26.6.3 Conceptualization of limits to the hominization of ecosystems

Many of the world's ecosystems are heavily hominized. That is to say
they have been shifted from their 'natural' condition to an 'artificial'
condition now typified by the presence of very large numbers of human
beings, the intensive action of human beings on their components, or
heavy energy throughputs, or by all three of these simultaneously. We
need to know how far we can go in thus 'artificializing' the ecosystems o
the various climatic zones of the biosphere. For example, how far can w
reorganize ecosystems to be designed for high production of certain kinds
of biomass and short food chains dependent on high energy throughput
without throwing them into conditions of instability? Progressively the
world system diminishes in its 'natural' component and increases in its
'hominized' component. We need some conceptualization of how to tack
the question of the limits that may exist to this changing mix. How do
we conceptualize the relationship between science–technology (what we
can do to hominize) and ecology (the understanding that all is a poised
dynamic system open to the possibility of 'degradation' and 'destruction'
The approach to this question raises major debate (see Neilands, 1976).

26.6.4 Additional concepts of the dynamics of socioeconomies

Socioeconomic concepts that deal with physical goods and services canno
handle other than the *commodity* aspect of information. As the informatic
society has a great deal of use for the noncommodity aspects of informatio
and since the information sector of the socioeconomies of developed
countries will be the growth area, revised or new concepts of productivity
ownership, utility, consumption, and transaction will be required. This mo
difficult area is only just beginning to make its presence felt. The enquiry
immediately leads to the nature and role of 'mind'. The development of
the concept of psychomass is intended as a contribution in this direction.
Some psychomass can be treated in the same way as physical goods; but
some cannot. A further area of conceptualization is needed to relate
our concepts along the perspective of physical goods and services to our
new concepts connected with 'mind', psychomass, and noosphere. Product
that are commodities (that is, are treated as such) I have described in the
aggregate as *manumass*—a word suggesting physical manufacture.

26.6.5 Monitoring of conditions of ecosystems

The ensuring of the viability of ecosystems will require that the condition
of and the trends within them are monitored continuously for signs of
particularly adverse change. The data collected and processed will need t
be made easily available to governments, business, planners, etc, and to
the public, much as we now make stock exchange information available.

We have seen that a beginning has been made at the global level with the distribution of data down to regions. There is not, however, as yet any widespread monitoring of ecosystems at the more local level, except for very crude recording of certain air and water pollutants. Automatic equipment for more sophisticated monitoring is now being developed, for satellite and ground use. Coupled with computer data-banking and processing capability and telecommunications for universal accessing, these developments could lead to the monitoring of ecosystems at a standard adequate for their guidance in accordance with policies for development and stabilization. To reach this level will, however, need a special socio-economic effort, the motivation for which is not as yet by any means adequately developed. Monitoring is still seen in its negative rather than its positive aspects. Work will be required to find the most effective indicators. These could be derived directly from our ecosystemic knowledge and be developed under the concepts of ecosystemic productivity (gross and net), diversity (species, spatial, biochemical), cyclicity (materials, land uses), stability (no change toward or away from the stable condition), etc. The monitoring of energy throughput in ecosystems would appear to be an important indicator of system condition.

26.6.6 Monitoring of the conditions of socioeconomies

Our present monitoring of socioeconomies in the developed countries is better than our monitoring of ecosystems. Governments monitor such key components as currency conditions, labour markets and manpower, the GNP, demographic matters, national deficits in trade, housing starts, etc. It may be doubted, however, whether some of the indicators used at present are the most appropriate that could be devised for emerging conditions in which reduction or stabilization of manumass growth will be likely to play a major role. We have seen how the conventional indicators used for employment have concealed the emergence of the information society in the USA. Another example of our possibly being misled is revealed by Boulding's suggestion that in a stabilizing situation the GNP might really be read as an indicator of *cost* (Boulding, 1972). We need to develop sophisticated indicators to show how the information sector develops, particularly with regard to the development of information outside our present conventional categories of production. We have to find these in order to be able to foster the growth of the superstructure of information. We also need a great deal of monitoring related to energy in the socioeconomy. At present we have little knowledge of how energy ratios change or how much energy the various physical products we manufacture consume in relation to such matters as their duration of life and their productivity. We need to know the *energy chains* of our socio-economies. As the management of stabilizing and stabilized socioeconomies will have to pay attention to both the growth-reduction or stabilized sector and the growth sector (mostly information), sophisticated and meaningful monitoring of both these sectors will be vital. The tele-communications–computer technology is well suited to providing the operational means for such monitoring. It is the organizational side that now presents the problem since the technology potentially offers universal access through packet-switching.

26.6.7 Development of telecommunications–computer technology for assisting control loops

The electronic technology can extensively serve the societal functions of monitoring, management, planning, production, increasing of transactions, and shaping of consciousness. It is therefore of importance to all the dynamics we have mentioned—population–food–energy, socioeconomic elements (global distribution, production–job–wages–consumption, mass-individual character profile), psychomass and noosphere growth—and is relevant to our foci of attention for action—global viability of ecosystems feedback control loops, development of psychomass and noosphere, reconstruction of the production–job–wages linkage, reconstruction of the mass-individual character profile, reduction of energy throughput in ecosystems, and increase in transactions. The technology also is an important servant for the development of new concepts and the monitoring functions just mentioned. The pervasiveness of the usefulness of the electronic technology strongly suggests that the development of the technology itself is of paramount cultural, societal, scientific, and technological importance.

Although most governments in the developed countries have paid attention to the growth of the technology the governmental response has not been commensurate with the pervasive and influential growth of the technology in conjunction with the emergence of the information society. By contrast, business and industry have been aggressive in their application of the technology to their own activities. As an example of this contrast, witness the vigorous use of TV for commercial advertising and the almost negligible effort of governments at using the media for developing autonomous controls within the mass individual. Developmental matters for the technology in its societal perspective include, in the present state of the technology:

easy public access to computer capability;
fostering public use of telecommunications to conserve energy;
stimulating the use of information accessed electronically to increase transactions;
bringing formal education up to the same high level of technique as is used in informal education, especially for children;
developing ways of forming necessary new control loops through the use of information;
developing the informational superstructure;

counteracting the systemically adverse aspects of the character profile
and sensibility of the mass individual;
increasing two-way electronic interaction;
increasing public participation in the use of all kinds of networks,
including public inputs into radio and TV programming;
increasingly relating the technology to the ongoing processes of
ecosystems.

26.6.8 Action for facing the control-loop question

The dilemma existing, in the present condition of the mass-individual
profile, as far as the use of the electronic technology for reshaping the
profile to create new control loops is concerned, lies in the nature of
saturation propaganda. Heavily propagandized, the mass individual will do
what is required by the propaganda. But this psychological fact offends
our sense of personal individual freedom to think our own thoughts and
decide our own actions. Some necessary control loops could very probably
be created by saturation propaganda and might conceivably hold for a
long time, but the price is the stifling of that very awareness and flexibility
of mind that direction of our psychosocial evolution essentially requires.
Yet the benefits of the technology for very rapidly shaping values and
attitudes in mass populations cannot be just thrown away. *Indeed, the
technology may conceivably now be the* only *means for keeping these
masses governable. The action required, therefore, seems to be to find out
how the electronic technology can be used to develop the loops and foster
their functioning while at the same time stimulating the awareness and
flexibility of the mass individual so that the growth potential of the
information society can be realized and the psychosocial evolutionary
process can move to new levels of complexity.*

The older, hoped-for resolution of this dilemma—that of the *philosophes*
and the theory and practice of the last century—was the raising of the
educational level of the masses. In our century that way of resolution has
been largely, but not entirely, superseded by belief in sociopolitical creeds.
Now these are failing as resolvers of the dilemma, and some new thinking
has to be done both in overall conceptualization and in detail. The
alternative to finding new acceptable resolutions is the application of
force—a path at the moment chosen by the majority of the world's
nations. The action required seems to include a reforging of our ideas of
freedom, government, sovereignty, and duty. Perhaps we might consider
the following:
encourage the sense of obligation as the corollary of rights to food,
shelter, free speech, etc;
rapidly develop the use of the electronic technology for making
possible—as it can—the much wider participation of the public in the
processes of government than now occurs;

set up bodies to endorse the accuracy and fairness of information—a
kind of information ombudsmanship;
reorganize the use of the electronic mass media to foster the psychic
growth of the mass individual, both as a self and as a member of the
group;
come to operational conclusions about how to deal with the question
of propaganda use, censorship, and the current 'by default' formation of
values and unintended offering of exemplars of behaviour, particularly
with regard to the young.

26.6.9 Basic psychomass needed for control loops

We have used Julian Huxley's word *psychosocial* to connote the idea that
current human evolutionary development is seen as being essentially in the
area of mind and society. When Huxley used the word, and still generally
today, the underpinning of this idea was that cultural and societal behaviour
is *learned* as a result of the individual's exposure to environmental factors,
with the possible exception of certain basic 'drives' or 'instincts'. Recent
scientific work has modified this emphasis and has reminded us that we
really know very little about the origins of human behaviour. One way of
dealing with this lack of firm knowledge in a key area necessary for
shaping our future development is to proceed experimentally. This is
essentially the way of propaganda. More refined, but still experimental, is
the operant behaviour approach of B F Skinner. Human beings can in
fact be trained in the same way as racehorses, without spending too much
effort on enquiring into how the process works in detail.

A line of enquiry now becoming very important is sociobiology. This is
the scientific study of all societal behaviour (nonhuman and human), that
applies Darwin's ideas of evolution to behaviour in societies of various
kinds—'colonial' animals (for example, coral), insects, vertebrates, and
human beings. The chief exponent of this emergent discipline is Wilson
(1975). He presents the view that hitherto we have mistakenly supposed
that our behaviour in society is to be accounted for either as culturally
generated or as resulting from individual or racial heredity. In Wilson's
view: "Social evolution is the outcome of genetic response of populations
to ecological pressure within the constraints imposed by phylogenetic
inertia" (Wilson, 1975, page 32). This is the underlying perspective that
I have used in this book in thinking about the dynamic relationship
emerging between our electronic technology and our ecological approach
to the life-support system.

In looking at human sociobiology the researcher is confronted with the
phenomenon of altruism in human beings. "Technically, the problem is to
explain how selfishness can evolve into altruism" (Calder, 1977, page 48).
The modern theory of altruism holds that apparent nonselfish behaviour is
enlightened self-interest in a survival perspective. This could be related to
the winning out of the individual and the survival of his particular genetic

characteristics as being a vigorous adaptation. T des Pres sums up the ideas of Wilson, as applicable to human development, as the first attempt to offer an empirical base for human identity and conduct, and to provide "... *empirical* guidelines for a cogent theory of social organization" (Calder, 1977, page 46). We need to think about the call for a new ethic by ecologists in the light of sociobiological thinking.

An important application of the ideas of sociobiology to our immediate concern lies in the area of the mass influence of propaganda. Wilson thinks that there is an evolutionary element in the human willingness to be propagandized or indoctrinated. We should not, perhaps, therefore necessarily regard this as particularly either a benign or a malign factor in our future evolution. We *tend* to think of it as malign, but we do not in fact know that it is necessarily operating in this way in our situation. We *tend* to assume that our inherited notions of liberty and freedom are benignly adaptive, but we do not *know* they are for sure.

With a somewhat different emphasis it is necessary to bear in mind that a key element in Darwinian evolutionary theory is the idea that the differences in individual genetic makeup are crucial to successful long-term adaptation. If this notion can be transferred into the psychosocial domain, then saturation propaganda, or even any propaganda, or anything else that produces a common mass 'mind' is a virus possibly lethal to our capacity for evolutionary adaptation. A society which may stabilize its relationship with the global life-support system through control loops generated by such means may forfeit the possibility of further psychosocial evolution.

On this gloomy note we have no alternative but to leave this question to the passage of time and the development of further knowledge. But we may bear in mind, on a more hopeful note, that in Calder's words "The chief message from Wilson's book is that an explanation of human behaviour is not only necessary but possibly within our grasp" (Calder, 1977, page 49).

26.6.10 Some specific areas for attention in the mass-individual profile
In spite of the present lack of knowledge and our condition of transition between one set of preferred assumptions and the development of another set, there are some aspects connected with the mass individual's profile that can be operationally tackled, whether by operant conditioning or by other means. In thinking about our main concern of how to bring individual and group behaviour into accord with each other for ensuring the well-being of the life-support system, the following three characteristics appear to need conscious attention.

Unwillingness toward self-discipline
If an external discipline which does violence to the individual's sense of self is to be rejected, an inner self-discipline must be required for obtaining the necessary behaviour when the action to be carried out cannot accord with the immediate desire. The mass individual is characteristically not

very good at generating and imposing any such discipline. Historically it has been possible for the individual to learn a considerable degree of discipline, but if George Steiner is right, our motivation to do so is now much weakened. Yet without it no generation of the necessary control loops is possible in acceptable form. Therefore the task is to find out how to motivate the mass individual to a greater self-discipline. Operant conditioning can work between humans and animals but has only limited possibilities in human societies where the 'trainer' and the 'trained' are, in the adult world, very tightly linked by control loops; governor and governed are a binary pair controlling each other.

Unintegrated psychomass
By this phrase is meant a condition of the psychomass possessed by the mass individual. In him a 'mind' is formed which is defective in its ability to integrate the elements of psychomass into a coherent whole at the level necessary for handling the complexities of our civilization. Instead of being a whole the 'mind' consists of a number of compartments which have few or no interrelations with each other. Psychomass in one compartment can be highly developed but have no effect on the psychomass in another. This inability to integrate even descends to the learning details of an academic discipline, such as mathematics or a language. The child may go through formal school without achieving any coherent idea of what mathematics or a language is really about, merely having performed the various mental tasks piecemeal. The devastating effect of this failure to integrate or form a whole 'mind' is a rapid and massive drop in the motivation to learn. If I have the psychomass that constitutes my 'mind' only in disconnected pieces of *fact* and have no *ideas* to bind them together shall I not eventually ask the question: What is the good of adding any more? That is the destruction of motivation. It is probably now widespread. As the information society will have to depend heavily on the use of information, the motivation to learn will be vital. *The unintegrated 'mind' of the mass individual is therefore antipathetic toward our emergent societal condition. The task is to find out how to motivate the mass individual toward the vigorous development of integration of the psychomass that makes up 'mind'. Perhaps we might start by putting facts into the context of ideas, and stimulate the young, in particular, to learn how to handle ideas. This means teaching synthesis and synergy—both neglected now because they are difficult to teach.* However, the electronic technology could be a great help. In common language to integrate means to make sense, to create a meaning for the individual *as person.* Mass individual is a creature for whom no meaning has been made. On this score he is worse off than the primitive Ortega y Gasset concluded he is, since in primitive societies there is plenty of evidence of created meaning. *To sum up, we might say the essential task here is to integrate psychomass so that it has meaning for the mass individual.*

Limits to psychic growth of the mass individual
The mass individual is characteristically truncated in his psychic growth
and does not reach Bateson's upper levels of learning capability (Bateson,
1972, page 287ff). He frequently remains juvenile, and is sometimes
infantile, although is perfectly capable of pushing the buttons and pulling
the levers that keep us running as a society. Indeed, in order to participate
in those functions it may be positively advantageous *not* to develop
psychically beyond a certain point. The effect is that the mass individual
is a good, often superb, technician but an immature person. This is often
very obvious. Although this state of affairs may be tolerated as a way of
getting the work done, it is scarcely acceptable since it offends our sense
of the individual's inherent right to full personality development, and not
merely to the meeting of his physical requirements. The task here is to
ensure that the mass individual is in a context which will not truncate his
development as a person. This would mean attack from both the individual
side and the societal end. If full development were made possible for
many mass individuals, would the achieving of control loops be more or
less likely? We have no means of knowing. Self-discipline in the interests
of society might be enhanced; or the individual might pursue personal
ends without inhibition, with the resultant failure of the society to ensure
its life-support base. It is clear that here we are deep within the psycho-
dynamics of the individual, whether bourgeois man, mass man, or other.
Perhaps there is only one ultimate control loop, and that is probably
unachievable in the mass—*ama et fac quod vis.* Love and do what you
wish. This is addressed to the individual. But the love must be of the
right kind or the loop that would hold individual and group together will
not work. This emphasis is in stark contrast to our century's belief in the
efficacy of reconstructing society according to preferred abstractions. I
have no competence to pursue this matter of the human heart further, but
would make the plea that conscious psychosocial development should
logically include the developmental aspects of the individual just as much
as those of the group. Why are we typically harbouring a bias toward the
reconstruction of society? Of our examples only Ryan takes the individual
way, with his interpretation of Peirce's firstness trying to develop the
necessary control loops internally to the individual.

26.6.11 Spatial planning
The spatial distribution of population in terms of residence, work activity,
and other activities will need to be approached with emphases that pay
serious attention to our dynamics and foci of attention for action.
Comments on some of the more important aspects follow.

Relationship between transaction and movement
Many transactions, including much work in the information society, that
at present require physical movement on daily or other time-interval basis
are capable of being done in part or totally by electronic means, provided

the necessary equipment is available. Some areas of activity are already well advanced into the process of transfer into a 'spaceless' mode: teleaccounting, telemedicine, teletuition, entertainment—to name a few, while some further bastions of physical movement are probably due to fall shortly, for example, postal services and methods for making payments by cheque. The trend to telecommunicate, that is, to move the data rather than the body, may be expected to increase because of the financial advantages it offers. An increasing number of work and other activities will be transferred, thus releasing the operator from the tie to a single location. This need not mean the worker sits at home on a terminal all his working hours. He may do this only part of the time. It does mean that shifts will occur in the physical distribution patterns of work and residential activities. It also means that specific policies could be developed to take advantage of this change in relationships so that particular objectives, such as reduction in municipal administrative and educational costs, control of urban air pollution and traffic congestion, and ecosystem management, could be achieved. Work on this question is only in the beginning phase, but already it indicates a very considerable potential (see Harkness, 1972; 1973; Day, 1973; Nilles et al, 1976a; 1976b; Weintraub, 1976a; 1976b; 1976c; Weintraub and Pye, 1976). This should now be a major area of spatial planning research and experimentation, as the electronic technology offers new compromises between the advantages and disadvantages of centralization and decentralization. The technology also offers the possibility of generating transactions and therefore of bringing many activities to a higher level of immediacy—important in food production, ecosystem control, control of physical movement, education, and commerce and industry (condition of markets, etc).

Land as work niche
This connects with the production–job–wages–consumption linkage. The progressive difficulties that are arising as the old industrial society falls astern may make reoccupation of agricultural land as a workplace necessary for a considerable fraction of the population. Pressure toward this change will increase as our numbers of urban unemployed swell in the developed countries. In the developing countries it is already clear that they cannot and should not attempt the degree of urbanization prevalent in the developed countries. Their populations will need to be 'niched' in jobs on the land to a very considerable extent. This view has already been widely diffused by Ward (1976). The change of trend that such a proposal involves is formidably difficult to manage, as is demonstrated by the example of the failure of such widely different cities as Moscow and Capetown to control inward migration. This links up with our ecological concern since higher-density resettlement of agricultural land might be expected to have both good and bad ecological effects. Todd's biological ark might prove very beneficial since it would require operators who were

very much aware of ecological matters. On the other hand, uninformed subsistence farming could cause a great deal of damage by way of decline in fertility, loss of topsoil, etc. *The considerable reoccupation of the land as workplace would seem to require very carefully framed ecological policies based on a sophisticated understanding of particular ecosystems. In a situation of such reoccupation the telecommunications–computer services could provide means of making essential information easily available. Such a service would need to be integrated with the monitoring services we have already mentioned.*

26.6.12 Ecological socioeconomic planning

Although there is now perception of the existence of the gap between these two areas of planning, they are at present far from reconciliation in aims and practices. If the general ecological view that we have to take thought for the continued viability of the life-support capability of the world's ecosystems is correct, then a number of narrowly based economic activities will need modification. Agribusiness is clearly one of these. The thoughtless use of limited fossil material for expendable energy purposes is another. As such activities are now bound into our socioeconomies to such an extent that their great mass populations could not be fed and serviced without them, the question of modifying narrow economic approaches is exceedingly difficult and is already causing bitter confrontations. As the world's population increases, this problem will become more acute. Better quality of information and improved access to it will be vital and the planning techniques [for example on-line planning (Sackman and Citrenbaum, 1972), crisis management (Kupperman et al, 1975), and computer conferencing (Turoff, 1976)] now emerging directly out of the capabilities of the electronic technology will be necessary and helpful. *Such techniques now need to be given the necessary forced development, particularly on experimental bases and in educational contexts so that a generation competent in them is produced as quickly as possible.* These techniques apply to all kinds of planning but perhaps centrally to this question of relating ecological planning to socioeconomic planning.

26.6.13 Organizational planning

The field of this application of planning has been widely explored by business and industry, and by some countries in the area of government. The problems and opportunities flowing from both our new ecological knowledge and our informational technology are already producing organizational change. Most of this is probably strongly *ad hoc* to the obvious effects of the new applications. So the electronification of the inventory processes of chain stores has led to staff reorganization, and in industry the changed relationship between the central and the branch plants due to telecommunications facilities means new human groupings. We seem only at the beginning of this process of organizational change.

New organizations having no spatial limitations are now possible, but we have little knowledge of how to establish them. Our extreme limitation in this area is demonstrated by the telephone. This is organizationally strictly of only two modes—the alphabetical index of subscribers giving addresses only for identification purposes, and the index of firms allowing the subscriber to find a service. The telephone cannot be used to *generate* organizations of common interests, similar age groups, etc. *Planning effort appears to be needed to explore what forms of organization would be useful and to find ways of using the electronic technology for both generating the organizations and running them when they are formed*[1].

26.6.14 Planning the uses of the regions of the electromagnetic spectrum

The regions of the electromagnetic spectrum are a vital resource for the development of information handling. There is already heavy pressure on this resource, and the allocation of it is causing serious problems in the developed countries and internationally, especially with regard to maritime activities. The allocating of rights to use various wave bands to various interests becomes very important if we look at the role of the tele-communications–computer technology in relation to the stabilization of socioeconomies, the substitution of some physical movement by data movement, the maintenance of transactions, and the generation of behavioural control loops in mass populations. Also, the intensification in the global working of electronic communications brings its own difficulties connected with wave-band allocation, power emitted, and the orbital location of satellites, etc. The planned allocation of the uses of the regions of the electromagnetic spectrum is very rapidly becoming sophisticated. As a planning function, side-by-side with other planned areas, however, it has not yet been generally acknowledged, and there is no attempt whatever to integrate it with such planning activities as those concerned with energy, transportation, land utilization, and renewable and nonrenewable resources allocation.

---

[1] Several of the foregoing areas of concern relate very closely to many of the interests of urban and regional planning as it is at present institutionalized, chiefly in urban planning. Urban planners are still struggling to sort out what they mean by 'planning'. If 'planners' eventually conclude that they are essentially 'land-use planners' in the historical meaning of the phrase, then they will have to review what this can possibly mean in the light of the radical changes made in our approach to time and space by the electronic technology and our ecological knowledge. The old land-use approach is no longer in accordance with our needs. If, on the other hand, the institutionalized planners come to see themselves as essentially 'corporate' planners— as facilitators of the societal process of holistically arriving at policies and programmes for communities—then they must reform their thinking and learn to use all that the electronic technology can offer. Information readily accessible, models, computer conferencing, on-line decisionmaking, etc become indispensable to the planning process, and systemic conceptualizations become the intellectual base.

26.6.15 Rendering processes transparent

A great benefit offered by the electronic technology is its ability to render complex processes more transparent—the bringing up-to-date of the information which must serve as the basis of decision. This capability of bringing the knowledge of the working of the ecosystem and the socio-economy into real time becomes ever more important as on-line management becomes necessary. Electronic monitoring, data processing, computer conferencing, and modelling now need to be planned integrally as support for the process of achieving increasing transparency.

26.7 A suggestion toward the integration of systems

This section gives some detail of a way in which the integration of the conceptualizations of 'natural' and 'human' systems can be fused so that we can think of a total system. Such a conceptualization would allow us to move freely between natural and human phenomena. This facility is urgently required if we are to avoid disasters arising either from attempts at reconstructing society without noticing what is happening to the life-support system, or from restricting the exploitation of our knowledge of how to obtain more food from ecosystems, or from the running wild of socioeconomies due to the psychic characteristics of the mass individual. The conceptualization is illustrated in figure 26.1.

As we have previously noted in diagramming the ecosystem (figure 5.1), it is difficult to combine everything in a single systemic diagram because of complexity. The method used previously for dealing with this difficulty was to provide several diagrams, each indicating a particular major aspect of the ecosystem—producer–consumer–decomposer, energy flow, etc. This method requires the reader to hold all the diagrams simultaneously in mind if he is to obtain a sense of what an ecosystem really is. Indeed, if he does not go through the exercise of synthesizing the several diagrams he cannot properly conceptualize the ecosystem. For our present purpose this technique of presentation will not suffice because all has to be brought together in an ultimate synthesis. The attempt to do this in a single diagram leads to necessary abbreviations and therefore some changes of approach within the diagram. So, for example, we find that an ambiguity about certain of the feedback loops appears: they work sometimes as negative controls to restrain the tendency toward running wild and sometimes positively to enhance the part of the process into which these feed; and sometimes the flow is reversed. The production of psychomass, for example, may refer to psychomass which works benignly to hold Consume D_1 to suitable limits in terms of the basic life-support output (A). Or, it may equally well operate to encourage the running wild of D_1—the consumption side overruns the production in A and C because of a certain psychomass production in, perhaps, F_4. The very attempt to integrate by diagram is fraught with such difficulties, but the diagram remains an absolutely essential tool for learning to think systemically.

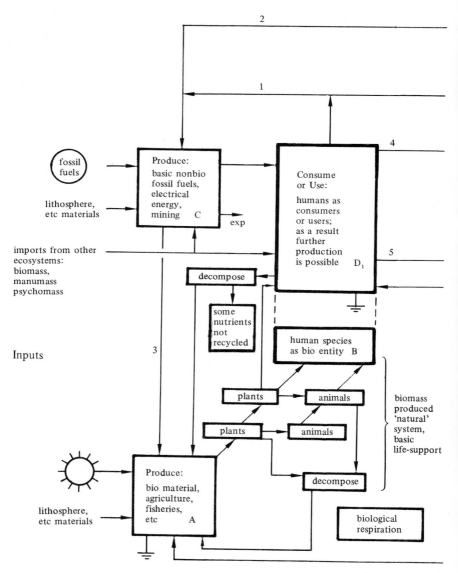

Figure 26.1. A possible way of diagramming an ecosystem dominated by a large human population. The bionic support of the human population is shown bottom left, producing biomass (including man himself and his food). Top left, human activity results in inputs of fossil fuels, assembly of natural materials for human purposes, etc. On these two areas of production secondary, tertiary, quaternary production are built. Secondary production (manumass) of goods and services is shown in the upper-right sequence of niches—upper levels being made possible by lower levels. The production

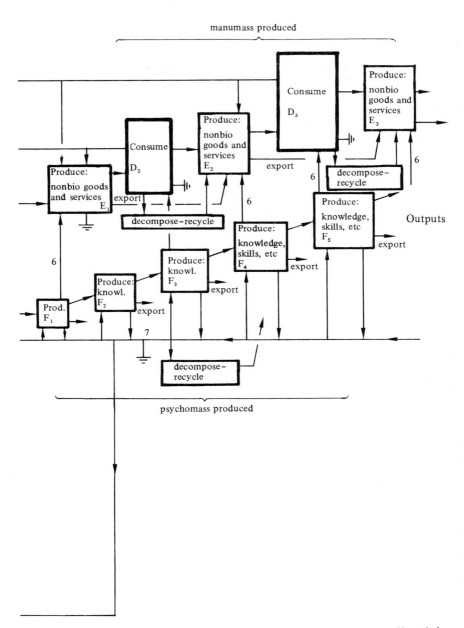

manumass produced

psychomass produced

of knowledge, etc (psychomass) is shown below the manumass production. Knowledge is built on knowledge by processes of synergy. The production of manumass and biomass has limits. There are none to the production of psychomass. The sequences of manumass and psychomass are diagrammed about the same size to acknowledge our present situation in the highly developed countries of about half the employment being information-based.

A description of the logic of the diagram now follows. This logic is an attempt at a synthesis which might be described as a component of a world view: it is a way of looking at major items which constitute our human condition in their basic relationships. The diagram should, however, be regarded as a tool for thinking about these things in this way rather than as a literal descriptive statement. It is intended as a learning aid.

If the reader will start at the bottom left-hand corner of the diagram he will quickly recognize a highly compressed statement of an ecosystem diagrammed with emphasis on the producer–consumer–decomposer ecosystemic cycle. Three trophic levels (niches) are shown, the top level occupied by human beings thought of as in the taxonomy of biology. This is basic to the whole conceptualization since *Homo sapiens* appears as a product, the top predator of the ecosphere. We must assume his appearance to be a phenomenon of 'nature', and it is basically, but not entirely, 'nature' which still feeds him. The original energy input to this part of the total system is from the sun in contemporary photosynthesis and the materials are those present naturally in the hydrosphere, lithosphere, and atmosphere.

In the next part of the diagram the emphasis shifts to the human capacity to consume. The rationale for this is that consumption takes precedence over production for the simple reason that the organism must consume to exist, irrespective of whether it produces: the human being has no choice but to continue to ingest the products of photosynthesis, or die. Hence he is consumer *par excellence*, but in order to increase the quantity of material for consumption he has developed a *psychic* capability to produce. The origin of the dynamic remains consume—shown as the large box D_1, which is inhabited in the developed countries by our friend the mass individual.

The drive to consume leads first directly through feedback 1, and later through feedback 2 as production process builds on production process, to tapping sources of stored biomass from ancient ecosystems—the fossil fuels. Some of the energy from these is fed back into the basic life-support part of the diagram, along line 3, in order to obtain more human-usable biomass from the ecosystems that are hominized. This 'extra' food allows the support of more human biomass—populations can be bigger. Some of the energy from fossil fuels goes directly into the box Consume D_1, to energize both Consume itself and the trophic levels of physical production—E_1, E_2, ... The primary-production box C also includes the manipulation of materials from the lithosphere and atmosphere, and biological material not used for food (the diagram here leaves out the ecosystemic relationship for nonfood bioproducts).

This basic nonbio production (C), through the Consume function D_1, generates upper levels of production which hierarchically ascend, each level making new possibilities available in a trophic level above it. Each upper level 'feeds' on the levels below it, as do the biota in the trophic levels of an ecosystem. Because we have learned how to make sheet steel we can build ocean liners—a simple example. More impressive, because we have learned how to achieve high refinement of certain elements we have been able to create electronic equipment capable of enormously enhancing our ability for mental process. Each of the levels of production, $E_1, E_2, ...,$ has its own special 'consume' level, $D_2, D_3, ...$. There are limits to the output of these trophic levels of physical production (manumass) and there are perhaps limits to the number of trophic levels. Consume $D_2, D_3, ...$ are restrained by feedback along lines 1 and 2 leading to the basic production C.

Consume D_1, as well as stimulating the trophic levels of the production and consumption of physical goods and services (manumass), stimulates the mental processes to discover *how* to produce. So Consume D_1 has a primary link, line 5, to the psychosupport part of the total system. This is the sequence of trophic levels which produce psychomass: knowledge, information, artistic production, expertise, etc. Although this sequence is also hierarchical, each upper level being made possible only by the levels below it, unlike the physical production sequence, it is without known upper limit. We do not at present fear that we shall encounter serious restriction of our ability to produce new knowledge at some point in the future. Knowledge, as a total psychomass, will grow whether or not a particular line of enquiry may reach a dead end. There are no limits to output as in an ecosystem, or to growth as understood in a socioeconomy. This area of psychosupport is a potentially inexhaustible growth area. No consume boxes are shown between the trophic levels because although psychomass is *used* it is not *consumed*, or destroyed by being used. It is used, of course, by all the Consume boxes, $D_1, D_2, D_3, ...$ etc and by all the produce boxes, A, C, $E_1, E_2, ...$ and by the boxes in its own trophic range, $F_1, F_2, F_3, F_4, F_5, ...$.

The control loops which relate the mass individual to the group are essentially in the trophic levels of the psychosupport and feed back into Consume D_1 along line 7, and into the trophic levels of manumass production through line 6.

Since for definition of thinking the system is best given some limits, the diagram can be thought of as imaging one of many global total subsystems which must be in relationship with other similar systems (including past ecosystems and psychosystems) and with the sun, whose energy constitutes an input from outside the system. We can therefore show inputs from outside—from other ecosystems as raw materials, energy, and biomass, from other total subsystems as manumass and psychomass. There will also be outputs in these same categories. These are shown at various points in the diagram as considered exported from the total system under consideration.

The diagram has some serious weaknesses, which are difficult to rectify. First, the element of change over time is hard to diagram. A diagram for illustrating the early period of human emergence, for example, would show quite a different weighting of the parts. The basic life-support would then be in much greater evidence. Produce A and the two sequences of trophic levels would be much less developed and emphasized. Looking to the future from where we are, the psychosupport may be expected to acquire greater prominence and the Produce E_1, E_2, ... somewhat less; as the information society develops still further, its information sector and the Produce E_1, E_2, ... tend to stabilize or have reduced growth.

Second, the notion of the working of what we may still call the socio-economy is a dynamic which does not show up in the diagram very strongly because it is essentially in the flow lines. The diagram is not organizational but records *functioning*—the words used are verbs. The flows are linkages of actions. To show this is to some extent to stress the dynamic and underplay the structure. This kind of problem, of course, bedevils all such diagramming techniques.

Third, the input–output aspect has difficulties. It implies that the system must be conceived as system within an environment. This is workable provided we remember that the environment is itself constituted of similar systems. That is not easy to conceptualize and may well be a cause of confusion. This is a particular case, perhaps, of the general difficulties which surround the concept *entity–environment*—difficulties which some, for example Bateson, try unsuccessfully to get around by saying the system is the system plus its environment!

In spite of these difficulties the diagram may provide some help in thinking out how to escape from some of the pitfalls inherent in raising ecological theory in its present form to serve as a theory for handling the conceptualization of a total system, or in structuring socioeconomies in biological vacuums, or in generating and maintaining a kind of mass-individual character profile which cannot survive long-term either biologically or societally. The essential purpose of the diagrammed conceptualization of a total system is simply to assist in improving the quality of the base on which we think about our approaches to action.

With a rather more emphatic operational approach the reader may find the discussion and theoretical framework for action in Jantsch (1975, page 207ff) useful. He struggles hard with the difficulties of synthesis: "... we ought to strive toward an intricately intermeshed way of thinking"— he is talking of goals and operational targets but he generally stresses the need to think multiply in various modes.

In the next chapter, however, another level of difficulty must be considered.

Some tightly tied knots

Although it is not unreasonable to attempt to identify key areas of the dynamics of our situation and from them to try to define areas of action, as we have done in the previous chapter, at best we have to admit that any such efforts must inevitably take place in the context of very serious gaps in our knowledge.

Some of these gaps might perhaps be filled if we were to recognize them and make determined efforts in the right directions. For example, we could very quickly obtain extremely valuable experience in integrating designed ecosystems with highly productive short food chains, after the Nissan example, with planned socioeconomic arrangements. The knowledge so obtained would almost certainly be of very great immediate value to the developing countries. Or, again, much faster development of teletuition— provided the purposes for increasing access to knowledge were properly thought out—would be likely to benefit developed and developing countries, since the process of human adaptation will now have to take place largely through the growth and diffusion of psychomass.

Some difficulties, however, cannot be described as gaps that we may hope to fill but rather as conundrums or enigmas. They are sometimes dilemmas in which taking either choice has very serious disadvantages. They are sometimes indicative of the need to change our thinking so drastically as to be virtually unacceptable, for example the possibility of a massive reduction in advertising in order to reverse consumerist attitudes. The difficulties of this kind, already exposed in this book, will now be listed together so that they can be seen as a group of a special type. They are perhaps usefully thought of as knots which we may hope to untie in time, or at least loosen, or which we may have to cut.

27.1 Limits to the hominization of ecosystems

One approach to what our attitude toward the global life-support system should be is to regard the biosphere as in a condition of 'nature' which will be stable as long as we do not interfere with it too much. The approach along this line is strongly supported by ideas of preservation and conservation: it sees the globe as a sort of Garden of Eden that we must be careful to keep in good order, as it was given to us.

This approach, which may lead to a very narrow concept of the human role of stewardship of the biosphere, has in it much which is clearly right, but also much that ignores the evolutionary development of many ecosystems under human influence. It also may lead to unrealistic action in the present condition of the total system. What is right is the attitude of respect for the dynamics of ecosystems that is generated. This respect is without doubt a necessary component of any viable attitude toward our life-support system. What is underplayed is the fact that human activity has been, and is, a major component in the making of the ecosystems in their contemporary condition. There really is no longer in existence a 'natural' system, at any rate on land in the world's temperate zones, and hardly in the tropical; only the Arctic and Antarctic might be claimed as still largely 'natural'.

The second item underplayed by this approach is that the attitudes it engenders with regard to the needs of human populations are characterized by a certain lack of realism. Hungry nations have a drive to eat *now*, and will sacrifice later ecosystem stability to satisfy that need. For the starving, good ecological behaviour is likely to be out of reach because it nearly always requires present constraint and restraint.

Rather by implication—attention to control loops and to various linkages—than by explicit statement this book has dismissed this approach to our stance toward human action in ecosystems. This dismissal leaves the field clear for other approaches, but does not therefore automatically lead to an unassailable logic for deciding our attitude.

An approach worthy of very serious consideration consists of admitting the threat that human numbers and their needs present to the contemporary condition of the world's ecosystems, in that increased throughputs of energy, in the mode of agribusiness, may well actually reduce their output of food. We are already aware of a situation of diminishing returns in this regard. In short, the continued application of technology in our present ways may not only be reaching its limits but may also be creating the conditions for ecosystemic regression. A suggested counterploy is to 'ecologize' technology. This means to insert our human intervention into ecosystemic processes—*as the ecosystems now exist in their present hominized condition and not conceived as totally 'natural' systems*—in ways that accord symbiotically with the ecosystem's dynamics. Thus we hope we may achieve both stability in the system and life support for very large human populations. So far, so good. We have looked at experiments that try to do this, with some success at very small scale. The difficulties that comprise this knot occur as soon as we think of applying the 'ecologization' of technology on the large scale demanded by the need to maintain our present mass populations. At once we are in head-on collision with our established developed socioeconomies.

These socioeconomies, whether free enterprise or other, run on the production–job–wages–consumption linkage in the developed countries. The individual must increasingly consume in order to be able to have the money necessary for buying food. In its present form this linkage drives in exactly the opposite direction from the ecologization of technology, and increasingly short-circuits the processes of ecosystems. The problem then appears in the light of the need to change the socioeconomies.

This seems to be a hopeful enough conclusion until we look at the various ways in which thinkers from different backgrounds underpin their arguments with largely unexamined assumptions. A paper by Neilands

(1976) is a compact demonstration. Neilands himself is an American. He thinks a steady-state biosphere must be reached by our going 'lean' and 'living lightly', the individual being considerably dependent on an increasing measure of self-support. This would achieve a reduction in the global rate of development. Such reduction is a presumed desideratum for most thinkers in the West. In contrast with this approach, which we recognize as stabilization, Soviet academician N P Fedorenko (quoted in Neilands, 1976) presses the view that it is not reduction of the rate of development which is necessary—that would be a very serious deprivation for some populations—but the development of "an ecologically efficient technology". In his perspective this will be achieved by "a socialist organization of the world". In other words, the socioeconomy in which technology is embedded will produce the ecologization of the technology, provided it is organized on socialist principles! There is, of course, no necessary logical connection between the two ideas, as is indeed indicated in real life when we look at the consistently poor output of Soviet agriculture, particularly when compared with the high level of output obtained in many countries dependent on private enterprise in agricultural production (see Ward, 1976, page 183ff). R Lother (Berlin, GDR; also quoted in Neilands, 1976) sees it with a different emphasis but along the same line. He criticizes Neilands' view for being a limited empirical approach within a context dominated by capitalist assumptions of profit and competition among monopolies. Stabilization is acceptable as a restraint to be imposed upon competitors! To Lother it is not technical progress which is the enemy but the nature of the capitalist socioeconomies. C Pawelzig (GDR) similarly insists that economic growth must not be restrained because there are so many people to feed but it must, and can be, carried out without degrading ecosystems. His conclusion is that: "The united planning, direction and control of the whole productive activities of society on a scientific basis and oriented to the fulfilment of the real needs of the people is on the agenda of history" (quoted in Neilands, 1976).

Enough has been given to illustrate the difficulty: what is technologically conceivable is not, at this operational level, necessarily societally achievable, at least partly because we have no common concept of society. For the first time in history we are aware that we ourselves are key components in a globally imaged physical, dynamic world system whose components and interactions we have learned how to alter. We *see* the possible danger of continued intervention along present lines, particularly in relation to our technologies. We *think* we could modify our development and application of technology to obtain improved life support from the world system without jeopardizing its viability. We might see this as stabilization of the rate of growth in manumass or as the ecologization of technology. Both of these require massive socioeconomic change as seen through the eyes of thinkers in the West. And they do not know how to achieve the change. The thinkers of the Eastern persuasion appear rather to place emphasis on a continuing vigorous rate of increase in socioeconomic development, including the output of manumass, and hope to keep ecosystems viable by doing this through an ecologization of technology. This in its turn is seen as achievable by already established 'scientific' structures for socioeconomies. Both approaches are roughly at the same place in seeing the matter as essentially a question of the structure and working of the socioeconomy. The East is perhaps relatively certain that it already has reached, or can reach, a solution to the question of what kind of socioeconomy will do the job. The West can be said to be searching and is perhaps opening to a variety of possibilities, including that of ecologizing technology.

Both approaches are perhaps guilty of some avoidance of the main question. This is the very practical matter of knowing how far we can safely go in hominizing any ecosystem. The extreme conservationists tend to say we cannot go very far. The developers tend to say we have to take some risks, even to accept some ecosystemic degradation so that we can eat. The need is obviously for more and better knowledge of specifics. The least useful approach is one of predetermined 'solutions' of whatever ideological colour.

A benefit which comes from the attempt to state the difficulty is an appreciation of the need to be altogether more subtle about the idea of stabilization than we have been so far. Stabilization in the sense of no-growth is simply unacceptable for the developing countries. The pressure on them to struggle for growth is obviously enormous. On the other hand, in the developed countries a reduction in the rate of that growth which merely adds to the physical 'luxury' equipment or unnecessarily increases the energy throughput (for example, by built-in obsolescence) seems eminently sensible as a contribution to conserving energy resources and achieving their global redistribution in ways more equitable for ensuring the necessities of life for all. So the debate becomes not one simply of stopping or slowing up development or accelerating it, but of doing both these on a discriminating basis. The socioeconomic organizational question remains unsolved, however, since at present growth is clearly only erratically and sporadically under societal control in both the East and the West. Attention to this question of what should be *forced* to grow, what *allowed* to grow, what *discouraged* from growing, and what *prevented* from growing is perhaps an important pragmatic approach to deciding how to act in relation to ecosystem viability. We have suggested that in the developed countries growth in the information sector should be a high priority, and that this implies fostering the growth of certain kinds of psychomass. Among the types of psychomass development to be fostered most urgently should be the development of knowledge capable of producing leads in this difficulty we have identified. The history of the twentieth century might suggest that ideological approaches certainly bring problems of their own, and that at least an empirical approach has the merit of flexibility.

As we have indicated, the question of conscious, organized change in socioeconomies cannot be considered without taking account of the character profile and sensibility of the mass individual. This matter is of great relevance to the debate on how to deal with the global problem of ensuring life support for a very large population within the limits of eco-systemic viability. There are rules about constructing viable socioeconomies, and *those* rules should be considered to include something about the limits of psychic tolerance in the individual. We shall see later that the relation of this question with the one we have outlined here is really the manifestation of another knot—perhaps the most difficult of all to loosen.

27.2 Regulation of ongoing system processes

If we visualize our totality as systemic, that is, that the whole can be imaged as socioeconomies and ecosystems forming components of the total system, the regulatory arrangements controlling the ongoing processes are of cardinal interest. (We may note the difficulty of conceptualizing a total system, or fusion of our ecological and socioeconomic understandings, other than by systems thinking.) In the 'natural' ecosystem the regulatory mechanisms operate unself-consciously. For example, Todd's bullhead fish regulate their numbers and the size to which they grow chemicosocially. As far as is known, fish do not have committee meetings. The regulation is chemical inasmuch as it relies on changes in the availability of nutritional material in the environment (the water) and signals provided by the effluents of the fish themselves. It is social inasmuch as it relates to groups of fish. But the fish do not design their regulatory mechanisms; whatever they consist of, they are supposed to have evolved and to operate unself-consciously.

For entirely 'natural' systems in which human beings play either no part at all or only a negligible role, this conceptualization is adequate and, on the basis of observation, appears to correspond well with everything we know about ecosystems. However, ecosystems are now widely dominated by human beings on a global scale. Characteristic of this domination is that the human beings act very considerably as specialized control groups or components of the ecosystems. This human controlling process is at any rate powerful enough to arrest the drive of ecosystems to reach their highest levels of succession and to repress them permanently into their 'young' phases. *Therefore the regulatory function is no longer generally diffused throughout the components and processes of the system as a whole.*

The model of the unself-conscious 'natural' evolutionary development of life-conserving regulatory processes in living systems is held by some thinkers to be appropriate for socioeconomies: Adam Smith's hidden hand. We have seen that Beer used this concept as an assumed underpinning for the 'Chilean process'. His basic idea was to make the production process, in particular, as transparent as possible in the expectation that increased transparency would allow the system itself to make its own 'natural' controls effective. This is to assist the hidden hand by giving it electronic capability. The assumption that the hand knows what it is doing remains the same—an as unsubstantiated assumption as it was before. The reasoning used by Beer is that, although we are able to understand the working of designed systems and can therefore devise controls for them, we do not understand very complex systems, such as the socioeconomy, and cannot regulate them in this way. Therefore it is necessary that we view these complex systems as self-regulatory and capable of developing internally their own control mechanisms. Such controls work by identifying pathological conditions, not by looking for the cause of the perturbation to be controlled (Beer, 1975, page 108ff).

Our century, however, has demonstrated a vigorous dissatisfaction with this unself-conscious control model for socioeconomic matters, however acceptable it may be ecologically. We have been emotionally moved by observing the clumsiness and injustice of the hidden hand. We will not tolerate in human societies the degree of individual suffering that is inherent in the processes of natural selection in nature. We therefore *consciously* generate specific control mechanisms to mitigate the harsher effects of unself-conscious regulation. Modern developed socioeconomies are very complex webs highly dependent on such specially designed controls. We forbid physical slavery, give protection against death by starvation, prevent physical death struggles for food and territory, develop cooperative activities, etc. It can be argued that it is precisely because human beings have been able to generate such 'artificial' regulatory elements through cultural and societal innovation that the human species has been able to be as successful as it is.

'Human' systems therefore differ fundamentally from 'natural' systems in that their control processes are at least in part consciously devised. Yet it is obvious that this conscious control is in harness with regulatory processes which we must still count as unself-conscious, if only because we do not understand them and therefore cannot manage them. One such of these, as we have suggested, lies in the region describable as the mass individual's behaviour in relation to ecosystem viability. This area of hitherto unself-conscious regulation may now have broken down so that large numbers of mass individuals may behave in ways aggregatively destructive of their physical life support. It does not matter for the present argument whether we diagnose this condition as an existing loop failing in its function or the 'abnormal' emergence of a malign loop. The dilemma is the unself-conscious–self-conscious nature of the regulatory mechanism, which is the knot.

The knot has to do with the problem of complexity of variables acknowledged by Beer and others. Yet we cannot leave things entirely to the hidden hand. If the hidden hand is making mistakes, electronification of its processes is as likely to do harm as good. We seem forced to the self-conscious construction of regulatory mechanisms, but in a context of only very limited knowledge of how the total system is designed and functions. Controls consciously devised are therefore always in danger of producing unanticipated effects that themselves become unacceptable components of the system. We seem forced to have to live with a mix of unself-conscious and self-conscious regulation.

What kind of a system is it in which one component—human beings—consciously continuously redesigns parts of the system's regulatory processes? It is no longer a 'natural' system, and yet human beings are still part of the totality of the natural world and can never stand outside it. (We have some familiarity with this difficulty in our wrestlings with the results of our having modelled our approaches in the societal disciplines on those used in the physical sciences.)

27.3 Dilemma of the cash socioeconomy in the ecological context

In the developed countries and progressively in many of the developing countries there is built in a major linkage between certain factors that makes changes connected with growth very difficult, regardless of the prevailing socioeconomic–political theory and practice. This is the production–job–wages–consumption nexus. Commodities, particularly food, can only be consumed through the exchange medium of money, which in its turn can be obtained by the adult population virtually only through having a job. A job means that products are generated, and these, if production is to be continued and jobs are to remain in being, must be consumed. Thus, in those socioeconomies which are heavily dependent on the production–job–wages–consumption linkage, we must consume goods and services in order to be able to eat.

In conjunction with other influences, technology in its general development, particularly because of the automated techniques available through the electronic technology, drives more and more toward the reduction of human inputs into a given production process even as it increases the product output. If we imagine the stabilization of the total physical output, we have to face the reduction in jobs, at any rate in connection with those activities devoted to generating physical goods. *This means that modifications have to be made to the production–job–wages–consumption linkage, or jobs have to be generated in a sector of socioeconomic activity which does not necessitate going beyond the stable state in physical output.*

The problem appears as two major squeezes coinciding in time in their pressures. We are under the necessity to modify our throughputs of energy in both biomass-producing and manumass-producing processes. Although in the former this could generate more jobs—on the land—it will not do so for some time. In the latter it means progressive reduction in the number of jobs available. The obvious socioeconomic 'solution' is the conscious development of new jobs which will confer the means to consume on some who do not have it. The socioeconomies must keep the production–job–wages–consumption linkage working at a reasonable level. To do this they are compelled, under the present arrangements, to accelerate the throughput. But for ecological stability throughput of energy ought to have some degree of reduction, if not stabilization.

This is a very terrible dilemma because breakdown of the linkage brings not only obvious socioeconomic difficulty but serious political troubles, 'solutions' to which may offer no guarantee whatever of relieving the key impasse.

As suggested in this book, perhaps we should be trying both to modify the linkage and to reinforce it. Modification would mean developing and running other linkages—production–consumption has been suggested—in parallel, and modifying the 'job' or the 'wages' component, or both, in relation to production and consumption. Reinforcement could be consciously attempted by forcing the development of the information sector so that it reverses its present *relative declining* growth rate and provides openings for workers becoming progressively redundant in the physical production sector. Further, this might be helped by using the electronic technology for increasing the number of transactions, enhancing the speed of transactions, and converting as many transactions as reasonably possible to electronic modes, and away from physical modes (for example, physical movement of the worker).

Whatever proposals may be offered, the dilemma seems likely to remain and will probably produce numerous cures worse than the disease. We no longer live in the kinds of socioeconomies which existed in the earlier part of this century when labour was a much more important component of the production process than it is now—we have shown the decline in the US from 1950. Nor, on the other hand, do we now live in an assumable situation of inexhaustible contemporary energy resources. In its present form, and in the present cultural–social–knowledge situation, the production–job–wages–consumption linkage is possibly a not very viable nexus as a component of the total world system. The operational difficulties surrounding attempts to alter it will be made the more intractable by the linkage already having reached a precarious state in some countries, for example, Britain, Italy, and Canada. Change in it cuts at the very base of life—food and shelter. The temptation to alleviate suffering by means that can be only short-term in ecosystem viability and resource utilization is very strong and may be expected to get stronger.

27.4 The propaganda pincer
The squeeze here is that, because we have mass populations composed of mass individuals with a certain character and sensibility profile, we could change behaviour and indeed the system itself by means of saturation propaganda. But in using this technique we would reinforce those very

qualities of the mass-individual profile which already inhibit needed action at the societal level.

The 'massification' of the individual is already strongly encouraged by the present ways of using the electronic technology, and by the role played by the massification process itself in holding together the production–job–wages–consumption linkage. We propagandize very heavily in order to sell ever more manufactured goods. The 'demand' for these in turn does something to maintain and generate job niches. To keep the society viable we need the mass individual to have a certain kind of personality profile which, among other things, is strongly oriented toward continuous consumption.

Unfortunately that profile, by very definition of the role it has to play, largely excludes the possibility of developing characteristics which would help generate and apply genuine solutions for other dilemmas. The mass individual can be propagandized into consuming less. But, if this ploy is successful, job opportunities must inevitably diminish, so that unless the production–job–wages–consumption syndrome can be modified or amplified simultaneously the nexus which holds society and individual together is endangered and government becomes enfeebled.

The pincer is that if we propagandize extensively we impair or fail to develop the individual responsibility essential for ecosystemic viability; if we do not propagandize we cannot link the mass individual to the mass society in permanently stable symbiosis.

The essence of the knot is perhaps that we have not found out how to have the mass individual behave both as a responsible person in terms of the society–individual nexus and as mass individual. In short, we do not know what are the real necessities or unavoidables of mass society. We do not, of course, even know that mass society has any long-term viability. We do not know, either, whether mass society, of our kind or any other kind, can exist permanently within the rules of ecosystemic viability. Worst of all, we may mistake a shortcut to disaster for a solution to perceived problems.

The two centuries previous to our own placed great faith in education as a way of at least partly cutting this kind of knot. Their thought gave sustained attention to the intelligent participation of the governed in the governing process. Obvious objections to this have been countered by stressing the need for a well-informed electorate. This has led to emphasis on education.

We must still hope along that line. But we now meet roadblocks that were invisible to earlier enthusiasts. We shall look at a major one in the next section. Strictly under the focus of attention of this section comes the difficulty that in the situation of which our knots are a part the education required is not that of learning chiefly facts—that of course has to be done—but of learning how to learn, and learning how to handle ideas. This is Bateson's (1972) deuterolearning or Lilly's (1974) metaprogramming. Unfortunately the mass individual's character profile and sensibility are not at all well suited to this kind of mature interior development. The mass individual is frequently *functionally successful* in our kind of socioeconomy precisely by being simultaneously factually knowledgeable and immature as a human being.

27.5 The outer–inner personality conflict in the mass individual
In reflecting on these matters, I have come to the conclusion that this is the most intractable difficulty of all because it is the most fundamental. So fundamental is it that we find it appearing under all sorts of guises, frequently unrecognized for what it is and without realization of the deadliness of its dynamics. It appears as failing motivation to learning or acting—*accidia*. It manifests itself as exaggeratedly emphatic adherence to esoteric cults and political doctrines. It comes in books that deal with science and society, and it is glimpsed in our occasional tentative speculations about how far rational action can safely be pushed.

We are now at the extreme opposite pole from that of the competence of the scientist and technologist as expert creators of ways of solving problems of a technical kind and are in the area in which it has to be decided *how* the technical knowledge is to be used, if at all. The problem is not necessarily that there is not a technical solution to a problem, but that we do not have a society–individual situation which permits the solution to be applied. Stafford Beer even believes that our thinking modes inhibit the creation of appropriate solutions. Among other factors, we are here in the area of will. We know how to correct a failing, but we do not have the will to carry it through. This is one way of expressing the difficulty. *The Limits to Growth* (Meadows et al, 1972) ended up underlining this dilemma.

Turning to science, we may see the human problem as a matter of developing the necessary knowledge, expertise, etc and applying it to shape our movement forward. "Our problem is to control our evolution, and this means to encourage freedom for the individual and provide an education for him to develop his power" (F H George, 1970b, page 165). George foresees the development and application of science to society as a whole as "... a new and overriding science of science ... science of systems" (page 156). This is a strong expression of the 'outer', the 'objective', the way of the discursive reason, of the ability to analyze and to assemble the findings into action.

In the next stage of looking at this area we have to record rising doubts about science. Doubts were not unknown before the diffusion of ecological knowledge, but it has been particularly in connection with our knowledge of ecosystems that science has, so to speak, been in some measure come to be questioned by science. This has led particularly to concern for some of the effects of applications of science where there is a strong relationship with the life-support system. There are many aspects to this question but the key point is perhaps that our technological applications frequently become widespread before firm scientific knowledge of the ecological impacts has been established (see Commoner, 1970, page 57ff). This has led to questionings about the integrity of science and technology and, to use Commoner's phrase, disquieting thoughts about "society versus science". Therefore the 'straight' approach of winning and applying scientific knowledge has suffered considerable erosion. We no longer feel ourselves to be in the innocent dawn of science and technology, but are assailed by doubts. This is a part of the present knot, but not the whole, and is not the deepest level at which it can be sensed.

The deepest level at which we need to give attention to the question of science and society is, in the light of what we have said about the mass individual, the relationship between knowledge and the will to action. There are two areas of dynamic: that of striving to know or learn, and that which has to do with carrying the knowledge out into action. The two are doubtless connected by many links, but most important must be a belief that the quest for knowledge and the effort of action are both worthwhile. The sense of worthwhileness is a product of the 'inner' or 'subjective' activity of the personality. We cannot pursue the development of science or promote its application to societal matters unless we feel it worthwhile to make the effort. There are various ways of describing what is required for the feeling of worthwhileness to be present: involvement, identification with the perceived need, a sense of personal worth, commitment, etc, but however it is said the key essential is that the total inner self, and not solely the discursive reason, must be properly engaged.

We have seen that the mass individual—that is, ourselves—has inner or subjective difficulties. The area of concern here is his progressive loss of affective relationship with the pursuit of 'objective' knowledge—that is, science. We have seen that characteristically he is now able to experience the discoveries of science and its technological applications only as remote and beyond his assimilative scope. He has come to take the offerings of science and technology for granted, as products of the natural order, and experiences himself as outside their creative processes. *This alienation from the best that we know erodes his inner sense of worth and fosters a feeling of helplessness in the face of unknown and unmanageable forces, whether natural or wielded by human beings.*

We may see the rise of the contemporary existentialist affirmation as a manifestation of our feeling that the inner or subjective has been squeezed out by the enormous pressure and material success of the outer or objective during the last two centuries. *It is a cry for the reinstatement of the core of the experiencing self as a partner in both knowing and acting.* Polanyi (1958) has said it by stressing that knowledge in the end is personal—inner—however objective it may be in its approach to the outer world. The best known expression of the emphasis is perhaps the 'I–Thou' or 'I-in-the-Thou' of Martin Buber (1968). Maslow (1969) has suggested that a new scientific approach to this question is necessary and perhaps possible. Rogers (in Wann, 1965) has said much the same thing. These last two writers are impressive because they reach their conclusions out of lifetimes of clinical experience.

This reaffirmation of the claims of the inner or subjective focus of the personality can be very well argued as an essential redressing of a long-standing imbalance, and the case made that this is a healthy and hopeful evidence of change in the personality structure of the mass individual. However, its more popular manifestations, as opposed to its more rarified intellectual variations, are anything but reassuring. We have seen what George Steiner thinks of them. The shift appears to reinforce rather than reduce the mass individual's sense of living in a world of alien 'powers', and hence to expose him to a recrudescence of belief in magic particularly dangerous in a society very heavily dependent on a certain kind of rationality for its continuance.

This brings us to the first circle of our present difficulty. This is that having recently come to understand the finiteness of our life-support system we now need the very rapid development of knowledge appropriate for handling our new situation. We know a good deal of the danger and human tragedy inherent in the syndrome population–food–energy viewed as a global dynamic. Tackling this situation is a matter of objective knowledge, will, and action. The inwards diversion, at this moment, of psychic attention to the psyche itself when so much effort is necessary towards the objective or outer direction of attention, at best will have some weakening effect and at worst may encourage a complete failure of will in mass populations. *The turning inwards, with its distrust of and aversion of the external facts of the objective, comes precisely at the moment when a great objective effort, necessarily backed up by the support of the mass individual* en masse, *appears essential for ensuring the viability of the life-support system.* George Steiner sees the strength of our existential concern in the perspective of an overturning of basic values: "... the value-structure of our civilization will alter, after at least three millenia, in ways almost unforeseeable" (Steiner, 1971, page 73). If this is indeed so, the great human concern is whether the degree of objective attention we shall be able to muster will be sufficient to keep the behaviour of the mass individual and the mass society in realistic relation with each other and with the workings of the life-support system.

The dilemma is that, if the objective or outer concern is now pushed too hard, further erosion of motivation towards it may be generated in the mass individual. If that occurs, objective attention to the life-support system will be further eroded. If, however, adequate objective attention is not paid to keeping the life-support system viable, society will be endangered through the human subsystems which ensure the material base of existence, themselves failing because of lack of the essentials of life.

The second round of this dilemma concerns our assumptions about the nature of knowledge, and our attitudes toward action. In general, our prevalent attitude to dealing with ecosystems is the sequence used above: find the necessary knowledge and apply it. This is the general assumption underlying all planning; it is typical of our time. Much of what we have looked at in this book proceeds from this largely unexamined assumption, including the suggestions put forward in the previous chapter. We think in terms of goals and means for achieving them; the intention and the instrumentality of its realization, as two clearly separated components.

In the light of what we have noted above about linkage between inner–outer and the mass individual in the contexts of mass society and the total global system, this assumption of how to proceed may be misleading, or even dangerous. Some analysts have expressed very serious doubts. The root of the doubt is precisely the question of what effect the application of objective knowledge to the individual has on the individual's own inner perception of himself and the world. If the effect produced turns out to be still further erosion of the individual's sense of self-worth and worthwhileness of the objective, we have to question whether the application of knowledge, especially knowledge derived from the social disciplines and applied to societal matters, in the end does not have a manipulative stigma and a corrosive outcome.

Bateson (1972, page 159ff) draws attention to this very serious difficulty "... the conflict is now a life-or-death struggle over the role which the social sciences shall play in the ordering of human relationships" (page 162). We might add that the difficulty is no less if we consider it in relation to the relationships between human beings and their life support. The issue may be seen as a moral choice—do we manipulate people in order to get society to function properly, or do we regard such manipulation as self-defeating of the very stability we are trying to achieve because it damages the individual's sense of the worthwhile?

Bateson refers to some observations along this same line by Margaret Mead (1942). She sees it as a question of how we have been acculturated to perceive means and ends; she would deemphasize goals-and-means thinking and stress *directions* of development. This, she thinks, would steer us away from the tendency towards totalitarianism inherent in our present perceptions and would enhance our democratic tendencies. The suggested focus of attention is, in Bateson's words, "... to find the value of a planned act implicit in and simultaneous with the act itself, not separate from it in the sense that the act would derive its value from reference to a future end or goal" (Bateson, 1972, page 160). This is difficult to grasp as an idea, let alone apply. But perhaps it cuts to the very centre of our knot, especially when we think of the enormous capability for manipulation already demonstrated by our electronic technology, and of the instrumentality emphasis inherent in most of our approaches to planning.

Matson (1966) gets to much the same point but from a different direction. He thinks that we have moved from seeing all nature as an extension of our own selves to seeing ourselves naturalistically; we have moved from anthropomorphism to mechanomorphism. Behaviourism, he thinks, is the attempt to perfect this switch. Across this cuts the fact of consciousness, which includes consciously planned behaviour, or planned societal organization, or planned intervention in 'natural' processes, such as those of ecosystems. The objective approach to behaviour, or action, may tell us much about a great deal, but it cannot tell us how to act as an inner decision, as a moral formulation. With considerable wit Matson goes on to comment that because we have embraced the mechanical–rational model so uncritically, when we see it fail we are driven to the conclusion that it is human behaviour which is irrational and not the model that is unreasonable (Matson, 1966, page 235).

A way of expressing this with different emphasis is to say that we do not know how far the 'objectivization' of knowledge about the human being himself is safe societally, is capable of further development, or is able to deliver genuine knowledge in its present modes.

Our difficulty is therefore a multiple one. We have the question of whether the mass individual can tolerate the objectivity necessary to ensure behaviour toward the life-support system adequate for its viability. If he cannot, the objective modes of knowledge will suffer some damage. We are by no means certain, however, that these modes themselves lead to the balance of knowledge and values required for continuing the human enterprise successfully. Policies developed as seemingly appropriate for the task may, in operation, prove to push matters precisely opposite to the desired direction. If, however, we welcome the tendency of the mass individual to appear to redress an imbalance that has overemphasized the objective, the outward-directed attention, we observe ourselves impaled upon the pike of the paralysed will to action in a systemic context demanding well-informed and vigorous action upon the outer world. We now see some of the difficulties connected with either accepting or rejecting the behaviourism of Skinner and the sociobiology of Wilson. Accepting alone and as sole explanation cannot give us guides to action, but to reject is to throw away the only path to action in which we have any present confidence. *Both approaches look at the human being naturalistically, which is exactly what the sensibility of the mass individual cannot tolerate. Yet it is this approach which has been so successful in giving us mastery over the natural world, the* outer *world*[1].

[1] The question of the degree of efficacy of reliance on the naturalistic approach to the study of human beings for understanding their behaviour is extremely complex. Suffice it to observe that it has for many in our age the emotional underpinning to sustain it as the only sound way to acquire such knowledge. Such a view does not, however, satisfy others as being even a component of an approach. I prefer the description 'naturalistic' to Matson's 'mechanomorphic' and the conventional 'dialectical

27.6 Regulation and the mass individual

In section 27.2 we noted the dilemma about conceptualizing the regulatory processes in a total systemic concept capable of dealing with both ecosystems and socioeconomies. For the present, it seems that we must admit controls that are both unself-conscious (not specifically designed by humans) and self-conscious (derived from human planning and intervention in the system's ongoing processes and evolutionary changes).

Amongst all the areas of regulation, that of the character profile and sensibility of the mass individual may be the most important. Regulation of these, or of the behaviour they lead to, will be necessary, especially if we considerably hold to the diffused and unself-conscious model of control. Regulation would have to be achieved to a considerable extent *within* the individual, since to regulate mostly from outside him would be to impose a self-defeating control, and therefore in effect to abandon the model. The meaning of this appears to be that if we assume the diffused model to be adequate we have to render a satisfactory description of how the 'inner' control is to be achieved in the mass individual. Ryan, we have seen (chapter 11), would expect this to be a product of the mass individual fully appreciating himself as a component of the total system, this appreciation being achieved by a technical process very much more sophisticated than Beer's assumption that the eudemony, the sense of well-being, expressed by the algedonic meters from the ground up in the society, will accord for certain with what is necessary for the survival of all. The weakness of Beer's use of the 'natural' ecosystemic conceptualization of diffused regulation lies precisely here. What if the general view of well-being consists of generally slacking off work or plundering the stores?

Beer, and others, are basically optimistic about the character profile and sensibility of the mass individual. Give him a chance to participate in the decisions that affect him, give him good material and mental conditions of life, and he will respond with the basic good that is in him. To say the least, this is an unproved affirmation; it is not a known fact. We therefore come to see that the assumptions or conceptualizations that we entertain about the nature of the mass individual will have a great deal to say about the model of society we shall generate and strive to operationalize.

materialistic', as being a simpler and more direct term. I am personally sympathetic to the naturalistic approach for describing certain aspects of both 'mind' and society, but leave open-ended the question of whether it can be a total description, since 'mind'—indeed a natural phenomenon—is also a systemic self-generator incapable, as yet, of adequate description. It is hard to see how the mass individual could wholeheartedly embrace the totally naturalistic view of his own interior workings, considering its inherent inability to satisfy his existential need. That human beings have developed 'mind' with several different basic underpinnings—animism, anthropomorphism, and the naturalistic approach (that is, reflecting what we have learned of the natural world onto ourselves as self-image of our own workings) is indication that 'mind' can operate successfully for long periods of time on a variety of different basic assumptions. We like to think that our own is nearest the 'truth', but outside the hard sciences we have no proof that it is.

Such an observation can scarcely claim novelty. Western thought has addressed a great deal of attention to this matter, demonstrating a swing from an older view that the human being would not behave as necessary for the good of the whole purely by reason of natural endowment, to the modern view, first articulately held by Rousseau, that human beings are inherently good; only circumstances make them behave badly. *What is new about the above observation is that this debate is given entirely new meaning by the application of our recently acquired knowledge of ecosystems, by our new-found ability to conceptualize society by means of systemic applications of knowledge and knowledge handling (models, simulations, computer assistance), and by our electronic capability for managing very large and complex systems. Our concept of the human being lies at the very root of how we shall conceptualize human society, therefore of how we shall construct our conceptualizations, and therefore of what it will be that we shall operationalize. That the view held of the human being was equally at the root of these things before we had access to our present knowledge is true. What is different is that we are moving towards a condition of greater transparency. This is the effect of improved knowledge. This is the 'difference that makes the difference'.*

The fundamental difficulty of the two basic views of the character and sensibility of the mass individual remains unsolved. The knot appears to be that, if the mass individual's profile is as described by Ortega y Gasset and others we have drawn upon, he is a component running wild in a system which is conceived as self-regulating through diffusion of control; and assumptions as to his behaving as is necessary for the safety of the whole are dangerous, unjustified optimism if we perceive the system as in considerable degree regulated by unself-conscious processes.

If, on the other hand, still assuming the given profile, we opt for a system containing highly specialized self-conscious control functions, must we abandon the idea of general democratic participation in the guidance and management of the whole—a vision indeed likely to be realizable through the use of the electronic technology and the conceptualizations its use encourages?

27.7 The double nature of information

Although we may demonstrate that the developed countries may be conceived as already in the information society, we have as yet little conceptualization of how an informational socioeconomy works. This is perhaps in considerable degree attributable to the very curious fact that information is an unexpendable economic 'good'. It can be used, consumed, yet it remains to be consumed again and again. This wreaks havoc with our conventional ways of looking at socioeconomies.

Information has been partly incorporated into our established patterns for handling physical commodities and services. Some information is bought and sold in familiar ways. A great deal is not, and an increasing number of occupations and activities or transactions have to do with information which is not seen primarily as commodity.

As improved information leads to increased automation of the production of physical goods *and* of the handling of information itself, there is the problem of how to conceptualize information and, having done that, of how to operationalize the conceptualization into a predominantly informational socioeconomy. Do we have to 'commoditize' it more — make it more of a market component? Or do we have to erect a superstructure of a different kind of 'upper' economy based on information? A useful thought may be the observation that socioeconomic development is essentially an operation in which a society raises itself by its own bootstraps. If this is so, the idea may hold for the information society just as well as for the industrial society which we have already transcended.

In what words one tries to describe this knot is perhaps not very important at this stage. The important thing is the realization that the knot is generated by the now dominant role of information in our society and our almost total lack of ability to conceptualize it.

27.8 An operational knot

Superficially examined, our ecological concern and our focus of attention on 'the environment' might appear to be the same from an operational standpoint. This is not so, and in terms of action the difference presents a possibly major future difficulty.

The concern for ensuring ecosystem viability stresses the systemic nature of the life-support process and emphasizes that the whole congeries of subprocesses must be maintained viable if the whole is to remain stable and therefore continue to support human beings. In this perspective pollution is the degradation of subsystems, or an excess of random matter which is not playing a life-maintaining role in the total system. In a fully viable ecosystem there is very little matter which is random in this sense. The system is either circulating matter or holding it in 'assemblies', such as organisms or consociations or communities.

Our focus on the environment, on the other hand, is not necessarily committed to any such systemic view. It may be satisfied with a narrowly human point of departure which simply concerns itself with 'not fouling the nest'. The idea is that it will be sufficient to clean up the mess we make with our industrial processes, our urban sprawl, our use of motor-cars, etc. The costs of cleaning up can be estimated and charged to the polluters. This approach appears through such activities as 'pollution abatement', 'environmental impact assessment', and 'environmental planning and control'.

The present operational situation is that the environmental approach is being considerably operationalized. This may be expected to increase. As likely to improve the experienced quality of the human environment, it is wholly to be applauded. Yet there is the difficulty that, if the full ecological approach is really the right one, our environmentalism offers no certainty of guaranteeing attention to maintaining the viability of ecosystems at the necessary new levels of productivity required to sustain the increasing global population. We have tried to show how complex are the relationships which have to be safeguarded to ensure this.

There is, therefore, the difficulty that decisionmakers will be satisfied with a cleanup approach and wholly miss the systemic necessities of the life-support process. In the field of operations this represents a formidable difficulty because the cleanup *appears* to satisfy the requirements.

Along the 'environmental' perspective there is the further complexity that a cleanup operation may require measures actually antagonistic to the welfare of the greater whole. For example, the control of the quality of emission from motor vehicles may be satisfactory from the point of view of achieving cleaner air in cities. But it can require an increase in fuel consumption that increases the total energy throughput precisely in the context of the need to reduce that throughput. There are also the obvious frictions within the socioeconomy (for example, reduction in jobs) if costs of pollution abatement, etc are more than the market will bear.

The knot appears essentially to be that of how to get the matter dealt with, in practical affairs, at the proper levels of conceptualization and operationalization.

Can we deal with the knots?

28.1 Necessity to act simultaneously with thinking

Attention to the existence of the knots or underlying difficulties considered in the previous chapter should not reduce our efforts to act to the best of our current knowledge. The knots will, perhaps, loosen only as a result of our both acting in the world of existing conditions and trying to grapple intellectually with the difficulties. It seems unlikely that they will be untied exclusively by thinking, although some loosening may be achieved thereby. Ecosystems are physical systems, and although we act upon them with 'mind', their performance is physically manifest. Degradation, output of human-usable biomass, and the numbers of human beings that can be carried are measurable.

The paucity of examples of sophisticated ecosystem management for human purposes within the systemic requirements of viability constitutes a very serious deficiency in the present phase and condition of the human enterprise. A very rapid acceleration of experiments in this field is necessary if the increasing world population is to be fed, even at present levels.

Theoretically, it would be very much better to have the knots untied before wholesale experiment takes place. In practice this is not possible. Therefore the two processes will have to go on simultaneously, with as much cross-fertilization as possible. In the meantime we can probe for ways of dealing with the knots.

28.2 Some tentative suggestions for dealing with the knots

The following are some directions we might explore. They are, of course, not intended as an all-inclusive list.

1 If we are going to admit the need for the consciously directed shaping of the character and sensibility of the mass individual (this assumes some passably acceptable solution to the propaganda pincer) we should try to reinforce his willingness toward the objective approach, but without unduly pressing against the manifest need for a larger place for the subjective sense of self. Operational areas of prime importance for doing this might be:

(a) Propagate the knowledge of ecosystems' organization and working with as much 'deobjectivization' as possible and a maximization of the sense of the individual being personally a functioning part of the ecosystemic process. This is, in a sense, a kind of 'descientized' scientific approach.

(b) Maximize the initiatory function of the mass individual in the operation of the applications of the electronic technology. This includes the acceleration of the development of the technology itself in order to get the mass individual as rapidly as possible away from the present passivity to the situation where he originates material, and the reorganization of broadcast TV, cable TV, access to computer capability, etc to assist this.

2 Concentrate on alternatives to our present assumptions of the all-purpose efficacy of technological rationality. This means developing other ways of approaching action than goals–policies–implementation or formulation of goals and the bringing to bear of means available. This implies trying to understand action as sometimes or in some degree *worthwhile in itself*, not solely for its degree of accomplishment of an aim. Operationally this might include:

(a) Deemphasize both purpose and instrumentality by strengthening those areas of the personality of the mass individual in which the action and the goal are fused. This means such things as the arts, sport, public affairs, etc in which the individual can participate actively, motivations of instrumentality being discouraged.

(b) Reconstruct the culture industry to help the above.

(c) Separate clearly the activity of science as free enquiry for its own sake, from science geared—entirely legitimately—to specific humanitarian and societal goals. Science has to be able to play fully both these roles and both must be given full cultural and societal approval.

3 Strenuous intellectual effort is required to reach conclusions about the degrees of validity of behaviourism and sociobiology for assisting the human enterprise in its new global context and for understanding what can be done along their perspectives for the character and sensibility of the mass individual in the context of electrobionic culture. Operationally the following appear important:

(a) increase of research in these areas, particularly practical experiments related to human behaviour;

(b) relating behaviourism and sociobiology to other modes of knowing, for example, experiential forms of acquiring and ordering knowledge;

(c) avoiding ideological entanglements arising from overemphasizing either empirical or theoretical assumptions of approach.

4 Develop as many ways of acquiring knowledge alternative to our present technological–rational mode as possible, particularly in regard to alternatives that deeply implicate the subjectivity of the knower, but with enlargement, not impairment, of our present objective mode of enquiry. There is an honourable lineage to this idea—Whitehead (1958), Conant (1965), Maslow (1969), Polanyi (1958)[1].

5 Operationally the above effort must be deeply implicated in action since the chief alternative mode is the experiential way of acquiring knowledge. We must, therefore, give attention to those who say what they know as a result of doing. This has some aspects antagonistic to science, seen as

[1] On this subject generally, many of the contributors to Bugental (1967) are helpful. Humanist and behaviourist thinkers take very different points of view. My own preference is for admitting the usefulness of some approaches of behaviourism, strictly within, however, a modified humanist framework.

itself practiced and as results applied in technology. Science – technology tries, generally by nonexperiential methods, to improve upon the results obtainable with accrued unaided experiential knowledge.

6 This leads to the need to continue in action, particularly with regard to experimenting in ecosystems in order to be able to obtain and evaluate the results of experience, since much is still unknown about the designed short food-chain sequences that hold promise of high capability for incorporating large numbers of human beings stably into ecosystems. The practical proposals now appearing—such as those brought forward in the Brussels conference (Laconte, 1976)—need to be vigorously pursued.

7 Intensive study is needed of the Janus nature of the emerging culture. Because we have large mass populations and an ubiquitous electronic technology which is eminently well suited to massive diffusion of the material—literature, drama, music, science, etc—of glyph cultures the developing electrobionic culture may carry forward values and attitudes inherited from glyph cultural and societal solutions to maintaining human populations. *Some of these values, attitudes, and solutions may not be suitable to our new population–food–energy situation and may not accord with the imperatives of our global ecological knowledge. It is therefore urgently necessary to know what values and attitudes from glyph cultures are being carried forward in the character profiles of mass populations, and to evaluate them in the context of our new condition.*

None of these suggested foci of attention should be thought of as standing alone. The message is that *systemic* relationships themselves are equally the focus for thought and action with the components.

28.3 A suggestion for thinking synergistically

In figure 28.1 an attempt is made to offer a way of thinking about these matters simultaneously. The diagram is simply a tool for this essential but very difficult task of learning how to think in synergistic ways. It is not, therefore, an operations diagram of how to proceed, critical-path style, nor is it at all an attempted description of the dynamics of society. It simply tries to indicate one way in which we may try to relate in thinking the substantive material dealt with in this book.

A diagram of this kind has to have a point of departure. Several perfectly effective ones are available. I have used the concept of 'costs'—cost of all kinds—because it is clear that changing ratios in costs is the way in which change is making itself felt, particularly in the developed countries. For example, energy supply difficulties appear as a shift in the cost of oil relative to the cost of telecommunications; the first rises while the second falls. Essentially also, it is changes in relative costs which chiefly influence the reallocation of resources, at any rate in the developed cash socioeconomies. This is therefore a very workable point of departure, since it is concrete and readily understood.

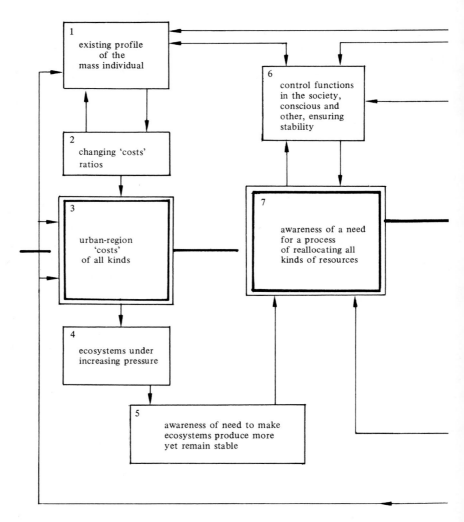

Figure 28.1. A suggested diagram of connections to be explored. Read from left to right. The main focus selected in terms of action (planning) is the awareness of the need to reallocate resources under the pressure of changing 'cost' ratios. The electronic technology may be expected to be an important tool for doing this. This is only one of many ways of attempting to diagram the systemic relationships of our emerging situation for purposes of thinking about it.

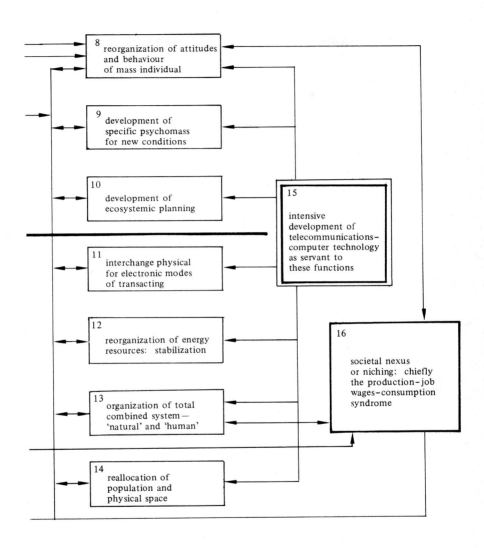

Costs are by no means to be restricted to measurement by monetary units. Costs in energy, human sense of well-being, ecosystem stability, intellectual effort, and resource depletion are also to be borne in mind. Some of these areas of cost now possibly ought to receive more attention than monetary costs, which, if used alone as measure, may be misleading and engender a false sense of security in our situation. Nor must we be bamboozled by the idea that all costs can be reduced to a monetary measure. The ecological and human costs of that mistake may indeed prove tragic.

On the left side of figure 28.1 we have the present state looked at with changing cost ratios as the underlying idea. Pressures toward required change in existing relationships come from both outside and inside the entity considered. The entity assumed here might be the greater metropolitan region. Pressures from outside are exerted by such elements as population increase, increasing difficulties with food and energy supplies, increasing demand for physical space, etc. From the inside, pressure comes from shifts in demands made on internal ecosystems, growth of the societal effects of automation, the mass-individual profile, etc.

The main stream of the diagram is horizontally through the middle of the diagram: blocks 3, 7, and 15. Block 7 is central: the awareness of the need to reallocate resources and the process of doing this. Three main areas are very important as inputs to this block: block 5 is the awareness of need with regard to ecosystems—the insistent pressure for more food instigated by increased population and humanitarian values, and the requirement of ensuring ecosystem viability in a situation of considerable ignorance about how near we may be to endangering that viability. Viability, of course, is in terms of the capability of the system to produce continuously a higher output of food. Block 16, the societal nexus, exerts pressure to reallocate resources, predominantly because of the failing ability of the present nexus to fit a sufficient proportion of the population into the production–job–wages–consumption linkage. Block 6 identifies the various control loops linking the society and the individual. These loops must ensure that the individual behaviour, when aggregated at the societal level, ensures a stable 'natural' and 'human' total system. If that block cannot contribute properly to the reallocation of resources, neither the ecosystems nor the society can be certain of survival.

In the next column the key specific areas of resource allocation are set out. The arrows suggest their interrelationships. Block 8, dealing with the character profile and sensibility of the mass individual, has in it the knot connected with propaganda in relation to behavioural control loops. Block 9 would require continuous attack on all the knots, as well as a relatively clearly perceived need for the rapid development of specific areas of psychomass, such as on-line societal management. Block 10 represents an extremely important present deficiency—the intensive operationalizing of the ecological knowledge we already possess. Block 11 has to do with transferring transactions to a greater degree than is already done, from physical to electronic modes so that energy may be conserved, urban physical congestion and pollution reduced, and the transacting process enhanced to provide the new growth sector. Block 12 may already be in operation. The uses of energy and the sources of energy have begun to change. An important allocative area here is the various regions of the electromagnetic spectrum, particularly in relation to other resource allocations. An assumption of some degree of 'stabilization' of growth rate, at least in the developed socioeconomies, is an important part of this block.

Block 13 is the most difficult of all since it requires the organization and operationalization of the concept of a combined total system fusing our present 'natural' system and 'human' system knowledge, attitudes, and assumptions. We may nourish the notion of the need for seeing the total system but we are at present far from knowing how to conceptualize its detail or organize it on the ground. Block 14 deals with physical space, both land space and built space, and has much to do with the total system since it is the base of both food supply and human transactional activity.

Block 15 requires the development of the telecommunications and computer technology not, as at present, so much in direct application to the societal status quo as in creative relationship to the items in blocks 8 to 14. It will relate closely to all these, but not to an equal degree. In some instances the role would be largely operational; in others it would rather be 'substitutional'; in yet others it would be productive of new dynamic.

As ever, there are plenty of objections that can be raised about the diagram. It should stand or fall by the test of whether it assists the process of thinking about the difficulty of identifying specifics and relating them to each other.

28.4 Conclusion

The very difficult knots or dilemmas we have looked at cannot be considered a total coverage of even the more important areas of the total range of difficulty emerging in culture and society since, because identification tends to vary with the original point of departure of the analyst, many attempts at analysis are required to achieve full coverage. But these six—the hominization-limit question in ecosystems, the regulation processes, the cash socioeconomy in the ecosystems context, the propaganda pincer, the inner–outer conflict in the mass individual, and regulation and the mass individual—do perhaps represent a considerable segment of the areas of very likely increasing difficulty where our ecological concerns and electronic technological practice intersect. Although this intersection is by no means the whole story, it can be argued that it is an indication of a key place to look.

If this is so, the essential question to raise is the extent to which our basic approach with its characteristic of weightings on the linear sequence of ends and means is workable in our population–biosphere situation, as at present understood. Culturally and societally this approach has great impetus behind it because of its short-term effectiveness in material matters during the past two or so centuries. Some very distinguished thinkers fear that it is of diminishing workability; we have looked at one example attempting to try something else (Ryan; chapter 11). If indeed the answer is negative, to question our dominant technological rationality will do good and not harm, as it will accelerate the quest for an alternative. If, however, this is still very much the way to go, questioning the route and encouragement of our existential anxiety will do damage, perhaps serious enough to impair the effective application of the objective knowledge we have already won.

According to the perspective of the mass individual along which we have looked, this brings us back to the problem of how far the emphasis on the objective or outer focus of attention can be pressed at the expense of the subjective or inner emphasis. This in its turn brings us to the question of how we think 'mind' is structured and functions. Of this little is known. I find conceptually useful the tentative view held by Bateson, McCulloch, Lilly, and others that 'mind' is a kind of ecological system which is considerably dependent on diversity for its stability. This concept would suggest that overemphasis on the outer will instigate a compensatory demand for the inner. As time is involved in such a process there would be a cyclical tendency producing overruns, as in a thermostat, on each side of the central position. This would mean swings of emphasis between the outer and the inner and vice versa.

If this is a concept which has some correspondence with what really happens, our question becomes that of asking whether confidence in the outer is now already waning, at any rate in the West, and whether we are now entering a period of preoccupation with the inner or subjective focus of attention in the mass individual. If so, a great fertile period of the Western human being looking outward with curiosity and intelligence, and eventually learning the workings of the system of which he is a component may be drawing to a close.

As a great deal of psychomass is very carefully stored in globally distributed locations, scientific and technological know-how might be preserved and maintained in a period of stasis, even if not added to. This might continue in use in the event of the general collapse of the ability to maintain the outward orientation in the mass population at large. This knowledge could be applied by a small elite who undertook to maintain the combined 'natural' and 'human' components of the total system by whatever means might prove to be necessary. I am here arguing a separation between those mass individuals who could maintain a fairly high degree of outward orientation and those who, being unable to do this, would sink into a timeless subjectivity which would be manageable for them but unfit them for any serious, other than routine, contribution to the business of maintaining the human enterprise. In the end, perhaps, the mass individual cannot for long tolerate the naturalistic view of himself which lies at the centre of our present approaches and success in objective action upon the world.

The working out of such a scenario would suggest a technocratic society in which a few have a fair knowledge of what goes on and the rest are kept brainwashed into a passive subjectivity maintained, doubtless, by astute manipulation of the electronic technology. The idea is repugnant, not new, but possible.

But we have no reason to conclude it is inevitable. The enhancement of transaction, and therefore of consciousness, through increase in human numbers, the global diffusion of the common use of the electronic technology, and the development of the noosphere thereby made possible give hope that the human species is capable of entering what von Foerster has called its compassionate phase (Calhoun, 1970; von Foerster et al, 1960).

28.5 Final comment on the theme of the book

In order to find ways of looking at our present and emerging condition, We started by examining two crucial and enormously influential areas of scientific knowledge recently developed—the exploration and utilization of the various regions of the electromagnetic spectrum, particularly those regions used for telecommunications and the computer, and our understanding of ecosystems and their life-support function.

We next looked at examples of applications of these bodies of knowledge, whether by way of general applications to society at large or by way of isolated experiments which might show directions for possible future developments. These applications and experiments were graded, beginning with obvious fitting to present societal arrangements, passing to joint applications in which both bodies of knowledge were relevant, next moving on to various attempts at visions of society incorporating extensive use of these bodies of knowledge, and culminating with focus on an example tackling the use of the electronic technology for a new mediation of the relationship between the individual and society (Ryan).

Out of examining these examples came the observation that certain key foci of attention deserved study in the light of these two bodies of knowledge and the forward thinking that was going on in connection with them. These foci included the cultural notion that a new stage of the human enterprise was beginning to be superimposed on the traditional literary culture of the West. This new stage we thought of as *electrobionic* and its predecessor as *glyph*. We looked at the emerging globalism in its electronic and ecological manifestations, and considered technological and other approaches to it. We next went to the human individual living out his life in this systemically conceptualized world, and used various sources to try to reach a composite picture of the character profile and sensibility of the mass individual. It began to become apparent that the inner landscape—

the way of seeing the world—of the mass individual would be of crucial importance to future action with regard to ecosystem viability simultaneous with societal stability, and that the electronic technology would have a very important role in shaping the values and attitudes of the mass individual.

From the foregoing it became clear that new conceptualizations and concepts will be necessary. We developed the conceptualization that physical and mental systems need concepts to join them and suggested that the concept of neuromass could be pivotal, leading to the concept of psychomass as the product of the noosphere. This allowed noosphere and biosphere to be conceptually linked as the base for thinking about total combined systems of 'nature' and human sociocultures. This was elaborated by looking at ecosystems and psychosystems in conjunction. Here we noted that ecosystems need to be considered in relation to each other because human beings move biomass and other materials, including energy, across ecosystem boundaries. And we concluded that psychomass is an important 'payment' made between ecosystems.

Into this perspective we again introduced the fact of the mass individual's role, trying to see mass societies in their function of components of ecosystems. The balance between the inner condition or profile of the individual and the outer need to act consciously in certain ways toward the life support turned out to be very important, particularly if some degree of reduction of energy throughput, or stabilization, in ecosystems is proved necessary. Among other things, this showed the need to examine the arrival of the information society in slightly more detail. Doing this, we concluded that analysis along this line did indeed show that we are already in the information society in North America and that we are in a very different situation with regard to the production–job–wages–consumption linkage from that which we generally imagine.

We next took the first step toward conscious action on the assumption of the humanist approach. Examination of this way of proceeding was shown to be unable to cope with the character profile and sensibility of the mass individual; it is impotent to energize him or control him by developing the necessary inner sanctions. He will not necessarily behave as may be ecologically necessary on the basis of being presented with *rational* arguments.

In the last part of the book we attempted to say something about integrating toward action. We looked at the importance of images and their relationship to concepts, and then brought what we found into conjunction with the mass-individual profile. That followed through to suggesting, first, major areas in which action should be considered and then some suggestions for action itself.

In the latter chapters we have raised basic philosophical questions about the assumptions underpinning our characteristic approaches to action, expressing these as dilemmas or knots. Although these may not be capable of being fully untied, the attempt to untie them is necessary as an effort to provide context for any action. This is the intended meaning of the gradient of the book.

By gradient of the book is meant the way in which it begins with objective knowledge of the physical world—radiation and ecological systems—and progressively moves to demonstrating that the *use* of this knowledge involves components that are neither physical nor necessarily to be treated with major objective emphasis; it then moves to the more complex level of looking at the approaches to the use of knowledge, until it poses questions at the deepest level of human concern.

The purpose of using this gradient is to suggest that we must think in this order. Flight into any single area of the gradient could well be fatal to both individual and society. The exercise is the very difficult one of holding many levels in mind at the same time, when considering any particular question. I hope that the book will have helped the development of the reader's ability in this exacting art. *The putting together of major ideas, side by side, is in my opinion now the most important area to be worked at in the next stage of psychomass development. Unfortunately we pay little attention to this need and particularly in formal education grossly neglect it. Yet, in the complexity in which we have to act, the ability to be able to do this fruitfully may well be crucial.*

In looking back over the book in its present form I regret that it has been necessary to omit certain areas of interest that were included in the two preliminary drafts. The reason for omission is simply that as the work progressed these items had to give way to other matters judged to be more significant. Among the areas I would have liked to have seen receive greater emphasis were the ideas of Calhoun and von Foerster dealing with the way in which interaction between groups and individuals has forced the growth of human consciousness. I suspect that this has greater relevance to our use of the electronic technology than I have indicated. Although the book has the limitations of a naturalistic or mechanomorphic approach— to use Matson's word—that I have indicated may always be a serious drawback, nevertheless this approach may still deliver important findings.

The other suppressed area, now omitted, contained specifics of psychomass and psychosystems. That section of a previous draft split up psychomass into various types and suggested models for thinking about psychosystems. This most important area of detailed probing will, it is hoped, see the light on another occasion.

References

● Reference not specifically quoted in the text but used as background for this book.

● Adler R, Baer W S, 1973 *Aspen Notebook: Cable and Continuing Education* (Praeger, New York)

● Allison A (Ed.), 1970 *Population Control* (Penguin Books, Harmondsworth, Middx)

Anderson P K, 1971 *Omega: Murder of the Ecosystem and Suicide of Man* (Brown, Dubuque, Ia)

● Armytage W H G, 1968 *Yesterday's Tomorrows: A Historical Survey of Future Societies* (Routledge and Kegan Paul, Henley-on-Thames, Oxon)

Arrow K, 1974 "Limited knowledge and economic analysis" *American Economic Review* **64**(1) 1-10

Ashby W R, 1960 *Design for a Brain: The Origin of Adaptive Behaviour* (Chapman and Hall, London)

Ashby W R, 1963 *An Introduction to Cybernetics* (John Wiley, New York)

Attinger E O (Ed.), 1970 *Global Systems Dynamics* (Karger, Basel)

Australian Telecommunications Commission, 1975 *Telecom 2000: An Exploration of the Long-Term Development of Telecommunications in Australia* (Australian Government Printing Unit, Melbourne)

● Awad E, 1973 *Automatic Data Processing* (Prentice-Hall, Englewood Cliffs, NJ)

● Bagdikian B H, 1971 *The Information Machines: Their Impact on Men and Media* (Harper and Row, New York)

● Barcelo M, Campbell H C, Young D A, 1971 *Information for Urban Affairs in Canada* (Canadian Council on Urban and Regional Research, Ottawa)

Bates M, 1960 *The Forest and the Sea* (Random House, New York)

Bateson G, 1971 "The cybernetics of 'self': a theory of alcoholism" *Psychiatry* **34**(2) 1-18

Bateson G, 1972 *Steps to an Ecology of Mind* (Ballantine, New York)

Bazewioz M, Mika T, 1977 "Some problems of computer network of Polish scientific centres" *Proceedings, Computer Networks and Teleprocessing Symposium, Budapest* (John von Neumann Society for Computing Sciences) volume 1, pp 285-395

● Bedford M T, 1972 *The Future of Communications Services in the Home* (Bell Canada, Montreal)

Beer S, 1974a *Cybernetics of National Development: Evolved from Work in Chile* (Zaheer Science Foundation, New Delhi)

Beer S, 1974b *Designing Freedom* (Canadian Broadcasting Corporation, Toronto)

Beer S, 1975 *Platform for Change* (John Wiley, New York)

● Bell C, 1928 *Art* (Chatto and Windus, London)

● Bell D, 1973 *The Coming of Post-Industrial Society* (Basic Books, New York)

Bell Canada, 1972 *Delphi: The Bell Canada Experience* (Business Planning Group, Bell Canada, Montreal)

Bertalanffy L von, 1952 *Problems of Life* (Watts, London)

Bertalanffy L von, 1968 *General System Theory* (George Braziller, New York)

Bhagwati J N (Ed.), 1974 *Economics and World Order from the 1970's to the 1980's* (Collier Macmillan, London)

● Blackham H J (Ed.), 1965 *Objections to Humanism* (Penguin Books, Harmondsworth, Middx)

● Bonner J T, 1965 *The Ideas of Biology* (Methuen, London)

● Borgstrom G, 1967 *The Hungry Planet* (Collier Books, New York)

Borgstrom G, 1973 *Harvesting the Earth* (Abelard-Schuman, New York)

Boulding K E, 1956 "General systems theory—the skeleton of science" *Management Science* **2**(3) 197-208

● Boulding K E, 1962 "After civilization what?" *Bulletin of the Atomic Scientists* **18**(8) 2-6

- Boulding K E, 1968 *The Organizational Revolution: A Study in the Ethics of Economic Organization* (Quadrangle Books, Chicago, Ill.)
- Boulding K E, 1971a "The economics of knowledge and the knowledge of economics" in *Economics of Information and Knowledge* Ed. D M Lamberton (Penguin Books, Harmondsworth, Middx) pp 21-36

  Boulding K E, 1971b "Environment and economics" in *Environment: Resources, Pollution, and Society* Ed. W W Murdoch (Sinauer Associates, Stamford, Conn.) pp 359-367

  Boulding K E, 1972 "The stationary state" *Resources* number 42, Institute of Behavioral Science, University of Colorado, Boulder, pp 19-20

  Bowen B A, Coll D C, George D A, 1971 *The Wired Scientific City* (Department of Communications Canada, Ottawa)
- Bronowski J, 1959 *Science and Human Values* (Harper and Row, New York)

  Bronowski J, 1970 "New concepts in the evolution of complexity" *Synthese* **21** (2) 228-246

  Bronowski J, 1973 *The Ascent of Man* (Little Brown, Boston)
- Brown J A, 1968 *Computers and Automation* (Arco, New York)

  Brown L R, 1975 "The world food prospect: the worldwide food shortages, assumed to be temporary, could become more or less chronic" *Science* **190** (4219) 1053-1059

  Brown L R, Eckholm E P, 1974 *By Bread Alone* (Praeger, New York)
- Brown L R, McGrath P L, Stokes B, 1976 *Twenty-two Dimensions of the Population Problem* (Worldwatch Institute, Washington, DC)

  Brubaker S, 1972 *To Live on Earth: Man and his Environment in Perspective* (Johns Hopkins University Press for Resources for the Future, Baltimore, Md)

  Brubaker S, 1975 *In Command of Tomorrow* (Johns Hopkins University Press, Baltimore, Md)

  Buber M, 1968 *Writings* selected by W Herberg (Cleveland World, Cleveland)
- Buckley W, 1967 *Sociology and Modern Systems Theory* (Prentice-Hall, Englewood Cliffs, NJ)

  Bugental J F (Ed.), 1967 *Challenges of Humanistic Psychology* (McGraw-Hill, New York)
- Burke J G (Ed.), 1968 *The New Technology and Human Values* (Wadsworth, Belmont, Calif.)

  Burkitt A, 1975 "Home data on trial" *Electronic Engineering* **47** (571) 56-57

  Cable Television Information Center, 1974 *Planning Interconnection Systems: Options for the Twin Cities Metropolitan Area* (The Urban Institute, Washington, DC)
- Calder N, 1969 *Technopolis: Social Control of the Uses of Science* (MacGibbon and Kee, London)

  Calder N, 1977 "Are we born to be good?" *Horizon* **19** (2) 43-49

  Caldwell L K, 1964 "Biopolitics: science, ethics and public policy" *Yale Review* **54** (1) 8-16

  Caldwell L K, 1972 *In Defense of Earth: International Protection of the Biosphere* (Indiana University Press, Bloomington)

  Calhoun J B, 1962a "A behavioral sink" in *Roots to Behavior* Ed. E L Bliss (Harper and Row, New York) pp 295-315
- Calhoun J B, 1962b "Population density and social pathology" *Scientific American* **206** (2) 139-148

  Calhoun J B, 1970 "Space and the strategy of life" *Ekistics* **29** (175) 425-437

  Calhoun J B, Wheeler G G, 1972 "Environmental behavior: origins and perspectives" *Journal of Environmental Health* **35** (3) 220-225
- California Institute of Technology, 1963 *Mariner: Mission to Venus* (McGraw-Hill, New York)

• Canada, Department of Communications, 1972 *Branching Out: Report of the Canadian Computer/Communications Task Force* (Information Canada, Ottawa)

Canada, Department of Communications, 1976a *A Computer/Communications-Based Health Information System for Prince Edward Island* (Information Canada, Ottawa)

Canada, Department of Communications, 1976b *Research Report on Teleconferencing* (Communications Research Centre, Ottawa) 2 volumes

• Canada, Ministry of Energy, Mines and Resources *Remote Sensing in Canada* (Information Canada, Ottawa) occasional publication

• Canada, Ministry of Energy, Mines and Resources, 1974 *Towards a Canadian Policy on Remote Sensing from Space: A Special Report to the Canadian Advisory Committee on Remote Sensing* (Information Canada, Ottawa)

• Canadian Advisory Committee on Remote Sensing, 1974 *Report* (Information Canada, Ottawa)

• Canadian Communications Research Information Centre, 1974-1975 *A Register of Communications Research in Canada 1974-1975* (Information Canada, Ottawa)

• Canadian Communications Research Information Centre *A Register of Communications Research in Canada 1975-1976* (Information Canada, Ottawa)

• Carpenter E, 1970 *They Became What They Beheld* (Outerbridge and Dienstfrey/Ballantine, New York)

Cassirer E, 1960 *The Logic of the Humanities* translated by C S Howe (Yale University Press, New Haven, Conn.)

• Chadwick G, 1971 *A Systems View of Planning* (Pergamon Press, Oxford)

Champness B G, 1974 *The Assessment of Users' Reactions to Confravision: Report of the Survey* (Communications Study Group, University College London)

Chan G, Saini B S, 1975 "Strategy for ecodevelopment of an island community: a case study of Nissan Island, Bougainville, New Guinea" *Ekistics* **40**(239) 232-240

Chapanis A, 1971 "Prelude to 2001: explorations in human communication" *American Psychologist* **26**(11) 949-961

Chapanis A, 1973 "The communication of factual information through various channels" *Information Storage and Retrieval* **9**(4) 215-231

Chapanis A, 1975 "Interactive human communication" *Scientific American* **232**(3) 36-42

• Chaplin G, Paige G D (Eds), 1973 *Hawaii 2000: Continuing Experiment in Anticipatory Democracy* (University Press of Hawaii, Honolulu)

• Cherry C, 1970 "Human communication: technology and urban planning" in *Communication and Energy in Changing Urban Environments* Ed. D J Jones (Butterworths, London) pp 117-130

Childe V G, 1951 *Man Makes Himself* (New American Library, New York) (originally published 1936)

Churchman C G, 1968 *The Systems Approach* (Delacorte Press, New York)

Clark J, Cole S, 1975 *Global Simulation Models: A Comparative Study* (Wiley-Interscience, New York)

Clarke R (Ed.), 1975 *Notes for the Future: An Alternative History of the Past Decade* (Thames and Hudson, London)

• Coleman G V, 1976 *Video Technology in the Courts* (The Mitre Corporation, McLean, Va)

Coll D C, 1973 *The Wired City Simulation Laboratory: Phase 1* (Department of Communications Canada, Ottawa)

Coll D C, George D A, Strickland L H, Paterson S A, Guild P D, McGown J M, Morris L R, Dakin A J, 1974 *The Wired City Laboratory: Studies in Interactive Broadband Communications* (Wired City Laboratory, Carleton University, Ottawa)

Commoner B, 1970 *Science and Survival* (Ballantine, New York)

Commoner B, 1972 *The Closing Circle: Nature, Man and Technology* (Bantam Books, New York)

Communications Study Group, 1973 "The scope for person-to-person telecommunication systems in government and business" Communications Study Group, University College London (mimeo)

Conant J B, 1965 *Two Modes of Thought: My Encounters with Science and Education* (Pocket Books, New York)

• Coulton G G, 1945 *Medieval Panorama: The English Scene from Conquest to Reformation* (Cambridge University Press, London)

• Cripps E L, 1970 *A Comparative Study of Information Systems for Urban and Regional Planning* (Urban System Research Unit, University of Reading, Reading, England)

• Cross N, Elliott D, Roy R (Eds), 1974 *Man-made Futures: Readings in Society, Technology and Design* (Hutchinson Educational, London)

• Cushman R H, 1972 "TOFT: a method for electronic doodling and a first step towards the use of computers on ill-defined problems" in *Proceedings of the 1972 International Conference on Cybernetics and Society* (Institute of Electrical and Electronic Engineers, Washington, DC)

• *Daedalus (Boston)*, 1973 "The No-Growth Society" *Daedalus* **102** (4) special issue

• Dakin A J, 1960 "Thoughts on theory-method in the planning process" *Plan Canada* **1** (3) 133–143

• Dakin A J, 1966 "Inhumanities of urban planning" *University of Toronto Quarterly* **35** (4) 321–356

• Dakin A J, 1972 *Telecommunications in the Urban and Regional Planning Process* (Department of Communications Canada, Ottawa)

Dakin A J, 1973 *Telecommunications and the Planning of Greater Metropolitan Regions* (Department of Communications Canada, Ottawa)

Dakin A J, 1974 *Telecommunications Experiments in Urban and Regional Planning* (Department of Communications Canada, Ottawa)

• Daniels F, 1974 *Direct Use of the Sun's Energy* (Ballantine Books, New York)

"Data management by RAP", 1976 *Engineering Forum* number 3 (June) (Faculty of Applied Science and Engineering, University of Toronto)

• DATAR (Délégation à l'Aménagement du Territoire et à l'Action Régionale), 1971 *Schéma Général d'Aménagement de la France: Prospective et Analyse de Systèmes* (Documentation Française, Paris)

DATAR, 1973 *Aménagement du Territoire: Décentralisation des Centres Informatiques* (Documentation Française, Paris)

Day L H, 1973 "An assessment of travel/communications substitutability" *Futures* **5** 559–572

• Deverell J and the Latin American Working Group, 1975 *Falconbridge: Portrait of a Canadian Mining Multinational* (Lorimer, Toronto)

• Dickson P, 1972 *Think Tanks* (Ballantine Books, New York)

• Dixon N F, 1971 *Subliminal Perception: The Nature of a Controversy* (McGraw-Hill, London)

• Dobzhansky T, 1967 *The Biology of Ultimate Concern* (New American Library, New York)

• Dolmatch K, 1974 *Cable Television Today: Policy and Practices in Europe, America and Japan* (Center for International Studies, Massachusetts Institute of Technology, Cambridge, Mass)

Doxiadis C A, 1967 *Ecumenopolis: The Settlement of the Future* (Athens Center of Ekistics, Athens)

Doyle F J, Goodwill D Z, 1971 *An Exploration of the Future in Educational Technology* (Bell Canada, Montreal)

DRCG, 1970 *Conceptual Design of a Regional Information System* (Denver Regional Council of Governments, Denver, Col.)

DRCG, 1971 *Regional Information System—Summary Implementation Recommendations* (Denver Regional Council of Governments, Denver, Col.)

Drucker P F, 1968 *The Age of Discontinuity: Guidelines to Our Changing Society* (Harper and Row, New York)

Dubos R J, 1961 *The Dreams of Reason: Science and Utopias* (Columbia University Press, New York)

Dubos R J, 1965 *Man Adapting* (Yale University Press, New Haven, Conn.)

The Ecologist, 1972 *A Blueprint for Survival* (Penguin Books, Harmondsworth, Middx)

Ehrlich P R, Ehrlich A H, 1970 *Population, Resources, Environment: Issues in Human Ecology* (W H Freeman, San Francisco, Calif.)

• Ehrlich P R, Ehrlich A H, Holdren J P, 1973 *Human Ecology: Problems and Solutions* (W H Freeman, San Francisco, Calif.)

Ehrlich P R, Hariman R L, 1971 *How to be a Survivor* (Ballantine, New York)

• *Ekistics*, 1973 "Networks: Information, Communication and Transportation" *Ekistics* **35**(211) special issue

• *Ekistics*, 1975 "Creating More with Less" *Ekistics* **40**(239) special issue

• Eklund S O, 1960 "Planning—a branch of civil engineering?" Southern Transvaal Regional Development Association, Johannesburg, South Africa (mimeo)

• Eldredge H W, 1975 *World Capitals: Toward Guided Urbanization* (Anchor Press/Doubleday, Garden City, NY)

Eliot T S, 1948 *Notes Towards the Definition of Culture* (Faber and Faber, London)

Ellul J, 1964 *The Technological Society* translated by J Wilkinson (Vintage Books, New York) (originally published in French, 1954)

Ellul J, 1973 *Propaganda: the Formation of Men's Attitudes* translated by K Keller, J Lerner (Vintage Books, New York)

Emery F E (Ed.), 1969 *Systems Thinking: Selected Readings* (Penguin Books, Harmondsworth, Middx)

• Environmetrics Inc, 1972 *The Urban Systems Model: A Design* (National Technical Information Service, Washington, DC)

• Esser A H (Ed.), 1971 *Behavior and Environment: The Use of Space by Animals and Men* (Plenum Press, New York)

• Etzioni A, 1968 *The Active Society: A Theory of Societal and Political Processes* (Free Press, New York)

• Evans (R W) Associates, 1975 *Should You Replace Your In-House Computer? EDP In-Depth Reports* **5**(1) [Evans (R W) Associates, Mississauga, Ontario]

Falk R A, 1972 *This Endangered Planet: Prospects and Proposals for Human Survival* (Vintage Books, New York)

Feibleman J K, 1954 "Theory of integrative levels" *British Journal of the Philosophy of Science* **5**(17) 59–66

Ferkiss V, 1974 *The Future of Technological Civilization* (George Braziller, New York)

Foerster H von, Mora P M, Amiot L W, 1960 "Doomsday: Friday 13 November, A.D. 2026" *Science* **132**(3436) 1291–1295

• Ford J M, Munro J E, 1971 *Living Systems: Principles and Relationships* (Canfield Press, San Francisco, Calif.)

Ford Foundation, 1974 *Exploring Energy Choices: A Preliminary Report of the Ford Foundation's Energy Policy Project* (Ford Foundation Energy Policy Project, Washington, DC)

Forrester J W, 1968 *Principles of Systems* (Wright-Allen, Cambridge, Mass)

Forrester J W, 1971 *World Dynamics* (Wright-Allen, Cambridge, Mass)

• Frisch O, 1972 *The Nature of Matter* (Thames and Hudson, London)

Fromm E, 1968 *The Revolution of Hope: Toward a Humanized Technology* (Bantam Books, New York)

Fuller R B, 1969 *Utopia or Oblivion: The Prospects for Humanity* (Bantam Books, New York)

● Furnas C C, 1936 *The Next Hundred Years: The Unfinished Business of Science* (Reynal and Hitchcock, New York)

● *The Futurist*, 1974 "The World of 1994" *The Futurist* **8** (3) special issue

The Futurist, 1975 "The future of computer conferencing: an interview with Murray Turoff" *The Futurist* **9** (4) 182-190, 195

Gabor D, 1969 *Inventing the Future* (Knopf, New York)

Gabor D, 1970 *Innovations: Scientific, Technological and Social* (Oxford University Press, London)

● Gabor D, 1972 *The Mature Society* (Secker and Warburg, London)

Galbraith J K, 1973 *Economics and the Public Purpose* (Houghton-Mifflin, Boston)

● Gasparski W W, 1975 "Systems methodology—its nature, structure and applications. Some remarks" in *Progress in Cybernetics and Systems Research* volume 2 (Hemisphere, New York) pp 308-320

George D A et al, 1975 *The Wired City Laboratory and Educational Communication Project* (Wired City Laboratory, Carleton University, Ottawa)

George F H, 1961 *The Brain as a Computer* (Pergamon Press, Oxford)

George F H, 1970a *Models of Thinking* (George Allen and Unwin, London)

George F H, 1970b *Science and the Crisis in Society* (Wiley-Interscience, New York)

● Glass B, 1962 "Information crisis in biology" *Bulletin of the Atomic Scientists* **18** (8) 6-12

Goddard J B, 1973 *Office Linkages and Location: A Study of Communications and Spatial Patterns in Central London* (Pergamon Press, Oxford)

● Goldmark P C, 1972 "Communications in a new and rural society" *Journal of the Society of Motion Picture and Television Engineers* **81** (7) 512-517

Goldsmith M, Mackay A (Eds), 1966 *The Science of Science* (Penguin Books, Harmondsworth, Middx)

● Goodman P, 1956 *Growing Up Absurd: Problems of Youth in the Organized Society* (Vintage Books, New York)

● Goodwill Z, 1971 *An Exploration of the Future in Business Information Processing Technology* (Bell Canada, Montreal)

● Gottlieb C C, Borodin A, 1973 *Social Issues in Computing* (Academic Press, New York)

● Gottmann J, 1961 *Megalopolis* (MIT Press, Cambridge, Mass)

Goudge T A, 1950 *The Thought of C. S. Peirce* (University of Toronto Press, Toronto)

● Goulet D, 1973 *The Cruel Choice: A New Concept in the Theory of Development* (Atheneum, New York)

● Graves C W, 1974 "Human nature prepares for a momentous leap" *The Futurist* **8** (2) 72-84

Grenet P, 1965 *Teilhard de Chardin: The Man and His Theories* (Souvenir Press, London)

● Hack W G et al, 1971 *Educational Futurism 1985* (McCutchan, Berkeley, Calif.)

● Häfele W et al, 1975 *Second Status Report of the IIASA Project on Energy Systems 1975* (International Institute for Applied Systems Analysis, Laxenburg, Austria)

● Hall A (Ed.), 1974 *Petersen's Book of Man in Space* (Petersen, Los Angeles, Calif.) 5 volumes

● Hall E T, 1969 *The Hidden Dimension* (Anchor Books/Doubleday, Garden City, NY)

Hall E T, 1973 *The Silent Language* (Anchor Books/Doubleday, Garden City, NY)

● Handel S, 1967 *The Electronic Revolution* (Penguin Books, Harmondsworth, Middx)

Hardin G, 1968 "The tragedy of the commons: the population problem has no technical solution: it requires a fundamental extension in morality" *Science* **162** (3859) 1243-1248

Harkness R C, 1972 "Communications innovation, urban form, and travel demand" research report 71-2, Urban Transportation Program, University of Washington, Seattle

Harkness R C, 1973 *Communications Substitute for Travel: A Preliminary Assessment of their Potential for Reducing Urban Transportation Costs by Altering Office Location Patterns* PhD Dissertation, University of Washington, Seattle (University Xerox Microfilms, Ann Arbor, Mich.)

Harman W W, 1976 *An Incomplete Guide to the Future* (San Francisco Book Company, San Francisco, Calif.)

Harman W W, 1977 "The coming transformation" *The Futurist* **11** (1) 5-12

Harper D, 1976 *Eye in the Sky: Introduction to Remote Sensing* (Multiscience, Montreal)

Hartshorne C, Weiss P, 1960 *Collected Papers of Charles Sanders Peirce. Volume 1* (Belknap Press: Harvard University Press, Cambridge, Mass)

• Hashida O, Kodaira K, 1976 "Digital data switching network configurations" *Review of the Electrical Communication Laboratories* **24** (1/2) 85-96

• Haynes P, 1974 "Towards a concept of monitoring" *Town Planning Review* **45** (1) 5-28

• Heilbroner R L, 1967 "Do machines make history?" *Technology and Culture* **8** (3) 335-345

Heilbroner R L, 1974 *An Enquiry into the Human Prospect* (Norton, New York)

• Hellman H, 1976 *Technophobia: Getting Out of the Technological Trap* (Evans, New York)

• Helmer J, Eddington N A (Eds), 1973 *Urbanman: The Psychology of Urban Survival* (Free Press, New York)

Helmer O, 1966 *Social Technology* (Basic Books, New York)

• Hencley S P, Yates J R, 1974 *Futurism in Education: Methodologies* (McCutchan, Berkeley, Calif.)

• Herbert G, 1975 "Holism, the ecosystem and architecture: towards a philosophy of environmental design" Annual Discourse, School of Architecture, University of Natal, Durban

• Hermansen T, 1969 "Information systems for regional development control" *Papers of the Regional Science Association* **22** 107-140

• Herrero M C, 1973 *New Communities and Telecommunications* (Center for Urban and Regional Studies, University of North Carolina, Chapel Hill)

Hertz H, 1893 *Electric Waves, Being Researches on the Propagation of Electric Action with Finite Velocity through Space* translated by D E Jones (Macmillan, London)

Hiltz S R, 1976 "Computer conferencing: assessing the social impact of a new communications medium" paper presented to the 71st Annual Meeting of the American Sociological Association (privately circulated)

Hirschleifer J, 1973 "Where are we in the theory of information?" *American Economic Review* **63** (2) 31-39

• HMSO, 1973 *The Dispersal of Government Work from London* (HMSO, London)

• Hollingdale S H, Tootill G C, 1970 *Electronic Computers* (Penguin Books, Harmondsworth, Middx)

Hollowell M L (Ed.), 1975 *Cable Handbook 1975-1976: A Guide to Cable and New Communications Technologies* (Communications Press, Washington, DC)

Human Futures: Needs, Societies and Techniques 1974, The Rome World Special Conference on Futures Research, 1973 (IPC Science and Technology Press, Guildford, Surrey)

Huxley J (Ed.), 1961 *The Humanist Frame* (George Allen and Unwin, London)

ICCC, 1976 *Proceedings of the Third International Conference on Computer Communication: Advancement Through Resource Sharing* Toronto, 3-6 August 1976, Ed. P K Verma (International Council for Computer Communication, Washington, DC)

• IEEE, 1975 "Social implications of Telecommunications" *IEEE Transactions on Communications* **23**(10) special issue

IIASA, 1977 *Study of the Potential Use of Informatics Technology on Problems of Scientific and Technological Cooperation* (The International Institute for Applied Systems Analysis, Laxenburg, Austria)

Ingram D J E, 1973 *Radiation and Quantum Physics* (Clarendon Press: Oxford University Press, London)

Institut de Recherche d'Informatique et d'Automatique, 1976 *Cyclades* (Rocquencourt, Paris)

• Interuniversity Communications Council, 1974 *Proceedings. North American Perspective: Computing and Networks in Canada and the United States* EDUCOM Fall Conference, Toronto 1974 (EDUCOM, Princeton, NJ)

Jamison P L, Friedman S M (Eds), 1974 *Energy Flow in Human Communities* Proceedings of a Workshop in New York, January-February 1974, Human Adaptability Coordinating Office of the US International Biological Program and the Committee on the Biological Bases of Social Behaviour of the Social Science Research Council, University Park, Pa

Jantsch E, 1967 *Technological Forecasting in Perspective: A Framework for Technological Forecasting* (OECD, Paris)

Jantsch E, 1975 *Design for Evolution: Self-Organization and Planning in the Life of Human Systems* (George Braziller, New York)

Japan Computer Usage Development Institute, 1972 *The Plan for Information Society— a National Goal Toward Year 2000* (Chiy-oda-ku, Tokyo)

• Johnson L L et al, 1972 *Cable Communications in the Dayton Miami Valley: Basic Report* (Rand Corporation, Santa Monica, Calif.)

The Journal of the New Alchemists 1974 (The New Alchemy Institute, Woods Hole, Mass)

The Journal of the New Alchemists 1976 (The New Alchemy Institute, Woods Hole, Mass)

• Jouvenel B de, 1963 "The political consequences of the rise of science" *Bulletin of the Atomic Scientists* **19**(10) 2-8

• Jouvenel B de, 1965 "Utopia for practical purposes" *Daedalus* (*Boston*) **95**(2) 437-453

• Jouvenel B de, 1967 *The Art of Conjecture* translated by N Lary (Basic Books, New York)

• Kahn H (Ed.), 1974 *The Future of the Corporation* (Mason and Lipscomb, New York)

• Kahn H, 1976 *The Next 200 Years: A Scenario for America and the World* (Morrow, New York)

• Kalba K, 1971 *Communicable Medicine: Cable Television and Health Services* (Sloan Commission, Bethesda, Md)

• Kalba K, 1973 "Telecommunications for future human settlements" *Ekistics* **35**(211) 329-336

• Key W B, 1972 *Subliminal Seduction: Ad Media's Manipulation of a Not So Innocent America* (Prentice-Hall, Englewood Cliffs, NJ)

• Khan A M, 1974 *Transportation and Telecommunications: A Study of Substitution, Simulation and Their Implications* (Canadian Transport Commission, Ottawa)

• Klir G, 1969 *Introduction to General Systems Theory* (Van Nostrand, New York)

• Kostelanetz R (Ed.), 1971 *Human Alternatives: Visions for Us Now* (Morrow, New York)

• Kraemer K, Mitchell W, Weiner M, Dial O, 1974 *Integrated Municipal Information Systems: The Use of the Computer in Local Government* (Praeger, New York)

Krebs C J, 1972 *Ecology: The Experimental Analysis of Distribution and Abundance* (Harper and Row, New York)

Kuhn T S, 1970 *The Structure of Scientific Revolutions* 2nd edition (University of Chicago Press, Chicago, Ill.)

Kupperman R H, Wilcox R H, Smith H A, 1975 "Crisis management: some opportunities" *Science* **187** (4175) 404-410

Laconte P (Ed.), 1976 *The Environment of Human Settlements. Human Wellbeing in Cities* (Pergamon Press, Oxford) 2 volumes

• Laing R D, 1967 *The Politics of Experience and the Bird of Paradise* (Penguin Books, Harmondsworth, Middx)

Laing R D, Esterson A, 1970 *Sanity, Madness and the Family* (Penguin Books, Harmondsworth, Middx)

• Lampl P, 1968 *Cities and Planning in the Ancient Near East* (George Braziller, New York)

• Laszlo E, 1972 *The Systems View of the World* (George Braziller, New York)

• Laszlo E, 1973 *Introduction to Systems Philosophy: Toward a New Paradigm of Contemporary Thought* (Harper Torchbooks, New York)

Laszlo E, 1975 "From crisis prevention to positive goals: new approaches to the world system" *New World Forum* **1** (1), n/p. (International Cultural Foundation, New York)

Laszlo E et al, 1977 *Goals for Mankind. A Report to the Club of Rome on the New Horizons of Global Community* (Dutton, New York)

Lehninger A L, 1965 *Bioenergetics: The Molecular Basis of Biological Energy Transformations* (Benjamin, New York)

Leontief W, Carter A P, Petri P A, 1977 *The Future of the World Economy* (Oxford University Press, New York)

Lévi-Strauss C, 1968 *Structural Anthropology* translated by C Jacobson, B G Schoepf (Penguin Books, Harmondsworth, Middx)

Lewis M, 1948 *The Navy of Britain: A Historical Portrait* (George Allen and Unwin, London)

Lilly J C, 1969 *The Mind of the Dolphin: A Nonhuman Intelligence* (Avon Books, New York)

Lilly J C, 1974 *Programming and Metaprogramming in the Human Biocomputer* (Bantam Books, New York)

• Linstone H A, Turoff M (Eds), 1973 *Delphi and Its Applications* (American Elsevier, New York)

Locker A, Coulter N A, 1975 "An outline of teleogenic systems theory" in *Progress in Cybernetics and Systems Research* volume 2, Eds R Trappl, F de P Hanika (Hemisphere, Washington, DC) pp 156-165

• Lofland L H, 1973 *A World of Strangers: Order and Action in Urban Public Space* (Basic Books, New York)

• Lowry I S, 1967 *Seven Models of Urban Development: A Structural Comparison* (Rand Corporation, Santa Monica, Calif.)

• Lyle J, Wodke M von, 1974 "Information system for environmental planning" *Journal of the American Institute of Planners* **40** (6) 394-413

Machlup F, 1962 *Production and Distribution of Knowledge in the United States* (Princeton University Press, Princeton, NJ)

Maddox J, 1972 *The Doomsday Syndrome* (Macmillan, London)

Man's Impact on the Global Environment 1970, report of the Study of Critical Environmental Problems (MIT Press, Cambridge, Mass)

●Manuel F E, Manuel F P, 1966 *French Utopias: An Anthology of Ideal Societies* (Free Press, New York)

●Marcuse H, 1967 *Reason and Revolution* (Routledge and Kegan Paul, Henley-on-Thames, Oxon.)

Marcuse H, 1969 *An Essay on Liberation* (Beacon Press, Boston)

Margalef R, 1968 *Perspectives in Ecological Theory* (University of Chicago Press, Chicago, Ill.)

●Marien M, 1972 *Alternative Futures for Learning: An Annotated Bibliography* (Educational Policy Research Center, Syracuse, NY)

Martin J, 1969 *Telecommunications and the Computer* (Prentice-Hall, Englewood Cliffs, NJ)

Martin J, 1971 *Future Developments in Telecommunications* (Prentice-Hall, Englewood Cliffs, NJ)

Martin J, Norman A R D, 1970 *The Computerized Society: An Appraisal of the Impact of Computers on Society over the Next Fifteen Years* (Prentice-Hall, Englewood Cliffs, NJ)

●Maruyama M, 1973 "Human futuristics and urban planning" *Journal of the American Institute of Planners* **39**(5) 346, 348–357

Maslow A H, 1969 *The Psychology of Science: A Reconnaissance* (Henry Regnery, Chicago, Ill.)

Maslow A H, 1970 *Motivation and Personality* (Harper and Row, New York)

●Maslow A H, 1972 *The Farther Reaches of Human Nature* (Viking Press, New York)

●Mason W F, 1971 "Full exploitation of the Wired City's potential requires a systems approach" *Electronics* **44**(20) 45–49

Mason W F et al, 1972 *Urban Cable Systems* (Mitre Corporation, Washington, DC)

●Massachusetts Institute of Technology, 1970 *Man's Impact on the Global Environment: Assessments and Recommendations for Action* (MIT Press, Cambridge, Mass)

Masuda Y, 1975 "The conceptual framework of information economics" *IEEE Transactions on Communications* **23**(10) 1028–1039

Matson F W, 1966 *The Broken Image: Man, Science and Society* (Anchor Books, New York)

●Matson F W, Montagu A (Eds), 1967 *The Human Dialogue: Perspectives on Communication* (Macmillan, New York)

●Mattyasovszky E, 1975 "Key principles in planning for environmental quality" *Plan Canada* **15**(1) 38–43

May R, 1967 *Man's Search for Himself* (New American Library, New York)

May R, 1969 *Love and Will* (Dell, New York)

McCulloch W S, 1965 *Embodiments of Mind* (MIT Press, Cambridge, Mass)

McHale J, 1971 *The Future of the Future* (Ballantine Books, New York)

●McHale J, 1972 *World Facts and Trends* (Collier, New York)

●McHale J, McHale M C, 1973 *World Trends and Alternative Futures* (East-West Center, University of Hawaii, Honolulu)

●McHale J, McHale M C, 1975 *Human Requirements, Supply Levels and Outer Bounds* (The Aspen Institute for Humanistic Studies, New York)

McHarg I L, 1969 *Design with Nature* (Natural History Press, New York)

McLuhan M, 1964 *Understanding Media: The Extensions of Man* (McGraw-Hill, New York)

McLuhan M, 1970 *Counterblast* (McClelland and Stewart, Toronto)

●McLuhan M, 1971 *From Cliché to Archetype* (Pocket Books, New York)

Mead M, 1942 "The comparative study of culture and the purposive cultivation of democratic values" in *Conference on Science, Philosophy and Religion in their Relation to the Democratic Way of Life* (Harper and Row, New York)

Meadows D H, Meadows D L, Randers J, Behrens W W, 1972 *The Limits to Growth: A Report for the Club of Rome's Project on the Predicament of Mankind* (New American Library, New York) (referred to as the first report to the Club of Rome)

Meier R L, 1962 *A Communications Theory of Urban Growth* (MIT Press, Cambridge, Mass)

• Meier R L, 1974 *Planning for an Urban World: The Design of Resource-Conserving Cities* (MIT Press, Cambridge, Mass)

• Menninger K, 1966 *Man Against Himself* (Harcourt, Brace and World, New York)

• Mercado J B de, 1973a "Interactive video networks" International Institute for the Management of Technology, Milan

• Mercado J B de, 1973b "The planning of cable television systems" International Telecommunications Union, Geneva

• Mercado J B de, Durr L, 1972 *Data Networks in Perspective: An Overview and Evaluation of Developments and Plans* (Department of Communications Canada, Ottawa)

Mesarovic M, Pestel E, 1974 *Mankind at the Turning Point: The Second Report to the Club of Rome* (Dutton/Reader's Digest Press, New York)

Mesarovic M, Reisman A (Eds), 1972 *Systems Approach and the City* (North-Holland, New York)

• Metropolitan Fund, Citizen Information Division, 1970 *Regional Urban Communications* (Metropolitan Fund, Detroit)

• Michael D N, 1962 *Cybernation: The Silent Conquest* (Center for the Study of Democratic Institutions, Santa Barbara, Calif.)

• Michael D N, 1970 *The Unprepared Society: Planning for a Precarious Future* (Harper Colophon Books, New York)

• Miller A, 1972 *The Assault on Privacy* (New American Library of Canada, Scarborough, Ontario)

• Monod J, 1972 *Chance and Necessity: An Essay on the Natural Philosophy of Modern Biology* translated by A Wainhouse (Vintage Books, New York)

Montagu A, 1970 *The Direction of Human Development* (Hawthorn Books, New York)

Morovitz H J, 1970 *Entropy for Biologists: An Introduction to Thermodynamics* (Academic Press, New York)

Moss M L, 1976 "Public service uses of cable television" paper presented to The Second Symposium on Research Applied to National Needs (National Science Foundation, Washington, DC)

• Mosse G L, 1975 *The Nationalization of the Masses* (Fertig, New York)

• Muller H J, 1952 *The Uses of the Past: Profiles of Former Societies* (New American Library, New York)

• Muller H J, 1966 *Freedom in the Modern World: The 19th and 20th Centuries* (Harper Colophon Books, New York)

Mumford L, 1961 *The City in History: Its Origins, Its Transformations, and Its Prospects* (Harcourt, Brace and World, New York)

Munn R E, 1973 *Global Environmental Monitoring System (GEMS): Action for Phase 1* SCOPE Report 3, United Nations Agency Work Group on Monitoring, Toronto

• Murdoch W W (Ed.), 1971 *Environment: Resources, Pollution and Society* (Sinauer Associates, Stamford, Conn.)

• Murdy W H, 1975 "Anthropocentrism: a modern version" *Science* **187** (4182) 1168–1172

Musil R, 1968 *The Man Without Qualities* translated by E Wilkins, E Kaiser (Panther Books, London)

• NASA, 1973 *Symposium on Significant Results Obtained from the Earth Resources Technology Satellite—1. Volume 1: Technical Presentations* SP-327 (National Aeronautics and Space Administration and Goddard Space Flight Center, Washington, DC)

NASA, 1974 *Third Earth Resources Technology Satellite Symposium* SP-356 (National Aeronautics and Space Administration and Goddard Space Flight Center, Washington, DC)

National Academy of Engineering, 1969 *Telecommunications for Advanced Metropolitan Form and Function* (Committee on Telecommunications, National Academy of Engineering, Washington, DC)

National Academy of Engineering, 1971 *Communications Techniques for Urban Improvement* (National Academy of Engineering, Washington, DC)

National Advisory Commission on Food and Fiber, 1967 *Food and Fiber for the Future* (Washington, DC)

• National Research Council of Canada. Second Man–Computer Communications Seminar, 1971 *Pre-Seminar Digest: Interactive Graphics* (National Research Council of Canada, Ottawa)

• National Research Council of Canada. Third Man–Computer Communications Seminar, 1973 *Proceedings* (National Research Council of Canada, Ottawa)

Neilands J B, 1976 "Science and the biosphere: coexistence or catastrophe?" *Scientific World* **20**(4) 20–23

Neumann J von, 1958 *The Computer and the Brain* (Yale University Press, New Haven, Conn.)

Newman P W G, 1975 "An ecological model for city structure and development" *Ekistics* **40**(239) 258–265

New York University/Reading, Pennsylvania, undated *Public Service Uses of Interactive Television: Interactive Telecommunications Research* (Alternate Media Center, New York University, New York)

• Nicol H, 1967 *The Limits of Man: An Enquiry into the Scientific Bases of Human Population* (Constable, London)

Nilles J M, Carlson F R, Gray P, Hanneman G J, 1976a *The Telecommunications Transportation Tradeoff* (Wiley-Interscience, New York)

Nilles J M, Carlson F R, Gray P, Hanneman G J, 1976b "Telecommuting—an alternative to Urban Transportation Congestion" *IEEE Transactions on Systems, Man, and Cybernetics* **6**(2) 77–84

Nippon Telegraph and Telephone, 1974 *Research and Development of a Digital Data Network* (Nippon Telegraph and Telephone, Tokyo)

Odum E P, 1969 "The strategy of ecosystem development" *Science* **164**(3877) 262–269

Odum E P, 1971 *Fundamentals of Ecology* 3rd edition (Saunders, Philadelphia)

Odum E P, 1975 *Ecology: The Link Between the Natural and the Social Sciences* (Holt, Rinehart and Winston, New York) (originally published 1963)

Odum H T, 1971 *Environment, Power and Society* (John Wiley, New York)

OECD, 1973 *Computers and Telecommunications* (Organization for Economic Co-operation and Development, Paris)

• Ohba H, Morino K, Haruta K, 1976 "On the interface between packet switches and computers" *Review of the Electrical Communication Laboratories* **24** (1/2) 97–105

O'Riordan T, 1976 *Environmentalism* (Pion, London)

Ortega y Gasset J, 1957 *The Revolt of the Masses* (Norton, New York) (originally published in Spanish, 1930)

• Owen B M, Waterman D, 1973 *Mass Communication and Economics: A Bibliography* (Center for Research in Economic Growth, Stanford University, Stanford, Calif.)

• Parker E B, 1973 "Technology assessment or institutional change?" in *Communications Technology and Social Policy: Understanding the New 'Cultural Revolution'* Eds G Gerbner, L P Gross, W H Melody (John Wiley, New York)

Parker E B, 1976a "Social implications of computer/telecoms systems" *Telecommunications Policy* **1** (1) 3–20

Parker E B, 1976b "Planning communication technologies and institutions for development" Institute for Communication Research, Stanford University, Stanford, Calif.

• Parker E B, Dunn D A, 1972 "Information technology: its social potential" *Science* **176** (4042) 1392–1399

Pask G, 1975 *The Cybernetics of Human Learning and Performance: A Guide to Theory and Research* (Hutchinson Educational, London)

Pasternak B, 1959 *Dr Zhivago* (Collet, London)

Pattee H H (Ed.), 1973 *Hierarchy Theory: The Challenge of Complex Systems* (George Braziller, New York)

Patterson W C, 1976 *Nuclear Power* (Penguin Books, Harmondsworth, Middx)

• Pekelis V, 1974 *Cybernetics A to Z* translated by M Samokhvolov (Mir, Moscow)

Perry R B, 1967 *General Theory of Value: Its Meaning and General Principles Construed in Terms of Interest* (Harvard University Press, Cambridge, Mass)

Phillipson J, 1966 *Ecological Energetics* (Edward Arnold, London)

• Piaget J, 1968 *Six Psychological Studies* translated by D Elkind (Vintage Books, New York)

• Piaget J, 1969 *The Mechanics of Perception* translated by G N Seagrim (Routledge and Kegan Paul, Henley-on-Thames, Oxon)

• Piaget J, 1970 *Structuralism* (Harper Torchbooks, New York)

• Piel G, 1963 "The acceleration of history" in *Fifty Great Essays* Eds E Huberman, E Huberman (Bantam Books, New York)

• Plumb J H, 1964 *Crisis in the Humanities* (Penguin Books, Harmondsworth, Middx)

Polanyi M, 1958 *Personal Knowledge* (University of Chicago Press, Chicago, Ill.)

• Polanyi M, 1959 *The Study of Man* (University of Chicago Press, Chicago, Ill.)

• Polanyi M, 1964 *Science, Faith and Society* (University of Chicago Press, Chicago, Ill.) (reissue)

Porat M U, 1976 *The Information Economy* unpublished PhD Dissertation, Stanford University, Stanford, Calif.

Porat M U, 1977 "The information economy" typescript privately circulated

• Porat M U et al, 1977 *The Information Economy* (Office of Telecommunications, US Department of Commerce, Washington, DC) nine volumes

Porter A, 1969 *Cybernetics Simplified* (Barnes and Noble, New York)

Post Office Telecommunications, 1974a *Business Telecommunications Applications: Field Trials of Television Conference Systems. Long Range Intelligence Bulletin 5* (Post Office Telecommunications Headquarters, London)

Post Office Telecommunications, 1974b *Evidence to the Government Enquiry into the Future of Broadcasting* (Post Office Telecommunications Headquarters, London)

• Post Office Telecommunications, 1975 *The Effectiveness of Person-to-Person Telecommunications Systems. Long Range Research Report 3* (Post Office Telecommunications Headquarters, London)

Potter V R, 1971 *Bioethics: Bridge to the Future* (Prentice-Hall, Englewood Cliffs, NJ)

• Pye R, Champness P G, Hollins H, Connell S, 1973 "The description and classification of meetings" Communications Study Group, University College London

Reiser O L, 1958 *The Integration of Human Knowledge* (Porter Sargent, Boston)

Richards I A, 1928 *Principles of Literary Criticism* (Harcourt, Brace and World, New York)

● Rosen S, 1976 *Future Facts: A Forecast of the World as We Will Know It Before the End of the Century* (Simon and Schuster, New York)

● Rubinoff M, Yovits M C, 1975 *Advances in Computers* volume 13 (Academic Press, New York)

● Russell B, 1931 *The Scientific Outlook* (Norton, New York)

● Russell B, 1960 *On Education, Especially in Early Childhood* (Unwin Books, London) (originally published 1926)

Russell B, 1968 *The Impact of Science on Society* (Unwin Books, London)

Ryan P, 1974 *Cybernetics of the Sacred* (Anchor Books, New York)

Ryan P, 1975 "Video as evolutionary tool: triadic relations" typescript privately circulated

● Ryerson R A, 1974 *High Altitude Imagery of Urban Areas in Canada: A Working Document* (Ministry of Energy, Mines and Resources Canada, Ottawa)

Sackman H, 1971 *Mass Information Utilities and Social Excellence* (Auerbach, Princeton, NJ)

Sackman H, Citrenbaum R L (Eds), 1972 *Online Planning: Towards Creative Problem-Solving* (Prentice-Hall, Englewood Cliffs, NJ)

Sagan C, 1973 *The Cosmic Connection: An Extraterritorial Perspective* (Doubleday, Garden City, NY)

Sagan C, 1975 *Other Worlds* (Bantam Books, New York)

● Sass M A, Wilkinson W D, 1965 *Computer Augmentation of Human Reasoning* (Macmillan, New York)

Schon D A, 1973 *Beyond the Stable State* (Norton, New York)

● Schramm W, 1964 *Mass Media and National Development* (Stanford University Press, Stanford, Calif.)

Schumacher E F, 1974 *Small is Beautiful: A Study of Economics as if People Mattered* (Sphere Books, London)

● Schwartz B N (Ed.), 1973 *Human Connection and the New Media* (Prentice-Hall, Englewood Cliffs, NJ)

● Science Council of Canada, 1972 *Lifelines: Some Policies for Basic Biology in Canada* (Information Canada, Ottawa)

Scientific American 1976 "Food and agriculture" *Scientific American* **235**(3) special issue

● Selye H, 1956 *The Stress of Life* (McGraw-Hill, New York)

Shannon C, Weaver W, 1949 *The Mathematical Theory of Communication* (University of Illinois Press, Urbana)

● Sharlin H I, 1963 *The Making of the Electrical Age, from the Telegraph to Automation* (Abelard-Shuman, London)

● Sharpe M R, 1969 *Living in Space: The Astronaut and His Environment* (Doubleday, Garden City, NY)

● Shepard P, McKinley D (Eds), 1969 *The Subversive Science: Essays Toward an Ecology of Man* (Houghton-Mifflin, Boston)

● Simon H A, 1969 *The Sciences of the Artificial* (MIT Press, Cambridge, Mass)

Simpson G G, 1964 *Biology and Man* (Harcourt, Brace and World, New York)

● Simpson G G, Beck W S, 1965 *Life: An Introduction to Biology* (Harcourt, Brace and World, New York)

Skinner B F, 1971 *Beyond Freedom and Dignity* (Knopf, New York)

Snow C P, 1954 *The New Men* (Macmillan, London)

Sorokin P A, 1957 *Social and Cultural Dynamics* (Porter Sargent, Boston)

Spence A M, 1974 "An economist's view of information" in *Annual Review of Information Science and Technology* volume 9, Eds C A Cuadra, A W Luke (American Society for Information Science, Washington, DC)

● Standing Conference on Broadcasting, 1973 *Cable: An Examination of Social and Political Implications of Cable Television* Report of the November 1973 conference on cable, Standing Conference on Broadcasting, London

● Starrs G, Stewart G, 1972 *Gone Today and Here Tomorrow* (Queen's Printer, Ontario)

Steiner G, 1971 *In Bluebeard's Castle: Some Notes Towards the Re-definition of Culture* (Faber and Faber, London)

Steiner G, 1974 *Nostalgia for the Absolute* (Canadian Broadcasting Corporation, Toronto)

● Steinhart J S, Steinhart C E, 1974 "Energy use in the U.S. food system" *Science* **184** (4134) 307-315

● Strom R, 1975 "Education for a leisure society" *The Futurist* **9** (2) 93-97

● Sweet D (Ed.), 1972 *Models of Urban Structure* (Lexington Books, Lexington, Mass)

Tama CCIS (Coaxial Cable Information System), 1974 *Experiment Project Plan for the Living Information System Development* (Living Information System Development Headquarters, Shinjuku, Tokyo)

Tansley A G, 1935 "The use and abuse of vegetational concepts and terms" *Ecology* **16** (3) 284-307

● Tate C, 1972 *Cable Television in the Cities: Community Control, Public Access, and Minority Ownership* (Urban Institute, Washington, DC)

● Taylor G R, 1971 *The Doomsday Book: Can the World Survive?* (Fawcett, Greenwich, Conn.)

Taylor G R, 1974 *Rethink: Radical Proposals to Save a Disintegrating World* (Penguin Books, Harmondsworth, Middx)

● Taylor G R, 1975 *How to Avoid the Future* (Secker and Warburg, London)

● Taylor J G, 1974 *The Shape of Minds to Come* (Penguin Books, Baltimore, Md)

Teilhard de Chardin P, 1970 *The Phenomenon of Man* translated by B Wall (Fontana Books, London) (originally published 1955)

Teilhard de Chardin P, 1971 *Man's Place in Nature* translated by R Hague (Fontana Books, London) (originally published 1956)

Télécable Vidéotron, 1976 *Catalogue pour Autoprogrammation: Télévision sur Demande* (Saint-Hubert, Montréal)

Telenet Communications Corporation, 1976 *A New Era in Data Communications: The Telenet Public Packet-Switched Network* (Telenet Communications Corporation, Washington, DC)

Theobald R, 1972 *Futures Conditional* (Bobbs-Merrill, New York)

● Theobald R, Scott J M, 1972 *Teg's 1994: An Anticipation of the Near Future* (Swallow Press, Chicago, Ill.)

● Thom R, 1969 "Topological models in biology" *Topology* **8** (3) 313-335

● Thompson G B, 1973 "Computers and visual literacy" in National Research Council of Canada Third Man-Computer Communications Seminar, Ottawa, 1973 *Proceedings* (National Research Council of Canada, Ottawa)

● Thompson W I, 1974 *Passages About Earth* (Harper and Row, New York)

● Thompson W I, 1975 "Lindisfarne: a planetary community" *The Futurist* **9** (1) 4-9

Tinbergen J et al, 1976 *Reshaping the International Order: A Report to the Club of Rome* (Dutton, New York)

Todd J H, Angevine R, Barnhart E, 1973 *The Ark: an Autonomous Fish Culture-Greenhouse Complex Powered by the Wind and the Sun and Suited to Northern Climates* (The New Alchemy Institute, Woods Hole, Mass)

Todd J H, Atema J, Bardach J E, 1967 "Chemical communication in social behaviour of a fish, the yellow bullhead, *Ictalurus natalis*" *Science* **158** (3801) 672-673

Toffler A (Ed.), 1972 *The Futurists* (Random House, New York)

● Toffler A (Ed.), 1974 *Learning for Tomorrow: The Role of the Future in Education* (Vintage Books, New York)

Toffler A, 1975 *The Eco-Spasm Report* (Bantam Books, New York)

Trans-Canada Telephone System, 1976a *Datapac Overview* (Computer Communications Group, Trans-Canada Telephone System, Ottawa)

Trans-Canada Telephone System, 1976b *Datapac: Standard Network Access Protocol Specification* (Computer Communications Group, Trans-Canada Telephone System, Ottawa)

●Trappl R, Pichler F R, 1975 *Progress in Cybernetics and Systems Research* (Hemisphere, New York)

Turn R, 1974 *Computers in the 1980's* (Columbia University Press, New York)

Turoff M, 1976 "How to participate in computer conferences" privately circulated brochure

●Tylor E B, 1958 *Primitive Culture* (Harper and Row, New York) (originally published 1871)

United Nations, 1970 *International Development Strategy: Action Programme of the General Assembly for the Second United Nations Development Decade* (United Nations, New York)

●United Nations, 1971 *The Application of Computer Technology for Development* (United Nations, Department of Economic and Social Affairs, New York)

●United States, Department of Housing and Urban Development, 1972 *Applying Systems in Urban Government: Three Case Studies* (Government Printing Office, Washington, DC)

●United States, Executive Office of the President, 1975-1976 *Activities and Programs 1975-1976* (Office of Telecommunications Policy, Washington, DC)

United States Congress, Office of Technology Assessment, 1976 *The Feasibility and Value of Broadband Communications in Rural Areas: A Preliminary Evaluation* (Government Printing Office, Washington, DC)

●Urban and Regional Information Systems Association, 1973 *Urban and Regional Information Systems* papers from the Tenth Annual Conference (Claremont College Printing Service, Claremont, Calif.) 2 volumes

●Vallee J, Johansen R, Spangler K, 1975 "The computer conference: an altered state of communication?" *The Futurist* 9(3) 116-121

●Vesper V D, 1975 "Epistemology, systems theory and the model of shells" in *Progress in Cybernetics and Systems Research* volume 2 (Hemisphere, New York) pp 303-307

●Vickers G, 1968 *Value Systems and Social Process* (Tavistock, London)

Vickers G, 1970 *Freedom in a Rocking Boat: Changing Values in an Unstable Society* (Penguin Books, Harmondsworth, Middx)

Volk J, 1971 *The Reston, Virginia Test of the Mitre Corporation's Interactive Television System* (Mitre Corporation, Washington, DC)

Waddington C H (Ed.), 1968-1972 *Towards a Theoretical Biology* (Edinburgh University Press, Edinburgh)

Wagar W W, 1963 *The City of Man: Prophecies of a World Civilization in Twentieth-Century Thought* (Houghton-Mifflin, Boston)

Walter W G, 1963 *The Living Brain* (Norton, New York)

Wann T W (Ed.), 1965 *Behaviorism and Phenomenology: Contrasting Bases for Modern Psychology* (University of Chicago Press, Chicago, Ill.)

Ward B, 1966 *Spaceship Earth* (Columbia University Press, New York)

Ward B, 1976 *The Home of Man* (McClelland and Stewart, Toronto)

Ward B, Dubos R J, 1972 *Only One Earth* (Penguin Books, Harmondsworth, Middx)

●Warren R (Ed.), 1972 *The Wired City of Los Angeles: Papers and Discussions from a Seminar on Urban Cable Television* (Center for Urban Affairs, University of Southern California, Los Angeles)

●Watt K E F, 1966 *Systems Analysis in Ecology* (Academic Press, New York)

●Watt K E F, 1971 "The environment crisis" in *Balance and Biosphere* (Canadian Broadcasting Corporation, Ottawa)

●Weinberg G M, 1975 *An Introduction to General Systems Thinking* (John Wiley, New York)

Weintraub P I, 1976a "Cost and ancillary services to organization and staff: impact paper to communications-transportation interactions—a technology assessment" Bell Canada, Montreal

Weintraub P I, 1976b "Staff availability and quality: impact paper to communications-transportation interactions—a technology assessment" Bell Canada, Montreal

Weintraub P I, 1976c "Reasons for business decentralization: impact paper to communications-transportation interactions—a technology assessment" Bell Canada, Montreal

Weintraub P I, Pye R, 1976 "Business travel: impact paper to communications-transportation interactions—a technology assessment" Bell Canada, Montreal

●Weizenbaum J, 1976 *Computer Power and Human Reason* (W H Freeman, San Francisco, Calif.)

●Westin A (Ed.), 1971 *Information Technology in a Democracy* (Harvard University Press, Cambridge, Mass)

●Westin A, Baker M, 1972 *Databanks in a Free Society: Computers, Record-Keeping and Privacy* (Quadrangle Books, New York)

Whitehead A N, 1958 *Modes of Thought* (Capricorn Books, New York) (originally published 1938)

Wiener N, 1967 *The Human Use of Human Beings: Cybernetics and Society* (Avon Books, New York) (originally published 1954)

Wills G, Wilson R, Manning N, Hildebrandt R, 1972 *Technological Forecasting: The Art and its Managerial Implications* (Penguin Books, Harmondsworth, Middx)

Wilson E O, 1975 *Sociobiology: The New Synthesis* (Belknap Press: Harvard University Press, Cambridge, Mass)

Wired City Laboratory, 1974 "The educational communications project" (Wired City Laboratory, Carleton University, Ottawa)

World Meteorological Organization, 1972 *World Weather Watch: The Plan and Implementation Programme* (World Meteorological Organization, Geneva)

●Young M, 1961 *The Rise of the Meritocracy 1870-2033* (Penguin Books, Harmondsworth, Middx)

Zolla E, 1968 *The Eclipse of the Intellectual* translated by R Rosenthal (Funk and Wagnalls, New York) (originally published in Italian 1956)

As certain areas of knowledge dealt with in this book, especially the electronic technology, are developing extremely rapidly it is necessary to add the following:

1 The following special issue gives a very useful review of certain aspects of universal packet-switching:

   IEEE Proceedings **66** (11) "Packet Communication Networks", 1978. See section 4.3.

2 The basic protocol (X.25) for accessing public packet-switching networks has now been amplified by additional protocol components, X.28; X.29; and X.75, which last is used additionally for networking between nations. See section 4.3.

3 During 1978 large-scale Confravision-type screens came into common use by the TV networks in the US. They are now used considerably for news broadcasts. Linkage is frequently by satellite service. See section 3.4.

4 During the last year or so the technology known as 'word processing' has developed rapidly. This is essentially the electronification of the techniques necessary for handling written material. Basically it consists of: manual (or terminal), display screen, microprocessor(s), memory, printout, and programmes for performing the various functions. Text can be 'typed out', revised, reorganized, stored, automatically printed out extremely rapidly (printout over 500 words per minute). No special technology is involved; emphasis is on the assembly of existing components.

5 The picking up of TV programmes by an earth receiving station from domestic satellite service (ANIK B) by cable TV companies began in early 1979 in Canada, for example, Victoria, BC Cablevision. There will be eventually between 50 and 100 such stations ($35 000 each). The decision to proceed with this service is Canadian Federal policy.

6 The 'Telidon' interactive system, using domestic TV sets, will be tested at Eli, near Winnipeg, Manitoba, during 1979. This project uses fibre optics techniques for allowing two-way communication between subscribers and includes access to computer data banks. See section 4.1.

7 The results of the projects carried out with the use of the Communications Technology Satellite ('Hermes') are now available:

   The Royal Society of Canada, 1978 *The Communications Technology Satellite: Its Performance and Applications* (The Royal Society of Canada, Ottawa).

   See section 3.2.

8 The Canadian Radio and Television Commission is now the Canadian Radio-Television and Telecommunications Commission.

9 In considering future world food supply it is noteworthy that there is
   considerable expert opinion which stresses that the last forty or so
   years have been abnormally benign in weather conditions, for example
   see:
   Gribbin J, 1978 *The Climatic Threat: What's Wrong with our
   Weather?* (Fontana/Collins, Glasgow)
   This opinion is important for aspects of the population–food–energy
   syndrome, as it implies that some of the recent improvement in
   agricultural output is attributable to favourable climatic conditions
   which may not obtain in the period we are now entering.   See
   section 26.3.
10 For various viewpoints on approaches to global developmental questions
   questions see:
   Dolman A J, Ettinger J van, 1978 *Partners in Tomorrow: Strategies
   for a New International Order* (Dutton, New York)
   See chapter 14.
11 Practical extension of the biosphere outwards will take place if we
   develop man-made space colonies (for producing electricity and
   for manufacturing). This will require some development of existing
   concepts. See on the possibility of space colonies, for example:
   O'Neill G K, 1978 *The High Frontier* (Bantam Books, New York).

Index of persons, organizations, places, and systems[1]

[1] Items in italics are figures or tables.

Index of subjects

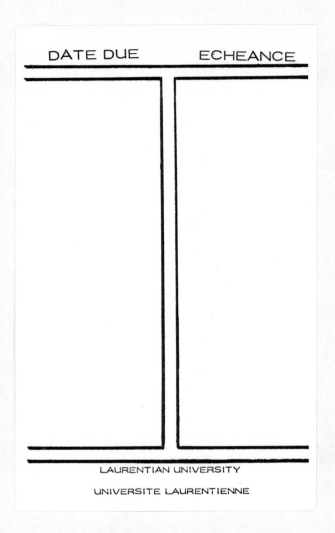

DATE DUE   ECHEANCE

LAURENTIAN UNIVERSITY

UNIVERSITE LAURENTIENNE